POLICY
ANALYSIS

POLICY ANALYSIS

CONCEPTS AND PRACTICE

David L. Weimer
University of Rochester

Aidan R. Vining
Simon Fraser University

PRENTICE HALL, Englewood Cliffs, N.J. 07632

Library of Congress Cataloging-in-Publication Data

WEIMER, DAVID L.
    Policy analysis : concepts and practice / David L. Weimer, Aidan
  R. Vining.
      p. cm.
    Includes index.
  ISBN 0-13-684044-2
      1. Policy sciences.   I. Vining, Aidan R.   II. Title.
  H97.W45 1989
  361.6´ 1—dc19   88-17839
                                                     CIP

Editorial/production supervision and
   interior design: Joseph Scordato
Cover design: Lundgren Graphics, Ltd.
Manufacturing buyer: Peter Havens

Printed in the United States of America
10   9   8   7   6   5   4   3   2   1

ISBN 0-13-684044-2

Prentice-Hall International (UK) Limited, *London*
Prentice-Hall of Australia Pty. Limited, *Sydney*
Prentice-Hall Canada Inc., *Toronto*
Prentice-Hall Hispanoamericana, S.A., *Mexico*
Prentice-Hall of India Private Limited, *New Delhi*
Prentice-Hall of Japan, Inc., *Tokyo*
Simon & Schuster Asia Pte. Ltd., *Singapore*
Editora Prentice-Hall do Brasil, Ltda., *Rio de Janeiro*

To Ulrike, Hal, Dolores, and Leo

CONTENTS

PREFACE

When we began our study of policy analysis at the Graduate School of Public Policy (GSPP), University of California at Berkeley, the field was so new that we seemed always to be explaining to people just what it was that we were studying. It is no wonder, then, that there were no textbooks to provide us with the basics of policy analysis. More than a dozen years later we found ourselves teaching courses on policy analysis but still without what we considered to be a fully adequate text for an introductory course at the graduate level. Our experiences as students, practitioners, and teachers convinced us that an introductory text should have at least three major features. First, it should provide a strong conceptual foundation of the rationales for, and the limitations to, public policy. Second, it should give practical advice about how to *do* policy analysis. Third, it should demonstrate the application of advanced analytical techniques rather than discuss them abstractly. We wrote this text to have these features.

We organize the text into four parts. In Part I we emphasize that policy analysis, as a professional activity, is client oriented and we raise the ethical issues that flow from this orientation. In Part II we provide a comprehensive treatment of rationales for public policy (market failures, broadly defined); we set out the limitations to effective public policy (government failures); and we catalogue generic policy solutions that can provide starting points for crafting specific policy alternatives. In Part III we give practical advice about doing policy analysis: structuring problems and solutions, gathering information, measuring costs and benefits, anticipating and influencing political and organizational feasibility, and designing programs with good prospects for successful implementation. Finally, in Part IV we present several extended examples illustrating how analysts have approached policy problems and the differences that their efforts have made.

We aim our level of presentation at students who have had, or are concurrently taking, an introductory course in economics. Nevertheless, students without a background in economics should find all of our general arguments and most of our technical points accessible. With a bit of assistance from an instructor, they should be able to understand the remaining technical points.

We believe that this text has several potential uses. We envision its primary use as the basis of a one-semester introduction to policy analysis for students in graduate programs in public policy, public administration, and business. We believe that our emphasis on conceptual foundations also makes it attractive for courses in graduate programs in political science and economics. At the undergraduate level, we think our chapters on market failures, government failures, generic policies, and benefit-cost analysis are useful supplements, and perhaps even replacements, for the commonly used public finance texts that do not treat these topic as comprehensively.

ACKNOWLEDGMENTS

A reviewer of this text told us that we had expounded what he takes to be the "GSPP approach to public policy." His comment surprised us. We had not consciously attributed our peculiar views of the world to any particular source. But in retrospect, his comment made us realize how much our graduate teachers contributed to what we have written. Although they may wish to disavow any responsibility for our product, we nevertheless acknowledge a debt to our teachers, especially Eugene Bardach, Robert Biller, Lee Friedman, C. B. McGuire, Arnold Meltsner, William Niskanen, and Aaron Wildavsky.

We offer sincere thanks to our many colleagues, in Rochester, Vancouver, B. C., and elsewhere, who gave us valuable comments on the drafts of this text: Gregg Ames, David Austen-Smith, Judith Baggs, Eugene Bardach, Larry Bartels, William T. Bluhm, Gideon Doron, Richard Fenno, Eric Hanushek, Richard Himmelfarb, Bruce Jacobs, Hank Jenkins-Smith, Mark Kleiman, David Long, Peter May, Charles Phelps, Paul Quirk, Peter Regenstreif, William Riker, Russell Roberts, Joel Schwartz, Fred Thompson, Scott Ward, Michael Wolkoff, Glenn Woroch, and Steven Wright. A special thanks to Stanley Engerman, George Horwich, and John Richards, who went well beyond the call of duty in offering extensive and helpful comments on every chapter.

We thank our research assistants, Eric Irvine, Murry McLoughlin, Katherine Metcalfe, and Donna Zielinski. We also thank Betty Chung, Mary Heinmiller, Jean Last, Dana Loud, Karen Mason, and Helaine McMenomy for logistical assistance at various times during preparation of this text.

DAVID L. WEIMER
University of Rochester

AIDAN R. VINING
Simon Fraser University

POLICY
ANALYSIS

1

WHAT IS
POLICY ANALYSIS?

The product of policy analysis is advice. It may be as simple as a statement linking a proposed action to a likely result: passage of bill A will result in consequence X. It may also be more comprehensive and quite complex: passage of bill A, which can be achieved with the greatest certainty through legislative strategy S, will result in aggregate social costs of C and aggregate social benefits of B, but with disproportionate costs for group one and disproportionate benefits for group two. At whatever extremes of depth and breadth, policy analysis is intended to inform some decision, either implicitly (A will result in X) or explicitly (support A because it will result in X, which is good for you, your constituency, or your country).

Obviously, not all advice is policy analysis. So to define it, we need to be more specific, though not overly rigid. We begin by requiring that the advice relate to public decisions, thereby excluding advice about purely private matters such as personal relationships and routine business activity. That is not to say that policy analysts do not work in private organizations. Businesses and trade associations often seek advice about proposed legislation and regulations that might affect their private interests—their employees provide policy analysis when they so advise. Of course, the majority of policy analysts are to be found in government and nonprofit organizations, where day-to-day operations inherently involve public decisions. Because our interest centers on policy analysis as a professional activity, our definition will require that policy analysts, in either public or private settings, have clients for their advice who can participate in public decision making. With these considerations in mind, we hazard the following simple definition: *policy analysis* is client-oriented advice relevant to public decisions.

A plethora of definitions of policy analysis already exists.[1] Why introduce this one? It will help us develop the practical approaches and conceptual foundations that will enable the reader to become an effective producer and consumer of policy analysis. We emphasize the development of a professional mind-set rather than the mastering of technical skills. If we keep central the idea of providing useful advice to clients, then an awareness of the importance of learning the various techniques of policy analysis and of gaining an understanding of political processes will naturally follow.

An appropriate starting place for our study is an overview of the emerging profession of policy analysis. How does policy analysis differ from the older professions to which it is related? Where are policy analysts to be found and what do they do? What skills are most essential for success?

POLICY ANALYSIS AND RELATED PROFESSIONS

If you are a student in a public policy analysis program, then you probably already have a good sense of what policy analysis is all about—you have by your educational choice purposely selected the profession. It is more likely, however, that you aspire to other professions such as public administration, business management, city and regional planning, law, and public health, where you may nevertheless be required to play the role of policy analyst from time to time. Perhaps you are reading this book as a student in an academic program in political science, economics, or political economy. We hope to put policy analysis in perspective by comparing it with some of the related professions and activities with which you may be more familiar.

A comparison of policy analysis with five other paradigms—academic social science research, policy research, classical planning, journalism, and the "old" public administration—appears in Figure 1.1. We focus our attention on similarities and differences in characteristics such as major objectives, client orientation, common style, time constraints, and general weaknesses. The comparison of paradigms emphasizes differences. As our discussion will indicate, however, the professions of planning and public administration have moved much closer to the policy analysis paradigm in recent years.

The common experience of higher education gives us all at least some famil-

---

[1]Some examples: "Policy analysis is a means of synthesizing information including research results to produce a format for policy decisions (the laying out of alternative choices) and of determining future needs for policy relevant information." Walter Williams, *Social Policy Research and Analysis* (New York: American Elsevier Publishing Company, 1971), p. xi; and "Policy analysis is an applied social science discipline which uses multiple methods of inquiry and argument to produce and transform policy-relevant information that may be utilized in political settings to resolve policy problems." William N. Dunn, *Public Policy Analysis* (Englewood Cliffs, N.J. Prentice Hall, 1981), p. ix. These definitions, as do most, lack the client orientation that distinguishes policy analysis as a professional activity. Descriptions of policy analysis closest to our definition are given by Arnold J. Meltsner, *Policy Analysts in the Bureaucracy* (Berkeley: University of California Press, 1976) and Norman Beckman, "Policy Analysis in Government: Alternatives to 'Muddling Through',' *Public Administration Review*, Vol. 37, No. 3, May/June 1977, pp. 221-22. For an extended discussion of the policy sciences, a broader conception of policy analysis, see Garry D. Brewer and Peter deLeon, *The Foundations of Policy Analysis* (Homewood, Ill.: Dorsey Press, 1983), pp. 6-17.

Paradigms	Major Objective	"Client"	Common Style	Time Constraints	General Weaknesses
Academic social science research	Construction of theories for under-standing society	"Truth" as defined by the disciplines; other scholars	Rigorous methodology to construct and test theories; often retrospective	Rarely external time constraints	Often irrelevant to information needs of decision makers
Policy research	Prediction of impacts of changes in "variables" that can be altered by government	Actors in the policy arena; the related disciplines	Applications of formal methodology to policy-relevant questions; prediction of consequences	Sometimes deadline pressure, perhaps mitigated by issue recurrence	Difficulty in translating findings into government action
Classical planning	Defining and achieving desirable future state of society	The "public interest" as professionally defined	Established rules and professional norms; specification of goals and objectives	Little immediate time pressure because deals with long-term future	"Wishful thinking" in plans when political process is ignored
The "old" public administration	Efficient execution of programs established by political processes	The mandated program	Managerial and legal	Routine decision making; budget cycles	Exclusion of alternatives external to program
Journalism	Focusing public attention on societal problems	General public	Descriptive	Must move while issue is topical	Lack of analytical depth
Policy analysis	Analyzing and presenting alternatives available to political actors for solving public problems	A specific decision maker or collective decision maker	Synthesis of existing research and theory to estimate consequences of alternative decisions	Completion of analysis usually tied to specific decision point	Myopia produced by client orientation and time pressure

Figure 1.1 Policy Analysis in Perspective

iarity with *academic research* in the social sciences. Its major objective is the development of theories that contribute to a better understanding of society. Because the client for the research is "truth," at least as recognized by other scholars, the social science disciplines have attempted to develop rigorous methods for logically specifying and empirically testing theories. Progress in the social sciences proceeds as much from the idiosyncrasy of researchers as from the demands of the larger society. The new theory or clever empirical test earns respect from social scientists whether or not it is immediately relevant to public policy. Nevertheless, the accumulation of empirical evidence, and the associated rise and fall of competing theories will eventually influence the "world views" of nonacademic policy makers.[2] Although academic research only fortuitously contributes to the debate over any particular policy issue, the development of social science knowledge forms a base for more narrowly specified research of greater potential relevance.

This research, which often directly employs the methods of the social science disciplines, can be described as *policy research*.[3] Whereas academic research looks for relationships among the broad range of variables describing behavior, policy research focuses on relationships between variables that reflect social problems and other variables that can be manipulated by public policy. The desired product of policy research is a more-or-less verified hypothesis of the form: if the government does X, then Y will result. For example, academic research into the causes of crime might identify moral education within the family as an important factor. Because our political system places much of family life outside the sphere of legitimate public intervention, however, there may be little that the government can do to foster moral education within the home. The policy researcher, therefore, may take moral education as a given and focus instead on factors partially under government control, such as the certainty, swiftness, and severity of punishment for those who commit crimes. The policy researcher may then be willing to make a prediction (a hypothesis to be tested by future events) that if the probability of arrest for a certain crime is increased by 10 percent, then the frequency of that crime will go down by, say, z percent.

A fine line often separates policy research and policy analysis. The strength of client orientation distinguishes them in our scheme. Policy researchers are less closely tied to public decision makers. While one or more decision makers may be interested in their work, policy researchers usually view themselves primarily as members of an academic discipline. Sometimes their main motivation for doing policy research is personal financial gain or the excitement of seeing their work influence policy; perhaps more often they do it to gain resources or attention for their academic research programs. Because they place primary importance on having the respect of others in their academic disciplines, policy researchers may be as concerned with the publication of their work as with its use by decision makers.

Disciplinary orientation contributes to a general weakness in policy research

---

[2] Within disciplines, new theories that better explain empirical anomalies are often accepted only after repeated failures of the older theories over an extended period. See Thomas S. Kuhn, *The Structure of Scientific Revolutions* (Chicago: University of Chicago Press, 1970).

[3] For a discussion of policy research, see James S. Coleman, *Policy Research in the Social Sciences* (New York: General Learning Press, 1972). Policy research, expanded to include the study of the policy process, is sometimes referred to as policy science. Harold D. Lasswell, "The Emerging Conception of the Policy Sciences." *Policy Sciences,* Vol. 1, No. 1, Spring 1970, pp. 3-30.

because the translation of research findings into policies that can be directly implemented often requires attention to practical considerations of little academic interest. Returning to our example, the policy researcher's prediction that an increase in the probability of arrest will decrease the crime rate is only the first step in developing and evaluating a policy option. How can the arrest rate be increased? How much will it cost? What other impacts will result? How can it be determined if the predicted reduction in the crime rate has actually occurred? The answers to questions such as these require information of a specific nature, often of little disciplinary interest. Consequently, policy researchers often leave these sorts of questions to the policy analysts, who will actually craft policy options for decision makers.

A very different paradigm is *classical planning,* a reaction to the apparent disorder and myopia resulting from private market behavior and pluralistic government. The general approach of planning is, first, to specify goals and objectives that will lead to a better society and, second, to determine the most efficient way of achieving them. Necessary for effective planning is a centralization of authority for the creation and execution of the plan.

As extreme cases, the centrally planned economies of Eastern Europe point to the inherent weaknesses of the planning paradigm. One weakness is the difficulty of specifying appropriate goals and objectives. The five-year plan may clearly specify what is to be produced, but it is unlikely that the production will closely match the wants of consumers. The other is the massive problem of cognition caused by the need to collect and process information for the comprehensive direction and monitoring of numerous economic actors.[4] Although central economic planning has had little currency in the American context, the planning paradigm has been important in narrower applications.

Urban planning in Great Britain and the United States developed from the belief that control of the use of land could be an effective tool for improving the aesthetics and efficiency of cities. The comprehensive master plan, which embodied professional norms about appropriate patterns of land use, became the statement of goals and objectives. Zoning and land-use ordinances were to serve as the mechanisms for implementing the master plans.

The impact of urban planning has been limited, however, by the autonomy of local governments that do not fully accept the professionally specified goals and objectives, and by the dynamic of local economic growth that often takes unanticipated forms. Recognizing the incongruence of the classical planning paradigm with the reality of democratic politics, many planners have urged their profession to adopt a more active interventionist role in public decision making.[5] Consequently, many urban and regional planning schools now require coursework in policy analysis.[6]

A more recent manifestation of the planning paradigm is *systems analysis.*

[4]For a discussion of the paradoxes inherent in planning, see Aaron Wildavsky, "If Planning Is Everything, Maybe It's Nothing," *Policy Sciences,* Vol. 4, No. 2, June 1973, pp. 127–53.

[5]For example, see Jerome L. Kaufman, "The Planner as Interventionist in Public Policy Issues," in Robert W. Burchell and George Sternlieb, eds., *Planning Theory in the 1980s: A Search for Future Directions* (New Brunswick, N.J.: The Center for Urban Policy Research, 1978), pp. 179–200.

[6]Some planning programs have become very much like policy analysis programs in basic structure if not in substantive focus. At Harvard University, for instance, the difference became so small that the graduate programs in public policy analysis and city and regional planning were recently merged.

The basic approach of systems analysis involves the construction of quantitative models that specify the links among the multitude of variables of interest in social or economic systems. The analytical objective is to maximize, or at least achieve lower bounds on, certain variables that represent goals by altering other variables that can be manipulated by government. By identifying the many possible interactions, the systems analyst hopes to avoid the myopia of incremental political decision making.

But systems analysis has tended to be overambitious.[7] Rarely is there adequate theory or data for the construction of reliable comprehensive models. Further, not all important factors are readily subject to quantification. In particular, the appropriate weights to place on the multiple goals that characterize public issues are usually not obvious; the analyst's choice may cloak value judgments in apparent objectivity. Additionally, the mystique of quantification may give simplistic models more attention than they deserve. Witness, for example, the public attention given to the report of the Club of Rome on the limits to world growth[8]—a report based on a model with virtually no empirical links to the real world.[9] An apparently rigorous model purported to show that continued economic growth would soon be unsupportable, leading to a dramatic decline in world living standards. Despite numerous arbitrary and questionable assumptions, the Club of Rome report was embraced by many whose worldview associated continued economic growth with unavoidable environmental degradation. The formality of the model tended to divert attention from its implicit assumptions.

A more focused application of systems analysis is the *planning, programming, budgeting system (PPBS)*, which shares some characteristics with policy analysis. The basic approach of PPBS is to identify all programs that have common objectives so that budget allocations to those programs can be compared in terms of their effectiveness in achieving the objectives. PPBS is like policy analysis in that it is directed at influencing specific decisions in the budget cycle. It differs in its attempt to force comprehensive and quantitative comparisons over a wide range of programs. After some apparent success in the Defense Department, President Lyndon Johnson ordered its use throughout the federal government in 1965. In 1971, however, its use was formally abandoned by President Richard Nixon's Of-

---

[7]For critiques of systems analysis, see Ida R. Hoos, *Systems Analysis in Public Policy: A Critique* (Berkely: University of California Press, 1972); and Aaron Wildavsky, "The Political Economy of Efficiency: Cost-Benefit Analysis, Systems Analysis, and Program Budgeting," *Public Administration Review*, Vol. 26, No. 4, December 1966, pp. 292–310. For a comparison of systems analysis and policy analysis, see Yehezkel Dror, "Policy Analysts: A New Professional Role in Government Service," *Public Administration Review*, Vol. 27, No. 3, September 1967, pp. 197–203.

[8]Donella H. Meadows, Dennis L. Meadows, Jorgen Randers, and William W. Behrens III, *The Limits to Growth: A Report for the Club of Rome's Project on the Predicament of Mankind* (New York: Universe Books, 1974).

[9]For critiques of the Club of Rome approach, see William D. Nordhaus, "World Dynamics: Measurement Without Data," *Economic Journal*, Vol. 83, No. 332, December 1973, pp. 1156–1183; Chi-Yuen Wu, "Growth Models and Limits-to-Growth Models as a Base for Public Policymaking in Economic Development," *Policy Sciences*, Vol. 5, No. 2, June 1974, pp. 191–211; and Julian L. Simon and Herman Kahn, eds., *The Resourceful Earth: A Response to Global 2000* (New York: Basil Blackwell, 1984).

fice of Management and Budget. Even this limited form of planning placed too great a strain on available knowledge and analytical resoures.[10]

The goal of the *"old" public adminstration* was more modest than that of planning: the efficient management of programs mandated by the political process. Its advocates sought to separate the management function from what they saw as the corruption of politics. The words of Woodrow Wilson provide an unequivocal statement of the basic premise of the old public administration: ". . . administration lies outside the proper sphere of politics. Administrative questions are not political questions. Although politics sets the tasks for administration, it should not be suffered to manipulate its offices."[11] The ideal is a skillful and loyal civil service free from political interference and dedicated to the implementation and efficient administration of politically mandated programs according to sound principles of management—the science of management insulated from the art of politics.

Both the old public administration and policy analysis are intended to bring greater expertise into public endeavors. Once organizational structures for programs have been created, public administrators turn their attention to the routine decisions concerning personnel, budgets, and operating procedures that help determine how well the programs will meet their mandated goals. Although policy analysts must concern themselves with questions of organizational design and administrative feasibility, they seek to influence the choice of programs by the political process. One focuses exclusively on doing well what has been chosen; the other also considers the choice of what is to be done.

Public adminstration has gradually come to include policy analysis among its professional activites. One reason is that the large bureaus and vague legislative mandates associated with an expanded public role in society require administrators to choose among alternatives policies—they thus become consumers and producers of policy analysis relevant to their own agencies. Another reason lies in the usual absence of a clean separation between politics and administration, Woodrow Wilson's vision not withstanding. The administrator must be able to secure resources and defend implementation decisions within the political process. Policy analysis may help accomplish these tasks.

The *"new" public administration* explicitly abandons the notion that administration should be separate from politics.[12] Its practitioners seek to influence the adoption as well as the implementation of policies. Professional training, therefore, must include methods both for predicting the consequences of alternative policies

[10]Consider the following assessment: "Although it may fail for many other reasons, such as lack of political support or trained personnel, it always fails for lack of knowledge, when and if it is allowed to get that far" in Aaron Wildavsky, *Budgeting: A Comparative Theory of Budgetary Processes* (Boston: Little, Brown, 1975), p. 354. See also Allen Schick, "A Death in the Bureaucracy: The Demise of Federal PPB," *Public Administration Review,* Vol. 33, No. 2, March/April 1973, pp. 146–156.

[11]Woodrow Wilson, "The Study of Administration," *Political Science Quarterly,* Vol. 2, No. 1, June 1887, pp. 197–222.

[12]Consider the following: "New Public Administration seeks not only to carry out legislative mandates as efficiently and economically as possible, but to both influence and execute policies which more generally improve the quality of life for all." H. George Frederickson, "Toward a New Public Administration," in Frank Marini, ed., *Toward a New Public Administration* (Scranton, Pa.: Chandler, 1971), p. 314.

so that informed choices can be made and for effectively participating in the political process so that the choices can be realized. Training in public administration thus often includes coursework in policy analysis even though its primary focus remains management and operational decision making.

The comparison of policy analysis with *journalism* may at first seem strange. Journalists typically concern themselves with recent events; they are rarely called upon to make predictions about the future. When they write about public policy, the need to attract a wide readership often leads them to focus on the unusual and the sensational rather than the routine and the mundane. Their contribution to the political process, therefore, is more often introducing policy problems to the public agenda than providing systematic comparisons of alternative solutions. Nevertheless, policy analysts and journalists share several goals and constraints.

Tight deadlines drive much of journalists' work. Because news quickly becomes stale, they often face the prospect of not being able to publish unless they make the next issue. Similarly, the advice of policy analysts, no matter how sophisticated and convincing, will be useless if it is delivered to clients after they have had to vote, issue regulations, or otherwise make decisions. Rarely will it be the case of better late than never.

Tight deadlines lead journalists and policy analysts to develop similar strategies for gathering information. Files of background information and networks of knowledgeable people often serve as extremely valuable resources. They may enable journalists to put events quickly in context. They play a similar role for policy analysts, but may also provide information useful for assessing technical, political, and administrative feasibility of policy alternatives when time does not permit systematic investigation. Policy analysts, like journalists, wisely cultivate their information sources.

Finally, communication is a primary concern. Journalists must be able to put their stories into words that will catch and keep the interest of their readers. Policy analysts must do the same for their clients. Effective communication requires clear writing—analysts must be able to explain their technical work in language that can be understood by their clients. Also, because the attention and time of clients are scarce resources, writing must be concise and convincing to be effective.

In summary: we gain a perspective on policy analysis by comparing it to related professions. Like policy research, policy analysis employs social science theory and empirical methods to predict the consequences of alternative policies. Like journalism, policy analysis requires skills in information gathering and communication. Policy analysis is neither so narrow in scope as the old public administration nor so broad in scope as classical planning. Yet planners and public administrators who explicitly recognize participation in the political process as professionally legitimate may at times become advice givers to various political actors, thus playing the role of policy analysts.

POLICY ANALYSIS AS AN EMERGING PROFESSION

As recently as fifteen years ago, few of those actually doing policy analysis would have identified themselves as members of the policy analysis profession; even fewer were filling positions labeled "policy analyst." Many who do policy analysis held, and continue to hold, positions as economists, planners, budget analysts, operations researchers, and statisticians. In recent years, however, the policy analysis profession has begun to emerge. Positions labeled policy analyst are now more common in government agencies, and often these positions are filled by people who have been trained in graduate programs in policy analysis. Many practicing analysts trained in a variety of disciplines have joined with academics to form a professional organization, the Association for Public Policy Analysis and Management.[13] Nevertheless, the profession is still young and those who consider themselves members represent only a fraction of those actually practicing the art of policy analysis.

Practicing policy analysts work in a variety of organizational settings, including federal, state, and local agencies and legislatures; consulting firms; research institutes; trade associations and other organizations representing interest groups; and business and nonprofit corporations. We focus here on the U.S. context, but policy analysts can be found in similar settings in all the major industrialized countries. The way analysts practice their craft is greatly influenced by the nature of their relationships with their clients and by the roles played by the clients in the political process. Because these relationships and roles vary greatly across organizations, we should expect to see a wide range of analytical styles. We consider the various analytical styles and their ethical implications in detail in the next chapter. For now, let us look at a few examples of organizational settings where policy analysts work.

First, consider the U.S. federal government. Where would we find policy analysts? Beginning with the executive branch, we could start our search right in the White House, where we would find small but influential groups of analysts in the National Security Council and Domestic Policy staffs. As presidential appointees in politically sensitive positions, they generally share closely the philosophy and goals of the administration. Their advice concerns the political, as well as economic and social, consequences of policy options. They often coordinate the work of policy analysts in other parts of the executive branch.

The Office of Management and Budget and, to a lesser extent, the Council of Economic Advisors also play coordinating roles in the federal government. Analysts in OMB are responsible for predicting the costs to the federal government of changes in policy. They also participate in the evaluation of particular programs. The major role that OMB plays in the preparation of the administration budget gives its analysts great leverage in disputes with the federal agencies; it also often leads the analysts to emphasize budgetary costs over social costs and benefits.[14] Analysts on the CEA do not play as direct a role in the budgetary process and therefore retain greater freedom to adopt the broad perspective of social costs and benefits. Without direct leverage over the agencies, however, their influence derives largely from the perception that their advice is based on the technical expertise of the discipline of economics.

---

[13]The Association for Public Policy Analysis and Management sponsors the *Journal of Policy Analysis and Management.* Membership information is available from Professor Philip J. Cook, APPAM Treasurer, Institute of Policy Sciences, Duke University, Durham, N.C. 27706.

[14]For a discussion of the institutional role of OMB, see Hugh Heclo, "OMB and the Presidency—The Problem of Neutral Competence," *Public Interest,* No. 38, Winter 1975, pp. 80–98. For a history of OMB, see Larry Berman, *The Office of Management and Budget and the Presidency 1921–1979* (Princeton, N.J.: Princeton University Press, 1979).

Policy analysts work throughout the federal agencies. In addition to small personal staffs, agency heads usually have analytical offices reporting directly to them. These offices have a variety of names that usually include some combination of the words "policy," "planning," "administration," "evaluation," "economic," and "budget."[15] For example, at various times the central analytical office in the Department of Energy has been called the "Office of the Assistant Secretary for Policy and Evaluation" and the "Policy, Planning, and Analysis Office." Often, the heads of agency subdivisions have analytical staffs that provide advice and expertise relevant to their substantive responsibilities.

Policy analysts also abound in the legislative branch. Both the Congress as a whole and its individual members serve as clients. Policy analysts work for Congress in the General Accounting Office, the Congressional Budget Office, the Congressional Research Service, and the Office of Technology Assessment.[16] The analytical agendas of these offices are set primarily by the congressional leadership, but sometimes by the requests of individual congressmen as well. Of course, congressmen have their own personal staffs, including legislative analysts. Most of the analysis and formulation of legislation, however, is done by committee staffs that report to committee chairmen and ranking minority members.[17] Committee staffers, often recruited from the campaign and personal staffs of congressmen, must be politically sensitive if they are to maintain their positions and influence. Congressional staff involved with legislation—and therefore to some extent working as policy analysts, even though often trained as lawyers—number in the thousands.[18]

Turning to state governments, we find a similar pattern. Governors and agency heads usually have staffs of advisors who do policy analysis. Most states have budget offices that play roles similar to that of OMB at the federal level.[19] Personal and committee staffs provide analysis in the state legislatures; in some

---

[15]As recently as the mid-1970s only a small fraction of the offices responsible for doing policy analysis actually had "policy" or "policy analysis" in their names. Arnold J. Meltsner, *Policy Analysts in the Bureaucracy* (Berkeley: University of California Press, 1976), pp. 173–77.

[16]The General Accounting Office and the Bureau of the Budget, the forerunner of OMB, were established in 1921 with the creation of an executive budget system. During much of its history, GAO devoted its efforts primarily to auditing government activities. In the late 1960s, however, GAO became a major producer of policy analysis in the form of program evaluations with recommendations for future actions. Because GAO must serve both parties and both legislative houses, and because its reports are generally public, it faces stronger incentives to produce politically neutral analyses than OMB. For a comparative history of these "twins," see Frederick C. Mosher, *A Tale of Two Agencies: A Comparative Analysis of the General Accounting Office and the Office of Management and Budget* (Baton Rouge: Louisiana State University Press, 1984).

[17]See Roger H. Davidson, "Congressional Committees: The Toughest Customers," *Policy Analysis,* Vol. 2, No. 2, Spring 1976, pp. 299–323. (The same issue of *Policy Analysis* contains six other articles dealing with various aspects of the use of policy analysis by Congress.)

[18]In 1979 approximately 1,500 personal staff had legislative designations; there were over 3,000 committee staff in 1979. Michael J. Malbin, *Unelected Representatives* (New York: Basic Books, 1980), pp. 252–56.

[19]For a survey, see Robert D. Lee, Jr., and Raymond J. Staffeldt, "Executive and Legislative Use of Policy Analysis in the State Budgetary Process: Survey Results," *Policy Analysis,* Vol. 3, No. 3, Summer 1977, pp. 395–405.

states such as California, the legislatures have offices much like the Congressional Budget Office to analyze the impact of proposed legislation.

At the county and municipal levels, legislative bodies rarely employ persons who work primarily as policy analysts.[20] Executive agencies, including budget and planning offices, usually do have some personnel whose major responsibility is policy analysis. Except in the most populous jurisdictions, however, most analysis is done by persons with line or managerial duties. Consequently, they usually lack the time, expertise, and resources for conducting analyses of great technical sophistication. Nevertheless, because they often have direct access to decision makers, and because they can often observe the consequences of their recommendations firsthand, policy analysts at the local level can find their work professionally gratifying despite the resource constraints they face.

What do public agencies do if their own personnel cannot produce a desired or mandated analysis? If they have funds available, then the agencies may be able to purchase an analysis from consultants. Local and state agencies commonly turn to consultants for advice about special issues, such as the contruction of new facilities or major reorganizations, or to meet evaluation requirements imposed by intergovernmental grant programs. Federal agencies not only use consultants for special studies, but also as routine supplements to their own staff resources. In extreme cases consulting firms may serve as "body shops" for government offices, providing the services of analysts who cannot be hired directly because of civil service or other restrictions.[21]

The importance of the relationship between client and analyst is extremely apparent to consultants. Usually, the consultants are paid to produce specific products. If they wish to be rehired in the future by their clients, then they must produce analyses that the clients perceive as useful. Consultants who pander to the prejudices of their clients at the expense of analytical honesty are sometimes described as "hired guns" or "beltway bandits." Consultants best able to resist the temptation to pander are probably those who have a large clientele, provide very specialized skills, or enjoy a reputation for providing balanced analysis; they will not suffer greatly from the loss of any one client and they will be able to find replacement business elsewhere if necessary.

Researchers in academia, "think tanks," and policy research institutes also provide consulting services. For example, although their work is usually not directly tied to specific policy decisions, researchers at places like the Rand Corporation, the Brookings Institution, the American Enterprise Institute for Public Policy Research, the Urban Institute, Resources for the Future, the Institute for Defense Analyses, and the Institute for Research on Public Policy (Canada) sometimes do produce analyses of narrow interest for specific clients. It is often difficult in practice to determine whether these researchers better fit the policy analysis or the policy research paradigms presented above.

Finally, large numbers of analysts neither work for, nor sell their services

[20]For a description of one exception, the San Diego County Office of Program Evaluation, see Gale G. Whiteneck, *Assessment of State and Local Government Evaluation Practices: An Evaluation Unit Profile* (Denver: Denver Research Institute/University of Denver, March 1977).

[21]For a study of the use of consultants by the federal government, see James D. Marver, *Consultants Can Help* (Lexington, Mass.: Lexington Books, 1979).

to, governments. They often work in profit-seeking firms in industries heavily regulated by government, in trade associations and national labor unions concerned with particular areas of legislation, and in nonprofit corporations that have public missions in their charters. For example, consider the proposal to make health insurance premiums paid by employers count as taxable income for employees. Private firms, trade associations, and labor unions would seek analysis to help determine the impact of the proposed change on the pattern and cost of employee benefits. The American Medical Association would seek analysis of the impact on the demand for physician services. Health insurance providers, such as Blue Cross and Blue Shield, would want predictions of the effect of the change on the demand for their policies and the cost of medical care. These interests might also ask their analysts how to develop strategies for supporting, fighting, or modifying the proposal as it moves through the political process.

It should be obvious from our brief survey that policy analysts work in a variety of organizational settings on problems ranging in scope from municipal refuse collection to national defense. What skills are common to successful analysts in this great diversity of roles?

BASIC PREPARATION FOR POLICY ANALYSIS

Policy analysis is as much an art and a craft as a science.[22] Just as the successful portraitist must be able to apply the skills of the craft of painting within an aesthetic perspective, the successful policy analyst must be able to apply basic skills within a reasonably consistent and realistic perspective on the role of government in society. In order to integrate effectively the art and craft of policy analysis, preparation in five areas is essential.

First, analysts must know how to gather, organize, and communicate information in situations where deadlines are strict and access to relevant people is limited. They must be able to develop strategies for quickly understanding the nature of policy problems and the range of possible solutions. They must also be able to identify, at least qualitatively, the likely costs and benefits of alternative solutions and communicate these assessments to their clients. Chapter 6 focuses on the development of these basic informational skills.

Second, analysts need a perspective for putting perceived social problems in context. When is it legitimate for government to intervene in private affairs? In the United States, the normative answer to this question has usually been based on the concept of *market failure*—a circumstance where the pursuit of private interest does not lead to an efficient use of society's resources or a fair distribution of society's goods. But market failures, broadly defined to include "unsatisfactory" distributions of economic and political resources, should be viewed as only necessary conditions for appropriate government intervention. Sufficiency requires that the form of the intervention not involve consequences that would inflict greater social costs than social benefits. Identification of these costs of intervention is facilitated by an understanding of the ways collective action can fail. In other

---

[22]For an excellent statement of this viewpoint, see Aaron Wildavsky, *Speaking Truth to Power: The Art and Craft of Policy Analysis* (Boston: Little, Brown, 1979), Chapter 16: "Analysis as Craft," pp. 385–406.

words, the analyst needs a perspective that includes *government failure* as well as market failure. The three chapters of Part II provide such a perspective. Chapter 3 analyzes the various market failures and other rationales that have been identified; Chapter 4 discusses the systematic ways that government interventions tend to lead to undesirable social outcomes; and Chapter 5 reviews generic policy solutions for correcting market and government failures. These chapters provide a "capital stock" of ideas for categorizing and understanding social problems and proposing alternative policies for dealing with them.

Third, analysts need technical skills to enable them to predict better and to evaluate more confidently the consequences of alternative policies. The disciplines of economics and statistics serve as primary sources for these skills. Although we introduce some important concepts from microeconomics, public finance, and statistics in the following chapters, those readers who envision careers in policy analysis would be well advised to take courses devoted to these subjects.[23] Even an introduction to policy analysis, however, should introduce the basics of benefit-cost analysis, the subject of Chapter 7. Chapters 11 and 12 illustrate the application of benefit-cost analysis and related techniques.

Fourth, analysts must have an understanding of political and organizational behavior in order to predict, and perhaps influence, the feasibility of adoption and successful implementation of policies. Also, understanding the worldviews of clients and potential opponents enables the analyst to marshal more effectively evidence and arguments. We assume that you have a basic familiarity with democratic political systems. Therefore, practical applications of theories of political and organizational behavior are integrated with subject matter throughout the text, but particularly in the context of thinking strategically about attaining goals (Chapter 8), information-gathering skills (Chapter 6), and government failure (Chapter 4), and in the case studies (especially chapters 10 and 11).

Finally, analysts should have an ethical framework that explicitly takes account of their relationships to clients. Analysts often face dilemmas when the private preferences and interests of their clients diverge substantially from their own perceptions of the public interest. Approaches to the development of professional ethics for policy analysts is the subject of the next chapter.

---

[23]There are three reasons why a solid grounding in economics and statistics is important for the professional policy analyst: (1) the techniques of these disciplines are often directly applicable to policy problems; (2) researchers in these fields are important sources of policy research—the ability to read their applied journals is therefore valuable; and (3) analytical opponents may use or abuse these techniques—self-protection requires a basic awareness of the strengths and limitations of the techniques.

2

TOWARD

PROFESSIONAL ETHICS

The policy analyst with a philosopher-king as a client would be fortunate in several ways. The analyst could prepare advice with the knowledge that it would be thoughtfully evaluated on its merits by a wise leader who placed the welfare of the kingdom above considerations of private or factional interest. Good advice would be adopted and implemented solely on the word of the king, without resort to complicated political or organizational strategies. Thus, as long as the king were truly wise, benevolent, and powerful, the analyst could expect that only reasoned and reasonable differences of opinion would come between recommendations and action. In other words, the analyst would not have to fear conflict between the professional ideal of promoting the common good and the practical necessity of serving a client.

Although we often discuss policy analysis as if all clients were philosopher-kings, reality is never so kind. In the Western democracies, many cooks contribute to the policy broth. The distribution of authority by constitution or tradition to elected officials, bureaucrats, legislators, and magistrates guarantees many their place at the kettle. Prevailing norms of democratic participation ensure that they receive a variety of advice and demands from their fellow citizens to whom they are accountable, either directly or indirectly, at the ballot box. Presidents and prime ministers may enjoy more favored positions than other participants; but, except for very mundane or exceptional circumstances, even they generally lack authority to select and to implement policies by simple directive.[1] Even in political systems where the authority of the chief executive verges on the dictatorial,

[1]Commenting on the U.S. executive, Richard E. Neustadt concludes, "Command is but a method of persuasion, not a substitute, and not a method suitable for everyday employment." Richard E. Neustadt, *Presidential Power* (New York: John Wiley, 1980), p. 25.

the limits of time and attention imposed by nature necessitate the delegation of discretion over many routine decisions to other officials.

Analysts must expect, therefore, that their clients will be players in the game of politics—players who not only have their own personal conceptions of the good society but who also must acknowledge the often narrow interests of their constituencies if they hope to remain in the game. The reality that, outside the classroom, policy analysis cannot be separated from politics has important practical and ethical implications. Analysis that ignores the interests of the client may itself be ignored; recommendations that ignore the interests of other key players are unlikely to be adopted or successfully implemented. In the extreme, if efficacy were the only professional norm, "good" analysts would be those who helped their clients become better players in the game of politics. But other norms, not always explicitly stated, lead to broader ethical considerations. Analysts should not only care that they influence policy, but that they do so for the better.

Much of the growing literature in the area of ethics and public policy concerns the values that we should consider in attempting to select better policies.[2] It reminds analysts that no single value, such as economic efficiency, can provide an adequate basis for all public decision making. We focus here on professional ethics rather than the comparative merits of substantive policies. Our objective in the following sections is to sketch a framework for thinking about the ethical responsibilities of the professional analyst. To do so, we must pay attention to the nature of the relationships between analysts and clients and the various contexts in which they evolve. Even if we fail to develop explicit and universally accepted ethical guidelines, we will at least become acquainted with the most common analytical environments and the dilemmas they sometimes raise for practitioners.

ANALYTICAL ROLES

Policy analysis, like life itself, forces us to confront conflicts among competing values. Often conflicts arise inherently in the substantive question being considered. For example: Should a policy that will yield a great excess of benefits over costs for society as a whole be selected even if it inflicts severe costs on a small group of people? Our answers will depend on the relative weights we give to the values of efficiency (getting the greatest aggregate good from available resources) and equity (fairness in the way it is distributed). These values, along with others, such as the protection of human life and dignity and the promotion of individual choice and responsibility, provide criteria for evaluating specific policy proposals.

[2]See, for example: Charles W. Anderson, "The Place of Principles in Policy Analysis," *American Political Science Review*, Vol. 74, No. 3, December 1979, pp. 711–23; Robert E. Goodin, *Political Theory and Public Policy* (Chicago: University of Chicago Press, 1982); Peter G. Grown, "Ethics and Policy Research," *Policy Analysis*, Vol. 2, No. 2, Spring 1976, pp. 325–40; Joel L. Fleishman and Bruce L. Payne, *Ethical Dilemmas and the Education of Policymakers* (New York: Hastings Center, 1980); Douglas J. Amy, "Why Policy Analysis and Ethics Are Incompatible," *Journal of Policy Analysis and Management*, Vol. 3, No. 4, Summer 1984, pp. 573–91; Thomas C. Schelling, "Economic Reasoning and the Ethics of Policy," *Public Interest*, No. 63, Spring 1981, pp. 37–61; and Daniel Callahan and Bruce Jennings, eds., *Ethics, the Social Sciences, and Policy Analysis* (New York: Plenum, 1983).

Rather than focusing on values from the unique perspectives of particular policy issues, here we consider values relevant to the general question of how analysts should conduct themselves as professional givers of advice. Three values seem paramount: analytical integrity, responsibility to client, and adherence to one's personal conception of the good society. Conflicts among these values raise important ethical issues for analysts.

To understand better the nature of these values and the contexts in which they become important, we consider three conceptions of the appropriate role of the analyst.[3] Each role gives priority to a different one of the three values, relegating the remaining two to a secondary status. We can anticipate, therefore, that none of the three roles provides an appropriate ethical standard in its pure form in all circumstances. Our task will be to search for appropriate balance.

Objective technicians hold analytical integrity as their fundamental value. They see their analytical skills as the source of their legitimacy. The proper role for the analyst, in their view, is to provide objective advice about the consequences of proposed policies. Objective technicians feel most comfortable applying skills with recognized standards of good practice. Therefore, they prefer to draw their tools from the disciplines of economics, statistics, and operations research, all of which employ well-established methods. They realize that they must often work under severe time constraints and data limitations. Nevertheless, they want to feel that researchers in the disciplines would approve of their work as methodologically sound under the circumstances.

As asserted in Figure 2.1, objective technicians view clients as necessary evils. Clients provide the resources that allow objective technicians to work on interesting questions. In return, clients deserve the most accurate predictions possible. The political fortunes of clients should take second place behind analytical integrity in the preparation, communication, and use of analyses. Analysts should try to protect themselves from interference by not becoming too closely associated with the personal interests of their clients. In general, they should select institutional clients because such clients are likely to provide greater opportunities for preparing and disseminating objective analyses. For example, one is likely to have greater latitude working for the Congressional Budget Office, which must be responsive to Congress as a whole, than working directly for a congressman who must run for reelection every two years.

The objective technician believes that values relevant to the choice of policies should be identified. When no policy appears superior in terms of all the relevant values, however, trade-offs among competing values should be left to the client rather than be implicitly imposed by the analyst. The analyst contributes to the good society, at least in the long run, by consistently providing unbiased advice even when it does not lead to the selection of personally favored policies.

The *client's advocate* places primary emphasis on his or her responsibility to the client. He or she believes that analysts derive their legitimacy as participants in the formation of public policy from their clients, who hold elected or appointed

---

[3]Our approach here benefits from Arnold J. Meltsner, *Policy Analysts in the Bureaucracy* (Berkeley: University of California Press, 1976), pp. 18–49, who developed a classification of styles to understand better how analysis is actually practiced; and from Hank Jenkins-Smith, "Professional Roles for Policy Analysts: A Critical Assessment," *Journal of Policy Analysis and Management*, Vol. 2, No. 1, Fall 1982, pp. 88–100, who developed the three roles we use.

Fundamental Values

	Analytical Integrity	Responsibility to Clients	Adherence to One's Concept of Good
Objective technician	Let analysis speak for itself. Primary focus should be predicting consequences of alternative policies.	Clients are necessary evils; their political fortunes should be secondary considerations. Keep distance from clients; select institutional clients whenever possible.	Relevant values should be identified but trade-offs among them should be left to clients.
Client's advocate	Analysis rarely produces definitive conclusions. Take advantage of ambiguity to advance clients' positions.	Clients provide analysts with legitimacy. Loyalty should be given in return for access to political process.	Select clients with compatible value systems; use long-term relationships to change clients' conceptions of good.
Issue advocate	Analysis rarely produces definitive conclusions. Emphasize ambiguity and excluded values when analysis does not support advocacy.	Clients provide an opportunity for advocacy. Select them opportunistically; change clients to further personal policy agenda.	Analysis should be an instrument for progress toward one's conception of the good society.

Figure 2.1 Three Views of the Policy Analyst's Role

office, or who represent organized political interests. In return for access, clients deserve professional behavior that includes loyalty and confidentiality. Like physicians, analysts should "do no harm" to their clients; like attorneys, they should vigorously promote their clients' interests.

To some extent the client's advocate views analytical integrity in the same way attorneys view their responsibility in the adversary system. Analysts have a primary responsibility never to mislead their clients through false statements or purposeful omissions. Once clients have been fully informed, however, analysts may publicly interpret their analyses in the best possible light for their clients. Because analysis rarely produces definitive conclusions, analysts can emphasize the possible rather than the most likely when doing so favors their clients. The client's advocate believes that analytical integrity prohibits lying, but it requires neither full disclosure of information nor public correction of misstatements by clients.

Clients' advocates must relegate their policy preferences to a secondary position once they make commitments to clients. Therefore, their selection of clients matters greatly. When analysts and clients share similar worldviews, less potential exists for situations to arise that require analysts to help promote policies that are inconsistent with their conceptions of the good society. Upon discovering that their clients hold very different worldviews, analysts may nevertheless continue such relationships if they believe that they will be able to make their clients' outlooks more like their own over periods of extended service. In fact, they may believe that they have a responsibility to educate before switching to new clients.

Issue advocates believe that analysis should be an instrument for making progress toward their conception of the good society. They focus on values inherent in policy outcomes rather than on values, like analytical integrity and responsibility to the client, associated with the actual conduct of analysis. They see themselves as intrinsically legitimate players in the policy process. They may also see themselves as champions for groups or interests, such as the environment, the poor, or the victims of crime, that they believe suffer from underrepresentation in the political process.

Issue advocates select clients opportunistically. Clients unable or unwilling to promote the advocates' personal policy agendas should be abandoned for clients who can and will. Analysts owe their clients only those duties spelled out in the contractual arrangements defining the relationships; loyalty to one's conception of the good society should take priority over loyalty to any particular client.

Like the client's advocate, the issue advocate believes in taking advantage of analytical uncertainty. When analysis does not support one's policy preferences, the issue advocate questions the simplifying assumptions that must inevitably be employed in dealing with complex issues, or challenges the choice of criteria used to evaluate alternatives. (The latter will almost always be a possible strategy when one does not agree with conclusions.) Though issue advocates desire the respect of other analysts, especially when it contributes to effectiveness, they may be willing to sacrifice respect to obtain important policy outcomes.

VALUE CONFLICTS

One can imagine each of these extreme roles being ethically acceptable in specific circumstances. For example, analysts on the White House staff enjoy privileged positions with respect to information and political access. An important factor in their selection was, undoubtedly, their perceived loyalty to the president. In accepting these positions, they were implicitly if not explictly committing themselves to a high degree of discretion in confidential matters. Except in the most extreme cases where failure to act would lead with reasonable certainty to significant violations of human rights or constitutional trust, honoring confidentiality and otherwise behaving as client's advocates seem to be ethically defensible. In contrast, a consultant hired by the Nuclear Regulatory Commission to analyze the risks associated with alternative policies for nuclear waste disposal might appropriately act as an objective technician, placing analytical integrity above the political interests of the commission. One might even argue that the consultant has an ethical duty to speak out publicly if the commission were to misrepresent the study to obtain a political outcome radically different from that which would otherwise have resulted.

In general, however, the analyst need not adopt any of the three roles in its extreme form. Rather than selecting one of the three fundamental values as dominant and sacrificing the other two as circumstances demand, the analyst should attempt to keep all three under consideration. The ethical problem, then, involves deciding how much of each value can be sacrificed when conflicts arise.

In any situation the range of ethical behavior will be bounded by the minimal duties the analyst owes to each of the values. The development of professional ethics, either collectively or individually, may be viewed as an attempt to discover these minimal duties. In the discussion that follows, we consider some of the common situations in which value conflicts arise and minimal duties must be determined. We begin by considering the range of actions the analyst has available for responding to severe conflicts in values.

Responses to Value Conflicts: Voice, Exit, and Disloyalty

The most serious ethical conflicts for policy analysts usually pit responsibility to the client against other values. A variety of factors complicate ethical judgment: continued access to the policy issue, the status of current and future employment, the personal trust of the client, and the analyst's reputation. Many of these factors involve implications that go well beyond the particular ethical issue being considered. For example, loss of employment directly affects the economic and psychological well-being of analysts and their families, as well as the sort of advice that will be heard on the issue at hand. It will also contribute to the sort of advice that will be offered in the analysts' organizations on similar issues in the future. We must be careful, therefore, to look for consequences beyond the particular issue at stake.

So far we have spoken of the analyst as if he or she were the direct employee of the client. Some analysts, such as consultants reporting directly to project managers or political appointees on the personal staffs of administrators and legislators, have clearly defined persons as clients. Analysts usually have immediate supervisors who can generally be thought of as clients. These supervisors, however, often operate in organizational hierarchies and therefore often have their own clients, who will also be consumers of the analysts' advice. Limiting the definition of the client to the immediate supervisor would unreasonably absolve analysts from responsibility for the ultimate use of their products. At the same time, we do not want to hold analysts accountable for misuse totally beyond their control. For our purposes, we consider the client to be the highest-ranking superior who receives predictions, evaluations, or recommendations attributable to the analyst. Thus, an analyst working in a bureau may have different persons as clients at different times. Sometimes the client will be the immediate supervisor; other times the client will be a higher-ranking official in the bureau.

Note that we have purposely adopted a narrow, instrumental conception of the client. There is some temptation to look for an ultimate client: analysts themselves as moral persons, the social contract as embodied in the constitution, or the public interest as reflected in national laws.[4] To do so, however, would assume away the essence of the professional role. Instead, we see personal morals,

---

[4]Many writers have chosen to approach professional ethics with the question: Who is the real client? See for example, E. S. Quade, *Analysis for Public Decisions* (New York: American Elsevier, 1975), pp. 273–75.

the constitution, and laws as the sources of other values that often conflict with responsibility to client.[5]

What are the possible courses of action for analysts when demands by their clients come in conflict with their sense of analytical integrity or their conception of the good society? We can begin to answer this question by considering the concepts of voice and exit developed by Albert O. Hirschman. In his book, *Exit, Voice, and Loyalty,* Hirschman explores how people can react when they are dissatisfied with the organizations in which they participate.[6] They may exercise voice by working to change the organization from within, or they may simply exit, leaving the organization for another. For example, parents dissatisfied with the quality of education provided by their local school district might exercise voice by attending school board meetings or even by standing for election to the board. Alternatively, they may put their children in private schools or move to another community with a better school district. In Hirschman's framework, loyalty helps determine how much voice is exercised before exit is chosen. Attachment to the community and commitment to public education, for example, will influence the parents' choice between voice and exit.

We find it useful to use Hirshman's concepts of voice and exit, and to add a third concept, disloyalty. An action is disloyal when it undercuts the political position or policy preferences of the client. Note that we thus abandon Hirshman's use of loyalty. Rather than being a contributing factor to the choice between voice and exit, we specify loyalty as another dimension of action.

Analysts can exercise various combinations of voice, exit, and disloyalty when they confront value conflicts. The logical possibilities are presented in Figure 2.2, where voice, exit, and disloyalty are represented by circles. Actions involving more than one of the dimensions are represented by intersections of circles. For example, we label voice alone as ''protest''; ''leak'' combines protest with disloyalty. We specify seven different actions for purposes of discussion.

Consider the following situation: You work in a government agency as a policy analyst. You have just been assigned the job of developing an implementation strategy for a policy that you believe is bad. After careful deliberation, you decide that the policy is sufficiently bad that you feel it would be morally wrong for you simply to follow orders. Under what conditions might you feel ethically justified in choosing each of the actions listed in Figure 2.2?

You might try to change the policy through *protest* within the agency. You would probably begin by informally discussing your objections to the policy with your supervisor. If your supervisor lacks either the inclination or the authority to reverse the policy, then you might next make your objections formally through memoranda to your supervisor and to successive superiors until you reach the lowest-ranking official with authority to change the policy. At the same time, you might speak out against the policy at staff meetings whenever you have the opportunity. You might also request that the assignment be given to someone else,

---

[5]John A. Rohr argues that public officials have a responsibility to inform their actions by studying the constitutional aspects of their duties through relevant court opinions and the substantive aspects through legislative histories. John A. Rohr, ''Ethics for the Senior Executive Service,'' *Administration and Society,* Vol. 12, No. 2, August 1980, pp. 203–16; and *Ethics for Bureaucrats: An Essay on Law and Values* (New York: Marcel Dekker, 1978).

[6]Cambridge, Mass.: Harvard University Press, 1970.

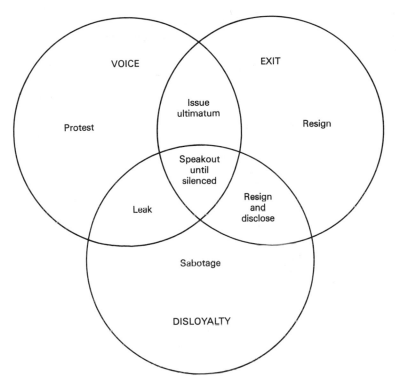

Figure 2.2   Alternative Responses to Value Conflicts

not only because you would feel morally absolved if someone else did it, but because the request helps to emphasize the intensity of your objections. At some point, however, you will have exhausted all the avenues of protest within the agency that are recognized as legitimate.

Although you remained loyal to the agency, your protest probably involved personal costs: the time and energy needed to express your opinions, the personal offense of your superiors, perhaps the loss of influence over the policy in dispute, and the potential loss of influence over other issues in the future. If you were successful in reversing the policy, then at least you can take comfort in having disposed of your ethical problem. If you were unsuccesful, then you must make a further assessment comparing the values you can achieve by remaining loyal to the agency with the values you give up by participating in the implementation of the bad policy.

A very different approach would be to *resign* when asked to prepare the implementation strategy. You decide that contributing to implementation would be so ethically objectionable that it justifies your leaving the agency. Your personal costs will depend largely on your employment opportunities outside the agency. If you are highly skilled and have a good reputation, then it may be possible for you to move directly to a comparable position. If you are less skilled and not well regarded in the professional network, then you may face unemployment or underemployment for a time.

But what are the ethical implications of your action? Only if your skills were essential to implementation would resigning stop the bad policy. If the policy goes forward, then the ethical value of your resignation is questionable. Although you were able simultaneously to remain loyal to the agency and to avoid contributing directly to the implementation, you forfeited whatever influence you might have had within the agency over the policy. You also may have betrayed the terms of your employment contract as well as some of the personal trust placed in you by your superiors and colleagues, and you may have jeopardized other worthy projects within the agency by withdrawing your contributions. If you believe that either the policy is very bad or you would have had a good prospect of overturning it from within the agency, then running away by resigning seems to lack fortitude.

Combining voice with the threat of exit by *issuing an ultimatum* is likely to be ethically superior to simply resigning. After employing the various avenues of protest within the agency, you would inform your superior that if the policy were not reversed you would resign. Of course, you must be willing to carry out your threat, as well as bear the costs of greater personal animosity than you would face from simple resignation. You gain greater leverage in your protest against the policy, but you lose influence over future decisions if you actually have to execute your threat.

Beyond your personal decision to resign, there may be a larger social issue at stake. Why do you find the policy so objectionable while others approve of it? Perhaps the answer is that you have a better-developed ethical sense; you are more principled. Is it good for society in the long run to have people such as yourself leave important analytical positions?[7] On the other hand, the reason for disagreement may be that both you and your superiors hold morally justifiable values that happen to conflict. Although we may have some concern about maintaining diversity within our public agencies, the danger of selective attrition seems less serious when it results from legitimate differences of opinion rather than from a clash between expediency, say, and basic principles.

Now consider actions that involve *disloyalty* to your client. You might *leak* your agency's plans to a journalist, congressman, interest group leader, or other person who can interfere with them.[8] You are taking your protest outside the agency and doing so surreptitiously. Even if you are not a pure Kantian, anytime you do not act openly and honestly, you should scrutinize closely the morality of your

---

[7] For an elaboration of this point, see Dennis F. Thompson, "The Possibility of Administrative Ethics," *Public Administration Review*, Vol. 45, No. 5, September/October 1985, pp. 555–61.

[8] In our discussion, *leaking* refers to the sharing of confidential information with the intention of undermining the client's decision or political position. The sharing of confidential information can also be instrumental to good analysis and to furthering the client's interest in systems where information is decentralized. Analysts may be able to increase their efficacy by developing relationships with their counterparts in other organizations—the exchange of information serves as the instrumental basis of the relationships. For a discussion of the importance of these professional relationships in the U.S. federal government, see William A. Niskanen, "Economists and Politicians," *Journal of Policy Analysis and Management*, Vol. 5, No. 2, Winter 1986, pp. 234–44. Even when the analyst believes that the revelation is instrumental to the client's interests, however, there remains the ethical issue of whether the analyst should take it upon himself to break the confidence.

actions. Further, an important moral tenet is that one take responsibility for one's actions.[9] By acting covertly, you hope to stop the bad policy without suffering any adverse personal consequences from your opposition beyond the moral harm you have done to yourself by betraying the trust of your client and by acting dishonestly.

You should not view the violation of confidentiality, by the way, solely as a betrayal of personal trust. Confidentiality often contributes to organizational effectiveness. The expectation of confidentiality encourages decision makers to seek advice beyond their closest and most trusted advisers and to consider potentially desirable alternatives that would attract political opposition if discussed publicly.[10] Your decision to violate confidentiality has implications not just for your client but also for the expectations others have about the confidentiality they will enjoy when considering good as well as bad policies.

You can at least avoid the dishonesty by speaking out publicly. One possibility is that you *resign and disclose* your former client's plans to potential opponents. Although you are being honest and taking responsibility for your actions, disclosure, by violating the confidentiality you owe to your client, is still disloyal. You also forfeit the opportunity of continuing your protest within the agency. Another possibility is that you *speak out until silenced*. This approach, often referred to as *whistle-blowing*, keeps you in your agency for a while at least. Your agency will probably move quickly to exclude you from access to additional information that might be politically damaging. You must expect that eventually you will be fired, or, if you enjoy civil service protection, exiled to some less-responsible assignment that you will ultimately wish to leave. Therefore, your approach combines voice and disloyalty with eventual exit.

Under what conditions is whistle-blowing likely to be ethically justified? Peter French proposes four necessary conditions: First, you must exhaust all channels of protest within your agency before bringing your objections to the attention of the media, interest groups, or other units in the government. Second, you must determine that "procedural, policy, moral, or legal bounds have been violated." Third, you must be convinced that the violation will "have demonstrable harmful immediate effects upon the country, state, or citizens." Fourth, you must be able to support specific accusations with "unequivocal evidence."[11]

French's conditions limit justifiable whistle-blowing to fairly exceptional circumstances. We might question whether they should all be viewed as necessary. For example, if great harm were at stake, we might view whistle-blowing as ethical even if the evidence brought forward were less than "unequivocal." We should

---

[9]We might think of leaking as a form of civil disobedience, a type of protest often considered ethically justified. The classification fails, however, because most definitions of civil disobedience include the requirement that the acts be public. See Amy Gutmann and Dennis F. Thompson, eds., *Ethics & Politics* (Chicago: Nelson-Hall, 1984), pp. 79–80. For a thoughtful discussion of personal responsibility in the bureaucratic setting, see Dennis F. Thompson, "Moral Responsibility of Public Officials: The Problem of Many Hands," *American Political Science Review*, Vol. 74, No. 4, December 1980, pp. 905–16.

[10]For a discussion of this point and whistle-blowing, see Sissila Bok, *Secrets: On the Ethics of Concealment and Revelation* (New York: Pantheon, 1982), pp. 175, 210–29.

[11]Peter A. French, *Ethics in Government* (Englewood Cliffs, N.J.: Prentice Hall, 1983), pp. 134–37.

also recognize that the conditions call for great judgment on the part of the potential whistle-blower, especially with respect to anticipating the harmful effects of inaction, and therefore constitute only general guidelines. Nevertheless, they seem appropriately to demand a careful weighing of all values including loyalty.

Consider again the appropriateness of leaking. In addition to whatever conditions you believe justify whistle-blowing, you must also have a moral reason for acting covertly. In some extreme situations, perhaps involving the reporting of criminal acts in democracies or the supporting of human rights in totalitarian states, you might feel justified in acting covertly because your life or that of your family would be jeopardized by open protest. You might also be justified acting covertly if you were convinced that you could prevent serious harm that might occur in the future by remaining in your position.

Finally, you might consider *sabotage*—disloyalty without voice or exit. In designing the implementation plan for the policy you abhor, you might be able to build in some subtle flaw that would likely force your agency to abandon implementation at some point. For example, you might select a pilot site in the district of a powerful congressman who will strongly oppose the policy once it becomes apparent. But such sabotage is morally suspect not only because it involves covert action, but also because it operates through obstruction rather than persuasion. Only the most extreme conditions, including all those needed to justify leaking plus the absence of any reasonable avenues for protest, justify sabotage. It is hard to imagine situations in democratic regimes that produce these conditions.

Some Examples of Value Conflicts

Clients, because they have political interests related to their own policy preferences, the missions of their agencies, or their own personal advancement, may refuse to accept the truthful reports of their analysts. In some situations clients may put pressure on analysts to "cook up" different conclusions or recommendations. In other situations the clients may simply misrepresent their analysts' results to other participants in the decision-making process. What are the minimal duties of analysts in these situations?

Demands for Cooked Results.   Most analysts desire at least the option to act as objective technicians. Faced with the task of evaluating alternative courses of action, they want the freedom to make reasonable assumptions, apply appropriate techniques, report their best estimates, and make logical recommendations. Unfortunately, clients sometimes hold strong beliefs that lead them to reject their analysts' findings not on the basis of method, but solely on the basis of conclusions. If the client simply ignores the analysis, the analyst will undoubtedly be disappointed but generally faces no great ethical problem—the analyst is simply one source of advice and not the final arbiter of truth. The ethical problem arises when the client, perhaps feeling the need for analytical support in the political fray, demands that the analyst alter the work to reach a different conclusion. Should the analyst ever agree to "cook" the analysis so that it better supports the client's position?

A purist would argue that analytical integrity requires refusal; issue an ultimatum and resign if necessary. Can less that complete refusal ever be ethical?

We should keep in mind that, because analysis involves prediction, analysts rarely enjoy complete confidence in their conclusions. Careful analysts check the sensitivity of their results to changes in critical assumptions and convey the level of confidence they have in their conclusions to their clients. We can imagine analysts developing plausible ranges of results. For example, although the analyst believes that the cost of some program is likely to be close to $10 million, the most conservative assumptions might lead to an estimate of $15 million and the most optimistic assumptions to an estimate of $5 million. After making the range and best estimate clear to the client, would it be ethical for the analyst to prepare a version of the analysis for public distribution that used only the most optimistic assumptions?

Analysts who view themselves as clients' advocates might feel comfortable preparing the optimistic analysis for public use; those who see themselves as issue advocates might also if they share their clients' policy preferences. After all, analysis is only one of many political resources, and it rarely encompasses all the relevant values. For analysts viewing themselves as objective technicians, however, the question is more difficult. Limiting the analysis to optimistic assumptions violates their conception of analytical integrity: in honest analysis, the assumptions drive the results rather than vice versa. Nevertheless, objective technicians may feel justified in going along if they are confident that their clients' political opponents will draw attention to the slanted assumptions.[12] When objective technicians believe that the aggregate of analysis reaching the political forum will be balanced, their acquiescence appears less serious in terms of ethics and more serious in terms of professional reputation.

Indeed, if we focus solely on consequences, might not analysts have a responsibility to slant their analysis to counter the slanted analyses of others? Imagine that the person making the final decision lacks either the time or the expertise to evaluate the technical validity of the analyses that are presented. Instead, the decision maker gives the results of each analysis equal weight. In our example, the final decision would be based on the average of the cost estimates presented by the various analysts. If one analyst gives a pessimistic estimate and another gives a realistic estimate, the final decision will be biased toward the pessimistic. If the second analyst gives an optimistic estimate instead, the final decision may be less biased. The broader consequences of compromising the procedural value of analytical integrity, however, may be to increase the professional acceptability of slanted analyses, and thus make it less likely that analysts will adopt the role of neutral technician in the future. Perhaps attacking the methodology of the slanted analysis directly rather than counterslanting, even if less effective for the issue at hand, would be better in the long run from the perspective of the social role of the profession.

[12]More generally, this example suggests that the appropriate role for the analyst will depend on the policy environment. In closed fora where the analysis is most likely to be decisive, the role of neutral technician seems most socially appropriate. In more open fora where all interests are analytically represented, advocacy may be the most socially appropriate role. For a development of this line of argument, see Hank Jenkins-Smith, *Politics and Policy Analysis: Efficiency and Democratic Norms in Tension*, dissertation at the University of Rochester, New York, 1985, pp. 357-63.

Misrepresentation of Results.   Analysts have less ethical room in which to maneuver when their clients try to force them out of the range of the plausible. Defense of analytical integrity would seem generally to require protest backed up with the threat of resignation. The analysts' predicament, however, becomes much more complicated when their clients do not actually try to force them to cook up results but misrepresent what they have already done.

An analyst facing such misrepresentation is in a position similar to the defense attorney in a criminal case in which the client insists on being given the opportunity to commit perjury as a witness. By actively participating in the perjury, the attorney would be clearly violating his or her responsibility as an officer of the court. A more interesting problem arises if the client switches attorneys, conceals the truth, and then commits the perjury. Hearing of the testimony, the first attorney knows that perjury has been committed. Must he or she inform the court? One value at stake is the integrity of judicial fact-finding. Another is the confidentiality of the communication between defendant and attorney that encourages defendants to be truthful so that their attorneys can give them the most vigorous defense. Although there seems to be a consensus among the U.S. legal profession that actually participating in perjury is unethical, there does not appear to be a consensus about the responsibility of attorneys when they know that former clients are committing perjury.[13]

Confidentiality probably plays a more important social role in the relationship between defense attorney and defendant than between analyst and client. The former contributes to a system of justice that rarely convicts or punishes the innocent; the latter to more inquisitive and open public officials. Further, the public official's obligation to honesty arises from a public trust as well as private virtue so that public dishonesty, unjustified by other overriding values, lessens the force of confidentiality. Therefore, the analyst's ethical burden seems to go beyond refusal to participate actively in the misrepresentation of the analysis.

Before taking any action, the analyst should be certain that the misrepresentation is intentional. Usually this involves confronting the client privately. Upon hearing the analyst's concern, the client may voluntarily correct the misrepresentation through private communication with relevant political actors or other remedial action. The client might also convince the analyst that some other value, such as national security, justifies the misrepresentation. If the analyst becomes convinced, however, that the misrepresentation is both intentional and unjustified, then the next step (following the guidelines for whistle-blowing) should be to determine the amount of direct harm that will result if the misrepresentation is left unchallenged. If little direct harm is likely to result, then resignation alone may be ethically acceptable. If the direct harm appears substantial, then the analyst bears a responsibility to inform the relevant political actors as well.

ETHICAL CODE OR ETHOS?

Professions often develop ethical codes to guide the behavior of their members. The codes typically provide guidelines for dealing with the most common ethical

---

[13]For general background, see Phillip E. Johnson, *Criminal Law* (St. Paul, Minn.: West, 1980), pp. 119–32.

predicaments faced by practitioners. The guidelines usually reflect a consensus of beliefs held by members of professional organizations. Established and dominant professional organizations with homogeneous memberships enjoy the best prospects for developing ethical codes that provide extensive and detailed guidance. Although a professional organization for policy analysts exists (the Association for Public Policy Analysis and Management), it is young, still relatively small, and seeks to serve a very diverse membership with strong ties to other, more established, professions. Not surprisingly, it has not yet tried to develop an ethical code. Even when it becomes more established, the great diversity of its members and the organizational contexts in which they work suggest the difficulty of developing a code that directly speaks to a wide range of circumstances.[14]

Students of the policy sciences, however, have suggested some general guidelines that deserve consideration. For example, Yehezkel Dror proposes that policy scientists not work for clients who they believe have goals that contradict the basic values of democracy and human rights, and that they should resign rather than contribute to the realization of goals with which they fundamentally disagree.[15] Obviously, the analyst who chooses only clients with similar worldviews and value systems is less likely to face conflicts between the values of responsibility to client and adherence to one's conception of good than analysts who are less selective. Unfortunately, analysts often find themselves in situations where selectivity is impractical. All analysts face the problem of inferring the values and goals of potential clients from limited information; in addition, analysts employed in government agencies may find themselves working for new clients when administrations change. We have already discussed the reasons why resignation is not always the most ethical response to value conflicts between analysts and clients.

Most of Dror's other proposals seem relevant to policy analysis. For example, he proposes that clients deserve complete honesty, including explicated assumptions and uncensored alternatives, and that analysts should not use their access to information and influence with clients to further their private interests. But these sorts of admonitions would follow from the moral system most of us would accept as private persons. In fact, some would argue that the moral obligations in most professions are not strongly differentiated from those of the nonprofessional.[16] A reasonable approach to professional ethics for policy analysts, therefore, may be to recognize a responsibility to the client and analytical integrity as values that belong in the general hierarchy of values governing moral behavior.

Rather than waiting for a code of ethics, perhaps we should, as Mark T. Lilla argues, work toward an ethos for the new profession of policy analysis.[17] As teachers and practitioners of policy analysis, we should explicitly recognize

[14]For a discussion of some of the problems of developing an ethical code, see Guy Benveniste, "On a Code of Ethics for Policy Experts," *Journal of Policy Analysis and Management*, Vol. 3, No. 4, Summer 1984, pp. 561–72, which deals with the conduct of scientists and others who provide expert advice on policy questions.

[15]Yehezkel Dror, *Designs of Policy Sciences* (New York: American Elsevier, 1971), p. 119.

[16]See, for example, Alan H. Goldman, *The Moral Foundations of Professional Ethics* (Totowa, N.J.: Rowman and Littlefield, 1980).

[17]Mark T. Lilla, "Ethos, 'Ethics,' and Public Service," *Public Interest*, No. 63, Spring 1981, pp. 3–17.

our obligations to protect the basic rights of others, to support our democratic processes as expressed in our constitutions, and to promote analytical and personal integrity. These values should generally dominate our responsibility to the client in our ethical evaluations. Nevertheless, we should show considerable tolerance for the ways our clients choose to resolve difficult value conflicts, and we should maintain a realistic modesty about the predictive power of our analyses.

3

RATIONALES FOR PUBLIC POLICY: MARKET FAILURES

Collective action enables society to produce, distribute, and consume a great variety and abundance of goods. Most collective action arises from voluntary agreements among people—within families, private organizations, and exchange relationships. The policy analyst, however, deals primarily with collective action involving the legitimate coercive powers of government: public policy encourages, discourages, prohibits, or prescribes private actions. Beginning with the premise that individuals generally act in their own best interest, we believe that policy analysts should bear the burden of providing rationales for any governmental interference with private choice. The burden should apply to the evaluation of existing policies as well as new initiatives. It should be an essential element, if not the first step, in any analysis; it will often provide the best initial insight into complex situations.

Our approach to classifying rationales for public policy begins with the concept of a perfectly competitive economy. One of the fundamental bodies of theory in modern economics deals with the properties of idealized economies involving large numbers of profit-maximizing firms and utility-maximizing consumers. Under certain assumptions, the self-motivated behaviors of these economic actors lead to patterns of production and consumption that are efficient in the special sense that it would not be possible to change the patterns in such a way so as to make some person better off without making some other person worse off.

Economists recognize several commonly occurring situations, referred to as *market failures*, that violate the basic assumptions of the idealized competitive economy and therefore interfere with efficiency in production or consumption. The traditional market failures—public goods, externalities, natural monopolies, and information asymmetries—provide widely accepted rationales for such public policies as the provision of goods and the regulation of markets by government agencies. Economists, until recently, have paid less attention, however, to the plausibility of some of the more fundamental assumptions about the behavior of consumers. For example, economic models usually treat the preferences of consumers as somehow exogenously determined. Is this reasonable? Do consumers always make the right calculations when faced with decisions involving such complexities as risk? Negative answers to these questions may also provide rationales for public policies.

Of course, efficiency is not the only societal value. Human dignity, economic opportunity, and political participation are values that deserve consideration along with efficiency. On occasion, public decision makers or ourselves, as members of society, may wish to give up some economic efficiency to protect human life, make the final distribution of goods more equitable, or promote fairness in the distribution process. As analysts we have a responsibility to confront these multiple values and the potential conflicts among them. The rationales for redistributive policies, for example, usually depend on values other than efficiency.

THE EFFICIENCY BENCHMARK: THE COMPETITIVE ECONOMY

Imagine a world where each person derives *utility* (one's perception of one's own well-being) from personally consuming various quantities of all possible goods including things, services, and leisure. We can think of each person as having a utility function that converts the list of quantities of the goods consumed into a utility index such that higher numbers imply greater well-being. We make several basic assumptions: First, other things equal, the more of any good a person has the greater that person's utility. (We can incorporate unpleasant things such as pollution within this framework by thinking of them as ''goods'' that decrease utility.) And, second, additional units of the same good give ever-smaller increases in utility, or, in other words, we have what economists call *declining marginal utility*.

Now make the following assumptions about the production of goods: Firms attempt to maximize profits by buying factor inputs (such as labor, land, capital, and materials) to produce goods for sale. The technology available to firms for converting factor inputs to final goods is such that, at best, an additional unit of output would require at least as many units of input to produce as the preceding unit. Firms behave competitively in the sense that they believe that they cannot change the prices of factor inputs or products by their individual actions.

Each person has a budget derived from selling labor and initial endowments of the other factor inputs. People maximize their well-being by using their incomes to purchase the combinations of goods that give them the greatest utilities.

In this simple world, a set of prices arises that distributes factor inputs to firms and goods to persons in such a way that it would not be possible for anyone to find a reallocation that would make at least one person better-off without making at least one person worse-off.[1] Economists refer to such a distribution as being *Pareto efficient*. It is a concept with great intuitive appeal: Shouldn't we be dissatisfied with an existing distribution if we could find an alternative one that

---

[1]For an overview of the history of general equilibrium theory, see E. Roy Weintraub, ''On the Existence of a Competitive Equilibrium: 1930–1954,'' *Journal of Economic Literature*, Vol. 21, No. 1, March 1983, pp. 1–39.

would make someone better-off without making anyone else worse-off? Although we would need other criteria for choosing between two distributions that were each Pareto efficient, we should, unless we are malevolent, always want to make Pareto-improving moves from inefficient distributions to efficient ones.

The ideal competitive economy is an example of a *general equilibrium model*—it finds the prices of factor inputs and goods that clear all markets in the sense that the quantity demanded exactly equals the quantity supplied. Although general equilibrium models can sometimes be usefully applied to policy problems, limitations in data and problems of tractability usually lead economists to evaluate policies in one market at a time.[2] Fortunately, a well-developed body of theory enables us to assess economic efficiency in the context of a single market.

MARKET EFFICIENCY: THE MEANING OF SOCIAL SURPLUS

Social surplus measures the net benefits consumers and producers receive from participation in markets. In the context of the ideally competitive economy, the Pareto-efficient allocation of goods also maximizes social surplus. When we look across markets, the set of prices and quantities that give the greatest social surplus is usually Pareto efficient. Moreover, differences in social surplus between alternative market allocations approximate the corresponding sum of differences in individual welfares.

Consumer Surplus

Imagine that you have the last five tickets to an opera. You walk into a room and announce to those present that you own all the remaining tickets to the opera and that you will sell one ticket to the highest bidder. Each person in the room decides the maximum amount (V_1) that he or she is willing to pay for a ticket. If this maximum amount must be paid, each person will be indifferent between buying and not buying the ticket. Figure 3.1 displays the valuations for the persons in the room in descending order from left to right. Someone in the room values the ticket at V_1, which is more than anyone else does. Value in this context means the maximum amount the person is willing to pay, given his or her budget and other consumption opportunities. In practice you should expect that the person who values the ticket at V_1 to make the winning bid at slightly over V_2, the maximum amount the person with the second highest valuation is willing to bid. You could now offer a second ticket, which you would expect the person with the second highest valuation to win with a bid slightly highter than V_3. Repeating this process, you should expect to sell the remaining three tickets at slightly higher prices than V_4, V_5, and V_6.

You were fortunate as a seller to get each person to pay almost the full amount he or she valued the ticket. If instead, you announced prices until you found one (say, V_* between V_5 and V_6) such that exactly five people wanted to buy tickets, then some of the purchasers would get tickets at prices substantially lower than

[2]For a review of general equilibrium models used in policy analysis, see John B. Shoven and John Whalley, "Applied General-Equilibrium Models of Taxation and International Trade: An Introduction and Survey," *Journal of Economic Literature*, Vol. 22, No. 3, September 1984, pp. 1007–51.

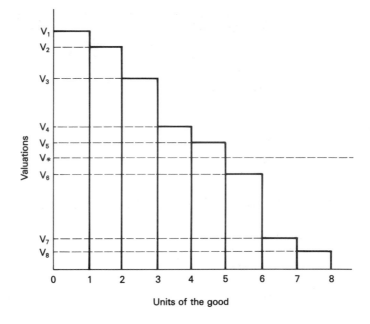

Figure 3.1   Consumer Values and Surpluses

the maximum amounts that they would have been willing to pay. For example, the person with the highest valuation would have been willing to pay up to V_1 but only had to pay V_*. The difference between the person's dollar valuation of the ticket and the price that he or she actually pays $(V_1 - V_*)$ can be thought of as the surplus value that the person gains from the transaction. Adding the surpluses realized by all persons yields a measure of the *consumer surplus* in the market.

The staircase in Figure 3.1 is sometimes called a *marginal valuation schedule* because it tells us how much successive units of a good are valued by consumers. If, instead of seeing how much would be bid for successive units of the good, we stated various prices and observed how many units would be purchased at each price, then we would obtain the same staircase but recognize it as a demand schedule. If we had been able to measure our good in small enough divisible units, the staircase would smooth out to become a curve.

The line labelled D in Figure 3.2 represents a person's demand schedule for some good X. The horizontal line drawn at P_0 indicates that she can purchase as many units of the good as she wishes at the constant price P_0. At price P_0 she purchases a quantity Q_0. Suppose, however, she purchased less than Q_0; then she would find that she could make herself better off by purchasing a little more because she would value additional consumption more than its cost. (The demand schedule lies above price for quantities less than Q_0.) Suppose, on the other hand, she purchased more than Q_0; then she would find that she could make herself better off by purchasing a little less because she would value the savings more than the lost consumption. The shaded area under the demand schedule but above

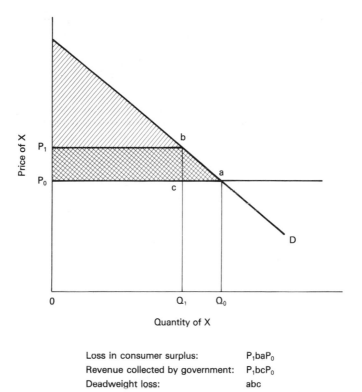

Loss in consumer surplus:	$P_1 ba P_0$
Revenue collected by government:	$P_1 bc P_0$
Deadweight loss:	abc

Figure 3.2 Changes in Consumer Surplus

the price line represents her consumer surplus from purchasing Q_0 units of the good at price P_0.

When evaluating alternative policies, we generally look at changes in consumer surplus. For example, how would consumer surplus change in Figure 3.2 if price rose from P_0 to P_1? It would fall by an amount equal to the area of the trapezoid inscribed by $P_1 ba P_0$ (the crosshatched region). We could interpret the area of the rectangle $P_1 bc P_0$ as the additional amount the consumer must pay for the units of the good that she continues to purchase and the area of the triangle abc as the surplus the consumer gives up by reducing consumption from Q_0 to Q_1.

Imagine that the price rise resulted from imposition of an excise (commodity) tax on each unit of the good in the amount of the difference between P_1 and P_0. Then the area of the rectangle would correspond to the revenue raised by the tax, which, conceivably, could be rebated to the consumer to exactly offset that part of the consumer surplus lost. The consumer would still suffer the loss of the area of triangle abc. Because there are no revenues or benefits to offset this reduction in consumer surplus, economists refer to it as the *deadweight loss* of the tax. As a net reduction in consumer surplus, it indicates that the equilibrium price and quantity under the tax are not Pareto efficient—if it were possible, the consumer would be better off simply giving the tax collector a lump-sum payment equal to the area of $P_1 ba P_0$ in return for removal of the excise tax and thereby avoiding the deadweight loss.

The loss of consumer surplus shown in Figure 3.2 approximates the most commonly used theoretical measure of changes in individual welfare: *compensating variation.*[3] The compensating variation of a price change is the amount by which the consumer's budget would have to be changed so that he or she would have the same utility after the price change as before.[4] It thus serves as a dollar measure, or "money metric," for changes in welfare. If the demand schedule represented in Figure 3.2 were derived by observing how the consumer varied purchases as a function of price, holding utility constant at its initial level (it thus would be what we call a *constant-utility demand schedule*), then the consumer surplus change would exactly equal the compensating variation. (We consider this distinction more fully in Chapter 7, when we take account of the income effects of price changes in benefit-cost analysis.)

But we almost never know the constant-utility demand schedule in practice. Instead, we usually work with empirically estimated demand schedules that hold constant the consumer's *income* (rather than utility) and all other prices. This *constant income*, or *Marshallian, demand schedule* involves decreases in utility as price rises (and total consumption falls) and increases in utility as price falls (and total consumption rises). In comparison with a demand schedule holding utility constant at the initial level, the Marshallian demand schedule is lower for price increases and higher for price reductions. Fortunately, as long as either the price change is small or expenditures on the good make up a small part of the consumer's budget, the two schedules are close together and estimates of consumer surplus changes using the Marshallian demand schedule are close to the compensating variations.[5]

Now consider a demand schedule that gives the relationship between price and quantity for of all consumers. We derive this market demand schedule by summing the amounts demanded by each of the consumers at each price. Graphically, this is equivalent to adding horizontally the demand schedules for all the individual consumers. The consumer surplus we measure using this market demand schedule would just equal the sum of the consumer surpluses of all the individual consumers. It would answer the questions: How much compensation

---

[3] For an excellent treatment of compensating variation, equivalent variation, and consumer surplus, see Lee S. Friedman, *Microeconomic Policy Analysis* (New York: McGraw-Hill, 1984), pp. 143–52.

[4] Alternatively, we might ask how much the consumer's initial budget would have to be changed so that he or she would have the same utility before the price change as after. This amount is called *equivalent variation.* It takes the utility $P_1 ba P_0$ after the price change rather than the initial utility as the reference level.

[5] In any event, the consumer surplus change measured under the Marshallian demand curve will lie between compensating variation and equivalent variation, the other commonly used theoretical measure of changes in individual welfare. For a more detailed discussion of the use of consumer surplus changes as a measure of changes in individual welfare, see Robert D. Willig, "Consumer Surplus Without Apology," *American Economic Review,* Vol. 66, No. 4, September 1976, pp. 589–97. For a more intuitive justification of the use of consumer surplus, see Arnold C. Harberger, "Three Basic Postulates for Applied Welfare Economics," *Journal of Economic Literature,* Vol. 9, No. 3, September 1971, pp. 785–97.

would have to be given in aggregate to restore all the consumers to their original utility levels after a price increase? How much could be taken from consumers in the aggregate to restore them all to their original utility levels after a price decrease?

Thus, if we can identify a change in price or quantity in a market that would produce a net positive increase in social surplus, then there is at least the potential for making a Pareto improvement. After everyone is compensated, there is still something left over to make someone better-off. Of course, the change is not actually Pareto improving unless everyone is given at least his or her compensating variations from the surplus gain.

Our primary use of consumer surplus in this chapter is to illustrate the inefficiencies associated with the various market failures. For this purpose, an exclusive focus on the potential for Pareto improvement is adequate. In the context of benefit-cost analysis, the Kaldor-Hicks compensation principle advocates a similar focus on net positive changes in social surplus as an indication of the potential for Pareto improvements. When we consider benefit-cost analysis as a tool for evaluating policies in Chapter 7, we discuss the implications of focusing on potential rather than actual improvements in the welfare of individuals.

Background on Pricing

In the ideal competitive model, we assume that marginal costs of production for individual firms are rising with increases in output beyond equilibrium levels. Because firms have some fixed costs that must be paid before any production can occur, the average cost of producing output first falls as the fixed costs are spread over a larger number of units, then rises as the increasing marginal cost begins to dominate. Consequently, some output level minimizes the average cost of the firm. The curve marked AC in Figure 3.3 represents a U-shaped *average cost* curve for the firm. The *marginal cost* curve is labeled MC; note that the marginal cost curve crosses the average cost curve at the latter's lowest point.[6]

Now imagine that the market price for the good produced by the firm is P_S. The firm would maximize its profits by producing Q_S, the quantity at which marginal cost equals price. Because average cost is less than price at output level Q_S, the firm would enjoy a profit equal to the area of rectangle $P_S ab AC_S$. (Note: We could measure the total cost of producing output level Q_S as either the area of rectangle $AC_S b Q_S O$ or the area under the marginal cost curve between output levels zero and Q_S—these areas are equivalent.) In the competitive model, these profits would be distributed to persons according to their initial endowments of ownership. But these profits would signal to others that profits could be made by simply replicating the firm. As more firms entered the industry, however, total output of the good would rise and, therefore, price would fall. At the same time the new firms would bid up the price of factor inputs so that marginal and average cost curves of the firms would shift up. Eventually, price would fall to P_L, the

---

[6]When marginal cost is lower than average cost, the latter must be falling. When marginal cost is higher than average cost, the latter must be rising. Only when marginal cost equals average cost does average cost remain unchanged. See, for example, James M. Henderson and Richard E. Quandt, *Microeconomic Theory* (New York: McGraw-Hill, 1971), pp. 70–75.

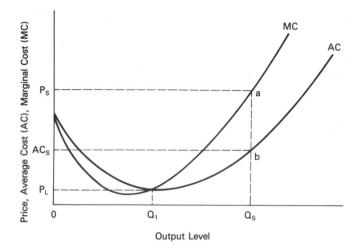

Figure 3.3 Average and Marginal Cost Curves

level at which the new marginal cost equals the new average cost. At P_L profits fall to zero, removing any incentive to enter the industry.

With no constraints on the number of identical firms that can arise to produce each good, the Pareto-efficient equilibrium in the competitive model is characterized by zero profits for all firms. (Note that we are referring to economic profits, not accounting profits. The latter is revenue minus expenditures.) Because the firm may not make an explicit payment to shareholders for the capital it uses, accounting profits may be greater than zero even when economic profits are zero. To avoid confusion, we refer to economic profits—any payments in excess of the minimum amounts needed to cover the cost of supply—as *rents.*

In the real economic world, unlike our ideal competitive model, firms cannot be instantaneously replicated; at any time some industries may thus enjoy rents. These rents, however, attract new firms so that over the long run we expect the rents to disappear. Only if some circumstance prevents the entry of new firms will the rents persist. Therefore, we expect the dynamic process of rent seeking to move the economy toward the competitive ideal.

To understand better the concept of rent, consider the case of an industry with a single firm that does not have to worry about future competition. This monopoly firm sees the entire demand curve for the good, labeled D in Figure 3.4. Associated with the demand curve is a *marginal revenue curve (MR),* which indicates how much revenue increases for each additional unit offered to the market. The marginal revenue curve lies below the demand schedule because each additional unit offered lowers the equilibrium price not just for the last, but for all, units sold. As long as marginal revenue exceeds marginal cost *(MC),* profits can be increased by expanding output. The profit-maximizing level of output occurs when marginal cost equals marginal revenue *(MC* intersects with *MR).* In Figure 3.4 this output level for the monopoly firm, Q_m, results in a market price P_m and profits equal to the area of rectangle $P_m abAC_m$—total revenue $(P_m \times Q_m)$ minus total cost $(AC_m \times Q_m)$. If the firm had been in a competitive industry, then it would have equated marginal cost with price (the intersection of *MC* and *D*), yielding price P_c and profits P_ccdAC_c. The difference in profit between monopoly and competitive pricing is the *monopoly rent*.

Remembering that the profits of the firm go to persons, we should take account of these rents in our consideration of economic efficiency. A dollar of consumer surplus (compensating variation) is equivalent to a dollar of distributed economic profit. If we set the price and quantity to maximize the sum of consumer surplus and rent, then we will generate the largest possible dollar value in the market, creating the prerequisite for a Pareto-efficient allocation.

The largest sum of consumer surplus and rent results when price equals marginal cost. A comparison in Figure 3.4 of the sums of consumer surplus and rent between the competitive and monopoly pricing cases illustrates this general proposition. The sum in the monopoly case, where marginal cost equals marginal revenue (*MC* = *MR*), is the area between the demand schedule and the marginal cost curve from quantity zero to Q_m; the sum in the competitive case, where

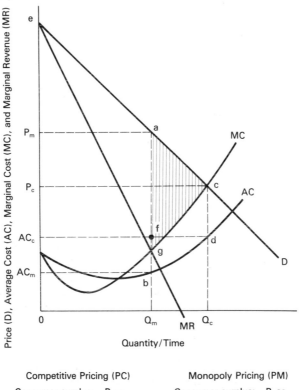

Competitive Pricing (PC)		Monopoly Pricing (PM)	
Consumer surplus:	P_cce	Consumer surplus:	P_mae
Total revenue:	P_ccQ_c0	Total revenue:	P_maQ_m0
Total cost:	AC_cdQ_c0	Total cost:	AC_mbQ_m0
Producer surplus:	P_ccdAC_c	Producer surplus:	P_mabAC_m
		Deadweight Loss:	acg

Figure 3.4   Monopoly Pricing and Rent

marginal cost equals price ($MC = P$), is the area between the demand schedule and the marginal cost curve from quantity zero to Q_c. Obviously, the sum under competitive pricing exceeds that under monopoly pricing by the shaded area between the demand schedule and the marginal cost curve form Q_m to Q_c. This difference is the deadweight loss caused by monopoly pricing. That this area is the deadweight loss follows directly from the observation that the marginal benefit (D) exceeds the marginal cost (MC) for each unit produced in expanding output from Q_m to Q_c.

Producer Surplus

We usually deal with markets where a large number of firms offer supply. We therefore desire some way of conveniently summing the rents that accrue to all the firms supplying the market. Our approach parallels the one we used to estimate compensating variations. First, we introduce the concept of a supply schedule. Second, we identify a quantity related to the supply schedule that corresponds to the sum of rents to firms in the market.

Imagine constructing a schedule indicating the number of units of a good that firms offer at various prices. In Figure 3.5, for example, at a price P_1 firms offer a total quantity Q_1. As price increases, firms offer successively greater quantities, yielding the standard upward-sloping *supply schedule*. The schedule results from the horizontal summation of the marginal cost curves of the firms. (For example, refer back to MC in Figure 3.3.) Each point on the supply curve tells us how much it would cost to produce another unit of the good. If we add up these marginal amounts one unit at a time, beginning with quantity equal to zero and ending at Q_0, we arrive at the total cost of producing the quantity Q_0. Graphically, this total cost equals the area under the supply curve from quantity zero to quantity Q_0.

The total revenue to the firms, however, equals price times quantity, corresponding to the area of rectangle P_0aQ_00. The difference between total revenue and total cost equals the total rent accruing to the firms. This difference, called *producer surplus,* is represented by the shaded area in Figure 3.5.

Note that producer surplus need not be divided equally among firms. Some firms may have unique advantages that allow them to produce at lower average cost than other firms, even though all firms must sell at the same price. For instance, a fortunate farmer with very productive land may be able to realize a rent at the market price of his crop while another farmer on marginal land just covers total cost. Because the quantity of very productive land is limited, both farmers face rising marginal costs that they equate with market price to determine output levels. The general point is that unique resources—such as especially productive land, exceptional athletic talent, easty-to-extract minerals—can earn rents in even competitive markets. Excess payments to such unique resources are usually referred to as *scarcity rents.* Unlike monopoly rents, which we discuss later in this chapter in the context of natural monopoly, they do not necessarily imply allocative inefficiency.

Changes in producer surplus represent changes in rents. For example, if we want to know the reduction in rents that would result from a fall in price from P_0 to P_1, we look at the change in producer surplus in the market. In Figure 3.5

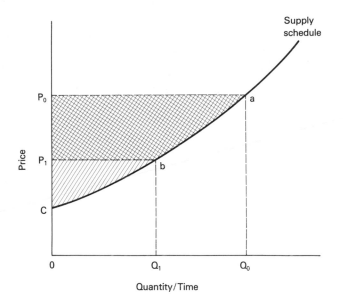

Loss in producer surplus resulting from a fall in price from P_0 to P_1:
P_0abP_1

Figure 3.5   A Supply Schedule and Producer Surplus

the reduction in rents would equal the crosshatched area P_0abP_1, the reduction in producer surplus.

Social Surplus

We now have the basic tools for anlyzing efficiency in specific markets. A necessary condition for Pareto efficiency is that it not be possible to increase the sum of compensating variations and rents through any reallocation of factor inputs or final products. But this is equivalent to maximizing *social surplus,* the sum of consumer and producer surpluses in all markets. For evaluating the efficiency implications of small changes in the price and quantity of any one good, it is usually reasonable to limit our analysis to changes in social surplus in its market alone. Not only is this approach useful in discussions of the traditional market failures, but in benefit-cost analysis as well.

THE TRADITIONAL MARKET FAILURES

The basic competitive model produces a Pareto-efficient allocation of goods. That is, the utility-maximizing behavior of persons and the profit-maximizing behavior of firms will, through the "invisible hand," distribute goods in such a way that no one could be better-off without making anyone else worse-off. Pareto efficiency arises through voluntary actions without any need for public policy. Economic reality, however, never corresponds perfectly with the assumptions of the basic competitive model. In the following sections we discuss violations of the assumptions that underlie the competitive model. These violations lead to market failures, that is, situations where individual behavior does not lead to Pareto efficiency. The four market failures (public goods, externalities, natural monopolies, and information asymmetries) that we consider have been extensively studied. They provide the traditional economic rationales for public participation in private affairs.

Public Goods

The term *public*, or *collective*, *goods* appears frequently in the literature of policy analysis and economics. The blanket use of the term, however, obscures important differences among the variety of public goods in terms of the nature of the market failure, and, consequently, the appropriate public policy response.

We begin with a basic question that should be raised when considering any market failure: Why doesn't the market allocate this particular good efficiently? The simplest approach to providing an answer involves contrasting public goods with private goods.

Defining Characteristics of Private and Public Goods.   Two characteristics define private goods: rivalry in consumption and excludability in ownership and use. *Rivalry* means that what one person consumes cannot be consumed by anyone else. *Excludability* means that some particular person has exclusive control over the good. For example, my shoes are private goods because when I wear them no one else can (rivalry in consumption) and, because I own them, I determine who gets to wear them at any particular time (excludability). Note that excludability has two elements: physical and legal. Obviously, others cannot wear the shoes while I have them on because I physically exclude them from doing so. Legal excludability refers to my right to control use of the shoes whether or not I am wearing them. We refer to this legal claim on control as a *property right*. If I can keep others from using my shoes without permission, then we say that I can effectively enforce my property right. A perfect private good is characterized by complete rivalry in consumption and fully effective property rights.

Public goods, on the other hand are, in varying degrees, *nonrivalrous* in consumption, *nonexcludable* in use, or *both*. In other words, we consider any good that is not purely private to be a public good. A good is nonrivalrous in consumption when more than one person can derive consumption benefits from a given level of supply at the same time. For example, a given level of national defense is nonrivalrous in consumption because all citizens benefit from it without reducing the benefits of others—a new citizen enjoys benefits without reducing the benefits of those already being defended. (Of course, each person values the commonly provided level of defense differently.) A good is nonexcludable if it is physically or legally impractical for one person to maintain exclusive control over its use. For example, species of fish that range widely in the ocean are usually nonexcludable in use because they move freely among regions where different people can exercise property rights.

In practice, a third characteristic, congestibility, is useful in describing public goods. A good is *congestible* if the marginal social cost of consumption can become positive beyond some level of consumption. A good is *congested* if the marginal social cost of consumption is positive. For example, a few people may be able to fish a stream without noticeably affecting each other's catches. As the number of fishermen increases beyond some level, however, they begin to interfere with each other so that each must fish longer to get the same catch.

Over the range where the marginal cost of consumption is zero, the amount consumed can be increased without reducing the consumption benefits of anyone. In the positive range, an increase in the consumption level reduces the consumption benefits of others. We can think of these reductions in consumer benefits as costs. Because these costs accrue to all consumers of the good, we refer to them as the *marginal social costs of consumption*. Congestion arises at the point where the marginal social costs of consumption become noticeable.

We must be careful to distinguish between the marginal social cost of consumption and the marginal cost of production. A purely nonrivalrous and noncongestible good exhibits zero marginal costs of consumption—additional consumption does not reduce the consumption benefits of anyone. Yet increments of the public good (unless they occur naturally) must be produced in the same way as a private good by utilizing various factor inputs. For instance, one way to increase the level of defense is to increase readiness, say by shooting off more ammunition in practice. But it takes labor, machines, and materials to produce the ammunition, things that could be used to produce other goods instead. Thus the marginal cost of production of defense is not zero; the marginal cost of consumption is zero, however, for a given level of supply.[7]

In our following discussions of goods involving congestion, we generally consider situations where supply is fixed and therefore the marginal cost of production is zero. Therefore, unless we indicate otherwise, we can equate the marginal social costs of consumption with the total marginal social cost of the production and consumption of the good. When marginal production costs are not zero, then the marginal social cost equals the sum of the marginal social cost of consumption and the marginal cost of production.

The three characteristics, then, that determine the specific nature of the public good (and hence the nature of the inefficiency that results from market supply) are first, the degree of rivalry in consumption; second, the extent of excludability, or exclusiveness, in use; and third, the existence of congestion. The presence of nonrivalry, nonexcludability, or congestion can lead to the failure of markets to achieve Pareto efficiency. The presence of either nonrivalry or nonexcludability is a necessary condition for the existence of a public good market failure.

Marginal Benefit Schedules for Rivalrous and Nonrivalrous Goods. As we concluded in our discussion of efficient pricing, the production of a private good, involving rivalrous consumption, will be in equilibrium at a level where price equals

---

[7]The picture may appear a bit more complicated because many goods that display nonrivalry in consumption also display "lumpiness" in supply. For example, one cannot simply add incremental units of bridge capacity. To provide additional units of capacity, one must typically either build a new bridge or "double-deck" the existing one. Either approach provides a large addition to capacity. But this "lumpiness" is irrelevant to the determination of congestion. The important consideration is whether or not the marginal social costs of consumption are positive at the *available* level of supply.

marginal cost ($P = MC$). On the demand side, the marginal benefits consumers receive from additional consumption must equal price ($MB = P$) in equilibrium. Therefore, marginal benefits equal marginal cost. Essentially the same principle applies to nonrivalrous goods. Because all consumers receive marginal benefits from the additional unit of the nonrivalrous good, however, it should be produced if the sum of all individual consumers' marginal benefits exceeds the marginal cost of producing it. Only when output is increased to the point where the sum of marginal benefits equals the marginal cost of production is the quantity produced efficient.

The sum of marginal benefits for any level of output of a purely nonrivalrous public good (whether excludable or not) can be obtained by vertically summing the marginal benefit schedules (demand schedules) of all individuals at that output level.[8] Repeating the process at each output level yields the entire social, or aggregate, marginal benefit schedule. This contrasts with the derivation of the social marginal benefit schedule for a private good—individual marginal benefit schedules (demand schedules) are added horizontally because each unit produced can only be consumed by one person.

Figure 3.6 illustrates the different approaches. The left panel represents the demand for a rivalrous good and the right panel the demand for a nonrivalrous good. In both cases the demand schedules of the individual consumers for the good appear as D_1 and D_2. The market demand for the rivalrous good results from the horizontal addition of individual demands D_1 and D_2. For example, at price P_0, person one demands Q_1 and person two demands Q_2 so that the total quantity demanded is Q_0 (equal to $Q_1 + Q_2$). Price P_0 also happens to be the price that equates marginal social benefits with marginal social costs (given by supply schedule S). The right-hand panel presents the equivalent situation for the nonrivalrous good, with the caveat that we are unlikely to be able to observe individual demand schedules for public goods (for reasons we discuss below). Here, the social marginal benefit at Q_S (MB) is the sum of the marginal benefits enjoyed by person one (MB_1) and person two (MB_2). Given the indicated supply schedule (S'), Q_S equates marginal social benefits with marginal social cost and therefore corresponds to the Pareto-efficient output level of the nonrivalrous good. Notice that in this example the upward-sloping supply schedule indicates that higher output levels have higher marginal costs (a brighter streetlight costs more to operate than a dimmer one); it is only the marginal cost of consumption that is equal, and zero, for each person (they can each look at what is illuminated by the light without interfering with the other). In other words, there are zero marginal social costs of consumption at each level of supply, but incremental levels of supply entail positive marginal costs of production.

A crucial distinction between rivalrous and nonrivalrous goods is that the valuations of individual consumers cannot directly tell us how much of the nonrivalrous good should be provided—only the sum of the valuations can tell us that. Additionally, once an output level has been chosen, every person must consume it. Hence no mechanism operates to reveal the various values different persons place on the chosen output level. Thus price neither serves as an allocative

---

[8]Paul A Samuelson, "Diagrammatic Exposition of a Theory of Public Expenditure," *Review of Economics and Statistics*, Vol. 37, No. 4, November 1955, pp. 350–56.

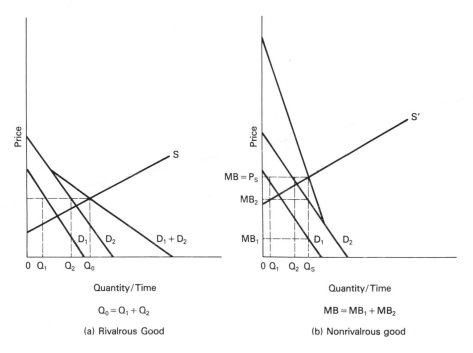

Figure 3.6 Demand Summation for Rivalrous and Nonrivalrous Goods

mechanism nor reveals marginal benefits as it does for a rivalrous good. Why won't the market supply the level of output that equates marginal cost with the sum of individual benefits? In contrast to the case of a rivalrous good, if the individual with demand D_2 (in the right-hand side of Figure 3.6) for the nonrivalrous good makes his own decision, he will purchase Q_2 (if price is P_S), which is less than the socially optimal output, while person one's demand (D_1) would be even less optimal at Q_1. But if person one knew that person two would provide Q_2, she would not find it in her own self-interest to purchase any of the nonrivalrous good. She would have an incentive to "free ride" on person two's consumption, which she gets to enjoy because of the nonrivalry in consumption. In other words, once person two purchases Q_2 units, she would not find it in her personal interest to purchase any additional units on her own because each unit she consumes above Q_1 (which is less than Q_2) gives her less benefit than P_S.

A market could still generate the optimal amount of the nonrivalrous good if all consumers would honestly reveal their marginal valuations. (Notice that one of the great advantages of the market for rivalrous goods is that consumers automatically reveal their marginal valuations with their purchases.) Consumers do not normally have an incentive to reveal honestly their marginal valuations, however, when they cannot be excluded from consumption of the good. This brings us to excludability.

We can almost always imagine some way of excluding some persons from consuming a good; these costs of exclusion range on a continuum from the trivial to the prohibitive. It is usually reasonable to assume that the costs of exclusion for a rivalrous good are zero (exclusive property rights can be maintained at no cost). But this is not always the case. As we discuss below, goods with rivalrous as well as nonrivalrous consumption characteristics may exhibit significant costs of excludability, or, as they are often termed, *attenuated property rights*. For property rights to provide effective exclusion, they must not only be allocated but also feasibly enforced. From a policy perspective, both aspects of property rights are important; excludability problems may arise from either the lack of allocation of property rights or the transaction costs of enforcing them.

A Classification of Public Goods.   Figure 3.7 presents the basic taxonomy of public goods with the rivalrous-nonrivalrous distinction labeling the columns and excludability-nonexcludability distinction labeling the rows. Additionally, the diagonals within the cells separate cases in which goods become congested at some relevant level from those that do not.

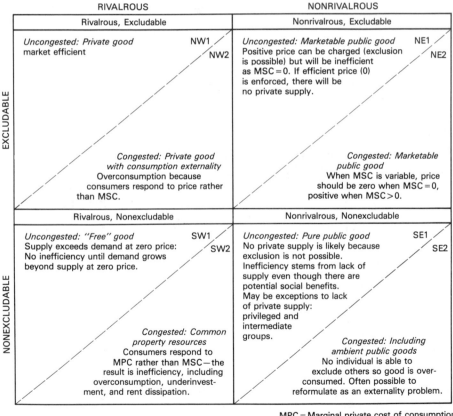

MPC = Marginal private cost of consumption
MSC = Marginal social cost of consumption

Figure 3.7   A Classification of Goods: Private and Public

Rivalry, Excludability: Private Goods.   The northwest (NW) cell defines private goods, characterized by both rivalry in consumption and excludability in use: shoes, books, bread, and the other things we commonly purchase and own. In the absence of congestion or other market failures, the self-interested actions of consumers and firms elicit and allocate these goods efficiently so that government intervention would have to be justified by some other rationale than the promotion of efficiency.

When the private good is congested (that is, it exhibits positive marginal social costs of consumption), market supply is generally not efficient. (In competitive markets the marginal social cost of the good equals not just the price—the marginal cost of production—but the sum of price and the marginal social costs of consumption.) Rather than consider such situations as public goods market failures, it is more common to treat them under the general heading of externality market failures. Consequently, we postpone consideration of category NW2 in Figure 3.7 to our discussion of externalities.

Nonrivalry, Excludability: Marketable Public Goods.   The northeast cell (NE) includes those goods characterized by nonrivalry in consumption and excludability. Prominent examples include bridges and roads that, once built, can carry significant levels of traffic without crowding. Other examples include natural recreation areas such as parks and lakes. Because exclusion is economically feasible, a private supplier might actually come forward to provide the good. For example, an enterprising individual might decide to build a bridge and charge a crossing toll that would generate a stream of revenue more than adequate to cover the cost of construction. Once the bridge is built, it requires no additional resources so that the marginal cost of production is effectively zero. Clearly, in this cell the problem is not supply per se. Rather, the problem is twofold. First, the private supplier may not provide the correct facility size to maximize social surplus (Q_S in Figure 3.6(b)). Second, the private supplier may not efficiently price the facility that is provided.

With respect to the pricing problem, first consider the case of no congestion (NE1), one in which we can be certain that the private supplier will not charge the efficient price. In the absence of congestion, the social marginal cost of consumption is zero, so that any positive price inappropriately discourages use of the bridge. The shaded triangular area Q_0ab in panel (a) of Figure 3.8 represents the deadweight loss that results from a positive price (or toll) P_0. From the diagram we can see that any positive price would involve some welfare loss. The reason is that if a positive price is charged, some individuals who "should" cross the bridge will be discouraged from doing so. Why? Because those individuals who would receive marginal benefits in excess of, or equal to, the marginal social cost of consumption should cross. Because the marginal social cost of consumption is zero (that is, lies along the horizontal axis), any individual who would derive any positive benefit from the crossing should cross. Those who obtain positive marginal benefits less than the price, however, would not choose to cross. The resulting deadweight loss may seem nebulous—the lost consumer surplus of the trips that will not take place because of the toll—but it represents a misallocation of resources that, if corrected, could lead to a Pareto improvement.

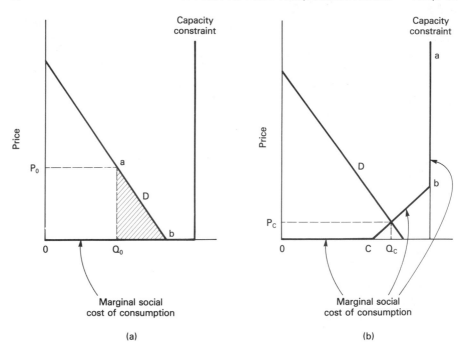

Figure 3.8 Excludable Nonrivalrous Goods (a) Social Surplus Loss with
Positive Price in the Absence of Congestion (b) Appropriate Positive Price
in the Presence of Congestion

The analysis just presented is complicated if the good displays congestion
over some range of demand (NE2). Return to the bridge example. We assumed
that capacity exceeded demand—this need not be the case. Consumption is typically uncongested up to some level of demand, but as additional people use the good,
the marginal social costs of consumption become positive. Goods such as bridges,
roads, and parks are potentially subject to congestion because of physical capacity constraints. Whether or not they are actually congested depends on demand
as well as capacity. The line cb in panel (b) of Figure 3.8 represents the marginal
social costs of consumption for goods that become congested. At low demand levels
(up to point c) the marginal cost of consumption is zero (in other words, consumption is uncongested), but additional consumption beyond point c imposes
marginal costs on all users of the good. Line segments $0c$, cb, and ba trace out
the marginal social cost of consumption for the good over the range of possible
consumption. Notice that these costs are imposed by the marginal consumer, not
by the good itself. In the case of the bridge, for instance, the costs appear as the
additional time it takes all users to cross the bridge. If additional users crowd
onto the bridge, quite conceivably marginal costs could become almost infinite:
"gridlock" prevents anyone from crossing the bridge until some users withdraw.
The economically efficient price is shown in panel (b) as P_C.

Let us take a closer look at the incentives that lead to socially inefficient
crowding. Suppose that there are 999 automobiles on the bridge experiencing an

average crossing time of ten minutes. You are considering whether your auto should be number 1,000 on the bridge. Unfortunately, given the capacity of the bridge, your trip will generate congestion—everyone crossing the bridge, including yourself, will be slowed down by one minute. In other words, the average crossing time of the users rises by one minute to eleven minutes. You will cross if your marginal benefits from crossing exceed your marginal costs (which in this case equal the new average consumption cost of eleven minutes for the group of users).[9] If you decide to cross, however, the marginal social costs of your decision will be 1,010 minutes! (the eleven minutes you bear plus the 999 additional minutes your use inflicts on the other users). Thus, from the social perspective, if everyone places the same value on time as you, then you should cross only if the benefits that you receive from crossing exceed the cost of 1,010 minutes of delay.

In practice, nonrivalrous, excludable public goods that exhibit congestion involve quite complex pricing problems; however, the basic principle follows readily from the above discussion. Let us assume that the congestion occurs at regular time periods (roads at rush hour, for instance). Efficient allocation requires that the price charged users of the good equal the marginal costs imposed on other users during each period of the day, implying a zero price during noncongested periods (more generally, price should equal the marginal cost of production in the absence of congestion) and some positive price during congested periods (so-called peak-load pricing). Here we have ignored questions relating to the optimal scale of the good (what size bridge to build), but obviously the congestion itself is a function of the scale chosen (for example, the number of road lanes).

Many nonrivalrous, excludable public goods are produced by private firms. The firms must pay the cost of producing the goods with revenues from user fees. That is, the stream of revenues from the fees must cover the cost of construction and operation. To generate the necessary revenues, the firms may have to set the user fees above the marginal social costs of consumption. Thus, market failure may result because the fees exclude users who would obtain higher marginal benefits than the marginal social costs that they impose. The magnitude of the forgone net benefits determines the seriousness of the market failure.

Nonrivalry, Nonexcludability: "Pure" and Ambient Public Goods. We now turn to those goods that exhibit nonrivalrous consumption and where exclusion is not possible—the southeast (SE) quadrant of Figure 3.7. When these goods are uncongestible, or at least uncongested, they are the "classic," or "pure," public goods, such as defense and lighthouses. With certain exceptions, to be discussed below, the pure public goods will not be supplied at all by private action. Contrast this with the NE quadrant, where there is likely to be market provision, but at a price that results in deadweight losses—some positive price generates revenues to cover costs but also discourages some use involving zero marginal social costs of consumption.

The number of persons who may potentially benefit from a pure public good can vary enormously, depending on the good: ranging from a particular

---

[9]We are assuming here that the marginal cost of production is zero. If each crossing inflicted noticeable maintenance costs on the bridge, then the full marginal social cost of a crossing would equal the sum of the marginal cost of production (maintenance) and the marginal social cost of consumption.

streetlight with only a few individuals benefiting to national defense, where all members of the polity presumably benefit. Because benefits normally vary spatially or geographically (that is, benefits decline monotonically as one moves away from a particular point on the map), we commonly distinguish among local, regional, national, international, and even global public goods. While this is a convenient way of grouping persons who receive benefits, it is only one of many potential ways. For example, persons who place positive values on wilderness areas in the Sierras may be spread all over North America—indeed, all over the world. Some, or even most, of those who actually reside in the Sierras may not be included in this category because their private interests depend upon commercial or agricultural development of the area rather than upon preservation.

We have already touched briefly on the major problem in the SE quadrant: the fact that the people who would actually receive some level of positive benefits if the good is provided, often do not have an incentive to reveal honestly the magnitude of these benefits: if contributions for the public good are to be based on benefit levels, then individuals generally have an incentive to understate their benefit levels; if contributions are not tied to benefit levels, then individuals may have an incentive to overstate their benefit levels to obtain a larger supply. Typically, the larger the number of beneficiaries, the less likely is any individual to reveal his or her preferences. In such situations, private supply is unlikely. As Mancur Olsen has pointed out, however, two specific situations can result in market supply of pure public goods.[10] He labels these situations the "privileged group" and the "intermediate group" cases.

The privileged group case is illustrated in Figure 3.9, where three consumers receive benefits from the good according to their marginal benefit schedules. For example, the three might be owners of recreational facilities in a valley and the good might be spraying to control mosquitoes. The marginal benefit schedule of person three (D_3) is high relative to the marginal benefit schedules of persons one and two. (By relatively high, we mean that at any quantity, person three places a much higher marginal value on having an additional unit than do the other two persons.) In fact, it is sufficiently high that person three will be willing to purchase Q_3 of the good no matter what the other two persons do. (Person three's demand schedule intersects with the supply schedule at quantity Q_3.) Of course, once person three purchases Q_3, neither person one nor person two will be willing to make additional purchases. In effect, they will "free ride" on person three's high demand. (We can speak of person three's marginal benefit schedule as a demand schedule because she will act as if the good were private, revealing her demand at various prices.) Despite the provision of Q_3 units of the public good, compared to the socially efficient level Q_0, social surplus is lower by the area of triangle *abc*.

In this case the demand of person three makes up such a large fraction of total demand that the amount purchased (Q_3) is fairly close to the economically efficient level (Q_0). In this sense, the three persons form a privileged group. Even when no one person has a sufficiently high demand to make a group privileged, however, *some* provision of the good may result if the group is sufficiently small

[10]Mancur Olson, *The Logic of Collective Action* (Cambridge, Mass.: Harvard University Press, 1973), pp. 43–52.

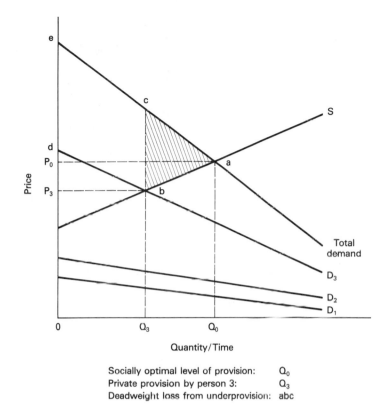

Socially optimal level of provision: Q_0
Private provision by person 3: Q_3
Deadweight loss from underprovision: abc

Figure 3.9   Private Provision of a Public Good: Privileged Group

so that members can negotiate directly among themselves. We recognize such a group as "intermediate" between privileged and unprivileged: two or more members may, for whatever reasons, voluntarily join together to provide some of the good, although usually at less than the economically efficient level. Intermediate groups are generally small or at least have a small number of members who account for a large fraction of total demand.

The reader who has some previous background in microeconomics may notice that the situation just described closely resembles a positive externality (benefits accruing to third parties to market transactions), which we discuss in detail in the next section. Clearly, if persons one and two did not agree to finance jointly the public good at the efficient level (Q_0), they would nevertheless receive benefits from Q_3, the amount purchased by person three. Through the purchase of Q_3, person three receives the private consumer surplus benefit given by the area of triangle P_3bd and confers an external (to herself) consumer surplus benefit of area bced on the other group members. For analytic convenience, however, we maintain a distinction between public goods and positive externalities. We restrict the definition of an externality to those situations where provision of a good necessarily requires the joint production of a private good and a public good. We reserve the public good classification for those cases where there is no joint production. So, for example, mosquito control poses a public good problem, while chemical waste produced as a by-product of manufacturing poses an externality problem.

In many situations large numbers of individuals would benefit from the provision of a public good where no small group receives a disproportionate share of total benefits. Such "large-number" cases present the free rider problem with a vengeance. In situations involving large numbers, each person's demand is extremely small relative to total demand and to the cost of provision. The rational individual compares his individual marginal benefits and costs. Taking as an example national defense, the logic is likely to be as follows: My monetary contribution to the financing of national defense will be infinitesimal; therefore, if I do not contribute and everyone else does, the level of defense provided, from which I cannot be effectively excluded, will be essentially the same as if I did contribute. On the other hand, if I contribute and others do not, national defense will not be provided anyway. Either way I am better off not contributing. (As we will discuss below, free riding arises in other contexts besides the market provision of public goods; it can also occur when attempts are made to supply the economically efficient quantity of the public good through public sector mechanisms.[11])

To summarize, then, the free rider problem exists because in the large numbers case it is usually impossible to get persons to reveal their true demand (marginal benefit) schedules for the good (it is even difficult to talk of individual demand schedules in this context because they are not generally observable). Even though all would potentially benefit if all persons agreed to contribute to the financing of the good so that their average contributions (in effect, the price they each paid per unit supplied) just equaled their marginal benefits, self-interest in terms of personal costs and benefits discourages honest participation.

The concept of free riding plays an important role in the theory of public goods. Recently, however, there has been considerable debate among economists about the practical significance of free riding. In the context of relatively small groups that permit face-to-face contact, such as neighborhood associations, social pressure may be brought to bear to make noncontribution unpleasant.[12] More generally, we would expect a variety of voluntary organizations with less individual anonymity to arise to combat free riding.[13] There has also been considerable in-

[11]As we will see below, free rider problems are also endemic in externality situations. Indeed, they may be worse because the potential for opportunistic behavior may be even greater.

[12]Thomas S. McCaleb and Richard E. Wagner, "The Experimental Search for Free Riders: Some Reflections and Observations," *Public Choice*, Vol. 47, No. 3, 1985, pp. 479–90.

[13]In addition to McCaleb and Wagner, p. 487, see P. Bohm, "Estimating Demand for Public Goods: An Experiment," *European Economic Review*, Vol. 3, No. 2, 1972, pp. 111–30; E. Brubaker, "Free Ride, Free Revelation, or Golden Rule?" *Journal of Law and Economics*, Vol. 18, No. 1, 1975, pp. 147–61; R. Issac, J. Walker, and S. Thomas, "Divergent Evidence on Free Riding: An Experimental Examination of Possible Explanations," *Public Choice*, Vol. 43, No. 2, 1984, pp. 113–49; O. Kim and M. Walker, "The Free Rider Problem: Experimental Evidence, "*Public Choice*, Vol. 43, No. 1, 1984, pp. 3–24; G. Marwell and R. Ames, "Economists Free Ride, Does Anyone Else?: Experiments on the Provision of Public Goods, IV," *Journal of Public Economics*, Vol. 15, No. 3, 1981, pp. 295–310.

terest lately in pricing mechanisms that encourage people to reveal their preferences truthfully.[14]

Thus far we have not considered the issue of congestion in this SE quadrant. Some goods are simply not congestible and can be placed to the left of the diagonal (SE1) within the SE quadrant. For instance, mosquito control, a local public good, involves nonexcludability, nonrivalry in consumption, and noncongestibility; no matter how many people are added to the area, the effectiveness of the eradication remains the same. Similarly, national defense, a national or international public good, in general is not subject to congestion.[15] In contrast, nature lovers may experience disutility when they meet more than a few other hikers in a wilderness area.

The most important class of goods that exhibit congestion and thus are appropriately placed into SE2 is what we call *ambient public goods*. Air and large bodies of water are prime examples of public goods that are exogeneously provided by nature. For all practical purposes, consumption (use) of these goods is nonrivalrous—more than one person can use the same unit for such purposes as disposing of pollutants.[16] In other words, consumption of the resource (via pollution) typically imposes no Pareto-relevant impact until some threshold, or ambient carrying capacity, has been crossed. Exclusion in many market contexts is impossible, or at least extremely costly, because access to the resources is possible from many different locations. For example, pollutants can be discharged into an airshed from any location under it (or even upwind of it!).

Relatively few goods fall into category SE2. The reason is that as congestion sets in, it often becomes economically feasible to exclude users so that goods that might otherwise be in SE2 are better placed in NE2 instead. For example, returning to wilderness hiking, once the density of hikers becomes very large, it may become economically feasible for a private owner to issue passes that can be enforced by spot checks. Wilderness in this context is an ambient public good only over the range of use between the onset of crowding and the reaching of a density where the pass system becomes economically feasible. The efficiency problems associated with many of the goods that do fall into category SE2 can alternatively be viewed as market failures due to externalities. So, for example, the carrying capacity of a body of water can be viewed as an ambient public good that suffers from overconsumption. Alternatively, the pollution that the body of water receives can be viewed as an externality of some other good that is overproduced.

[14]See Edward H. Clarke, *Demand Revelation and the Provision of Public Goods* (Cambridge, Mass.: Ballinger, 1980).

[15]Of course, few pure public goods are completely uncongestible. Even a lighthouse may conceivably be subject to congestion if there are so many ships using it that view of the beam becomes blocked for some ships. As long as such goods are not actually subject to congestion over the relevant range of demand, however, they can be placed in SE1 for analytical purposes.

[16]Some sorts of consumption may be rivalrous. For example, taking water from the body of water for irrigation is rivalrous—assuming congestion (positive marginal social costs of consumption), the water should be treated as a common property resource (SW2 in Figure 3.7) rather than as an ambient public good. The same body of water, however, generally would be nonrivalrous with respect to its capacity to carry away wastes.

Rivalry, Nonexcludability: Common Property Resources and "Free" Goods. Finally, we turn to goods in the southwest quadrant, where consumption is rivalrous, but where exclusion is not economically feasible—in other words, there is "open access" to the good. For example, consider the migrating fish we already mentioned. No immediate market failure appears in those cases where the good is naturally occurring, where supply exceeds demand at zero price, and where there is no congestion. In situations without excess supply, we have what are usually referred to as *common property resource* problems. We should stress that in this quadrant we are dealing with goods that are rivalrous in consumption. Trees, fish, buffalo, oil, and pasture land are all rivalrous in consumption: if you take the hide from a buffalo, for instance, it is no longer available for someone else to take.

The market failure arises in the common property resource case from the "unfeasibility" of exclusion. Why the quotation marks? Because, as we will see, the common property resource problem often occurs in situations where institutional factors rather than the inherent nature of the goods make exclusion unfeasible. For example, in most countries oil does not suffer from the common resource problem because governments keep and enforce exclusive property rights to subsurface resources. In the United States, however, oil has often suffered from the common property resource problem because of the "rule of capture," a legal doctrine that gives most subsurface rights to the owner of the surface property. When different people own separate pieces of property over the same pool of oil, the rule of capture prevents exclusion. Unless all the owners agree to treat their combined property as a unit, the common reservoir of oil will be extracted too quickly.

Nonexcludability leads to economically inefficient overconsumption of rivalrous goods. Naturally occurring resources are especially susceptible to the common property problem. Persons with access to the resource realize that what they do not consume will be consumed by someone else. Each person, therefore, has an incentive to consume the resource at a faster rate than if he or she had exclusive ownership. For instance, deforestation often results when a population relies on a common forest as a source of firewood. In addition to overconsumption, inefficiency may also result from misuse of the resource in consumption and underinvestment in its management.[17] With respect to common forests, the availability of underpriced firewood does not give consumers the appropriate incentive to invest in stoves that use less wood; further, the fact that anyone can cut and gather wood discourages individuals from replanting or nurturing trees.

Figure 3.10 illustrates the efficiency losses associated with overconsumption when there is open access to a resource. The marginal social benefit schedule *(MSB)* represents the horizontal summation (remember, we are dealing with a rivalrous good) of all the marginal benefit schedules of individuals. The economically efficient level of consumption, Q_0, results when marginal social cost *(MSC)* equals marginal social benefit. Each individual, however, takes account of only the costs that he or she directly bears, that is, marginal private costs *(MPC)*. This private marginal cost turns out to be the average cost for the group if marginal social cost is borne equally (that is, averaged) among consumers. With everyone rationally treating average group cost as their marginal cost, equilibrium consump-

[17]See Michael B. Wallace, "Managing Resources That Are Common Property: From Kathmandu to Capitol Hill," *Journal of Policy Analysis and Management*, Vol. 2, No. 2, Winter 1983, pp. 220–37.

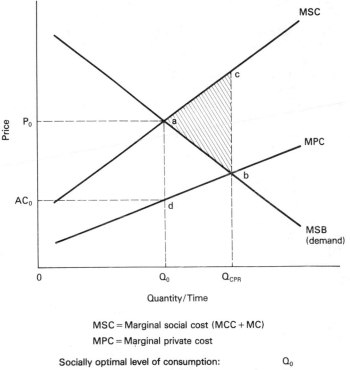

MSC = Marginal social cost (MCC + MC)
MPC = Marginal private cost

Socially optimal level of consumption: Q_0
Common property resource level of consumption: Q_{CPR}
Deadweight loss from overconsumption: abc

Figure 3.10   Overconsumption of Common Property Resources

tion will be at Q_{CPR}, which is greater than the economically efficient level Q_0. The shaded triangle *abc* measures the loss in social surplus that results from the overconsumption.

    A simple example may help clarify why individuals in common property situations have an incentive to respond to marginal private cost rather than marginal social cost. Imagine that you are in a restaurant with a group of ten people who have agreed to split the bill evenly. If you were paying your own tab, then you would not order the fancy dessert costing ten dollars unless you expected to get at least ten dollars' worth of value from eating it. But because the actual cost to you of the dessert will be one dollar (the average increase in your bill and for the bills of everyone else in the group, you would be rational (ignoring calories, your remaining stomach capacity, and social pressure) to consume it as long as it would give you at least one more dollar in value. You might continue ordering desserts until the value you placed on one more fell to one dollar. In other words, the individual's out-of-pocket cost for an additional dessert is the increment to his or her bill that is determined by the consumption averaged over the group. But this result is clearly inefficient because you and everyone else in the group could be made better off if you refrained from ordering the last dessert in return for a payment from the others of an amount between one dollar (your marginal private cost) and nine dollars (the difference between the marginal social cost and the marginal private cost that you perceive). Remember that the problem arises here because you have access to items on the menu at below their prices, which equal their social marginal costs.

Notice the similarity between the restaurant example and the bridge congestion example considered in our discussion of marketable public goods (quadrant NE2). In each case the inefficiency arises because individuals do not face prices that reflect the full social costs of their actions.

Natural resources (both renewable and nonrenewable) have the potential for yielding scarcity rents—returns in excess of the cost of production. If, because of open access, they are treated as common property, these rents may be completely dissipated. In Figure 3.10, for instance, consumption at the economically efficient level Q_0 would yield rent equal to the area of rectangle P_0adAC_0. The economically efficient harvesting of salmon, for example, requires catch limits that keep the market price above the marginal costs of harvesting. In the absence of exclusion, however, these rents may well be completely dissipated.[18] (At consumption level Q_{CPR} in Figure 3.10 there is no rent.) The reason is that fishermen will continue to enter the industry (and those already in will fish more intensively) as long as marginal private benefits—the rents they can capture—exceed marginal private costs. Just as in the restaurant example, each fisherman will ignore the marginal costs that his behavior imposes on other fishermen. If every fisherman is equally efficient, then his marginal private cost equals the average cost for the fishermen as a group. The question of how rent should be distributed is usually one of the most contentious issues in public policy. For example, how should the catch limits for salmon be divided among commercial, sport, and native fishermen? Nevertheless, from the perspective of economic efficiency someone should receive the scarcity rent, rather than allowing it to be wasted.

Of course, if a particular good is in excess supply at zero price, it does not make sense to talk of overconsumption. Goods in this category (SWI) are essentially "free." Thus, although they are theoretically rivalrous in consumption, for practical purposes, they are not.

Historically, free goods have been fairly common in North America, including such resources as buffalo, forests, aquifer water, and rangeland. Typically, however, the free goods eventually disappeared as demand increased and excess supply was eliminated.[19] Open access often led to rapid depletion and, in some cases, near destruction of the resource before effective exclusion was achieved. For example, open access permitted destruction of the Michigan, Wisconsin, and

---

[18]See, for example, L. G. Anderson, *The Economics of Fishery Management* (Baltimore: Johns Hopkins University Press, 1977).

[19]In the case of the American buffalo, the opening of the railroad facilitated the hunting and transportation of hides at much lower costs so that what had previously been a free good became a common property resource. For an economic analysis, see John Hanner, "Government Response to the Buffalo Hide Trade, 1871–1883," *Journal of Law and Economics,* Vol. 24, No. 2, October 1981, pp. 239–71.

Minnesota pine forests.[20] Nonexcludibility continues to be at the heart of many water use problems in the western United States.[21] When animal populations are treated as common property resources, the final result of overconsumption may be species extinction; such a result has already occurred with certain birds, and other animals with valuable skin or fur.

Thus far we have not specified the meaning of "feasible" exclusion. Many of the goods we have given as examples appear not to be inherently nonexcludible. Indeed, one of the most famous historical examples of a common property resource—open-access sheep and cattle grazing on the medieval English pasture—was "solved," willy-nilly, without overt government intervention, by the enclosure movement, which established property rights for estate holders. Similar enclosures appear to be currently taking place on tribal, historically open-access, lands in parts of Africa.

Although it simplifies a complex continuum, it is useful to dichotomize common property resource problems into those that are *structural* (where aspects of the goods preclude economically feasible exclusion mechanisms) and those that are *institutional* (where economically efficient exclusion mechanisms are feasible but the distribution of property rights precludes their implementation). The averaging of restaurant bills, which we previously discussed, serves as an excellent illustration of an institutional common property problem. We can imagine an obvious exclusion mechanism that we know from experience is economically feasible: separate bills for everyone. Institutional common property resource problems are usually not fundamentally market failures. Rather, they are most often due to the failure of government to allocate enforceable property rights.

Typically, the crucial factor in making a distinction between structural and institutional common property problems is whether or not the good displays *spatial stationarity*. Trees are spatially stationary, salmon are not, and bodies of water may or may not be. When resources are spatially stationary, their ownership can easily be attached to the ownership of land. Owners of the land will usually be able to monitor effectively all aspects of ownership and, consequently, ensure exclusive use. Given exclusion, common property resources become private resources that will be used in an economically efficient manner. Without spatial stationarity, ownership of land will not be a good proxy for low monitoring costs and the viability of enforcing exclusion. It does not necessarily follow that the common property problem could not be dealt with by some form of private ownership, but it does suggest that ownership of a defined piece of land or water will not be adequate to ensure exclusion. Allocating fishing rights to specific water acreage where the fish stock moves over considerable distances, or associating the rights to oil extraction to ownership of land when the oil pool extends under a large number of parcels, illustrate the difficulty of creating effective property rights for nonstationary resources.

[20]Andrew Dana and John Baden, "The New Resource Economics: Toward an Ideological Synthesis," *Policy Studies Journal,* Vol. 14, No. 2, December 1985, pp. 233–43.

[21]B. Delworth Gardner, "Institutional Impediments to Efficient Water Allocation," *Policy Studies Review,* Vol. 5, No. 2, November 1985, pp. 353–63. See also William Blomquist and Elinor Ostrom, "Institutional Capacity and the Resolution of a Commons Dilemma," *Policy Studies Review,* Vol. 5, No. 2, November 1985, pp. 283–93.

In summary, a stationary good may have common property resource characteristics simply because its ownership is not well defined, perhaps because of the historical accident that at one time supply exceeded demand at zero price. Nonstationary goods generally require more complex policy interventions to achieve efficiency because the linking of property rights to land ownership will not serve as an effective proxy for exclusive resource ownership of the resource.

Summary.   Returning to Figure 3.7, we summarize the efficiency implications of the various types of market failures involving public goods. To reprise, the major problem in the NE quadrant (nonrivalry, excludibility) is underconsumption arising from economically inefficient pricing rather than a lack of supply per se. Congestion usually further complicates these problems by introducing the need for variable pricing. In the SE quadrant (nonrivalry, nonexcludibility), the pervasiveness of free riding generally leads to no market supply at all. In specific circumstances (a privileged or intermediate group where one or a few persons account for a large fraction of demand), however, there may be some, and perhaps even nearly efficient, market supply. In the SW quadrant (rivalry, nonexcludibility), inefficiency results because individuals do not equate marginal benefits, but rather marginal private costs and marginal benefits; hence they overconsume common property resources.

Externalities

An *externality* is any valued impact (cost or benefit) resulting from any action (whether related to production or consumption) that affects someone who did not fully consent to it. We have already encountered a variety of externalities in our discussion of public goods—private supply of nonrivalrous goods by privileged and intermediate groups (a positive externality) and the divergence between private and social marginal cost in the use of congestible resources (a negative externality). We reserve the label *externality problem* for those situations where the good conveying the valued impact on nonconsenting parties is the by-product of either the production or consumption of some good.

As is the case with common property resources and ambient public goods, externality problems involve attenuated property rights because either the rights to exclusive use are incompletely specified or the costs of enforcing the rights are high relative to the benefits. Secure and enforceable property rights often permit private transactions to eliminate the economic inefficiency associated with externalities. We will return to this point after discussing a few examples.

Common examples of negative externalities include the air and water pollution generated by firms in their production activities, the cigarette smoke that nonsmokers must breathe in public places, and the unsightliness generated by a dilapidated house in a well-kept neighborhood. Persons who suffer these externalities place different values on them. For instance, I simply dislike the smell of cigarette smoke, but you may be allergic to it. Whereas I would be willing to pay only a small cost to avoid sitting near a smoker—say, waiting an extra ten minutes for a restaurant table in the nonsmoking section—you might be willing to pay considerably more—say, waiting thirty minutes or leaving the restaurant altogether. Note that we can think of placing a value on these externalities in the same way we do for the goods we voluntarily consume.

Economists often cite the pollination benefits that orchard owners derive from being located near beekeepers as an example of a positive externality. An example closer to home is the benefits that neighbors receive from a homeowner's manicured lawn and frequently painted house. (Although, to the extent it puts social pressure on one to pay more attention to these domestic activities than one would otherwise desire, the fastidious neighbor may be a source of negative externality!)

Externalities can arise in either production or consumption. Production externalities affect either firms (producer-to-producer externalities) or consumers (producer-to-consumer externalities); consumption externalities may also affect the activities of firms (consumer-to-producer externalities) or those of other consumers (consumer-to-consumer externalities). In this context, consumers as recipients of externalities includes everyone in society. Figure 3.11 provides simple examples of each type of externality. (Keep in mind that sometimes the same activity may constitute a positive externality for some but a negative externality for others.) Classifying a situation that potentially involves an externality is often a good way to begin considering its efficiency implications, distributional impacts, and, most importantly, possible remedies.

	Positive	Negative
Producer-to-producer	Warm water from nuclear power plant used by downstream fish farmers	Toxic chemical pollution harming downstream commercial fishing
Producer-to-consumer	Private timber forests providing scenic benefits to nature lovers	Air pollution from factories harming lungs of people living nearby
Consumer-to-consumer	Immunization by persons against contagious disease helping protect others	Cigarette smoke from one person reducing enjoyment of meal by another
Consumer-to-producer	Unsolicited letters from consumers providing information on product quality	Disturbing of domestic farm animals by game hunters

Figure 3.11   Examples of Externalities

Efficiency Losses of Negative and Positive Externalities.   Figure 3.12 illustrates the resource allocation effects of a negative externality in production. In the presence of a negative externality, firms will produce too much of the private good that generates the externality. The market supply schedule for the private good, S, indicates the marginal costs borne directly by the firms producing it. For example, if the private good were electricity, S would represent the marginal amounts firms have to pay for the coal, labor, and other things that show up in

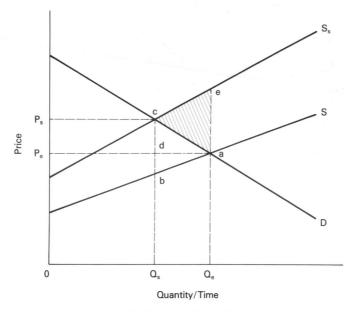

Social Surplus at Q_e Relative to Q_s

Consumer surplus from private good: larger by $P_s caP_e$
Producer surplus of firms producing private good: smaller by ($P_s cdP_e$ – abd)
Consumer surplus of those bearing externality: smaller by abce
Net social surplus loss from overproduction of private good: ace

Figure 3.12   Overproduction with a Negative Externality

their ledgers. But S does not reflect the negative impacts of the pollution that results from burning the coal. If somehow we could find out how much each person in society would be willing to pay to avoid the pollution at each output level, then we could add these amounts to the marginal costs actually seen by the firms to derive a supply schedule that reflected total social marginal costs. We represent this more inclusive supply schedule as S_S.

Economic efficiency requires that social marginal benefits and social marginal costs be equal at the selected output level—this occurs at quantity Q_s where supply (S_s) and demand (D) intersect. But because firms do not consider the external costs of their output, they choose output level Q_e at the intersection of S and D. Relative to output level Q_5, consumers of the private good being produced gain surplus equal to area $P_s caP_e$ (because they get quantity Q_e at price P_e rather than quantity Q_s at price P_s) and producers lose surplus equal to area $P_s cdP_e$ minus area *abd* (the first area captures the effect of the lower price, the second the effect of greater output). Those who bear the external costs, however, suffer a loss given by the area *abce* (the area between the market and social supply curves over the output difference—remember, the vertical distance between the supply curves represents the external marginal cost). The net loss in social surplus is the area of triangle *ace,* the algebraic sum of the surplus differences for the consumers and producers of the private good and the bearers of the externality. (This net social surplus loss is simply the deadweight loss due to the overproduction—the area between S_s and D from Q_s to Q_e.) In other words, Pareto efficiency requires a reduction in output from the equilibrium level in the market (Q_e) to the level where marginal social costs equal marginal social benefits (Q_s).

Turning to positive externalities, we can think of the private good generating benefits that cannot be captured by the producer. For example, firms that plant trees for future harvesting may provide a scenic benefit for which they receive no compensation. In Figure 3.13 we illustrate the demand schedule for the private good (trees for future harvest) as D. At each forest size, however, the social marginal benefit schedule would equal the market demand plus the amounts that viewers would be willing to pay to have the forest expanded by another unit. D_s labels the social marginal benefit schedule, which includes both the private and external marginal benefits. Equilibrium results at output level Q_e, where the market demand schedule and the supply schedule intersect. But if output were raised to Q_s, consumer surplus would increase by area acd (resulting from increased consumption from Q_e to Q_s) minus area $P_s cbP_e$ (due to the price rise from P_e to P_s), and producer surplus would increase by area $P_s abP_e$. The net increase in social surplus, therefore, would be area abd. Again, we see that in the case of an externality we can find a reallocation that increases social surplus and thereby offers the possibility of a Pareto improvement.

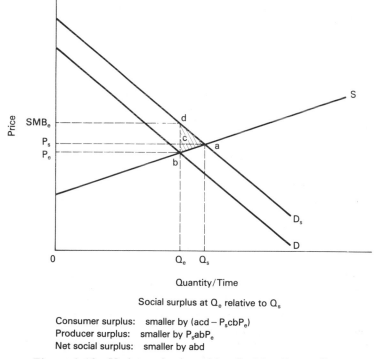

Social surplus at Q_e relative to Q_s

Consumer surplus: smaller by (acd − $P_s cbP_e$)
Producer surplus: smaller by $P_s abP_e$
Net social surplus: smaller by abd

Figure 3.13 Underproduction with a Positive Externality

Market Responses to Externalities.   Will the market always fail to provide an efficient output level in the presence of externalities? Just as pure public goods will sometimes be provided at efficient, or nearly efficient, levels through voluntary private agreements, so too may private actions counter the inefficiency associated with externalities. The relevance of such private responses was first pointed out by Ronald Coase in a seminal article on the externality problem.[22] He argued that in situations where property rights are clearly defined and costless to enforce, bargaining among participants will lead to an economically efficient level of external effect. Of course, the distribution of costs and benefits resulting from the bargaining depends on who owns the property rights.

Before exploring the issue further, we must stress a very restrictive assumption of Coase's model that limits its applicability to many actual externality situations. Namely, Coase assumes zero transaction costs in the exercise of property rights. In many real-world situations, transaction costs are high usually because those producing or experiencing the externality are numerous. With large numbers of actors, the bargaining that produces the Coasian outcome becomes impossible because of the high costs of coordination in the face of opportunities for a free ride.

Nevertheless, Coase's insight is valuable. He pointed out that in the case of small numbers (he assumes one source and one recipent of the externality), the allocation of property rights alone would lead to a negotiated (that is, private) outcome that is economically efficient. Efficiency results whether a complete property right is given to the externality generator (one bears no liability for damages caused by one's externality) or to the recipient of the externality (one bears full liability for damages caused by one's externality). Either rule should lead to a bargain being reached at the same level of externality; only the distribution of wealth will vary, depending on which rule has force.

A moment's thought should suggest why large numbers will make a Coasian solution unlikely. Bargaining would have to involve many parties, some of whom would have an incentive to engage in strategic behavior. For example, in the case of a polluter with no liability for damages, those experiencing the pollution may fear free riding by others. In addition, firms may engage in opportunistic behavior, threatening to generate more pollution to induce payments. Under full liability, individuals would have an incentive to overstate the harm they suffer. Other things equal, we expect that the greater the number of parties experiencing the externality, the greater will be the costs of monitoring damage claims.

Nevertheless, private cooperation appears effective in some situations. For instance, neighborhood associations sometimes do agree on mutually restrictive covenants, and individual neighbors occasionally do reach contractual agreements on such matters as light easements (which deal with the externalities of the shadows cast by buildings).

Moreover, there is an important case where Coase-like solutions do arise, even with large numbers of parties—namely, where (1) property rights become implicitly established by usage; (2) the value of the externality (whether positive or negative) is captured by (more technically, "capitalized into") land values; (3) considerable time has passed such that the initial stock of external parties has "rolled over"; and (4) externality levels remain stable. The relevance of these

---

[22]"The Problem of Social Cost," *Journal of Law and Economics*, Vol. 3, No. 1, 1960, pp. 1–44.

conditions can best be explained with an example. Suppose that a factory has been polluting the surrounding area for many years without anyone challenging its owners' rights to do so. It is probable that the pollution will result in lower property values. Residents who bought before the pollution was anticipated will have to sell their houses for less—reflecting the impact of the pollution. New homeowners, however, will not be bearing any Pareto-relevant externality, because the negative impact of the pollution will be capitalized into house prices. The lower prices of the houses will reflect the market's (negative) valuation of the pollution. In other words, through the house price it is possible to get a proxy dollar measure of the disutility of pollution. Notice that a second generation of homeowners (that is, those who bought houses after the pollution was known and capitalized into prices) would receive a bonus if the existing allocation of property rights were changed so that the factory had to compensate current homeowners for existing levels of pollution. Of course, if there are unexpected changes in the level of pollution (or new information about the harmful impacts of the pollution—see our discussion of information asymmetry below), there will be in effect new (either positive or negative) impacts; in these situations, considerable argument is likely to occur over who has right to compensation for the changes.

Natural Monopoly

Natural monopoly occurs when the fixed costs of providing a good are high relative to the variable cost so that average cost declines over the relevant range of demand. Note the two elements of the definition of natural monopoly: declining average cost, and relevant range of demanded output. The second condition distinguishes natural monopoly from situations involving economies of scale per se. If both these conditions are met, then a single firm can produce the particular output, or set of outputs, at lower cost than any other market arrangement, including competition.

While the cost-and-demand conditions establish the existence of a natural monopoly situation, the *price elasticity of demand* determines whether or not the natural monopoly has important implications for public policy. The price elasticity of demand measures how responsive consumers are to price changes. Specifically, the price elasticity of demand is defined as the percentage change in the quantity demanded (measured in percentage points) that results from a one-percentage-point change in price.[23] If the absolute value of the price elasticity of demand is less than one (a one-percent change in price leads to less than a one-percent reduction in the quantity demanded), then we say that demand is inelastic and an increase in price will increase total revenue. A good is unlikely to have inelastic demand if there are other products that, while not exactly the same, are close substitutes. In such circumstances, the availability of substitutes greatly limits the economic inefficiency associated with natural monopoly. For example, although local cable television markets seem to have the cost-and-demand characteristics

---

[23]Mathematically, if the demand schedule is continuous, the price elasticity of demand at some quantity equals the slope of the demand schedule at that quantity times the ratio of quantity to price. For example, with linear demand schedule, $Q = a - bP$, the slope of the demand schedule (the derivative dQ/dP) is $- b$. Therefore, the price elasticity of demand is $e = -bQ/P$. Note that the elasticity of a linear demand schedule varies over quantity.

of natural monopolies, many substitute products, including conventional over-the-air television, video tape recorders (and, arguably, all other forms of entertainment) may prevent the cable television companies from realizing large monopoly rents.

We should also keep in mind that, although we stated the basic definition of natural monopoly in static terms, markets in the real world are dynamic. Thus, if market conditions alter—say because technological change leads to different cost characteristics or high prices bring on better substitutes—the natural monopoly conditions may disappear.

We show a cost structure leading to natural monopoly in Figure 3.14. Marginal cost *(MC)* is shown as constant over the range of output. Fixed cost *(FC)*, which is not shown on the figure, must be incurred before any output can be supplied. Because of the fixed cost, average cost starts higher than marginal cost and falls toward it as the output level increases. *(AC = MC + FC/Q*, where *Q* is the output level.) Although marginal cost is shown as constant, the same analysis would apply even if marginal cost were rising or falling, provided that it remains small relative to fixed cost.

Allocative Inefficiency under Natural Monopoly.   Figure 3.14 shows the incongruity between the firm's profit-maximizing behavior and economic efficiency. Let us first consider the economically efficient price and output. Efficiency requires, as we have already discussed, that price be set equal to marginal cost (that is, $P = MC$). Because marginal cost is below average cost, the economically efficient output level, Q_0, results in the firm suffering a loss equal to *FC*. Obviously, the firm would not choose this output level on its own. Instead, it would maximize profits by selecting output level Q_m, which equates marginal revenue to marginal cost *(MR = MC)*. At output level Q_m, the market price will be P_m and profits equal to the area of rectangle $P_m cbP_0$ − *FC* will result. Relative to output level Q_0, consumer surplus is lower by the area of $P_m caP_0$, but the profit of the firm is larger by $P_m cbP_0$. The net loss in social surplus due to the underproduction just equals the area of the shaded triangle *abc,* the deadweight loss to consumers. (As noted in our discussion of Figure 3.4, units of forgone output would have offered marginal benefits in excess of marginal costs—a total loss equal to the area between the marginal benefit, or demand schedule, and the marginal cost curve. In Figure 3.14, this loss is the area of triangle *abc.*)

Natural monopoly presents a curious outcome. An unconstrained market process results in the good being supplied by only one firm that could not survive if it produced at the economically efficient level. We might briefly consider what would happen if the firm priced at average, rather than marginal, cost; that is, if the firm priced at P_{AC} and produced Q_{AC} in Figure 3.14. Clearly, under these circumstances the firm can survive because its costs are now being just covered. (Note that FC equals P_{AC} *efP$_0$.*) Although the deadweight loss under average cost pricing is much lower than under monopoly pricing (areas *aef* versus area *abc*), it is not eliminated.

Restraints When Markets Are Contestable.   We can imagine circumstances where the natural monopoly firm might, in fact, be forced to price at

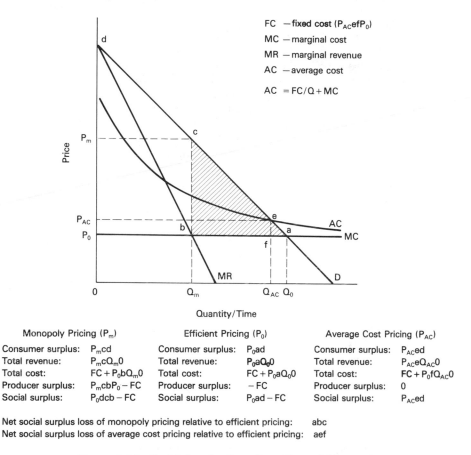

<table>
<tr><td>FC</td><td>—fixed cost ($P_{AC}efP_0$)</td></tr>
<tr><td>MC</td><td>—marginal cost</td></tr>
<tr><td>MR</td><td>—marginal revenue</td></tr>
<tr><td>AC</td><td>—average cost</td></tr>
<tr><td>AC</td><td>$= FC/Q + MC$</td></tr>
</table>

Monopoly Pricing (P_m)		Efficient Pricing (P_0)		Average Cost Pricing (P_{AC})	
Consumer surplus:	$P_m cd$	Consumer surplus:	$P_0 ad$	Consumer surplus:	$P_{AC} ed$
Total revenue:	$P_m cQ_m 0$	Total revenue:	$P_0 aQ_0 0$	Total revenue:	$P_{AC} eQ_{AC} 0$
Total cost:	$FC + P_0 bQ_m 0$	Total cost:	$FC + P_0 aQ_0 0$	Total cost:	$FC + P_0 fQ_{AC} 0$
Producer surplus:	$P_m cbP_0 - FC$	Producer surplus:	$- FC$	Producer surplus:	0
Social surplus:	$P_0 dcb - FC$	Social surplus:	$P_0 ad - FC$	Social surplus:	$P_{AC} ed$

Net social surplus loss of monopoly pricing relative to efficient pricing: abc
Net social surplus loss of average cost pricing relative to efficient pricing: aef

Figure 3.14   Social Surplus Loss from Natural Monopoly

average cost because of the threat of competition from potential entrants. The crucial requirement is that entry to, and exit from, the industry be relatively easy. Whether or not the firm has in-place capital that has no alternative use usually determines the viability of potential entry and exit. If the established natural monopoly has a large stock of productive capital that cannot be sold for use in other industries, it will be difficult for other firms to compete because they must first incur cost to catch up with the established firm's capital advantage. The in-place capital serves as a barrier to entry; the greater the replacement cost of such capital, the higher the barrier to entry. For example, once a petroleum pipeline is built between two cities, its scrap value is likely to be substantially less than the costs a potential competitor would face in building a second pipeline. The greater the difference, the greater is the ability of the established firm to fight off an entry attempt with temporarily lower prices. Of course, keep in mind that the ability of the firm to charge above the marginal cost level will be influenced by the marginal costs of alternative transportation modes such as truck and rail.

Much recent economic research considers industries with low barriers to entry and decreasing average costs, which, because of the threat of potential entry, are said to be in *contestable markets*.[24] We expect markets that are contestable to exhibit pricing closer to the efficient level. One of the most important debates in the literature arising from the contestable market framework concerns the empirical significance of in-place capital as effective barriers to entry.[25] Most natural monopolies appear to enjoy large advantages in in-place capital, raising the question of whether or not they should be viewed as being in contestable markets.

As we have seen, the "naturalness" of a monopoly is determined by decreasing average cost over the relevant range of output. In many situations it appears that average cost declines over considerable ranges of output, but then flattens out. What happens if demand shifts to the right (for example, with population increases) such that the demand curve intersects the flat portion of the average cost curve? There may be considerable room for competition under these circumstances.[26] Figure 3.15 illustrates such a situation. If demand is only D_1 (the "classic" natural monopoly), only one firm can survive in the market. If demand shifts outward beyond D_2 to, say, D_3, then two or more firms may be able to survive.

Simply because several firms could survive at D_3 does not mean that three competing firms will actually emerge as demand expands. If the original natural-monopoly firm expands as demand moves out, it may be able to forestall new entrants and capture all of the market. Nevertheless, we are again reminded of the importance of looking beyond the static view.

When considering natural monopoly from a policy perspective, we sometimes find that legal and regulatory boundaries do not correspond to the boundaries delineating natural monopoly goods. Most discussion of industrial issues tends to be within the framework of product "sectors," such as the electric and the telephone industries. Unfortunately, the economic boundaries of natural monopolies are not likely to conform to these neat sectoral boundaries. Historically, regulation has often not recognized this unpleasant fact. In addition, the existence, or extent, of a natural monopoly can change as production technology or demand changes.

The telecommunications industry illustrates these definitional problems. In

---

[24]William J. Baumol, John C. Panzar, and Robert D. Willig, *Contestable Markets and the Theory of Industry Structure* (New York: Harcourt Brace Jovanovich, 1982); and William J. Baumol, "Contestable Markets: An Uprising in the Theory of Industry Structure," *American Economic Review*, Vol. 72, No. 1, March 1982, pp. 1–15. For a discussion of *imperfect contestability*, see Steven A. Morrison and Clifford Winston, "Empirical Implications and Tests of the Contestability Hypothesis," *Journal of Law and Economics*, Vol. 30, No. 1, April 1987, pp. 53–66.

[25]For evidence that the U.S. Postal Service, for example, may have few natural monopoly characteristics, see Alan L. Sorkin, *The Economics of the Postal Service* (Lexington, Mass.: Lexington Books, 1980), Chapter 4; Leonard Waverman, "Pricing Principles: How Should Postal Rates Be Set?" in *Perspectives on Postal Services Issues,* Roger Sherman, ed., (Washington, D.C.: American Enterprise Institute, 1980), pp. 7–26.

[26]William G. Shepherd, "Public Enterprises: Purposes and Performance," in W. T. Stanbury and Fred Thompson, eds., *Managing Public Enterprises* (New York: Praeger, 1982), pp. 13–50 at 34.

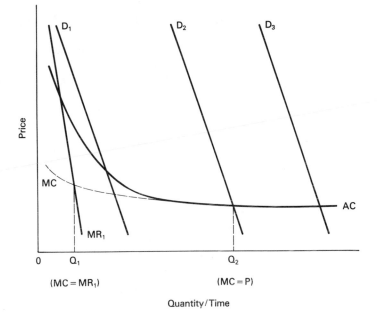

Figure 3.15   Shifting Demand and Multiple Firm Survival. *Source:* William G. Shepherd, *The Economics of Industrial Organization* (Englewood Cliffs, N.J.: Prentice Hall, 1979), fig. 3.4, p. 59.

1982 the U.S. Justice Department and AT&T agreed on a plan for the breakup of the corporation. The agreement called for a division into two parts: that part which could be expected to be workably contestable and that part which had strong natural monopoly elements. Both long-distance services (contestable) and equipment manufacture and supply (competitive) were largely deregulated, while local telephone exchanges were deemed to be regional natural monopolies.[27] Similar problems with sectoral definitions have not been well recognized in other contexts, however. For example, electricity generation and transmission have typically been treated as part of an electrical utility natural monopoly, although the evidence suggests that in many circumstances only transmission has the required cost-and-demand characteristics to be considered a natural monopoly.[28] (Running multiple sets of transmission lines across the countryside would generally be inefficient; having multiple firms generating electricity would not be.)

[27]Kenneth Robinson, "Maximizing the Public Benefits of the AT&T Breakup," *Journal of Policy Analysis and Management,* Vol. 5, No. 3, Spring 1986, pp. 572–97. For discussion of technological change that eroded the natural monopoly characteristics of telephone services, see Irwin Manley, *Telecommunications America: Markets Without Boundaries* (Westport, Conn.: Quorum, 1984).

[28]For the case against treating any aspects of the electric industy as a natural monopoly, see Robert W. Poole, Jr., *Unnatural Monopolies: The Case for Deregulating Public Utilities* (Lexington, Mass.: Lexington Books, 1985).

Another dimension, apart from the sectoral, where the problem of defining natural monopoly arises is the spatial. Over what spatial area does the natural monopoly exist? Almost all natural monopoly regulation corresponds to existing city, county, state, or federal boundaries; but the economic reality of a natural monopoly knows no such bounds—it is purely an empirical question how far (spatially) the natural monopoly extends. Again, the appropriate spatial boundaries of a natural monopoly can change with changes in technology.

X-Inefficiency Resulting from Limited Competition.   Thus far we have described the potential social costs of natural monopoly, whether it prices to either maximize profits or cover cost, in terms of deadweight loss caused by allocational inefficiency. The social costs, however, may be larger because natural monopolies do not face as strong incentives as competitive firms to operate at minimum cost. One of the greatest advantages of a competitive market is that it forces firms to keep their costs down—in other words, the whole average cost curve is as low as it can possibly be. In the absence of competition, firms may be able to survive without operating at minimum cost. Harvey Leibenstein has coined the phrase *X-inefficiency* to describe the situation in which a monopoly does not achieve the minimum costs that are technically feasible.[29] (As we shall see, X-inefficiency is not fully descriptive because transfers as well as technical inefficiencies are often involved.)

In Figure 3.16 we incorporate X-inefficiency into the basic analysis of monopoly pricing. But first suppose that we ignore X-inefficiency for a moment. The deadweight loss associated with a profit-maximizing natural monopoly appears as the shaded triangular area *abc* (already discussed in Figure 3.14 above). If we take X-inefficiency into account, however, the minimum possible marginal cost curve is lower than that observed from the behavior of the firm. The actual deadweight loss, therefore, is the triangular loss *abc* plus a portion of the other shaded area *abtl*.

Additionally, the shaded area *ubtv* represents unnecessary cost that should be counted as either producer surplus or deadweight loss. If marginal costs are higher than the minimum because the managers of the firms employ more real resources such as hiring workers who stand idle, then the shaded area should be thought of as a social surplus loss. If, on the other hand, costs are higher because the managers pay themselves and their workers higher than necessary wages, we should consider the shaded area as rent—it represents unnecessary payments rather than the misuse of real resources. If, however, potential employees and managers spend time or other resources attempting to secure the rent (say, by enduring periods of unemployment while waiting for one of the overpaid jobs to open up), the rent may be converted to deadweight loss. We will encounter the problems of X-inefficiency and rent seeking again in our discussion of government failures in the next chapter.

In summary, natural monopoly inherently involves the problem of undersupply by the market. The extent of undersupply depends on the particular cost-and-demand conditions facing the monopolist, and the extent to which the market

---

[29]For a full analysis of X-inefficiency, see Harvey J. Leibenstein, *Beyond Economic Man* (Cambridge, Mass.: Harvard University Press, 1976).

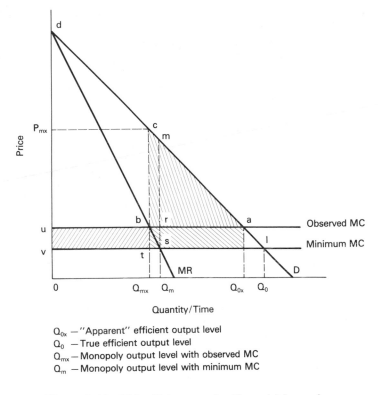

Price

Quantity/Time

Q_{0x} — "Apparent" efficient output level
Q_0 — True efficient output level
Q_{mx} — Monopoly output level with observed MC
Q_m — Monopoly output level with minimum MC

Figure 3.16   X-Inefficiency under Natural Monopoly

can be contested. Natural monopoly may involve additional social surplus losses because the absence of competition permits production at greater than minimum cost to persist.

Information Asymmetry

Please note that we do not use the title "information costs" or "imperfect information" in this section. The reason is that information is involved in market failure in at least two distinct ways. First, information itself has public good characteristics. Consumption of information is nonrivalrous—one person's consumption does not interfere with another's; the relevant analytical question is primarily whether exclusion is or is not possible. Thus, in the public goods context we are interested in the production and consumption of information itself. Second—and the subject of our discussion here—there may be situations where the amount of information about the characteristics of a good varies in relevant ways across persons. The buyer and the seller in a market transaction, for example, may have different information about the quality of the good being traded. Similarly, there may be differences in the level of information relating to the attributes of an externality between the generator of the externality and the affected party—workers, for instance, may not be as well informed about the health risks of industrial chemicals as their employers. Notice that in this context we are not primarily interested in information as a good, but in the degree of asymmetry in the information relevant parties have about any good. We thus distinguish between information *as* a good (the public good case) and information *about* a good's attributes as distributed between buyer and seller or between externality generator and affected party (the *information asymmetry* case).

Inefficiency Due to Information Asymmetry.   Figure 3.17 illustrates the potential social surplus loss associated with information asymmetry.[30] D_U represents the quantities of some good that a consumer would purchase at various prices in the absence of perfect information about its quality. It can therefore be thought of as the consumer's uninformed demand schedule. D_I represents the consumer's informed demand schedule—the amounts of the good that would be purchased at various prices if the consumer were perfectly informed about its quality. The quantity actually purchased by the uninformed consumer is determined by the intersection of D_U with the supply schedule, S. This amount, q_U, is greater than q_I, the amount that the consumer would have purchased if fully informed about the quality of the good. The shaded area *abc* equals the deadweight loss in consumer surplus resulting from the over-consumption. (For each unit purchased beyond q_I, the consumer pays more than its marginal value as measured by the height of the informed demand schedule.) This over consumption also results in a higher equilibrium price (P_U) which transfers surplus equal to the area $P_U baP_I$ from the consumer to the producer of the good. Figure 3.17 signals the presence of information asymmetry if the producer could have informed the consumer about the true quality of the good at a cost less than the deadweight loss in consumer surplus resulting when the consumer remains uninformed. More generally, we have market failure due to information asymmetry when the producer does not supply the amount of information that maximizes the difference between the reduction in deadweight loss and the cost of providing the information.

The same sort of reasoning would apply if the consumer underestimated rather than overestimated the quality of the good. The consumer would suffer a deadweight loss resulting from consuming less than q_I. The incentives that the producer faces to provide the information, however, can be quite different in the two cases. In the case where the consumer overestimates quality, providing information results in a lower price and therefore a smaller transfer of surplus from the consumer to the producer—an apparent disincentive to provide the information. In the case where the consumer underestimates quality, providing information results in a higher price that increases producer surplus—the prospect of this gain may encourage the producer to supply information. As we discuss later,

---

[30]The basic analysis was introduced by Sam Peltzman, "An Evaluation of Consumer Protection Legislation: The 1962 Drug Amendments," *Journal of Political Economy*, Vol. 81, No. 5, September/October 1973, pp. 1049–91. For a discussion of the empirical problems one encounters in using this approach when some consumers overestimate and others underestimate the quality of some good, see Thomas McGuire, Richard Nelson, and Thomas Spavins, " 'An Evaluation of Consumer Protection Legislation: The 1962 Drug Amendments': A Comment," *Journal of Political Economy*, Vol. 83, No. 3, June 1975, pp. 655–61.

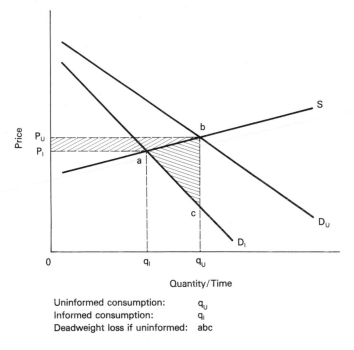

Uninformed consumption: q_U
Informed consumption: q_I
Deadweight loss if uninformed: abc

Figure 3.17   Consumer Surplus Loss from Uninformed Demand

however, this incentive to provide information can be muted if producers are unable to get consumers to distinguish their products from those of competitors.

Diagnosing Information Asymmetry.   Our first task in deciding when information asymmetry is likely to lead to market failure is to classify goods into useful categories. Economists have generally divided goods into two categories: *search goods* and *experience goods*.[31] A good is a search good if consumers can determine its characteristics with certainty prior to purchase. For example, a chair is a search good because consumers can judge its quality through inspection prior to purchase. A good is an experience good if consumers can determine its characteristics only after purchase; examples include meals, hair styling, concerts, legal services, and used automobiles. We add a third category, which we call *post-experience goods*, to distinguish those goods for which it is difficult for consumers to determine quality even after they have begun consumption. For example, people may fail to associate adverse health effects with drugs that they are consuming. Experience goods and post-experience goods differ primarily in terms of how effectively consumers can learn about quality through consumption. After some period of consumption, the quality of the experience goods generally becomes ap-

---

[31]The distinction between search and experience goods was introduced by Philip Nelson, "Information and Consumer Behavior," *Journal of Political Economy*, Vol. 78, No. 2, March/April 1970, pp. 311–29. His work followed the pioneering work on price dispersion of George J. Stigler, "The Economics of Information," *Journal of Political Economy*, Vol. 69, No. 3, June 1961, pp. 213–25.

parent; in contrast, continued consumption does not necessarily reveal to consumers the quality of the post-experience good.

Within these three categories, a number of other factors help determine whether information asymmetry is likely to lead to serious market failure. The effectiveness of any information-gathering strategy, other things equal, generally depends on the *variance in the quality* of units of a good (heterogeneity) and the *frequency* with which consumers make purchases. The potential costs of the information asymmetry to consumers depend on the extent to which they perceive the *full price* of the good, including imputed costs of harm from use.[32] The *cost of searching* for candidate purchases and the full price determine how expensive and potentially beneficial it is for consumers to gather information.

Search Goods.   Searching can be thought of as a sampling process in which consumers incur costs to inspect units of a good. A consumer pays a cost C_s to see a particular combination of price and quality. If the price exceeds the consumer's marginal value for the good, no purchase is made and the consumer either again pays C_s to see another combination of price and quality or stops sampling. If the consumer's marginal valuation exceeds price, then the consumer either makes a purchase or pays C_s again in expectation of finding a more favorable good in terms of the excess of marginal value over price. When C_s is zero, the consumer will find it advantageous to take a large sample and discover the complete distribution of available price and quality combinations so that the pre-search information asymmetry disappears. For larger C_s, however, the consumer will take smaller samples, other things equal, so that information asymmetry may remain. Additionally, because the range in price for a given quality is likely to be positively correlated with price, optimal sample sizes will be smaller the larger the ratio of C_s to expected price.

The more heterogeneous the available combinations of price and quality, the more likely that the consumer will fail to discover a more favorable choice for any given sample size. In contrast, even small samples will eliminate information asymmetry if the price and quality combinations are highly homogeneous. Once consumers realize that nearly identical units are offered at the same price, the optimal sample size falls to one.

Going beyond a static view, the frequency of purchase becomes important in determining whether information asymmetry remains. If the frequency of purchase is high relative to the rate at which the underlying distribution of combinations of price and quality changes, then consumers accumulate information over time that reduces the magnitude of the information asymmetry. If the frequency of purchase is low relative to the rate of change in the underlying distribution, then accumulated information will not necessarily lead to reductions in informa-

---

[32]A formal specification of the concept of full price is provided by Walter Oi, "The Economics of Product Safety," *Bell Journal of Economics and Management Science,* Vol. 4, No. 1, Spring 1973, pp. 3–28. He considers the situation where a consumer buys X units of a good at price P per unit. If the probability that any one unit is defective is 1-q, then on average the consumer expects $Z = qX$ good units. If each bad unit inflicts on average damage equal to W, then the expected total cost of purchase is $C = PX + W(X - Z)$ which implies a full price per good unit of $P^* = C/Z = P/q + W(1 - q)/q$.

tion asymmetry. In either case, however, frequent purchasers may become more experienced searchers so that C_s falls and larger samples become efficient.

Thus, if search costs are small relative to the expected purchase price *or* the distribution of price and quality combinations is fairly homogeneous *or* the frequency of purchase is high relative to the rate of change in the distribution of price and quality combinations, then information asymmetry is unlikely to lead to significant inefficiency. In the case where search costs are high relative to the expected purchase price, the distribution of price and quality combinations is very heterogeneous, and the frequency of purchase is relatively low, information asymmetry may lead to significant inefficiency. But, if it is possible for producers to distinguish their products by brand, they have an incentive to undertake informative advertising that reduces search costs for consumers. When brands are difficult to establish, as in the case of, say, farm produce, retailers may act as agents for consumers by advertising prices and qualities. Because the veracity of such advertising can be readily determined by consumers through inspection of the goods, and because retailers and firms offering brand name products have an incentive to maintain favorable reputations, we expect the advertising generally to convey accurate and useful information.

In summary, search goods rarely involve information asymmetry that leads to significant and persistent inefficiency. When inefficiency does occur, it takes the form of consumers' forgoing purchases that they would have preferred to ones that they nevertheless found beneficial. From the perspective of public policy, intervention in markets for search goods can rarely be justified on efficiency grounds.

Experience Goods: Primary Markets.   Consumers can determine the quality of experience goods with certainty only through consumption. To sample, they must bear the search costs, C_s, and the full price, P^*, (the purchase price plus the expected loss of failure or damage collateral with consumption).[33] The full price of consuming a meal at an unfamiliar restaurant, for instance, is the sum of purchase price (determined from the menu) and the expected cost of any adverse health effects (ranging from indigestion to poisoning) from the meal being defective. Of course, even when the expected collateral loss is zero, prior to consumption, the marginal value that the consumer places on the meal is not known with certainty.

In contrast to search goods where, holding search costs constant, consumers optimally take larger samples for more expensive goods, they optimally take smaller samples for more expensive experience goods. Indeed, for all but the very inexpensive experience goods, we expect sampling (equivalent to the frequency of purchase for experience goods) to be governed primarily by durability. For example, sampling to find desirable restaurants will generally be more frequent than sampling to find good used automobiles.

As is the case with search goods, the more heterogeneous the quality of an experience good, the greater is the potential for inefficiency due to information

---

[33]In our discussion of information asymmetry, we assume that consumers cannot sue producers for damages. (In other words, they do not enjoy a property right to safety.) As we discuss in Chapter 5 under "framework regulation," tort and contract law often reduce the inefficiency of information asymmetry by deterring parties from withholding relevant information in market transactions.

asymmetry. The consumption of an experience good, however, may involve more than simply forgoing a more favorable purchase of the good. Once consumption reveals quality, the consumer may discover that the good provides less marginal value than its price and therefore regret having made the purchase regardless of the availability of alternative units of the good. The realized marginal value may actually be negative if consumption causes harm.

Learning from the consumption of experience goods varies in effectiveness. If the quality of the good is homogeneous and stable, then learning is complete after the first consumption—consumers know how much marginal value they will derive from their next purchase including the expected loss from product failure or collateral damage. If the quality is heterogeneous or unstable, then learning proceeds more slowly. Unless consumers can segment the good into more homogeneous groupings, say by brands or reputations of sellers, learning may result only in better *ex ante* estimates of the mean and variance of their *ex post* marginal valuations. When consumers can segment the good into stable and homogeneous groupings, repeated sampling helps them discover their most preferred sources of the good in terms of the mean and variance of quality. For example, national motel chains with reputations for standardized management practices may provide travelers with a low variance alternative to independent motels in unfamiliar locales.

In what situations can informative advertising play an important role in reducing information asymmetry? Generally, informative advertising can be effective when consumers correctly believe that sellers have a stake in maintaining reputations for providing reliable information. A seller who invests heavily in developing a brand name with a favorable reputation is more likely to provide accurate and useful information than an unknown firm selling a new product or an individual owner selling a house or used automobile.

When consumers perceive that sellers do not have a stake in maintaining a good reputation, and marginal cost of supply rises with quality, then a "lemons" problem may arise: consumers perceive a full price based on average quality so that only sellers of lower than average quality goods can make a profit and survive in the market.[34] In the extreme, producers offer only goods of low quality.[35]

When reliability is an important element of quality, firms may offer warranties that promise to compensate consumers for a portion of replacement costs, collateral damage, or both. The warranties thus provide consumers with insurance against low quality: higher purchase prices include an implicit insurance premium and the potential loss from product failure is reduced. The quality of a warranty may itself be uncertain, however, if consumers do not know how readily firms honor their promises. Further, firms may find it impractical to offer extensive warranties in situations where it is costly to monitor the care taken by consumers.

---

[34]The "lemons" argument originated with George Akerlof, "The Market for Lemons," *Quarterly Journal of Economics,* Vol. 84, No. 3, August 1970, pp. 488–500.

[35]Economists have recently considered the role of expenditures to establish reputation as a means for high quality producers to distinguish themselves. See, for instance, Benjamin Klein and Keith B. Leffler, "The Role of Market Forces in Assuring Contractural Performance," *Journal of Political Economy,* Vol. 89, No. 4, August 1981, pp. 615–41; and Paul Milgrom and John Roberts, "Price and Advertising Signals of Product Quality," *Journal of Political Economy,* Vol. 94, No. 4, August 1986, pp. 796–21.

Nevertheless, warranties serve as a common device for reducing the consequences of information asymmetry for experience goods.

Experience Goods: The Role of Secondary Markets.   Producers and consumers often turn to private third parties to help remedy information asymmetry problems. Certification services, agents, subscription services, and loss control by insurers are the most common market responses that arise.

Certification services "guarantee" minimum quality standards in processes or products. Professional associations, for instance, often set minimum standards of training or experience for their members—the broad certified specialities in medicine are examples. Perhaps closer to most people's experience, the Better Business Bureau requires members to adhere to a code of fair business practices. Underwriters Laboratory tests products against minimum fire safety standards before giving its seal of approval. When such services establish their own credibility, they help producers to distinguish their goods satisfying the minimum standards from goods that do not.

Agents often sell advice about the qualities of expensive, infrequently purchased, heterogeneous goods. These agents combine expertise with learning from being participants in a large number of transactions between different pairs of buyers and sellers. For example, most people do not frequently purchase houses, which are expensive and heterogenous in quality. Because owners typically enjoy an informational advantage by virtue of their experiences living in their houses, prospective buyers often turn to engineers and architects to help assess structural integrity. Art and antique dealers, jewelers, and general contractors provide similar services.

The public good problem limits the supply of agents for goods that are homogeneous—one consumer can easily pass along information that the agent provides to prospective purchasers of similar units of the good. Inexpensive goods are unlikely to provide an adequate incentive for consumers to pay for the advice of agents. (Note that the full price is the relevant measure—one might very well be willing to pay for a visit to a doctor to get advice about a drug with a low purchase price but a high potential for harm to one's health.) Finally, agents are less likely to be relatively attractive for goods with high frequencies of purchase because consumers can often learn effectively on their own.

Consumers often rely on the experiences of friends and relatives to gather information about the quality of branded products. They may also be willing to pay for published information about such products. But such subscription services, which have public good characteristics, are likely to be undersupplied from the perspective of economic efficiency because nonsubscribers can often free ride on subscribers by interrogating them and by borrowing their magazines. (The very existence of subscription services such as *Consumer Reports* suggests that a large number of consumers see the marginal costs of mooching or using a library as higher than the subscription price.)

Insurers sometimes provide information to consumers as part of their efforts to limit losses. For example, Health Maintenance Organizations, which provide medical insurance, often publish newsletters that warn members of potentially dangerous and unhealthy goods such as diet products and tanning salons. Casualty insurers may signal warnings through their premiums as well as through direct information. Fire insurance underwriters, for instance, set premiums based on the types of equipment businesses plan to use; they also often inspect commercial properties to warn proprietors of dangerous equipment and inform them about additions that could reduce their risks of fire.

Experience Goods: Summary. By their very nature, experience goods offer the potential for serious inefficiency caused by information asymmetry. Secondary markets, however, limit the inefficiency for many experience goods by facilitating consumer learning and providing incentives for the revelation of product quality. Nevertheless, problems are likely to remain in two sets of circumstances: first, when quality is highly heterogeneous, branding is ineffective, and agents are either unavailable or expensive relative to the full price of the good; and second, where the distribution of quality is unstable so that consumers and agents have difficulty learning effectively. In these fairly limited circumstances, market failure may justify public intervention on efficiency grounds.

Post-Experience Goods. Consumption does not perfectly reveal the true quality of post-experience goods. Quality remains uncertain because the individual consumer has difficulty recognizing the causality between consumption and some of its effects. Some effects of consumption may be unexpected. For example, consumers may not recognize that the fumes of a cleaning product cause severe headaches because they do not expect the product to have such an effect. Often, the effects of consumption only appear after great delay so that consumers do not connect them with the product. An extreme example is DES, a drug that increases the risk of cancer in mature daughters of women who used it during pregnancy. Many other drugs require extended periods before all their effects are manifested. Young smokers, for instance, may fully appreciate the addictive power of tobacco only after they are addicted. Beyond drugs, many medical services appear to be post-experience goods—patients often cannot clearly link the state of their health to the treatments that they have received.

In terms of our earlier discussion, the consumer of a post-experience good may not have sufficient knowledge of the product to form reasonable estimates of its full price even after repeated consumption. In other words, whereas experience goods involve risk (known contingencies with known probabilities of occurrence), post-experience goods involve uncertainty (unknown contingencies or unknown probabilities of occurrence). Further, repeated consumption of a post-experience good does not necessarily lead to accurate estimates of risk.

Obviously, the potential for substantial and persistent inefficiency due to information asymmetry is greater for post-experience than experience goods. Other things equal, frequent purchases are less effective in eliminating information asymmetry for post-experience goods. In contrast to the case of experience goods, information asymmetry can persist for an extended period for even homogeneous post-experience goods.

Turning to private responses to the information asymmetry inherent in the primary markets for post-experience goods, we expect secondary markets in general to be less effective than they are for experience goods because of learning problems. Nevertheless, secondary markets can play important roles. For example, consider the services that are, or have been, privately offered to provide information about pharmaceuticals. The *Medical Letter on Drugs and Therapeutics*, one of the few medical periodicals that covers its costs through subscriptions rather than advertising, provides independent assessments of all new drugs approved by the FDA. Many hospitals, and some insurers, have formulary committees that review information about drugs for participating physicians. Between 1929 and 1955, the American Medical Association ran a seal-of-acceptance program that subjected all products advertised in the *Journal of the American Medical Association* to committee review. The National Formulary and the United States Pharmacopoeia were early attempts at standardizing pharmaceutical products. Of course, most of these information sources are directed at physicians and pharmacists who commonly serve as agents for consumers of therapeutic drugs. Although their learning from direct observation may not be effective, they can often determine if advertising claims for products are based on reasonable scientific evidence.

Summary. The potential for inefficiency due to information asymmetry between buyers and sellers can be found in many markets. The potential is rarely great for search goods, often great for experience goods, and usually great for post-experience goods. The extent to which the potential is actually realized, however, depends largely on whether public goods problems hinder the operation of secondary market mechanisms that provide corrective information. Thus, market failure is most likely in situations where information asymmetry in primary markets occurs in combination with public good problems in secondary markets.

OTHER LIMITATIONS OF THE COMPETITIVE FRAMEWORK

Although the four traditional market failures—public goods, externalities, natural monopolies, and information asymmetries—represent violations of the ideal competitive model, we nevertheless were able to illustrate their efficiency consequences with the basic concepts of producer and consumer surplus. The consequences of relaxing other assumptions of the competitive model, however, cannot be so easily analyzed with the standard tools of microeconomics. This in no way reduces the importance of considering them. They often serve as rationales, albeit implicitly, for public policies.

We begin by considering two of the most fundamental assumptions of the competitive model—namely, that participants in markets behave competitively and that individual preferences can be taken as fixed and exogenous. We then look at the assumptions that must be made to extend the basic competitive model to uncertain and multiperiod worlds. Finally, we consider the assumption that the economy can costlessly move from one equilibrium to another.

Markets with Few Sellers or Few Buyers

Participants in markets behave competitively when they act as if their individual decisions do not affect prices. In other words, they take prices as given. It is reasonable to assume competitive behavior when no seller accounts for a noticeable fraction of supply and no buyer accounts for a noticeable fraction of demand—usually the case when there are many buyers and many sellers. In markets with either few sellers or few buyers, imperfect competition can lead to prices that differ from the competitive equilibrium and hence result in Pareto-inefficient allocations of inputs and goods.

We have already considered one important example of noncompetitive behavior—natural monopoly. In the case of natural monopoly, declining average cost over the relevant range of demand makes supply by more than one firm inefficient. Yet the single firm, if allowed to maximize its profits, will produce too little output from the perspective of economic efficiency. Whether or not a firm is a natural monopoly, it can at least temporarily command monopoly rents when it is the only firm supplying a market. The monopoly rents, however, will attract other firms to the market.[36] Unless technological, cost, or other barriers block the entry of new firms, the monopoly will eventually lose its power to set price and command rents.

Noncompetitive behavior can also occur on the demand side of the market. In the case of pure monopsony, a single buyer faces competitive suppliers and therefore can influence price by choosing purchase levels. When supply is not competitive, the monopsonist may be able to extract some of the rents that would otherwise go to suppliers. The resulting allocation of rents, however, will not necessarily be more efficient than that without the exercise of monopsony power.

Intermediate between cases of perfect competition and monopoly is oligopoly. In an oligopolistic industry two or more firms account for a significant fraction of output. (A common rule of thumb is that when the four-firm concentration ratio—the percentage of industry sales by the four leading firms—reaches about 40 percent, the leading firms begin to realize their mutual dependence.[37]) The belief that oligopoly often leads to monopoly pricing, either through collusive agreements to limit output (cartelization) or through "cutthroat" competition to drive firms from the industry to obtain an actual monopoly, has motivated much of antitrust law. A full evaluation of antitrust policy requires a critical review of the various models of oligopoly—a task beyond the scope of this text.[38] It is sufficient for our purposes to note that imperfect competition often serves as a rationale for public intervention.

The Source and Acceptability of Preferences

In the basic competitive model, we assume that each person has a fixed utility function that maps his or her consumption possibilities into an index of happiness.

---

[36]Of course, firms are always looking for opportunities to be able to price above competitive levels. An extensive literature on business strategy has grown over the last decade analyzing the ways in which firms can create and preserve rents. See, for example, Michael E. Porter, *Competitive Strategy: Techniques for Analyzing Industries and Competitors* (New York: Free Press, 1980); and Arnoldo C. Hax and Nicholas S. Majluf, *Strategic Management* (Englewood Cliffs, N.J.: Prentice Hall, 1984).

[37]F.M. Scherer, *Industrial Pricing: Theory and Evidence* (Chicago: Rand McNally, 1970), p. 3. In recent years, many economists have argued that high concentration per se does not necessarily lead to collusion. For a review of this argument, see Yale Brozen, *Concentration, Mergers, and Public Policy* (New York: Macmillan, 1982), p. 9.

[38]For an introduction, see Hal R. Varian, *Intermediate Microeconomics* (New York: Norton, 1987), Chapter 26. For an advanced treatment, see James W. Friedman, *Oligopoly and the Theory of Games* (New York: North-Holland, 1977).

We make no assumption about how the particular utility functions arise, just that they depend only on the final bundles of consumed goods. But the preferences underlying the utility functions must come from somewhere. Either people have fully developed preferences at birth, or preferences are formed through participation in society.[39] If the latter, then they either arise in a sphere of activity totally independent of all economic exchange, or, in violation of the assumption of fixed preferences, depend upon what goes on in the economic world.

Endogenous Preferences. Historically, the perception that preferences can be changed has been the basis for many public policies. The specific rationales usually involved arguments that, without instruction or correction, certain persons would engage in behavior that inflicted costs on others. In other words, the outcomes of certain preferences had negative external effects. Such policies as universal education, which was supposed to supplement the formation of values in the home and community, and criminal rehabilitation, which was intended to alter the willingness of some to harm others, were responses to the external effects of preferences. Although we may now despair in finding particular education and rehabilitative programs that actually impart values in the intended ways, we may nevertheless continue to view these public efforts as conceptually, if not practically, valid.

The question of preference stability also arises in debates over the social implications of private advertising. Does advertising ever actually change preferences or does it simply provide information that helps people better match available goods to the preferences they already hold? If advertising actually does change preferences, then we can imagine situations in which private advertising leads to economic inefficiency. For example, if advertising convinced me that, holding other consumption and my income constant, I now additionally need a Cabbage Patch doll to maintain my level of happiness, I have been made worse off by the advertising. Further, the gains to the makers of Cabbage Patch dolls cannot be large enough to make the advertising even potentially Pareto improving.

Can advertising actually change preferences? Although some empirical evidence suggests that advertising may increase the total demand for specific products, it appears that the primary effect of advertising is to influence the market shares of different brands.[40] Even for those cases in which advertising does ap-

[39]Gary Becker proposes that we think of persons having fairly stable and uniform utility functions over the direct consumption of fundamental "household goods," such as health and recreation, that result when market goods and time are combined according to individual production functions. Gary Becker, *The Economic Approach to Human Behavior* (Chicago: University of Chicago Press, 1976). Although this formulation preserves the properties of the competitive equilibrium, it begs the question of how the different production functions arise. For an interesting discussion of the normative implications of Becker's approach, see Alexander Rosenberg, "Prospects for the Elimination of Tastes from Economics and Ethics," *Social Philosophy & Policy*, Vol. 2, No. 2, Spring 1985, pp. 48–68. For an example of an explicit model of utility change, see Michael D. Cohen and Robert Axelrod, "Coping with Complexity: The Adaptive Value of Changing Utility," *American Economic Review*, Vol. 74, No. 1, March 1984, pp. 30–42.

[40]For reviews of the empirical evidence, see Mark S. Albion and Paul W. Farris, *The Advertising Controversy: Evidence on the Economic Effects of Advertising* (Boston: Auburn House, 1981); and William S. Comanor and Thomas A. Wilson, "The Effect of Advertising on Competition: A Survey," *Journal of Economic Literature*, Vol. 17, No. 2, June 1979, pp. 453–76.

pear to increase market demand, we have no methodology for clearly separating behavior that results from better information about available choices from behavior that results from changes in preferences. Only the latter potentially involves economic inefficiency.

Preferences may also change as a result of the consumption of addictive goods. Repeated use of cocaine and tobacco, for example, may produce physical dependencies that increase the relative importance of these goods in people's utility functions. People who are not able to appreciate fully the consequences of the dependency may overconsume to the detriment of their future happiness. In a sense, we encounter the sort of information asymmetry that we have already discussed. The addictive substance is a post-experience good, perhaps with an irreversible consequence—namely, a change in the person's utility function. Thus, public intervention offers at least the potential for Pareto improvement.

Utility Interdependence. Going beyond the question of how preferences arise, we next confront the implications of relaxing the assumption that the utility of individuals depends only upon the goods that they personally consume. Most of us do care about the consumption of at least some others—we give gifts to those we know and donations to charities that help those we do not know. This sort of altruistic behavior is most obvious in the context of the family. Parents typically care deeply about the consumption of their children. We can accommodate this interdependence in the competitive model by taking the household, rather than the individual, as the consuming unit. As long as we are willing to think of the household as having a utility function that appropriately reflects the preferences of household members, the competitive equilibrium will be economically efficient. Unfortunately, parents are not always adequately paternal. In cases of abuse, for instance, most of us would agree that public intervention is justified to ensure that the utilities of the children are being adequately taken into account in the distribution of goods (including safety).

Interdependence causes much greater conceptual difficulty when utilities depend not only on the absolute quantities of goods people consume, but also on the relative amounts.[41] In the basic competitive model, increasing the goods available to one person without decreasing the goods available to anyone else is always a Pareto-efficient redistribution. The redistribution may not be Pareto improving, however, if some people care about their relative consumption positions. For instance, if your happiness depends to some extent on your income being higher than that of your brother-in-law, then when your brother-in-law receives a salary increase that puts his income above yours, you will feel worse off even though your consumption possibilities have not changed. Although many people do undoubtedly care to some extent about their relative standings among colleagues, friends, or some other reference group, the implications of such interdependence for the economic efficiency of the competitive economy are as yet unclear. If nothing else, preferences based on relative consumption limit the straightforward, intuitive interpretation of the Pareto principle.

---

[41]For a provocative discussion of the implications of this sort of interdependence, see Robert H. Frank, *Choosing the Right Pond: Human Behavior and the Quest for Status* (New York: Oxford University Press, 1985).

Legitimacy of Preferences. This brings us to an important general question about preferences: Are all preferences equally legitimate?[42] In the competitive model we treat all preferences as legitimate, all consumers as sovereign. Almost all would agree, however, that certain preferences leading to behaviors that directly harm others should not be considered legitimate from the social perspective. For example, our criminal laws prohibit us from taking out our anger on others through assault on their persons. Of course, we can think of this as simply prohibiting one from inflicting nonvoluntary transactions, which directly violate the Pareto principle, on others.

But our laws and customs also prohibit the exercise of other preferences that do not seem to harm others directly. For instance, some people get pleasure from having sexual intercourse with animals, an activity that, if carried out in private with one's own animal, would seem not to influence directly the utility of others. Why is it not, therefore, Pareto inefficient to prohibit bestiality? Although the reason may not be obvious, in most societies there is a consensus favoring prohibition. Sometimes we can identify external effects that seem to justify such prohibitions. For example, rationales presented for restrictions on prostitution include preventing several external effects: the undermining of family stability, the exploitation of prostitutes by pimps, and the spread of venereal diseases. Perhaps disease and family stability are also relevant to the prohibition of bestiality. It may also be, however, that the prohibition rests as much on some widely shared conception of what behaviors violate human dignity. Of course, even accepting the undesirability of the behavior, the question still remains as to whether public restriction or private suasion is more appropriate.

Summary. Preferences in the real world are neither as stable nor as simple as assumed in the competitive model. The extent to which this divergence keeps the economy from achieving Pareto efficiency remains unclear. We should tread carefully, therefore, in using perceived problems with preferences to justify public policies.

The Problem of Uncertainty

Without great conceptual difficulty we can extend the basic competitive model to incorporate multiple periods and uncertainty. Instead of assuming that people have utility functions defined over the goods consumed in a single period with complete certainty, we assume that they have utility functions over all goods in all periods and under all possible contingencies. In effect, we simply distinguish goods by time of consumption and "state of nature" (or contingency) as well as by physical characteristics. In a two-period world (this year versus next) with two possible states of nature (heavy versus light snow), for example, a physical com-

---

[42]Peter Brown sees this question, along with ones concerning whose utilities should count and how much, as providing the basic framework for the consideration of the ethics of substantive public policy. Peter G. Brown, "Ethics and Education for the Public Service in a Liberal State," *Journal of Policy Analysis and Management*, Vol. 6, No. 1, Fall 1986, pp. 56–68; also see Dale Whittington and Duncan MacRae, Jr., "The Issue of Standing in Cost-Benefit Analysis," *Journal of Policy Analysis and Management*, Vol. 5, No. 4, Summer 1986, pp. 665–82; and S. C. Littlechild and J. Wiseman, "The Political Economy of Restriction of Choice," *Public Choice*, Vol. 51, No. 2, 1986, pp. 161–72.

modity such as rented cross-country skis enters the utility functions of consumers as four different goods: skis this year if snow is light, this year if snow is heavy, next year if snow is light, and next year if snow is heavy. With the crucial assumption that efficient markets exist for all these goods at the beginning of the first time period, the resulting equilibrium allocation of goods will be Pareto efficient.[43]

Availability of Insurance. The assumption that efficient markets exist for all goods under all contingencies means that it must be possible to buy actuarially fair insurance so that each person's utility will remain constant no matter what state of nature actually occurs. Insurance is actuarially fair when the premium exactly equals the expected payout. Of course, to know the expected payout, one must know the probabilities of each of the possible contingencies as well as their associated payouts. In standard terminology, *risk* involves contingencies with known probabilities and *uncertainty* involves contingencies with unknown probabilities.

Do efficient and complete insurance markets exist in the real world? Of course, insurers must routinely charge something more than the actuarially fair price to cover their administrative costs. More importantly, however, two sets of factors limit the range of contingencies that can be insured at even approximately actuarially fair prices: characteristics of the contingencies themselves and behavioral responses to the available insurance. In order to set actuarially fair prices, insurers must know the probabilities of the covered contingencies. The most common types of casualty insurance protect against contingencies that occur frequently enough to allow reliable estimation of the probabilities from experience. For example, by observing the accident records of the large number of drivers, insurers can make fairly accurate predictions of the probability that any one with specific characteristics (such as sex, age, and driving environment) will have an accident over the next year. "Experience rating" of this sort, however, is not possible, or at least not accurate, for very rare events such as major earthquakes. Consequently, insurers are unable to offer actuarially fair insurance against rare events. Further, the price of the insurance they do offer will likely include a *risk premium*, which is an addition to the estimated actuarially fair price to reflect their lack of confidence in the estimates of probabilities.

An additional premium above the actuarially fair price may also be demanded in situations where individual risks are not independent, so that after pooling, some collective, or social, risk remains.[44] If the probability that any one

---

[43]This extension of the basic model is in the spirit of Kenneth J. Arrow and Gerard Debreu, "Existence of an Equilibrium for a Competitive Economy," *Econometrica,* Vol. 22, No. 3, July 1954, pp. 265–90. The model can be generalized in a number of ways, including allowance for consumers and firms having different estimates of the probabilities of the states of nature. Roy Radner, "Competitive Equilibrium under Uncertainty," *Econometrica,* Vol. 36, No. 1, January 1968, pp. 31–58.

[44]For a discussion of this problem and a general review of issues in the economics of uncertainty, see J. Hirshleifer and John G. Riley, "The Analytics of Uncertainty and Information: An Expository Survey," *Journal of Economic Literature,* Vol. 17, No. 4, December 1979, pp. 1375–1421. For thoughtful discussions of the limitations of insurance markets, see Richard J. Zeckhauser, "Coverage for Catastrophic Illness," *Public Policy,* Vol. 21, No. 2, Spring 1973, pp. 149–72; and "Resource Allocation with Probabilistic Individual Preferences," *American Economic Review,* Vol. 59, No. 2, May 1969, pp. 546–52.

policyholder will have an accident is independent of the probabilities that other policyholders will also have accidents, then as the number of policyholders gets larger, the actual payouts by the insurers will get closer to the expected payouts. For instance, for all practical purposes the probability that any driver will have an accident is independent of the probabilities that other drivers will have accidents; insurers are able, therefore, to predict their annual losses confidently. The convergence between observed frequencies and underlying probabilities, which is known as the Law of Large Numbers, breaks down when individual probabilities are not independent. In the absence of independence, insurers may demand an additional premium to guard against the probability that losses in any period will greatly exceed expected losses. For instance, the probabilities of individual losses from flooding are clearly not independent if all policyholders live in the same river valley.

In all but extreme situations, insurers generally are able to mitigate social risk through some sort of diversification. For example, insurers may be able to spread coverage over several different floodplains. When geographic diversification is not possible, insurers may be able to shift some of the risk to reinsurers, who balance it against other types of risk. If the probability of loss correlates negatively with other risky holdings, then the total risk held by the reinsurer will fall.[45] Some social risks, however, such as nuclear war or the presumed melting of the polar icecaps due to the "greenhouse effect," would involve sufficiently large and widespread negative impacts so that diversification would not be possible.

Adverse Selection, Moral Hazard, and Underinsuring. Turning to the behavioral responses to available insurance, we consider adverse selection, moral hazard, and underinsuring of irreplaceable commodities.

We have already encountered the concept of *adverse selection* (of goods) in our discussion of the 'lemons' problem. In the insurance context, it pertains to insured individuals and arises when insurers cannot costlessly classify potential policyholders according to risk categories. Within each category some will have higher-than-average probabilities of loss and some lower than average. Those with higher-than-average probabilities will tend to find the insurance attractive; those with lower-than-average probabilities will not. As more of the former buy policies and more of the latter decline to buy, the average for the group must rise. This in turn drives the insurance price higher above the actuarially fair level for the group as a whole. Eventually, only those with the highest probabilities choose to remain covered. Insurers can sometimes limit adverse selection by offering inclusive policies to groups such as company employees, for which insurance is only one attraction of membership. In general, however, information asymmetries tend to keep the prices of many types of insurance above actuarially fair levels. One rationale for public insurance programs is that they can be made mandatory so that adverse selection can be avoided.

Moral hazard refers to the reduced incentive that insurees have to prevent compensable losses. If fully insured, they can make themselves better off, and

---

[45]In managing portfolios of assets, investors usually try to balance the expected value and variance of the rate of return. Adding a new asset with comparable variance but with an expected rate of return that is negatively correlated with the expected rate of return of the existing portfolio reduces the overall variance in the rate of return. So too does adding a stock with a lower variance.

perhaps society in the aggregate worse off, by spending less of their own resources on loss prevention than they would in the absence of insurance.[46] Actual reductions in loss protection are more likely to occur the more costly it is for insurers to monitor behavior. Insurers try to limit moral hazard by requiring insurees to pay a fraction of the suffered loss through copayments.

People may underinsure for contingencies involving the loss of irreplaceable goods that cannot be exactly replicated. For many plausible utility functions, economically rational people will only wish to purchase actuarially fair insurance to cover the monetary part of their losses.[47] Thus, in a world filled with irreplaceable goods such as good health, beloved spouses, and unique works of art, people will not necessarily choose to purchase adequate insurance to give them constant utility under all contingencies. Of course, in light of the experience rating and moral hazard problems we have already discussed, insurers might not be willing to offer actuarially fair insurance for all irreplaceable goods anyway. For example, insurers might worry about the dangers of moral hazard if you claimed that you needed one million dollars to compensate yourself fully for the supposed accidental death of your dog.

Subjective Perception of Risk.   So far we have assumed that people effectively evaluate and use information to arrive at rational decisions in situations involving risk. A growing body of experimental research in social psychology, however, suggests that people tend to make several systematic errors in assessing probabilities.[48] In order to deal economically with a great variety of information in a complex world, people tend to employ heuristics (rules of thumb) that sometimes lead to correct decisions but nevertheless involve predictable biases. For instance, it appears that people often estimate the probabilities of events by the ease with which instances or occurrences can be brought to mind.[49] Recall, however, depends on a number of factors, such as the personal salience of events that tends to systematically bias estimates of relative probabilities. For example, in a study of flood and earthquate insurance coverage, Howard Kunreuther and

---

[46]Moral hazard also describes risky actions by the insured to qualify for compensation. See, for example, the study of the behavior of air traffic controllers under the Federal Employees Compensation Act by Michael E. Staten and John R. Umbeck, "Close Encounters in the Skies: A Paradox of Regulatory Incentives," *Regulation*, May/April 1983, pp. 25–31.

[47]See Philip J. Cook and Daniel A. Graham, "The Demand for Insurance and Protection: The Case of Irreplaceable Commodities," *Quarterly Journal of Economics*, Vol. 91, No. 1, February 1977, pp. 141–56; and Richard Zeckhauser, "Procedures for Valuing Lives," *Public Policy*, Vol. 23, No. 4, Fall 1975, pp. 419–64.

[48]For general overviews, see Amos J. Tversky and Daniel Kahneman, "Judgment under Uncertainty: Heuristics and Biases," *Science*, Vol. 185, 27 September 1974, pp. 1124–31; Daniel Kahneman, Paul Slovic, and Amos Tversky, eds., *Judgment under Uncertainty: Heuristics and Biases* (New York: Cambridge University Press, 1982).

[49]Tversky and Kahneman call this the *heuristic of availability* (p. 1127). They also identify the *heuristic of representativeness*, which is often used when people have to estimate conditional probabilities (given some observed characteristics, what is the probability that the object belongs to some class); and the *heuristic of anchoring*, which refers to the tendency of people not to adequately adjust their initial estimates of probabilities as more information becomes available (Tversky and Kahneman, pp. 1124 and 1128).

colleagues found that knowing someone who suffered flood or earthquake loss was the single most important factor for distinguishing between purchasers and nonpurchasers.[50]

The growing dissatisfaction among economists with use of the expected utility hypothesis for predicting individual behavior also raises questions about our understanding of the way people make risky choices and hence shakes our confidence somewhat in the rationality of private behavior involving risk.[51] The *expected utility hypothesis* states that people choose among alternative actions to maximize the probability-weighted sum of utilities under each of the possible contingencies. For example, if a person's utility, $U(w)$, depends only on his wealth (w), and the probability that his wealth will be w_a is p and the probability that his wealth will be w_b is $(1 - p)$, then his expected utility is $pU(w_a) + (1 - p)U(w_b)$. The expected utility hypothesis is consistent with the competitive model and lies at the heart of most economic analysis of individual responses to risk. Laboratory experiments have identified several situations in which the expected utility hypothesis seems to be systematically violated. Although individuals tend to underestimate the probabilities of very infrequent events, for instance, they tend to be overly sensitive to small changes in the probabilities of rare events relative to the predictions of the expected utility hypothesis.[52] These findings have led social psychologists and economists to begin to explore other formulations of behavior under uncertainty.[53] As yet the full implications of the alternative formulations for our evaluation of economic efficiency remain unclear.

Summary.   These observations about insurance markets and individual responses to risk suggest that public policies may have potential for increasing economic efficiency in circumstances involving uncertainty. Public assessments of risks, for example, may be an appropriate response when people make important systematic errors in their private assessments, and public insurance may be justified when private coverage is significantly incomplete. Until we have a better understanding of how individuals actually deal with uncertainty, however, our evaluation of economic efficiency in circumstances involving uncertainty must itself remain uncertain.

Intertemporal Allocation: Are Markets Myopic?

As we have already indicated, the competitive model can be extended to the intertemporal allocation of goods. If we assume that it is possible to make contracts in the current period for the production and delivery of goods in all future

[50]H. Kunreuther, R. Ginsberg, L. Miller, P. Sagi, P. Slovic, B. Borkin, and N. Katz, *Disaster Insurance Protection: Public Policy Lessons* (New York: John Wiley, 1978), pp. 145–53.

[51]See Kenneth J. Arrow, "Risk Perception in Psychology and Economics," *Economic Inquiry*, Vol. 20, No. 1, January 1982, pp. 1–9.

[52]For an excellent review of these issues, see Mark J. Machina, " 'Expected Utility' Analysis without the Independence Axiom," *Econometrica*, Vol. 50, No. 2, March 1982, pp. 277–323.

[53]For a review of variants of the expected utility hypothesis, see Paul J. H. Schoemaker, "The Expected Utility Model: Its Variants, Purposes, Evidence, and Limitations," *Journal of Economic Literature*, Vol. 20, No. 2, June 1982, pp. 529–63.

periods (in other words, forward markets exist for all goods), then the competitive equilibrium will be Pareto efficient.[54] One "price" that emerges in the intertemporal context is the *social rate of time preference*, the rate at which everyone is indifferent between exchanging current for future consumption. For example, if people were indifferent between giving up one unit of current consumption for an additional 1.06 units next year and giving up 1.06 units of consumption next year in return for an additional unit this year, then they would be exhibiting a rate of time preference of 0.06. In the ideal competitive equilibrium, the social rate of time preference will equal the interest rate at which people can borrow and lend—that is, the market interest rate.

To see why the social rate of time preference and the market rate of interest must be equal in equilibrium, consider what would happen if someone's rate of time preference was either smaller or larger than the market interest rate. If it were smaller (say 0.06 compared to a market interest rate of 0.08), giving up one unit of current consumption by lending at the interest rate would yield an additional 1.08 units of consumption next year, which is more than the 1.06 needed to keep the consumer as well off as before the temporal reallocation. The consumer would be able to make himself better off by continuing to shift consumption to the future until his time preference has risen to the market rate of interest and no further gains are possible. If the market interest rate were lower than the consumer's rate of time preference, then the consumer could make himself better off by borrowing until his rate of time preference has fallen to the rate of interest.

Capital Markets.   What determines the rate of interest? In equilibrium the demand for borrowing must just equal the supply of loans. The resulting rate of interest is the price that clears this "capital market." Of course, in the real world the financial institutions that make up the capital market cover their administrative expenses by lending at higher rates than they borrow. They may also demand premiums for riskier loans.

Just as the theoretical efficiency of the competitive equilibrium depends upon the existence of complete insurance markets to accommodate uncertainty, it depends upon complete, or perfect, capital markets to accommodate intertemporal allocation. Perfect capital markets allow anyone to convert future earnings to current consumption through borrowing. But in reality, the anticipation by lenders of moral hazard greatly reduces the amount people can actually borrow against future earnings. Borrowers who owe large percentages of their incomes may be tempted to reduce their work effort because they realize smaller net returns to their labor than if they were debt free. With the almost now-universal prohibition against slavery and the existence in most countries of bankruptcy laws, borrowers have no means of convincing lenders that they will maintain full work effort. Therefore, at least with respect to labor income, capital markets appear to be imperfect. It is at least conceivable that some public policies, such as subsidized loans for education, might be justified on the grounds of imperfect capital markets.

---

[54]We can distinguish three types of markets: *Spot markets* encompass transactions involving immediate delivery of goods. *Forward markets* encompass contracts that specify future delivery at a specified price. *Futures markets* are specially organized forward markets in which clearinghouses guarantee the integrity of the contracts.

At a more fundamental level, scholars have long debated whether or not capital markets lead to appropriate levels of saving and investment for future generations.[55] No one lives forever. How then, can we expect the decisions of current consumers to take account adequately of the unarticulated preferences of those yet to be born? One response recognizes that generations overlap. Most of us consider the welfare of our children and our grandchildren, who we hope will outlive us, in our economic decisions. Rather than attempting to consume all of our resources before the instant of death, most of us plan on bequeathing at least some of our savings to family or charity. Even when we do not intentionally plan to leave unconsumed wealth behind, we may do so unintentionally through untimely death.

Despite intentional and unintentional bequests, positive market interest rates prevail in most societies. Some philosophers and economists object on normative grounds to interpreting positive interest rates as appropriate social rates of time preference.[56] They argue that there is no ethical basis for any social rate of time preference other than zero; that is, they argue that consumption by someone in the future should be given the same weight from the social perspective as consumption by someone today. Their argument implies that any investment yielding a positive rate of return, no matter how small, should be undertaken. Because investment in the competitive economy demands rates of return at least as high as the rate of interest, they generally advocate public policies to increase investment.

The underinvestment argument seems to ignore the legacy of capital from one generation to the next. Net investments increase the available capital stock. Most forms of capital do, of course, depreciate over time. A bridge, for instance, needs maintenance to keep it safe, and eventually may have to be abandoned. But perhaps the most important element of our capital stock is knowledge, which does not depreciate. Improvements in technology not only increase current productive options but those in the future as well. This legacy helps explain the growing wealth of successive generations in countries like the United States that rely primarily on private investment. The underinvestment argument loses force, therefore, if the total capital stock, including nontangible capital such as knowledge, can be expected to continue to grow in the future.

One variant of the underinvestment (or overconsumption) argument deserves particular attention. It concerns the irreversible consumption of natural resources such as animal species, wilderness, and fossil fuels. When an animal species becomes extinct, it is lost to future generations. Likewise, fossil fuels consumed today cannot be consumed tomorrow. Although it may be technically possible to restore wilderness areas that have been developed, the cost of doing so may make it practically unfeasible. Will markets save adequate shares of these resources for future generations?

The answer is almost certainly yes for resources such as fossil fuels that have value as factor inputs rather than final goods. As long as property rights

[55]For a variety of economic approaches to the issue, see Robert C. Lind, ed., *Discounting for Time and Risk in Energy Policy* (Washington, D.C.: Resources for the Future, 1982).

[56]For a review of the objections, see Robert E. Goodin, *Political Theory & Public Policy* (Chicago: University of Chicago Press, 1982), Chapter 8, pp. 162–83.

are secure, owners of resources will hold back some of the resources in anticipation of future scarcity and the higher prices the scarcity will command.[57] As higher prices are actually realized, substitutes will become economically feasible. Although generations in the distant future will be consuming less fossil fuel, they undoubtedly will produce energy from alternative sources and use energy more efficiently to produce final goods. There is no particular reason to believe, therefore, that any collective decision about how much to save for future generations will be any better than allocations made by private markets.

Resources that are themselves unique goods, such as wilderness areas and animal species, raise more serious doubt about the adequacy of market preservation. When owners have secure property rights and can anticipate selling their resource as a private good in the future, they must base their decisions about the extent of development on their estimates of future demand.[58] If they maximize the expected value of profits, the standard assumption of the competitive model, they may develop too much of the resource from the social perspective.[59] This is because as more information becomes available about future demand, and hence about the opportunity cost of development, it will be possible for the owners to increase the extent of development, but not decrease it because restoration of the unique asset is unfeasible. Errors of underdevelopment are correctible; errors of overdevelopment are not. From the social perspective, somewhat slower development may be justified to reduce the risk of inappropriately losing in perpetuity the option to preserve.[60]

A final point, which we address more fully later in the context of benefit-cost analysis, concerns the validity of interpreting the market interest rate as the social rate of time preference even if we accept use of the latter as appropriate

---

[57]In a world with secure property rights, competitive firms will maximize the present value of profits (the maximum amount they could borrow today against all future profits) from extraction of the finite resource by choosing production rates that lead to the net price (market price minus marginal extraction costs) rising at the rate of interest. The basic model of *exhaustible resources* was first set out by Harold Hotelling, "The Economics of Exhaustible Resources," *Journal of Political Economy*, Vol. 39, No. 2, April 1931, pp. 137–75. For a recent review of the subsequent literature, see Shantayanan Devarajan and Anthony C. Fisher, "Hotelling's 'Economics of Exhaustible Resources': Fifty Years Later," *Journal of Economic Literature*, Vol. 19, No. 1, March 1981, pp. 65–73.

[58]We are assuming that a market mechanism exists for articulating the demand. This is often not the case for natural areas, even when exclusion is possible, because there is usually no way to secure contributions from people who would be willing to pay something to keep the resource in place so as to retain the option of visiting it sometime in the future. This willingness of nonusers to contribute to maintenance of the resource is called *option demand*. See Burton A Weisbrod, "Collective-Consumption Services of Individual Consumption Goods," *Quarterly Journal of Economics*, Vol. 78, No. 3, August 1964, pp. 471–77; and C. J. Cicchetti and A. M. Freeman III, "Option Demand and Consumer Surplus: Further Comment," *Quarterly Journal of Economics*, Vol. 85, No. 3, August 1971, pp. 528–39.

[59]Kenneth J. Arrow and Anthony C. Fisher, "Environmental Preservation, Uncertainty, and Irreversibility," *Quarterly Journal of Economics*, Vol. 88, No. 2, May 1974, pp. 312–19.

[60]Environmental quality is probably a *normal good*—other things equal, the higher our income the greater the amount of environmental quality we collectively want to consume. Ironically, the larger the legacy of economic wealth we leave to future generations, the less satisfied they may be with the level of environmental quality we bequeath!

when comparing current and future consumption. Lenders generally charge higher rates of interest for riskier investments. But when we look across the full set of investment projects, the aggregate risk will be much less than the risk associated with any individual project because the circumstances that tend to make some projects fail tend to make others succeed. For example, the low energy prices that, ex post, make synthetic fuel plants appear to be bad investments may make recreational facilities requiring long road trips appear to be good investments. The market interest rate, therefore, will tend to exceed the social rate of time preference, which should only reflect the social risk and not the risk to individual lenders. Although a problem caused by public policy rather than inherent in markets, a similar wedge is introduced by taxes on profits.[61] If, for whatever reason, the market interest rate exceeds the social rate of time preference, private investment will fall short of the economically efficient level.

In summary, specific reservations about the efficiency of capital markets and general concerns about the adequacy of the weight given to the preferences of future generations may serve as plausible rationales for public policies intended to improve the intertemporal allocation of resources and goods.

Adjustment Costs

The competitive model is static. For any given set of assumptions about utilities, production functions, and factor endowments, a unique allocation of factor inputs and goods constitutes an equilibrium in the sense that, at the prevailing prices, no consumers can make themselves better off by changing the quantities of goods they purchase and no firms can increase their profits by changing input mixes or output levels. If any of the assumptions change, then a new equilibrium distribution will arise. We can assess welfare changes by comparing allocations in the two equilibria (economists call this *comparative statics*). In doing so we implicity assume, however, that the economy can move costlessly from one equilibrium to another.

In reality, the economy is never static. Changing incomes, the introduction of new products, the growing work force and capital stock, good and bad harvests, and numerous other factors necessitate continual adjustments toward efficient allocation. In most circumstances, as long as prices are free to move in response to changes in supply and demand, the adjustment process itself occurs costlessly: persons change their consumption to maximize utility and firms their factor inputs to maximize profits in response to the new prices. Some persons may be worse off under the new allocation, but this will be fully reflected in the comparison of social surpluses before and after the reallocation. For example, an epidemic that decimates the population of chickens and drives up the price of eggs will,

---

[61]This is an example of what is sometimes referred to as the *theory of the second best*. In a world with many market failures and government distortions, correcting a single price may not improve efficiency. For example, in our discussion of the traditional market failures, we learned that, from the social perspective, monopolies underproduce and firms with negative production externalities overproduce. What then should we do about a polluting monopolist? In the context of our current discussion, what is the appropriate social rate of time preference when the government distorts interest rates with profits taxes? See R. G. Lipsey and K. Lancaster, "The General Theory of the Second Best," *Review of Economic Studies*, Vol. 24, No. 1, 1956, pp. 11–32.

other things equal, make egg consumers worse off. The consumer surplus loss measured in the egg market serves as a good approximation for the reduction in welfare they suffered.

The picture changes if institutional or psychological factors constrain the free movement of prices. Constraints on price movements keep the economy from immediately reaching the new Pareto-efficient equilibrium. As a result, comparing the old and new equilibria may overstate social surplus gains and understate social surplus losses. The larger the needed adjustment and the more rigid are prices, the greater are the adjustment costs that do not show up in the comparative statics.

Consider, for example, the effects of an oil price shock of the sort experienced during the Arab oil embargo (1973-74) and the Iranian revolution (1979-80).[62] A dramatic rise in oil prices makes petroleum a much more expensive factor input. The supply schedules for goods that require petroleum as a factor input will shift up—marginal costs of production will rise. The market clearing product price will be higher and the market clearing quantity will be lower than before the price shock. Therefore, at any wage rate firms will demand less of all factor inputs, including labor, than before the shock. If all factor prices were flexible, we would expect this shift to result in a reduction both in the quantity of labor demanded and in the wage rate. But contracts and custom often keep firms from immediately lowering wage rates. Firms, therefore, will reduce the quantity of labor they use more than they would if wages were free to fall. Either underemployment (employees cannot work as many hours as they want at the prevailing wage rate) or, more likely, again for reasons of contract and custom, involuntary unemployment will result.

Wage rigidities due to either implicit or explicit contracts should not necessarily be interpreted as market failures.[63] They may be the result of attempts by firms and workers to share the risks associated with fluctuations in the demands for products; workers may accept lower-than-market clearing wages during good times to secure higher-than-market clearing wages during bad times. The picture is complicated, however, not only by all the limitations to complete insurance markets that we have already discussed, but also by the prevalence of collective bargaining that tends to give greater protection to workers with longer tenure. Incomplete markets for risk spreading make it at least possible that public programs, such as unemployment insurance, may contribute to greater economic efficiency.

The business cycle poses a sort of social risk that may justify public stabilization polices.[64] The economy is dynamic and tends to go through cycles of expan-

---

[62]For a detailed discussion of how the economy adjusts to oil price shocks, see Chapter 2 of George Horwich and David Leo Weimer, *Oil Price Shocks, Market Response, and Contingency Planning* (Washington, D.C.: American Enterprise Institute, 1984).

[63]For a review, see Sherwin Rosen, "Implicit Contracts: A Survey," *Journal of Economic Literature*, Vol. 23, No. 3, September 1985, pp. 1144-75. For the argument that labor contracts of long duration involve negative externalities, see Laurence Ball, "Externalities from Contract Length," *American Economic Review*, Vol. 77, No. 4, September 1987, pp. 615-29.

[64]For an overview of economic thought on the business cycle, see Victor Zarnowitz, "Recent Work on Business Cycles in Historical Perspective: A Review of Theories and Evidence," *Journal of Economic Literature*, Vol. 23, No. 2, June 1985, pp. 523-80.

sion and recession. During recessions unemployed labor and underutilized capital indicate inefficiency in the economy-wide use of factor inputs. The government may be able to dampen recessions through its fiscal and monetary policies. *Fiscal policies* involve taxation and expenditures. During recessions, for instance, the government may be able to stimulate demand by spending in excess of revenues. *Monetary policy* refers to manipulation of the money supply. In general, the money supply must continually increase to accommodate the growing economy. During recessions, the government may increase the money supply at a faster rate to lower interest rates, at least temporarily, thereby stimulating investment and current consumption.

Unfortunately, there is no consensus among economists about either the causes of business cycles or the most appropriate policies for reducing their adverse effects. Although fiscal and monetary policies undoubtedly have potential for improving the dynamic efficiency of the economy, we must await advances in the field of macroeconomics before we can have confidence in anyone's ability to use them for anything approaching fine tuning. Fortunately, in the vast majority of situations, policy analysts can take monetary and fiscal policies as given and still provide good advice about economic efficiency.

BEYOND EFFICIENCY: DISTRIBUTIONAL RATIONALES

The traditional market failures and other limitations of the competitive framework summarized in Figure 3.18 identify circumstances in which private economic activity may not lead to Pareto efficiency. Thus, they indicate the potential for Pareto improvements through public policies. Values other than efficiency, however, warrant consideration in our assessments of the extent to which any particular combination of private and public activity achieves the "good society." As individuals we turn to philosophy, religion, and political ideology to help ourselves develop systems of values to guide our assessments. Absent a consensus over the values to be considered and their relative importance when they conflict, our political institutions must unavoidedly play a role in selecting the specific values that will have weight in collective decision making. Nevertheless, we sketch here some of the more common rationales for public policies that are based on values other than efficiency.

Human Dignity: Equity of Opportunity and Floors on Consumption

We begin with the premise that all people have intrinsic value, which derives from the very fact that they are human beings rather than from any measurable contribution they can make to society. Our own dignity as human beings requires us to respect the dignity of others. Although the meaning of dignity ultimately rests with the individual, it involves, at least to some extent, one's freedom to choose how one lives. A good society must have mechanisms for limiting the extent to which any person's choices interfere with the choices of others. It also should facilitate broad participation in the institutions that determine the allocation of private and public goods.

I. **Traditional market failures**

  A. Public goods
     1. Nonrivalrous, excludable: marketable public goods (undersupply)
     2. Nonrivalrous, nonexcludable: pure public goods (undersupply)
     3. Rivalrous, nonexcludable: common property resources
       (overconsumption, underinvestment)

  B. Externalities
     1. Positive externalities (undersupply, underconsumption)
     2. Negative externalities (oversupply, overconsumption)

  C. Natural monopoly (undersupply, X-inefficiency)

  D. Information asymmetry: over- or underestimation of quality
     (overconsumption or underconsumption)

II. **Other limitations of the competitive framework**

  A. Markets with few sellers or few buyers (undersupply)

  B. Endogenous or unacceptable preferences
     1. Endogenous preferences (typically overconsumption)
     2. Utility interdependence (distributional inefficiency)
     3. Unacceptable preferences (overconsumption)

  C. Problems of uncertainty
     1. Incomplete insurance markets: adverse selection, moral hazard, and unique
      assets (under- or overconsumption, undersupply)
     2. Misperception of risk (either overconsumption or underconsumption)

  D. Intertemporal problems: nontraded assets and bankruptcy
     (incomplete capital markets, underinvestment)

  E. Adjustment costs (underemployed resources)

Figure 3.18   A Summary of Market Failures and Their Implications for Efficiency

We have focused on market exchange as a mechanism for translating the preferences of individuals into allocations of private goods. But to participate in markets one must have something to exchange. In the competitive framework one has a set of endowments—ownership of labor and other factor inputs. Someone who has no endowments would be effectively barred from participating in the market process. With very small endowments, people have very little choice; without any endowments, people cannot express their choices of private goods at all. Because survival depends upon the consumption of at least some private goods (food and protection from exposure), we might find a Pareto-efficient allocation that results in the premature deaths of some people.

Most of us would not consider such extreme allocations as appropriate. In many societies, people take it upon themselves to mitigate the most drastic consequences of extreme allocations through voluntary contributions to charities or individuals. For example, until the role of the federal government expanded greatly during the 1930s, private charity was a major source of assistance for widows, orphans, and the disabled in the United States[65] Concern that charity may not adequately reach these vulnerable populations serves as a widely accepted rationale for public assistance.

More generally, we might agree that viable participation in market exchange requires some minimal endowment of assets. Because most people can sell their own labor, one approach to increasing the number of people with the minimal endowment is to increase their effectiveness and marketability as workers. Public policies intended to provide remedial education, job training, and physical rehabilitation may play an important role in increasing effective participation in the private sector. So too might policies that protect against discrimination by employers on the basis of factors not relevant to performance on the job. Direct public provision of money or in-kind goods, however, may be the only way to ensure minimal participation of those, such as the severely disabled, who have little or no employment potential.

Increasing participation in decisions over the provision and allocation of public goods also merits consideration as an appropriate value in the evaluation of public policies. As we previously discussed, markets will generally not lead to efficient levels of provision of public goods. Although we can conceive of the efficient level of provision, in practice, limitations in information about the true preferences of individuals force us to leave the actual choice to the political system. Public policies that broaden political participation may be desirable, therefore, in terms of respect for individual preferences for public goods. We support universal adult suffrage, for instance, not because we expect it necessarily to lead to greater efficiency in the provision of public goods, but rather because it recognizes the inherent value of allowing people some say over the sort of society in which they will live.

Finally, we must consider situations in which people are incapable of rationally exercising choice. For example, most of us would not consider preventing either young children or the mentally impaired from seriously harming themselves to be a violation of their human dignity. On the contrary, we might feel an affirmative duty to act paternalistically. The problem, from the perspective of public policy, is deciding the point at which individual choices should be overriden.

Increasing the Equality of Outcomes

Respect for human dignity seems to justify public policies that ensure some minimum level of consumption to all members of society. Most of us would agree that the minimum level should be high enough to ensure the commonly recognized needs for dignified survival. The level is absolute but not fixed. It is absolute in the sense that it does not explicitly depend on the wealth, income, or consumption of others in society. It is not fixed because the collective assessment of what constitutes dignified survival will undoubtedly reflect the aggregate wealth in society. For example, the U.S. government regularly estimates how much in-

[65]It may be that public transfer programs displace private charity dollar for dollar. See Russell D. Roberts, "A Positive Model of Private Charity and Public Transfers," *Journal of Political Economy*, Vol. 92, No. 1, February 1984, pp. 136–48.

come families must have to consume a set of basic goods thought necessary for decent survival in 1965. The number of persons in families raised above this *poverty line* often serves as a measure of success of government programs. As the United States has become wealthier, however, there has been a growing tendency to use multiples, such as 125 percent, of the poverty line in evaluations, suggesting change in our collective assessment of the decent minimum.[66]

Rather than looking just at the absolute consumption levels of the poorest members of society, we might also consider the entire distribution of wealth. Personal attributes, family circumstances, and chance lead to a wide dispersion in the levels of wealth enjoyed as outcomes in a market economy. Several conceptual frameworks seem to support equality in outcomes as an important social value.

For example, John Rawls argues that policies should work to the "greatest benefit of the least advantaged members of society," on the basis of a provocative thought experiment intended to free us from our particularistic values.[67] Imagine a group of people who must decide on a system of social institutions without knowing what their own attributes and endowments will be. Behind this "veil of ignorance" people can deliberate as equals. Not knowing where one will be in society encourages one to consider the fairness of the entire system. Rawls argues that people would select the system that raises the position of the least advantaged, leading to greater equality of outcomes. If we accept his argument, we must worry about relative as well as absolute wealth levels.

A more traditional argument for viewing equality of outcomes as a social value is based on the assumption that marginal utility declines with wealth. That is, individuals get less additional happiness from additional units of wealth as their levels of wealth increase. If we are willing to make interpersonal comparisons by assuming that everyone has the same utility function over wealth, then it follows that, holding the total wealth of individuals constant, the more equal the distribution of wealth the greater is the sum of utilities across individuals. In terms of tax policy, for instance, this argument leads to the notion of *vertical equity*—those with greater wealth should pay higher taxes so that everyone gives up the same amount of utility. (The related notion of *horizontal equity* requires that those in similar circumstances be treated alike.)

Although we might challenge the reasonableness of the assumption that utility functions are identical with respect to wealth, a much more important factor comes into play in thinking about equality of outcomes as a social value. The argument assumes that the amount of wealth to be distributed among individuals is constant. This may be true for an initial unexpected reallocation. Once people anticipate reallocation, however, they will begin to change their behaviors in ways that reduce the total amount of wealth that will be available. In the extreme, where everyone received the same share of wealth, the incentives for work, investment, and entrepreneurship would be greatly reduced. Costly and intrusive control mechanisms would have to be put in place to get people to work and invest as

[66]For a discussion of this trend with respect to the economic well-being of the elderly, see Bruce Jacobs, "Ideas, Beliefs, and Aging Policy," *Generations,* Vol. 9, No. 1, Fall 1984, pp. 15–18.

[67]John Rawls, "Justice as Fairness: Political not Metaphysical," *Philosophy & Public Affairs,* Vol. 14, No. 3, Summer 1985, pp. 223–50, p. 227; and John Rawls, *A Theory of Justice* (Cambridge, Mass.: Harvard University Press, 1971).

much as they would have in the absence of the redistribution. Undoubtedly, the result would be a less wealthy society.

In general, we should expect the total available wealth to shrink more the greater the amount of redistribution attempted. Arthur Okun uses the analogy of transfering water with a "leaky bucket."[68] If we try to transfer a little water we will lose a little; if we try to transfer a lot we will lose a lot. The key question, therefore, is how much current and future wealth are we collectively willing to give up to achieve greater equality in distribution? In practice, we must rely on the political process for an answer.

OVERVIEW AND CONCLUSION

We have set out two broad classes of rationales for public policies: the correction of market failures to improve efficiency in the allocation of resources and production of goods, and the reallocation of opportunity and goods to achieve distributional values. We devoted the majority of our discussion to market failures, not because distributional values are any less important than efficiency, but because the basic analytics of welfare economics serve as useful tools for positive prediction as well as normative evaluation. That is, the various market failures can often serve as models for understanding how unsatisfactory social conditions arise and how they might be remedied. Figure 3.18, therefore, can serve as a starting point for diagnosing public policy problems.

Market failures and unsatisfied distributional goals are necessary but not sufficient grounds for public intervention. We must always consider the costs of the proposed intervention. Just as markets fail in fairly predictable ways, we can identify generic government failures that either contribute indirectly to the costs of policy interventions or cause them to fail outright. We discuss these limits to public intervention in the next chapter.

[68]Arthur M. Okun, *Equality and Efficiency: The Big Tradeoff* (Washington, D.C.: Brookings Institution, 1975), pp. 91–100.

4

LIMITS
TO PUBLIC INTERVENTION:
GOVERNMENT FAILURES

Every society produces and allocates goods through some combination of individual and collective choice. Most individual choice, expressed through participation in markets and other voluntary exchanges, furthers such social values as efficiency and liberty. But some individual choice, like that arising in situations we identify as market failures, detracts from social values in predictable ways. Collective choice exercised through governmental structures offers at least the possibility for correcting the perceived deficiencies of individual choice. But just as individual choice sometimes fails to promote social values in desired and predictable ways, so too does collective choice. Public policy, therefore, should be informed not only by an understanding of market failure but of *government failure* as well.

The social sciences have yet to produce a theory of government failure as comprehensive or widely accepted as the theory of market failure. In fact, we must draw on several largely independent strains of research to piece one together.[1] From social choice theory, which focuses on the operation of voting rules and other mechanisms of collective choice, we learn of the inherent imperfectibility of democracy. From a variety of fields in political science we learn of the problems of representative government. Public choice theory and studies of organizational behavior help us understand the problems of implementing collective decisions in decentralized systems of government and of using public agencies to produce and distribute goods. Together, the insights from these fields help us

---

[1]Charles Wolf, Jr., is one of the few social scientists to try to develop a theory of government ("nonmarket" in his terms) failure that could complement the theory of market failure. His typology includes problems of government supply and policy implementation but largely ignores the more fundamental problems of social choice. For a summary, see Charles Wolf, Jr., "A Theory of Nonmarket Failures," *Journal of Law and Economics*, Vol. 22, No. 1, April 1979, pp. 107–39.

realize that even governments blessed with the most intelligent, honest, and dedicated public officials cannot be expected to promote the social good in all circumstances.

As policy analysts we should exercise caution in advocating public intervention into private affairs. Some market failures are simply too costly to correct; some distributional goals are too costly to achieve. More fundamentally, we do not know just how government intervention will work out. That government often fails to advance the social good is clear, but the theory of government failure is yet neither as comprehensive nor as powerful as the theory of market failure. While it raises important warnings about the general problems likely to be encountered in pursuing social values through public policies, the theory of government failure is not yet well developed enough to allow us always to predict the particular consequences of specific government interventions. Enthusiasm for perfecting society through public intervention, therefore, should be tempered by an awareness that unintended consequences will often arise.

In the following discussion we classify government failures as problems inherent in four general features of political systems: direct democracy, representative government, bureaucratic supply, and decentralized government. In addition to their conceptual importance, these features have varying degrees of practical relevance for policy analysts. At one extreme are the characteristics of direct democracy, which simply warn analysts to be skeptical of claims that the results of elections and referenda provide unambiguous mandates for specific policies. At the other extreme are the characteristics of bureaucratic supply and decentralized government, which help analysts anticipate the problems likely to be encountered during the implementation of public policies. An understanding of the characteristics of representative government can help analysts determine and improve the political feasibility of their preferred policy alternatives. Although we note some of these practical implications of government failure along the way, our primary purpose in this chapter is to provide a conceptual framework that will be useful for analysts who must operate in a politically complex world.

PROBLEMS INHERENT IN DIRECT DEMOCRACY

Over the course of history, societies have employed a variety of mechanisms for making social choices. Monarchies and dictatorships, where the preferences of one or a small number of people dominate social choice, have to some extent given way to systems with broader bases of participation. Universal adult suffrage has come to be viewed as an essential element of democracy, which itself is an important social value in many national traditions. In democracies, voting serves as the mechanism for combining the preferences of individuals into social choices.

If voting were a perfect mechanism for aggregating individual preferences, then the job of the policy analyst would be much easier. Questions about the appropriate levels of public goods provision, redistribution, and public regulation of private activity could be answered either directly through referenda or indirectly through the election of representatives who serve as surrogate decision makers. The vast number of issues arising in a large industrial country, however, make reliance on referenda impractical for all but the most important issues. Even if improvements in communication technology greatly reduce the logistical costs of voting, the time and other costs citizens face in learning about issues limit the attractiveness of direct referenda. But reliance on referenda for the revelation of social values suffers from a more fundamental problem: no method of voting is both fair and consistent.

The Paradox of Voting

Imagine that a referendum were held in the United States to determine foreign policy toward Nicaragua. The issue has been structured so that a policy will be selected through a series of pairwise votes among three alternatives: declare war, support the Contra rebels trying to overthrow the Nicaraguan government, and stop supporting the rebels and work toward friendly relations. After much public debate, all voters fall into one of three categories. Hawks, who comprise 10 percent of voters, fear that Nicaragua will support subversion in other Central American countries. Their preferred policy is to declare war; their second choice is to support the Contras. Pragmatists, who make up 45 percent of voters, want to discourage Nicaragua from pursuing its current policies but do not want to fight a war with U.S. troops. Their preferred policy, therefore, is to support the Contras; their second choice is friendly relations. Finally, constitutionalists, who represent 45 percent of voters, prefer friendly relations. If aggressive action is to be taken against Nicaragua, however, they prefer it to be through a declaration of war rather than through support for the Contras.

Figure 4.1 summarizes the voters' policy choices under three different agendas. Agenda A first offers declared war and support for the Contras as alternatives. The hawks and constitutionalists rank war ahead of support of the Contras, so war wins with 55 percent of the vote. Next, voters are offered a choice between

Hypothetical Groups	1st Choice	Preferences 2nd Choice	3rd Choice	% of Voters
Hawks	War	Contras	Peace	10
Pragmatists	Contras	Peace	War	45
Constitutionalists	Peace	War	Contras	45

Agenda A (Result: Peace)

    Round 1: War versus Contras   War wins 55% to 45%
    Round 2: War versus Peace   Peace wins 90% to 10%

Agenda B (Result: Contras)

    Round 1: War versus Peace   Peace wins 90% to 10%
    Round 2: Peace versus Contras   Contras wins 55% to 45%

Agenda C (Result: War)

    Round 1: Peace versus Contras   Contras wins 55% to 45%
    Round 2: Contras versus War   War Wins 55% to 45%

Figure 4.1   An Illustration of the Paradox of Voting

war and peace. Both pragmatists and constitutionalists prefer peace to war, so peace wins with 90 percent of the vote under Agenda A.

Agendas B and C involve different sequences of pairings. Under Agenda B, voters first choose between war and peace. Because peace wins, they next choose between peace and the Contras. Because hawks and pragmatists prefer support of the Contras to peace, the Contras win with 55 percent of the vote. Under Agenda C, voters first choose the Contras over peace. In the following vote both hawks and constitutionalists prefer a declaration of war to support of the Contras, so war wins with 55 percent of the vote. Thus, each agenda results in a different social choice!

The situation is even more perplexing if we allow for the possibility that some people will be opportunistic in their voting. For example, consider how hawks might try to manipulate the outcome under Agenda A. If they have reasonable estimates of the percentages of voters who are pragmatists and constitutionalists, then they can anticipate that war will lose overwhelmingly to peace in the second round. If instead support for the Contras is paired with peace in the second round, then the Contras would win. The hawks, who prefer support for the Contras to peace, might decide to vote for the Contras over war even though they prefer war. If the other voters continued to vote their true preferences, then the Contras would be selected in the first round and defeat peace in the second round. Consequently, by voting in this opportunistic manner, the hawks would be able to avoid their least-preferred alternative, peace, which otherwise would have resulted. Because this opportunistic voting requires one to realize that a more favorable final outcome can sometimes be achieved by voting against one's true preferences in the preliminary rounds, political scientists usually refer to its as *sophisticated voting*.

Of course, others voters may also attempt to manipulate the outcome by voting against their true preferences in the first round. The final social choice would depend, therefore, not only on the agenda but also on the extent to which people engage in sophisticated voting. At the heart of this indeterminacy lies what is often referred to as the *paradox of voting*. It brings into question the common interpretation of voting outcomes as "the will of the people."

The paradox of voting was first discovered by the French mathematician and philosopher Condorcet in the eighteenth century. Although later rediscovered by Charles Dodgson (Lewis Carroll) and others, its relevance to the study of democracy was not widely recognized until after the Second World War.[2] As long as the paradox of voting was viewed as a peculiar result of a particular voting scheme, it could be dismissed by scholars as a curiosity. But in 1951, Kenneth Arrow proved that any voting rule that satisfies a basic set of fairness conditions may produce illogical results.[3]

Arrow's *General Possibility Theorem* applies to any rule for choice where two or more persons must select a policy from among three or more alternatives. It assumes that we require any such scheme to satisfy at least the following conditions to be considered fair: First, each person is allowed to have any transitive

[2]The paradox of voting was rediscovered by Duncan Black in the 1940s. For an overview, see William H. Riker, *Liberalism Against Populism* (San Francisco: Freeman, 1982), pp. 1–3.

[3]Kenneth Arrow, *Social Choice and Individual Values*, 2nd ed. (New Haven, Conn.: Yale University Press, 1963). For a treatment that can be followed with minimal mathematics, see Julian H. Blau, "A Direct Proof of Arrow's Theorem," *Econometrica*, Vol. 40, No. 1, January 1972, pp. 61–7.

preferences over the possible policy alternatives.[4] Second, if one alternative is unanimously preferred to a second, then the rule for choice will not select the second. Third, the rule is not arbitrary in the sense that it will always select the same alternative when faced with the same collection of individual preferences and the same set of alternatives. Fourth, the rule must not allow any one person dictatorial power to impose his or her preferences regardless of the preferences of others. Arrow's theorem states that any fair rule for choice (one that satisfies the four conditions above) will fail to ensure a transitive social ordering of policy alternatives. In other words, cyclical (intransitive) social preferences like those appearing in the paradox of voting can arise from *any* fair voting system.[5]

What are the implications of Arrow's theorem for the interpretation of democracy? First, because cycles can arise with any fair voting scheme, those who control the agenda will have great opportunity for manipulating the social choice. Referring back to Figure 4.1, note that even though only 10 percent of the voters prefer war over the other alternatives, war will result if voting follows Agenda C. More generally, it appears that, in a wide range of circumstances involving policy alternatives with more than one dimension (for example, choosing tax rates and deductions in a tax bill), once a cycle arises anywhere in the social ordering, a person with control of the agenda can select a series of pairwise votes to secure any of the alternatives as a final choice.[6] Thus one would have to know how a final vote was reached before one could evaluate the extent to which it reflects the will of the majority.

Second, the introduction of alternative policies that create cycles is often an attractive strategy for voters who would otherwise face an undesirable social choice. For instance, William H. Riker argues persuasively that the introduction of slavery as an important national issue in the United States after 1819 can be interpreted as the ultimately successful method in a series of attempts by Northern Whigs (later Republicans) to split the nationally strong Democratic party.[7] Riker goes on to offer a fundamentally important generalization: Persistent losers have an incentive to introduce new issues in an attempt to create voting cycles that offer an opportunity to defeat the dominant coalitions during the resulting periods of disequilibrium. Because of this incentive, we should expect voting cycles to be more frequent than if they simply resulted unintentionally from chance combinations of individual preferences. In other words, political disequilibrium, and

---

[4] *Transitivity* requires that if alternative one is preferred to alternative two and alternative two is preferred to alternative three, then alternative one is preferred to alternative three.

[5] Further, other scholars have proven that sophisticated voting (manipulation of outcomes by voting against one's true preferences) is an inherent feature of all fair voting systems. Allan Gibbard, "Manipulation of Voting Schemes: A General Result," *Econometrica*, Vol. 41, No. 4, July 1973, pp. 587–601; and Mark Satterthwaite, "Strategy Proofness and Arrow's Conditions," *Journal of Economic Theory*, Vol. 10, No. 2, April 1975, pp. 187–217.

[6] In particular, if the agenda setter has full information about the preferences of the voters, who vote sincerely, then he can reach any desired alternative through a series of pairwise votes. Richard D. McKelvey, "Intransitivities in Multidimensional Voting Models and Some Implications for Agenda Control," *Journal of Economic Theory*, Vol. 12, No. 3, June 1976, pp. 472–82; and Norman Schofield, "Instability of Simple Dynamic Games," *Review of Economic Studies*, Vol. 45, No. 4, October 1978, pp. 575–94.

[7] William H. Riker, *Liberalism Against Populism* (San Francisco: Freeman, 1982), pp. 213–32.

the attendant problem of interpreting the meaning of social choices, is especially likely when the stakes are high.

Preference Intensity and Bundling

Imagine a society that decides every public policy question by referendum. If everyone votes according to his or her true preferences on each issue, social choices may result that are both Pareto inefficient and distributionally inequitable. For example, consider a proposal to build an express highway through a populated area. If we were able to elicit truthful answers from each person about how much he or she would value the road, we might find that a majority of people would each be willing to pay a small amount to have the road built, while a minority, perhaps those living along the proposed route, would require a large amount of compensation to be made as well-off after the construction of the road as before. If the total amount the majority would be willing to pay falls short of the total amount needed to compensate the minority, then the project is not Pareto efficient nor even potentially Pareto efficient. Further, most would view the project as inequitable because it concentrates costs on a minority. Nevertheless, the project would be adopted in a majority rule referendum if all voted their true preferences.

Of course, not everyone in the majority will necessarily vote according to strict private interests. Some may vote against the project out of a sense of fairness. Others may fear setting a precedent that might be used to justify unfair policies when they are in the minority. Absent these constraints, however, direct democracy can lead to *tyranny by the majority*, whereby either a permanent majority consistently inflicts costs on a minority or a temporary majority opportunistically inflicts very high costs on a temporary minority.[8]

Majorities may also inadvertently inflict high costs on minorities because voting schemes do not allow people to express the intensity of their preferences. No matter how much someone dislikes a proposed project, he or she only gets one vote. Even if the majority wishes to take the interests of the minority into consideration, they have no guarantee that the minority will be truthful in revealing the intensity of their preferences. In fact, the minority would have an incentive to overstate the intensity of their dislikes, perhaps checked only by the need to maintain some level of credibility. We can contrast this characteristic of collective choice with markets for private goods that allow people to express the intensity of their preferences by their willingness to purchase various quantities at various prices.

The danger of tyranny by the majority makes democracy by referendum generally undesirable; the complexity of modern public policy makes it impractical. Perhaps the closest a society could come to direct democracy would be the election of a decision maker who would serve subject to recall. The decision maker

---

[8]In situations where individual preferences create a voting cycle, we might describe the social choice that results from agenda control as *tyranny by the minority*. For example, consider the hawks in Figure 4.1. They may be able to achieve a temporary majority for a declaration of war even though a majority would prefer peace. No matter which policy is selected, a majority would prefer some other policy if given the choice.

would at least have some opportunity to fashion policies that took into consideration the intense preferences of minorities. He or she would have an incentive to
do so if the composition of intense minorities changed with issues. Otherwise,
two or more intense minorities might form a new majority in favor of recall.

Candidate decision makers would stand for office on platforms consisting
of positions on important policy issues. Voters would have to evaluate the bundle
of positions offered by each candidate. Different voters may vote for the same
candidate for different reasons. In fact, a candidate holding the minority position
on every important issue may still win the election. For example, one-third of
the electorate may vote for a candidate because of her position on trade policy,
which they believe to be most salient, even if they dislike her positions on all the
other issues. Another one-third may dislike her position on trade policy but vote
for her because of her position on defense spending, which they view as the most
important issue. Thus, she may win the election even though a majority of voters
opposes her positions on all issues including trade and defense policies. The general
implication for democracy is that whenever people must vote on a bundle of
policies, it is not necessarily the case that any particular policy in the winning
bundle represents the will of a majority. Even a landslide victory may not represent a "mandate from the people" for the winner's proposed policies.

Democracy as a Check on Power

The paradox of voting, the possibility of minorities with intense preferences,
and the problem of bundling show the imperfection, and imperfectibility, of
democracy as a mechanism of social choice. As policy analysts, we must recognize
that democratic processes will not always give us a true assessment of social values.
Perhaps no consistent social values exist; perhaps voting will not discover them.
Hence governments apparently following the "will of the people" will not always
be doing good.

Despite these inherent problems, direct democracy offers several advantages.
The opportunity for participation encourages citizens to learn about public affairs. Actual participation may make citizens more willing to accept social choices
that they opposed because they had an opportunity to be heard and to vote. Indeed, referenda may provide a means of putting divisive political issues to rest.
For example, the 1980 Quebec referendum on sovereignty association seems to
have defused what otherwise might have been an explosive issue. The 1975 referendum in Great Britain on the question of membership in the European Economic
Community, for instance, seems to have settled the issue in favor of continued
participation despite strong opposition.[9]

It is another feature of democracy, however, that makes it preferable to other
systems of social choice: it provides a great check on the abuse of power by giving
the electorate the opportunity to overturn onerous policies and remove unpopular
decision makers. It is this ability to "throw the bastards out" that fundamentally

---

[9]Austin Ranney, ed., *The Referendum Device* (Washington, D.C.: American Enterprise Institute,
1981), pp. xii, 1–18. Also, for a discussion of the disadvantages of referenda, see David Butler and
Austin Ranney, *Referendums: A Comparative Study of Practice* (Washington, D.C.: American Enterprise
Institute, 1978).

gives democracy its intrinsic social value. Democracy does not always lead to good, let alone the best, policies, but it provides an opportunity to correct the worst mistakes. Although we cannot count on democratic processes to produce enlightened public policies, as policy analysts we should nevertheless recognize their essential role in the preservation of liberty. They may deny us the full benefits of a truly benevolent and wise government, but they help protect us from the harm of one that is either evil or foolish.

PROBLEMS INHERENT IN REPRESENTATIVE GOVERNMENT

In modern democracies, representatives of the electorate actually make and execute public policy. Although the particular constitutional arrangements vary considerably across countries, in most democratic systems voters choose representatives to legislative or executive, and sometimes judicial, branches. The legislature typically plays a dominant role in establishing public policy by passing laws, but also often plays an administrative role by monitoring budgets and overseeing government operations. The chief executive exercises administrative responsibility, including the appointment of high-ranking officials in government agencies. Members of the executive branch make public policy when they interpret legislation, as, for example, when agency heads issue rules under broadly delegated authority to regulate some aspect of commerce. In addition, they may make proposals that influence the legislative agenda. The members of the judicial branch also interpret laws as well as determine their constitutionality. These legislators, executives, and judges, often referred to as "public servants," represent the rest of society in the numerous governmental decisions that constitute public policy.

Representatives often face the dilemma of choosing between actions that advance their conception of the good society and actions that reflect the preferences of their constituencies.[10] For example, a legislator may believe that construction of a safe nuclear waste facility is socially desirable and that the best location would be in her district. Should she support construction of the facility even if the residents of her district are almost unanimously opposed to it? On the one hand, we might approve of her support of the facility as consistent with increasing aggregate social welfare. On the other hand, we might approve of her opposition as consistent with protecting a segment of society from bearing disproportionate costs of collective action. The very fact that we have no clear-cut way of resolving this sort of dilemma suggests the difficulty we face in evaluating the behavior of representatives.

Two factors greatly influence the way representatives actually behave. First, representatives have their own private interests. It would be naive to believe that

---

[10]Political philosophers distinguish between the roles of the representative as a *trustee* (who should act on behalf of what he believes to be his constituency's interest) and as a *delegate* (who should act in accordance with the desires of a majority of his constituency). They also distinguish between representation of a local constituency and the entire nation. For a review, see J. Rolland Pennock, *Democratic Political Theory* (Princeton, N.J.: Princeton University Press, 1979), pp. 321–34. Pennock argues that the proper role of a representative falls somewhere between that of trustee and delegate (p. 325).

they do not consider their own well-being and that of their families. Elected representatives, motivated perhaps by the status and perquisites of office, usually seek either reelection or election to higher office. Candidates often behave as if they are trying to maximize the percentage of votes they will receive. This strategy, which maximizes the probability that they will actually gain a majority, requires them to pay more attention to the interests of the most responsive citizens than to those who are either unlikely to vote or who are likely to vote according to party, ethnicity, or other general considerations. Public executives, elected and appointed, similarly seek career security and advancement as well as circumstances that make it easier to manage their agencies. In general, the personal interests of representatives tend to push them toward responsiveness to their constituencies and away from concern for broader social welfare. Legislators tend to emphasize benefits to their districts over social costs; public executives tend to value resources for use by their agencies beyond their contribution to social benefits.

Second, individuals must incur costs to monitor the behavior of their representatives. Given financial and time constraints, individuals will usually not find it in their private interests to articulate policy preferences or to monitor closely the actions of their representatives. The broader the scope of government, the more costly is comprehensive articulation and monitoring. Those who do monitor typically have strong policy preferences based upon either ideology or financial interests. Consequently, representatives tend to be most closely evaluated by groups that have preferences very different from their broader constituencies. These ''interest groups'' may thus enjoy more influence with representatives than they would in a world with perfect information and costless monitoring.

In the following sections we explore some of the implications of self-interested representatives who are not fully monitored by their constituencies. These implications should be thought of as general tendencies. Not all representatives will act in their own narrow self-interest all of the time. Some will have strong policy preferences that lead them occasionally to take stands that are politically costly. (Of course, in so doing they run an increased risk of being turned out of office.) Analysts can sometimes make common cause with such representatives on the basis of principle. More generally, however, analysts find allies among representatives whose private interests happen to lead them to what the analysts believe to be good policies.

Rent Seeking: Diffuse and Concentrated Interests

In a world where most people pay little attention to their representatives, the politically active few have an opportunity to wield influence disproportionate to their number. By providing information, activists may be able to persuade representatives to support their positions and advocate them more effectively in the political arena. By promising to help secure the votes of constituency groups and by providing campaign funds, they may be able to alter the way representatives concerned with reelection view the social good—at least as revealed by the representatives' policy choices.

Who is likely to become politically active? Undoubtedly, some people have a strong sense of duty to promote the social good and therefore feel obliged to express their views on public policy issues whether they stand to gain or lose personally. In general, however, private self-interest plays an important role in motivating political participation. If we believe that most people are economically rational, then the greater the expected net benefits one expects to reap from some political activity, the more likely that one will undertake the activity. Policies that would spread large aggregate benefits widely and uniformly among the electorate may not elicit active political support because, for any individual, the costs of political activity exceed the expected benefits (which are the individual's private gains if the policy is adopted weighted by the probability that political action will result in adoption). Similarly, no individuals may find it in their own self-interests to protest policies that spread costs widely. In contrast, at least some people will likely find it in their self-interest to become politically active when policies involve concentrated costs or benefits. Assuming that representatives respond at least somewhat to political activity, the consequence of individual rationality will be collective choices biased toward policies with concentrated benefits and away from policies with concentrated costs. This bias opens the door for the adoption of policies for which total costs exceed total benefits.

Concentrated economic benefits (and diffuse economic costs) often arise when governments intervene in markets. The interventions generally create economic benefits in the form of rents—payments to owners of resources above those which the resources could command in any alternative use. Lobbying for such interventions is called· rent seeking.[11]

The effort to use government to restrict competition is perhaps the oldest form of rent seeking. In earlier times kings gained revenue by sharing the rents that resulted from monopolies given to favored subjects. In more modern times, bribery by those seeking local monopolies, such as cable television franchises, has contributed to the corruption of local public officials. Professions often attempt to keep wages high by restricting entry through government-sanctioned licensing—if the restricted entry does not provide offsetting benefits, such as reductions in informational asymmetry (as described in Chapter 3), the professionals gain rents at the expense of consumers. Domestic manufacturers often lobby for tariffs and quotas on foreign imports so that they can sell their products at higher prices. By limiting foreign competition, tariffs and quotas extract rents for domestic manufacturers from domestic consumers.

Firms within an industry may seek regulation as a way of limiting competition.[12] For instance, each of the three major laws that expanded federal regulation of the U.S. pharmaceutical industry was supported by firms that believed they would be able to meet standards more easily than their competitors.[13] Even when industries initially oppose regulation, their concentrated interests give them an incentive to lobby the regulators; the result may be "capture." For example, the U.S. Interstate Commerce Commission was originally created largely in

---

[11]James M. Buchanan, Robert D. Tollison, and Gordon Tullock, eds., *Toward a Theory of the Rent-Seeking Society* (College Station: Texas A&M University Press, 1980).

[12]George Stigler, "The Theory of Economic Regulation," *Bell Journal of Economics and Management Science*, Vol. 3, No. 1, Spring 1971, pp. 3–21.

[13]David Leo Weimer, "Organizational Incentives: Safe—and Available—Drugs," in LeRoy Graymer and Frederick Thompson, eds., *Reforming Social Regulation* (Beverly Hills, Calif.: Sage Publications, 1982), pp. 19–69.

response to anticompetitive practices by the railroads.[14] By the 1920s, however, the ICC so identified with the interests of the railroads that it tried to protect them from the growing competition from trucking.[15]

Sometimes governments generate rents for producers by directly setting prices in markets. For example, many countries set price floors on certain agricultural products like wheat, milk, and honey. Figure 4.2 illustrates the rent transfers and deadweight losses that result. Without a price floor, quantity q_e will be supplied and demanded at market clearing price P_e. At an imposed floor price of P_s, the quantity demanded falls to q_D. Those who are able to sell their output extract a rent from consumers equal to the area of rectangle $P_s P_e cd$. A deadweight loss equal to the area of triangle abd also results from the losses in consumer and producer surplus associated with lower consumption levels. Of course, at floor price P_s, farmers will want to supply q_s. To maintain the price floor, therefore, the government must take the excess supply off the market. It may try to do so by forcing farmers to destroy the excess, by inducing farmers to grow less, or by buying up the surplus and holding it off the market. In the latter case, the revenue going to farmers from consumers and the government equals the area of rectangle $P_s P_e fg$, $P_s P_e ag$ of which is rent; efficiency losses equal to the area of triangle aeg result.

Programs like price supports often produce only temporary rent transfers. If farmers believe that the government will permanently guarantee a price above the market clearing level, the price of land will rise to reflect the higher value of its output. Specifically, the price of land will reflect the present value of future rents. A farmer who sells his land after the introduction of the price supports therefore captures all the rent. The new owner, who must service the debt on the purchase amount, does not realize any profits above the normal rate of return. In effect, as the original farmers extract their shares of the rent by selling their land, the supply curve shifts up to the level of the support price. Attempts to regain efficiency and reduce government expenditures through elimination of the price supports will force many of the current owners into bankruptcy.[16]

Even the initial beneficiaries of the market intervention may fail to realize the full rents because of the costs of the rent-seeking activity. Direct lobbying and campaign contributions can be costly, especially if they must be spread over a large number of representatives to secure adoption of the intervention. In the extreme, all the rents may be dissipated, leaving the rent seekers no better off than they were in the absence of the intervention.

[14]Some scholars argue that the railroads welcomed regulation as a way of rescuing faltering cartels. See Gabriel Kolko, *Railroads and Regulation, 1877-1916* (Princeton, N.J.: Princeton University Press, 1965); and Paul W. MacAvoy, *The Economic Effects of Regulation: The Trunk-Line Railroad Cartels and the Interstate Commerce Commission Before 1900* (Cambridge, Mass.: MIT Press, 1965).

[15]Samuel P. Huntington, "The Marasmus of the ICC: The Commission, the Railroads, and the Public Interest," *Yale Law Review*, Vol. 61, No. 4, April 1952, pp. 467-509.

[16]For a general discussion of the problem of one-time rent gains see Gordon Tullock, "The Transitional Gains Trap," in Buchanan, Tollison, and Tullock, eds., *Rent-Seeking Society*, pp. 211-21. For an interesting case study that illustrates the transitional gains trap by comparing the highly regulated egg industry in British Columbia with the less-regulated industry in Washington State, see Thomas Borcherding (with Gary W. Dorosh), *The Egg Marketing Board: A Case Study of Monopoly and Its Social Cost* (Vancouver, B.C.: Fraser Institute, 1981).

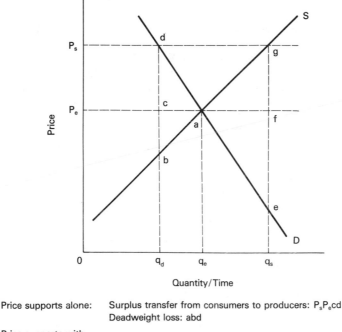

Price supports alone: Surplus transfer from consumers to producers: P_sP_ecd
                         Deadweight loss: abd

Price supports with
government purchases: Surplus transfer from consumers and government to producers: P_sP_eag
                         Surplus loss from overproduction: aeg

Figure 4.2   Surplus Transfers and Deadweight Losses under Price Supports

Rents can be realized directly from government as well as through the marketplace. Outright grants can sometimes be secured if a plausible public rationale can be offered. Because they tend to be more hidden from public view, exemptions from regulations and taxes are often more attractive targets for rent seekers. Sometimes tax loopholes provide large benefits to small numbers of firms. For example, the transition rules of the 1986 U.S. tax reform law create about $10 billion in loopholes, some written with restrictions so specific that they benefited single companies.[17]

Despite the advantages concentrated interests enjoy in mobilizing for political activity, they do not always prevail over diffuse interests. If those with similar interests are already organized, then they may be able to use the existing organizational structure to overcome the free riding problem that would keep them from expressing their interests individually. For instance, people join the National Rifle Association primarily because of their interests in hunting, shooting, and gun collecting. While very few individual members would find it in their personal interests to lobby on their own, most support expenditures by the NRA for lobbying

[17]Mark D. Uehling and Rich Thomas, "Tax Reform: Congress Hatches Some Loopholes," *Newsweek*, September 29, 1986, p. 22.

on such issues as gun control. In effect, organizations like the NRA provide public goods for their members.

Diffuse interests may also enjoy access to representatives by virtue of their distribution. For example, the National Education Association appears to enjoy success in lobbying not only because it has a large, well-educated, and politically active membership, but also because its membership is spread fairly evenly over congressional districts.[18] Similarly, organizations of local governments are often effective at the national level because their members generally have access to at least their own representatives.[19] The extent to which such diffuse interests can become politically effective usually depends on the existence of an organization to mobilize the contributions of individual members.

Even without the advantage of prior organization, however, diffuse interests can sometimes overcome highly concentrated interests. Experience suggests that two factors facilitate the success of diffuse interests: attention to the policy issue from a large segment of the electorate and low public trust in the concentrated interests. These factors often hold in situations where key goods rise dramatically in price. For example, rapidly rising rental prices often attract widespread attention in communities with low rates of home ownership and generate animosity toward landlords who appear to be profiting at the expense of tenants. Representatives may respond with rent control programs that provide modest short-run savings to current tenants at the expense of landlords.

The regulation of petroleum prices in Canada and the United States during the 1970s also shows diffuse interests dominating concentrated ones. The quadrupling of world oil prices during the Arab oil embargo drew public attention to the "energy crisis" and raised widespread suspicion that oil companies were profiteering. Each country instituted extensive regulation of its petroleum industry, including price ceilings on petroleum products.

It is worth noting that those who successfully organize diffuse interests may enjoy concentrated private benefits. They may draw salaries as staff members and enjoy access to the political process. These entrepreneurs thus face incentives to search for issues that will enable them to maintain support for their organizations.

Mobilizations of diffuse interests that simply impede the rent seeking of concentrated interests probably advance the social good. Sometimes, however, they facilitate rent seeking. When they result in price ceilings, for instance, they generally reduce economic efficiency and rarely lead to greater equity. Figure 4.3 illustrates these points. The price ceiling, P_c, lies below the unrestrained market price, P_e. At price P_c, consumers demand q_D but producers supply only q_s. In the "best case," consumers gain a surplus equal to the area of rectangle, P_eP_cbc, which corresponds to the producers' loss of rents on the q_s units they sell; the social cost of the transfer, however, is a deadweight loss of social surplus from reduced consumption equal to the area of triangle abd.

[18]Richard A. Smith, "Advocacy, Interpretation, and Influence in the U.S. Congress," *American Political Science Review*, Vol. 78, No. 1, March 1984, pp. 44–63.

[19]Robert H. Salisbury, "Interest Representation: The Dominance of Institutions," *American Political Science Review*, Vol. 78, No. 1, March 1984, pp. 64–76.

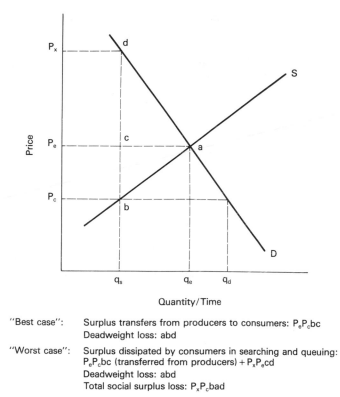

Quantity/Time

"Best case": Surplus transfers from producers to consumers: P_eP_cbc
Deadweight loss: abd

"Worst case": Surplus dissipated by consumers in searching and queuing:
P_eP_cbc (transferred from producers) $+ P_xP_ecd$
Deadweight loss: abd
Total social surplus loss: P_xP_cbad

Figure 4.3 Surplus Transfers and Deadweight Losses under Price Ceilings

In the "worst case," consumers dissipate the surplus they gain from producers as well as surplus equal to the area of rectangle P_xP_ecd. When supply is limited to q_s, consumers value the last unit available at P_x. Therefore, consumers will be willing to pay up to $P_x - P_c$ in nonmonetary costs such as queuing, searching, and perhaps even bribing to obtain shares of the limited supply. These costs have the effect of dissipating the benefits consumers enjoy from the lower monetary cost.

In order to achieve the "best case," an efficient rationing scheme is needed. For example, the distribution of coupons entitling consumers to shares of the available supply, coupled with an efficient "white market" for buying and selling coupons, could secure the surplus transfer for consumers without substantial dissipation. Coupon rationing can be administratively costly, however, because it requires creation and distribution of an entirely new currency. In addition, in most markets rationing schemes become obsolete because the shortages induced by ceiling prices eventually disappear as producers reduce product quality and consumers shift their demand to other markets.[20]

[20]For a detailed discussion of the impact of price ceilings, see George Horwich and David Leo Weimer, *Oil Price Shocks, Market Response, and Contingency Planning* (Washington, D.C.: American Enterprise Institute, 1984), pp. 57–110.

Advocates of price ceilings usually defend their positions on equity grounds. They argue that the poor have a better chance at obtaining a "fair share" of the good if allocation is not done solely on the basis of price. But the mechanisms of nonprice allocation do not always favor the poor. Queuing for gasoline, for instance, involves less hardship for two-adult families with flexible professional work hours than for single parents working fixed hours. More importantly, price ceilings tend to create a number of big losers. For example, by reducing economic efficiency, price ceilings on petroleum products contribute to higher levels of unemployment and lower wages during oil price shocks. Another example is the effect of rent control on future residents: by locking-in current tenants and by discouraging investment in rental housing, rent control hurts those who would like to live in the area some day. Because the identities of the big losers are generally not revealed until after implementation of the price ceilings, their interests rarely receive consideration at the time of adoption.

The accumulation of rent-seeking organizations can have adverse effects on economic growth. Mancur Olsen argues that in stable societies rent-seeking "distributional coalitions" shift resources toward cartel activity and lobbying and away from production.[21] Aside from this direct effect on economic efficiency, attempts by coalitions to protect their rents reduces the capacities of societies to adopt new technologies and reallocate resources to meet changing conditions. Consequently, in Olsen's view, the greater is the accumulation of distributional coalitions, the slower the rate of economic growth.

Problems of the District-Based Legislature

Legislatures rely on voting to reach collective decisions. As we have already discussed, no method of voting is both fair and consistent. Procedural rules concerning such things as agenda setting and permissible amendments may prevent cyclical voting, but cannot eliminate opportunities for sophisticated voting and agenda manipulation. An additional collective choice problem arises in legislatures because the members usually represent constituencies with heterogeneous preferences. Specifically, under majority voting, certain distributions of preferences can result in social choices opposed by a majority of the total electorate.[22]

For example, consider a legislature made up of 100 members, each representing the same number of constituents. Assume that representatives vote according to the preferences of a majority of their constituents. Imagine that 51 percent of the voters in 51 of the constituencies favor a particular policy, while none of the voters in the other 49 favor it. Majority voting in the legislature would result in adoption of the policy, even though it is favored by only a little more than one-quarter of the total electorate.

Because such extreme distributions of preferences are likely to be somewhat rare, the problem of minority choice under representative government probably

---

[21]Mancur Olson, *The Rise and Decline of Nations: Economic Growth, Stagflation, and Social Rigidities* (New Haven, Conn.: Yale University Press, 1982), p. 69.

[22]James M. Buchanan and Gordon Tullock, *The Calculus of Consent* (Ann Arbor: University of Michigan Press, 1962), pp. 220–22.

has limited practical significance in political systems with only two parties.[23] A much more important social choice problem arises from the efforts of representatives to serve the narrow interests of their constituencies.

In most countries legislators represent geographically defined districts. While they may sincerely wish to do what is in the best interests of the entire country, their self-interest in terms of reelection encourages them to pay special attention to the interests of their districts. This often leads to policy choices that do not contribute to aggregate national welfare.

The problem goes well beyond legislators emphasizing the social benefits that accrue to their own constituencies in deciding how to vote. Certain social costs sometimes appear as benefits to districts.[24] For example, a benefit-cost analysis of a weapons system from the social perspective would count expenditures on components as costs. A legislator, however, might very well count expenditures on components manufactured in her own district as benefits because they contribute to the vitality of the local economy. What from the social perspective might be a cost of say $10 million might be viewed by the legislator as a benefit of perhaps $5 million. For example, observers have attributed the ultimate political success of the U.S. B-1 bomber program partly to the fact that major subcontractors are located in a large number of congressional districts.[25]

District-oriented valuation of expenditures often leads to adoption of policies with net social costs as legislators bargain with each other to get their share from the "pork barrel." This process, sometimes called "logrolling," involves assembling a collection of projects that provide sufficient locally perceived benefits to gain adoption of the packages as a whole.[26] When coupled with an unwillingness on the part of representatives to bear the political costs of raising taxes, logrolling for district "pork" contributes to deficit spending.

The legislative process generally favors policies that spread perceived benefits over a majority of districts. Although this tendency may contribute to regional equality, it also makes targeting and policy experimentation difficult. Some programs produce net social benefits only in special circumstances and limited scope.

---

[23]In systems with more than two parties, the problem of minority rule is more common. For example, the Conservatives in Great Britain have won control of Parliament with a minority of votes in their last three elections. In the 1987 election, for instance, the Conservatives won 59.4 percent of the seats in Parliament with only 43.3 percent of total votes cast.

[24]For a formal development of this idea, see Kenneth A. Shepsle and Barry R. Weingast, "Political Solutions to Market Problems," *American Political Science Review*, Vol. 78, No. 2, June 1984, pp. 417–34; and Barry R. Weingast, Kenneth A. Shepsle, and Christopher Johnsen, "The Political Economy of Benefits and Costs: A Neoclassical Approach to Distributive Politics," *Journal of Political Economy*, Vol. 89, No. 4, August 1981, pp. 642–64.

[25]Michael R. Gordon, "B-1 Bomber Issue No Longer Whether to Build It But How Many, at What Price," *National Journal*, Vol. 15, No. 36, September 3, 1983, pp. 1768–72. ". . . Rockwell has aggressively lobbied for the B-1B program, notifying members of Congress about the jobs at stake, many of which are spread among contractors throughout the United States" (p. 1771).

[26]See, for example, William H. Riker and Steven J. Brams, "The Paradox of Vote Trading," *American Political Science Review*, Vol. 67, No. 4, December 1973, pp. 1235–47. Riker and Brams see logrolling as leading to reductions in social welfare. It is worth noting, however, that logrolling can also lead to socially beneficial results by allowing minorities with intense preferences to form majorities.

For instance, one or two centers for the study of educational innovation might offer positive expected net benefits; on the other hand, because skilled researchers and good ideas are scarce resources, twenty such centers offer net social costs. Nevertheless, legislative approval might be easier to obtain for the more dispersed program because it provides expenditures in more districts. The U.S. Model Cities program fit this pattern.[27] Originally proposed by President Johnson to demonstrate the effects of concentrated and coordinated federal aid on a small number of cities, it was expanded to include a large number of small and medium-sized cities to gain the support of congressmen who represented rural and suburban districts. As a result, resources were widely disbursed so that the effects of concentration could not be determined.

Limited Time Horizons: Electoral Cycles

Representatives must often make decisions that will have consequences extending many years into the future. From the perspective of economic efficiency, the representatives should select policies for which the present value of benefits exceeds the present value of costs. In making the comparison, each representative should apply the same social discount rate to the streams of benefits as to costs. Self-interest operating in an environment of imperfect monitoring, however, creates incentives for representatives to discount excessively costs and benefits that will not occur in the short-run.

Consider a representative who must stand for reelection in, say, two years. Because his constituency does not fully monitor his behavior, he faces the problem of convincing the electorate that his actions have contributed to their well-being. He will undoubtedly realize that it will be easier to claim credit for effects that have actually occurred than for ones expected to occur in the future. Now, imagine him choosing between two projects with different benefit and cost profiles. Project A offers large and visible net benefits over the next two years but large net costs in subsequent years so that, overall, it offers a negative net present value. Project B incurs net costs over the next two years but growing net benefits in subsequent years so that overall it offers a positive net present value. From the social perspective, the representative should select project B; from the perspective of his own self-interest, however, he can enhance his chances for reelection by selecting project A and claiming credit for the benefits that are realized prior to the election.

Under what circumstances will such myopic judgment be most likely to occur? One factor is the representative's perception of his vulnerability in his reelection bid. The more threatened he feels, the more likely he is to select projects with immediate and visible benefits for which he can claim credit. Representatives either not standing for reelection or running in "safe" districts are likely to place less value on short-term political gains and therefore will be more likely to act as "statesmen" with respect to the time horizon they use in evaluating projects. Another factor is the ease with which an opponent can draw the attention of the electorate to the yet-unrealized future costs. The more easily an opponent can

---

[27]Bryan D. Jones, *Governing Urban America: A Policy Approach* (Boston: Little, Brown, 1983), p. 410.

alert the electorate to these costs, the less likely is the incumbent to overdiscount the future.

To what extent does the myopia induced by the electoral cycle actually influence social choice? The common wisdom that legislatures rarely increase taxes in the year before an election, for instance, appears to be empirically verified by the pattern of tax changes observed across states within the United States.[28] At the national level, several studies suggest a link between general fiscal policy and election cycles for a number of countries.[29] These latter findings obviously bring into question the ability of national governments to manage efficiently macroeconomic activity even when reliable policy tools are available.

Posturing: Public Agendas, Sunk Costs, and Precedent

Candidates for public office must compete for the attention of the electorate. Most of us focus our attention on our families, careers, and other aspects of our private lives. While we certainly care about public policy, especially when it directly affects us, we generally do not devote great amounts of our time to learning about issues and about how our representatives handle them. Because gathering and evaluating detailed information on public affairs is costly, we usually rely on newspapers, magazines, radio, and television to do it for us. We should not be surprised, therefore, that representatives consider how their actions and positions will be portrayed in the mass media.

The media offer opportunities for representatives to reach the public. When the news media draw public attention to some undesirable social condition like drug abuse, representatives may be able to share the limelight by proposing changes in public policy. These attempts to convert undesirable and highly visible conditions to public policy problems amenable at least to apparent solution help determine the policy agenda. As newly "discovered" conditions push older ones from the media, the agenda changes. Representatives and analysts who prefer specific policies may have to wait for an appropriate condition to arise to gain a "policy window" into the agenda.[30] For example, advocates of urban mass transit in the United States enjoyed a policy window initially when the media reflected public concern about traffic congestion, another when the environmental movement drew attention to pollution, and a third when the energy crisis raised concern about

---

[28]The year of the governor's term also appears to influence the pattern of tax changes. John Mikesell, "Election Periods and State Tax Policy Cycles," *Public Choice*, Vol. 33, No. 3, 1978, pp. 99–105.

[29]See, for example, William D. Nordhaus, "The Political Business Cycle," *Review of Economic Studies*, Vol. 42(2), No. 130, 1975, pp. 169–90; C. Duncan MacRae, "A Political Model of the Business Cycle," *Journal of Political Economy*, Vol. 85, No. 2, April 1977, pp. 239–63; Edward R. Tufte, *Political Control of the Economy* (Princeton, N.J.: Princeton University Press, 1978); and Henry W. Chappell, Jr., and William R. Keech, "Welfare Consequences of the Six-Year Presidential Term Evaluated in the Context of a Model of the U.S. Economy," *American Political Science Review*, Vol. 77, No. 1, March 1983, pp. 75–91.

[30]For an excellent treatment of the ideas discussed in this paragraph, see John W. Kingdon, *Agendas, Alternatives, and Public Policies* (Boston: Little, Brown, 1984), pp. 205–218.

the conservation of fuel.[31] They made some progress in spreading their preferred solution when each of these windows opened.

A policy agenda strongly influenced by the pattern of media coverage is not necessarily consistent with the concept of public policy as a rational search for ways to improve social welfare. The policy agenda only reflects appropriate priorities if the media happen to cover conditions in proportion to their worthiness as public policy problems—a dubious assumption because undesirable social conditions, no matter how unamenable to correction by public policy, still may make good stories. Street crime, for instance, depends most heavily on local rather than national law enforcement policies. Nevertheless, it may elicit a national response when it commands national media attention, as was the case in the United States in the late 1960s.[32]

A media-driven policy agenda discourages the careful evaluation of alternatives. Representatives who take the lead in proposing policy responses are most likely to benefit from the wave of media coverage. Thus, they face an incentive to propose something before the crest passes. If they wait too long, the policy window may close. Further, adoption of any policy response may hasten the decline in media coverage by giving the appearance that something has been done about the problem. Consequently, more comprehensive and, perhaps, better-analyzed policy responses may not have time to surface. Even if they are held in reserve for the next policy window, they may no longer be the most desirable in light of the new conditions.

Whether or not representatives are attempting to exploit policy windows, they seek to put their actions and positions in a favorable light.[33] Their previous positions often constrain their current options. For example, politicians and economists often view *sunk costs* differently.[34] To an economist, resources committed to a project in the past and no longer available for other uses are ''sunk'' and irrelevant when deciding to either continue or terminate the project. The politician who advocated the project initially, however, may be loath to terminate it for fear that opponents will point to abandonment as an admission of a mistake. He may even use the earlier expenditures as a justification for continuation: ''If we stop now, we will have wasted the millions of dollars that we have already spent.'' While a statement of this sort is true, and perhaps politically significant, it makes a point that is irrelevant from the social perspective when deciding whether additional resources should be invested in the project.

---

[31]Ibid., p. 181.

[32]In the early 1970s James Q. Wilson reflected, ''Nearly ten years ago I wrote that the billions of dollars the federal government was then preparing to spend on crime control would be wasted, and indeed might even make matters worse if they were merely pumped into the existing criminal justice system. They were, and they have.'' *Thinking about Crime* (New York: Basic Books, 1975), p. 234.

[33]William Riker has coined the word *heresthetics* to refer to the art of political strategy. It includes such things as agenda control, sophisticated voting, and the introduction of new issues to split dominant majorities. It also encompasses the use of rhetoric, the art of verbal persuasion, for political purposes. William H. Riker, *The Art of Political Manipulation* (New Haven; Conn.: Yale University Press, 1986), pp. ix, 142–52. The limited attention of the electorate gives representatives ample scope for the use of rhetorical heresthetics.

[34]See Robert D. Behn, ''Policy Analysis and Policy Politics,'' *Policy Analysis*, Vol. 7, No. 2, Spring 1981, pp. 199–226.

Precedents often provide opportunities for representatives to gain favorable public reaction to their proposals. By pointing to apparently similar policies adopted in the past, representatives can appeal to people's sense of fairness: "We gave a loan guarantee to firm X last year, isn't it only fair that we do the same for firms Y and Z now?" Without close examination, it may not be clear that the circumstances that made the guarantee to firm X good policy do not hold for firms Y and Z. Policy analysts should anticipate the possibility that any new policies they recommend may serve as precedents for actions in the future. A subsidy, waiver, or other action that, when considered in isolation, appears socially desirable, may not actually be so if it increases the likelihood that representatives will inappropriately adopt similar actions in the future.

Representatives and Analysts

The characteristics of representative government that we have described suggest that the political system generally does not base public policy on the careful weighing of social costs and social benefits. To the extent that this failure either results from, or is facilitated by, limited information, policy analysts may be able to contribute to better social choices by providing assessments of the likely consequences of proposed policies. To the extent that inattention to social costs and benefits is tied to the self- interest of representatives, analysts may be able to contribute to the social good by helping to craft politically feasible alternatives that are better than those that would otherwise be adopted. In any event, analysts should try to anticipate the limitations of representative government when they propose and evaluate public policies.

PROBLEMS INHERENT IN BUREAUCRATIC SUPPLY

Governments often create publicly funded organizations to deal with perceived market failures.[35] Armies, court systems, and a variety of other agencies provide public goods that might be undersupplied by private markets. Other agencies regulate natural monopolies, externalities, and information asymmetries. Like private firms, they use labor and other factor inputs to produce outputs. Unlike private firms, however, they need not pass a market test to survive. Consequently, the extent to which their continued existence contributes to aggregate social welfare depends greatly upon the diligence and motivations of the representatives who determine their budgets and oversee their operations. The very nature of public agencies, however, makes monitoring difficult and inefficiency likely.

[35]In our discussion we use the term *public agency* to denote organizations that are staffed by government employees and that obtain the majority of their revenues from public funds rather than the sale of outputs. We distinguish public agencies from organizations that are owned by governments but generate the majority of their revenues from sales. Such publicly owned corporations (Crown Corporations in Canada, for instance) will not necessarily suffer from the problems we describe in this section. For a conceptual overview of publicly owned corporations, see Catherine Eckel and Aidan R. Vining, "Elements of a Theory of Mixed Enterprise," *Scottish Journal of Political Economy,* Vol. 32, No. 1, 1985, pp. 82–94.

The monitoring problem is not unique to public agencies. In fact, a growing "principal-agent" literature attempts to explain why principals (such as stockholders) employ agents (such as managers) to whom they delegate discretion. In other words, why do we have firms consisting of hierarchical relationships between principals and agents rather than sets of contracts that exactly specify the services to be provided and the payments to be made by every participant in the productive process? The answer lies in the fact that contracting involves negotiation costs. Rather than continuously recontracting, it may be less costly in terms of negotiation and performance-monitoring activities to secure services under fairly general labor contracts. When this is the case, we expect to observe production organized by hierarchical firms rather than by collections of independent entrepreneurs.[36]

The principal-agent problem arises because employers and employees do not have exactly the same interests and because it is costly for employers to monitor the behavior of their employees. For example, although employees generally want their firms to do well, they also enjoy doing things like reading the newspaper on the job. Managers must expend time, effort, and goodwill to keep such shirking under control. More generally, because agents have more information about their own activities than do their principals, agents can pursue their own interests to some extent. The principal faces the task of creating organizational arrangements that minimize the sum of the costs of the undesirable behavior of agents and of the activity undertaken to control it. These costs, which are measured relative to a world with perfect information, are referred to as *agency loss*.

Agency loss is inherent in all organizations, whether private or public. Three factors, however, make agency loss a more serious problem for public bureaus than for privately owned firms: the difficulty of valuing public outputs (and, therefore, performance), the lack of competition among bureaus, and the inflexibility of civil service systems. After discussing each of these factors, we focus on public executives as agents for political representatives.

The Necessity to Impute the Value of Output

In the absence of market failures, the marginal social value of the output of a competitive firm equals the market price. Customers reveal this marginal value by their willingness to pay. Most public agencies, however, do not sell their output competitively. In fact, many were undoubtedly created in the first place because markets appeared not to be functioning efficiently. Representatives thus face the problem of having to impute values to such goods as national security,

[36]Much of the intellectual underpinning for the theory of economic organization was provided by Ronald H. Coase, "The Nature of the Firm," *Economica*, Vol. 4, No. 16, November 1937, pp. 386–405. For a review of the literature that approaches the organization question from the perspective of the distribution of property rights, see Louis De Alessi, "The Economics of Property Rights: A Review of the Evidence," *Research in Law and Economics*, Vol. 2, No. 1, 1980, pp. 1–47. See also Armen A. Alchian and Harold Demsetz, "Production, Information Costs, and Economic Organization," *American Economic Review*, Vol. 62, No. 5, 1972, pp. 777–95; Oliver E. Williamson, *The Economics of Discretionary Behavior: Managerial Objectives in the Theory of the Firm* (Englewood Cliffs, N.J.: Prentice Hall, 1964); John C. McManus, "The Costs of Alternative Economic Organization," *Canadian Journal of Economics*, Vol. 8, No. 3, 1975, pp. 33–50; and Terry Moe, "The New Economics of Organization," *American Journal of Political Science*, Vol. 28, No. 4, November 1984, pp. 739–77.

law and order, and health and safety. Even when representatives are sincerely interested in estimating the true social benefits of such goods, analysts can rarely provide convincing methods for doing so.

The absence of reliable benefit measures makes it difficult to determine the optimal sizes of public agencies. For instance, most observers would agree that adding an aircraft-carrier battle group to the U.S. Navy would increase national security by some amount. Would it contribute enough to national security to justify its multibillion-dollar cost? This is a very difficult question to answer. Some progress toward an answer might be made by trying to assess how the additional battle group furthers various objectives of national security such as keeping the sea lanes open in time of war and projecting military capability to vital regions. Analysts might then be able to find alternative force configurations that better achieve the objectives or achieve them equally well at lower cost. In the end, however, these analyses do little to address the appropriateness of such politically established input goals as the "600-ship navy."

Often distributional goals further complicate the valuation problem. Private firms generally need not be concerned about which particular people purchase their products. In contrast, public agencies are often expected to distribute their output in accordance with principles such as horizontal and vertical equity. Crime reduction, for example, might be thought of as the major output of a police department. At the same time, however, the distribution of crime reduction across neighborhoods is also important—most of us would not favor aggregate reductions in crime gained at the expense of abandoning crime control in some neighborhoods altogether. The valuation of outputs when goals are multiple and conflicting requires consensus about how progress with respect to one goal should be traded off against retrogression with respect to another. Such consensus rarely exists.

Effects of Limited Competition on Efficiency

Competition forces private firms to produce output at minimum cost. Firms that do not use resources in the most efficient manner are eventually driven from the market by firms that do. Because public agencies do not face direct competition, they can survive even when they operate inefficiently.

We have already discussed the consequences of an absence of competition in our discussion of natural monopolies in the preceding chapter. Natural monopolies can maintain economic profits even if they operate above the minimum achievable average cost curve. The resulting X- inefficiency represents some combination of the opportunity cost of wasted resources and rent transfers in the form of excess payments to factor inputs. Because competition is absent, X-inefficiency can also arise in public agencies.

The absence of competition also affects the dynamic efficiency of public agencies.[37] Public agencies usually face inappropriate incentives for innovation. Usually public agencies have weaker incentives to innovate than private firms. The profit motive provides a strong incentive for firms to find new production methods (technological innovations) that will cut costs. When one firm in an in-

---

[37] See David L. Weimer, "Federal Intervention in the Process of Innovation in Local Public Agencies," *Public Policy*, Vol. 28, No. 1, Winter 1980, pp. 83–116.

dustry successfully innovates, others must follow or eventually be driven from the industry. Additionally, firms may be able to capture some of the industry-wide benefits of their innovations through patents. In comparison, public agencies are generally neither driven from existence if they do not innovate, nor capable of fully capturing the external benefits if they do.

Incentives for innovation do operate. Some agency heads seek the prestige and career advancement that might result from being perceived as innovators. Agency heads may also seek cost-reducing innovations at times of budgetary retrenchment to try to maintain output levels to their clienteles. These incentives, however, do not operate as consistently as the profit motive and threats to firm survival.

Public agency heads who do wish to innovate face several disadvantages relative to their private sector counterparts. They have no competitors to imitate. While they can sometimes look to agencies with similar functions in other jurisdictions, they face the valuation problem in deciding whether a new technology has actually produced net benefits elsewhere. Unlike managers of firms, they cannot borrow funds from banks to cover start-up costs. Instead, they must seek funds from their budgetary sponsors, who may be unwilling to allocate funds for uncertain research and development projects, especially when difficult-to-value improvements in output quality are the anticipated benefits. Finally, as we will discuss below, civil service rules may make it difficult to secure specialized expertise needed to implement innovations.

The absence of competition raises the possibility that public agencies can survive even if they fail to operate efficiently. Whether inefficiency actually results or not depends on the system of incentives that budgetary sponsors actually impose on public executives.

Inflexibility Caused by Civil Service Protections

The modern civil service provides career opportunities within public agencies. Typically, only high-ranking officials serve at the pleasure of the ruling political power. The remaining employees belong to the civil service, which, in theory, determines their employment tenure and salary independent of the political parties. This separation of most government employees from partisan politics provides continuity in expertise when ruling parties change as well as insulation against attempts to use agencies for partisan purposes.

Continuity and nonpartisanship, however, must be purchased at the expense of a certain amount of inflexibility in agency staffing. The same rules that make it difficult to fire employees for political purposes make it difficult to weed out the incompetent and unproductive. Fixed pay schedules, which provide less opportunity for undue political leverage over employees, tend to underreward the most productive and overreward the least productive. As the former leave for higher-paying jobs in the private sector, the agencies are left with a higher proportion of the latter.[38]

---

[38]For a brief discussion of the implications of this process for policy analysis offices, see Hank Jenkins-Smith and David L. Weimer, "Rescuing Policy Analysis from the Civil Service," *Journal of Policy Analysis and Management*, Vol. 5, No. 1, Fall 1985, pp. 143–47.

A civil service system that makes it difficult to fire employees must also take great care in hiring them if quality is to be maintained. But a slow and complicated hiring system reduces the ability of managers to implement new programs quickly. The problem is particularly severe for the public manager who fears losing allocated slots if they are not filled within the budget period. Rather than waiting for the civil service to give approval for hiring the most appropriate employee, the safer course of action may be simply to take someone less qualified who already is in the civil service system. The more often these sorts of decisions are made for expediency, the more difficult it is for agencies to operate efficiently in the long run.

Finally, consider the commonly heard complaint that bureaucracies are unresponsive. Because agencies usually enjoy monopoly status, consumers usually cannot show their displeasure by selecting another supplier. Of course, elected representatives have an incentive to be responsive to the constituent-consumers. But by shielding the civil service from undue political interference, the role politicians can play in informing agencies about public wants is also reduced. Threatening budget cuts and badgering agency executives may not be very effective ways of influencing behavior by the employees at the lowest level of the bureau, who, in most cases, actually deal with the public. Again, the necessity for some separation between politics and administration limits the capability of public agencies to meet consumer wants effectively.

The Public Executive as Agent

Public executives generally operate in environments characterized by great asymmetry of information, not just with respect to the general public but with respect to other representatives as well. The executive (agent) is generally in a much better position to know the minimum cost of producing any given level of output than either the public or its representatives (principals) who determine the agency's budget. For example, consider the U.S. Department of Defense. The public tends to pay attention primarily to sensational circumstances—the revelation that some toilet seats were purchased at $600 apiece, for instance. The Office of Management and Budget and the relevant congressional oversight committees look at the entire budget, but usually do so in terms of such billion-dollar elements as entire weapon systems. Limitations in time and expertise preclude extensive review of the ways available resources are actually used within the agency.[39] Even the secretary of defense suffers from an informational disadvantage relative to the heads of the many units that constitute the department.

We can see the implications of the asymmetry in information by introducing the concept of the *discretionary budget*: the difference between the budget that the agency receives from its sponsor and the minimum cost of producing the out-

---

[39]See William A. Niskanen, *Bureaucracy and Representative Government* (Chicago: Aldine-Atherton, 1971); Albert Breton and Ronald Wintrobe, "The Equilibrium Size of a Budget-Maximizing Bureau," *Journal of Political Economy*, Vol. 83, No. 1, February 1975, pp. 195–207; and Jonathan Bendor, Serge Taylor, and Ronald Van Gaalen, "Bureaucratic Expertise versus Legislative Authority: A Model of Deception and Monitoring in Budgeting," *American Political Science Review*, Vol. 79, No. 4, December 1985, pp. 1041–60.

put level that will satisfy the sponsor.[40] The executive enjoys the greatest freedom of action when the size of the discretionary budget is both large and unknown to the sponsor. It would be economically efficient for the executive to produce output at minimum cost so that he can return the discretionary budget to the sponsor. If he does so, however, he reveals information to the sponsor about the minimum cost—information that the sponsor can use in deciding how much to allocate to the agency in next year's budget. The observation that agencies rarely fail to spend their budgets, sometimes exhorting employees to spend faster as the end of the fiscal year approaches, suggests that few executives view revelation of their discretionary budgets as an attractive management strategy.[41]

If the agency were a private firm with sales revenue as the source of the budget, the owner-executive would simply keep the discretionary budget as profit.[42] In most countries, however, civil service laws keep public executives from converting discretionary budgets to personal income. Executives not wishing to return their discretionary budgets have an incentive to find personally beneficial ways to use their discretionary budgets within their agencies to make their jobs as managers easier. With extra personnel, executives can tolerate some shirking by employees that would be time consuming and perhaps unpleasant for the executive to eliminate. The added personnel might also make it easier for them to respond to unexpected demands faced by their agencies in the future. Increased spending on such things as travel and supplies might contribute to morale and thereby make managing more pleasant. These uses of the discretionary budget are the realization of X-inefficiency. They also represent what Charles Wolf calls *internalities*—the socially inappropriate inclusion of private and organizational considerations in social decision making.[43]

Analysts and Bureaucracy

Policy analysts who do not anticipate the problems inherent in bureaucratic supply risk giving bad advice about policy alternatives. The risk arises not only in considering such fundamental issues as the scope of government, but also in

[40]The concept of the discretionary budget allows Niskanen to generalize his earlier and seminal study of bureaucracy to objective functions beyond simple budget maximization. William A. Niskanen, "Bureaucrats and Politicians," *Journal of Law and Economics*, Vol. 18, No. 3, December 1975, pp. 617–44. For an excellent discussion of how Niskanen's work relates to earlier organizational theory concepts like *organizational slack*, see Bruce Jacobs, *The Political Economy of Organizational Change* (New York: Academic Press, 1981), pp. 18–30.

[41]For a brief discussion of the advantages and disadvantages of not spending allocated funds, see Aaron Wildavsky, *The Politics of the Budgetary Process*, 3rd ed. (Boston: Little Brown, 1979), pp. 31–32.

[42]In firms where chief executive officers are not the owners, they usually receive part of their compensation in the form of stock options to increase their incentives to maximize the present value of the firm. The design of such contractual arrangements in the face of information asymmetry is an important principal-agent problem. See, for example, Michael C. Jensen and William H. Meckling, "Theory of the Firm: Managerial Behavior, Agency Costs, and Ownership Structure," *Journal of Financial Economics*, Vol. 3, No. 4, 1976, pp. 305–60; and Eugene F. Fama, "Agency Problems and the Theory of the Firm," *Journal of Political Economy*, Vol. 88, No. 2, 1980, pp. 288–307.

[43]Charles Wolf, Jr., "A Theory of Nonmarket Failures," *Public Interest*, No. 55, Spring 1979, pp. 114–33 at pp. 21–23.

more instrumental issues like the choices of organizational forms for providing public goods. Of course, analysts who work in bureaucratic settings must be careful to keep their personal and organizational interests in perspective when called upon to give advice about the social good. At the same time, an understanding of the incentives others face in their organizational setting is often essential for designing policy alternatives that can be adopted and successfully implemented.

PROBLEMS INHERENT IN DECENTRALIZATION

Canada, the United States, and many other democratic countries have highly decentralized and complex systems of government. Separate and independent branches exercise legislative, executive, and judicial authorities. Some powers are exercised by the central government while others are reserved for the governments of local jurisdictions such as provinces, states, counties, cities, and towns. Within the executive branches of these various levels of government, agency executives often enjoy considerable discretion over policy and administration.

Strong normative arguments support several forms of decentralization. Distribution of authority among branches of government provides a system of "checks and balances" that makes abuse of authority by any one official less damaging and more correctible and that reduces the opportunity for tyranny by the majority.[44] Assigning different functions to different levels of government facilitates both the production of public goods at efficient levels and the matching of local public goods to local preferences.[45] Decentralization to lower levels of government is generally desirable because it brings citizens closer to public decisions, usually making it easier for them to exercise "voice" about the quantities and qualities of public good. More important, geographic decentralization is generally desirable because it permits citizens to exercise "exit" those dissatisfied with the policies of a jurisdiction have the opportunity to "vote with their feet" by moving to jurisdictions offering more preferred policies. Adherence to these normative principles, however, leads to governments that are not only decentralized but also complex.

The highly desirable benefits of decentralization come at a price. Decentralization tends to hinder implementation of policies. It also allows for fiscal externalities to occur in association with the supply of local public goods. Thus, while decentralization is a desirable, if not essential, structural feature of government, it sometimes limits the effectiveness of public policies.

The Implementation Problem

Adopted policies gain force through implementation. The passage of a law, the adoption of an administrative rule, or the issuance of a judicial order establish policy goals and specify the means thought necessary to achieve them. *Implementation* describes the efforts made to execute the means—efforts that do not always achieve the established goals.

---

[44]James Madison sets out the normative arguments for separation of powers in Nos. 47 to 51 of *The Federalist Papers* (New York: New American Library, 1961), pp. 300–25.

[45]See Wallace Oates, *Fiscal Federalism* (New York: Harcourt Brace Jovanovich, 1972), pp. 3–20.

Eugene Bardach provides an excellent metaphor for implementation: the process of assembling and keeping in place all the elements needed for a machine.[46] Of course, just as a machine may not work as intended if its design is flawed, a policy based on an incorrect theory may also produce unintended consequences. But an effective design (correct theory) is only a necessary, but not a sufficient, condition for a working machine (effective policy). If necessary parts (essential policy elements) are either not available or unreliable, the machine (policy) will not work effectively.

The essence of the implementation problem lies in the distribution of necessary elements. The greater the potential for either persons or organizations to withhold necessary contributions, the greater is the possibility of failure. Those who oppose the goals of the policy and those who do not view the goals as sufficiently beneficial to justify their own costs of compliance may purposely withhold contributions.[47] Others may do so simply because their resources and competence are too limited to allow them to comply.

In decentralized political systems, many officials have the capability to withhold contributions. They thereby enjoy bargaining power that may enable them to extract things from those who need their contributions. For example, consider the implementation of the U.S. strategic petroleum reserve program, which is intended to reduce the vulnerability of the U.S. economy to petroleum price shocks.[48] Approval from the governor of Louisiana was needed for essential facilities; before he would give it, he secured a number of concessions from the Department of Energy, including a promise that nuclear wastes would not be stored in his state. The DOE also was forced to make concessions to the Environmental Protection Agency, another federal agency, even though the petroleum reserve enjoyed the enthusiastic support of the president and Congress.

The problem of interorganizational cooperation also arises when central governments must rely on lower levels of government for contributions. Even when the central government enjoys nominal authority over units of the lower-level government, it faces the problem of monitoring the compliance of multiple jurisdictions that may have very different local conditions. For example, the central government may have the constitutional authority to order local school districts to end racial segregation. Systematic monitoring of compliance, however, may require an extended period of investigation because of the large number of jurisdictions involved. Further, the reasons for noncompliance may vary greatly across jurisdictions, making it difficult for the central government to employ a uniform enforcement strategy.

Implementation of policies requiring cooperation from lower-level governments becomes even more difficult when the central government does not have the authority to coerce. In order to induce cooperation successfully, the central

[46]Eugene Bardach, *The Implementation Game: What Happens after a Bill Becomes Law* (Cambridge, Mass.: MIT Press, 1977), pp. 36–38.

[47]Pressman and Wildavsky argue that means rather than ends are more likely to be the actual focus of conflicts during the implementation process. Jeffrey L. Pressman and Aaron Wildavsky, *Implementation* (Berkeley: University of California Press, 1973), pp. 98–102.

[48]David Leo Weimer, *The Strategic Petroleum Reserve: Planning, Implementation, and Analysis* (Westpoint, Conn.: Greenwood Press, 1982), pp. 39–62.

government must offer sufficient rewards to secure voluntary compliance. When the lower-level jurisdictions are highly diverse, the central government may offer more compensation than necessary to some and not enough to others, especially if either norms of fairness or legal restrictions force the central government to offer the same opportunities to all. For example, a grant program intended to induce local governments to improve their sewage treatment plants might very well fund some plants that would have been constructed by local governments anyway (the problem of displacement) and some plants that should not be built from the social perspective (the problem of targeting).[49]

Finally, we should note that many of the problems inherent in bureaucratic supply contribute to the implementation problem. The difficulty representatives have in monitoring costs often leaves them uncertain about the size of contributions that agencies actually can and do make, and sometimes gives public executives opportunities to avoid compliance that is in conflict with their own interests. When executives do wish to comply, they may have difficulty motivating subordinates who face attenuated rewards and punishments within the civil service. These problems introduce uncertainties that complicate interorganizational bargaining over compliance.

Fiscal Externalities

Decentralization permits local public goods to be better matched to local demands. It also gives people some opportunity to choose the bundles of public goods they consume through their selections of jurisdictions. The greater the variation in public goods bundles across jurisdictions, the greater is the opportunity for people to exercise choice by voting with their feet.[50] In the extreme, we can imagine migration working to sort people into groups with homogeneous preferences for local public goods. Because the number of jurisdictions is always limited and because people consider private factors, such as employment, as well as public goods in locational choice, the sorting process is never complete in reality. Further, jurisdictions have an incentive to discourage some migrants and encourage others.[51]

---

[49]For a discussion of the incentives that can operate to lead to inappropriate responses to inducements, see David Leo Weimer, *Improving Prosecution? The Inducement and Implementation of Innovations for Prosecution Management* (Westpoint, Conn.: Greenwood Press, 1980), pp. 5–26.

[50]The interpretation of locational choice as a method of demand revelation for local public goods was first suggested by Charles M. Tiebout, "A Pure Theory of Local Expenditures," *Journal of Political Economy*, Vol. 64, No. 5, October 1956, pp. 416–24. A similar but more general model of demand revelation through choice of membership was provided by James M. Buchanan, "An Economic Theory of Clubs," *Economica*, Vol. 32, No. 125, February 1965, pp. 1–14.

[51]See James M. Buchanan and Charles J. Goetz, "Efficiency Limits of Fiscal Mobility: An Assessment of the Tiebout Model," *Journal of Public Economics*, Vol. 1, No. 1, April 1972, pp. 25–42. For an application to international migration, see Norman Carruthers and Aidan R. Vining, "International Migration: An Application of the Urban Location Model," *World Politics*, Vol. 35, No. 1, October 1982, pp. 106–20. For a detailed application to metropolitan government in California, see Gary J. Miller, *Cities by Contract: The Politics of Municipal California* (Cambridge, Mass.: MIT Press, 1981), pp. 183–89.

Migrants who pay above-average tax shares and place below-average demands on public services are particularly desirable because they lower tax shares for everyone else in the jurisdiction without reducing service levels. In other words, they impart a positive fiscal externality to the established residents. In contrast, migrants who pay below-average tax shares and place above-average demands on public services are particularly undesirable because they impart a negative fiscal externality to established residents. Because tax shares are usually linear functions of property values at the local level, jurisdictions have an incentive to try to exclude those who would have below-average property values. The incentive leads to such local policies as minimum lot sizes, restrictions on multiple-unit dwellings, and restrictive building codes that inflate construction costs. One social cost of these policies is a reduction in housing opportunities for low- and middle-income families.

In competing for wealthier residents, local jurisdictions may inflict fiscal externalities on each other—families with low incomes and high service demands tend to be left behind in poorer jurisdictions. Similarly, local jurisdictions often inflict fiscal externalities on each other in competition for industry. Many local jurisdictions offer incentives such as tax reductions and site preparation to lure firms that will provide jobs to residents. These incentives are probably not large enough to influence the level of investment in the country as a whole. Therefore, the jurisdictions compete for a fixed amount of investment.

Local jurisdictions face a "prisoner's dilemma" in their decisions concerning incentives for industrial development. Consider two similar jurisdictions courting a single firm. If neither offered tax abatements to attract the firm, one of the jurisdictions would get the firm and receive full tax revenues. If one jurisdiction thought it would lose the competition, however, it might offer a tax abatement to change the firm's decision. Of course, the other jurisdiction would be in the same situation. The result is likely to be both jurisdictions offering abatements up to a level that would leave them indifferent between having the firm and not having it. As a consequence, neither jurisdiction gains from the competition.

Analysts in Decentralized Political Systems

Political decentralization poses challenges for policy analysts. By complicating the implementation process, it greatly increases the difficulty analysts face in trying to predict the consequences of alternative policies. Because analysts have clients throughout the political system, they often encounter conflicts between their own conception of what promotes the social good and the personal interests of their clients. Even the most basic question of whose costs and benefits should count often arises. For example, how should an analyst who works for the mayor of a city count costs and benefits that accrue outside of the city? From the social perspective, we would generally regard these spillovers as relevant to the determination of net social benefits, but what would be the consequences of taking them into account when other jurisdictions do not take into account the externalities of their policies? We will address these and other questions that arise as a consequence of political decentralization when we study the art and craft of policy analysis in Part III.

Problems inherent in direct democracy

Paradox of voting
(meaning of mandate is ambiguous)

Preference intensity and bundling
(minorities bear costs of inefficient social choices)

Problems inherent in representative government

Influence of organized interests
(rent seeking)

Geographic constituencies
(pork-barrel allocations)

Limited time horizon induced by electoral cycles
(underinvestment)

Posturing to public attention
(restricted agendas)

Problems inherent in bureaucratic supply

Difficulty valuing output
(X-inefficiency)

Limited competition
(X-inefficiency)

Civil service protections
(inflexibility)

Agency problem
(diversion of resources)

Problems inherent in decentralization

Diffuse authority
(implementation problems)

Fiscal externalities
(unequal distribution of local public goods)

Figure 4.4   Sources of Government Failure: A Summary

CONCLUSION

Governments, like markets, sometimes fail to promote the social good. We often cannot accurately predict the exact consequences of government failures (indeterminacy itself is sometimes a predictable consequence!). We must be aware, however, that they can occur if we are to avoid the most ineffective and unwise interferences with private choices. Figure 4.4 summarizes the basic sources of government failure. Our next task in developing conceptual foundations for policy analysis is to consider the various generic policies that can be used to deal with market and government failure.

5

CORRECTING MARKET AND GOVERNMENT FAILURES: GENERIC POLICIES

Our discussion of the ways private and collective actions lead to socially unsatisfactory conditions provides a conceptual framework for diagnosing public policy problems. We now turn our attention to policy solutions. We focus on what we call *generic policies*—the various types of actions that government can take to deal with perceived policy problems. They represent a range of general strategies. Because policy problems are usually complex and always contextual, generic policies normally must be tailored to specific circumstances to produce viable policy alternatives. Nevertheless, familiarity with generic policies encourages a broad perspective that helps the analyst craft specific solutions.

Policy problems rarely have perfect solutions, but some policies are better than others. A primary task of the policy analyst is to identify those policies that have the best prospects for improving social conditions. To facilitate this task, we indicate the market failures, government failures, or equity concerns that each generic policy most appropriately addresses, as well as the most common limitations and undesirable consequences associated with the use of each. In other words, we provide a checklist for systematically searching for candidate policies.

There are two caveats concerning our discussion of generic policies. First, we do not wish to imply that all policy analyses compare and evaluate across generic policies. Much policy analysis is relatively incremental. For example, you may be asked to compare the efficiency and equity impacts of a variety of voucher schemes. Familiarity with a broad range of generic policies helps you *know* that you are examining relatively incremental alternatives; it may also enable you to exploit opportunities for introducing alternatives that are less incremental. Second, there is an enormous literature on each of the generic policies—too much material for us to review in any depth here. In order to prepare you to examine further the issues relating to each generic policy, however, we provide samplings of references to relevant literatures.

We group generic policies into five general categories: (1) freeing, facilitating, and simulating markets; (2) using taxes and subsidies to alter incentives; (3) establishing rules; (4) supplying goods through nonmarket mechanisms; and (5) providing insurance and cushions (economic protection). In the following sections we consider specific policies within each of these groups.

FREEING, FACILITATING, AND SIMULATING MARKETS

Market failures, government failures, and distributional concerns underlie perceived policy problems. Markets offer the potential for efficiently allocating goods. Markets, therefore, provide the yardsticks against which to measure the efficiency of government interventions. If we determine that there is no market failure, then we should consider the establishment (or reestablishment) of a market as a candidate solution for our policy problem. Of course, other values besides efficiency may lead us to reject the market solution as a final policy choice. Nevertheless, letting markets work should be among the policies we consider if market failure does not appear inherent in the policy problem.

It is not the case, however, that governments can always create viable markets by simply allowing private transactions. Often, government must play a more affirmative role in enabling the market to function. In other circumstances, although an operational market per se cannot be introduced, market outcomes can be simulated with the use of marketlike mechanisms.

As shown in Figure 5.1, we distinguish three general approaches for taking advantage of private exchange in dealing with policy problems: freeing markets, facilitating markets, and simulating markets. The second column of Figure 5.1 notes the perceived problems that the generic policies might appropriately address, while the third column presents the typical limitations and collateral consequences. The second column of Figure 5.1 emphasizes that generic policies cannot be addressed until you have reached a conclusion on the nature and extent of market and government failure.

Freeing regulated markets should be considered in those situations where an effective market can be expected to reemerge with relatively minor efficiency distortions—in other words, where there is no inherent market failure. Keep in mind, however, that there may be relatively major windfall, or distributional, gains or losses once the current government intervention is eliminated. In addition, at this general level of discussion, we are not considering the possibility that other goals, such as national security, may be relevant. The absence of markets when there is no inherent market failure suggests either government failure or as yet unaccommodated changes in preferences or technology. Accommodation may require the affirmative establishment of property rights by government, an example of facilitating markets. Finally, even when the complete withdrawal of government may be neither feasible nor desirable, there may be opportunities to simulate markets via various auction processes.

Freeing Markets

Unfortunately, a wide range of terminology is used to describe the process of freeing markets, the broadest and most popular being deregulation. We have chosen to distinguish among deregulation, legalization, and privatization.

Generic Policies	Perceived Problems	Typical Limitations and Collateral Consequences
Freeing markets		
Deregulate	G.F.: Allocative inefficiency and rent seeking	Distributional effects: Windfall losses and gains, wage decreases, bankruptcies
Legalize	L.C.F.: Changed preferences	
Privatize	G.F.: Bureaucratic supply	Transitional instability
Facilitating markets		
Allocating existing goods (establish property rights)	M.F.: Public goods, especially emergence of common property problems	
	M.F.: Negative externality	Distributional effects: Windfall gains and losses
Create new marketable goods (tradable permits, financial instruments)	M.F.: Negative externality	Thin markets
	M.F.: Public goods, especially ambient public goods or common property resources	
Stimulating markets		
Auctions	M.F.: Natural monopoly	Collusion by bidders, opportunistic behavior by winning bidder, political pressure to change rules "ex post"
	M.F.: Public goods	
	D.I.: Transference of scarcity rents	

M.F.: Market Failure   D.I.: Distributional Issue
G.F.: Government Failure   L.C.F.: Limitation of Competitive Framework

Figure 5.1   Freeing, Facilitating, and Simulating Markets

Deregulation.   Clearly, it is difficult to justify government interference with private affairs on efficiency grounds in the absence of evidence of market failure. Historically, in the United States and many other countries, governments have engaged in price, entry, and exit regulation of competitive markets. (We consider these various forms of regulation, themselves generic policy solutions, in a later section.) Economists have been almost uniformly critical of the regulation of competitive industries: ". . . if economics has any scientifically settled issues, one is surely that price and entry regulation in perfectly competitive industries generates economic inefficiencies."[1]

We can usually identify various forms of government failure—especially legislators responding to rent seeking by industries—along with sometimes legitimate distributional concerns, as the primary explanations for government regulation of competitive markets. In other cases, changes in technology or patterns of demand may have radically altered the structure of an industry and, therefore, the need for regulation. As we saw in Chapter 3, the natural monopoly characteristics of an industry that justify regulation may erode over time— computer advances facilitating competition in telecommunications, for instance. In these situations, the efficiency rationale for regulation may no longer hold at some point.

Whatever the putative rationale for regulation, deregulation almost inevitably involves complex efficiency and distributional issues. This should not be surprising in light of our discussion of rent seeking in Chapter 4. Deregulation may be problematic from an efficiency perspective in those industries where only a small number of firms operate—a legacy of regulation may be entrenched firms with a temporary competitive advantage. Martha Derthick and Paul Quirk have argued, however, that efficiency alone is rarely the determinative issue in deregulation. Vested interests—the workers and managers of protected firms, consumers enjoying cross-subsidies, sometimes the regulators themselves—have an incentive to fight to retain the advantages they enjoy under regulation. Consequently, successful deregulation often requires vigorous advocacy that details the failures of the regulatory regime and allays fears about distributional effects.[2]

The evidence from the recent deregulation of the U.S. trucking and airline industries suggests that, as expected, large gains in social surplus result.[3] It is also apparent that deregulation has been traumatic and costly for many of the stakeholders (those with a direct economic interest) in these industries. Remember, however, that firm failure is not synonymous with market failure; the evidence suggests that consumer gains more than offset employee and shareholder losses.[4] Further, keep in mind that industries may be subject to more than one type of regulation so that deregulation need not apply to all the activities of the industry—

---

[1]Paul L. Joskow and Roger G. Noll, "Regulation in Theory and Practice: An Overview," in Gary Fromm, ed., *Studies in Public Regulation* (Cambridge, Mass.: MIT Press, 1981), p. 4.

[2]Martha Derthick and Paul Quirk, *The Politics of Deregulation*, (Washington, D.C.: Brookings Institution, 1985). On trucking deregulation, see Dorothy Robyn, *Braking the Special Interests: Trucking Deregulation and the Politics of Regulatory Reform* (Chicago: University of Chicago Press, 1987).

[3]For the evidence on airlines, see Steven Morrison and Clifford Winston, *The Economic Effects of Airline Deregulation* (Washington, D.C.: Brookings Institution, 1986). With respect to trucking, see Donald V. Harper, "Consequences of Reform of Federal Economic Regulation of the Motor Trucking Industry," *Transportation Journal*, Vol. 21, No. 4, Summer 1982, pp. 35–58, at p. 42.

[4]For a discussion of these distributional impacts in the U.S. trucking industry, see Thomas Gale Moore, "The Beneficiaries of Trucking Regulation," *Journal of Law and Economics*, Vol. 21, 1978, pp. 327–43. For evidence in Canada, see Moshe Kim, "The Beneficiaries of Trucking Regulation, Revisited," *Journal of Law and Economics*, Vol. 27, No. 1, April 1984, pp. 227-41.

pricing and scheduling within the U.S. airline industry were largely deregulated while safety, traffic control, and landing rights were not.[5]

Legalization. *Legalization* refers to freeing a market by removing criminal sanctions. The impetus for legalization often stems from changing social attitudes (for example, in regard to sexual behavior and drug use). Moves to legalize the market for prostitution fall into this category.[6] Sometimes *decriminalization* is advocated as a partial form of legalization: criminal penalties are replaced with civil fines.[7] Decriminalization lessens the stigma and punishment associated with the previously criminal actions, but does not fully sanction the actions as socially acceptable.

Privatization. The word *privatization* is used in several different ways: (1) the switch from agency subventions to user fees (to be discussed below as uses of subsidies and taxes to alter incentives); (2) the contracting-out of the provision of a good that was previously produced by a government bureau (to be discussed below as a method of supplying goods through nonmarket mechanisms); (3) denationalization, or the selling of state-owned enterprises to the private sector; (4) demonopolization, the process by which the government relaxes or eliminates restrictions that prevent private firms from competing with government bureaus or state-owned enterprises.[8] Only these latter two types of privatization are directly related to the freeing of markets. Even denationalization, however, may not result in free market outcomes if other private firms are restricted from competing against the newly privatized firm. Restrictions on competitors has been one of the major criticisms of the privatization of British Telecom, for instance.[9]

---

[5]Deregulation may also bring to the fore latent market or government failures. For example, when U.S. airline scheduling was closely regulated, the allocation of landing and takeoff rights was not a serious problem. With increased competition, however, airlines try to crowd scheduled flights at the times most attractive to consumers, resulting in long delays at major airports. We would diagnose the problem as due to the fact that airlines do not pay for the congestion costs their scheduling imposes on others (a common property resource problem). Higher peak-hour fees, or perhaps an auction of time slots, are possible solutions to the delay problem.

[6]Barbara Yondorf "Prostitution as a Legal Activity: The West German Experience," *Policy Analysis*, Vol. 5, No. 4, Fall 1979, pp. 417–33. For a discussion on cannabis, see R. Solomon, E. Single, and P. Erickson, "Legal Considerations in Canadian Cannabis Policy," *Canadian Public Policy*, Vol. 9, No. 4, December 1983, pp. 419–33.

[7]For an argument that prostitution should be decriminalized rather than legalized (in Canada), see Frances M. Shaver, "Prostitution: A Critical Analysis of Three Policy Approaches," *Canadian Public Policy*, Vol. 11, No. 3, September 1985, pp. 493–503.

[8]See David Heald, "Privatisation: Analysing its Appeals and Limitations," *Fiscal Studies*, Vol. 5, No. 1, February 1984, pp. 36–46. Also see E.S. Savas, *Privatization: The Key to Better Government* (Chatham, N.J.: Chatham House, 1987).

[9]For a discussion of this issue, see Tom Sharpe, "Privatisation: Regulation and Competition," *Fiscal Studies*, Vol. 5, No. 1, February 1984, pp. 47–60.

The presence or absence of market failure is the crucial issue in evaluating privatization. Most public corporations in the United States are in sectors for which there is at least some prima facie evidence of market failure. To many other countries, however, the linkage between market failure and the provision of goods via state-owned enterprises appears to be much more tenuous.[10] A major trend towards privatization, or partial privatization, has developed over the last decade in a wide range of countries, including the United Kingdom, France, Canada, and New Zealand.

Facilitating Markets

If a market has not existed previously, then it does not make sense to talk of freeing it. Rather, the process is one of facilitating the creation of a functioning market, by either establishing property rights to existing goods or creating new marketable goods.[11]

Allocating Existing Goods.   We saw in Chapter 3 that as demand increases a free good can begin to shift into the common property resource category (or put another way, move from the SW1 cell to the SW2 cell in Figure 3.7). Obviously, it will not be feasible to allocate property rights effectively if the problem is structural in nature, but it may well be possible if the problem is institutional. For example, while a national government cannot allocate effective property rights to internationally migrating fish, it could allocate effective property rights to its national forests. The allocation of effective property rights is usually extremely contentious, however. Those who previously enjoyed use at below-efficient prices will undoubtedly oppose any distribution of property rights that makes them worse off. Remember that the Coase theorem suggests that from an ex post efficiency point of view it does not matter who receives a property right—as long as the right is secure and enforceable. From an distributional point of view, however, it does matter who gets a property right. People may therefore expend resources on political activity to gain larger allocations (that is, they engage in rent seeking). From an ex ante efficiency perspective, we want allocation mechanisms that limit the political competition for new property rights. Auctions (which we discuss below) and lotteries can sometimes serve this purpose.

The allocation of property rights is an important issue in water policy in the western United States. State legislatures have increasingly come to recognize the importance of establishing property rights. For example, in 1982 the California legislature stated: ''The Legislature hereby finds . . . that the growing water needs of the state require the use of water in a more efficient manner and that

[10]For a review of the ''reach'' of the state-owned enterprise, see Howard Thomas and K. L. K. Rao, eds., *Multinational Corporations and State-Owned Enterprises: A New Challenge in International Business* (Greenwich, Conn.: JAI Press, 1986).

[11]For a discussion of this issue in a somewhat broader context, see Elizabeth S. Rolph ''Government Allocation of Property Rights: Who Gets What?'' *Journal of Policy Analysis and Management*, Vol. 3., No.1, Fall 1983, pp. 45–61.

efficient use of water requires greater certainty in the definition of property rights to the use of water and greater transferability of such rights.''[12] Several recent studies have also documented the legal, administrative, political, social, and distributional barriers to the establishment of such property rights.[13]

The Creation of New Marketable Goods.   In certain circumstances it may be possible for the government to create new marketable goods. The most common form of these goods is tradable permits, usually for environmental emissions.[14] In theory, the allocation of tradable emissions permits ensures that a specified level of air or water quality is achieved at a minimum total cost (including direct abatement costs and regulatory costs). Under such a tradable permit system, firms maximize profits by restricting emissions to the point where the price of an additional emissions permit equals the marginal cost of abatement. If all firms in the industry can buy and sell permits (including potential entrants), then each firm faces the same price for the last unit of pollution produced and it would not be possible to find a less costly way of meeting the specified level of total emissions.

Thomas H. Teitenberg, among others, concludes that tradable permits are superior to emissions standards in terms of the informational burden, the speed of compliance, and in making appropriate trade-offs between economic growth and environmental protection.[15] Clearly, tradable permits have intuitive appeal from an efficiency perspective, yet there have been few implemented examples in the environmental area.[16] Several recent critics emphasize the formidable institutional barriers, such as thin markets (few buyers and sellers), to the practical use of tradable permits.[17]

Simulating Markets

In situations where efficient markets cannot operate, it may be possible for the government to simulate market processes. Chadwick in 1859 was the first to argue that, even when competition *within* a market cannot be guaranteed, com-

---

[12]California Assembly Bill 3491, Chapter 867, Statutes of 1982.

[13]For a sample of the literature on this topic, see Terry L. Anderson, *Water Rights, Scarce Resource Allocation, Bureaucracy and the Environment* (Cambridge, Mass.: Ballinger, 1983); and B. Delworth Gardner, ''Institutional Impediments to Efficient Water Allocation,'' *Policy Studies Review*, Vol. 5, No. 2, November, 1985, pp. 353–63.

[14]The argument for tradable permits was first extensively analyzed by John Dales, *Pollution, Property Rights, and Prices* (Toronto: University of Toronto Press, 1968).

[15]Thomas H. Tietenberg, *Emissions Trading* (Washington, D.C.: Resources for the Future, 1985).

[16]Some countries have had considerable experience with using tradable permits to implement import quotas and other policies where government restrictions create rents. As was the case with the U.S. Mandatory Oil Import Control Program, well-organized markets for the permits can develop. For a history of the Mandatory Oil Import Control Program, see Craufurd B. Goodwin, ed., *Energy Policy in Perspective* (Washington, D.C.: Brookings Institution, 1981), pp. 251–61.

[17]Robert W. Hahn and Roger G. Noll, ''Implementing Tradable Emissions Permits'' in LeRoy Graymer and Frederick Thompson, eds., *Reforming Social Regulation* (Beverly Hills, Calif.: Sage Publications, 1982), pp. 125–58. For a more sceptical view of the feasibility of permits, see W. R. Z. Willey, ''Some Caveats on Tradable Emissions Permits,'' pp. 165–70 in the same volume.

petition *for* the market may be possible.[18] In other words, the right to provide the good can be sold through an auction.[19]

One context where it has been suggested that an auction can appropriately simulate a market is in the provision of goods with natural monopoly characteristics—cable television, for example. It is not efficient to auction the right to operate the natural monopoly to the highest bidder, however. In a competitive auction, the winning bidder would be prepared to pay up to the expected value of the excess returns from operating the natural monopoly. The winning bidder would then be forced to price accordingly, resulting in the allocative inefficiency we described in Chapter 3. Rather, a more efficient approach is to require bidders to submit the lowest retail price at which they will supply customers. While no bidder will be able to offer to supply the good at marginal cost (as you saw in Chapter 3, this would result in negative profits), the winning bidder should be forced to bid close to average cost.

Oliver Williamson has pointed out a potentially serious problem with the use of auctions to allocate the right to operate natural monopolies. The winning bidder has both an incentive and opportunity to cheat by reducing the quality of the good. To avoid this outcome, specifications for the good must be fully delineated and enforced. Yet it is difficult to foresee all contingencies and costly to monitor contract performance. Williamson has documented how many of these specification, monitoring, and enforcement problems actually arose in the case of a cable television network in Oakland, California.[20] The end result of the interaction between government and franchisee may be quite similar to more traditional regulation.[21]

Auctions are used extensively in the allocation of rights for the exploitation of publicly owned natural resources. As described in Chapter 3, these resources often generate scarcity rents. If the government simply gives away exploitation rights, the rents accrue to the developers rather than the public (of course, we should not forget that who receives the rent is a distributional, rather than efficiency, issue).

An auction also has advantages relative to setting a fixed price for the exploitation rights. Most importantly, selling at a fixed price requires the government to estimate the value of the resource, which, in turn, requires estimates of the quality of the resource, future demand and prices for the resource, and future demand and prices for substitutes. An auction, on the other hand, allows the

[18]Edwin Chadwick, "Research of Different Principles of Legislation and Administration in Europe of Competition for the Field as Compared with Competition within the Field," *Journal of the Royal Statistical Society*, Series A, Vol. 22, 1859, pp. 381–420.

[19]It is beyond our scope to look at design of auctions. For a starting point in the theoretical and experimental literature, see Vernon L. Smith, Arlington W. Williams, W. Kenneth Bratton, and Michael G. Vannoni, "Competitive Market Institutions: Double Auctions vs. Sealed Bid-Offer Auctions," *American Economic Review*, Vol. 72, No. 1, March 1982, pp. 58–77; and R. Preston McAfee and John McMillan, "Auctions and Bidding," *Journal of Economic Literature*, Vol. 25, No. 2, June 1987, pp. 699–738.

[20]Oliver E. Williamson, "Franchise Bidding for Natural Monopolies: In General and with Respect to CATV," *Bell Journal of Economics*, Vol. 7, No. 1, Spring 1976, pp. 73–104.

[21]This point has been made by Victor Goldberg, "Regulation and Administered Contracts," *Bell Journal of Economics*, Vol. 7, No. 1, Autumn 1976, pp. 426–48.

market, and therefore all information available in the market, to determine the appropriate value. Problems can arise, however, if there are few bidders. If the number of bidders is small, there is danger that they will collude to limit price. Even if the number of bidders is fairly large, they may not generate competing bids if the number of units being offered is large.[22]

Auctions may be useful allocative tools in situations where governments must allocate *any* scarce resource. The Bank of Zambia, for example, allocates foreign exchange to the highest bidders. When the auctions were first started in 1985, the winning bidders had to pay approximately 50 percent more *kwacha* for each dollar, suggesting that the previous allocation system substantially overvalued the local currency.[23] Auctions have been used in a variety of policy areas;[24] they might be usefully employed in other areas as well.[25]

USING SUBSIDIES AND TAXES TO ALTER INCENTIVES

Freeing, facilitating, or simulating markets may prove inadequate if market failure is endemic or values other than efficiency are important. More interventionist approaches may be necessary. The first major class of these more intrusive policies that we examine consists of subsidies and taxes.[26] They aim to induce behavior rather than command it. Subsidies and taxes, therefore, are market-compatible forms of direct government intervention.

In recent years policy analysts, bureaucrats, and politicians have been engaged in a heated debate on the relative merits of incentives versus other generic policies.[27] While policy analysts, especially those trained in economics, generally view incentives favorably, bureaucrats and politicians tend to be less enthusiastic. In the United States, this debate has primarily focused on the advantages and

[22]One possible solution is to only accept bids on some fraction of the total units offered. For a discussion of this topic, see Lee S. Freedman, *Microeconomic Policy Analysis* (New York: MacGraw-Hill, 1984), pp. 582–83.

[23]"The IMF's Africa Model," *Economist*, Oct. 19, 1985, pp. 78–84.

[24]For example, since the 1950s the U.S. government has leased exploration and development rights to offshore oil and gas through *bonus bidding*—cash bids for the right to a lease with fixed royalty shares for the government (usually 12.5 percent). The Outer Continental Shelf Lands Act Amendments of 1978 opened up the possibility of experimentation with other bidding systems: fixed bonus with variable bidding on the royalty rate, fixed bonus and royalty rate with bidding on exploration expenditures, and fixed bonus and royalty rates with bidding on the rate of profit sharing. Obviously, these systems have different implications for the sharing of risk between the government and the bid winner.

[25]For example, emissions permits could be distributed by auction. See Randolph Lyon, "Auctions and Alternative Procedures for Allocating Pollution Rights," *Land Economics*, Vol. 58, No. 1, February 1982, pp. 16–32.

[26]The basic case for the greater use of incentives can be found in Charles Schultze, *The Public Use of the Private Interest* (Washington, D.C.: Brookings Institution, 1977), pp. 1–16.

[27]For an overview of the debate, see Steven E. Rhoads, *The Economist's View of the World: Government, Markets, and Public Policy* (New York: Cambridge University Press, 1985), pp. 39–58.

disadvantages of incentives relative to direct regulation. This terminology is confusing because incentives also require governmental intervention and, therefore, involve regulation. To clarify, we distinguish between incentives and rules.[28]

We are primarily concerned with using taxes and subsidies in situations where the intention is to correct market failures or achieve redistribution. We are not concerned with taxation intended mainly to raise revenue—even though these taxes induce behaviors that are relevant to policy issues. Indeed, taxes designed to raise revenue inevitably involve economic inefficiency: for example, by altering the trade-off between leisure and labor or the choice between savings and consumption. (Of course, the *net* effect of these taxes on efficiency depends on how the revenues are ultimately used. If they help correct market failures, then the combined tax and expenditure programs may enhance efficiency.) We also are not concerned with efforts to raise incomes generally (this is dealt with below under cushions). Our concern here is with taxes and subsidies that change incentives by altering the *relative* prices of goods. Put simply, we are considering the use of taxes to raise the prices of things that are too abundant from the social perspective and the use of subsidies to lower the prices of things that are too scarce from the social perspective.

In general, taxes and subsidies can have one of three possible impacts on efficiency. First, where taxes and subsidies are aimed at correcting for externalities in particular markets, their impact may enhance efficiency. It is usually difficult in practice to estimate accurately either total social marginal benefits or total social marginal costs—measures needed to gauge the magnitude of positive and negative externalities. If social marginal costs and benefits are inaccurately assessed, there may be no efficiency gains and, indeed, net efficiency losses may occur. Second, where the objective of taxes and subsidies is purely redistributive, there is inevitably some net deadweight loss. Of course, redistribution may itself enhance efficiency if there is utility interdependance between donors and recipients (remember our discussion of preferences in Chapter 3). Rarely, however, do we have sufficient information to make such assessments confidently. Third, taxes may be used in an attempt to extract scarcity rents such as those that arise in the extraction of natural resources such as oil. In theory, such taxes can be designed to transfer rents without losses in efficiency; in practice, limited information about the magnitude of rents generally leads to market distortions.

In order to make our discussion of taxes and subsidies more concrete, we divide them into four general categories: (1) supply-side taxes, (2) supply-side subsidies, (3) demand-size subsidies, and (4) demand-side taxes. These categories are summarized in Figure 5.2. Note that some policies fall in more than one category. For example, a tax on gasoline can be thought of as either a supply-side or a demand-side tax—the effect of the tax does not depend on whether it is collected from refiners or consumers. Nevertheless, we find these categories useful because they emphasize the behavior that is the target of the policy.

---

[28]Many writers use the term *command-and-control* to describe rule-oriented policies. Lester C. Thurow distinguishes between *p-regulations* (incentives) and *q-regulations* (rules). *Zero-Sum Society* (New York: Basic Books,1980), Chapter 6.

Generic Policies	Perceived Problems	Typical Limitations and Collateral Consequences
Supply-side taxes		
Output taxes	**M.F.**: Negative externality **D.I.**: Transference of scarcity rent	Frequent adjustment of tax levels may be required—politically and administratively difficult
Tariffs	**L.C.F.**: Noncompetitive behavior by foreign exporters	Deadweight losses for domestic consumers, rent seeking by domestic producers
Supply-side subsidies		
Matching grants	**M.F.**: Positive externality **M.F.**: Negative externality **M.F.**: Natural monopoly **M.F.**: Public goods (information) **D.I.**: Equity	Often promotes opportunistic behavior
Tax expenditures (business deductions and credits) expenditures	**M.F.**: Positive externality **M.F.**: Negative externality **M.F.**: Public goods (information)	Often generates intra-industry and inter-industry misallocation of resources and inequity
Demand-side subsidies		
In-kind subsidies	**M.F.**: Positive externality **L.C.F.**: Utility interdependence **D.I.**: Equality of outcome	Restricts consumer choice, resulting in deadweight losses Bureaucratic supply failures Because of "lumpiness" often restricted to a subset of eligible-inequitable or a "lottery"
Vouchers	**M.F.**: Positive externality **D.I.**: Equity	Does not deal with informational asymmetry (market failure) Strong bureaucratic and institutional resistance (government failure) Short-run supply inelasticity transfers subsidy in the short run to suppliers rather than consumers

Figure 5.2   Using Subsidies and Taxes to Alter Incentives

Figure 5.2 (continued)

Generic Policies	Perceived Problems	Typical Limitations and Collateral Consequences
Tax expenditures (personal deductions and credits)	**M.F.:** Positive externality **D.I.:** Equity	} Targets poorly subsidized } Increased regressivity of } tax system
Demand-side taxes		
Commodity taxes and user fees	**M.F.:** Negative externality	} Deadweight losses and } black markets
	M.F.: Information asymmetry	
	M.F.: Public goods, especially common property resources	} Deadweight losses }

M.F.: Market Failure
G.F.: Government Failure
D.I.: Distributional Issue
L.C.F.: Limitation of Competitive Framework

Supply-Side Taxes

We consider supply-side taxes under two broad categories: output taxes and tariffs.

Output Taxes. As we saw in Chapter 3, markets with negative externalities overproduce goods from the social perspective (see Figure 3.12). When transaction and coordination costs prevent Coasian market solutions through negotiation among the affected parties, government intervention is desirable to equalize marginal social benefits and costs. Theoretically, the appropriate tax raises price to the level of marginal social cost, thereby internalizing the externality.

The idea that an appropriate per unit tax can lead to an efficient internalization of a negative externality is usually credited to A. C. Pigou and is often referred to as the *Pigovian tax solution.*[29] The major advantage of using taxes to correct for negative externalities is that they allow firms (or consumers) the choice of how much to reduce production (or consumption) to limit their tax payments. As long as each firm sees the same tax, the industry as a whole reduces the quantity of the externality in the least costly way to society.[30]

The implementation of externality taxes has proven to be extremely difficult, however. The major problem is that the government needs to know the shapes of the social benefit and social cost schedules. The estimation of social benefits

[29]Arthur Cecil Pigou, *The Economics of Welfare*, 4th ed. (London: Macmillan, 1946). For a discussion of taxes and subsidies, see Paul Burrows, "Pigovian Taxes, Pollutor Subsidies, Regulation, and the Size of a Polluting Industry," *Canadian Journal of Economics*, Vol. 12, No. 3, August 1979, pp. 494–501.

[30]For a more detailed discussion, see Allen Kneese and Charles Schultze, *Pollution, Prices and Public Policy* (Washington, D.C.: Brookings Institution, 1975).

from the reduction of a negative externality requires the determination of a damage function—a difficult task because it depends on the impact of a complex set of physical and biological forces upon human beings.[31] Information on the marginal costs of firms, needed to determine the difference between private and social marginal cost, may not be easily determined.[32] Many critics have pointed out that if such information *were* available on private and social marginal costs and benefits, the government would be able to specify the appropriate level of production directly without having to deal with taxes at all.[33] In practice, these problems, along with objections to firms receiving a "license to pollute,"[34] have limited the political acceptability of taxes on pollutants.

While lack of information usually makes it impossible to set optimal tax rates initially, it may be possible to approximate such rates by trial and error after observing how firms respond. Trial-and-error experiments have serious drawbacks, however, including uncertainty, opportunistic behavior by externality producers, and political infeasibility.[35] Trial-and-error experiments may also involve substantial monitoring and administrative costs.

Despite these disadvantages, the potential for efficiency gains should be kept in mind: (1) lower cost—the same outcome can be achieved but at lower cost than with standards; (2) innovation—taxes encourage appropriate innovation as innovation continues until the marginal costs of new technology equal the marginal benefits of forgone taxes; (3) informational requirements—firms face incentives to acquire appropriate information; (4) intrusiveness—government intervention is minimized; (5) administrative complexity—economic incentives are self-enforcing and require the minimum level of administrative intervention; (6) transaction costs—economic incentives avoid many of the hidden costs of bureaucratic regulation, such as negotiation and lobbying.[36]

Thus far we have discussed supply-side taxes as a way of dealing with externalities, a context in which they have been much advocated but little used. The use of such taxes in transferring rent has been much more common. As we saw in Chapter 3, many natural resources generate scarcity rents—that is, pure economic surpluses, independent of the labor and capital employed. The distribu-

[31]See Peter Nemetz and Aidan R. Vining, "The Biology-Policy Interface: Theories of Pathogenesis, Benefit Valuation, and Public Policy Formation," *Policy Sciences*, Vol. 13, No. 2, April 1981, pp. 125–38.

[32]For a discussion of this issue, see Thomas C. Schelling, "Prices as Regulating Instruments," in Thomas Schelling, *Incentives for Environmental Protection* (Cambridge, Mass.: MIT Press, 1983), pp. 1–40.

[33]For a discussion of the administrative problems associated with the use of effluent charges, see Clifford S. Russell "What Can We Get from Effluent Charges?" *Policy Analysis,* Vol. 5, No. 2, Spring 1979, pp. 156–80.

[34]On the importance of this perception to environmentalists, see Steven Kelman, *What Price Incentives? Economists and the Environment* (Boston: Auburn House, 1981), p. 44.

[35]Russell has reviewed these issues at length; see Russell, "What Can We Get from Effluent Charges?" pp. 164–78.

[36]Stephen L. Elkin and Brian J. Cook, "The Public Life of Economic Incentives," *Policy Studies Journal*, Vol. 13, No. 4, June 1985, pp. 797–813.

tion of these rents is often a contentious public issue. Ideally, any efforts to capture these rents for the public would not disturb the harvesting or extraction decisions of the private owners of the resources. Many different types of taxes have been used to transfer scarcity rents: flat-rate gross royalties (on the physical output), profit taxes, resource rent taxes, corporate income taxes, cash flow taxes, and imputed profit taxes.[37] While in theory some of these mechanisms could capture a portion of the scarcity rent without distorting private decisions about the use of the resource, in practice none is likely to be completely neutral because of limited information.[38] For example, a one-time tax on the value of the resource (a resource rent tax) would not interfere with the owners' decisions about future extraction of the existing resource. It would require, however, accurate information about future extraction costs and market prices. Further, its imposition may reduce the incentive for firms to explore for new stocks of the resource.[39]

Tariffs.　A *tariff* is a tax on imported goods. Like any other taxes, tariffs generate deadweight losses in the absence of market failures. The usual argument used to justify tariffs is that there are positive externalities from protecting a fledgling industry (the so-called infant industry argument). Several recent studies have argued, however, that the major impetus in the United States for tariffs, and protectionism in general, has stemmed from redistributional politics and is best understood in terms of government failure. One recent study estimates that the annual welfare losses caused by U.S. import restraints is approximately $8 billion, with the cost to consumers per job saved ranging from a low of approximately $25,000 to a high of approximately $1 million per job saved.[40]

Monopsony effects have also been used to justify tariffs. If a country accounts for a large share of world demand for some good, then that country may be able to affect world price by restricting its demand through tariffs (or quotas).[41] Depending on the magnitude of the domestic and world elasticities of supply and demand, the imposition of a tariff may actually increase domestic social

---

[37]Lawrence Copithorne, Alan MacFadyen, and Bruce Bell, "Revenue Sharing and the Efficient Valuation of Natural Resources," *Canadian Public Policy*, Vol. 11, Supplement, July 1985, 465–78.

[38]For a discussion of the information requirements of the various approaches to rent extraction, see Thomas Gunton and John Richards, "Political Economy of Resource Policy," in Thomas Gunton and John Richards, eds., *Resource Rents and Public Policy in Western Canada* (Halifax, N.S.: Institute for Research on Public Policy, 1987), pp. 1–57.

[39]For an illustration of the efficiency effects of taxes on natural resources, see Jerry Blankenship and David L. Weimer, "The Double Inefficiency of the Windfall Profits Tax on Crude Oil," *Energy Journal*, Vol. 6, Special Tax Issue, 1985, pp. 189–202.

[40]Gary Clyde Hufbauer, Diane T. Berliner, and Kimberly Ann Elliott, *Trade Protectionism in the United States* (Washington, D.C.: Institute for International Economics, 1986)

[41]Quotas and tariffs are usually thought of as being equivalent: the same outcome can be achieved by either imposing a tariff or auctioning import permits. The equivalence breaks down, however, if world supply is not competitive. When world suppliers have market power, the imposition of a quota may actually result in an increase in world price. See George Horwich and Bradley Miller, "Oil Import Quotas in the Context of the International Energy Agency Sharing Agreement," in George Horwich and David L. Weimer, eds., *Responding to International Oil Crises* (Washington, D.C.: American Enterprise Institute, 1988), pp. 134–78.

surplus by depressing the world price.[42] The monopsony effect is one of the rationales advanced in support of a U.S. oil import tariff—although recent supporters from oil-producing states seek the higher prices for domestic oil that would result.

Supply-Side Subsidies

One way to increase the supply of goods is to give direct subsidies to the suppliers of the goods. The subsidies may be directed at either private firms or lower levels of government. Intergovernmental subsidies are usually referred to as *grants-in-aid*, or simply *grants*.[43] In most respects subsidies to internalize positive externalities are analytically symmetrical with the taxes on negative externalities described above. Broadly speaking, therefore, if there is a positive externality, an appropriately designed per unit subsidy to the supplier generates an increased supply of the good, reducing the undersupply caused by the externality and thereby increasing social welfare.

Matching Grants.   In Figure 5.3 we illustrate how a subsidy might be used by a central government to induce a local government to supply more of some public good X. The vertical axis measures the local government's expenditure on all goods other than X. The horizontal axis measures the quality of X that the local government provides. For example, X might be remedial classes for children who are slow learners. Given a total budget of B, the local government could spend nothing on X and B on other services, nothing on other services and purchase B/P_x of X where P_x is the price of X, or any point on the line connecting these extremes. Given this budget line, assume that the local government chooses to provide x_0 units of X. The indifference curve labeled I_0 gives all the combinations of X and expenditures on other goods that would be as equally satisfying to the local government (say the mayor) as x_0 and y_0.

Now imagine that the central government offers to pay s dollars to the local government for each unit of X that the local government provides. (We would refer to this as a *matching grant* because it matches local expenditures at some fixed percentage. We would also call it *open-ended* because there is no cap on the total subsidy that the local government can receive.[44]) The effective price that the local government sees for X falls from P_x to $P_x - s$ because of the subsidy. As a result, the budget line for the local government swings to the right. The local government now buys x_1 units of X, reaching the higher level of satisfaction indicated

[42]See Douglas R. Bohi and W. David Montgomery, *Oil Prices, Energy Security, and Import Policy* (Washington, D.C.: Resources for the Future, 1982), pp. 20–29.

[43]For a review of this topic, see Wallace Oates, *Fiscal Federalism* (New York: Harcourt Brace Jovanovich, 1972), pp. 65–94; Martin McGuire, "Notes on Grants-in-aid and Economic Interactions among Governments," *Canadian Journal of Economics*, Vol. 6, No. 2, May 1973, pp. 207–21; and Neville Topham, "Local Government Economics" (Chapter 4), in Robert Millward, et al., ed., *Public Sector Economics* (New York: Longman, 1983).

[44]When a central government offers a local government a fixed amount to be spent on some good, we say the central government is providing a *block grant*. The in-kind subsidies we analyze in Figure 5.4 can be thought of as block grants to individuals.

If a matching grant is closed-ended, it becomes equivalent to a block grant once the cap is reached.

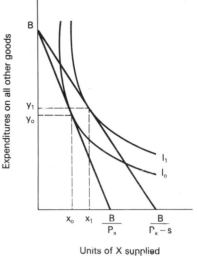

Figure 5.3   The Effect of a Matching
Grant on the Local Provision of Good X

by indifference curve I_1. Note that the local government also spends more on other goods as well—some of the subsidy for X spills over to other goods. In the terminology of grants, part of the categorical grant has been "decategorized."

To counter this spillover, the subsidy could be given with a *maintenance-of-effort requirement*: only units beyond x_0 would be subsidized. The budget line under the maintenance-of-effort requirement follows the original budget line up to x_0 then rotates to the right so that it becomes parallel to the budget line for the subsidy without maintenance-of-effort requirements. The local government responds by purchasing more units of X and by spending less on other goods than they would in the absence of the subsidy.[45] Thus, maintenance-of-effort provisions may be useful in targeting subsidies so that given expenditure levels have the greatest desired impact. Unfortunately, analysts in central governments do not always have sufficient information to design effective maintenance-of-effort requirements.

Subsidies can also be used to deal with negative externalities.[46] Instead of taxing the good generating the externality, firms can be paid for reducing the level of the externality itself. Such subsidies, however, are vulnerable to opportunistic behavior on the part of suppliers. Unless the government knows how much of the externality the firms would have produced in the absence of the subsidy,

---

[45]For an analysis of an alternative maintenance-of-effort requirement, see Lee S. Friedman, *Microeconomic Policy Analysis*, pp. 104–7.

[46]Empty containers left in public places are a negative externality of beverage consumption. Many states have tried to internalize this externality by requiring consumers to pay a deposit at the time of purchase that is refunded when the empty container is returned to the place of purchase. For a discussion of an alternative subsidy program that may offer several advantages over deposit systems, see Eugene Bardach, Curtis Gibbs, and Elliott Marseille, "The Buyback Strategy: An Alternative to Container Deposit Legislation," *Resource Recovery and Conservation,* Vol. 3, 1978, pp. 151–64. Also see Peter Bohm, *Deposit-Refund Systems* (Baltimore: The Johns Hopkins University Press, 1981).

the firms have an incentive to increase their externality levels in anticipation of the subsidy. For example, if a firm expects a subsidy program to be implemented for reducing emissions of some pollutant, then it may temporarily increase emissions to qualify for greater levels of future subsidies. It would be particularly difficult to monitor such behavior if the firms simply slowed the introduction of reductions that they were planning to adopt anyway.

Subsidies also have different distributional consequences than taxes. While taxing goods with externalities usually generates revenue, subsidies must be paid for with other taxes. When negative externalities are internalized with taxes, consumers of the taxed good share some of the costs of the reduction in output; when negative externalities are reduced through subsidies, consumers of the good generating the externality generally bear a smaller burden of the reduction. Indeed, sufficiently large subsidies may induce shifts in technology that lead to reductions in the externality without reductions in the supply of the good.

Subsidies can sometimes be effective mechanisms for dealing with market failures other than externalities. For instance, an alternative to auctioning the right to operate a natural monopoly is to induce the natural monopolist to price efficiently (where price equals marginal cost) by providing a subsidy that gives the monopolist a positive rate of return.[47] While this approach has some appeal, it has not been utilized much in practice. One reason is that it requires information about the firm's marginal cost schedule. Another reason is that government has to pay for the subsidy with revenue raised from somewhere.

Sceptics argue that most supply-side subsidies are provided for inappropriate distributional reasons. While such direct help is relatively uncommon at the federal level in the United States—although the Chrysler bailout demonstrates that it is not unknown—it is extremely common both in other countries and at the state level. Such help may take the form of direct grants, loan forgiveness, loan guarantees, or tax expenditures. Such subsidies are frequently directed at declining, or "sunset," industries. They are likely to be especially inefficient if they simply slow the exit of unprofitable firms from the industry.

Tax Expenditures.   Probably the most common form of supply-side subsidy is through *tax expenditures* such as deductions to taxable income and credits against taxes otherwise owned under corporate income taxes.[48] You can best understand a tax expenditure by realizing that a cash gift and a forgiven debt of the same amount are equivalent. If we assume that there is some benchmark tax system (or comprehensive tax base) that treats all taxpayers similarly no matter what their expenditures, we would have a system without tax expenditures. If one is forgiven a tax payment (i.e., debt) from this benchmark rate, it is equivalent to being given a subsidy of the same amount. We classify tax expenditures as subsidies because they change relative prices by making certain factor inputs less expensive. For example, allowing firms to deduct fully investments in energy-saving equipment from their current tax liabilities makes such equipment appear less expensive than if they had to depreciate it over its useful life as they

---

[47]See William S. Vickrey, "Economic Efficiency and Pricing," in Selma J. Mushkin, ed., *Public Prices for Public Products* (Washington, D.C.: Urban Institute, 1972), pp. 53–72.

[48]For a general overview, see Stanley S. Surrey and Paul R. McDaniel, *Tax Expenditures* (Cambridge, Mass.: Harvard University Press, 1985).

must for other capital goods. Again, to the extent that the tax expenditures do not correct for market failures, inefficiency results, including interindustry and intraindustry misallocation of resources.[49]

The public good nature of certain aspects of *research and development* may also serve as a rationale for subsidies. The U.S. government, as well as the governments of nearly every other industrial nation, directly and indirectly provides research and development assistance. Indeed, these subsidies are viewed as the cornerstones of industrial policies in several countries.

Research and development will be supplied at inefficient levels to the extent that they have the characteristics of public goods. First, where exclusion of competitors from access to findings is not possible, private firms tend to underinvest in research and development.[50] The argument is that no market mechanism can ensure that some of the benefits of the innovation will not be captured by other firms. Some of the benefits will accrue to users as consumer surplus, while some of the producer surplus will go to other producers. The typical policy approach has been to subsidize private research and development in an attempt to raise it to socially optimal levels. Second, where exclusion is possible—through patents or effective industrial secrecy—firms tend to restrict information concerning their research and development to suboptimal levels. Consequently, private firms may wastefully duplicate research.

Kenneth Arrow also suggests that there may be underinvestment because of problems in adequately spreading risks. Research is an inherently risky activity. If the returns on various projects are independent, however, as the number of projects approaches infinity, the risk of a portfolio of projects approaches zero. Research should be conducted to the point where marginal social benefits equal marginal social costs, regardless of the risk of individual projects. Yet in a competitive market private firms generally cannot hold an adequate portfolio of independent projects.

The underinvestment argument is not without its critics. Gordon McFetridge has questioned whether the public sector is more effective than the private sector in dealing with risk. He argues that risk avoidance is demanded by individuals in the market and that mechanisms, such as venture capital, are available for pooling such risks. He also points out that the stock market itself is a mechanism for risk pooling (of projects) and risk spreading (for individuals).[51]

Do public subsidies actually affect the efficiency and dissemination of research and development? Richard Nelson and a team of researchers conducted case analyses of seven industries: aviation, semiconductors, computers, agriculture, automobiles, and residential construction. Their study attempts to deal with the question of allocative efficiency as well as with distributional and implementation issues. Nelson concludes that government supply or funding of basic and generic research incrementally increases the aggregate of research and development ac-

[49]For a review of some of these inefficiencies, see Michael T. Sumner, "The Incentive Effects of Taxation," in Robert Millward, ed., *Public Sector Economics*, pp. 6-77.

[50]Kenneth Arrow, "Economic Welfare and Invention," in National Bureau of Economic Research, *Rate and Direction of Inventive Activity* (Princeton, N.J.: Princeton University Press, 1962), pp. 609-25.

[51]Gordon McFetridge, *Government Support of Scientific Research and Development: An Economic Analysis* (Toronto: University of Toronto Press, 1977).

tivities and encourages the wide dissemination of information. On the other hand, the evidence on applied research and development was less clear.[52]

Demand-Side Subsidies

Demand-side subsidies aim at increasing the consumption of particular goods by reducing their prices to final consumers. There are two basic methods of providing demand-side subsidies: in-kind subsidies (vouchers) and personal deductions and credits (tax expenditures). As with all generic policies, the crucial issue is the rationale for intervention. Two major efficiency rationales for intervention, each involving arguments about positive externalities, may be offered. In other cases, demand-side subsidies are justified primarily on redistributional grounds. In many debates about such subsidies, confusion arises because the efficiency and equity dimensions are not clearly distinguished.

The distributional argument alone for such subsidies is weak because the recipients would always be better off (from their own perspective at least) with straight cash transfers (which would not alter relative prices directly). Therefore, the rationale for such transfers is often put in terms of *merit goods*.[53] While the term has no precise and generally accepted meaning, it usually incorporates a mix of redistribution and market failure arguments (most frequently positive externalities, but also information asymmetry and nontraditional market failures such as unacceptable or endogeneous preferences).

In-Kind Subsidies.   *In-kind grants* subsidize the consumption of specific goods. Strictly speaking, in-kind grants refer to the direct provision of a commodity to consumers. For example, the government may purchase food and distribute it directly to people. In the United States and Canada, however, most in-kind grants are distributed through vouchers that allow recipients to purchase the favored goods in markets. For example, the U.S. food stamp program distributes food vouchers free to those meeting income requirements. In contrast, U.S. programs to distribute surplus agricultural products like cheese are literally in-kind grants. So too are public housing programs (in contrast to rent and construction subsidies); recipients receive housing services directly from the government at a subsidized rent.

Figure 5.4 illustrates the impact of a lump-sum in-kind subsidy of Z^* units of some good Z. The introduction of the subsidy moves the budget line from Bc to Bbd. If it is possible for the recipient to sell the subsidized good to others, then the effective budget line is abd, which, for quantities greater than Z^*, is identical

---

[52]Richard R. Nelson, "Government Support of Technical Progress: Lessons from History," *Journal of Policy Analysis and Management*, Vol. 2, No. 4, 1983, pp. 499–514. There is a vast literature on the effect of government tax expenditures on research and development; for a sample, see Barry Bozeman and Albert Link, "Public Support for Private R&D: The Case of the Research Tax Credit," *Journal of Policy Analysis and Management*, Vol. 4, No. 3, Spring 1985, pp. 370–82; Edwin Mansfield and Lorne Switzer, "Effects of Federal Support on Company-Financed R&D: The Case of Energy," *Management Science*, Vol. 30, No. 5, May 1984, pp. 562–71; and by the same authors, "How Effective are Canada's Direct Tax Incentives for R and D?" *Canadian Public Policy*, Vol. 11, No. 2, June 1985, pp. 241–46.

[53]On merit goods, see J. G. Head, "Public Goods and Public Policy," *Public Finance*, Vol. 17, No. 3, 1962, pp. 197–220.

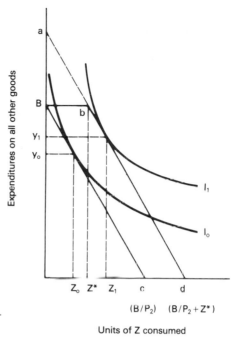

Figure 5.4   Effect of an In-Kind Subsidy on Consumption

to the budget line resulting from a cash grant of P_z times Z^* where P_z is the price of the subsidized good. Even if resale were not possible, the subsidy level is sufficiently small so that the consumption level Z_1 is the same as would result from a cash grant of P_z times Z^*. Note that, in this particular illustration, the equivalence results even though the in-kind subsidy is larger than the presubsidy consumption level. Put in blunt and somewhat pejorative terms, the disconcerting conclusion under these circumstances is that one may as well give the recipient booze as soup.[54]

If the subsidy is sufficiently large and nonmarketability can be enforced, consumption of the subsidized good can be increased above the level that would result from an equivalent cash grant. What rationales might justify large in-kind subsidies and the necessary enforcement efforts to prevent trading of the subsidized good in black markets? One putative rationale for effective (large and nontradable) in-kind subsidies based on efficiency grounds is that the givers of the subsidies derive utility from the specific consumption patterns of recipients (another way of describing this interdependence is that taxpayers receive a positive consumption externality from seeing recipients consume particular goods.)[55] For exam-

---

[54]See Mark Pauly, "Efficiency in the Provision of Consumption Subsidies," *Kyklos*, Vol. 23, Fasc. 1, 1970, pp. 33–57.

[55]See Harold M. Hochman and James D. Rodgers, "Pareto Optimal Redistribution," *American Economic Review*, Vol. 59, No. 4, 1969, pp. 542–57. The approach has recently been modified by Russell D. Roberts, "A Positive Model of Private Charity and Public Transfers," *Journal of Political Economy*, Vol. 92, No. 1, February 1984, pp. 136–48. See also Edward M. Gramlich, "Cooperation and Competition in Public Welfare Policies," *Journal of Policy Analysis and Management*, Vol. 6, No. 3, Spring 1987, pp. 417–31.

ple, many people place a positive value on knowing that the children of the poor arc fed adequately; others see work as important in developing responsible habits of self-sufficiency and therefore place a positive value on programs that induce work effort through subsidies. In the presence of utility interdependence, in-kind transfers may be more efficient than unconstrained (cash) transfers. This should not be surprising in light of our discussion of internalizing externalities—cash grants do not internalize the externality associated with the specific goods.[56]

Another possible rationale is that the good in question generates positive externalities. There has been considerable debate about the existence, and magnitude, of positive externalities associated with the consumption of housing, education, health services, and food. Obviously, these are empirical issues that must be considered on a case-by-case basis.

Vouchers.   In-kind grants are often administered through *vouchers*, which allow consumers to purchase marketed goods at reduced prices. Typically, the vouchers are distributed to selected consumers at prices lower than their face value. Suppliers who sell the favored goods for vouchers, or consumers with receipts for purchase, then cash the vouchers at their face value. If the vouchers are distributed in fixed quantities at zero price to consumers, then they are conceptually identical to the lump-sum in-kind grants analyzed in Figure 5.4.

The voucher system in the United States with the greatest participation is the food stamp program. One study has suggested that food stamps did actually generate additional spending on food. Subsequent amendments to the Food Stamp Act, however, almost completely eliminated this increase.[57] Food stamps currently, therefore, may be little more than an administratively costly form of cash transfer that nonetheless seems to enjoy political popularity.

Vouchers have typically been proposed for subsidizing such other goods as primary and secondary education, day care, and housing. If the vouchers provide large subsidies, they will stimulate market demand for these goods. Because these goods are usually purchased in local markets where short-run supply schedules are upwardly sloping, they may cause the prices of the subsidized goods to rise. For example, if the short-run supply schedule of housing in a locality were perfectly inelastic, the introduction of housing vouchers would simply drive prices up for all renters without increasing supply. These higher prices would, however, eventually induce new construction and the splitting of structures into more rental units. The price effects of housing vouchers were tested through the Housing Allowance Program, a more than $160 million experiment sponsored by the U.S. Department of Housing and Urban Development.[58] Unfortunately, researchers

[56]For a comprehensive discussion of this issue, see Leslie Rosenthal "Subsidies to the Personal Sector", Chapter 3 in Robert Millward, ed., *Public Sector Economics*.

[57]See Teh-Wei Hu and Norman L. Knaub, "Effects of Cash and In-Kind Welfare on Family Expenditures," *Policy Analysis*, Vol. 2, No. 1, Winter 1976, pp. 71–92; Judith A. Barmack, "The Case Against In-Kind Transfers: The Food Stamp Program," *Policy Analysis*, Vol. 3, No. 4, Fall 1977, pp. 509–30; and Norman L. Knaub, "The Impact of Food Stamps and Cash Welfare on Food Expenditures; 1971–1975," *Policy Analysis*, Vol. 7, No. 2, Spring 1981, pp. 169–82.

[58]For a description, see Harvey S. Rosen, "Housing Behavior and the Experimental Housing Allowance Program: What Have We Learned?" in Jerry A. Hausman and David A. Wise, eds., *Social Experimentation* (Chicago: University of Chicago Press, 1985), pp. 55–75.

disagree with the experimental findings that the housing vouchers did not increase local housing prices.[59]

Many analysts have advocated vouchers as devices for increasing access to private primary and secondary education, for increasing parental choice, and for introducing competition among public schools.[60] The primary rationale for public support of education is that individuals do not capture all the benefits of their educations—others benefit from having educated citizens and workers around them. Many see the direct provision of education through public institutions, however, as suffering from the government failures that result from lack of competition. Advocates see vouchers as simultaneously permitting public financing and competitive supply. Critics counter that competitive supply suffers from information asymmetry (parents may not discover the quality of the education their children receive until they have fallen far behind) so that vouchers could not be effectively used without the direct regulation of quality.

There have been limited experiments with educational vouchers in the United States, but they have not really tested the central tenet of voucher programs: that consumer-driven competition will improve school performance. For example, in the Alum Rock experiment in California, teachers in schools that lost students could not be fired.[61] The major unanswered question, however, is whether consumers can judge quality effectively. If they cannot, then it is unlikely that any demand-driven scheme such as vouchers will be allocatively efficient. Information asymmetry is less likely to be a serious problem in higher education, where career opportunities can be more closely linked to educational programs.[62]

Tax Expenditures.   Tax expenditures are commonly used to stimulate individual demand for housing, education, medical care, and child care. Other tax expenditures stimulate demand for goods produced by certain kinds of nonprofit agencies such as charitable, cultural, or political organizations. Tax expenditures have their effect by lowering the after-tax price of the preferred good. For example, being able to deduct the interest payments on mortgages from taxable income makes home ownership less expensive.

Tax expenditures are an important source of subsidy in the United States. For example, the forgone revenue from allowing mortgage interest and property tax deductions in 1981 was estimated to be $35 billion; the exclusion of social security and other benefits that could be regarded as income may involve in ex-

[59]For a summary, see Gregory K. Ingram, "Comment," in Hausman and Wise, eds., ibid., pp. 87–94. For an extensive treatment, see Katharine L. Bradbury and Anthony Downs, eds., *Do Housing Allowances Work?* (Washington, D.C.: Brookings Institution, 1981).

[60]One of the earliest advocates was Milton Friedman. See his *Capitalism and Freedom* (Chicago: University of Chicago Press, 1962), pp. 85–107. For a detailed discussion of the related issues, see John E. Coons and Stephen D. Sugarman, *Education by Choice: The Case for Family Control* (Berkeley: University of California Press, 1978).

[61]Rand Corporation, *Education Vouchers: The Experience at Alum Rock* (Washington, D.C.: National Institute of Education, December 1973).

[62]Recently in Canada, the McDonald Commission recommended the introduction of vouchers for higher education. *The Royal Commission on the Economic Union and Development Prospects for Canada* (Ottawa: Minister of Supply and Services, 1985), Vol. 2, p. 749.

cess of $50 billion in forgone taxes.[63] Additionally, the taxation imputed income (an increase in wealth that does not directly accrue as a money payment) is not normally treated as a tax expenditure. For example, federal estimates of tax expenditures do not include the imputed income on equity in owner-occupied housing.[64]

Most Western countries have now come to recognize the importance of the magnitude of tax expenditures. The United States, West Germany, Great Britain, Japan, and Canada all now require the annual presentation of tax expenditure accounts.[65]

Critics argue that tax expenditures are less desirable than direct subsidies for two reasons. First, because tax expenditures emerge from relatively hidden debates on the tax code, their role as subsidies is not rigorously analyzed—consequently various forms of government failure like rent seeking are encouraged. Second, tax expenditures are notorious for their inequitable distributional consequences. Higher-income individuals are much more able to take advantage of tax expenditures than members of lower-income groups, who, not surprisingly, pay little or no tax in the first place.[66] Deductions, which reduce taxable income, avoid tax payments as the payer's marginal tax rate and thus favor higher-income persons in progressive tax systems. Credits, which directly reduce the tax payment, are worth the same dollar amounts to anyone who can claim them. Therefore, credits generally preserve progressivity more than deductions costing the same amount in forgone revenue.

Demand-Side Taxes

We divide demand-side taxes into two major categories: commodity taxes and user fees. Be warned, however, that other analysts may use other terminology and the distinction between the two is often unclear.

Commodity Taxes.   The terms *commodity tax* and *excise tax* are frequently used interchangeably. We can think of commodity taxes as internalizing the impacts of goods with negative externalities. The most common applications are to reduce consumption of so-called demerit goods like alcohol (see our earlier discussion of merit goods under demand-side subsidies). The use of taxes in these con-

[63]Theodore J. Eismeier, "The Power Not to Tax: The Search for Effective Controls," *Journal of Policy Analysis and Management*, Vol. 1, No. 3, Spring 1982, pp. 333–45.

[64]See Michael Krashinksy, "Limitations on the Use of Tax Expenditures: Some Comments," *Canadian Public Policy*, Vol. 8, No. 4, Autumn 1982, pp. 615–20.

[65]Kevin McLoughlin and Stuart B. Proudfoot, "Giving by Not Taking: A Primer on Tax Expenditures, 1971–75," *Policy Analysis*, Vol. 7, No. 2, Spring 1981, pp. 328–37. For discussion of the tax expenditure reporting system in California, see Karen M. Benker, "Tax Expenditure Reporting: Closing the Loophole in State Budget Oversight," *National Tax Journal*, Vol. 39, No. 4, December 1986, pp. 403–17.

[66]For a review of this argument, see Neil Brooks, "The Tax Expenditure Concept," *Canadian Taxation*, Vol. 1, No. 1, January 1979, pp. 31–35. Daniel Weinberg estimates that in FY1985 over one-half of the $250 billion dollars in U.S. tax expenditures given through the individual income tax system went to the one-fifth of families with the highest incomes. Daniel H. Weinberg, "The Distributional Implications of Tax Expenditures and Comprehensive Income Taxation," *National Tax Journal*, Vol. 40, No. 2, June 1987, pp. 237–53.

texts often appears to display a certain amount of schizophrenia. Will taxes only minimally affect demand and raise lots of revenue, or will taxes substantially decrease demand and generate much less revenue? Presumably the idea in this context is to dampen demand, but the revenue goal often appears to displace it. Obviously, the price elasticity of demand determines the balance between reduced consumption and revenue generation in each particular policy context.[67]

User Fees.   The technical terms often used by policy analysts for *user fees* include congestion taxes, marginal social cost pricing, and optimal tolls. In more common bureaucratic parlance, they are usually known as license fees, rental charges, fares, and other synonyms for price. There are two efficiency arguments for user fees: first, (once again!) to internalize externalities; second, to price public goods appropriately, specifically in the context of nonrivalrous, excludable, congested public goods (see NE2 in Figure 3.7) like bridges and common property resource public goods (see SW2 in Figure 3.7) like fishing grounds. We already reviewed the appropriate price for excludable public goods in Chapter 3 (see Figure 3.8). Efficient allocation requires that the price charged users of the good equal the marginal costs they impose on other users, implying a zero price during noncongested periods and a positive price during congested periods.

Often the central problem faced by policy makers is the feasibility of such peak-load prices. One context where the feasibility of such pricing may be changing rapidly because of technological advances is road congestion. While road pricing has been considered in many jurisdictions,[68] it is not likely to be widely implemented until electronic monitoring is introduced. Hong Kong is now experimenting with a system whereby an electronic license plate is sensed by detector loops. These loops transmit vehicle movement information to a central computer facility, where monthly billing statements can be generated.[69]

ESTABLISHING RULES

Rules pervade our lives. Indeed, they are so pervasive that we tend not to think of them as instruments of government policy. Our objective here is to emphasize that rules are like other generic policies, with advantages and disadvantages. Government uses rules to coerce, rather than induce (through incentives), cer-

[67]For example, what is the effect of high taxes on tobacco consumption? There is some evidence that the price elasticity of demand for smoking is somewhat elastic so that higher tobacco taxes would be effective in reducing smoking. See Edwin T. Fujii, "The Demand for Cigarettes: Further Empirical Evidence and Its Implications for Public Policy," *Applied Economics*, Vol. 12, No. 4, 1980, pp. 479–89. For evidence that youth price elasticities are much larger than adult elasticities, see Eugene M. Lewit, Douglas Coate, and Michael Grossman, "The Effects of Government Regulation on Teenage Smoking," *Journal of Law and Economics*, Vol. 14, No. 3, December 1981, pp. 545–69.

[68]In 1964 the Smeed Commission in the U.K. recommended road use pricing, *Road Pricing: The Economic and Technical Possibilities* (Ministry of Transport, London: Her Majesty's Stationery Office, 1964).

[69]Hong Kong Transport Branch, *Electronic Road Pricing Pilot Scheme: Results, Brief & Consultation Document* (Hong Kong: Hong Kong Government, 1985). For an introduction to the general topic of road pricing, see Martin Wohl, "Congestion Toll Pricing for Public Transport Facilities," in Selma Mushkin, ed., *Public Prices for Public Products*, pp. 243–66.

tain behaviors. Compliance may be enforced by either criminal or civil sanctions. We cannot always clearly distinguish between rules and incentives in terms of their practical effect, however. For instance, should one view small fines imposed by the criminal courts as rules or as implicit taxes (in other words, negative incentives)?

While it is fashionable to focus on the disadvantages of rules (for example, relative to incentives), rules may provide the most efficient method for dealing with market failures in some contexts.

We divide rules into two major categories: (1) framework rules, encompassing both civil and criminal law; and (2) regulations, including restrictions on price, quantity, quality, and information, as well as more indirect controls relating to registration, certification, and licensing of market participants. Figure 5.5 sets out these generic policies.

Frameworks

We should not forget that it is meaningless to talk of competitive markets, *except* within a rule-oriented framework. Lester Thurow states the point strongly:

> There simply is no such thing as the unregulated economy. All economies are sets of rules and regulations. Civilization is, in fact, an agreed upon set of rules of behavior. An economy without rules would be an economy in a state of anarchy where voluntary exchange was impossible. Superior force would be the sole means for conducting economic transactions. Everyone would be clubbing everyone else.[70]

The genesis of this idea goes back to Adam Smith, who recognized the need for frameworks when he pointed out that the first inclination of people in the same line of business when they gather together is to collude and subvert the operation of a competitive market.[71] The competitive market itself, then, can be thought of as a public good that will be undersupplied if left entirely to private activity.[72] Contract law, tort law, commercial law, labor law, and antitrust law can all be thought of as *framework rules*.

Although there is little dispute that a system of criminal and civil rules is in and of itself efficiency enhancing, there is considerable debate on the most efficient structure of such rules. In civil law, for example, the exact nature of optimal liability rules (say negligence versus strict liability standards) is conten-

[70]Lester Thurow, *The Zero-Sum Society*, p. 129. See also Richard A. Posner, "Theories of Economic Regulation," *Bell Journal of Economics and Management Science*, Vol. 5, No. 2, Autumn 1974, pp. 335–58. For an extensive discussion of this issue, see Robert D. Cairns, "Rent Seeking, Deregulation, and Regulatory Reform," *Canadian Public Policy*, Vol. 11, No. 3, September 1985, pp. 592–99.

[71]Adam Smith, *The Wealth of Nations*, 1st ed., 1776 (New York: Penguin Books, 1977), Book One, Chapter X, Part II, pp. 232–33.

[72]Richard Dales argues that the market should be thought of as a common property resource type of public good; see "Beyond the Marketplace," *Canadian Journal of Economics*, Vol. 8, No. 4, November 1975, pp. 483–503.

Generic Policies	Perceived Problems	Typical Limitations and Collateral Consequences
Frameworks Civil laws (especially liability rules)	**M.F.:** Public goods **M.F.:** Negative externality **M.F.:** Information asymmetry **D.I.:** Equity (equal opportunity)	Bureaucratic supply failure
Criminal law	**M.F.:** Public goods **M.F.:** Negative externality **L.C.F.:** Illegitimate preferences	
Regulations Price regulation	**M.F.:** Natural monopoly **D.I.:** Equity (scarcity rent extraction) **D.I.:** (distribution)	X—inefficiency and allocative inefficiency
Quantity regulation	**M.F.:** Negative externality **M.F.:** Public goods, common property resources	Distorted investment, black markets
Direct information provision (disclosure and labeling)	**M.F.:** Information asymmetry **M.F.:** Negative externality	Cognitive limitations of consumers
Indirect information provision (registration, certification, and licensing)	**M.F.:** Information asymmetry **M.F.:** Negative externality	Rent seeking (cartelization)

M.F.:   Market Failure   **D.I.:**   Distributional Issue
G.F.:   Government Failure   **L.C.F.:**   Limitation of Competitive Framework

Figure 5.5   Establishing Rules

tious.[73] Much of the burgeoning literature on "law and economics" is concerned with the specification of such optimal rules in various contexts.

[73]Much of this literature attempts to analyze the specific nature and extent of market failure in particular contexts, such as product liability, in order to develop optimal liability rules. For recent discussions of some of these issues, see Gary Schwartz, "The Vitality of Negligence and the Ethics of Strict Liability," *Georgia Law Review*, Vol. 15, Summer 1981, pp. 963–1005; and George Priest, "The Invention of Enterprise Liability: A Critical History of the Intellectual Foundations of Modern Tort Law," *Journal of Legal Studies*, Vol. 14, No. 3, December 1985, pp. 461–527. The *Journal of Legal Studies* and the *Journal of Law and Economics* regularly carry articles that address the efficiency of liability systems.

For an overview of the evolution of U.S. tort law see Richard A. Epstein, *Modern Products Liability Law* (Westport, Conn.: Quorum Books, 1980).

One of the most basic public goods is the establishment and enforcement of property rights, including the rights to health and safety. In the United States, Canada, and other countries with roots in English common law, tort systems allow those who have suffered damages to seek compensation through the courts. Depending on the particular rules in force, the possibility of tort lowers the expected loss that consumers see from collateral damage and deters some risky behavior by producers in situations involving information asymmetry. Because tort often involves substantial transaction costs, however, it may not work effectively as a deterrent or compensation mechanism when the damage suffered by individual consumers is relatively small. (Small claims courts and class action suits are attempts to deal with this problem.) Because the liability of corporations is generally limited to their assets, tort may be ineffective when large losses result from products produced by small corporations. In addition, we expect tort to be least effective in limiting the inefficiency of information asymmetry in cases of post-experience goods because of the difficulty of establishing links between consumption and harmful effects.

Contract law can also be formulated to reduce the consequences of information asymmetry. For example, insurance law places the burden of informing the insured of the nature and extent of coverage on the insurer.[74] Even when contracts state explicit and contradictory limits, the reasonable expectations of the insured are generally taken by the courts in the United States as determining the extent of coverage. Indeed, most insurance agents carry their own errors and omissions insurance to cover their liability when the impressions they convey to clients diverge from the coverage implied by contracts. In many jurisdictions, other types of agents, such as those selling real estate, have a duty to disclose certain product characteristics related to quality. Such rules, however, may create an incentive for firms not to discover negative characteristics of their products. To be effective, therefore, they may have to be coupled with "standard of care" rules.

Framework rules can also be used to counter some of the problems associated with government failures. For example, individual rights given as constitutional guarantees can protect minorities from tyranny of the majority under direct democracy. Similarly, restrictions on gifts and perquisites that can be given to representatives may help avoid the most blatant abuses of rent seeking.

Regulations

Whereas framework rules facilitate private choice in competitive markets, *regulations* seek to alter choices that producers and consumers would otherwise make in these markets. Regulations generally operate through "command and control": directives are given, compliance is monitored, and noncompliance is punished.

Price Regulation. In Chapter 4 we analyzed the efficiency costs of imposing either price ceilings or price supports on a competitive market (see Figures 4.2 and 4.3). The conclusion that price regulation leads to inefficiency can be generalized to wage and price controls and income policies, which have frequent-

---

[74]See Kenneth S. Abraham, *Distributing Risk: Insurance, Legal Theory, and Public Policy* (New Haven: Yale University Press, 1986), pp. 31–6.

ly been adopted by Western governments, including the United States.[75] The extent of the inefficiency is often difficult to determine, however.

If the quality of a good is variable, then the imposition of price floors often results in firms competing on the basis of quality rather than price. The result may be excessive quality and higher prices, but only normal rates of return. In contrast, price ceilings often lead to declines in product quality, enabling firms to sell at a price closer to the competitive level for the lower-quality product. In other words, social surplus analysis (assuming that quality remains constant) does not always tell the full story of the impact of price regulation.

Price regulation is frequently used as a method of preventing monopolies from charging rent-maximizing prices. As we saw in Chapter 3, if a natural monopoly can be forced to price at average cost, then deadweight losses are much lower than under rent-maximizing pricing. Many regulatory regimes attempt to force natural monopolies to price at average cost by regulating prices. Large sectors of our energy, transportation, communication, and urban services sectors are, or have been, regulated in this way. Typically, the statutes authorizing regulations speak of "reasonable" prices and profits. In practice, however, it is often not clear what is the relative importance of efficiency and equity in defining reasonableness.

There have been two major lines of criticism to the use of price regulation to limit undersupply by natural monopolies. First, in line with various forms of government failure, George Stigler and others have argued that the regulators are quickly "captured" by the firms that they are supposed to be regulating, such that the outcome may be worse than no regulation at all.[76] Second, such regulation induces inefficient and wasteful behavior. Two well-documented outcomes of such incentives are X-inefficiency and an overuse of capital under rate-of-return regulation.[77]

Notice that using price regulation to correct for market failure caused by natural monopoly is only one alternative—we have already considered the alternative possibilities of dealing with natural monopoly through auctions and subsidies; we will consider government ownership below. Here we see the

[75]See D. Quinn Mills, "Some Lessons of Price Controls in 1971-1973," *Bell Journal of Economics*, Vol. 6, No. 1, Spring 1975, pp. 3-49; and John Kraft and Blaine Roberts, *Wage and Price Controls: The U.S. Experiment* (New York: Praeger, 1975).

[76]George Stigler, "The Theory of Economic Regulation," *Bell Journal of Economics and Management*, Vol. 2, No. 1, Spring 1971, pp. 3-21; Richard A. Posner, "Theories of Economic Regulation," *Bell Journal of Economics and Management*, Vol. 5, No. 2, Autumn 1974, pp. 335-58; and Sam Peltzman, "Toward a More General Theory of Regulation," *Journal of Law and Economics*, Vol. 19, No. 2, August 1976, pp. 211-40.

[77]For an extensive discussion of all of these issues, see William G. Shepherd, *Public Policies Toward Business* (Homewood, Ill.: Richard D. Irwin, 1985), particularly Part 3, "Utility Regulation and Deregulation," pp. 323-428. On the overuse of capital, see the seminal article by Harvey Averch and Leland L. Johnson, "Behavior of the Firm under Regulatory Constraint," *American Economic Review*, Vol. 53, No. 5, December 1962, pp. 1052-69. For empirical tests of the Averch-Johnson hypothesis, see Robert M. Spann, "Rate of Return Regulation in Production: An Empirical Test of the Averch and Johnson Thesis," *Bell Journal of Economics and Management*, Vol. 5, No. 1, 1974, pp. 38-54; and Leon Courville, "Regulation and Efficiency in the Electric Utility Industry," same issue, pp. 53-74.

substitutability of generic policies. Analysis of the specific context is needed to determine which generic policy is most appropriate.

Price ceilings are sometimes used in an attempt to transfer scarcity rents from resource owners to consumers. For example, during the 1970s ceilings kept the wellhead price of U.S. (and Canadian) crude oil well below world market levels. While these controls transferred rents from the owners of oil reserves to refiners and consumers, they reduced the domestic supply of oil, increased demand for oil, and contributed to higher world oil prices.[78] In general, the use of price ceilings to transfer scarcity rents involve efficiency losses.

Quantity Regulation. We have already mentioned quantity regulation as a means of controlling negative externalities in our discussion of taxes and subsidies. While quantity regulation is less flexible and generally less efficient than market incentives, it usually provides greater certainty of outcome. Therefore, it may be desirable in situations where the cost of error is great. For example, if an externality involves post – experience goods with catastrophic and irreversible consequences, directly limiting it may be the most desirable approach. Should we be prepared to use economic incentives to control the use of fluorocarbons, which have the potential of destroying the ozone layer? If, in the first taxing iteration, we overestimate the price elasticity of demand, the cost and difficulty of achieving reductions later may be great. Other planet-threatening dangers, such as the greenhouse effect, raise similar issues.[79]

In the United States, quantity regulation of pollutants has often taken the form of specifications for the type of technology that must be used to meet standards. For example, the 1977 Clean Air Act Amendments require that all new coal-fired power plants install flue gas scrubbers to remove sulfur emissions, whether the plant uses low- or high-sulfur coal.[80] This approach was appealing to representatives from states that produce high-sulfur coal, to owners of old plants whose new competitors would enjoy less of a cost advantage, and to many environmentalists, who saw it as a way of gaining reductions with minimal administrative costs.[81] By raising the cost of new plants, however, the scrubber requirement may actually have slowed the reduction of aggregate sulfur emis-

---

[78]For an overview, see Kenneth J. Arrow and Joseph P. Kalt, *Petroleum Price Regulation: Should We Decontrol?* (Washington, D.C.: American Enterprise Institute, 1979). For a more detailed treatment, see Joseph P. Kalt, *The Economics and Politics of Oil Price Regulation* (Cambridge, Mass.: MIT Press, 1981). For a discussion of the particular problems associated with domestic oil price ceilings in the context of oil price shocks in the world market, see George Horwich and David Leo Weimer, *Oil Price Shocks, Market Response, and Contingency Planning* (Washington, D.C.: American Enterprise Institute, 1984), pp. 57–110.

[79]For background on the greenhouse effect, see Gordon J. MacDonald, "Scientific Basis for the Greenhouse Effect," *Journal of Policy Analysis and Management*, Vol. 7, No. 3, Spring 1988, pp. 425–44. Other articles in the same issue deal with possible policy responses to the greenhouse effect.

[80]See Robert W. Crandall, "An Acid Test for Congress?" *Regulation,* Vol. 8, September/December 1984, pp. 21–28. Also, see Bruce A. Ackerman and William T. Hassler, *Clean Coal/Dirty Air* (New Haven, Conn.: Yale University Press, 1981).

[81]Robert W. Crandall, "An Acid Test for Congress?" pp. 21–22.

sions by reducing the speed at which electric utilities replace older plants. In general, regulating how standards are to be met reduces flexibility and thus makes the standards more costly to achieve.

The use of quotas in international trade is another illustration of quantity regulation, albeit one that has been vigorously criticized. As we have already discussed, tariffs and quotas differ little in theory: in the case of tariffs, prices are raised until imports are reduced to a certain level; in the case of quotas, the government limits the import level directly and prices adjust accordingly. In practice, tariffs have the advantage of being more accommodating than quotas to changes in supply and demand. Additionally, tariffs are generally easier to implement than quotas because the latter require the government to distribute rights to the limited imports.

Jose Gomez-Ibanez, Robert Leone, and Stephen O'Connell have recently examined the impact of quotas on the U.S. automobile market.[82] Their analysis is generalizable to import quotas for footwear, textiles, steel, and many other products. They estimate that the short-run consumer losses are in excess of $1 billion per annum and that "it is apparent that under most assumptions the economy as a whole is worse off because of restraints."[83] They also point out that the longer-run "dynamic" efficiency costs may be even more significant than the short-run costs, as the Japanese automobile producers adjust their behavior in the face of quotas.

The most extreme form of quantity regulation is an outright ban on usage or ownership, usually enforced via criminal sanctions. For example, in 1984 the U.S. National Organ Transplant Act banned the sale or purchase of human organs.[84] More familiar prohibitions include bans on gambling, liquor, prostitution, and drugs such as heroin and cocaine. Again, countries have chosen to use this policy instrument differently. Many countries ban the private ownership of handguns, while most jurisdictions in the United States allow sale and ownership. On the other hand, no country that we know of has banned the use or sale of cigarettes, although it could be argued that they should be a prime target for such treatment.[85] There has not been a consensus on these types of prohibitions among the analytic community. This is not surprising because many of the issues relate to strongly held ethical values. As we saw in our discussion of legalization, changes in such values often lead to calls for freedom of choice. If there is extensive consumer demand for such products, the usual result is black markets.

One context in which criminal sanctions are now being used more extensively is the regulation of toxic chemicals. Recently several Illinois businessmen were convicted of murder and sentenced to twenty-five years imprisonment for

---

[82]Jose Gomez-Ibanez, Robert Leone, and Stephen O'Connell, "Restraining Auto Imports: Does Anyone Win?" *Journal of Policy Analysis and Management*, Vol. 2, No. 2, Winter 1983, pp. 196–219.

[83]Ibid., p. 205; see Table 2.

[84]National Organ Transplant Act, October 4, 1984, Public Law 98–507, 98 Stat. 2339.

[85]Recently there have been numerous calls for a ban on advertising, as opposed to selling, cigarettes. See Kenneth E. Warner, et al., "Promotion of Tobacco Products: Issues and Policy Options," *Journal of Health Politics, and Law*, Vol. 11, No. 3, Fall 1986, pp. 367–92; Rebecca Arbogost, "A Proposal to Regulate the Manner of Tobacco Advertising," same issue, pp. 393–422.

the toxic-chemical-related death of an employee.[86] While such severe criminal sanctions may provide a powerful deterrent, they also may discourage firms from reporting accidents where they may have been negligent.

The design of efficient standards requires that noncompliance be taken into account. If we want those subject to standards to make efficient decisions, then they should see an expected punishment equal to the external costs of their externality. For example, if dumping a toxic substance causes $10,000 in external damage, and the probability of catching the dumper is 0.01, then the fine should be on the order of $1 million to internalize the externality. The political system, however, may not be willing to impose such large fines. Nor may it be willing to hire enough inspectors to increase the probability that noncompliance will be detected. In general, the problem of noncompliance limits the effectiveness of standards.[87]

Direct Information Provision. We discussed information asymmetry extensively in Chapter 3. We noted there that the quality of many goods cannot be evaluated until long after they are consumed (for example, post – experience goods like asbestos insulation and certain medical treatments). As products become more technologically complex, product quality is likely to become an increasingly important area of policy concern.

The presence of information asymmetry suggests a relatively simple policy: provide the information! An important question is whether it is more effective for government to supply such information to consumers or to require the suppliers of goods to provide the information. Few studies directly address this important question. In practice, governments tend to engage in both strategies. For instance, the U.S. government, through the National Institutes of Health, provides information concerning the health impact of cigarette smoking as well as requires cigarette manufacturers to place warning labels on their products.

The practice of requiring firms to supply information about various attributes of product quality is becoming increasingly common.[88] Examples of requiring information disclosure have recently included appliance energy-efficiency labeling, automobile mileage ratings, clothing care labeling, mortgage loan rate facts, nutrition and ingredient labeling, octane value labeling, truth-in-lending provisions, warranty disclosure requirements, and health warnings on cigarette packages.[89] Additionally, federal, state, and local governments have devoted much effort to instituting so-called plain language laws to make contracts readable.[90]

---

[86]See Daniel Riesel, "Criminal Prosecution and Defence of Environmental Wrong," *Environmental Law Reporter*, Vol. 15, No. 3, 1985, pp. 10065-81; and Mark Schneider, "Criminal Enforcement of Federal Water Pollution Laws in an Era of Deregulation," *Journal of Criminal Law and Criminology*, Vol. 73, No. 2, Summer 1982, pp. 642-74.

[87]W. Kip Viscusi and Richard J. Zeckhauser, "Optimal Standards with Incomplete Enforcement," *Public Policy*, Vol. 27, No. 4, Fall 1979, pp. 437-56.

[88]For an overview, see Susan Hadden, *Read the Label: Reducing Risk by Providing Information* (Boulder, Colo.: Westview Press, 1986).

[89]Joel Rudd, "The Consumer Information Overload Controversy and Public Policy," *Policy Studies Review*, Vol. 2, No. 3, February 1983, pp. 465-73.

[90]For a review of this topic, see Stephen M. Ross, "On Legalities and Linguistics: Plain Language Legislation," *Buffalo Law Review*, Vol. 30, No. 2, Spring 1981, pp. 317-63.

A final variation on the theme of requiring suppliers of goods to provide information is to facilitate the provision of information by employees.[91] Currently airline employees can communicate safety problems to federal regulators presumably without being exposed to employer reprisals. Clearly, airline pilots have a more direct incentive to report safety problems than do airline executives. Of course, this policy approach can be applied to government itself—by facilitating the protection of whistle-blowing employees who report inefficiency or corruption.

Direct information provision is likely to be a viable policy response to "pure" information asymmetry problems. It is an attractive policy option because the marginal costs of both providing the information and enforcing compliance are low. It may be less viable when information asymmetry is combined with other market imperfections such as limited consumer attention, endogenous preferences, or addictive products. For example, providing information about the adverse health effects of smoking may not be an adequate policy response because of the addictive properties of tobacco. If we believe that many smokers are incapable of rationally evaluating the health risks, then further regulation may be appropriate, including perhaps the imposition of quality standards.

Standards provide information to consumers by narrowing the variance in product quality. For example, the premarketing clearance procedures of the Food and Drug Administration require that scientific evidence of efficacy and safety be presented before a new drug can be sold. These quality standards provide at least some information to consumers about marketed drugs.

The effective use of quality standards may be limited by government failure. Regulatory bureaus often lack the expertise to determine appropriate quality standards. They may also operate in political environments that undervalue some errors and overvalue others. For example, when the Food and Drug Administration allows a harmful product to reach the market, it is likely to come under severe criticism from congressmen, who can point to specific individuals who have suffered. In contrast, it receives virtually no congressional criticism when it prevents a beneficial product from reaching the market, even though large numbers of (generally unidentified) people forgo benefits.[92]

Programs of quality regulation and information disclosure run the risk of regulatory capture. Firms in the regulated industry that can more easily meet quality and disclosure standards may engage in rent seeking by attempting to secure stringent requirements that inflict disproportionate costs on their competitors and create barriers that make it more difficult for new firms to enter the industry. In addition to reducing competition in the industry, stringent standards may also impede innovation by forcing excessive uniformity.[93] The retarding of innova-

[91]Eugene Bardach and Robert A. Kagan propose that information provision by employees not just be facilitated but mandated in some circumstances. They also view rules that define the authority of professionals, such as health and safety inspectors, within corporations to be a form of "private regulation" worthy of consideration. Eugene Bardach and Robert A. Kagan, *Going by the Book: The Problem of Regulatory Unreasonableness* (Philadelphia: Temple University Press, 1982), pp. 217–42.

[92]For a more detailed discussion of the asymmetry in oversight of the Food and Drug Administration, see David Leo Weimer, "Safe—and Available—Drugs," in Robert W. Poole, Jr., ed., *Instead of Regulation* (Lexington, Mass.: Lexington Books, 1982), pp. 239–83.

[93]See the discussion of the dairy industry by Eugene Bardach and Robert A. Kagan, *Going by the Book*, pp. 260–62.

tion is likely to be especially serious when the standards apply to production processes rather than to the quality of final products.

Indirect Information Provision.   Unfortunately, direct information about the quality of services, as opposed to physical products, usually cannot be provided. Typically, service quality is not fixed: it may change over time either with changes in the level of human capital or the amount of input effort. Because the quality of services may vary over time, providing reliable information about their quality directly may be impractical.

The infeasibility of providing such direct information has led policy makers and analysts to search for indirect information substitutes. A common policy approach is to license or certify providers who meet some standard of skill, training, or experience.

Licensure can be defined as "a regulatory regime under which only the duly qualified who have sought and obtained a license to practice from an appropriate agency or delegate of the state are legally permitted to perform or to take responsibility for given functions."[94] It can be distinguished from *certification* "under which qualified practitioners receive special designations or certifications which other practitioners cannot legally use; however, uncertified practitioners are legally permitted to provide the same functions, provided they do so under some other designation. Certification involves exclusive rights to a professional designation but not to practice."[95]

Milton Friedman has succinctly summarized the weakness of using these approaches: "The most obvious social cost is that any one of these measures, whether it be registration, certification, or licensure, almost inevitably becomes a tool in the hands of a special producer group to obtain a monopoly position at the expense of the rest of the public."[96] Criticism has focused particularly on licensure.

While the rationale for providing indirect information through licensure does not necessarily imply *self*-regulation, this is the route that almost all states have gone with occupational licensure. The typical steps are: members form a professional association, the association sets up a system of voluntary licensure, and the profession petitions the legislature for mandatory licensure under the auspices of its association.[97]

Occupational licensure suffers from a number of weaknesses: the correlation between training or other measurable attributes and performance may be low; the definition of occupations may lock-in skills that become outmoded in dynamic markets; high entry standards deny consumers the opportunity to choose low-quality, but low-price, services; and when professional interests control the

---

[94]Michael J. Trebilcock and Barry J. Reiter, "Licensure in Law," Chapter 3 in Robert G. Evans and Michael J. Trebilcock, *Lawyers and the Consumer Interest* (Toronto: Butterworth, 1982), pp. 65–103, at p. 66.

[95]Michael Trebilcock and Barry Reiter, "Licensure in Law," p. 66.

[96]Milton Friedman, *Capitalism and Freedom* (Chicago: University of Chicago Press, 1962), p. 148.

[97]William D. White and Theodore R. Marmor, "New Occupations, Old Demands," *Journal of Policy Analysis and Management*, Vol. 1, No. 2, Winter 1982, pp. 243–56.

licensing standards, the standards may be set unduly high to restrict entry so as to drive up the incomes of the existing practitioners.[98]

While all of these problems deserve serious attention, economists have tended to concentrate on the social costs of entry barriers and the resulting monopoly pricing—perhaps because it is one of the easier licensure impacts to measure. There is certainly strong empirical evidence that professional cartels do indeed raise prices and restrict competition.[99] In light of the existence of these excess returns and what you have already learned about rent seeking, you should not be surprised to hear that many professional and quasi-professional groups continue to seek licensure.[100]

We should therefore be cautious in advocating licensure as a policy alternative. When we do, we should consider alternatives to professional *self*-regulation. Yet we believe it is fair to say that the critics of professional regulation have not been particularly imaginative in proposing alternative policies.[101]

Licensure is now spreading beyond its traditional boundaries. Numerous paraprofessional occupations are winning the right to license and self-regulate. One recent proposal even suggests that prospective parents should be licensed before having children![102]

SUPPLYING GOODS THROUGH NONMARKET MECHANISMS

Surprisingly, policy analysts have had relatively little to say about when government provision of goods through public agencies is an appropriate response to market failure. Peter Pashigian puts it as bluntly:

> Public production of goods and services is somewhat of an embarrassment to most economists. It exists, and will in all likelihood increase in importance, but it is difficult to explain. An acceptable theory of public production has not yet appeared.[103]

[98]We take these points from Michael Trebilcock and Barry Reiter, "Licensure in Law," pp. 67–70. They develop these points in depth and raise a number of others.

[99]For just a small sample of this large literature, see Alex Maurizi, "Occupational Licensing and the Public Interest," *Journal of Political Economy,* Vol. 82, No. 2, March/April 1974, pp. 399–413; James W. Begun, "The Consequences of Professionalism for Health Services: Optometry," *Journal of Health and Social Behavior,* Vol. 20, No. 4, December 1979, pp. 376–86; Lee Benham, "The Effects of Advertising on the Price of Eyeglasses," *Journal of Law and Economics,* Vol. 15, No. 2, October 1972, pp. 337–52; Ronald Bond, et al., Effects of Restrictions on Advertising and Commercial Practice in the Professions: The Case of Optometry (Washington, D.C.: Federal Trade Commission, 1980).

[100]William D. White and Theodore R. Marmor, "New Occupations, Old Demands," pp. 249–52.

[101]For one proposal, see Aidan R. Vining, "Information Costs and Legal Services," *Law and Policy Quarterly,* Vol. 4, No. 4, October 1982, pp. 475–500.

[102]John E. Tropman, "A Parent's License," *Journal of Policy Analysis and Management,* Vol. 3, No. 3, Spring 1984, pp. 457–59.

[103]Peter Pashigian, "Consequences and Causes of Public Ownership of Urban Transit Facilities," *Journal of Political Economy,* Vol. 84, No. 6, December 1976, pp. 1239–59.

Indeed, the choice between government provision and other generic policies is one of the least well understood public issues. Perhaps the reason is that, while we have a convincing theory of market failure and an (emergingly) convincing theory of government failure, we have no overreaching theory that delineates the efficiency trade-offs between market failure and government failure.[104]

It is tempting to believe that the theory of market failure itself resolves this dilemma: direct government provision is appropriate when there is endemic market failure. A moment's thought should convince you of the weakness of such an argument: it ignores the fact that market failures can be addressed with other generic policies. Therefore, market failure provides a rationale generally for government intervention, rather than specifically for direct provision by government. For example, consider the possible responses to natural monopoly: auctions to take advantage of competition for markets, subsidies to facilitate marginal cost pricing, and direct regulation. These approaches are alternatives to government ownership of the monopoly.

William Baumol provides the beginnings of a moral hazard theory of government production.[105] His insight is best introduced with an example: the provision of national defense. The common rationale for the provision of national defense by government rests on the argument that it is a public good. But this is only an argument for government intervention, not a public army per se. Baumol's case for a *public* army is made in terms of moral hazard. A government intends to use its armed forces only when needed for its own purposes. An army provided by the market to the government under contract may have very different incentives that bring into question its loyalty and reliability.

We suggest that the moral hazard problem can be viewed more broadly in the context of principal-agent theory. Again, we can illustrate the crux of the problem using the example of national defense: armies cannot be trusted to carry out the contracts because the government does not have an independent mechanism of enforcement. In other words, the armies are in a position to engage in opportunistic behavior, like the soldiers in the Thirty Years' War who were lured from one side to the other with bonuses and higher wages.[106] Even if a particular private army does not engage in such behavior, the state will inevitably be forced into costly monitoring. For instance, the government would at least have to establish an office of inspector general to make sure that the contractor can actually muster the promised forces. We have already discussed many of these principal-agent problems in our discussion of government failure in Chapter 4. Ironically, in this context it is more a form of market failure than government failure.

Although the danger of strategic behavior is most starkly revealed in the area of national defense, it is by no means unique to it. The collection of taxes,

[104]For this argument, see Lee S. Friedman, "Public Institutional Structure: The Analysis of Adjustment," in John P. Crecine, ed,, *Research in Public Policy Analysis and Management*, Vol. 2 (Greenwich, Conn.: JAI Press, 1981), pp. 303–25.

[105]William J. Baumol, "Toward a Theory of Public Enterprise," *Atlantic Economic Journal*, Vol. 12, No. 1, March 1984, pp. 13–20. Baumol actually proposes his theory in terms of public enterprise rather than government supply, but throughout uses the term *public sector employee*.

[106]André Corvisier, *Armies and Societies in Europe, 1494–1789*, trans. Abigail T. Siddall (Bloomington: Indiana University Press, 1979), p. 45.

the printing of money, the administration of justice, all could potentially face serious principal-agent problems if supplied by private firms.

Our analysis suggests a *double market-failure test* for the use of public agencies: first, evidence of market failure or a redistributive goal; second, evidence either that a less-intrusive generic policy cannot be utilized or that an effective contract for private production cannot be designed to deal with the market failure (that is, evidence of a principal-agent problem). While we believe that this double market-failure approach provides a rationale for government production, little progress has been made in delineating the range of circumstances in which government production is likely to be the best generic policy.[107] The task is especially difficult because public agencies themselves, as we saw in Chapter 4, are prone to serious principal-agent problems (in the intragovernment context this is government, rather than market, failure).

In spite of these theoretical difficulties, we can at least provide an overview of alternative forms of nonmarket supply. Broadly speaking, once a decision has been made to supply goods publicly, governments can do so either directly or indirectly. Direct supply involves production and distribution of goods by government bureaus. As outlined in Figure 5.6, the major means of indirect supply are independent agencies (usually government corporations or special districts) or various forms of contracting out. Although these distinctions are theoretically clear, in practice they are often less so.

Direct Supply by Government Bureaus

The direct production of goods by government bureaus is as old as government itself. Karl Wittfogel argues that the stimulus for the development of many early civilizations in semiarid regions (e.g., Egypt, Mesopotamia, and parts of China and India) came from the need to construct and manage water (hydraulic) facilities collectively. This, in turn, tended to generate direct government supply of nonhydraulic construction: "under the conditions of Pharaonic Egypt and Inca Peru, direct management prevailed."[108]

The U.S. government provides a vast array of goods through such agencies as the Army Corps of Engineers, the Bureau of the Mint, the National Forest Service, and the Cooperative Extension Service of the Department of Agriculture. Even in the early days of the republic, direct supply was extensive when the activities of the states are included.[109] Christopher Leman finds that domestic government production can be divided into ten functional categories: (1) facilitating commerce; (2) managing public lands; (3) constructing public works and managing real property; (4) research and testing; (5) technical assistance; (6) laws and

---

[107]The best treatment we know of is provided by David E. M. Sappington and Joseph E. Stiglitz, "Privatization, Information, and Incentives," *Journal of Policy Analysis and Management*, Vol. 6, No. 4, Summer 1987, pp. 567–82.

[108]See Karl Wittfogel, *Oriental Despotism* (New Haven, Conn.: Yale University Press, 1957), p. 45. See also his Table 1 on government management in agriculture and industry, p. 46.

[109]Carter Goodrich, ed., *The Government and the Economy, 1783–1861* (Indianapolis: Bobbs-Merrill, 1967), pp. xv–xviii.

Generic Policies	Perceived Problems	Typical Limitations and Collateral Consequences
Direct supply Bureaus	**M.F.**: Public goods **M.F.**: Positive externality **M.F.**: Natural monopoly **D.I.**: Equity **D.I.**: Equity (scarcity rent distribution	Bureaucratic supply failure
Independent agencies Government corporations	**M.F.**: Natural monopoly **M.F.**: Positive externality **D.I.**: Equity **D.I.**: Equity (scarcity rent extraction)	Bureaucratic supply failure Principal-agent problems
Special districts	**M.F.**: Natural monopoly **M.F.**: Local public goods **M.F.**: Negative externality	
Contracting out Direct contracting out	**M.F.**: Public goods (especially local public goods) **G.F.**: Bureaucratic supply failure	Opportunistic behavior by suppliers
Indirect contracting out (nonprofit corporations)	**M.F.**: Positive externality **D.I.**: Equity	

M.F.: Market Failure
G.F.: Government Failure
D.I.: Distributional Issue
L.C.F.: Limitation of Competitive Framework

Figure 5.6 Supplying Goods Through Nonmarket Mechanisms

justice; (7) health care, social services, and direct cash assistance; (8) education and training; (9) marketing; and (10) supporting internal administrative needs.[110] The "nondomestic" functions of government include national defense and the administration of foreign policy.

A perusal of these categories suggests that all could be justified by some market failure or redistributive rationale. This, however, does not address the question of whether these goods could be efficiently provided by other generic policies, or provided *indirectly* by government. Clearly, some of these goods (or at least close substitutes) can be supplied using other generic policies; for instance,

[110]Christopher K. Leman, "The Forgotten Fundamental: Successes and Excesses of Direct Government," in Michael Lund and Lester Salamon, eds., *The Tools of Public Policy* (Washington, D.C.: Urban Institute Press, forthcoming).

elements of health care can be variously provided in free markets, through market incentives, and under rules.

Leman also points out that other interventionist generic policies inevitably involve some level of *direct* government provision.[111] Some examples: the provision of in-kind subsidies requires a bureau to dispense the goods and vouchers; the use of rules requires agencies to monitor and enforce compliance; and even the creation of tradable property rights may require agencies to act as banks and clearinghouses.

Our discussion in Chapter 4 of the various forms of government failure, especially those of bureaucratic supply, suggests that government supply is not a panacea. The policy pendulum appears to have swung against the use of public agencies, as shown by the current interest in privatization and various forms of public contracting for private goods.

Independent Agencies

The range and type of independent agencies is enormous. The British have coined the term quango (quasi-nongovernmental organization) to describe the myriad range of semiautonomous bodies that are not explicitly government departments. Such autonomous "off-budget" agencies have grown explosively in almost all countries around the world. The United States has not been exempt. Annmarie Walsh has identified over 1,000 domestic state and interstate authorities as well as over 6,000 substate authorities.[112] These regional, state, and local agencies construct and operate a wide range of facilities, including dams, airports, industrial parks, and bridges, and provide a wide range of services, including water, gas, and electricity. Because there is no broadly recognized nomenclature, however, even identifying and classifying such entities is problematic. Many authorities appear to have considerable independence but are not corporate in form, while others are corporate but are formally included in government departments. Even more confusingly, formal inclusion in a bureau does not necessarily subject the corporation to departmental supervision or regulation.[113] Here we will briefly review two forms of independent agency: government corporations and special districts.

Government Corporations. In the United States the corporate form tends to be used for the delivery of tangible and divisible goods in sectors that at least appear to be natural monopolies. *Government corporations* generally operate with their own source of revenue under a charter that gives them some independence from legislative or executive interference in their day-to-day operations. For ex-

---

[111]Ibid.

[112]Annmarie H. Walsh, *The Public's Business: The Politics and Practices of Government Corporations* (Cambridge, Mass.: MIT Press, 1978), p. 6. See also Neil W. Hamilton and Peter R. Hamilton, *Governance of Public Enterprises: A Case Study of Urban Mass Transit* (Lexington, Mass.: Lexington Books, 1981).

[113]See Harold Seidman, "Public Enterprises in the United States," *Annals of Public and Co-operative Economy*, Vol. 54, No. 1, January-March 1983, pp. 3–18.

ample, electric utilities owned by municipalities generate revenue from the electricity that they sell. Usually, their charter requires them to do so at the lowest prices that will cover operating costs and allow for accommodation of growth.

Although government corporations are less important in the United States than in many other countries, their presence is not insignificant. The Tennessee Valley Authority had assets of over $14 billion in 1982, making it the largest electrical utility in North America; other important federally owned electricity producers include the Bonneville Power Administration, the Southeastern Federal Power Program, and the Alaska Power Administration. Major federal corporations include Conrail, AMTRAK, the Federal National Mortgage Association, the Postal Service, the Federal Deposit Insurance Corporation, and the Corporation for Public Broadcasting. At the subnational level, major enterprises include the Port Authority of New York and New Jersey, the New York Power Authority, and the Massachusetts Port Authority.

What is the rationale for government corporations? Most government corporations, at least in the United States, meet the *single market-failure test*—that is, they are in sectors where natural monopoly or other market failure suggests the need for government intervention. In our view, the critics of government corporations are implicitly arguing that few meet the double market-failure test.

The superficial appeal of government corporations is that they can correct market failures while presumably retaining the flexibility, autonomy, and efficiency of private corporations. Are government corporations less prone to principal-agent problems than government bureaus?

Louis De Alessi and other critics contend that government corporations, like government bureaus, are more prone to principal-agent problems than private firms: "the crucial difference between private and political firms is that ownership in the latter effectively is nontransferable. Since this rules out specialization in their ownership, it inhibits the capitalization of future consequences into current transfer prices and reduces owners' incentives to monitor managerial behavior."[114] The theoretical force of this argument is somewhat weakened by the growing realization that large private firms are also subject to principal-agent problems, especially if shareholding is dispersed.[115] The majority of empirical studies do, indeed, find that dispersed shareholding results in lower profitability and higher costs.[116]

Are public firms less efficient than private firms? The evidence is quite mixed. Several recent surveys of empirical studies that compare private and public performance find some "edge" for the private sector, but several others find no con-

---

[114]Louis De Alessi, "The Economics of Property Rights: A Review of the Evidence," in R. Zerbe, ed., *Research in Law and Economics*, Vol. 2 (Greenwich, Conn.: JAI Press, 1980), pp. 1–47, 27–28.

[115]For a comprehensive review of this issue, see the special issue of the *Journal of Law and Economics*, "Corporations and Private Property," Vol. 26, No. 2, June 1983, especially Eugene F. Fama and Michael C. Jensen, "Separation of Ownership and Control," pp. 301–26; "Agency Problems and Residual Claims," pp. 327–50 by the same authors; and Oliver E. Williamson, "Organization Form, Residual Claimants, and Corporate Control," pp. 351–66.

[116]For a review of these studies, see Douglas F. Greer, *Industrial Organization and Public Policy*, 2nd ed. (New York: Macmillan, 1984), pp. 222–24.

sistent differences.[117] In Appendix 5A we summarize the results of a large number of empirical studies.

Many of these studies, in fact, suggest that the degree of competition in a given market is a better predictor of efficient performance than ownership per se. This is not surprising. The private firms that are most comparable to public firms typically also operate in sectors characterized by natural monopoly where we would expect X-inefficiency resulting from limited competition. In some other cases, a single public firm has been compared to a single (usually heavily regulated) private firm; again, not surprisingly, performance differences appear to be small.

One recent study does suggest that public firms (and mixed firms) are less efficient than private firms in globally competitive markets. Aidan Vining and Anthony Boardman compared the performance of public, private, and mixed firms among the 500 largest non-U.S. firms. After controlling for important variables such as industry and country, they found that public and mixed firms appeared to be less efficient than the private firms.[118]

Certainly many countries have, at least until recently, utilized government corporations in an extremely broad range of sectors where there is little evidence of market failure. In France, for example, machine tools, automobiles, and watches are all produced by state firms. Until 1987, the French government even controlled one of the largest advertising agencies in the country! In Sweden, there is even a government corporation that makes beer.

Special Districts. *Special districts* are single-purpose governmental entities, usually created to supply goods that are believed to have natural monopoly, public goods, or externality characteristics. Such goods are typically local in nature, but may extend to the state or region. By far the most common use of special districts in the United States is to provide primary and secondary schooling. Other examples include air pollution, water, and transportation districts. What are the advantages and disadvantages of special districts relative to cities and counties? Indeed, we might ask why we have cities at all. One advantage of special districts is that they allow consumers to observe the relationship between service provision and tax-price clearly. Another advantage is that they can be designed to internalize externalities that spill across the historically evolved boundaries of local governments. A major disadvantage is the costs that consumers face in monitoring a whole series of "minigovernments" for different services: " . . . only for

---

[117]Louis De Alessi makes the strongest claim for superior private firm performance in "The Economics of Property Rights: A Review of the Evidence." Tom Borcherding appears to find a slight edge for the private sector in "Toward a Positive Theory of Public Sector Supply Arrangements," in J. Robert S. Prichard, ed., *Crown Corporations in Canada* (Toronto: Butterworth, 1983) pp. 99–184. Two reviews that find no difference are Colin C. Boyd, "The Comparative Efficiency of State-owned Enterprises," in A. R. Negandhi, H. Thomas, and K. L. K. Rao, eds., *Multinational Corporations and State-Owned Enterprises: A New Challenge in International Business* (Greenwich, Conn.: JAI Press, 1986), pp. 221–44; and Robert Millward and David M. Parker, "Public and Private Enterprise: Comparative Behavior and Relative Efficiency," in Robert Millward, ed., *Public Sector Economics*, pp. 199–274.

[118]Anthony E. Boardman and Aidan R. Vining, "Ownership and Performance in Competitive Environments: A Comparison of the Performance of Private, Mixed and State-Owned Enterprises," *Journal of Law and Economics* (forthcoming).

the most important collective functions will wholly independent organization be justified on cost grounds . . . the costs of organizing each activity separately would be greater than the promised added benefits from alternative organization."[119]

An important consideration is that collections of special districts prevent logrolling across issue areas. As we discussed in Chapter 4, logrolling often leads to inefficient pork-barrel spending. But it also permits minorities to express intense preferences that are not registered in majority voting on single issues where the social choice only reflects the preferences of the median voter. The more issues that are handled independently in special districts, the fewer that remain for possible inclusion in logrolls. Whether the reduction in logrolling contributes to efficiency and equity depends on the distribution of preferences in the population.

Contracting Out

We divide contracting out into direct contracting for goods used by government and indirect contracting for consumer goods provided by nonprofit organizations.

Direct Contracting Out.   Government frequently finances or "provides" services that are delivered by profit-making firms (if the services were previously delivered by government, this is a version of privatization). We should not underestimate the importance of direct contracting. The U.S. government, for example, contracts for the construction of almost all military matériel. It also purchases about $36 billion annually in regular commercial services like maintenance.[120] Direct contracting is an important component of the health care system and is becoming increasingly important in some sectors of government activity traditionally associated with direct supply, such as corrections.[121] A recent International City Management Association survey found that contracting for a wide range of services has increased rapidly in the 1980s, especially at the local level.[122]

What is the evidence on efficiency of direct supply vis-à-vis contracting out? Here, the empirical evidence does seem to suggest that contracting out is frequently more efficient than either market delivery (private subscription) or direct government supply: ". . . the empirical studies have found that contracting out tends to be less costly than government provision. . . cover[ing] a number of distinct

---

[119]James M. Buchanan and Marilyn R. Flowers, *The Public Finances*, 4th ed. (Homewood, Ill.: R. D. Irwin, 1975), p. 440.

[120]Congressional Budget Office, *Contracting Out: Potential for Reducing Federal Costs* (Washington, D.C.: Congress of the United States, June 1987), p. vii.

[121]On some of the thorny issues in this particular context, see Ira P. Robbins, "Privatization of Corrections: Defining the Issues," *Federal Probation*, September 1986, pp. 24–30; and Connie Mayer, "Legal Issues Surrounding Private Operation of Prisons," *Criminal Law Bulletin*, Vol. 22, No. 4, July/August 1986, pp. 309–25.

[122]Reported in Robert W. Poole, Jr., and Philip E. Fixler, Jr., "The Privatization of Public Sector Services in Practice: Experience and Potential," *Journal of Policy Analysis and Management*, Vol. 6, No. 4, Summer 1987, pp. 612–25.

services and pertain[ing] to a variety of geographical areas."[123] The limitations of these findings, however, should be kept in mind. Most important, the services examined usually have tangible, easily measurable outputs, such as are found in highways, garbage disposal, transportation, and food provision. Consequently, monitoring the quality of output is relatively straightforward. In addition, while opportunistic behavior is possible, even at its worst, it is likely to be limited in nature. The usefulness of direct contracting for health care and corrections is less clear and will depend on the extent to which quality, quantity, and eligibility can be effectively monitored and the possibilities for opportunistic behavior.[124]

Indirect Contracting Out. The double market-failure rationale has been most clearly used to explain the role of nonprofit organizations (although using somewhat different language). Nonprofits typically provide public goods (the first market failure) in a context where potential contributors (governments or private individuals) do not have the information to assess whether their contribution is actually used to produce the public good (the second, or principal-agent, market failure). Henry Hansmann argues that, as a result of the principal-agent problem, profit-making firms are able to divert funds to owners because contributors have neither the incentive nor the information to monitor diversion. In addition, because of the difficulty of monitoring performance (i.e., information asymmetry), the profit-making firm may provide inferior goods at excessive prices. In other words, donors may "trust" nonprofits because they are not allowed to make a profit. Perhaps donors also see certain nonprofits as having a strong sense of mission that leads them to maximize the output of desired goods. Against this must be set the possibility that nonprofits, given the lack of information, may transfer or dissipate (for example, through higher salaries or less work) the excess of revenue over costs.[125]

You will notice that this analysis compares indirect contracting to provision via profit-making firms; it does not compare indirect contracting to direct government supply. Yet nonprofit organizations can be thought of as being somewhere between market supply and direct government supply. Why might nonprofit supply be preferable to direct government provision? One advantage is that the nonprofit form allows for voluntary contributions—those who value the supplied good can make additional contributions to expand its supply. Another is that it allows for great flexibility in the mix of services provided, a feature especially important where the recipients of the services have heterogeneous preferences. Of course, the relative independence of nonprofit firms sometimes makes it difficult for the government sponsor to select the exact set of services that will be supplied. Indeed, it may be difficult for government to stimulate the creation of nonprofits where they do not already exist.

[123]Ibid., p. 615.

[124]Randall R. Bovbjerg, Philip J. Held, and Mark V. Pauly, "Privatization and Bidding in the Health Care Sector," *Journal of Policy Analysis and Management,* Vol. 6, No. 4, Summer 1987, pp. 648–66.

[125]Henry Hansmann, "The Role of Non-Profit Enterprise," in Susan Rose-Ackerman," ed., *The Economics of Non-Profit Institutions* (New York: Oxford University Press, 1986), pp. 57–84.

Generic Policies	Perceived Problems	Typical Limitations and Collateral Consequences
Insurance		
Mandatory insurance	L.C.F.: Incomplete insurance markets	} Moral hazard
Subsidized insurance	M.F.: Information asymmetry	} Moral hazard
	L.C.F.: Adverse selection	} Deadweight losses
	L.C.F.: Consumer myopia	
Cushions		
Stockpiling	L.C.F.: Adjustment costs	} Rent seeking by suppliers and consumers
	G.F.: Price controls, cartelization	
Transitional assistance (buy-outs and grandfathering)	L.C.F.: Adjustment costs	} Inequality in availability
Cash grants	D.I.: Equality of outcome	} Reduction in work effort, dependency
	L.C.F.: Utility interdependence	

M.F.: Market Failure   D.I.: Distributional Issue
G.F.: Government Failure   L.C.F.: Limitation of Competitive Framework

Figure 5.7   Providing Insurance and Cushions

PROVIDING INSURANCE AND CUSHIONS

Some government interventions provide shields against the "slings and arrows of outrageous fortune." We divide these into two general categories: insurance and—for want of a better word—cushions. Figure 5.7 presents a summary of these generic policies: mandatory and subsidized insurance, stockpiles, transitional assistance, and cash grants.

Insurance

The essence of insurance is the reduction of individual risk through pooling. Insurance can be purchased in private markets to indemnify against loss of life, damage to property, cost of health care, and liability for damages caused to others. As we discussed in Chapter 3, factors such as moral hazard, adverse selection, and limited actuarial experience can lead to incomplete insurance markets. Further, people do not always make optimal decisions about purchasing insurance coverage because of biases inherent in the heuristics commonly used to estimate and interpret probabilities. Therefore, there may be an appropriate role for public intervention in some insurance markets. More generally, insurance can be used in conjunction with liability laws to deal with problems caused by information asymmetry.

In designing public insurance programs, care must be taken to limit moral hazard. By making certain outcomes less costly, insurance may induce people to take greater risks or bear greater compensable costs than they otherwise would.[126] One way to limit moral hazard is to invest in monitoring systems. Another is to design payment structures that reduce the incentive for beneficiaries to inflate compensable costs. For example, requiring beneficiaries to pay a fraction of their claimed costs through copayments reduces their incentive to incur unnecessary expenses. The general point is that in analyzing proposals for public insurance programs, it is necessary to anticipate how participants will respond to the availability of benefits.

Mandatory Insurance. When people have better information about their individual risks than insurers, adverse selection may limit the availability of insurance. For example, health insurance is sold primarily through group plans because they are less prone to adverse selection than individual policies. Because the premiums for individual policies are set on the assumption that the worst risks will self-select, good risks who do not have access to group coverage may decide not to insure. Government can use its authority to mandate universal participation in insurance plans to prevent adverse selection from operating. Many proposals for national health insurance in the United States would mandate broader workplace coverage and require those not covered in the workplace to participate in public insurance programs.

Does the mere existence of an incomplete insurance market justify mandatory insurance? Usually, the rationale for mandatory insurance is based on the argument that the losses suffered by those left uncovered involve negative externalities. For example, the personal assets of many drivers are insufficient to cover the costs of property damage and personal injury that they inflict on others in serious accidents. Therefore, many states mandate liability coverage for all drivers so that those injured have opportunities to obtain compensation through tort law.

Paternalism may also serve as a rationale for mandatory insurance. For example, one function of the Old Age, Survivors, Disability and Health Insurance Program, the U.S. social security system, is to insure against the possibility that people have insufficient savings for retirement because of myopia, misinforma-

---

[126]For example, Robert Topel attributes one-third or more of all unemployment spells among full-time participants in unemployment insurance programs to the benefits provided. Robert Topel, "Unemployment and Unemployment Insurance," *Research in Labor Economics*, Vol. 7, annual, 1985, pp. 91–135.

.ion, miscalculation, bad luck, or simple laziness.[127] People who do not save an adequate amount will either consume at low levels in retirement or receive assistance from private or public charity. It is worth noting that social security is not a pure insurance program but rather involves considerable transfers from high-income workers to low-income workers and from current workers to current retirees.[128] Mandatory insurance programs typically combine actuarially based risk pooling with income transfers. Of course, if the programs were not mandatory, those paying the subsidies through higher premiums or lower benefits would be unlikely to participate.

Mandatory insurance can also be used to privatize regulation. One reason why legal liability alone cannot fully remedy information asymmetries and negative externalities is that firms often have inadequate assets to pay damages. This is especially likely for the short-lived fly-by-night firms that often exploit information asymmetries. By requiring that they carry minimum levels of liability insurance, the government can guarantee that at least some assets will be available for compensating those who have been harmed. Perhaps more important, the insurance companies have an incentive to monitor the behavior of the firms with an eye to reducing liability.[129]

Subsidized Insurance.   Rather than mandating insurance, the government can provide it at subsidized premiums when myopia, miscalculation, or other factors appear to be contributing to underconsumption. For example, in the United States the Federal Emergency Management Agency provides subsidized flood insurance under the Flood Disaster Protection Act of 1973. As might be expected, restrictions on coverage are necessary to prevent those who suffer losses from rebuilding in flood plains.

Fairness often serves as a rationale for subsidizing premiums. For example, residents and businesses in poor neighborhoods may find actuarily fair premiums for fire insurance to be so high that they forgo coverage. A perception that they are unable to move to other locations with lower risks may serve as a rationale for subsidy. Rather than pay the subsidies directly, governments often force private insurers to write subsidized policies in proportion to their total premiums. Such *assigned risk pools* have been created to provide subsidized premiums for fire insurance in many urban areas. They are also commonly used in conjunction with mandatory insurance programs.

[127]Laurence J. Kotlikoff, "Justifying Public Provision of Social Security," *Journal of Policy Analysis and Management*, Vol. 6, No. 4, Summer 1987, pp. 674–89. For a detailed history of analyses dealing with social security issues, see Lawrence H. Thompson, "The Social Security Reform Debate," *Journal of Economic Literature*, Vol. 21, No. 4, December 1983, pp. 1425–67.

[128]For calculations for representative age and income groups, see Anthony Pellechio and Gordon Goodfellow, "Individual Gains and Losses from Social Security Before and After the 1983 Amendments," *Cato Journal*, Vol. 3, No. 2, Fall 1983, pp. 417–42.

[129]For example, regulation of manufacturing practices by the Food and Drug Administration might be replaced with a mandatory insurance program. See David Leo Weimer, "Safe—and Available—Drugs," in Robert W. Poole, Jr., ed., *Instead of Regulation* (Lexington, Mass.: Lexington Books, 1982), pp. 239–83, at p. 270.

Cushions

Whereas insurance schemes reduce the variance in outcomes by spreading risk, *cushions* reduce the variance in outcomes through a centralized mechanism. From the perspective of beneficiaries, the consequences may appear identical. The key difference is that with insurance individuals make ex ante preparations for the possibility of unfavorable outcomes, while with cushions they receive ex post compensation for unfavorable outcomes that occur.

Stockpiling. In an uncertain world we always face the potential for supply disruptions or "price shocks," whether as a result of economic or political cartelization, unpredictable cyclicity of supply, or man-made and natural disasters. These shocks are unlikely to cause major problems unless they involve goods without close substitutes that are central to economic activity. In practice, the most serious problems arise with natural resources and agricultural products.

With respect to natural resources, if they are geographically concentrated, then the owners may be able to extract monopoly rents (as well as scarcity rents) from consumers. In a multinational context, cartels, whether they have primarily economic or political motives, may attempt to extract rents. While the long-run prospects for successful cartelization are limited because higher prices speed the introduction of substitutes, cartels may be able to exercise effective market power in the short run. In addition, the supply of concentrated resources may be subject to disruption because of revolution, war, or natural disaster.

The adverse consequences of these supply disruptions can be dampened with *stockpiling programs* that accumulate quantities of the resource during periods of normal market activity so that they can be released during periods of market disruption. For example, the United States has long maintained government stockpiles of critical minerals like chromium, platinum, vanadium, and manganese, for which production is concentrated in South Africa, the Soviet Union, and other countries of questionable political reliability.[130] Experience with the program suggests that political pressure from domestic producers tends to keep items in stockpiles long after they have lost their critical nature and that there is a reluctance to draw down stocks at the beginning of supply disruptions when they are most valuable to the economy.[131]

The most prominent U.S. resource stockpiling program is the Strategic Petroleum Reserve, which stores over 500 million barrels of crude oil for use during oil supply disruptions.[132] Because much of the world's low-cost reserves of crude oil are located in the politically unstable Middle East, the possibility exists for sharp reductions in supply that would cause steep rises in the price of oil and

---

[130]Michael W. Klass, James C. Burrows, and Steven D. Beggs, *International Mineral Cartels and Embargoes* (New York: Praeger, 1980).

[131]See Glenn H. Snyder, *Stockpiling Strategic Materials: Politics and National Defense* (San Francisco: Chandler, 1966).

[132]For a history of the program, see David Leo Weimer, *The Strategic Petroleum Reserve: Planning, Implementation, and Analysis* (Westport, Conn.: Greenwood Press, 1982).

consequent losses to the U.S. economy. Drawdown of the Strategic Petroleum Reserve would offset a portion of the lost supply, thereby dampening the price rise and reducing the magnitude of economic losses.

Because private firms could make an expected profit by buying low during normal markets and selling high during disruptions, we might ask why the government should stockpile.[133] One reason is government failure: based on past experience, firms might anticipate the possibility that the government will institute price controls, preventing them from realizing speculative profits. Another is market failure: acquisition and drawdown decisions by private firms have external effects on the economy. (We consider these rationales in more depth in Chapter 11.)

In ancient times agricultural stockpiles served primarily as hedges against scarcity; in modern times they serve mainly as hedges against abundance. For example, the U.S. Commodity Credit Corporation in effect buys surpluses of grain from farmers to help support prices. While stockpiles of agricultural commodities provide security against widespread crop failures, they are costly to maintain. Further, modest price swings can probably be adequately accommodated by private stockpiling and by risk-diversification mechanisms like private futures markets.[134]

State and local governments, which typically must operate with a balanced budget, can prepare for revenue shocks by stockpiling financial resources. These reserves are sometimes called *rainy day funds*.[135] They serve as a form of self-insurance for governments that have difficulty borrowing on short notice. As with stockpilings of physical commodities, an important question is whether political interests permit efficient decisions concerning acquisition and use. In particular, we might expect the pressures of the election cycle to lead to inefficient decisions concerning use.

Transitional Assistance.   Policy analysts and politicians have increasingly come to realize that efficiency-enhancing policy changes are strongly resisted by those who suffer distributionally. This may result from the elimination of existing benefits or the imposition of new costs. Indeed, if there have only been transitional gains (as discussed in Chapter 4), the elimination of a benefit can impose real economic loss. Resistance to the elimination of benefits is likely to be especially bitter in these circumstances. Government may also wish to pay compensation when its projects would increase aggregate welfare, but would impose disproportionate costs on particular individuals or localities.

Compensation may take either monetary or nonmonetary forms. Monetary compensation is typically in the form of a *buy-out*, whereby government purchases,

[133]For a detailed discussion of this question, see George Horwich and David Leo Weimer, *Oil Price Shocks, Market Response, and Contingency Planning* (Washington, D.C.: American Enterprise Institute, 1984), pp. 111–39.

[134]Brian D. Wright, "Commodity Market Stabilization in Farm Programs," in Bruce L. Gardner, ed., *U.S. Agricultural Policy* (Washington, D.C.: American Enterprise Institute, 1985), pp. 257–76.

[135]Michael Wolkoff, "An Evaluation of Municipal Rainy Day Funds," *Public Budgeting and Finance,* Vol. 7, No. 2, Summer 1987, pp. 52–63; and Richard Pollock and Jack P. Suyderhud, "The Role of Rainy Day Funds in Achieving Fiscal Stability," *National Tax Journal,* Vol. 39, No. 4, December 1986, pp. 485–97.

at a fixed price, a given benefit. Examples of cash payments include relocation assistance payments to homeowners and renters displaced by federal urban renewal and highway construction projects.[136]

Nonmonetary payment usually takes the form of either a *"grandfather" clause* or a *"hold harmless" provision*, both of which allow a current generation to retain benefits that will not be available to future generations. Grandfather clauses can increase political feasibility, but they can also reduce effectiveness.[137]

Cash Grants. The most direct way to cushion people against adverse economic circumstances is through *cash grants.* This generic term covers such programs in the United States as Aid to Families with Dependent Children (welfare) and Supplemental Security Income (aid to the blind and disabled). The 1974 Health, Education, and Welfare, "megaproposal" summarizes the situations in which cash grants are preferable to vouchers: "the provision of cash benefits is an appropriate public action when the objective is to alter the distribution of purchasing power in general and when the recipient of the benefit is to be left free to decide how to spend it . . .," while ". . . the provision of vouchers is appropriate when the objective is to alter the distribution of purchasing power over specific goods and services when the supply of these can be expected to increase as the demand for them increases."[138]

The advantage (or disadvantage) of cash grants is that they do not interfere with the consumption choices of a target population. Clearly, this is a valuable attribute if the goal is simply to raise incomes. On the other hand, if the objective is to *alter* consumption patterns, then cash grants are less-effective instruments. While cash grants do not restrict consumption behavior, they may affect other behavior, most importantly, the "leisure-labor" trade-off. Increases in unearned income—whether through cash grants, in-kind grants, or other subsidies— generally increase the demand for all goods, including leisure, so that the amount of labor supplied falls.[139]

A fundamental trade-off between transferring income and discouraging work effort arises in designing cash grant programs. For example, consider the goals of a negative income tax: (1) to make any difference, the transfer should be substantial; (2) to preserve work incentives, marginal tax rates should be relatively low; and (3) the break-even level of income (the point at which the transfer reaches zero) should be reasonably low to avoid high program costs. Unfortunately, at

[136]Joseph J. Cordes and Burton A. Weisbrod, "When Government Programs Create Inequities: A Guide to Compensation Policies," *Journal of Policy Analysis and Management*, Vol. 4, No. 2, Winter 1985, pp. 178–95.

[137]For a discussion of these issues, see Christopher Leman, "How to Get There from Here: The Grandfather Effect and Public Policy," *Policy Analysis*, Vol. 6, No. 1, Winter 1980, pp. 99–116.

[138]Laurence Lynn and John Michael Seidl, "Policy Analysis at H.E.W.: Story of Mega-Proposal—Introduction," *Policy Analysis*, Vol. 1, No. 2, Spring 1975, pp. 232–73.

[139]For a review of empirical evidence on the income elasticity of the labor supply, see George Borjas and James Heckman, "Labor Supply Estimates for Public Policy Evaluation," in *Proceedings of the Thirty-First Annual Meeting* (Chicago: Industrial Relations Research Association, 1979); and Robert A. Moffitt and Kenneth C. Kehrer, "The Effect of Tax and Transfer Programs on Labor Supply," *Research in Labor Economics*, Vol. 4, annual, 1981, pp. 103–50.

least to some extent, the three are incompatible.[140] For example, if a negative income tax guaranteed every family a floor on income of $4,000 through a cash grant, then a tax rate of 20 percent on earned income would imply that only when earned income reached $20,000 would net payments to families be zero. Raising the tax rate to, say, 50 percent would lower the break-even earned income to $8,000. The higher tax rate, however, would reduce the after-tax wage rate and thereby probably reduce work effort.

If recipients reduce their work effort, their chances of becoming dependent on the cash grants increase. For some categories of recipients, such as the permanently disabled, the increased risk of dependence may not be a serious concern. For others, however, there may be a trade-off between the generosity of short-term assistance and the long-run economic vitality of recipients. Work requirements may be one way to improve the terms of the trade-off.[141] Unfortunately, they are typically costly and difficult to implement, especially for single-parent families with young children.

Cash grants can also influence choices about living arrangements and family structure. For example, Aid to Families with Dependent Children often makes it financially possible for young unmarried mothers to set up their own households. The less-generous are state benefit levels, the more likely it is that these mothers will stay with their parents.[142] Indeed, the opportunity to gain independence may encourage some teenage girls to have children. The general point is that the availability of cash grants may influence a wide range of behaviors.

CONCLUSION

A variety of generic policies can be used to address market and government failures. Figure 5.8 indicates the generic policy categories that are most likely to provide candidate solutions for each of the major market failures, government failures, and distributional concerns. In many cases, more than one generic policy can provide potential solutions for the same problem. But the solutions are never perfect. They must be tailored to the specifics of the situation and evaluated in terms of the relevant goals.

Our discussions of general problems and generic policy solutions lay the foundations for actually doing policy analysis. An understanding of market and government failure helps us to understand the nature of public policy problems. Being aware of the generic policies and their collateral consequences helps us to begin our search for solutions to our specific policy problems. In the next chapter, we turn to the process of policy analysis that enables us to use these foundations effectively.

[140]For a more extensive discussion of these problems, see Robin W. Boadway and David E. Wildasin, *Public Sector Economics* (Boston: Little, Brown, 1984), pp. 445–96.

[141]Lawrence W. Mead, "The Potential for Work Enforcement: A Study of WIN," *Journal of Policy Analysis and Management*, Vol. 7, No. 2, Winter 1988, pp. 264–88.

[142]David T. Ellwood and Mary Jo Bane, "The Impact of AFDC on Family Structure and Living Arrangements," *Research in Labor Economics*, Vol. 7, annual, 1985, pp. 137–207.

	Market Mechanisms	Incentives	Rules	Nonmarket Supply	Insurance and Cushions
Traditional market failures					
Public goods	S	S	S	P	
Externalities	S	P	P	S	
Natural monopoly	S	S	P	P	
Information asymmetry			P	S	S
Other limitations of the competitive framework					
Noncompetitive behavior			P		
Preference-related problems	S	S	P		
Uncertainty problems			P		S
Intertemporal problems			S		P
Adjustment costs					P
Distributional concerns					
Equity of opportunity		S	S		P
Equality of outcomes			S		P
Governmental failures					
Direct democracy			P		
Representative government	P		S		
Bureaucratic supply	P	S	S	S	
Decentralization	S	P		S	

P: Primary source of policy solutions*
S: Secondary source of policy solutions*
*Remember, this framework is primarily normative (the generic policies that "make sense"), rather than positive (the generic policies most often adopted).

Figure 5.8 Searching for Generic Policy Solutions

APPENDIX 5A

EMPIRICAL EVIDENCE ON THE RELATIVE EFFICIENCY OF PUBLIC CORPORATIONS AND PRIVATE FIRMS

Sector	Public Corporation More Efficient	No Difference or Ambiguous Results	Private Company More Efficient

Electric utilities	Meyer (1975)
	 Neuberg (1977)
	 Pescatrice &
	   Trapani (1980)
		Mann (1970)
		 Junker (1975)
		 Spann (1977)
		 Färe et al. (1985)
		 Atkinson & Halvorsen
		   (1986)
			Shepherd (1966)
			 Moore (1970)
			 Peltzman (1971)
			 Tilton (1973)
			 De Alessi (1974)
			 De Alessi (1977)

Refuse	Pier et al. (1974)	Hirsch (1965)
		 Kemper & Quigley
		   (1976)
		 Collins & Downes
		   (1977)
			Kitchen (1976)
			 Savas (1977)
			 Pommerehne & Frey
			   (1977)
			 Stevens (1978)
			 Edwards & Stevens
			   (1978)

Water	Mann & Mikesell
	   (1971)
	 Bruggink (1982)
		Feigenbaum &
		   Teeples (1983)
			Hausman (1976)
			 Morgan (1977)
			 Crain & Zardkoohi
			   (1978, 1980)

Health-related services		Becker & Sloan (1985)	Clarkson (1972)
			 Rushing (1974)
			 Lindsay (1976)
			 Frech (1976)
			 Bays (1979)
			 Frech (1980)
			 Bishop (1980)*
			 Frech & Ginsburg
			   (1981)
			 Finsinger (1982)
			 Wilson & Jadlow
			   (1982)
			 Schlesinger & Dorwart
			   (1984)

Sector	Public Corporation More Efficient	No Difference or Ambiguous Results	Private Company More Efficient
Airlines		Forsyth & Hocking (1980) Morrison (1981) Jordan (1982)	Davies (1971) Davies (1977)
Railroads		Caves & Christensen (1980) Caves et al. (1982)	
Financial institutions		Lewin (1982)	Davies (1981)
Fire services			Ahlbrecht (1973)
Nonrail transit			Pashigan (1976) Palmer et al. (1983) McGuire & Van Cott (1984)

* Review of ten other studies.

**Vis-à-vis public, not vis-à-vis not for profit.

NOTE: See bibliography for complete citations.

Source: Anthony Boardman and Aidan Vining, "Ownership and Performance in Competitive Environments: A Comparison of the Performance of Private, Mixed and State-Owned Enterprises," *Journal of Law and Economics* (forthcoming).

AHLBRECHT, ROGER. "Efficiency in the Provision of Fire Services," *Public Choice*, Vol. 16, Fall 1973, pp. 1–15.

ATKINSON, SCOTT E., and ROBERT HALVORSEN. "The Relative Efficiency of Public and Private Firms in a Regulated Environment: The Case of U.S. Electric Utilities." *Journal of Public Economics*, Vol. 29, No. 1, April 1986, pp. 281–94.

BAYS, CARSON. "Cost Comparisons of For-profit and Nonprofit Hospitals." *Social Science and Medicine*, Vol. 13C, No. 3, 1979, pp. 219–25.

BECKER, EDMUND R., and FRANK A. SLOAN. "Hospital Ownership and Performance." *Economic Inquiry*, Vol. 23, No. 1, January 1985, pp. 21–37.

BISHOP, CHRISTINE. "Nursing Home Cost Studies and Reimbursement Issues." *Health Care Financing Review*, Vol. 1, No. 4, Spring 1980, pp. 47–64.

BRUGGINK, THOMAS H. "Public Versus Regulated Private Enterprise in the Municipal Water Industry: A Comparison of Operating Costs." *Quarterly Review of Economics and Business*, Vol. 22, No. 1, Spring 1982, pp. 111–25.

CAVES, DOUGLAS, and LAURITS R. CHRISTENSEN. "The Relative Efficiency of Public and Private Firms in a Competitive Environment: The Case of Canadian Railroads." *Journal of Political Economy*, Vol. 88, No. 5, October 1980, pp. 958–76.

CAVES, DOUGLAS W., LAURITS R. CHRISTENSEN, JOSEPH A. SWANSON, and MICHAEL W. TRETHEWAY. "Economic Performance of U.S. and Canadian Railroads." In W. T. Stanbury and F. Thompson, eds., *Managing Public Enterprises*. New York: Praeger, 1982, pp. 123–51.

ARKSON, KENNETH W. "Some Implications of Property Rights in Hospital Management." *Journal of Law and Economics*, Vol. 15, No. 2, October 1972, pp. 363–84.

COLLINS, JOHN, and BRIAN DOWNES. "The Effect of Size on the Provisions of Public Services: The Case of Solid Waste Collection in Smaller Cities." *Urban Affairs Quarterly*, Vol. 12, 1977, pp. 333–45.

CRAIN, W. MARK, and ASGHAR ZARDKOOHI. "A Test of the Property Rights Theory of the Firm: Water Utilities in the United States." *Journal of Law and Economics*, Vol. 21, October 1978, pp. 395–408.

DAVIES, DAVID. "Property Rights and Economic Behavior in Private and Government Enterprises: The Case of Australia's Banking System." *Research in Law and Economics*, Vol. 3, 1981, pp. 111–42.

_____. "The Efficiency of Public Versus Private Firms: The Case of Australia's Two Airlines." *Journal of Law and Economics*, Vol. 14, No. 1, April 1971, pp. 149–65.

_____. "Property Rights and Economic Efficiency: The Australian Airlines Revisited." *Journal of Law and Economics*, Vol. 20, No. 1, April 1977, pp. 223–26.

DE ALESSI, LOUIS. "An Economic Analysis of Government Ownership and Regulation: Theory and the Evidence from the Electric Power Industry." *Public Choice*, Vol. 19, Fall 1974, pp. 1–42.

_____. "Ownership and Peak-Load Pricing in the Electric Power Industry." *Quarterly Review of Economics and Business*, Vol. 17, No. 4, Winter 1977, pp. 7–26.

EDWARDS, FRANKLIN, and BARBARA STEVENS. "The Provision of Municipal Sanitation by Private Firms: An Empirical Analysis of the Efficiency of Alternative Market Structures and Regulatory Arrangements." *Journal of Industrial Economics*, Vol. 27, No. 2, December 1978, pp. 133–47.

FÄRE, R., S. GROSSKOPF, and J. LOGAN. "The Relative Performance of Publicly Owned and Privately Owned Electric Utilities." *Journal of Public Economics*, Vol. 26, February 1985, pp. 89–106.

FEIGENBAUM, SUSAN, and RONALD TEEPLES. "Public Versus Private Water Delivery: A Hedonic Cost Approach." *Review of Economics and Statistics*, Vol. 65, No. 4, November 1983, pp. 672–78.

FINSINGER, JORG. "The Performance of Public Enterprises in Insurance Markets." Paper presented at a conference of the Performance of Public Enterprise, Liége, Sart Tilman, Belgium, 1982.

FORSYTH, ? J., and R. D. HOCKING. "Property Rights and Efficiency in a Regulated Environment. The Case of Australian Airlines." *Economic Record*, Vol. 56, No. 153, June 1980, pp. 182–5.

FRECH, U E., III. "Property Rights, the Theory of the Firm, and Competitive Markets for Top Decision-Makers.' In R. Zerbe, ed., *Research in Law and Economics*, Vol. 2, (Greenwich, Conn.: JAI Press, 1980) pp. 49–63.

_____. "The Property Rights Theory of the Firm: Empirical Results from a Natural Experiment." *Journal of Political Economy*, Vol. 84, February 1976, pp. 143–52.

FRECH, H. E., III, and PAUL L GINSBURG. "The Cost of Nursing Home Care in the United States: Government Financing, Ownership, and Efficiency." In Jacques van der Gaag and Mark Perlman, eds., *Health, Economics, and Health Economics*. New York: North-Holland, 1981. Pp. 67–81.

HAUSMAN, JEAN M. "Urban Water Services Pricing: Public vs. Private Firms." Ph.D. thesis, Department of Economics, George Washington University, 1976.

HIRSCH, WERNER Z. "Cost Functions of an Urban Government Service: Refuse Collection." *Review of Economics and Statistics*, Vol. 47, No. 1, February 1965, pp. 27–92.

JORDAN, WILLIAM A. "Performance of North American and Australian Airlines." In W. T. Stanbury and F. Thompson, eds., *Managing Public Enterprises*. New York: Praeger, 1982. Pp. 161-99.

JUNKER, J. A. "Economic Performance of Public and Private Utilities: The Case of U.S. Electric Utilities." *Journal of Economics and Business*, Vol. 28, No. 1, Fall 1975, pp. 60-67.

KEMPER, PETER, and JOHN QUIGLEY. *The Economics of Refuse Collection*. Cambridge, Mass.: Ballinger, 1976.

KITCHEN, HARRY. "A Statistical Estimation of an Operating Cost Function for Municipal Refuse Collection." *Public Finance Quarterly*, Vol. 4, No. 1, January 1976, pp. 56-76.

LEWIN, ARIE Y. "Public Enterprise, Purposes and Performance." In W. T. Stanbury and F. Thompson, eds., *Managing Public Enterprises*. New York: Praeger, 1982. Pp. 51-78.

LINDSAY, COTTON M. "A Theory of Government Enterprise." *Journal of Political Economy*, Vol. 84, No. 5, October 1976, pp. 1061-77.

MANN, PATRICK C. "Publicly Owned Electric Utility Profits and Resources Allocation." *Land Economics*, Vol. 46, No. 4, November 1970, pp. 478-84.

MANN, PATRICK C., and JOHN L. MIKESELL. "Tax Payments and Electric Utility Prices." *Southern Economic Journal*, Vol. 38, No. 1, July 1971, pp. 69-78.

McGUIRE, ROBERT A., and T. NORMAN VAN COTT, "Public Versus Private Economic Activity: A New Look at School Bus Transportation." *Public Choice*, Vol. 43, No. 1, 1904, pp. 25-43.

MEYER, ROBERT A. "Publicly Owned vs. Privately Owned Utilities: A Policy Choice." *Review of Economics and Statistics*, Vol. 57, No. 4, November 1975, pp. 391-99.

MOORE, THOMAS G. "The Effectiveness of Regulation of Electric Utility Prices." *Southern Economic Journal*, Vol. 36, No. 4, April 1970, pp. 365-75.

MORGAN, DOUGLAS W. "Investor Owned vs. Publicly Owned Water Agencies: An Evaluation of the Property Rights Theory of the Firm." *Water Resources Bulletin*, Vol. 13, No. 4, August 1977, pp. 775-81.

MORRISON, STEPHEN. "Property Rights and Economic Efficiency: A Further Examination of the Australian Airlines." Unpublished paper, faculty of Commerce and Business Administration, University of British Columbia, 1981.

NEUBERG, LELAND GERSON. "Two Issues in the Municipal Ownership of Electric Power Distribution Systems." *Bell Journal of Economics*, Vol. 8, No. 1, Spring 1977, pp. 303-23.

PALMER, JOHN P., JOHN QUINN, and RAY RESENDES. "A Case Study of Public Enterprise: Gray Coach Lines Ltd." In J. Robert S. Prichard, ed., *Crown Corporations in Canada: The Calculus of Instrument Choice*. Toronto: Butterworths, 1983.

PASHIGAN, B. PETER. "Consequences and Causes of Public Ownership of Urban Transit Facilities." *Journal of Political Economy*, Vol. 84, No. 6, December 1976, pp. 1239-60.

PELTZMAN, SAM. "Pricing in Public and Private Enterprises: Electric Utilities in the United States." *Journal of Law and Economics*, Vol. 14, No. 1, April 1971, pp. 109-47.

PESCATRICE, DONN R., and JOHN M. TRAPANI. "The Performance and Objectives of Public and Private Utilities Operating in the United States." *Journal of Public Economics*, Vol. 13, No. 2, April 1980, pp. 259-76.

PIER, WILLIAM J., ROBERT B. VERNON, and JOHN H. WICKS. "An Empirical Comparison of Government and Private Production Efficiency." *National Tax Journal*, Vol. 27, No. 4, December 1974, pp. 653-56.

POMMEREHNE, WERNER, and B. S. FREY. "Public vs. Production Efficiency in Switzerland: A Theoretical and Empirical Comparison." In Vincent Ostrom and Robert Bish, eds., *Comparing Urban Service Delivery Systems, Urban Affairs Annual Review*. Beverly Hills, Calif.: Sage Publications, 1977. Pp. 221-41.

RUSHING, WILLIAM. "Differences in Profit and Nonprofit Organizations: A Study of Effectiveness and Efficiency in General Short-Stay Hospitals." *Administrative Science Quarterly*, Vol. 19, No. 4, December 1974, pp. 474–84.

SAVAS, E. S. "Policy Analysis for Local Government: Public vs. Private Refuse Collection." *Policy Analysis*, Vol. 3, No. 1, Winter 1977, pp. 49–74.

SCHLESINGER, MARK, and ROBERT DORWART. "Ownership and Mental Health Services." *New England Journal of Medicine*, Vol. 311, No. 13, October 1984, pp. 959–65.

SHEPHERD, WILLIAM G. "Utility Growth and Profits under Regulation." In William G. Shepherd and Thomas G. Gies, eds., *Utility Regulation: New Directions in Theory and Practice*. New York: Random House, 1966.

SPANN, ROBERT M. "Public Versus Private Provisions of Governmental Services." In T. E. Borcherding, ed., *Budgets and Bureaucrats*. Durham, N.C.: Duke University Press, 1977. Pp. 71–89.

STEVENS, BARBARA J. "Scale, Market Structure, and the Cost of Refuse Collection." *Review of Economics and Statistics*, Vol. 60, No. 3, August 1978, pp. 438–48.

TILTON, JOHN E. "The Nature of Firm Ownership and the Adoption of Innovations in the Electric Power Industry." Paper presented at the Public Choice Society, Washington, D. C., March 1973.

WILSON, GEORGE W., and JOSEPH M. JADLOW. "Competition, Profit Incentives and Technical Efficiency in the Nuclear Medicine Industry." *Bell Journal of Economics*, Vol. 13, No. 2, Autumn 1982, pp. 472–82.

6

LANDING ON YOUR FEET:
HOW TO CONFRONT
POLICY PROBLEMS

The previous chapters have been concerned with the conceptual foundations of policy analysis: how to diagnose problems, how to develop policy alternatives, how to think about efficiency and other policy goals, and how to measure some of the costs and benefits of either intervening in markets or altering existing public interventions. Upon these foundations the analyst must build a structure—one that is useful and appropriate for the environment. In this chapter we focus on the construction process: How should one plan and execute a policy analysis? Our answer keeps central the notion that policy analysis as a process involves *formulating* and *communicating* useful advice.[1]

Getting started on a written analysis is often difficult. We emphasize, therefore, how to go about developing a strategy for doing analysis (in other words, the "analysis of the analysis," or, if you like, "meta-analysis"). We suggest, however, that, before you begin trying to do analysis, you analyze yourself.

ANALYZING YOURSELF: META-ANALYSIS

Your self-analysis should influence the way you go about doing policy analysis. You may base the self-analysis either on your first attempt at a policy analysis

---

[1] Some pieces we find particularly helpful on the *process* of policy analysis include: Christopher Leman and Robert Nelson, "Ten Commandments for Policy Economists," *Journal of Policy Analysis and Management*, Vol. 1, No. 1, 1981, pp. 97–117; Alain Enthoven, "Ten Practical Principles for Policy and Program Analysis," in Richard Zeckhauser, ed., *Benefit-Cost and Policy Analysis Annual, 1974* (Chicago: Aldine, 1975), pp. 456–65; James M. Verdier, "Advising Congressional Decision-Makers: Guidelines for Economists," *Journal of Policy Analysis and Management*, Vol. 3, No. 3, 1984, pp. 421–38; and Robert D. Behn and James Vaupel, "Teaching Analytic Thinking," *Policy Analysis*, Vol. 2, No. 4, Fall 1976, pp. 663–92.

(the preferred method), or on your experience in writing academic papers (less preferable).

Students (and most others as well) tend to fall into one of two broad categories of thinkers and writers: linear and nonlinear.[2] Linear thinkers tend to solve problems by moving sequentially through a series of logical steps. Nonlinear thinkers tend to view problems configuratively, moving back and forth over steps as various pieces of the puzzle become apparent and begin to fall into place. We should stress that, for our purposes, neither is better or worse—*both* have strengths and weaknesses. Your particular weakness (or strength) may not have been revealed in other courses that were more structured and dealt with greater substantive certainty.

This last point is crucial. Most of you are familiar with course assignments, especially problem sets in mathematics, statistics, and economics, where right and wrong answers can be specified. Policy analysis is rarely so certain. This does *not* mean that there are not good or bad analyses, but that your answer, the recommendation you make to a client, rarely by itself determines the quality of your analysis. Good analysis asks the right questions and creatively but logically answers them. The approach that you choose should allow you to eliminate, minimize, or at least mitigate your particular weaknesses in thinking and writing.

How can you diagnose your weaknesses? We have found that students who are linear thinkers and writers tend to suffer from "analysis paralysis." Linear thinkers, not surprisingly, like to start at the beginning of an analytic problem and to work step by step through to the end, following what is sometimes called a rationalist approach.[3] If they cannot complete these steps sequentially, however, they tend to become paralyzed. In contrast, many others do not like to approach analysis sequentially. They have many ideas that they wish to get down on paper; they have difficulty communicating these ideas in a well-organized, sequential mode, which, put bluntly, often results in written products that look like a "regurgitated dog's dinner."

The first meta-analysis rule is that *linear thinkers should adopt nonlinear **think- ing** strategies, while nonlinear thinkers should adopt linear **writing** strategies.* The format of this book should assist linear thinkers in adopting a nonlinear thinking approach because it compartmentalizes the analytic process. For example, you do not need to understand the problem fully to sketch out some generic policy alternatives. The previous chapters of the book—together with the next section—should also assist nonlinear thinkers in organizing analyses so that they can be communicated more clearly. Nonlinear thinkers can, and should, continue to think nonlinearly, but they must *write* linearly and comprehensively. Linear thinkers, on the other hand, will find that they will be more productive and less vulnerable to analysis paralysis if they also adopt nonlinear work strategies. Therefore, the second meta-

---

[2]There is growing evidence that the distinction between the linear and the nonlinear corresponds to the differential abilities of the right and left sides of the brain. The evidence suggests that the left hemisphere is used for logical, sequential processes, while the right hemisphere is used for processes requiring intuition and creativity. Jan Ehrenwald has recently proposed that "geniuses" are those individuals best able to "shift gears" from one hemisphere to the other as required. See Jan Ehrenwald, *Anatomy of Genius: Split Brains and Global Minds* (New York: Human Sciences Press, 1984).

[3]Because the rationalist, or linear, approach is not necessarily the best way to get a good analysis, we do not wish to call such an approach rational per se.

analysis rule is that *analysts should simultaneously utilize linear and nonlinear modes when conducting policy analyses.*

Our admonition to use linear and nonlinear modes is by no means new. Grover Starling quotes English novelist Laurence Sterne as writing: ". . . the ancient Goths of Germany had all of them a wise custom of debating everything of importance to their state twice: that is—once drunk, and once sober; drunk—that their councils might not want vigor; and sober—that they might not want discretion."[4] We interpret this as ensuring that the Goths examined their problems both linearly and nonlinearly. Subsequent sections of this chapter lay out the seven steps in the rationalist, or linear, mode. Later we will return to how nonlinear strategies can be translated into practical techniques for conducting analysis. Before proceeding through these analytic steps, we must first reiterate the importance of the client orientation.

THE CLIENT ORIENTATION

In the introductory chapters we emphasized that policy analysis is client-driven, and we considered some of the ethical issues relating to the relationship between analysts and clients. Our concern here is more with the practical consequences of having a client. The first client heuristic may seem obvious, but it is often neglected: *you must address the issue that the client (or the surrogate—your professor) poses.* Academic training (especially in nonquantitative courses) often does not prepare one for this reality because one has considerable discretion as to topic and approach. This is reasonable because when a professor is the client, he or she is most interested in your cognitive development. Real clients are more interested in getting their question answered. An important heuristic flows from this unpleasant fact: *it is almost always better to answer with uncertainty the question that was asked than to answer with certainty a question that was not asked.* Another heuristic follows as a corollary: *good analysis does not suppress uncertainty,* whether with respect to facts or theories.

We all like neatness, and most of us have been rewarded for unambiguous answers. In policy analysis, however, it is more effective to *highlight* ambiguities than to suppress them. Remember that if your client does not hear of these ambiguities from you, he or she will normally hear of them from analytic, or political, opponents—a much more unpleasant way for your client to be informed. As an analyst you bear an essential responsibility to keep your client from being "blind sided" as a result of your advice.

Highlighting ambiguity should not be seen as an excuse for vague, wishy-washy, or unresearched analysis. Indeed, you will have to work harder to arrange the competing theories and facts intelligently. Additionally, highlighting ambiguity does not absolve you from drawing analytic conclusions. For example, if, for a given policy problem, it is unclear whether there is a market failure, you should succinctly summarize evidence on both sides of the issue and *then* reach your conclusion. Thus your client will be aware of both the arguments and your conclu-

[4]Quoted in Grover Starling, *The Politics and Economics of Public Policy: An Introductory Analysis with Cases* (Homewood, Ill.: Dorsey Press, 1979), p. 490.

sions. It is particularly important to make your client aware of the weaknesses of the relevant data and evidence. As Max Singer notes, although the facts used in policy debates are often inaccurate or at least unverified, they nonetheless remain unchallenged. He calls this the "vitality of mythical numbers."[5] To pick one recent example, Douglas Besharov has demonstrated the wholesale deceptive use of statistics in analyses of the child abuse problem.[6]

What should you do if you become convinced that your client has asked the wrong question? We offer no definitive advice on how to deal with this difficult situation. One clear rule, however, is that *you must fully explain to your client why you believe that he or she has asked the wrong question.* Clients are often ambiguous about their goals and they sometimes appear to have goals that you may consider inappropriate. You may be able to help your client ask a better question by identifying ambiguity and by indicating why you believe that certain goals are inappropriate. In general, you should try to do so at the early stages of your analytical effort rather than waiting until you deliver what your client expects to be the answer to the original question.

Clients often ask questions that are not wrong but rather just poorly formulated. Many times you will be presented "symptoms" that your client finds troubling. ("My constituents are complaining about the rising cost of day care.") Other times you may be presented with a policy alternative rather than a policy problem.[7] ("Should the state subsidize liability insurance for day-care centers?") Your task as an analyst is to reformulate expressions of symptoms and statements of policy alternatives into coherent analytical frameworks. ("Does the day-care industry under current regulations provide an efficient and equitable supply of services? If not, why not?") The following discussion of problem analysis provides guidance for doing so.

STEPS IN THE RATIONALIST MODE

The word *analysis* comes from the Greek word meaning to break down into component parts. Teachers of policy analysis usually specify the components of the analytical process as a series of steps along the lines of the following: define the problem, establish evaluation criteria, identify alternative policies, display alternatives and select among them, and monitor and evaluate the policy outcomes.[8] Such lists usually begin with "defining the problem" so that all the following steps can be described as "solving the problem." These formulations, we believe, often

[5]See Max Singer, "The Vitality of Mythical Numbers," *Public Interest*, No. 23, 1971, pp. 3–9. See also Peter Reuter, "The Social Costs of the Demand for Quantification," *Journal of Policy Analysis and Management*, Vol. 5, No. 4, Summer 1986, pp. 807–12.

[6]Douglas Besharov, "Unfounded Allegations—A New Child Abuse Problem," *Public Interest*, No. 83, 1986, pp. 18–33.

[7]For a discussion of the importance of stripping away the prescriptive elements of problem definitions, see Eugene Bardach, "Problems of Problem Definition in Policy Analysis," *Research in Public Policy Analysis and Management*, Vol. 1, 1981, pp. 161–71.

[8]See, for example, Carl V. Patton and David Sawicki, *Basic Methods of Policy Analysis and Planning* (Englewood Cliffs, N.J.: Prentice Hall, 1986), p. 26. Others provide lists that include implementation as a step. For example, Grover Starling, *Politics and Economics of Public Policy*, p. 10.

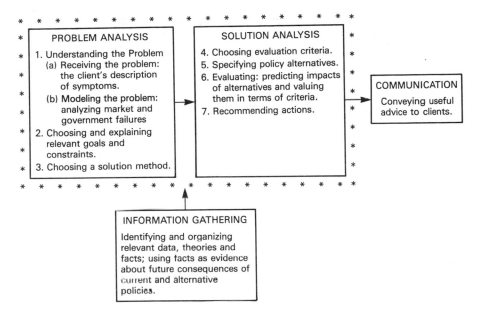

Figure 6.1 A Summary of Steps in the Rationalist Mode

incorrectly suggest to the inexperienced student that defining, or explaining, the problem is a relatively short and simple part of the analytical process. In practice, analysts usually encounter the greatest difficulty and often expend the most time in trying to define, explain, and model the problem in a useful way.[9] These tasks are very important because they largely determine which goals and methods should be used to judge the desirability of alternative solutions. This in turn tends to drive the selection of policy alternatives.

A better perceptual balance is achieved by representing the policy analysis process as in Figure 6.1, which breaks the process into two major components: problem analysis and solution analysis. Both are vital. For example, an analysis that devotes 90 percent of its pages to analyzing the problem inevitably will not be credible in terms of the policy alternatives it presents or the reasons for choosing among them. Therefore, such an analysis may portray the nature of the problem convincingly, but not the solution. Because most clients seek solutions, such an imbalance typically diminishes the value of an analysis. Conversely, your recommendation will carry little weight unless you convince the client that you have framed the problem correctly, thought carefully about the potentially relevant goals, and considered an array of alternatives.

Our experience suggests that some students (and analysts) suffer in the extreme from looking only at solutions. Those suffering from such "recommendationitis" try to cram their complete analysis into their recommendations. If you suffer from this syndrome (or the tendency to cram all your analysis into any one

[9]For an in-depth and thoughtful treatment of problem definition in the organizational context, see David Dery, *Problem Definition in Policy Analysis* (Lawrence: University Press of Kansas, 1984).

step of the analytical process), then you are probably a nonlinear thinker who should take especially seriously the steps in the rationalist mode.

You will find it necessary to gather information throughout your problem and solution analyses. Both documents and people serve as sources. As students you already have considerable experience in locating documents in libraries. You probably have less experience in eliciting information directly from people. To help you develop your skills in information gathering, we provide an overview of gathering information for policy analysis in Appendix 6A, "Gathering and Organizing the Data, Facts, and Evidence." We recommend that you skim Appendix 6A before you begin the next section and read it more carefully after you complete the body of this chapter. We think you will find it very useful to reread Appendix 6A before you begin your first "live" analysis.

PROBLEM ANALYSIS

Problem analysis consists of three major steps: (1) understanding the problem—assessing the conditions that concern your client and modeling their causes as market failures, government failures, or market and government failures; (2) choosing and explaining relevant policy goals and constraints; and (3) choosing a solution method.

Understanding the Problem: Market and Government Failure

Clients generally experience problems as conditions that some group perceives as undesirable. They tend to specify problems to analysts in terms of these undesirable conditions, or symptoms, rather than as underlying causes. The analyst's task is to assess the symptoms and provide an explanation (model) of how they arise.

Assessing symptoms involves determining their empirical basis. In a narrow sense, this means trying to locate data that help you put the symptoms in quantitative perspective. For example, if your client is concerned about automobile accidents in your county caused by drunk drivers, then you might try to locate data to help you estimate the number of such accidents, how the number has changed over time, what percentage of total accidents they comprise, and other measures that help you determine the magnitude, distribution, and time trend of the symptom. In a broader sense, you should become familiar with current public discussion about the symptom (read the newspaper!) and the history of existing policies that are generally perceived as being relevant to it. For example, you may find that, although there has been a steady decline in the number of alcohol-related accidents in recent years, a particularly tragic accident has focused public attention on the dangers of drunk driving. Viewed in the perspective of the favorable trend, drunk driving may seem less deserving of attention than other conditions of concern to your client.

Your assessment of symptoms generally appears as background in your problem analysis—it conveys the relative importance and urgency of the problem, and it begins to establish your credibility as someone who is knowledgeable about it. But the assessment of symptoms alone provides an inadequate basis for your analysis. You must identify causal relationships that link the symptoms to factors that can be changed by public policy. In other words, you must model the problem.

Potentially any positive, or predictive, social science model can be used as the basis for problem analysis. The major focus of explanation here is a specification of the expected deviation between individual self-interest (utility maximization) and aggregate social welfare. While we believe that this focus is usually the best starting point for framing policy problems, we also believe that several caveats need to be noted.

First, we must avoid the danger of reductionism in such an approach. Although for many purposes we can treat wealth maximization and utility maximization as synonymous, saying that people maximize wealth is not the same as saying that people care only about money. Clearly, they care about many other things as well. Also, as we saw in the examination of nontraditional market failure, economics tends to treat preferences as fixed, and therefore deals primarily with utility articulation rather than utility formation. Other social sciences have devoted considerably more effort to examining how preferences are formed. Consequently, considerable room exists for such "noneconomic" social sciences as anthropology, psychology, and sociology to play a part in framing the issues of market and government failure.[10]

Second, and this is obviously related, we have not claimed that efficiency is the only appropriate goal of public policy. Therefore, any realistic problem-analysis framework must enable the analyst to integrate other goals or constraints into the analytical process. The framework should also allow the analyst to set out the goals in a coherent way: ". . . good policy analysis . . . requires a clear statement and defense of the value judgments that combine with the analysis to lead to specific conclusions."[11] In the next section we suggest how to incorporate these goals into policy analysis. We believe, however, that you should begin by focusing your attention on efficiency. Figure 6.2 shows how to approach the question of efficiency through consideration of market and government failures.

As Figure 6.2 indicates, the first step involves deciding whether there is market failure. This requires that you decide whether a market operates to accommodate individual preferences. This may itself be a difficult decision—there is a complex continuum from free, unfettered markets to the complete absence of markets. We recommend the following working rule: if prices legally exist as signaling mechanisms (no matter how extensively regulated), treat the situation as if it involves an operational market. Where prices are not legally permitted—for example, if only black market transactions take place—start with the assumption

[10]Amitai Etzioni has eloquently argued that policy analysis should not be restricted to economic analysis. He offers, by way of comparison, medical knowledge which eclectically incorporates political, social, cultural, psychic, and environmental factors. See "Making Policy for Complex Systems," *Journal of Policy Analysis and Management*, Vol. 4, No. 3, Spring 1985, pp. 383–95. See also Jack Hirschleifer, who has argued, "There is only one social science. . . .Ultimately, good economics will also have to be good anthropology and sociology and political science and psychology." In "The Expanding Domain of Economics," *American Economic Review*, Vol. 75, No. 6, December 1985, pp. 53–68, at p. 53.

[11]Helen Ladd goes on to point out that economic analysts often forget this: "The failure of some of the authors to spell out and defend their value judgments in some cases leaves the misleading impression that the policy conclusion follows logically from the analysis alone." Review of John M. Quigley and Daniel L. Rubinfeld, *American Domestic Priorities: An Economic Appraisal*, in *Journal of Economic Literature*, Vol. XXIV, No. 3, September 1986, pp. 1276–77, at p. 1277.

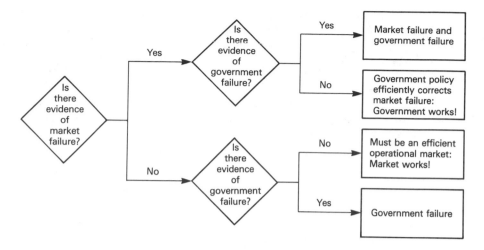

Figure 6.2   Problem Analysis: Market Failure and Government Failure

that the market is not operational. Of course, if, on closer inspection, a black market appears to involve low-cost transactions, then legalization itself may be adequate to create what we call an operational market.

If you decide that the market *is* operational, then you should next consider the theory, evidence, data, and facts relevant to market failure. A close familiarity with Chapter 3 should give you a sound basis for your investigation. (We provide practical advice on gathering information on the appendix to this chapter.) If neither theoretical arguments nor empirical evidence suggests market failure, then it is reasonable to assume that the existing market will allocate scarce resources in the most *efficient* way. You must next consider, however, the possibility of government failure as outlined in Chapter 4. If you cannot identify any government failure, then the logical conclusion must be that the existing market is operating efficiently. If you are interested only in efficiency, then the market should be left alone! If, on the other hand, you identify government failure (that is, an operating market, no market failure, government failure), then the focus of your subsequent analysis should be on government failure.

If theory and evidence suggest market failure, then you should again assess whether, additionally, there is government failure. The combination of market and government failures typically arises when government recognizes market failure but chooses an intervention that is itself inefficient. But government failures are also often manifested as forgone opportunities for efficient interventions rather than as inefficient interventions. In the context of representative government, an interest group may be able to stop correction of a market failure. For example, a polluting industry may be able to lobby successfully to block policies that would internalize its externality.

If you do not identify a government failure, then you are concluding that the existing government intervention corrects the market failure to the greatest extent practical. In other words, you can identify no changes in current policy that could increase efficiency. It may help to keep in mind the distinction between conditions and problems. The fact that a particular interest group is complaining about a policy does not necessarily mean that there is a policy problem. Interest groups may dislike efficient policies, perhaps because it keeps them from realizing rents or desired redistribution. In such cases, it may be appropriate to tell your client, "Don't panic, the current policy is at least efficient; therefore, the question is whether other values are at stake."

If a market *is not* operational, then you should work through Figure 6.2, asking if a market could be made operational and the extent to which it would likely fail; in other words, the concept of market failure is relevant here, even though no market is currently operational. Notice that, as this is a "what if" question, direct evidence may not exist to inform your answer. In these circumstances, you must draw upon theory (such as found in Chapter 3), evidence available from other jurisdictions (for example, other cities, states, and countries), or analogous problems. Obviously, you face the difficult task of deciding the applicability of such evidence to the particular problem at hand.

If your analysis suggests that a market could operate without serious flaws, then you may assume a priori that significant *efficiency* costs are probably associated with the existing government intervention, whether it be an outright prohibition, a displacement of private supply by public provision, or simply a failure to establish property rights or other rules needed to facilitate private transactions. Thus, if there is no operational market and no evidence of market failure, then you can logically conclude that there must be government failure.

Notice the relative simplicity of the analysis if the only goal is the maximization of aggregate social welfare. In the absence of market failure, government intervention will almost always be inefficient. Multiple goals make such a simple analysis inappropriate. It may be worth bearing losses in net social surplus (in other words, enduring some inefficiency) in order to achieve other social goals.

Most importantly, decision makers usually care about distributional (equity or equality) considerations, whether in terms of socioeconomic, racial, or other status characteristics. You should explicitly decide whether distributional concerns are relevant to your particular policy problem. While in most situations you will be familiar with client preferences, other times the client may be unaware of the facts and evidence relating to particular target groups. In the latter case, you may wish to argue to the client that greater equity should be a goal. After making a decision on equity, you should consider other goals and constraints. For instance, does the client expect that public revenue would or should be generated? Thus, the absence of market failure is not, in and of itself, determinative. Government intervention that interferes with nonfailing markets is not necessarily undesirable—other goals may justify the losses in efficiency.

Before considering how to deal with goals, it is worth reiterating that your analysis of market and government (nonmarket) failures plays a vital role in "framing" your subsequent solution analysis. John Brandl, an economist and a member of the Minnesota Senate, has succinctly summarized the value of such an approach for the decision maker:

> To view an issue as an instance of market (or nonmarket) failure is
> to transform what was bewildering into a solvable problem. An im-
> mense variety of issues can be approached in this fashion. Tuition

policy becomes pricing policy, airplane noise is an externality, a utility is a natural monopoly, research yields public goods. This application of economic theory is much more than a translation of English into jargon. In each case the economist has advice to offer aimed at rectifying the wrong implicit in market imperfection. (Currently a new economic theory . . . is being created to explain . . . nonmarket institutions.)[12]

Choosing and Explaining Goals and Constraints

Probably the most difficult step in any policy analysis is deciding on appropriate goals. As Jeanne Neinbauer and Aaron Wildavsky put it, ". . . of objectives [goals] it can be said that they invariably may be distinguished by these outstanding qualities: they are multiple, conflicting, and vague."[13] Only when you recognize this uncomfortable reality can you deal systematically and successfully with goals.

Even with the advice we offer, you are likely to find goal selection and delineation an inherently difficult task as most of you will have had little experience in your academic careers in choosing goals. In most contexts you will have been given one or more goals to achieve. In policy analysis you face a much more difficult problem because you must determine the relevant goals. Specifying goals requires you to be normative: you often must decide what *should* be wanted. This is both difficult and inherently controversial. It is controversial because it means being overt about value systems. Nonetheless, we can suggest some ways that you may be able to assist your clients in establishing appropriate goals—ones that make trade-offs apparent and that realistically reflect the available policy alternatives. Our advice falls under two headings: (1) accepting that goals are outputs of analysis as well as inputs to analysis, or, in other words, dealing with the vagueness, multiplicity, and conflict among goals as part of the analytical process; and (2) clarifying the distinction between goals and policies.

Goal Vagueness: Goals as Outputs.   The problem analysis framework laid out in Figures 6.1 and 6.2 should warn you to expect goal vagueness at the beginning of a policy analysis. Even if a particular client has clear goals, there may be good reasons why the client will not reveal them. Obviously, where clients do not have clear goals, they are unlikely to have measures in mind that can readily identify achievement of those goals. (Such measures, which "operationalize" goals, serve as the criteria for evaluating policy alternatives.) The revelation of this reality probably generates more analysis paralysis among novice analysts than anything else.

Novices often try to elicit goals from clients at the beginning of their efforts. Our advice: *resist this temptation.* After you have provided your own initial explana-

---

[12]John E. Brandl, "Distilling Frenzy from Academic Scribbling," *Journal of Policy Analysis and Management*, Vol. 4, No. 3, Spring 1985, pp. 344–53, at p. 348.

[13]Jeanne Neinbauer and Aaron Wildavsky, *The Budgeting and Evaluation of Federal Recreation Programs* (New York: Basic Books, 1973), p. 10.

tion of the problem, eliciting goals from your client will probably be valuable and perhaps essential, but it is rarely so at the outset. There are two reasons why it is usually futile to ask for goals before starting the analysis: First, the client may not have decided on the appropriate goals in a particular policy context. Even if the client has decided on the appropriate set of goals, he or she will almost certainly not have decided on the appropriate trade-offs between pairs of these goals. Second, a client may have goals but be unwilling to reveal them. Let us deal with each in turn.

Many observers argue that individuals preparing to make complex decisions do not have predetermined goals.[14] In fact, it may be desirable that decision makers not have rigid goals when dealing with complex, unstructured problems until after the problems have been analyzed.[15] Put another way, it does not make sense to want something until you have some explanation of what is going on. For example, your client may not recognize the efficiency costs (and therefore the importance of efficiency as a goal) of a particular government intervention until you have explained it.

It may seem surprising that a client might not reveal goals to his or her policy analyst, but there may be good reasons for such a tactic. Wise decision makers realize that explicit goals often crystalize conflict—and opposition. It may be that your client wishes to use *you* as a "stalking horse" in presenting and explicating controversial but worthy goals.

How should you formulate goals in these situations? We suggest, whether or not your client has suggested a particular goal or set of goals, that you explicitly consider the relevance of efficiency and equity. Clearly, in this textbook, the focus on both market and government failure suggests that policy analysis should always be centrally concerned with aggregate social surplus, or efficiency. Indeed, some policy analysts (mostly economists) argue that, in general, aggregate efficiency should be the primary concern of policy analysis and that distributional and other goals are rarely appropriate in evaluating alternative policies. They argue that seeking efficiency leads to the largest total of goods and therefore provides the greatest opportunity for redistribution. They advocate that distributional goals be met through purely redistributional programs, such as the tax system.

[14]See Henry Mintzberg, Gurev Raisinghani, and Andre Theoret, "The Structure of Unstructured Decision Processes," *Administrative Science Quarterly*, Vol. 21, No. 2, June 1976, pp. 246–75. As James March puts it, ". . . it seems to me perfectly obvious that a description that assumes goals come first and action comes later is frequently radically wrong. Human choice behavior is at least as much a process of discovering goals as for acting on them." James March, "The Technology of Foolishness," in James C. March and J. P. Olsen, *Ambiguity and Choice in Organizations* (Bergen, Norway: Universitetsforlaget, 1976), p. 72.

[15]As Aaron Wildavsky puts it, "We learn to choose by knowing what we cannot do as well as by what we might wish to try. Ends and means are chosen simultaneously." Aaron Wildavsky, "Policy Analysis Is What Information Systems Are Not," Working Paper 53, Graduate School of Public Policy, University of California, Berkeley, 1976, p. 1. Laurence H. Tribe has made essentially the same point, ". . . no system of thought that takes values and ends as externally 'given' and purports only to assess the comparative efficacy of alternative means can offer a satisfactory way of evaluating actions insofar as they are pursued as ends, or insofar as their consequences include the alterations of the ultimate ends sought by various persons in the society." L. Tribe, "Technology Assessment and the Fourth Discontinuity," *Southern California Law Review*, Vol. 46, No. 617, 1973, p. 637.

While we sympathize with the view that policy analysts should provide a voice for efficiency, especially because there is rarely an organized constituency in the political arena for maximizing aggregate social welfare, we presume that other goals are also important. Henry Rosen makes the case for routinely including equity considerations:

> Should equity issues be dealt with in each policy decision, or should they be dealt with through a separate income redistribution policy? . . . In specific cases there usually is no way to identify all of the gainers and losers, and the information costs of attempting such identifications are often high. Moreover, the mechanisms for compensating losers are weak or nonexistent. . . . An analysis which omits distributional effects and discusses only aggregate efficiency deals with a part of the decision maker's problem, and only a small part.[16]

Essentially similar arguments have been made for including other goals of public policy. We cannot tell you in general whether a particular goal should be included in your analysis, but we urge you to assume a priori that other goals as well as efficiency are relevant. This approach forces you to present reasoned arguments for either *including* or *excluding* a particular goal.

Whether or not you ultimately decide to include equity and other goals in the solution analysis, we also encourage you *to take seriously* the question of other appropriate goals, whether substantive or instrumental. Thus, if your analysis is not going to include goals that various stakeholders in the policy environment hold important (implicitly or explicitly), you should explain why. In the next section, we will argue that equity, or any other goal, can be usefully viewed in terms of trade-offs with efficiency. But the fact remains that analytic technique cannot tell your client or you what you should want. Ultimately, the client, the analyst, and the political process must decide how much efficiency should be given up to achieve a given amount of redistribution or some other objective.

Other goals can be broken down into two broad categories: substantive and instrumental. *Substantive goals* represent values, like equity and efficiency, that society wishes to secure for their own sake. These include considerations of human dignity, self-perception, and self-actualization. For instance, a recent Hastings Center report on organ transplants argued that, apart from efficiency, the relevant goals of public policy should include "the moral values and concerns our society has regarding individual autonomy and privacy, the importance of the family, the dignity of the body, and the value of social practices that enhance and strengthen altruism and our sense of community."[17]

Instrumental goals are conditions that make it easier to achieve substantive goals. Commonly relevant instrumental goals include political feasibility and budget availability. Keep in mind that such instrumental goals are often stated

---

[16]Henry Rosen, "The Role of Cost-Benefit Analysis in Policy making," in Henry M. Peskin and Eugene P. Seskin, eds., *Cost Benefit Analysis and Water Pollution Policy* (Washington, D.C.: Urban Institute, 1975), pp. 367–68.

[17]The Hastings Center, *Ethical, Legal, and Policy Issues Pertaining to Solid Organ Procurement: A Report on Organ Transplantation*, October 1985, p. 2.

as constraints rather than as goals. A constraint is simply a goal that must be satisfied.[18] Once again, the appropriateness of including political feasibility as a policy goal can be disputed. As one perceptive commentator has put it, "[T]he motive may be defensive or offensive—to prevent the abuse of their analysis, or to make their analytic voices more influential—but analysts still need to increase their political sophistication."[19] A recent example of political feasibility as an instrumental goal (or constraint) was the 1986 U.S. tax reform bill. While many analysts argued that mortgage interest deductibility is both inefficient *and* inequitable, it was undoubtedly retained because any attempt to eliminate the deduction would have made the whole concept of tax reform politically unfeasible.

Policy analysis is the art of the possible. Resource constraints, therefore, are of central importance. While budgetary limitations are usually the preeminent resource constraint, other resource constraints such as administrative infrastructure and availability of skilled personnel may also be critical. More generally, *the list of constraints should include any resources that are essential for either maintaining the status quo or implementing alternative policies.*

Your list of goals for a given problem might include efficiency, equity, human dignity, political feasibility, and budget availability. It is impossible, however, to describe the relevant goals for all policy problems. As you research a problem, you should always be aware of the importance of identifying potential goals. As you become familiar with specific policy areas you will become aware of the typical goals that are advocated. For example, in considering energy policy, security against the economic costs of oil supply disruptions is often an important policy goal that sometimes conflicts with short-run efficiency.

Keep in mind that selecting goals per se may be relatively noncontroversial. After all, it is easy to agree that distributional considerations should play *some* role in almost any policy problem. As we will see, it is the *trade-offs* between goals that is, in practice, more difficult and controversial. Additionally, the posited relationships between means (policy alternatives) and ends (goals) are also likely to be tenuous because they often require highly uncertain predictions.

It should be becoming clear that specifying goals and the appropriate trade-offs among them is an important *output* of policy analysis. This is not the only way in which goals are important outputs, however. The process of explaining relationships between goals and policies may itself alter the choice of goals. This point can be illustrated with the notion of an *indifference curve*—those combinations of values that give the decision maker the same level of utility.

Figure 6.3 illustrates a situation where two goals—efficiency and equity— are represented on the axes. Assuming that the decision maker wants both greater equity and efficiency, but values additional units of each less at higher levels of attainment, other things remaining equal, he or she will have indifference curves like I_A and I_B in the figure. The decision maker would prefer a combination of equity and efficiency on I_B, the "higher" indifference curve. Assume, however, that the decision maker is limited to choices that lie within the budget constraint indicated by line XX_1 so that the highest utility can be achieved by point x on

---

[18]Readers familiar with linear programming will have had experience switching goals (which are represented in the objective function) and contraints to form the "duals" of problems.

[19]Robert D. Behn, "Policy Analysis and Policy Politics," *Policy Analysis*, Vol. 7, No. 2, Spring 1981, pp. 199–226, at p. 216.

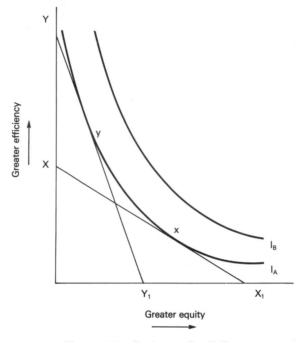

Figure 6.3   Goals and Feasibility

indifference curve I_A. (Of course, in reality the budget constraint may not be a straight line because, as we will see below, we may not be able to trade equity and efficiency at a fixed ratio.)

Unfortunately, in many analytical situations, the actual position of the budget constraint may be uncertain. For example, the budget constraint might be either XX_1 or YY_1 as shown. If YY_1 were the constraint, then the decision maker would choose point y on I_A. Thus, information on the nature of the "true" budget constraint will be valuable in choosing between goals x and y. The focus of much public policy research and analysis is devoted to clarifying such issues. For example, in the area of welfare policy, an important consideration is the trade-off between benefit levels and work effort by recipients. Notice that preferences, per se, are not "changed" by providing such information (the decision maker's preferences are still represented by the indifference curves), but the levels of efficiency and equity selected do change, along with the rates at which the decision maker would be willing to make marginal trades between them.

The relationship between goals and program feasibility may also change how goals are weighted. Figure 6.4, which shows benefit levels to various groups as vertical bars, illustrates a situation where such an outcome might occur. It presents three alternative programs or policies, each of which is *predicted* to provide a different combination of efficiency and equality to three different groups in the population. In this example, equality is defined in terms of the variance across the three groups, while efficiency is defined as the total benefits received by all groups. (In other contexts equality might be measured in terms of the maximum

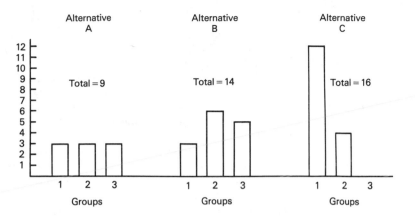

Figure 6.4 Program Feasibility and Weighting of Goals

difference between any two groups.) Suppose that one client had specified before the analysis that she is interested only in efficiency (an economist, no doubt!) Another client has declared that he is interested only in equality. Notice their choices, given the distribution of benefits in Figure 6.4. The client who claims to be interested only in efficiency will choose policy C, which yields the highest efficiency (16 units). The client interested in equality (as defined above) would choose policy A, which is most equitable (but least efficient). If each client were presented with the actual trade-offs as revealed in Figure 6.4, however, either or both might well choose policy B. While policy B is not as equitable as policy A, it is considerably more efficient, although notice that each group is at least as well off under policy B as under policy A. Notice that while policy B is somewhat less efficient than policy C (14 as opposed to 16), it is much more equitable.

The crucial lesson that emerges from observing Figure 6.4 is that the revelation of the trade-offs may alter the choice of policies. Therefore, we have an important heuristic: *specifying the appropriate weights for goals is more commonly an output of, rather than an input to, policy analysis.*

The Distinction Between Goals and Policies. Probably the most confusing semantic difficulty you will come across in policy analysis is in the distinction between goals (the values we seek to promote) and policies (the alternatives and strategies for promoting them). This semantic confusion arises because, in everyday language, policies (concrete sets of actions) are often stated as goals: "Our goal is to add 100,000 barrels of oil per day to the strategic petroleum reserve," or "Our goal is to complete deregulation of the airline industry by the end of next year."[20] While this everyday use of such language is harmless, it can

---

[20] In the context of choosing implementation strategies, it is often reasonable to take already-decided policies as goals. For example, if the secretary of energy has already made a final decision that adding 100,000 barrels of oil per day to the strategic petroleum reserve will be the policy, then it may be reasonably taken as a goal by those in the Department of Energy who must decide how the additions will actually be made. Unfortunately, however, other goals, such as minimizing cost and maximizing reliability, would be introduced as relevant to the choice of implementation strategies. Indeed, one might question the wisdom of the secretary's decision if it were made without consideration of these instrumental goals.

easily derail the neophyte analyst. Goals should be used to *evaluate* alternative policies, but if a policy is stated as a goal, how can one evaluate it? Indeed, stated this way, any policy is self-justifying. In order to avoid this confusion, one must keep in mind a clear separation between goals and policies. We suggest that you do this by following another of our heuristics: *start by formulating goals as abstractly as possible and policy alternatives as concretely as possible.* Keep in mind that goals must ultimately be *normative*, a reflection of human values. Policy alternatives, on the other hand, are the concrete methods to achieve these goals; they only have relevance to the extent that they achieve a "bundle" of goals.

At this level of analysis, the distinction may appear clear. As a typical policy analysis proceeds, the distinction often becomes cloudy. The primary reason is that, in spite of the very abstractness of goals, we must develop concrete, quantitative proxies to measure their achievement. For example, in benefit-cost analysis, we may be ultimately interested in efficiency, but we attempt to measure this by willingness to pay and ultimately by a dollar valuation. It is often easy to forget that these quantitative criteria are, in fact, proxies for measuring the achievement of goals. They become objectives. We suggest that you overtly ask yourself what value (efficiency, equity, human dignity) lies behind the criteria and objectives you employ. This tends to become increasingly difficult as one moves to such "nuts and bolts" issues as sanitation, police patrol, and emergency services often found at the municipal and county levels. Indeed, clients sometimes claim that these sorts of issues are purely technical in nature and do not involve such value-laden considerations as efficiency and equity.

Our experience suggests, however, that such problems require goal frameworks to assure that the criteria and objectives used correspond to appropriate values. For instance, researchers have found little evidence that changes in preventive patrol levels by police have measurable effects on the total crimes committed in a city.[21] Therefore, maximizing hours of police patrol may be a poor objective if the underlying goal is reducing the costs of crime.

Choosing a Solution Method

You must decide which goals are relevant to your analysis before you can begin to consider solutions systematically. Figure 6.5 distinguishes three general circumstances: First, efficiency is the only relevant goal. Second, efficiency and one other goal are relevant. Third, efficiency and two or more other goals are relevant. The number of relevant goals determines the appropriate solution method.

There are five basic approaches to policy analysis: (1) standard benefit-cost analysis, (2) qualitative benefit-cost analysis, (3) modified benefit-cost analysis, (4) cost-effectiveness analysis, and (5) multigoal policy analysis. Figure 6.5 indicates when each approach is most appropriate.

Benefit-Cost Analysis. As indicated in Figure 6.5, benefit-cost analysis should be your primary solution method when you believe that efficiency is the

---

[21]For a general review, see Lawrence W. Sherman, "Patrol Strategies for Police," in James Q. Wilson, ed., *Crime and Public Policy* (San Francisco: Institute for Contemporary Studies, 1983), pp. 145–63.

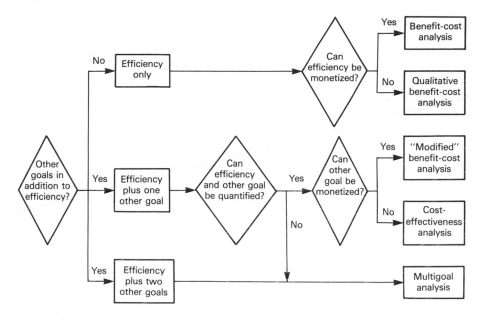

Figure 6.5 Choosing a Solution Method

only relevant goal. Conceptually, benefit-cost analysis is relatively simple. If you have either flipped through our chapter on benefit-cost (Chapter 7) or you have already been exposed to benefit-cost analysis elsewhere, then you may be surprised to hear it described as being relatively simple. Consider, however, what benefit-cost analysis attempts to do. It reduces *all* the impacts of a proposed alternative to a common unit of impact, namely dollars. Of course, once all impacts have been measured in dollars they can be aggregated—a dollar is a dollar is a dollar. If individuals would be willing to pay dollars to have something, presumably it is a benefit; if they would pay to avoid it, it is a cost. Once all the impacts have been reduced to dollars, the evaluation rule is relatively straightforward: choose that alternative that generates the largest aggregate net benefits (in dollars). Thus, in benefit-cost analysis, although we have different "goals," in the conventional usage of the word, they can all be reduced to positive efficiency impacts (benefits) or negative efficiency impacts (costs) that, in turn, can all be reduced to dollars.

As we will see in the benefit-cost chapter, market prices often do not reflect marginal social costs becuase of the distortions caused by market failures and government interventions. There are also many classes of impacts such as waiting time that usually cannot be "monetized" through estimations based on direct observation of markets. Considerable skill and judgment must be exercised to assess the costs and benefits of these impacts in a reasonable way.

Keep in mind that you will need some practice before you will feel comfortable deciding if all the relevant goals can really be viewed as elements of efficiency. Consider an example. You are confronted with a problem: a crowded freeway. Let us suppose for the sake of simplicity that your client is interested in policy alternatives that will reduce commuting time and save fuel. Superficially these are different goals (and they certainly may differ in importance to different clients), but both can be translated into a common impact: dollar-cost savings. As we will see, this is conceptually straightforward, although in practice quite difficult.

Qualitative Benefit-Cost Analysis.   As shown in Figure 6.5, even when you decide that efficiency is the only relevant goal, you must still determine whether all efficiency impacts can be reasonably monetized. If not, then qualitative benefit-cost analysis is the appropriate solution method. Like standard benefit-cost analysis, it begins with a prediction of impacts. Some of the impacts may be expressed in natural units (say, for example, hours of delay or tons of pollutants), while others may be qualitative (for example, a despoiled scenic view). If you are unable to monetize one or more of these impacts, then you cannot directly calculate the dollar value of net benefits. Instead, you must make qualitative arguments about the orders of magnitude of the various nonmonetized impacts.

Often impacts cannot be monetized because of technical difficulties in making valuations. When standard procedures do exist for inferring such values, limitations of time, data, and other resources frequently make monetization impractical. Even professional economists sometimes resort to qualitative benefit-cost analyses when they write about policy issues. Rather than attempt difficult and time-consuming valuations, they fall back on theoretical arguments to put orders of magnitude on efficiency impacts.

When you cannot confidently monetize important efficiency impacts to within even orders of magnitude, you may find it useful to work with the non-monetized impacts as if they were separate goals. For example, you may have to decide how to compare certain program costs with highly uncertain benefits. Thus, your qualitative benefit-cost analysis takes the form of the multigoal analysis we describe below.

Modified Benefit-Cost Analysis.   In a particular analysis you may conclude that efficiency and one other goal (most frequently equality) are appropriate As indicated in Figure 6.5, you can employ modified benefit-cost analysis if you are able and willing to monetize both efficiency and the other goal. In other words, you must be willing to assign dollar values to various levels of achievement of the other goal. For example, if the other goal is equality, modified benefit-cost analysis involves weighting costs and benefits accruing to different groups.[22] The advantage of such an approach should be clear. By incorporating distributional issues into a benefit-cost analysis, you can come up with a single metric for ranking alternatives. This is obviously attractive. The disadvantage should also be clear from our discussion above: namely, that the metric is only achieved by forcing efficiency and equality to be commensurable. As we will see below, you must implicitly engage in such an exercise in order to recommend a particular policy. The danger of modified benefit-cost analysis is that it merges the distributional weights into the aggregate net benefit measure. Consequently, special care must

[22]See Edward M. Gramlich, *Benefit-Cost Analysis of Government Programs* (Englewood Cliffs, N.J.: Prentice Hall, 1981), Chapter 7.

be taken to communicate clearly to the client the significance of the particular weights used.

Cost-Effectiveness Analysis: Achieving Goals Efficiently.   It might seem reasonably to assume that if a client is concerned only with equality, or any other single nonefficiency goal, then efficiency is irrelevant. In fact, a moment's thought should convince you that the exact opposite is true. Again, this can be most clearly illustrated for the case where equality is putatively the only goal. Any intervention in the market to finance redistribution (absent utility interdependence and market failure) must inevitably result in *some* deadweight loss. Even if we are primarily concerned with achieving a given redistribution, we should seek to minimize the deadweight loss; in other words, we should attempt to carry out the redistribution as efficiently as possible.

Cost-effectiveness is appropriate where both efficiency and the other goal can be quantified, but where the other goal cannot be monetized. (See Figure 6.5.) Put another way, the two goals are still treated as noncommensurable. Contrast this with modified benefit-cost analysis, where both goals are measured in dollars and thus made commensurable.

We can approach cost-effectiveness analysis in one of two ways. The first method is to choose a given level of expenditures (say, $10 million) and find the policy alternative that will provide the greatest benefits (such as, the largest redistribution gain). The second method is to specify a given level of benefit (however defined) and then to choose the policy alternative that achieves the benefit at the lowest cost. Both of these methods are cost-effectiveness procedures.

Keep in mind the crucial distinction between benefit-cost analysis and cost-effectiveness analysis. Benefit-cost analysis can assess both (1) whether any of the alternatives is worth doing (that is, whether social benefits exceed social costs), and (2) how alternatives should be ranked if more than one generates net social benefits. Cost-effectiveness cannot tell the analyst whether a given alternative is worth doing (this requires a benefit-cost analysis), but if a decision is made to redistribute or achieve some other goal, it can help in deciding which policy alternative will do so most efficiently (with minimum losses of social surplus).

Edward Gramlich and Michael Wolkoff have provided an excellent illustration of both this distinction and how to do cost-effectiveness studies. They suppose that we wish to raise the income of some group of people. They compare a negative income tax alternative, minimum wage legislation, and a public employment plan. Each intervention involves costs that may or may not exceed benefits. For example, the negative income tax is likely to discourage some individuals from working who would normally do so. The public employment plan is likely to *attract* low-income individuals. In short, all *may* generate net costs (that is, fail the benefit-cost test). If we are determined to go ahead with some program for redistributional purposes, however, which would make most sense? Gramlich and Wolkoff adopt the "given level of expenditures" approach and seek to find the most beneficial policy alternative, given an arbitrary $5 billion expenditure. Notice, in this context, benefit is used in a special sense. It does not aggregate social benefits, but rather counts benefits going to specific low-income groups. Given this, the authors developed a weighting scheme that ranks these impacts. They found that the negative income tax was much more successful at redistributing income per $5 billion expenditure than either minimum wage or public employment programs.[23]

Multigoal Analysis.   When three or more goals are relevant, multigoal analysis is the appropriate solution method. As indicated in Figure 6.5, it is also the appropriate method when one of two goals cannot be quantified.

Because all of the other solution methods can be viewed as special cases of multigoal analysis, the remaining steps in the rationalist mode (all within the solution analysis phase) lay out how to conduct multigoal analysis. Specifically, they indicate how and when goals can be converted to criteria, objectives, and constraints and how alternatives can be compared.

SOLUTION ANALYSIS

Policy problems rarely involve only one value. Multigoal policy analysis, therefore, usually serves as the appropriate solution method. As we have indicated, however, sometimes efficiency will appear to be the only relevant goal, so that you can evaluate current and alternative policies solely with benefit-cost analysis. Other times, you may decide that only efficiency and one other goal are relevant, so that cost-effectiveness analysis seems appropriate. Yet even in these cases, it is usually best to begin with the presumption that some other goals may be relevant. If your initial assessment that either benefit-cost or cost-effectiveness analysis alone provides an appropriate evaluation rule remains unchanged, then you can easily treat either of these solution methods as a special case of multigoal analysis. Our discussion of solution analysis, therefore, deals with the general case of multiple goals.

We decompose solution analysis into four steps: (1) the choice of evaluation criteria, (2) the specification of policy alternatives, (3) the evaluation of alternatives in terms of their predicted impacts on the criteria, and (4) the presentation of recommendations.

Choosing Criteria: Converting Goals to Objectives and Constraints

The first step in solution analysis involves moving from general goals to more specific criteria for evaluating the desirability of alternative policies. Criteria can be stated as objectives or constraints. For example, the general goal of equality in the distribution of some service might be operationalized by an objective such as "minimize the variance in service consumption across income groups." Alternatively, it might be operationalized as a constraint such as "families with incomes below the poverty line should be given full access to the service."

A good criterion provides a basis for measuring progress toward achieving a goal. Not every goal can be reasonably quantified as a single objective or constraint, however. For example, the goal of police investigation is to contribute

[23]Edward M. Gramlich and Michael Wolkoff, "A Procedure for Evaluating Income Distribution Policies," *Journal of Human Resources*, Vol. 14, No. 3, Summer 1979, pp. 319–50.

to the arrest, conviction, and punishment of those who have committed crimes. Police departments often try to operationalize this goal by the objective, "maximize the number of reported offenses for which a suspect has been identified." These identifications, sometimes called clearances, accumulate with little cost to the police when someone arrested for one offense confesses to many others. If too much weight is placed on getting clearances, then investigators may help suspects get lenient sentences in return for admissions that clear reported offenses. The end result may be what Jerome Skolnick describes as a reversal of the hierarchy of penalties found in the substantive law, whereby those who have committed more crimes receive less-severe punishments.[24] Of course, investigators may also be tempted to make inappropriate arrests.

Rather than emphasize a single objective that only measures one dimension of a goal, you should try to specify criteria that cover all the important dimensions. With respect to investigation, for instance, maximizing the number of convictions and the sum of sentences given to those convicted as well as clearances might together serve as an appropriate set of criteria. Of course, having three objectives rather than one forces you to consider the appropriate weights for deciding which policy is best for achieving the underlying goal. This added complexity is an unavoidable cost of trying to represent a broad goal quantitatively.

As these examples suggest, you should exercise considerable care in selecting criteria to measure the achievement of goals. Always ask yourself: How closely do high scores on the criteria correspond to progress toward goals? Asking this question is especially important because analysts and clients tend to focus attention on those criteria that can be easily measured.[25] A sort of Gresham's law operates: *easily measured criteria tend to drive less easily measured criteria from analytical attention.* This tendency may lead us astray when the easily measurable criteria fail to cover all the important dimensions of the goal. For example, casualties inflicted on the enemy is one criterion for measuring success in war. It may be secondary to other criteria—the relative morales of the opposing sides, their respective capabilities for protracted struggle, or the control of disputed populations—for measuring progress toward the goal of ultimate victory. Yet during the height of the Vietnam War, "body counts" became the primary measure of U.S. success because they could be easily reported as a number on a weekly basis. This emphasis made search-and-destroy missions appear relatively more effective than efforts to establish stable political control over the population, even though the latter might very well have contributed more to the chances of victory.[26]

Overemphasis of easily measurable criteria is not the only danger you must guard against in moving from goals to criteria. The policy arena in which you operate may place pressures on you to select a skewed set of criteria. As we discussed in Chapter 4, the political process often gives more weight to impacts that are concentrated, tangible, certain, and immediate than to impacts that are diffuse,

---

[24]Jerome H. Skolnick, *Justice Without Trial: Law Enforcement in Democratic Society* (New York: John Wiley, 1966), p. 174-79.

[25]As Vincent N. Campbell and Daryl G. Nichols state, ". . . there is a tendency to undermine the purpose of stating objectives (to make clear what you want) by stating only those things that can be measured easily." *Policy Analysis,* Vol. 3, No. 4, Fall 1977, pp. 561-78, at pp. 561-62.

[26]Alain C. Entoven and K. Wayne Smith, *How Much Is Enough? Shaping the Defense Program, 1961-1969* (New York: Harper & Row, 1971), pp. 295-306.

intangible, uncertain, and delayed. For example, public discussions of trade policy tend to emphasize employment effects in easily identifiable domestic industries directly competing with imports rather than diffuse employment effects in the larger economy (including firms that use imported inputs to produce goods for export) that result from changes in import prices. One of your responsibilities as an analyst is to propose criteria that provide a more comprehensive treatment of effects.

Some goals are so difficult to operationalize that they themselves are best taken as criteria. For example, improving community relations is almost certainly a relevant goal in evaluating alternative patrol policies for police departments. Although you might think of measuring changes in community relations by looking at changes in the number of citizen complaints, such a quantification may miss much less tangible but perhaps more important aspects of community relations, like the willingness of people to cooperate with police in investigations. Rather than adopt quantitative measures as criteria, it may be better to keep community relations as a qualitative criterion. You would then rate policies with terms such as "excellent," "good," or "poor."

Limited time, information, or resources also may lead you to keep broad goals as criteria. If you have no hope of quantifying the impacts of alternative policies in the time available, you have to make qualitative assessments. Nevertheless, you should spend at least some time thinking about possible ways of operationalizing your general goals to make sure that you have not overlooked quantitative measures readily at hand. Also, you may find thinking about more specific criteria useful in deciding whether a more thorough analysis would likely be productive in the future. Of course, do not let yourself be distracted from completing a "quick and dirty," but timely and useful, analysis with qualitative criteria.

In conclusion, we state what should be your cardinal rule for selecting criteria: *the set of criteria should capture all the important dimensions of the relevant goals*. While quantitative objectives and constraints are highly desirable as criteria because they facilitate more precise ex ante comparisons of effects and because they suggest yardsticks for ex post evaluations of adopted policies, they should not be used unless they satisfy the cardinal rule. Obviously, you should choose qualitative criteria that closely match goals over quantitative criteria that match goals poorly or incompletely.

Specifying Policy Alternatives

We have already presented a set of generic policy solutions in Chapter 5. They provide "templates" for examining policy alternatives. The specification of policy alternatives is one component of policy analysis where nearly everyone agrees one can, and should, be "creative." When told this, many of our students have replied, "Give us a hint." Here we attempt to do so.

There are really four sources of developing policy alternatives: (1) existing policy proposals; (2) generic policy solutions, as outlined in the previous chapter; (3) "modified" generic policy solutions; and (4) custom-made solutions.

Existing policy proposals, including the status quo policy, should be taken seriously. Not because they necessarily represent the best set of alternatives, but rather because other analysts have found them to be plausible responses to policy problems. Proposals already on the table sometimes are the product of earlier analyses; other times they represent attempts by interest groups or by policy entrepreneurs to draw attention to policy problems by forcing others to respond to concrete proposals. (Indeed, you can sometimes work backwards from policy proposals to infer some of the perceptions and goals of the proposers.[27])

It is rare, although not impossible, that you will end up considering a set of purely generic policy alternatives. Nonetheless, generic policy solutions often provide a good starting point. For example, if you model the apparent overexploitation of a resource as a common-property problem, then it is natural to look first at such generic policy solutions as private ownership, user fees, and restrictions on access. Although the particular technical, institutional, political, and historical features of the problem may limit their direct applicability, the generic solutions can provide a framework for crafting and classifying more complex alternatives.

Once you develop a portfolio of generic alternatives, you can begin to modify them to fit the particular circumstances of the policy problem. For example, a common-property resource like salmon has value to sport and commercial fisherman. Selling exclusive harvesting rights to a private firm might create appropriate incentives for efficient long-term management of the salmon. The firm would probably find it difficult to control sport fishing, however, because it would face high transaction costs in using the civil courts to protect its property rights against individual poachers. A hybrid policy that reserved an annual catch of fixed size for licensed sportsmen might deal more effectively with the poaching problem by bringing the police powers of the government to bear. Modified alternatives of this sort can often be formed by combing elements of generic solutions or by introducing new features.

Finally, in the course of your analysis, you may come up with a unique, or custom-made, policy alternative. Its elements may be lurking in the literature or it may be the product of your imagination. Certainly this is one area of policy analysis in which you should stretch your imagination. Much of the intellectual fun of policy analysis arises in trying to come up with creative alternatives. Be brave! You can always weed out your failures when you begin your systematic comparison of alternatives. Indeed, you may not be able to identify your failures until you begin your comparative evaluation.

As an example of a creative policy alternative, consider a proposal by Richard Schwindt and Aidan Vining for improving the supply of body organs for transplant operations.[28] They propose a future delivery system for transplant organs whereby people could sell their organs to the government for a cash pay-

---

[27]This is a useful type of nonlinear (or, perhaps more precisely, reverse-linear) thinking. Richard Elmore uses the term "backward mapping" to describe a similar process. "Backward Mapping: Implementation Research and Policy Decisions," in Walter Williams, ed., *Studying implementation* (Chatham, N.J.: Chatham House, 1982), pp. 18–35.

[28]For more details, see Richard Schwindt and Aidan R. Vining, "Proposal for a Future Delivery Market for Transplant Organs," *Journal of Health Politics, Policy, and Law*, Vol. 11, No. 3, Fall 1986, pp. 483–500.

ment today in return for promising delivery upon death. They argue that such a system would both increase supply and encourage its efficient allocation.

Be warned that your creative alternatives are likely to be controversial, so be prepared to take the heat! (Sometimes you can launch trial balloons in order to get a sense of how hostile the reception will be. For example, you might try to get informal reactions to alternatives during interviews with people who have interests in the policy area.)

Keeping these sources in mind, we can suggest some heuristics for crafting policy alternatives.[29] First, *you should not expect to find a dominant or perfect policy alternative*. Policy analysis generally deals with complex problems and, most importantly, multiple goals. It is unlikely that any policy is going to be ideal in terms of *all* goals. Rarely is the best policy also a totally dominant policy.

Further, *do not contrast a preferred policy with a set of "dummy" or "straw man" alternatives*. It is often very tempting to make an alternative, which for some reason you prefer, look more attractive by comparing it to unattractive alternatives—almost anyone can look good if compared to a Frankenstein. This approach usually does not work and, moreover, it misses the very point of policy analysis. It rarely works because even relatively inexperienced clients are usually aware of the extant policy proposals advanced by interested parties. Your credibility can be seriously eroded if the client realizes that the alternatives have been faked. It misses the point of policy analysis because such an approach assumes that *the* critical component of analysis is the recommended alternative. As we have stressed, however, the *process* of policy analysis is equally important. You achieve the process goal of policy analysis by considering the best possible set of alternatives. Of course, comparing viable candidates makes determination of the best policy alternative more difficult and less certain, but as we have already pointed out, it is better to have an ambiguous reality than a fake certainty.

Another heuristic may help you to avoid dummy alternatives: *don't have a "favorite" alternative until you have evaluated all the alternatives in terms of all the goals*. This may seem too obvious to state. Yet many neophyte analysts sprinkle their analyses with hints that they have accepted or rejected a policy alternative before they have formally evaluated it. Make your primary investment in the analysis and only marginally in the particular recommendation. Anyway, good analysis will produce good recommendations; the reverse is not necessarily true.

Having ensured that your policy alternatives are not straw men, you should *ensure that your alternatives are mutually exclusive*; they are, after all, *alternative* policies. Alternatives are obviously not mutually exclusive if you could combine all the features of alternative A with all the features of alternative B and come up with alternative C. In such circumstances, A and B may be too narrow and perhaps should be eliminated from the set of alternatives. For example, imagine a series of alternatives that specify fees for different classes of users of a public facility. If the adopted policy is very likely to set fees for all the classes, then it probably would be appropriate to combine the set of fees into a single alternative that can then be compared to other combinations that also cover all the classes of users.

---

[29]Several of the ideas in the section are drawn from Peter May, "Hints for Crafting Alternative Policies," *Policy Analysis,* Vol. 7, No. 2, Spring 1981, pp. 227–44.

You almost always face an infinite number of potential policy alternatives. If one of your policy alternatives is to build 10,000 units of low-income housing, mutually exclusive alternatives include building 9,999 units or 10,001 units. An infinite number of policy alternatives is a few too many. Given clients' limited attention span (and analysts' limited time), somewhere between three and seven policy alternatives is a reasonable number.[30] Keep in mind that one of the alternatives should be current policy—otherwise you introduce a bias for change.

It is preferable to provide a reasonable contrast in the alternatives examined. Unless there are important discontinuities, it is analytically wasteful to make three of your alternatives 9,999 housing units, 10,000 housing units, and 10,001 housing units. The alternatives should provide real choices.

You should *avoid "kitchen sink" alternatives*—that is, "do-everything" alternatives. Such alternatives are often incomprehensible and unfeasible. If you find yourself proposing a kitchen sink alternative, take a close look at all the constraints your client faces. Does your client have the budgetary, administrative, and political resources to pay for it? If not, then it is probably not a valid alternative.

More generally, *alternatives should be consistent with available resources, including jurisdictional authority and controllable variables.* If your client is a mayor, there is usually little point in proposing alternatives that require new federal resources. If you believe that such an alternative should be formulated, you must recast it as a call for mobilization, coordination, or lobbying. In other words, it must be oriented around a set of steps that your client can take to generate the appropriate federal action.

Remember that *policy alternatives are concrete sets of actions.* (Remind yourself of the distinction between goals and policies.) Generic policy solutions are abstract statements. Thus, while it is useful for analytic purposes to think of a given alternative as the "demand-side subsidy alternative," this abstraction should be converted to a concrete proposal (for example, housing vouchers worth X, going to target population Y) in your policy analysis. Alternatives should be well-specified sets of instructions so that the client knows exactly what she is choosing and how it will be executed. To prepare these instructions, you must determine what resources will be needed during implementation and how these resources are to be secured from those who control them. In effect, you must be able to create a scenario that shows how the policy can be moved from concept to reality. (In Chapter 8 we deal with this important aspect of analysis in greater depth.)

Predicting and Valuing: Putting Goals and Alternatives Together

Once you have specified the relevant evaluation criteria and policy alternatives, you must bring them together in a way that facilitates choice. You face three tasks: (1) predicting, or forecasting, the impacts of the alternatives; (2) valuing the impacts in terms of criteria; and (3) comparing alternatives across disparate criteria.

---

[30]On the question of attention span, see G. A. Miller, "The Magical Number Seven, Plus or Minus Two: Some Limits on Our Capacity for Processing Information," *Psychological Review*, Vol. 63, 1956, pp. 81–97.

You should confront these tasks explicitly. By doing so, you make clear the assumptions inherent in your analysis. For example, consider benefit-cost analysis: A prediction of impacts underlies the estimation of the stream of future costs and benefits. Valuation is relatively simple because all the impacts are already expressed in dollars, which, with appropriate discounting, can be weighted to produce a common metric representing the value of a dollar at the present time. Because efficiency is the only relevant goal, the choice rule is simply to select the alternative that gives the greatest excess of discounted benefits over discounted costs.

In the decisions we make in our everyday lives, we often predict, value, and choose implicitly and incompletely. Indeed, our goals and alternatives often remain unspecified. When decisions are routine, our experience allows us to take these shortcuts with little risk of serious error. When the decision problems are novel or complex, however, we run the risk of missing important considerations when we do not explicitly value all of our alternatives in terms of all of our goals.

To be more specific about how to evaluate alternatives systematically, we focus our attention on the *criteria/alternatives matrix*, a useful device for forcing us to be comprehensive in our comparisons of alternatives.[31] For reasons that we discuss in the following section, it is advisable to prepare an impacts/alternatives matrix as a preliminary step to valuation.

Predicting Impacts.   Before you can evaluate alternatives in terms of criteria, you must predict their impacts. Here is where your model of the policy problem (Step 1 of problem analysis) becomes especially important. Your model helped you understand and explain current conditions, which are observable. It should also help you predict what will happen in the future under current policy. For example, assume that the policy problem is rush-hour traffic congestion in the central business district, and that your model is that crowding results because people base their commuting decisions on the private costs and benefits of the various transit modes. Because drivers do not pay for the delay costs that their presence inflicts on everyone else driving in the central business district during rush hour, too many people commute by automobile from the perspective of total social costs and benefits. Your model suggests that changing conditions, such as growing employment in the central business district, that alter the costs and benefits of various transit modes will affect future congestion. By projecting changes in conditions, therefore, you can predict future congestion levels under current policy. You would make predictions about congestion under alternative policies by determining how they would alter the costs and benefits of different transit modes. Higher parking fees, for instance, would raise the private costs of commuting by automobile.

Consider how you might actually go about making the link between higher parking fees and congestion. Ideally, you would like to know the price elasticity of demand for automobile commuting in your city. That is, by how many percentage points will automobile use for commuting change as a result of a one-point percentage change in price? Starting with estimates of the current price and level

[31]There are several terminologies for this approach. Patton and Sawicki call it the *matrix (scoreboard) display system* (p. 275), while Easton calls it *ordering multivalued alternatives*. Allan Easton, *Complex Managerial Decisions Involving Multiple Objectives* (New York: John Wiley, 1973), p. 168.

of automobile commuting, you could use the elasticity to predict levels under various parking fee increases. It is unlikely that you would have the authority, time, or resources to run an experiment to determine the elasticity. You may be able to take advantage of natural experiments, however. For example, your city may have raised parking fees for other reasons in the past. What effect did this have on automobile use? Do you know of any other cities that raised parking fees? What happened to their congestion levels? If you cannot find answers to these questions, then you might be able to find some empirical estimates of the price elasticity of automobile commuting in the literature on transportation economics. As a last resort, you might ask some experts to help you make an educated guess or simply make a best guess yourself.

Policies almost always have multiple impacts. We recommend a two-stage procedure for making predictions. First, use your model, your specification of the alternative, and your common sense to list as many different impacts as you can. For example, with respect to a parking fee increase: What will be the impact on automobile use for commuting? On the price and quantity of private parking in and near the central business district? On city revenues from parking fees and parking tickets? On the use of other transit modes? On off-peak driving in the central business district? On resident and commuter attitudes toward city hall? Each of the impacts you identify should be relevant to at least one of your criteria. If an impact does not seem relevant to any of your criteria, then your set of criteria is probably too narrow. For instance, once you start thinking about how commuters might respond to the higher parking fees, you may realize that some will park in nearby residential neighborhoods and ride public transit to the downtown. If you had not already considered on-street parking congestion in near-by residential neighborhoods as an evaluation criterion, then you should add it to your list.

Second, go through your criteria to make sure that you have a prediction for each one. If a policy does not seem to have an impact relevant to a particular criterion, then predict "no difference from current policy." The key point is that *you should predict the effects of each alternative on **every** criterion.* After you have worked through all the alternatives, you will be able to compare them across each of the evaluation criteria.

You can force yourself to be comprehensive in your prediction of impacts by constructing a matrix that lists alternatives on one dimension and impact criteria on the other. The cells of the matrix serve as a worksheet for making predictions. Figure 6.6 shows what your worksheet might look like for the parking congestion problem. The columns are labeled with the three alternatives: current policy, a doubling of parking fees at city-owned lots in the central business district, and the establishment of bus-only lanes on certain major traffic arteries. Only by filling in all the cells do you make a complete set of predictions. As you gather more information, you can refine the cell entries until you are either satisfied with their accuracy or you have no hope of improving them further with available time and resources.

Do not try to suppress the uncertainty in your predictions. You need not fill in cells with single numbers (point estimates). Instead, ranges (confidence intervals) may be appropriate. For example, you may be fairly confident that the average number of vehicles entering the central business district at rush hour on workdays will be very close to 50,000 under current policy over the next year because this has been the average over the last two years. In contrast, you may be very uncertain about the average number of vehicles that would enter if parking fees were doubled. Perhaps you believe that it is unlikely that the number would be either less than 45,000 or greater than 48,000. Rather than fill the appropriate cell with a specific number, you should indicate this range. Later you can use these upper and lower bounds to come up with "best" and "worst" cases for each alternative.

Many times your uncertainty will be so great that a qualitative rather than quantitative entry is appropriate. For instance, consider the criterion, "Change in CBD business activity," in Figure 6.6. Although it would be natural to measure this change in dollars, you probably have no basis for making quantitative predictions. Cell entries such as "slight increase" or "moderate decrease" may be the most realistic predictions you can make.

Often it is necessary to predict impacts far into the future. To do so, you must make assumptions about how general conditions of relevance will change. For example, consider Figure 6.7, which presents the prediction matrix for three alternative regulatory programs intended to reduce sulfur emissions from older U.S. coal-burning electric power plants. The estimates were made by analysts at the Congressional Budget Office, using the National Coal Model developed by the Department of Energy. The model, which predicts the pattern of coal use from 1986 to 1995, requires numerous assumptions that range from the growth rate in electricity demand to the future cost of equipment for "scrubbing" sulfur out of smoke from burned coal. The analysts undoubtedly based the predictions in Figure 6.7 on what they believed to be the most reasonable set of assumptions. To test the sensitivity of their predictions to any particular assumption, they could have kept unchanged all assumptions except the one of interest and constructed a new prediction matrix. Each set of assumptions would represent a different scenario. If the relative impacts of alternatives differed greatly under different scenarios, then the analysts could (and should) have retained more than one prediction matrix through the valuation stage.

Valuing Impacts.   A prediction matrix typically expresses impacts in units that are not readily comparable. By introducing a common metric for several impacts, you can make them directly comparable. In this way, the impact criteria can be reduced to a smaller number of evaluation criteria. Benefit-cost analysis serves as an extreme example—it requires that all impacts be valued in dollars. More generally, some, but not all, impacts can be expressed in the same units. *You should try to make the impact criteria as comparable as possible without distorting their relationships to the underlying goals.* By combining impact criteria that are truly commensurate, you may be able to specify a more manageable set of evaluation criteria.[32]

We illustrate the valuation process by returning to the prediction matrix shown in Figure 6.6. Four criteria are associated with the goal, Access to the Central Business District: the number of vehicles entering the CBD during rush hour

---

[32]For a discussion of transformation issues, see Clyde Coombs, *A Theory of Data* (New York: John Wiley, 1964), Chapter 13, "Comparing Incomparables: Compressing Partial Orders to Form Decisions," pp. 284–91.

		Alternatives		
Goals	Criteria	Current Policy	Double CBD Parking Fees	Express Bus Lanes
Access to CBD	1. Number of rush-hour vehicles (per workday)	50,000	45,000 to 48,000	44,000 to 48,000
	2. Average rush-hour delay for vehicles (minutes)	12	6 to 10	14 to 18
	3. Number of commuter-bus riders (per workday)	30,000	31,000 to 33,000	32,000 to 36,000
	4. Average rush-hour delay for bus commuters (minutes)	12	6 to 10	3
Fiscal health	1. Revenues from parking fees and bus fares in excess of current policy (millions of dollars per year)	0	13.00 to 20.80	−0.52 to −0.13
	2. Direct costs in excess of current policy (millions of dollars per year)	0	0.12	3.50
Citywide social & economic well-being	1. Change in CBD business activity	none	slight decrease?	slight increase?
	2. Change in profits of private parking firms (millions of dollars per year)	0	13.00	−2.60 to −0.91
	3. Parking congestion in nearby residential neighborhoods	moderate	high	moderate
Public acceptability	Public acceptability	diffuse complaints	drivers and business owners oppose; private parking firms favor	drivers oppose; bus riders favor

Figure 6.6 Worksheet for Predicting Impacts of Alternative Policies for Dealing with Central Business District (CBD) Traffic Congestion

and the average delay they face, and the number of commuter-bus riders and the average delay they face. As long as we consider an hour of delay faced by an automobile-commuter to be equivalent to an hour of delay faced by a bus-commuter, then we could calculate the total commuter-hours of delay under each

Policy Alternatives:	• No subsidies • No restrictions on fuel switching • No taxes		• No subsidies • 80% of 1995 coal purchase must be same type as purchased in 1985 • No taxes		• Scrubber subsidy: 90% of annual capital cost & 50% operating cost through 2015 • No restrictions on fuel switching • 1.0 mill per kilowatt-hour tax on fossil-fuel electricity production	
Effects:						
1995 SO$_2$ emissions reductions from 1980 level (in millions of tons)	8.0	10.0	8.0	10.0	8.0	10.0
Total program costs (in billions of discounted 1985 dollars)[b]	20.4	34.5	23.1	50.8	30.0	41.5
Cost-effectiveness (in discounted 1985 dollars per ton of SO$_2$ reduction)[c]	270	360	306	528	389	431
Reductions in coal-mining employment in four key high-sulfur coal states[d]	14,000	21,900	11,600	12,800	4,500	11,200

[a]Reduction allocated across states in proportion to the total SO$_2$ discharged by plants discharging more than 1.2 pounds of SO$_2$ per million British Thermal Units in 1980.

[b]Present value of the sum of annual utility costs incurred over the 1986–2015 period, using a real discount rate of 3.7 percent.

[c]Discounted program costs divided by present value of annual SO$_2$ reductions over 1986–2015 period.

[d]Difference between option and current policy in 1995 for Illinois, Indiana, Ohio, and Pennsylvania.

Figure 6.7 Regulatory Options for Reducing SO$_2$ Emissions from Electric Utilities in Operation Prior to 1980.[a] *Source:* Congressional Budget Office, *Curbing Acid Rain: Cost, Budget, and Coal Market Effects* (Washington, D.C.: GPO, June, 1986), Summary Table 1, pp. xx–xxiii.

of the alternatives. We would thus have a single criterion associated with the general goal of access to the CBD.

The criterion, commuter-hours of delay, is still not directly comparable to the other criteria in Figure 6.6. Note that the criteria under the goal, Fiscal Health, are measured in dollars and, therefore, could be combined to form a single criterion we could call "net program costs." If we wanted to compare directly commuter-hours of delay with net program costs, then we would have to find a way of putting a dollar value on delay. One approach, often used by economists, is to assume that people value leisure time, which delay reduces, at their wage rate. You can make a dollar estimate of the value of improved access relative to current policy by multiplying the reduction in hours of delay by an average wage rate. You might call the resulting criterion, "monetized value of reductions in delays."

For example, using an average wage rate of eight dollars per hour, the dollar cost of delay would be $33.3 million per year under current policy, between $16.2 million and $27.4 million under alternative two (the doubling of parking fees), and between $26.3 million and $33.3 million under alternative three (the creation of express bus lanes). Compared to current policy, therefore, alternative two would reduce the monetized cost of delay by between $5.9 million and $17.1 million; alternative three would reduce the monetized cost of delay by between zero and $7.0 million.

You could next add your estimate of avoided delay costs to net program costs to create a new criterion, "net monetized benefits," which implicitly assumes a one-to-one trade-off between the dollar measures of access to the CBD and fiscal health. Is "net monetized benefits" an appropriate amalgamation of the two goals? From the perspective of the city government, the answer might very well be No for a number of reasons: First, the delay encountered by bus commuters may not be as important to the city council as delay encountered by drivers because a higher proportion of the latter are city residents. Second, the city council may be unwilling to trade program costs and revenues, which show up in the budget, dollar-for-dollar against monetized delay costs, which are diffuse and indirect. Indeed, if bus service were provided by an independent agency, the city council undoubtedly would want to see a separate listing of bus fares and parking fees in the revenue estimates.

"Net monetized benefits" would not be an appropriate criterion from the social welfare (efficiency) perspective. While program expenditures generally represent payments for real resources that could have been used to produce goods elsewhere in society, program revenues include transfers of money from parkers to the city. These transfers would not be counted in a standard benefit-cost analysis done from the perspective of society as a whole. (We explore such issues in greater depth in Chapter 7.)

Given these considerations, "net monetized benefits" would not be an appropriate criterion for valuing impacts in terms of the goals of "access to the CBD" and "fiscal health." You might reasonably report it as one of your summary measures, however, as long as you keep "monetized value of reductions in delays" and "net program costs" as separate evaluation criteria.

In summary, you should look for ways to make impact criteria comparable. In doing so, however, you should not lose sight of the underlying goals. Remember that your purpose in valuing impacts is to facilitate, rather than obscure, explicit comparison.

Comparing Alternatives Across Incommensurable Criteria. Choosing the best alternative is trivial when you have either a single criterion or an alternative that ranks highest on all criteria. Unfortunately, reality is rarely so kind. Although you may sometimes be pleasantly surprised, you should expect to find different alternatives doing best on different criteria. Your task is to make explicit the trade-offs among criteria implied by various choices, so that your client can easily decide the extent to which she shares the values you brought to bear in choosing what you believe to be the best alternative. In other words, *you should continue to be overt about values in the final phase of evaluation.*

For example, return to Figure 6.7, which compares regulatory options for reducing SO_2 emissions from existing coal-fired power plants. Consider the regulatory options that cut emissions by 10.0 million tons (columns two, four, and six). Note the trade-off between employment reductions in the four high-sulfur states and total program costs. Relative to the basic option (column two), restrictions on fuel switching (column four) involve an additional $16.3 billion in program costs but a loss of 9,100 fewer jobs; relative to the basic option, the tax-supported subsidies for scrubbers (column six) involve an additional $7.0 billion in program costs but a loss of 10,700 fewer jobs. If you restrict your attention to program costs and employment reductions, then the tax-supported subsidies option clearly dominates the restrictions on fuel-switching option—the former involves both lower program costs and a loss of fewer jobs. Yo must still decide, however, whether the additional $7.0 billion in program costs to save the 10,700 jobs justifies the choice of the tax-supported subsidies option over the basic option. Whatever your decision, you should make an explicit statement of how you reached it.

You should also be explicit about uncertainty. Rarely will you be able to predict and value impacts with great certainty. The scores you give alternatives on the evaluation criteria usually constitute your best guesses. If your predictions are based on statistical or mathematical models, then your best guesses may correspond to sample means or expected values and you may be able to estimate or calculate variances as measures of your confidence in them.[33] More often your best guesses and your levels of confidence in them will be based on your subjective assessment of the available evidence. In situations where you are generally confident about your best guesses for the major evaluation criteria, a brief discussion of the range of likely outcomes may suffice.

We have already discussed some ways of organizing your evaluation when you are not very confident about your best guesses. When lack of confidence springs from uncertainty about relevant conditions in the future, you can construct a number of scenarios that cover the probable range. You can then choose the best alternative under each scenario. If one appears to dominate under all scenarios,

[33]The *sample mean* is simply the average of a number of observations. The *expected value* is the sum of all possible outcomes weighted by their respective probabilities. The *sample variance* measures how tightly the observations are distributed around the sample mean—the greater the sample variance, the more likely it is that any new observation (what actually results under the adopted policy) will be far from the sample mean (your prediction or best guess). Similarly, the *mathematical variance* indicates how tightly around the expected value random draws from a probability distribution are likely to fall.

then you can choose it without worry. If no alternative dominates, then you can make your choice either on the basis of the best outcomes under the most likely scenarios or on the basis of avoiding the worst outcomes under any plausible scenario.[34] In either case, you should discuss why you think your approach is the most appropriate one.

Sometimes your confidence in your best guesses will vary greatly across alternatives. You may be very certain about your valuations of some alternatives, but very uncertain about others. One approach is to conduct a "best case" and "worse case" evaluation for each of the alternatives with very uncertain outcomes. You must then decide which case is most relevant for comparisons with other alternatives. Another approach is to create a new evaluation criterion, perhaps labeled "likelihood of regret," that gauges how probable it is that the actual outcome will be substantially less favorable than the best guess. You could then treat this new criterion as just another incommensurable.

No matter from what source, as the number of criteria deserving prominence rises, the complexity of comparison becomes greater. For example, our previous discussion of regulations on SO_2 emissions was limited to options involving 10.0 million ton reductions (columns two, four, and six in Figure 6.7). By also considering the options that yield 8.0 million ton reductions (all six columns in the figure), we move from comparing three alternatives in terms of two criteria to comparing six alternatives in terms of three criteria. Further, while the tax-supported subsidies option dominates the fuel-switching restrictions option for 10.0 million ton reductions, it does not do so for 8.0 million ton reductions. The possibility of this sort of scale effect argues for comprehensive comparisons.

In the face of such complexity, it may be tempting to resort to a more abstract decision rule. For instance, you might begin by scoring the alternatives on a scale of one to ten for each of the criteria (say ten points for fully satisfying the criterion, zero points for not satisfying it all). One possible decision rule is to select the alternative that has the highest sum of scores; another is to select the alternative with the highest product of scores. Of course, if you had a basis for doing so, you could give extra weight to scores earned on one or more of the scales.

Although rules such as these can sometimes be useful, we recommend that you not use them as substitutes for detailed comparisons of the alternatives. Simple decision rules tend to divert attention from trade-offs and the values implied in making them. Also, they invariably impose arbitrary weights on incommensurate criteria. In other words, we urge caution in their use because they tend to obscure rather than clarify the values underlying choice.

One abstract decision rule that we believe is often appropriate for simplifying choice is the *"go, no go" rule*. To apply it, you must set a threshold level of acceptability for each criterion. For example, if a criterion is "minimize SO_2 emissions," the threshold might be a reduction of at least 8.0 million tons per

[34]Avoiding the worst outcomes is similar to the *minimax strategy* in game theory. The minimax strategy involves determining the worst possible outcome that could result under each alternative policy and then choosing the best of these worst outcomes. Keep in mind that the minimax strategy is very conservative— the worst outcome, no matter how unlikely, determines the ranking of the alternative. It is most appropriate in situations where the stakes for either your client or society are very high. It is least appropriate for decisions where "bad luck" can be easily accommodated by the affected parties.

year. Once you have established thresholds for all the criteria, you simply eliminate those alternatives that fail to pass any of the thresholds. If a single alternative remains, then you can accept it as the only one that has a "go" on every criterion. If two or more alternatives remain, then you can focus your attention on them, making detailed comparisons in terms of trade-offs among criteria. The difficult case arises when no alternative, including current policy, gets a "go" on every criterion. You must then either develop better alternatives or lower some of the threshold levels!

Presenting Recommendations

The final step in the rationalist mode of analysis is to give advice. Specifically, you should clearly and concisely answer three questions: First, what do you believe your client should do? Second, why should your client do it? And third, how should your client do it? Answers to the first two questions come directly from your evaluation of alternative policies. Your answer to the third should include a list of the specific actions that your client must take a secure adoption and implementation of the recommended policy.

We offer several heuristics to help guide your presentation of recommendations. First, *your recommendations should follow from your evaluation of the alternatives (step 6)*. While this may seem obvious, we think it is worth stating. Sometimes what seem to be good ideas for policy solutions take form only as your deadline gets near. Resist the temptation to introduce these new alternatives as recommendations. The proper approach is to redo your specification and evaluation of alternatives so that the new candidate is systematically compared with the others. Otherwise you risk giving advice that you may later regret. One reason that we advocate working in a nonlinear way along with following the steps in the rationalist mode is that doing so increases the chances that good ideas arise early enough to be treated seriously.

Second, *you should briefly summarize the advantages and disadvantages of the policy that you recommend*. Why should your client accept your recommendation? What benefits can be expected? What will be the costs? Are there any risks that deserve consideration? By answering these questions you appropriately draw your client's attention to the consequences of following your advice.

Finally, *you must provide a clear set of instructions for action*. Exactly what must your client do to realize the policy that you recommend? Sometimes the set of instructions can be very short. For example, if your client is a legislator, then the instruction, "vote for bill X," may be adequate. Often, however, adoption and implementation of your recommendation require a much more complex set of actions by your client. For example, imagine that you recommend to the director of the county social services department that funds be shifted from one day-care vendor to another. When and how should approval be secured from the county manager? Is it necessary to consult with the county's legal department? When and how should the vendors be notified? When and how should participating families be notified? Should any members of the county legislature be briefed in advance? Which staff members should be assigned to monitor the transition? These questions may seem mundane. Nonetheless, with a little thought, you should be able to imagine how failing to answer any one of them might jeopardize the successful implementation of the recommended policy.[35]

COMMUNICATING ANALYSIS

The format of your policy analysis plays an important part in determining how effectively you communicate your advice to your client. Clients vary greatly in their levels of technical and economic sophistication; you should write your analysis accordingly. Generally, however, clients share several characteristics: (1) they usually want to play some role in shaping the analysis (but they do not want to *do* the analysis); (2) they are busy and they face externally driven timetables; and (3) they are nervous about using the work of untested analysts when they have to "carry the can" for it in the policy arena. These generalizations suggest some guidelines on how to present your work.

Structuring Interaction

Often you can involve your client in the analysis productively by sharing a preliminary draft. You should do so early enough so that you can make use of your client's comments, but not so early that you appear confused or uninformed. By trying to prepare full drafts of your analysis at regular intervals over the course of your project, you force yourself to identify the major gaps that you must yet fill. Giving your client the opportunity to comment systematically on one of these intermediate drafts will usually be more effective than ad hoc oral interactions. Of course, if you believe that your client is a better listener than reader (perhaps because you can only claim your client's time and attention through an appointment), you may find oral progress reports, perhaps structured by a prepared agenda, to be more effective. Be flexible! Use whatever type of communication that seems to work best.

You can improve the effectiveness of your written interaction by carefully structuring your draft. You should follow two general guidelines: first, decompose your analysis into component parts; and second, make the presentation within the components clear and unambiguous. These guidelines are not only appropriate for your final product, but they also promote effective communication at intermediate stages by allowing your client to focus on those components that seem weak or unconvincing. Decomposition and clarity also tend to crystallize disagreement between you and your client. Although this may seem like a disadvantage, it usually is not. By crystallizing disagreement at an early stage of your project, your draft analysis helps you determine which of your client's beliefs might be changed with further evidence and which are rigid. In this way your preliminary drafts and other structured interaction with your client reduce the chances that your analysis will ultimately be rejected.

[35]Your list of questions should come from thinking of all the possible things that could go wrong during implementation. Some observers describe people particularly skilled in anticipating the actions of interested parties as having "dirty minds." Martin Levin and Barbara Ferman, "The Political Hand: Policy Implementation and Youth Employment Programs," *Journal of Policy Analysis and Management*, Vol. 5, No. 2, Winter 1986, pp. 311–25. In Chapter 8 we try to help you develop a "dirty mind."

The steps in the rationalist mode, shown in Figure 6.1, provide a general outline for decomposing your analysis. While your final analysis must be written as if you began with the problem description (step 1) and moved sequentially to your recommendations (step 7), you should not necessarily try to write (as opposed to present) the components of your preliminary drafts in strict order lest you encounter the analysis paralysis we mentioned earlier. Obviously, the steps cannot be treated as if they were completely independent. For example, the operational criteria you choose for evaluating your alternatives (step 4) cannot be finalized until you have specified the relevant goals (step 2). But very early in your project you should try to write a draft of each of the components as best you can. This effort forces you to think configuratively and anticipate the sort of information you will need to make the final draft effective. This may be particularly valuable in helping you move from problem to solution analysis so that you do not end up with an overdeveloped description of the status quo and an underdeveloped analysis of alternative policies.

Keeping Your Client's Attention

Clients are typically busy people with limited attention spans. Reading your analysis will be only one of many activities that compete for your client's attention. You bear the burden of producing a written analysis that anticipates your client's limited time and attention.[36]

While most of our suggestions stress presentational issues, timeliness is by far the most important element. If you are trying to inform some decision, you must communicate your advice before the decision must be made. Sometimes clients can delay decisions. Often, however, the need to vote, choose a project, approve a budget, or take a public stand places strict deadlines on clients and therefore on their analysts. While you should always strive for excellence, keep in mind that an imperfect analysis delivered an hour before your client must make a decision will almost always be more valuable to your client than a perfect analysis delivered an hour after the decision has been made.

You can facilitate more effective communication with busy clients by following a few straightforward rules: provide an executive summary and a table of contents; set priorities for your information; use headings and subheadings that tell a story; be succinct; and carefully use diagrams, tables, and graphs.

Your analysis should not read like a mystery. Rather than holding your client in suspense, tell her your recommendations at the very beginning in an *executive summary*. The executive summary should be a concise statement of the most important elements of your analysis including a clear statement of your major recommendations. In a short analysis of a few pages, your first paragraph can serve as an executive summary. An analysis of more than a few pages should have a separate executive summary that stands on its own. That is, it should be a statement that conveys the essence of your advice.

A *table of contents* enables your client to see at a glance where your analysis is going. It presents the structure of your decomposition so that your client can

---

[36]For an interesting discussion of policy communication in organizational contexts, see Arnold J. Meltsner and Christopher Bellavita, *The Policy Organization* (Beverly Hills, Calif.: Sage Publications, 1983), pp. 29–57.

focus on aspects of particular interest. Together with the executive summary, the table of contents enables your client to skip portions of your analysis without losing the major points. While we all want people to read what we write, you should consider yourself successful (at least in a presentational sense) if your client takes your advice on the basis of your executive summary and table of contents alone.

You should arrange your material so that a client who reads sequentially through your analysis encounters the most important material first. Usually a ten-page analysis is not nearly as useful to the busy client as a five-page analysis with five pages of appendices. But doesn't the client still have to read ten pages of material? Only if she wants to! By breaking the analysis into five pages of text and five pages of appendices, you have taken the responsibility for prioritizing the information. As you and your client develop an ongoing relationship, your client may find it unnecessary to check the background facts and theoretical elucidations provided in the appendices.

Headings and subheadings allow your client to move through an analysis much more quickly. As a general rule, headings should approximately correspond to the steps in the rationalist mode. They should, however, be concise *and* tell a story. For example, rather than the heading "Market Failure," a section of your analysis might be titled "Smokers Do Not Bear the Full Social Costs of Smoking." Similarly, rather than "Government Failure," a preferable heading might be "Why State Price Ceilings Are Leading to Undersupply and Inefficiency." Use headings and subheadings freely—even a few pages of unbroken text can lose your client's attention.

Other presentational devices can also be helpful in making your analysis readily useful to your client. Indenting, selective single spacing, numbering, and judicious underlining can all be used to highlight and organize important points in your analysis. The key is to make sure that they draw attention to the material that deserves it. A long series of points or "bullets," especially if expressed in sentence fragments without verbs, not only denies the reader adequate explanation but also fails to highlight the really important points.

Diagrams, graphs, and *tables* can be very useful for illustrating, summarizing, and emphasizing information. Use them, but use them sparingly so that they draw attention to important information. Like headings, their titles should tell a story. All their elements should be labeled completely so that they can be understood with little or no reference to the text. We offer Figure 6.8 as a summary of our major suggestions on communication.

Be succinct! Keep the text focused on the logic of your analysis. Relegate tangential points and interesting asides to your files; or, if you think they might be useful in some way to your analysis, put them in either footnotes or appendices. Be careful not to cut corners with jargon; only use technical terms that your client will understand. (Sometimes you might purposely include unfamiliar technical terms to prepare your client for debate with others—your task is then to explain the terms in the clearest possible manner.)

Try to write crisp text. Start paragraphs with topic sentences. Favor simple over complex sentences. To keep your text lively use the active rather than passive voice: "I estimate the cost to be. . ." rather than "The cost was estimated to be. . . ." Allow yourself time to edit your own text, especially if you tend to be wordy.

Do: *Remember the client!* Keep in mind that policy analysis has little meaning without a client.

Set priorities! Organize your information carefully (essential material in text, supporting material in appendices).

Decompose your analysis into component parts.

Use headings that tell a story. Avoid abstract headings such as market failure (these are to organize your analysis, not to write your report).

Be balanced! If 90% of your analysis is on "the problem," or 90% on "the solution," it fails this test.

Acknowledge ambiguity but then make sure you provide *your* resolution of the ambiguity. (Provide sensitivity analysis where appropriate.)

Be credible by documenting as extensively as possible.

Be smart on the margin! In other words, first make sure you're competent before you try to be brilliant.

Be succinct and only use as much jargon as is needed to communicate the point; clearly explain technical terms.

Be value overt: rather than implying some goal is important, argue its importance explicitly.

Write crisp text. Favor short and direct sentences; use the active voice.

Don't: *Write an essay!* The differences between an essay and a policy analysis should be clear to you by now.

Tell the client everything you know as it comes into your head. It's fine to think nonlinearly, but write linearly.

Write a mystery! Instead, state your important conclusions up front in an executive summary.

Figure 6.8 The Do's and Don'ts of Communicating Policy Analysis

Establishing Credibility

Until you have established a track record as a reliable analyst, you should expect your clients to be somewhat nervous about relying on your analysis. After all, they are the ones who will bear the political and career risks from following your advice. Therefore, if you want your advice to be influential, you must establish the credibility of your analysis.

You can enhance the credibility of your analysis in several ways. First, make sure that you cite your sources completely and accurately. Of course, you will find it easier to do so if you have kept clear notes on your library and field research.

Second, flag uncertainties and ambiguities in theories, data, facts, and predictions. You do a great disservice to your client by hiding uncertainty and ambiguity, not just because it is intellectually dishonest, but also because it may set your client up to be blind-sided by others in the policy arena who have more sophisticated views. After flagging uncertainties and ambiguities, you should resolve them to the extent necessary to get on with the analysis. (Perhaps a "balance of evidence" will be the best you can do.) You should always check the implications of your resolution for your recommendations. Where your recommendations are very sensitive to the particular resolution, you should probably report on the implications of making a range of resolutions. For example, instead of just working through your evaluation of policy alternatives under your "base case" assumptions, you might present evaluations under "best case" and "worse case" assumptions as well.

Finally, as we have already argued, you should be "value overt." Clearly set out the important goals and explain why you believe that they are important. Also, explain why you have rejected goals that others might believe important. Your explication of goals is especially important if you wish to argue to your client that she should alter her goals or give them different weights.

META-ANALYSIS ONCE AGAIN: COMBINING LINEAR AND NONLINEAR APPROACHES

What we have called the rationalist mode of policy analysis consists of seven sequential steps beginning with understanding the policy problem (step 1) and ending with presenting recommendations (step 7). These steps promote logical and comprehensive analysis. Rather than viewing them as the sequence that you should follow to produce analysis, however, you should think of them more as the outline for your final product. Someone who just reads your final report should be left with the impression that you followed the steps in sequence, even if someone else following your efforts from start to finish observed you jumping and iterating among them. Indeed, we believe that you generally should jump and iterate, working nonlinearly toward your linear product.

Briefly reflecting on our discussions of gathering information, specifying goals, and designing alternatives, should make apparent why we urge you to work nonlinearly. Rarely do you know what information is available before you start gathering it—one source leads to another. You may not be able to specify realistic goals until you have considered the range of feasible policy alternatives. Ideas for new alternatives may not emerge until you start to evaluate the ones you have initially designed. As we have noted, the policies advocated by interested parties can help you determine how they view "the problem," perhaps helping you understand it better yourself.

We offer a practical hint for helping you combine the linear and nonlinear approaches: begin your analysis by starting a file (a separate page will do) for each of the seven steps in the rationalist mode—descriptions and models of the problem, goals, solution methods, criteria, alternatives, evaluation, and recommendations. As you gather information, insights will come to you. Write them down in the appropriate file. Even if they do not survive in your final analysis, they not only help you get started but also provide a record of how your own thinking has progressed, something that may be useful when you think about how to communicate effectively your analysis to others.

Working with parallel files may have the added advantage of reducing the anxiety you face in writing to meet deadlines. If you already have a start at each of the components, then putting together the complete analysis will be less traumatic.[37] You can help yourself even more by occasionally going through the files to convert your insights and information into paragraphs. Doing so forces you to confront the weak links in your arguments, thereby helping you focus your attention on critical questions and required information. Also, some of the paragraphs may survive to your final draft, thus sparing you the anxiety of facing a blank page as your deadline approaches.

Once you have had some experience doing policy analysis, take some time to reanalyze yourself. If you find yourself getting paralyzed at one step or another, then you should probably try to force yourself to work more configuratively. (You may find it helpful to try to draft a full analysis about midway to your final deadline.) If you have trouble organizing and presenting your analyses, then you should probably try to follow the steps in the rationalist mode more closely.

CONCLUSION

Our focus in this chapter has been on policy analysis as the process of providing useful written advice to a client. We set out a series of sequential steps, the rationalist mode, that should help you structure your written product. We emphasized, however, that you should think configuratively about the steps as you gather information and work toward a final product. Although we have provided considerable practical advice, the analytical process cannot be reduced to a simple formula—that is why doing policy analysis is so interesting and doing good policy analysis is so challenging. The stylized analysis of Canadian airline deregulation we present in Chapter 9 provides a template for policy reports. The case studies in Chapters 10, 11, and 12 should help you to get a better feel for the process of policy analysis in real settings. But first, in the next two chapters, we discuss doing benefit-cost analysis (Chapter 7) and thinking strategically about policy adoption and implementation (Chapter 8).

---

[37]If you do find yourself with writer's block, then you might want to look at Martin H. Krieger, "The Inner Game of Writing," *Journal of Policy Analysis and Management*, Vol. 7, No. 2, Winter 1988, pp. 408–16, for encouragement.

APPENDIX 6A

GATHERING AND ORGANIZING THE DATA, FACTS, AND EVIDENCE

Very few policy problems are truly unique. Invariably there is *some* theory or data "out there" that will assist you in some aspect of your policy analysis. But it may be difficult to pull the relevant information from the great mass of data that is available. Often you must tap data originally collected for some purpose very different from yours. In dealing with some policy analysis problems, however, you will have the mandate, time, and resources to conduct field research that you can direct at gathering directly relevant data. Your field research may involve taking a firsthand look at some policy problem or it may be limited to gaining expert advice about relevant theories and data sources.

In conducting policy analyses, you face the crucial tasks of developing explanations or models of what is going on and what will happen if any particular alternative is implemented. What, then, is the relevance of facts? Theories and models can tell us a great deal about broad trends and the general directions of expected impacts, but they can rarely tell us about magnitudes. For example, at any given moment, we can only observe a single point on a demand curve. It is relatively easy to predict, as we have done, that imposing a tax will decrease consumption of a good. It is basically an empirical question, however, whether the reduction in the quantity consumed will be large (that is, if demand is elastic) or small (if demand is inelastic). Yet predicting the size of impacts is essential for evaluating alternative policies. In criminal justice, for instance, policy makers may be correct in assuming that increasing penalties for drug possession will decrease consumption of a given drug; but if demand for the drug is considerably more inelastic than they predict or hope, the policy may be quite ineffective— perhaps leading to more street crime to support more expensive habits.

Facts are relevant, therefore, in estimating the extent and nature of existing market and government failures and to predicting the impacts of policy alternatives. Data can often help us discover facts. For example, the total budgetary costs of a program might be calculated by identifying and summing all the expenditures for program elements. It can also enable us to make inferences that we are willing to treat as facts. Returning to the drug example, we might statistically infer the magnitude of the elasticity of demand with respect to punishment by analyzing data on drug consumption in jurisdictions with different levels of punishment. By using standard statistical techniques to make our inferences, we can generally say something about their probable accuracy—for example, with confidence bounds or significance levels. The facts we assemble, either through direct observation or inference, and organize by theories constitute our evidence for supporting our assertions about current and future conditions.

Two points warrant note: First, what one considers to be a fact will often depend upon the theory one brings to bear. The elasticity estimate we treat as a fact depends on the assumptions embedded in the statistical model we employed. A different, but perhaps equally plausible, model might have led to a very different inference. Second, virtually all the facts we bring to bear will to some extent be uncertain. Therefore, we are almost never in a position to prove any assertion with logic alone. Rather, we must balance sometimes inconsistent evidence to reach conclusions about appropriate assertions.

Gathering evidence for policy analysis can be usefully divided into two broad categories: (1) document research and (2) field research. Or, as Eugene Bardach puts it, "In policy research, almost all likely sources of information, data and ideas fall into two general classes: documents and people."[1] Within field research, we include conducting interviews and gathering original data (including survey research). Document research includes reviewing relevant literature, both theory and evidence, and locating existing raw data sources.

DOCUMENT RESEARCH

Relevant literature is generally easier to identify and more usable the greater the extent to which the policy problem is universal rather than particular, national rather than local, strategic (major) rather than tactical, and inherently important rather than unimportant. Thus, broadly speaking, the bigger the problem, the more likely it is that there will be an extant literature of potential usefulness. Unfortunately, we note one major caveat to this comforting assertion: often little relevant literature will be available on major but newly emergent problems (for example, on the policy aspects of Acquired Immune Deficiency Syndrome in the mid-1980s). When confronting either these problems or others with scarce literatures, you will be forced to be bold in the application of theory and creative in your search for analogous policy problems.

Literature Review

Four general categories of documents deserve consideration in the search for policy-relevant information: (1) journal articles, books, and dissertations; (2) publications and reports of interest groups, consultants, and think tanks; (3) government publications and research documents; and (4) the popular press.

If this text had been written twenty years ago, we would have recommended two approaches to accessing relevant journal articles and books: first, by topic, sector, or field[2] (for example, housing, energy, or education); second, by discipline (for example, economics, political science, or sociology). Both approaches are still valid and, indeed, essential. In addition, however, there has arisen in the last two decades a literature with a direct public policy focus. This overtly public policy literature now overlaps with each of the other two approaches and, to some extent, supersedes them. For most purposes, it makes sense to look first

---

[1]Eugene Bardach, "Gathering Data for Policy Research," *Urban Analysis*, Vol. 2, 1974, pp. 117–44, at p. 121.

[2]We avoid the term "subject," which is used in most indexes because it includes both fields (for example, housing) and disciplines (for example, anthropology) as headings.

Journal of Policy Analysis and Management
Policy Sciences
The Public Interest
Policy Studies Review
Policy Studies Journal
Journal of Public Policy (U.K.)
Canadian Public Policy
Applied Economics
Yale Journal of Regulation
Law and Policy
Law and Contemporary Problems
Harvard Civil Liberties Review
Philosophy and Public Affairs
Public Finance Quarterly
Antitrust Bulletin
Public Administration Review
The Bureaucrat
Administration and Society
Fiscal Studies (U.K.)
Canadian Public Administration
National Tax Journal
Journal of Law, Economics and Organization

Figure 6A.1   Policy Journals and Near-Policy Journals

at the policy literature in journals such as *Journal of Policy Analysis and Management, Policy Sciences, Policy Studies Review, The Public Interest, Canadian Public Policy,* and *Journal of Public Policy* (Great Britain).[3] Many professional policy analysts find it worthwhile to subscribe to several of these journals. Many other journals deal with public policy in particular substantive areas. The *Journal of Health Politics, Policy and Law,* for instance, which concentrates on health-related issues, has a strong policy orientation. Similarly, many disciplinary journals have acquired a strong policy emphasis. For example, the *Yale Journal of Regulation* and *Law and Contemporary Problems,* normally found in law libraries, are among those law journals that have a particularly strong emphasis on public policy. Figure 6A.1 provides a listing of policy and near-policy journals.

An obvious starting point for a literature review is the particular topic area of your problem: housing, energy, criminal justice, health, transportation, for example. Figure 6A.2 provides an illustrative listing of journals in three substantive areas. Be cautioned that such journals and periodicals come and go; you should regularly review libraries that carry periodicals to ensure that you are up to date.

The major strength of topic-oriented journals and periodicals is also their weakness. They tend to be concerned with what is *unique* about the topic. They can sometimes leave the impression, however, that the topic is completely unique, thereby blinding the policy analyst to the possibilities of examining analogies and similarities in *other* policy areas. Keep in mind that this text—with its emphasis on market and government failure—asserts that many aspects of policy analysis are common across substantive areas. Another problem is that many topic-oriented journals have a specific disciplinary perspective that may be relatively hidden. It is important for you to understand whether a particular journal is primarily

---

[3]Even though no longer published, back issues of *Public Policy* and *Policy Analysis* can also be extremely useful.

Labor and Employment

Journal of Labor Economics
Journal of Industrial Relations
Journal of Human Resources
Industrial Relations
Journal of Labor Research
Monthly Labor Review
Journal of Occupational Behavior

Labour Research
British Journal of Industrial Relations
European Industrial Relations Review
Industrial and Labor Relations Review
Labor Law Journal
International Labor Review
Social Security Bulletin

Energy

Energy Journal
Energy Policy
Energy Systems and Policy
Energy and Development
Resources and Energy
Journal of Environmental Systems

Nuclear Technology
Public Utilities Fortnightly
Oil and Gas Journal
Journal of Environmental Economics and
Management

Health

Inquiry
New England Journal of Medicine
Journal of Health Economics
Journal of Health Politics, Policy and Law
Medical Care
Journal of Medicine and Philosophy

Public Health Reports
The Lancet
Journal of the American Medical
Association
American Journal of Public Health
Milbank Memorial Fund Quarterly
Hastings Center Report

Figure 6A.2   Illustrative Set of Three Sectors and Associated Publications

concerned with, say, the efficiency of employment issues rather than some other aspect.

Finally, one must distinguish between journals and periodicals. Journals are usually run by editorial boards with a high percentage of academics with scholarly norms, and their articles are usually refereed by experts or professional peers. While this does not eliminate and may even contribute to disciplinary bias, it does ensure that the vast majority of articles in such journals meet basic standards of competence and honesty. Periodicals, on the other hand, may be put out by individual firms, industry associations, and other interest groups, so that one must be cautious in using their articles as sources. Another major advantage of using journals is that they, unlike periodicals, usually provide extensive references. Thus, articles lead to other articles.

Simultaneously, the literature can be approached from a disciplinary perspective. With the growth of specialized professional schools devoted to such topics as education, social welfare, and criminology, the distinction between disciplinary and topical research has, to some extent, become blurred. Nevertheless, it is still relevant for major disciplines such as economics, political science, sociology, psychology, and anthropology.

Because of the importance of efficiency considerations in almost any type of policy analysis, economics journals are an obvious starting point. Probably the most useful one is the *Journal of Economic Literature* (*JEL*). The *JEL* provides three useful services for the policy analyst. First, it provides literature reviews of both specific fields[4] and theoretical issues.[5] Second, it provides a subject or topic index of recent articles in economic journals (fortunately for the analyst, broadly defined). Third, it provides the titles of articles in recent issues of economic journals. All three of these functions are extremely useful. The first, literature reviews, can save the analyst a tremendous amount of work in preparing comprehensive reviews and bibliographies. The second, the subject index of recent economic articles, allows one to search for current research by field. Computer access to the *JEL* index of articles from 1969 to the present is available from DIALOG Information Retrieval Service. The data base can be searched, using the four-digit subject classification code used in *JEL*; or by author, journal, title, geographic area, or date.[6] The third, the listing of articles in recent issues of economics journals, facilitates browsing across substantive areas that may turn up analogous problems.

Other valuable guides to the literature include *Public Affairs Information Service, The Reader's Guide to Periodical Literature, Ulrich's International Periodicals Directory,*[7] *The Social Science Citation Index, Index to Legal Periodicals,*[8] and *Simpson's Guide to Library Research in Public Administration.*[9] There are also numerous specialized sources. In the criminal justice field, for example, the National Criminal Justice Research Service (NCJRS) of the National Institute of Justice (U.S.) provides a microfiche index to the approximately 20,000 publications it holds. Copies of any of these documents can be obtained on microfiche from NCJRS. An example in the energy field is *Energy Abstracts for Policy Analysis*, put out by the Office of Scientific and Technical Information (U.S. Department of Energy), which includes abstracts of documents from congressional committees, government departments, conference proceedings, firms, journals, and other sources.[10]

[4]See, for example, Eric A. Hanushek's review of economics research in education as an excellent primer for policy analysts interested in the economic approach to this topic. "The Economics of Schooling," *Journal of Economic Literature*, Vol. XXIV, No. 3, September 1986, pp. 1141-77.

[5]See, for example, Rodney Maddock and Michael Carter, "A Child's Guide to Rational Expectations," *Journal of Economic Literature*, Vol. XX, No. 1, March 1982, pp. 39-51.

[6]See Drucilla Ekwurzel and Bernard Saffran, "Online Information Retrieval for Economists— The Economic Literature index," *Journal of Economic Literature*, Vol. XXIII, No. 4, December 1985, pp. 1728-55.

[7]New York and London, R. R. Bowker Co.

[8]New York, W. W. Wilson Company.

[9]New York: Center for Productive Public Management, John Jay College of Criminal Justice, 1977.

[10]See also ERIC (Educational Resources Information Center), which abstracts unpublished material relating to education (research findings, conference proceedings, and so on); JPRS (Joint Publications Research Service), which translates approximately 30,000 articles and books a year at the request of government agencies, covering scientific, economic, industrial, medical, and other topics. JPRS material is indexed in Readex Microprint's *U.S. Government Publications* (see below).

Analogous to journal articles are master's and doctoral dissertations. These are often extremely useful information sources because they usually delve into a problem in considerable detail and they often contain detailed bibliographies. Information on dissertations can be found in *Dissertation Abstracts International* and *Master's Abstracts*. A major problem with dissertations is that they are usually not available in libraries and therefore cannot be used for "quick and dirty" analyses. When time allows, copies of dissertations can usually be obtained from University Microfilms in Ann Arbor, Michigan.

It is impossible to describe exhaustively all the useful economic journals. Figure 6A.3 provides an illustrative list of economic journals that do not have a specific topic or subject orientation. It provides similar lists for political science and sociology.

Apart from journals and theses, a large number of books are annually published on a wide range of public policy topics. These books are reviewed on a continuing basis in journals such as the *Journal of Policy Analysis and Management*. The *JEL* is again a valuable source of information on books published in economics. Each issue of the *JEL* provides brief reviews of thirty to forty of the more recent economics books. As libraries are turning to computerized indexing of all material, it is becoming much simpler to conduct a comprehensive library search for relevant books. Also valuable for policy analysts are annual reviews published in many disciplines as well as in fields such as criminal justice; especially valuable are the annuals in policy studies and benefit-cost analysis. Another annual worthy of note is the Brookings Institution's *Setting National Priorities*, which focuses on U.S. issues from the perspective of federal budgetary policy.

The second source of literature is interest groups, think tanks, and consulting firms. We consider these organizations together because they perform overlapping functions. *Interest groups* usually provide unsolicited information on policy issues, but they occasionally do contract research. *Consulting firms* produce mainly narrowly focused analyses, but sometimes they do policy research of more general scope. *Think tanks* tend to emphasize broader policy research, but many of the newer ones are closely tied to interest groups.

Even experienced analysts face difficulty in identifying and accessing the mass of potentially relevant material produced by interest groups, think tanks, and consulting firms. Some of this written material is published, but not easy to get hold of; some is not officially published, but reasonably accessible; and most problematically, some is not published and not easily accessible, although it can be "dug up" (if you know where to dig).[11]

Much of the interest group and think tank "action" in the United States is concentrated in Washington, D.C., although organizations producing policy-relevant studies can be found in most major cities such as New York and Los Angeles, and state capitals such as Sacramento, Austin, and Albany. In many other countries that have both more concentrated political power and the seat

---

[11]In the age of the word processor and desktop publishing, the distinction between "published" and "unpublished" is vanishing. For the policy analyst, the crucial consideration is accessibility.

Economic Journals

Applied Economics
American Economic Review
Economic Journal
Journal of Political Economy
Rand (Bell) Journal of Economics
Journal of Economic Literature
Public Choice
Review of Economics and Statistics
Economic Inquiry
Economic Issues
Southern Economics Journal
Journal of Economic Behavior and Organization
Scottish Journal of Political Economy
Journal of Economic Perspectives
Journal of Law and Economics
Kyklos

Political Science Journals

American Political Science Review
World Politics
Journal of Politics
Annals of American Academy of Political and Social Science
British Journal of Political Science
Canadian Journal of Political Science
American Journal of Political Science

Sociology and Organizational Behavior

Social Forces
Social Problems
American Sociological Review
American Journal of Sociology
Administrative Science Quarterly
Organizational Behavior and Human Performance
Human Relations

Figure 6A.3   Illustrative List of Disciplinary Journals

of government in the largest city, almost all important policy organizations can be found in one place.[12]

A valuable guide to the myriad interest groups and think tanks that are a potential source of policy-relevant analysis in Washington, D.C., is *The Capital Source*, published twice yearly by the *National Journal*. It provides relevant names of individuals and organizations, addresses, and telephone numbers. The index of *The Capital Source* is itself a valuable checklist of public and private organizations that are worth considering as sources of policy-relevant material.

---

[12]London, Paris, and Rome fall into this category. Canada, West Germany, and Australia, in contrast, have the seat of government in relatively small cities (respectively, Ottawa, Bonn, and Canberra).

Many organizations have sections that function as interest groups. Corporations, labor unions, trade and professional associations, and consultants often provide information to the political process. Often various governmental agencies operate in the manner of interest groups. For example, foreign embassies often do so in matters of international trade, and commerce offices at the state and local level do so with respect to economic development.

A vast range of interest groups—corporate, consumer, professional, regional, political, issue-specific, and others—produce various kinds and quantities of policy analysis, or at least policy-relevant information. These organizations range from Common Cause and the Sierra Club to the Conservative Caucus and the National Rifle Association. Among professional and trade associations can be found the Tobacco Institute, the Natural Gas Supply Association, and the Solar Energy Institute of North America. Often direct contact, either writing or telephoning, is the only way to identify and obtain the written material available from these sources.

Why should the analyst consult these sources if their objectivity is suspect? A substantive reason is that these analyses almost always explicitly or implicitly propose public policy goals and policy alternatives. Therefore, they provide valuable sources of *potential* goals and alternatives for your analysis even if you decide to reject them ultimately. Another reason is that these sources may help you prepare for political opposition. If a particular interest group does not agree with the policy recommendations of your analysis, it is likely to be a major critic. It is usually more effective to deal preemptively with these disagreements in your own analysis rather than to attempt to deal with them later.

Think tanks can be a major source of policy information, research, and analyses. Only a decade ago this would have been a relatively simple topic to discuss. A small number of think tanks—including the Brookings Institution, the Rand Corporation, and the American Enterprise Institute for Public Policy Research—dominated policy debate. The number of think tanks has increased rapidly in the last few years, including many that are more specialized and more overtly ideological.[13]

In addition to think tanks that function as independent organizations, many institutes and research centers are more or less loosely associated with universities and colleges around North America, ranging from the Policy Center on Aging at Brandeis University to the Western Illinois University Public Policy Research Institute. An invaluable guide to both nonuniversity and university think tanks and related organizations in North America is the *Research Centers Directory*, which provides addresses and information on the fields covered, publications, and budgets.[14]

The third major source of written material is government publications: national, state, regional, and local. The United States government is one of the world's most prolific publishers—perhaps as many as 100,000 documents yearly.

---

[13]See Amy Wilentz, "On the Intellectual Ramparts," *Time*, September 1, 1986, pp. 18–19.

[14]Detroit, Michigan: Gale Research Co., 1985. See especially the directory section on Private and Public Policy Affairs.

These documents are mainly published by either the Government Printing Office (GPO), which deals with congressional and agency materials, or the National Technical Information Service (NTIS), which deals with a wide range of technical and other reports. In addition, many government agencies publish materials directly and will make them available if asked.

The major governmental source to this material is the *Monthly Catalog of United States Government Publications*, published by the U.S. Superintendent of Documents. This is essentially the government's "sales catalogue."[15]

Several commercial firms also provide indices and abstracts of governmental material, including the Congressional Information Service. Figure 6A.4 provides a summary of important guides, catalogues, bibliographies, manuals, and directories. These serve as good starting points for general searches.

Figure 6A.5 lists the key documents published by the U.S. government, what they tell you, and how to use them. The documents are divided into congressional sources, presidential sources, and judicial sources.

The Readex Microprint Corporation publishes on microformat all material listed in the Government Printing Office's *Monthly Catalog* since 1958. These are available at most libraries. Finally, the National Technical Information Service (NTIS) acts as a clearinghouse of government-funded research, including scientific, economic, and behavioral sciences material.

Selected state and local government materials can be researched through the *Index to Current Urban Documents*, the *Public Affairs Information Service Bulletin (PAIS)*, the *Municipal Yearbook*, the *County Yearbook, Council of Planning Librarians Bibliographies*,[16] and the *Monthly Checklist of State Publications*. Keep in mind two things when conducting your literature review. First, a knowledgeable research librarian can assist you tremendously in accessing material; our review of the potential information sources is by no means complete. Second, finding, synthesizing, and presenting the relevant literature is often one of the valuable tasks that you can perform for a client.

Finally, the popular press can be a valuable source of background information, especially when you are confronting a new issue. Newspaper and magazine articles rarely provide detailed information and analysis, but they often mention and quote experts, stakeholders, organizations, documents, and other sources of potential value. These leads are particularly valuable because they often appear in the popular press long before they do in other published sources. They also may be the only published references to many local issues. For these reasons, it is often useful to begin any new investigation with a quick search through the popular press.

---

[15]New publications are listed by authoring agency with an annual cumulative subject index. Since computerization in 1976, the *Monthly Catalog of United States Government Publications* has become considerably more detailed with additional indexes.

[16]Council of Planning Librarians, 1313 East 60th Street, Chicago, Illinois 60637. These bibliographies are often quite detailed and focused. For example, see Gregory P. Ames, "Recreational Reuse of Abandoned Railroad Rights-of-Way: A Bibliography and Technical Resource Guide for Planners," Council of Planning Librarians, No. 66, November 1981.

1. GENERAL

Andriot, J. L. *Guide to U.S. Government Publications.* 1976– . McLean, Va.,
Document Index, Irregular.
"Annotated guide to important series and serials . . .very useful."

Morehead, J. *Introduction to United States Public Documents.* Littleton, Colo.: Libraries
Unlimited, 1975.
"Clear and straightforward."

Schmeckebier, L.F., and R. B. Eastin. *Government Publications and Their Use,* 2nd rev.
ed. Washington, D.C.: Brookings Institution, 1969.
"The Bible."

U.S. Library of Congress, Serials Division. *Popular Names of U.S. Government Reports:
A Catalog,* 3rd ed. Washington, D.C.: 1976.

U.S. Superintendent of Documents. *Monthly Catalog of United States Government
Publications.* 1895– . Washington, D.C.
"A sales catalogue."

2. CONGRESS

Congressional Research Service. *C.I.S. Annual.* 1970– . Washington, D.C.
"Congressional hearings, reports, and prints are exhaustively annotated and
cross-indexed."

Zwirn, J. *Congressional Publications: A Research Guide to Legislation, Budgets, and
Treaties.* Littleton, Colo.: Libraries Unlimited, 1983.
"A path through the maze; a light to lighten the darkness."

3. THE CONSTITUTION

McCarrick, E. M. *U.S. Constitution: A Guide to Information Sources.* Detroit: Gale,
1980.
"Annotated bibliography of primary and secondary sources."

4. STATUTES

U.S. Office of the Federal Register. *How to Find U.S. Statutes and U.S. Code Citations,* 3rd rev. ed. Washington, D.C.: Government Printing Office, 1977.
"Easily used charts."

5. REGULATIONS

U.S. Office of the Federal Register. *The Federal Register: What It Is and How to Use It.*
Washington, D.C.: 1980.

Figure 6A.4 U.S. Government Documents: Guides, Catalogues,
Bibliographies, Manuals, and Directories. *Source:* Simon Fraser University,
U.S. Government Publications. Abbreviated, rearranged, edited. All comments
in quotations are from this document.

Figure 6A.4 (continued)

6. THE PRESIDENCY

Davison, K. E. *The American Presidency: A Guide to Information Services*. Detroit: Gale, 1983.

U.S. Library of Congress, Manuscript Division. *Presidents' Papers Index Series*. "Indexes to the microfilmed MS groups of presidential papers."

7. FOREIGN RELATIONS

Plischke, E. *U.S. Foreign Relations: A Guide to Information Sources*. Detroit: Gale, 1980.
"Detailed, comprehensive, valuable."

8. ORGANIZATION MANUALS

Information U.S.A. Ed. by M. Lesko. New York: Viking Press/Penguin Books, 1983.
"Government programs are briefly outlined."

United States Government Organization Manual. Vol. 1, 1935– . Washington, D.C.: Government Printing Office, annual.
"Describes the organization and functions of agencies in the legislative, judicial, and executive branches of government. Includes a number of organization charts."

9. PEOPLE

Congressional Staff Directory. Vol. 1, 1959– . Washington, D.C.: Government Printing Office, annual.
"Biographies of senators, congressmen, and members of the Supreme Court; lists of committees and members; lists of foreign diplomatic representatives and consular offices in the United States."

Barone, Michael, and Grant Ujifusa. *The Almanac of American Politics 1988*. Washington, D.C.: National Journal, 1987.

Data and Statistical Sources

In many analyses it is useful to present and analyze new data. A major source of both raw and analyzed data is likely to be the articles, books, and documents described above. But you also may wish to examine primary data sources. Once again, an excellent source is the United States Government.[17] An excellent desk . reference is the *Statistical Abstract of the United States*, which is published yearly by the Bureau of the Census.[18] Figure 6A.6 summarizes the major available sources of guides, catalogues, and bibliographies to these data. A particularly valuable

[17]The Canadian government also provides many useful sources—for example, *Canada Yearbook* (Ottawa: Minister of Supply and Services Canada, 1985).

[18]Another useful, privately published, desk reference is Harold W. Stanly and Richard G. Niemi, *Vital Statistics on American Politics* (Washington, D.C.: Congressional Quarterly Press, 1988).

1. CONGRESS

A. Background

Goehlert, R. U., and J. R. Sayre. *The United States Congress: A Bibliography*. New York: Free Press, 1982.
"200 years of scholarly research on the history, development, and legislative process of Congress."

B. Debates

U.S. Congress. *Congressional Record*. 1983– . Washington, D.C.
"A daily record of the proceedings in the Senate and the House. Includes a complete history of all legislation as well as much extraneous material."

C. Journals

U.S. Congress. House. *Journal of House of Representatives*. 1789–   Washington, D.C., annual.
"The minutes: motions, action taken, votes on roll calls or divisions."
U.S. Congress. Senate. *Journal of Senate*. 1789– . Washington, D.C.: annual.
"The minutes: motions, action taken, votes on roll calls or divisions."

D. Bills and Resolutions

"Bills and resolutions are introduced by a member of Congress and usually referred immediately to a committee. They are numbered in eight series with the beginning of each Congress and retain that number until they become laws, at which time they are printed as slip laws and given a new number. The slip laws are later republished as the *U.S. Statutes at Large*." See also *Digest of Public Bills and Resolutions*.

E. Voting

Congress and the Nation: A Review of Government and Politics. Washington, D.C.: Congressional Quarterly, 1965– .
"Key Senate and House votes. Summary of all major legislation in historical perspective with a chronology of legislative action."

Congressional Quarterly Almanac. Vol. 1, 1945– . Washington, D.C., annual.
"Includes a record of every roll-call vote in the House and Senate, texts of presidential messages to Congress, and a lobby round-up."

F. Committees

"A bill or resolution introduced in Congress is usually referred to a committee. The testimony given by witnesses appearing before the committee is published as *hearings*. The committee concludes its work with the publication of a *report*."
"Since 1970 committee publications have been abstracted and indexed in the *CIS Annual* and the material is available on microfiche."

Figure 6A.5 Key U.S. Government Documents. *Source:* Simon Fraser University, *U.S. Government Publications*. Abbreviated, rearranged, edited. All comments in quotations are from this document.

Figure 6A.5 (continued)

G. Keeping Up with Congress

Congressional Digest. 1921– . Washington, D.C.: monthly.
"Each issue deals with a particular topic currently being discussed in Congress. Indexed in *P.A.I.S.* and *Reader's Guide.*"

Congressional Quarterly Guide to Current American Government. Washington, D.C., semiannual.

Congressional Quarterly Weekly Report. Vol. 1, 1945– . Washington, D.C.
"Digests congressional and political activity for the current week. Includes full text of presidential press conferences, major statements, messages, and speeches, and a lobby report. Indexed in *P.A.I.S.*"

Editorial Research Reports. Vol. 1, 1923– . Washington, D.C., weekly.
"Objectively assembles and documents the basic facts on major issues currently receiving public attention. Indexed in *P.A.I.A.*"

2. THE PRESIDENCY

U.S. President. *Public Papers of the Presidents of the United States.* Washington, D.C.: Government Printing Office, 1958– . (In progress.)
"Messages to Congress, public speeches, new conferences, radio and TV broadcasts, informal remarks, public letters."

U.S. Department of State. *Bulletin.* Vol. 1, 1939– . Washington, D.C., monthly.
"Includes presidential news conferences, speeches, and statements. Indexed in *P.A.I.S.* and *Reader's Guide.*"

3. LAWS

A. Statute Law

"Each law as passed by Congress is first published in pamphlet form and known as a 'slip law.' At the end of each session of Congress all slip laws just enacted are republished in numerical order as part of the set *United States Statutes at Large.*"

"Beginning in 1926, the *United States Code*, a codification of the *Statutes at Large*, has been issued every six years. In the *U.S. Code* public and general law current as of a specific date is arranged into fifty broad subject groupings (called 'titles'). The most recent edition of the *U.S. Code*, all its annual supplementing volumes, and the newly enacted 'slip laws,' comprise the current law."

United States Code. 1982 ed. 10th ed. Washington, D.C.: Government Printing Office, 1983.
Cited as *U.S.C., 1982 ed.* "A codification of the general and permanent laws of the United States in force on January 14, 1983, arranged under fifty titles (i.e., subjects)."

United States Statutes at Large . . . 1789–1873; 1873– . Boston: Little, Brown, 1945-73; Washington, D.C.: Government Printing Office, 1875–
"Includes the 'Little, Brown' edition, titled *Statutes at Large*, covering the first forty-two Congresses, 1789–1873 and ending with Volume 17. This series was taken over by the federal government with Volume 18."

Figure 6A.5 (continued)

B. Regulations

"Regulatory documents with general applicability and legal effect, proposed rules, and documents required to be published by statute are published in the daily gazette, the *Federal Register*. The *Code of Federal Regulations* is an annual codification of the general and permanent rules published in the *Federal Register*. The *Code* is divided into fifty broad titles (i.e., subjects). The *Code* is kept up to date by the later individual issues of the *Federal Register*."

C. Court Reports

Congressional Quarterly Almanac. Vol. 1, 1945– . Washington, D.C.
   "Includes reviews of major Supreme Court decisions."

Supreme Court Review. 1960– . Chicago: University of Chicago Press, annual.
   "Authoritative essays on important Supreme Court decisions. Indexed in *Index to Legal Periodicals.*"

U.S. Supreme Court. *United States Reports. Cases Adjudged in the Supreme Court.* Vol. 1, 1790– . Washington, D.C.: Government Printing Office.

---

1. GENERAL

Congressional Information Service. *American Statistics Index*, Vol. 1, 1973– . Bethesda, Md., annual.
   "A comprehensive guide and index to the statistical publications of the U.S. Government."

Congressional Information Service. *Statistical Reference Index: A Selective Guide to American Statistical Publications from Private Organizations and State Government Sources*, Vol. 1, 1980– . Bethesda, Md., annual.

Directory of Federal Statistical Data Files. 1981– . Washington, D.C., Department of Commerce, annual.
   "Machine-readable data files."

Hoel, A. A. et al. *Economics Sourcebook of Government Statistics.* Lexington, Mass.: Lexington Books, 1983.
   "Describes about fifty key U.S. statistical measures such as the prime rate, CPI, etc., noting their limitations and biases and where they are published."

Lesko, Matthew. *The Computer Data and Database Source Book.* New York: Avon Books, 1984.

Statistics Sources, ed. P. Wasserman, et al., 9th ed. 2 vols. Detroit: Gale, 1984.
   "Frequently revised and valuable subject index to statistical publications. . . . Start here."

U.S. Bureau of the Census. *Catalog of Publications.* Washington, D.C.: Government Printing Office, annual.

Figure 6A.6 Data and Statistics: Guides, Catalogues, and Bibliographies. *Source:* Simon Fraser University, *U.S. Government Publications.* Abbreviated, rearranged, edited, amended. All comments in quotations are from this document.

Figure 6A.6   (continued)

U.S. Bureau of the Census. *Directory of Computerized Data Files*. (Loose-leaf vol.) Washington, D.C., 1979.
"Machine-readable data files."

U.S. Government Accounting Office. *GAO Documents: Catalog of Reports, Decisions and Opinions, Testimonies and Speeches*. Washington, D.C., monthly.

2. BUSINESS AND INDUSTRY

Directory of Industry Data Sources: United States of America and Canada, 2nd ed. Cambridge, Mass.: Ballinger, 1982.

3. FOREIGN TRADE

U.S. Bureau of the Census. *U.S. Foreign Trade Statistics. Classifications and Cross-classifications, 1980*. Washington, D.C., 1981.
"The basic schedules of commodity and geographic trade classifications currently being used in the compilation of U.S. foreign trade statistics."

---

and easy-to-use index is the *American Statistics Index: A Guide to the Statistical Publications of the U.S. Government*.[19]

The U.S. Census provides much useful data. The 1980 census provides an immense amount of disaggregated data on the population (race, sex, age, occupation, and so forth) and housing. Particular departments and agencies also produce their own statistical data.

Several publications of the U.S. Bureau of the Census are especially useful for making comparisons across state and local jurisdictions: the *County and City Data Book*, the *Congressional District Data Book*, and the *State and Metropolitan Area Data Book*. Other federal agencies also publish data disaggregated at the state and local levels. For example, the *Sourcebook of Criminal Justice Statistics*, published by the U.S. Department of Justice, provides a fairly comprehensive collection of comparative data on crime and criminal justice system expenditures.

Once we move away from the federal government, even illustratively cataloguing the available data and statistics is impractical. *Statistical Reference Index: A Selective Guide to American Statistical Publications from Private Organizations and State Government Sources* is the best general index for locating sources other than federal agencies.[20] A variety of private and public sources publish data on particular states and their local jurisdictions.[21] States, counties, municipalities, special districts, and local governmental departments all collect and, more or less, make available such data. While libraries sometimes catalogue annual reports and special studies from state and local agencies, usually such documents must be obtained directly from the agencies themselves. Keep in mind that the quality of such data is highly variable.

[19]Congressional Information Service, Inc., Bethesda, Maryland. Also, from the same source, see the *Index to International Statistics: A Guide to the Statistical Publications of International Intergovernmental Organizations*.

[20]Congressional Information Service, Inc., Bethesda, Maryland.

[21]For example, *New York State Statistical Yearbook* (Albany: Nelson A. Rockefeller Institute of Government, State University of New York, 1987).

Often universities are another important source of data, especially universities with institutes or departments involved in survey research and economic forecasting. To the extent that these data are unpublished and raw—essentially in the form of agency files—it is necessary to engage in some field research to identify and obtain them.

FIELD RESEARCH

Field research consists of talking to people and gathering raw or semiraw data. These tasks are often related because it is usually difficult to get such data without interviewing and impossible to judge its reliability, validity, and comprehensiveness without talking to those who actually gathered it.

How should you decide to whom to talk? Your literature review will often suggest some key people. Our discussion in the previous section, however, necessarily concentrated on the national branches of government. If you work on state or local problems, you should make sure that you have relevant directories and organizational charts. Such directories for the legislative and executive branches of government are usually readily available. Most analysts quickly develop their own directories of local interest groups, professional bodies, regulatory agencies, consulting firms engaged in policy research, quasi-public agencies, and law firms that deal with public issues.

Do not limit your consideration to people currently in relevant organizations. In particular, recently retired employees are often valuable sources. Retired employees offer several advantages: they usually have time for interviews; they have had some time to reflect on their experiences; and they no longer have to worry about agency politics or retribution. Consequently, they may well be more forthright and more analytic. The only problem is that the "shelf life" of their information may be quite short.

Interviews need not be in person. Use the telephone to check whether someone who appears to be an appropriate source (judging by title, department, or organizational role) is likely to be helpful. On projects with short time frames, you may be forced to do both preliminary spadework and interviewing over the telephone.

Here we cannot provide a comprehensive guide to interviewing—several complete books deal with this topic alone.[22] Instead, we provide some basic advice on the major issues relating to interviewing: (1) What kind of information does interviewing elicit most effectively? (2) How can you judge the efficacy of the information you do get? (3) How do you get interviewees to talk? (4) Whom should you interview when?

In the following list we reproduce, with some modification, the advice offered by other writers:[23]

[22]See Lewis A. Dexter, *Elite and Specialized Interviewing* (Evanston, Ill.: Northwestern University Press, 1970); and Jerome T. Murphy, *Getting the Facts: A Fieldwork Guide for Evaluators and Policy Analysts* (Santa Monica, Calif.: Goodyear, 1980). For an excellent treatment of gathering information through direct observation, see Richard F. Fenno, Jr., *Home Style: House Members in Their Districts* (Boston: Little Brown, 1978), pp. 249–95.

[23]Questions 1 and 2 are drawn (in a modified way) from Patton and Sawicki, *Policy Analysis and Planning*; questions 3 and 4 (again modified) from Bardach, "Gathering Data for Policy Research."

1. *What information will interviewing elicit most effectively?*
   a. Historical background and context. The narrative of what has happened.
   b. Basic facts, whether directly through interviews or the raw data provided by interviewees.
   c. Political attitudes and resources of major actors. (These may not be committed to paper anywhere. Interviews may be the only source for this kind of information.)
   d. Projections about the future; extrapolations of current trends.
   e. Other potential interviewees and written materials.

2. *How can the efficacy of an interview be judged?*
   a. The plausibility, reasonableness, and coherence of answers.
   b. The internal consistency of answers.
   c. The specificity and detail of answers.
   d. Correspondence to known facts.
   e. Firsthand familiarity of the interviewee with the facts described.
   f. The interviewee's motivation, bias, and position.
   g. Reasons that the interviewee might withhold information.
   h. The self-critical nature of the interviewee.

3. *How do you get interviewees to talk?*
   a. The "energy" must come from the analyst, not the interviewee. Be prepared to ask questions.
   b. The analyst should not pretend to be neutral, but should avoid dogma and hostility.
   c. Demonstrate that you have other sources of information that interpret events differently from the current interview.
   d. Demonstrate reasonable tenacity on important questions.
   e. Point out other views on a topic and indicate that this is the interviewee's chance to tell her side of the issue.

4. *Whom should you interview when?*
   Approach *early* in the interview sequence:
   a. Those who are likely to be rich sources of information.
   b. Individuals who have power. (They can provide access, either directly or indirectly, to other sources of information.)
   c. Knowledgeable persons who can give you information that will induce others to talk more freely.
   d. Friendly expert interviewees who will contribute to the credibility of the analysis.
   e. Potential opponents, to the extent that they can be assessed.
   f. Retired employees.[24]
   Approach relatively *late*:
   a. Those interviewees who are likely to be hostile or defensive. (Use earlier interviews to acquire leverage.)
   b. Interviewees whom you may not be able to speak to again because they are busy, remote, or otherwise difficult to reach. (Especially if you want their reactions to policy alternatives that you cannot fully specify until the later stages of your project.)

[24]Added by authors, not on Bardach's original list.

  c. Powerful political opponents who could prevent you from gaining access
     to other interviewees.[25]
  d. Administrators who may not identify critical issues even though they have
     the requisite knowledge.
  e. "Expert" interviewees, especially academics, who may be more
     theoretically oriented.[26] (If you interview them too early, you may not
     know enough to frame questions that take full advantage of their
     expertise.)

Most of these points speak for themselves, yet some additional considerations deserve mention. The responses to question 1 suggest that interviews are likely to be most useful for facts, history, and projections. As a corollary, they are likely to be less useful for either a theoretical explanation of what is going on (that is, a model) or a clear and reasoned delineation of goals. These must usually come from your own familiarity with theory and your literature review. There are two exceptions to this general observation, however. First, academic interviewees are usually more comfortable with models and theory. Indeed, they are unlikely to be familiar with program budgets, organizational structures, and institutional history. Second, many governmental agencies have their own analysts and researchers. These government employees are often more comfortable dealing with theoretical issues than either program administrators or regular staff.

A major point to note with respect to the second question is that the reliability and value of an interview can often be judged only by conducting apparently redundant interviews. To the extent that the information from a particular interview is vital to your analysis, you should conduct "insurance" interviews when possible.

Undoubtedly, the hardest issue to deal with is getting interviewees to talk (question 3). One general hint is not to demonstrate that you don't know what you're talking about. Why do we use the double negative? Because demonstrating that you are not ignorant is sometimes not the same as demonstrating knowledge. Put another way: if you know something, flaunt it subtly! If done skillfully, your knowledge can be one way of introducing some reciprocity into the interview. This is especially useful if you are likely to need additional interviews. This is just one aspect of the art of interviewing. More broadly, the trick, to paraphrase Bardach, is to be fair-minded, discreet, intelligent, and self-possessed and to avoid appearing to be partisan, a tale-bearer, a dope, or a dupe.[27]

In situations where you think you have discovered information that is particularly important or controversial, you may want to write a follow-up letter to the interviewee restating the information. Conclude with a request that the interviewee let you know if you have misinterpreted anything. Interviewees will sometimes respond with useful elaborations as well as corrections. The record of communication can also be useful in avoiding arguments about what was said. Of course, common courtesy suggests that you send a brief thank-you note to people who have given you more than a few moments of their time.

---

[25]Bardach is aware of the contradiction of recommending both early and late interviews for potential opponents.

[26]Added by authors, not on Bardach's original list.

[27]Bardach, "Gathering Data for Policy Research," p. 131.

Final practical tips on interviewing: Always do your homework—plan a se quence of questions but be flexible in following it. Don't ask questions that you can answer from documents or from interviews with more accessible people. Make sure that you write up interview notes as soon as possible after an interview. When practical, do not schedule too many interviews in a given day.[28] Don't schedule lunch meetings if you expect to take extensive notes. Ask about other potential interviewees. And ask about potentially useful documents and data.

PUTTING DOCUMENT REVIEW AND FIELD RESEARCH TOGETHER

Bardach suggests four basic ways of expanding the scope of information gathering: documents lead to documents,[29] documents lead to people, people lead to people, and people lead to documents. Figure 6A.7 sets out one way in which Bardach's heuristics might unfold. The flowchart indicates that it is usually advisable to conduct a literature review initially, although starting with telephone interviews often is more appropriate for short-term projects. While the literature review may involve some searching, once you gain access to the relevant literature, the initial documents, references, and bibliographies will quickly lead you to other literature (that is, documents lead to documents). As the initial literature search progresses, it is likely to suggest specific people as potential interviewees or, at least, the role or type of potentially desirable interviewees (that is, documents will lead to people). The objective of the initial literature review is to give you enough background to conduct intelligent interviews. The gist of this advice can be boiled down to a simple heuristic: *know something before you talk to people.*

Once you have a broad sense of the issue, moving to an initial phase of field research is often productive. The first phase may productively consist largely of telephone "mini-interviews." Alternatively, or additionally, it may consist of interviews with potential early interviewees (for example, friendly experts). Especially attractive are potentials who are located nearby. It is less costly (both in terms of time and money) to interview them than others farther away, and you can usually be much more flexible in scheduling the interviews.

Once the initial field research is completed, you should have enough direction to engage in both further literature reviews (that is, people have led to documents) and more extensive and systematic field research (that is, people have led to people and data).

THE MOST IMPORTANT COMPONENT: THINK!

Robert Behn and James Vaupel have pointed out that most students spend 99 percent of their time gathering and processing information (or conducting the

---

[28]If you do, you're likely to appear flushed and rushed. It also makes it less practical to write up notes, and interviews start to merge into each other.

[29]Bardach's "documents" include both published (e.g., journals) and unpublished material.

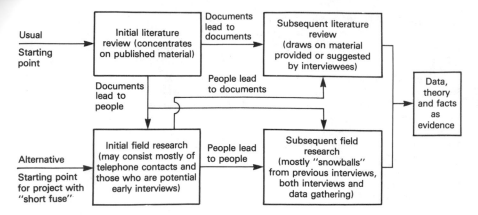

Figure 6A.7 A Strategy for Combining Literature Review and Field Research

literature review and field research).[30] They suggest that instead students should spend at least half their time thinking. The heuristic they suggest is: *model simple; think complex.*[31] We agree. Yet, it is easier said than done. A critical point is to make sure that you don't get into a position where you can't see the forest for the trees. We suggest that "the forest" is keeping the mind focused on market and government failure and the relevant steps in the analytic process (outlined in Figures 6.1 and 6.2). Keep in mind that the mass of data that you are collecting is useful only if it can be placed into an analytic framework. Always ask yourself where the facts you have fit in and what facts you would like to have.

[30]Robert D. Behn and James W. Vaupel, "Teaching Analytical Thinking," *Policy Analysis,* Vol. 2, No. 4, Fall 1976, pp. 661–92, at p. 669.

[31]Attributed by Behn and Vaupel, ibid., p. 669, to Gary Brewer from a talk given at Duke University on December 3, 1973.

7

BENEFIT-COST ANALYSIS

Benefit-cost analysis, a technique for systematically estimating the efficiency impacts of policies, came into common use in the evaluation of flood control projects in the 1930s.[1] It has since been applied, with variable success, across the broad spectrum of public policies.[2] Its appropriateness as a decision rule depends on whether efficiency is the only relevant value and the extent to which important impacts can be monetized. When values other than efficiency are relevant, benefit-cost analysis can still be useful as a component of multigoal policy analysis. When important impacts cannot be reasonably monetized, the first step of benefit-cost analysis—identifying impacts and categorizing them as costs or benefits—can nevertheless serve as the starting point for a more accommodating analytical approach. Thus, the value to analysts of familiarity with the basic elements of benefit-cost analysis goes beyond its direct use as a decision rule.

In this chapter we introduce the basic elements of benefit-cost analysis. A thorough treatment of all of the relevant theoretical and practical issues requires

[1]The U.S. Flood Control Act of 1936 required that water resource projects be evaluated in terms of the difference between estimated benefits and estimated costs. (Earlier requirements for the estimation of costs and benefits appeared in the River and Harbor Act of 1902 and the Flood Control Act of 1926.) The 1950 report of the Inter-Agency Committee on Water Resources, *Proposed Practices for Economic Analysis of River Basin Projects* (known as the Green Book), tried to bring practice in line with economic theory. The Bureau of the Budget set out its own criteria in 1952 in *Budget Circular A-47*. For an overview, see Peter O. Steiner, "Public Expenditure Budgeting," in Alan S. Blinder, et al., *The Economics of Public Finance* (Washington, D.C.: Brookings Institution, 1974), pp. 241–357.

[2]Executive Order 12291 (February 17, 1981) requires U.S. regulatory agencies to prepare regulatory impact analyses for any regulations that are likely to result in annual effects on the economy of $100 million or more. These analyses must identify social costs and benefits and attempt to determine if the proposed regulation maximizes net benefits to society.

ʌtire text—several good ones are already available.[3] So here we focus on the concepts for doing benefit-cost analyses, as well as evaluating those done by ʌhers.

A PREVIEW: INCREASING ALCOHOL TAXES

Would a higher excise tax on alcohol be efficient? This is the sort of question that we try to answer with benefit-cost analysis. We begin by identifying all the impacts of the tax. The direct impacts include higher prices of alcohol for consumers and revenue for the government. But the higher prices lead to reduced consumption of alcohol. Lower levels of consumption produce several indirect effects: fewer fatalities and injuries and less property damage from alcohol-related automobile accidents; and perhaps better health and productivity for people who reduce their consumption of alcohol.

The next task we face in doing our benefit-cost analysis of an increased alcohol tax is to put dollar values on its impacts. For example: How much money would we have to give consumers to make them willingly accept the higher price of alcohol? (The answer is one of the costs of the tax increase.) How much would people be willing to pay to reduce their risks of being in automobile accidents? (The answer is one of the benefits of the tax increase.) After answering questions such as these for all of the impacts, we then compare the marginal benefits of the tax increase with its marginal costs. If benefits exceed costs, then we conclude that the tax increase is *efficient*—it would at least be possible to compensate fully all those who bear net costs and still have some excess left to make some people better-off.

Later in this chapter we present a benefit-cost analysis of an increased tax on alcohol. First, however, we set out the basic concepts that help us correctly identify, measure, and compare costs and benefits.

THE BASIC CONCEPTS

Benefit-cost analysis proceeds in four steps: (1) identifying relevant impacts, (2) monetizing impacts, (3) discounting for time and risk, and (4) choosing among policies. We organize our discussion of the basic concepts underlying benefit-cost analysis according to these steps.

[3]We recommend Edward M. Gramlich, *Benefit-Cost Analysis of Government Programs* (Englewood Cliffs, N.J.: Prentice Hall, 1981); and Robert Sugden and Alan H. Williams, *The Principles of Practical Cost-Benefit Analysis* (New York: Oxford University Press, 1978). Other possibilities include: E. J. Mishan, *Cost-Benefit Analysis* (New York: Praeger, 1976); Mark S. Thompson, *Benefit-Cost Analysis for Program Evaluation* (Beverly Hills, Calif.: Sage Publications, 1980); Lee G. Anderson and Russell F. Settle, *Benefit-Cost Analysis: A Practical Guide* (Lexington, Mass.: Lexington Books, 1977); and Arnold C. Harberger, *Project Evaluation* (Chicago: Markham, 1972). For survey articles, see A. R. Prest and R. Turvey, "Cost-Benefit Analysis: A Survey," *Economic Journal*, Vol. 75, No. 300, 1965, pp. 685–705; and Richard A. Musgrave, "Cost-Benefit Analysis and the Theory of Public Finance," *Journal of Economic Literature*, Vol. 7, No. 3, 1969, pp. 797–806.

Identifying Relevant Impacts

The first step in benefit-cost analysis is to identify all the impacts of the policy under consideration and categorize them as either costs or benefits for various groups. This immediately raises a key issue: Who has standing?[4] That is, whose utility should we consider when assessing costs and benefits? The question almost always arises in the context of choosing geographic boundaries. It also arises, however, when persons either cannot articulate their preferences or articulate preferences that society considers invalid.

Geographic Extent. The most inclusive definition of society encompasses all people, no matter where they live or to which government they owe allegiance.[5] Analysts working for the United Nations or some other international organization might very well adopt such a universalistic perspective. Analysts employed by their national governments, however, would most likely view their countrymen, perhaps including residents of their countries who are not citizens, as the relevant societies for considering economic efficiency. Impacts that accrue outside national boundaries are typically ignored for purposes of measuring changes in economic efficiency. Of course, these external impacts may have political implications—for instance, Canadians would undoubtedly voice strong opposition to any U. S. policies that further exacerbate their acid rain problem. Because the political importance of externalities cannot always be readily determined, it is usually best to begin by listing *all* identifiable impacts, whether they are internal or external to the national society. Explicit judgments can then be made about which externalities should be ignored, which monetized (usually a heroic task!), and which highlighted as "other considerations."

The issue of geographic standing often arises for analysts working for subnational governments. For example, consider a city that is deciding whether to build a convention center. Assume that a benefit-cost analysis from the social perspective (giving standing to everyone in the country) predicts that the project will generate costs in excess of benefits of $1 million. Also assume, however, that the central government will pay $2 million of the costs of this particular project through an intergovernmental grants program. Because the residents of the city contribute a negligible fraction of the total taxes collected by the central government, the grant appears to city residents as a $2 million benefit offsetting $2 million in costs. Thus, from the perspective of the city, the convention center appears to generate $1 million in net benefits rather than $1 million in net costs.

A variety of externalities, or spillovers, can cause a divergence between aggregate social welfare and the welfare of local governments. We can divide them into two broad categories: fiscal and economic.

[4]Our treatment of this topic benefited greatly from Dale Whittington and Duncan MacRae, Jr., "The Issue of Standing in Cost-Benefit Analysis," *Journal of Policy Analysis and Management*, Vol. 5, No. 4, Summer 1986, pp. 665–82. The term *standing* has its origins in the legal doctrine "standing to sue": plaintiffs have standing if they have a legally protectible and tangible interest at stake in the litigation. See *Black's Law Dictionary*, 5th ed., 1979, p. 1260.

[5]Some would argue that even future generations should be included in the definition of society. We will address the implications of this in our discussion of discounting.

Fiscal externalities, like the intergovernmental grant in the example, transfer wealth, or rents, across the boundaries of local jurisdictions. In a benefit-cost analysis from the perspective of aggregate social welfare, a fiscal externality appears as offsetting costs and benefits to different groups in society and therefore does not influence the final calculation of net benefits. For example, a program that lured a firm from one city to another typically involves costs for one city that offset the gross benefits accruing to the other.

Economic externalities, as discussed in Chapter 3, directly affect the capability of some persons outside of the jurisdiction to either produce or consume. For example, if an upstream city upgrades its sewage treatment plant, then cities downstream enjoy cleaner water, which may enhance the recreational value of the river and perhaps reduce the cost of producing potable water. Although the upstream city might not count these downstream benefits in its benefit-cost analysis of the treatment plant, they should be included in a benefit-cost analysis from the perspective of social welfare.

How should analysts treat costs and benefits that are external to their clients' jurisdictions? We believe that analysts should estimate costs and benefits from the perspectives of their clients *and* society. The benefit-cost analysis from the perspective of society indicates what should be done in an ideal world. The benefit-cost analysis from the perspective of the local jurisdiction indicates what should be done to serve the direct interests of the client's constituency and, therefore, the political interests of the client. As an analyst, if you do not note significant externalities, you are failing in your duty to inform your client about appropriate values; if you do not clearly indicate the costs and benefits accruing to your client's constituency, you are probably failing in your responsibility to represent your client's interests.

Persons and Preferences.   Should all persons within a jurisdiction have standing? Beyond citizens, almost everyone would agree that costs and benefits incurred by legal residents should be counted. What about those incurred by illegal aliens? The answer may depend on the nature of the costs and benefits. For example, if they result from direct changes in health and safety, we might be more inclined to count them than if they result from changes in incomes. The same reasoning probably applies to citizens convicted of serious crimes. Obviously, however, such questions about standing raise difficult ethical issues. Indeed, when such questions are central to the identification of relevant impacts, multigoal, rather than benefit-cost, analysis is likely to be the more appropriate method.

The issue of standing also arises with respect to the expression of preferences. Do families and other institutions adequately articulate what would be the informed preferences of children, the insane, and other persons with limited ability to reason? Do markets and other institutions adequately express the preferences of future generations for such amenities as environmental quality? In other words, should we give special attention to impacts on any particular groups within society? Also, should we accept all preferences as valid? For example, burglars would undoubtedly view reductions in the monetary take from their crimes as a cost of an enforcement policy. Yet most analysts would not include this cost in their evaluation of the policy.[6] As with the other questions about standing, when these issues become central, we should carefully reconsider the appropriateness of benefit-cost analysis as the method of evaluation.

Summary.   The first step in benefit-cost analysis is to identify all relevant impacts and classify them as either costs or benefits for various groups. It is best to start out by being inclusive of any affected groups. Reasoned arguments can then be made to exclude those groups that you believe should not have standing. When a client has a subnational constituency, it is usually desirable to estimate costs and benefits from the perspectives of both the national society and the constitutency. If it appears that issues of standing will be central to your analysis, then you should consider switching from the benefit-cost framework to multigoal analysis.

Monetizing Impacts

The basic principle underlying benefit-cost analysis is the Kaldor-Hicks criterion: a policy should be adopted only if those who will gain could fully compensate losers and still be better-off.[7] In other words, when efficiency is the only relevant value, a *necessary* condition for adopting a policy is that it have the potential to be Pareto improving. As we discussed in Chapter 3, policies that increase social surplus are potentially Pareto improving and therefore meet the Kaldor-Hicks criterion. Further, when considering mutually exclusive policies, the one that produces the greatest increase in social surplus should be selected because, if adopted, it would be possible through the payment of compensation to make everyone at least as well-off as they would have been under any of the alternative policies.

Many economists treat the move from the Pareto-improving criterion to the *potentially* Pareto-improving criterion as if it were a minor step. It is not. Actual Pareto-improving exchanges are voluntary and, by definition, make someone better-off without making anyone else worse-off. Potential Pareto-improving moves do not guarantee that no one is made worse-off—just that everyone could be made better-off with appropriate redistribution following the move. Thus, while the Kaldor-Hicks criterion is ingenious in that it is Pareto-like, it is also controversial. As Richard Posner, among others, forcefully argues, benefit-cost analysis

---

[6]Some analysts would count a part of the reduction in monetary returns from crime as a cost. See, for example, David A. Long, Charles D. Mallar, and Craig V. D. Thornton, "Evaluating the Benefits and Costs of the Job Corps," *Journal of Policy Analysis and Management*, Vol. 1, No. 1, Fall 1981, pp. 55-76.

[7]N. Kaldor, "Welfare Propositions of Economics and Interpersonal Comparisons of Utility," *Economic Journal*, Vol. 49, No. 195, September 1939, pp. 549-52; and J. R. Hicks, "The Valuation of the Social Income," *Economica*, Vol. 7, No. 26, May 1940, pp. 105-124. The principle can also be stated as suggested by Hicks: adopt a policy only if it would not be in the self-interest of those who will lose to bribe those who will gain not to adopt it. Although these formulations are not conceptually identical (Kaldor's is based on compensating variation; Hick's is based on equivalent variation), they usually lead to the same result when applied in practical situations. Consequently, they are usually discussed as a single criterion.

based on the Kaldor-Hicks criterion contains elements of utilitarianism ("the surplus of pleasure over pain—aggregated across all of the inhabitants of society") that the pure Pareto criterion avoids.[8] Most fundamentally, the aggregation underlying the Kaldor-Hicks criterion implicitly compares utility across individuals.[9] Nevertheless, it provides a good test for determining if policies could be efficient, if not a fully acceptable rule for choosing among policies.

In practice, two related concepts serve as guides for estimating changes in social surplus and, therefore, for applying the Kaldor-Hicks criterion: opportunity cost and willingness to pay. They provide ways of monetizing costs and benefits.

Valuing Inputs: Opportunity Cost. Public policies usually require resources (factor inputs) that could instead be used to produce other goods. Some examples: public works projects such as dams, bridges, and highways require labor, materials, land, and equipment; social service programs typically require professional services and office space; and wilderness preserves, recreational areas, and parks require at least land. The resources used to implement these policies cannot be used to produce other goods. The values of the forgone goods measure the costs of policies. In general, the *opportunity cost* of a policy is the value of the required resources in their best alternative use.

The nature of the market for a resource determines how we go about measuring its opportunity cost. Three situations arise: (1) the market for the resource is efficient (no market failures), and purchases for the project will have a negligible effect on price (constant marginal costs); (2) the market for the resource is efficient, but purchases for the project will have a noticeable effect on price (rising or falling marginal costs); and (3) the market for the resource is inefficient (market failure).

Efficient Markets and Negligible Price Effects. In an efficient market the equilibrium price equals the marginal social cost of production. The amount that must be paid to purchase one additional unit exactly equals the opportunity cost of that unit. Because marginal cost is constant (the supply curve is perfectly elastic), we can continue to purchase additional units at the original price. The opportunity cost of the marginal units is simply the total amount we spend to purchase them.

Panel (a) in Figure 7.1 illustrates the opportunity cost of purchases in efficient factor markets with constant marginal cost. Purchasing q' units of the factor for a public project can be thought of as shifting the demand schedule for the factor, D, to the right by a horizontal distance of q'. (Strictly speaking, D is a derived demand schedule—it represents the marginal valuations of various quantities of the factor that derive from their use in producing goods that consumers directly demand.) Because marginal cost (MC) is constant, price remains at P_0. The total amount spent on the factor used by the project is P_0 times q', which

[8]Richard Posner, *The Economics of Justice* (Cambridge, Mass.: Harvard University Press, 1983), p. 49. For a discussion of the same point from a very different perspective, see Steven Kelman, "Cost-Benefit Analysis: An Ethical Critique," *Regulation*, January/February 1981, pp. 33–40.

[9]For a fuller discussion of this issue, see Walter Hettick, "Distribution in Benefit-Cost Analysis: A Review of the Theoretical Issues," *Public Finance Quarterly*, Vol. 4, No. 2, April 1976, pp. 123–51.

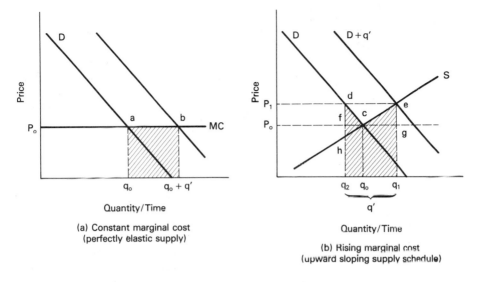

Figure 7.1 Measuring Opportunity Cost in Efficient Factor Markets

equals the area of the shaded rectangle ab $(q_0 + q')$ q_0, the total social cost of using q' units of the factor for the public project. If the q' units are not used for the project, then P_0 times q' worth of goods could be produced elsewhere in the economy. Thus, this public expenditure exactly equals the opportunity cost of using q' units of the factor for the project.

Because most factors have neither steeply rising nor declining marginal cost schedules, interpreting expenditures as opportunity costs is usually reasonable when the quantity purchased makes a small addition to the total demand for the factor. For example, consider a proposed remedial reading program for a school district. The textbooks, which are purchased in a national market, undoubtedly represent only a small addition to total demand for textbooks and hence result in a negligible increase in their price. In contrast, to hire qualified reading teachers for the program in the local labor market may require higher salaries than those being paid to the reading teachers already employed.

Efficient Markets with Noticeable Price Effects.   Panel (b) in Figure 7.1 illustrates the effect of factor purchases when marginal costs are increasing so that the supply schedule is upward sloping. As in panel (a), purchase of q' units of the factor for use by the public project shifts the demand schedule to the right. Because the supply schedule (S) is upward sloping, the equilibrium price rises from P_0 to P_1. The total expenditure on the q' units of the factor needed for the project is P_1 times q', which equals the area of rectangle $q_2 d e q_1$.

Unlike the case in which marginal costs are constant, this expenditure is not the opportunity cost of using q' units of the factor for the project. When purchases for a project induce a price change in a factor market, the effects of the price change on social surplus within the market must be taken into account when calculating opportunity cost. *The general rule is that opportunity cost equals expenditure less (plus) any increase (decrease) in social surplus occurring in the factor market itself.* In other words, expenditures do not accurately represent opportunity costs when purchases cause social surplus changes in factor markets.

Referring again to panel (b) in Figure 7.1, we can identify the changes in producer and consumer surplus that result from the increase in price from P_0 to P_1. Producer surplus increases by the area of trapezoid $P_1 ecP_0$ (the increase in the area below price and above the supply schedule). At the same time consumer surplus decreases by the area of trapezoid $P_1 dcP_0$ (the decrease in the area above price and below the demand schedule). Subtracting the loss in consumer surplus from the gain in producer surplus leaves a net gain in social surplus in the factor market equal to the area of triangle *cde*. Subtracting this social surplus gain from the expenditure on the q' units of the factor needed for the project yields the opportunity cost represented by the shaded area within the geometric figure $q_2 dceq_1$. Note that calculation of this area is straightforward when the supply and demand schedules are linear—it is the amount of the factor purchased for the project, q', multiplied by the average of the old and new prices, $1/2(P_1 + P_0)$.[10]

An alternative explanation may be helpful in understanding why the shaded area represents opportunity cost. Imagine that the government obtains the q' units of the output by first restricting supply to the market from q_0 to q_2 and then ordering the firms in the industry to produce q' for the government at cost. The social surplus loss resulting from restricting market supply to q_2 is the area of triangle *cdh*, the deadweight loss. The total cost of producing the q' units for the government is the area of trapezoid $q_2 heq_1$. Adding these areas gives the same opportunity cost as calculated under the assumption that the government purchases the factor like any other participant in the market. It is interesting to note, however, that while public expenditures on the factor exceed opportunity cost when the government purchases it like everyone else, expenditure falls short of opportunity cost when government obtains the factor through directives. In other words, budgetary cost can either understate or overstate social opportunity cost.

Inefficient Markets.   In an efficient market, price equals marginal cost. Whenever price does not equal marginal cost, allocative inefficiency results. As we saw in Chapters 3 and 4, a variety of circumstances can lead to inefficiency: absence of a working market, market failures (public goods, externalities, natural monopolies, and information asymmetries), markets with few sellers, and distortions due to government interventions (such as taxes, subsidies, price ceilings, and price floors). Any of these distortions can arise in factor markets, complicating the estimation of opportunity cost.

Consider a proposal to establish more courts so that more criminal trials can be held. Budgetary costs will include the salaries of judges and court attendants, rent for courtrooms and offices, and perhaps expenditures for additional correctional facilities (because the greater availability of trial capacity may permit more vigorous prosecution). The budget may also show payments to jurors. Usually, however, these payments just cover commuting expenses. Compensa-

---

[10]Exactly one-half of the area of rectangle *degf* is shaded (with a bit of geometry one can show that the area of triangle *cdf* plus the area of triangle *ceg* equals the area of triangle *cde*). Therefore, the total shaded area equals $1/2(P_1 - P_0) \times q'$ plus $P_0 \times q'$, which equals $1/2 (P_1 + P_0) \times q'$, the average price times the quantity purchased.

tion paid to jurors for their time is typically not related to their wage rate, but rather set at a nominal per diem rate. Thus, the budgetary outlay for payments to jurors almost certainly understates the opportunity cost of the jurors' time. A better estimate of opportunity cost would be commuting expenses plus the number of juror-hours times either the average or the median hourly wage rate for the locality. The commuting expenses estimate the resource costs of transporting the jurors to the court; the hourly wage rate times the hours spent on jury duty estimates the value of goods forgone because of lost labor.

Assessing opportunity costs in the presence of market failures or government interventions requires a careful accounting of social surplus changes. For example, let us examine the opportunity costs of labor in a market where either minimum wage laws or union bargaining power keeps the wage rate above the market clearing level. In Figure 7.2, the preproject demand schedule for labor, D, and the supply schedule for labor, S, intersect at P_e, the equilibrium price in the absence of the wage floor, P_m. At the wage floor, L_s units of labor are offered but only L_d units are demanded so that $L_s - L_d$ units are "unemployed." Now imagine that L' units are hired for the project. This shifts the demand schedule to the right by L'. As long as L' is less than the quantity of unemployed labor, price will remain at the floor. The total expenditure on labor for the project is P_m times L', which equals the area of rectangle abL_tL_d. But the trapezoid $abcd$ represents producer surplus enjoyed by the newly hired and hence should be subtracted from the expenditure to obtain an opportunity cost equal to the shaded area inside trapezoid cdL_dL_t. Alternatively, we can think of the shaded area as the value of the leisure time (a good) given up by the newly hired workers.[11]

Other market distortions affect opportunity costs in predictable ways: In factor markets where supply is taxed, expenditures overestimate opportunity costs; in factor market where supply is subsidized, expenditures underestimate opportunity costs. In factor markets exhibiting positive externalities of supply, expenditures overestimate opportunity costs; in factor markets exhibiting negative externalities of supply, expenditures underestimate opportunity costs. In monopolistic factor markets, expenditures overestimate opportunity costs. To determine opportunity costs in these cases, apply the general rule: *opportunity cost equals expenditures on the factor plus (minus) gains (losses) in social surplus occurring in the factor market.*

A final point on opportunity costs: the relevant determination is what must be given up today and in the future, *not* what has already been given up. For instance, suppose that you are asked to reevaluate a decision to build a bridge after construction has already begun. What is the opportunity cost of the steel and concrete that is already in place? It is not the original expenditure made to purchase them. Rather, it is the value of these materials in the best alternative use—most likely measured by the maximum amount that they could be sold for as scrap. Conceivably, the cost of scrapping the materials may exceed their value in any alternative use so that salvaging them would not be justified. Indeed, if salvage is necessary, say for environmental or other reasons, then the opportunity cost of the material will be negative (and thus counted as a benefit) when calculating the net benefits of *continuing* construction. In situations where resources that have already been purchased have exactly zero scrap value (the case of labor

[11]For a more detailed treatment of the problem of assessing the opportunity costs of unemployed labor, see Edward M. Gramlich, *Benefit-Cost Analysis of Government Programs*, pp. 61–67.

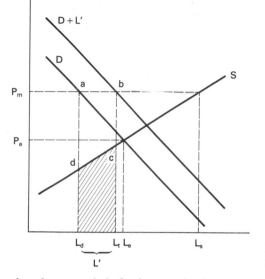

Figure 7.2 Opportunity Cost in a Factor Market with a Price Floor

already expended, for instance), the costs are *sunk* and are not relevant to our decisions concerning future actions.

Valuing Outcomes: Willingness to Pay. The valuation of policy outcomes is based on the concept of willingness to pay: *Benefits are the sum of the maximum amounts that people would be willing to pay to gain outcomes that they view as desirable; costs are the sum of the maximum amounts that people would be willing to pay to avoid outcomes that they view as undesirable.* Of course, estimating changes in social surpluses that occur in relevant markets enables us to take account of these costs and benefits. Three situations deserve consideration: (1) valuation in efficient market, (2) valuation in distorted markets, and (3) valuation in secondary markets that undergo substantial effects.

Efficient Markets. Valuation is relatively straightforward when the policies under consideration will affect the supply schedules of goods in efficient markets. A general guideline holds for assessing benefits: *the benefits of a policy equal the net revenue generated by the policy plus the social surplus changes in the markets in which the effects of the policy occur.* Note that the benefits can be either positive or negative. We generally refer to those that are negative as costs. Indeed, if we think of the use of factor inputs as an impact, then this statement of benefit calculation encompasses opportunity costs. In other words, depending on how we initially categorize policy impacts, we may measure any of them either as a cost or as a negative benefit.

Two situations are common: First, the policy may directly affect the quantity available to consumers. For example, opening a publicly operated day-care center shifts the supply schedule to the right—more day care is offered to consumers at each price. Second, the policy may shift the supply schedule by altering the price or availability of some factor used to produce the good. For example, deepening a harbor so that it can accommodate large, efficient ships reduces the costs of transporting bulk commodities to and from the port.

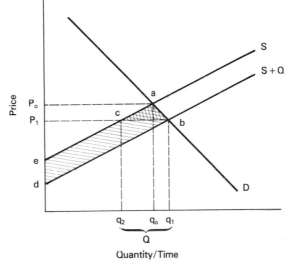

Social surplus charge:

(a) Direct supply of Q by project: gain of triangle abc
    plus project revenue equal to area of rectangle q_2cbq_1

(b) Supply schedule shift through cost reduction: gain
    of trapezoid abde

Figure 7.3   Measuring Benefits in an Efficient Market

Figure 7.3 shows the social surplus changes that result from additions to supply. The intersection of the demand schedule, D, and the supply schedule, S, indicates the equilibrium price, P_0, prior to the project. If the project directly adds a quantity, Q, to the market, then the supply schedule as seen by consumers shifts from S to $S + Q$, and the equilibrium price falls to P_1. If consumers must purchase the additional units from the project, then the gain in consumer surplus equals the area of trapezoid P_0abP_1. Because suppliers continue to operate on the original supply schedule, they suffer a loss of surplus equal to the area of trapezoid P_0acP_1 so that the net change in social surplus equals the area of triangle abc, which is darkly shaded. In addition, however, the project enjoys a revenue equal to P_1 times Q, the area of rectangle q_2cbq_1. So that the sum of project revenues and the change in social surplus in the market equals the area of trapezoid q_2cabq_1, which is the total benefits from the project selling Q units in the market.

What benefits accrue if the Q units are instead distributed free to selected consumers? If the Q units are given to consumers who would have purchased an identical or greater number of units at price P_1, then the benefit measure is exactly the same as when the project's output is sold. Even though no project revenues accrue, consumers enjoy a surplus that is greater by the area of rectangle q_2cbq_1, which exactly offsets the revenue that would accrue if the project's output is sold.

If the Q units are distributed to consumers in greater quantities than they would have purchased at price P_1, then area q_2cabq_1 will be the project's benefit only if these recipients can and do sell the excess quantities to those who would have bought them. If the recipients keep any of the excess units, then area q_2cabq_1

will overestimate the project's benefit in two ways. First, in contrast to the situation in which the Q units are sold, some consumers will value their marginal consumption at less than P_1. (If they valued it at or above P_1, they would have been willing to purchase at P_1.) Second, their added consumption shifts the demand schedule to the right so that the market price after provision of Q units by the project will not fall all the way to P_1. Even if the recipients do not keep any of the excess, the project's benefits may be smaller than the area of q_2cabq_1 because of transactions costs.

For example, suppose that the project provides previously stockpiled gasoline to low-income consumers during an oil supply disruption (an in-kind subsidy). Some of the recipients will find themselves with more gasoline than they would have purchased on their own at price P_1; therefore, they will try to sell the excess. Doing so will be relatively easy if access to the stockpiled gasoline is provided through legally transferable coupons; it would be much more difficult if the gasoline had to be physically taken away by the recipients. If the gasoline can be costlessly traded among consumers, then we would expect the outcome to be identical to the one that would result if the gasoline were sold in the market, with the revenue given directly to the low-income consumers.

Next suppose that the project, like the harbor deepening, lowers the cost of supplying the market. In this case, the supply schedule as seen by both consumers and producers shifts to $S + Q$, not because the project directly supplies Q to the market, but rather because reductions in the marginal costs of firms allow them to offer Q additional units profitably at each price along $S + Q$. As with the case of direct supply of Q, the new equilibrium price is P_1 and consumers gain surplus equal to the area of trapezoid P_0abP_1. Producers gain surplus equal to the difference in the areas of triangle P_0ae (the producer surplus with supply schedule S) and triangle P_1bd (the producer surplus with supply schedule $S + Q$). Area P_1ce is common to the two triangles and therefore cancels, leaving the area $ecbd$ minus the area P_0acP_1. Adding this gain to the gain in consumer surplus, which can be stated as area P_0acP_1 plus abc, leaves areas abc plus $cbde$. Thus, the gain in social surplus resulting from the project equals the area of trapezoid $abde$. Because no project revenue is generated, area $abde$ alone is the benefit of the project.

The straightforward measurement of willingness to pay illustrated in Figure 7.3 depends on two important assumptions: that the market is efficient and that effects in other markets can be ignored. We next relax these assumptions.

Distorted Markets. If market failures or government interventions distort the relevant product market, then the determination of the benefits and costs of policy effects is more difficult. Although the same general rule for measuring benefits continues to apply, complications arise in determining the correct social surplus changes in distorted (inefficient) markets. For example, a program that subsidizes the purchase of rodent extermination services in a poor neighborhood probably has an external effect: the fewer rodents in the neighborhood, the easier it is for residents in adjoining neighborhoods to keep their rodent populations under control. Thus, in Figure 7.4 we show the market demand schedule, D_m, as understating the social demand schedule, D_s so that the market equilibrium price (P_0) and quantity (q_0) are too low from the social perspective. What are the social benefits of a program that makes vouchers worth v dollars per unit of extermina-

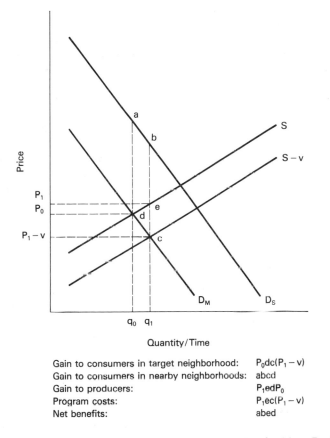

Gain to consumers in target neighborhood: $P_0dc(P_1 - v)$
Gain to consumers in nearby neighborhoods: abcd
Gain to producers: P_1edP_0
Program costs: $P_1ec(P_1 - v)$
Net benefits: abed

Figure 7.4 Social Benefits for Direct Supply of a Good with a Positive Externality

tion service available to residents of the poor neighborhood? When the vouchers become available, residents of the poor neighborhood see a supply schedule that is lower than the market supply schedule by v dollars. Consequently, they increase their purchases of extermination services from q_0 to q_1, and they see an effective price equal to the new market price less the per unit subsidy $(P_1 - v)$. Consumers in the targeted neighborhood enjoy a surplus gain equal to the area of trapezoid $P_0dc(P_1 - v)$; producers, who now see a price of P_1, receive a surplus gain equal to the area of trapezoid P_1edP_0; and people in the surrounding neighborhoods, who enjoy the positive externality, gain surplus equal to the area of parallelogram *abcd*, the area between the market and social demand schedules over the increase in consumption. Ignoring administrative costs, the program must pay out v times q_1, which equals the area of rectangle $P_1ec(P_1 - v)$. Subtracting this program cost from the gain in social surplus in the market yields net program benefits equal to the area of trapezoid *abed*.

Effects in Secondary Markets.   Many goods have important complements and substitutes. That is, a change in price of one good noticeably affects the demand for another. For example, stocking a lake near a city with game fish lowers the effective price of access to fishing grounds for the city residents. They will not only fish more but also demand more bait and other fishing equipment. We say that access to fishing grounds and fishing equipment are complements because a decrease (increase) in the price of one will result in increases (decreases) in the demand for the other. In contrast, fishing might very well be a substitute for golfing in the local market, so that as the price of fishing goes down (up) the demand for golfing goes down (up).

When should we ignore the secondary effects of policies on the markets for complements and substitutes? *We should ignore effects in a secondary market when two conditions hold: (1) price does not change in the secondary market **and** (2) the secondary market is undistorted.* When these conditions hold, attributing costs or benefits to secondary markets leads to double-counting errors. If we have no reason to believe that the fishing equipment market is distorted, and the supply schedule for fishing equipment is flat so that the price of fishing equipment remains unchanged when the demand schedule for fishing equipment shifts to the right, then the increased consumption of fishing equipment is not relevant to our benefit-cost analysis of a program to increase access to fishing grounds.

A closer look at the fishing example should make the rule for the treatment of secondary markets clearer. Panel (a) in Figure 7.5 shows the market for "fishing days." Prior to the stocking of the nearby lake, the effective price of a day of fishing (largely the time costs of travel) was P_{F0}, the travel cost to a lake much farther away. Once fishing is available at the nearby lake, the effective price falls to P_{F1}, and the number of days spent fishing by local residents rises from q_{F0} to q_{F1}. The resulting increase in social surplus equals the area of trapezoid $P_{F0}abP_{F1}$, the gain in consumer surplus. We measure this gain in consumer surplus using the demand schedule for fishing, D_F.

Now consider the market for fishing equipment. The decline in the effective price of fishing days shifts the demand schedule for fishing equipment from D_{E0} to D_{E1} as shown in panel (b) of Figure 7.5. If the supply schedule is perfectly elastic, the likely case when the local market accounts for only a small fraction of demand in the regional or national market, then the shift in demand will not increase the price of fishing equipment. Does the shift in demand for fishing equipment represent any change in consumer welfare? The answer is No. The entire change is measured in the fishing market using the demand schedule for fishing days, which gives consumers' valuations of increasing levels of fishing while holding the price of other goods, including fishing equipment, constant. As long as price does not change in the equipment market, the social surplus change in the fishing market is the entire benefit from the stocking project.[12]

[12]In situations where we cannot measure social surplus changes in primary markets, we may try to infer them from the demand shifts in secondary markets. For example, imagine that we have no information to help us determine the demand schedule for fishing days, but that we do have information to help us predict how the demand schedule for fishing equipment will change. For lack of a direct measure of benefits, we might take the difference between the social surplus in the fishing equipment market after the project (based on demand schedule D_{E1}) and the social surplus in the equipment market prior to the project (based on demand schedule D_{E0}). We would then apply some scaling factor to correct for underestimation that results from the fact that not all the consumer surplus from fishing will be reflected in the equipment market. (Some fishermen will fish with old equipment and self-collected bait—their surplus will not appear in the equipment market.)

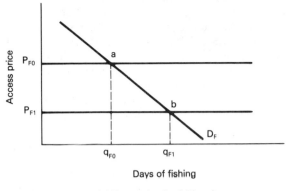

(a) The market for fishing days

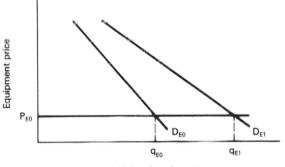

(b) The market for fishing equipment; perfectly elastic supply schedule

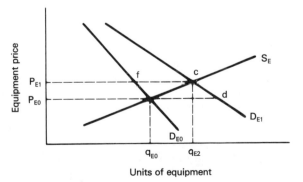

(c) The market for fishing equipment: upward sloping supply schedule

Figure 7.5   Valuation of Effects in Secondary Markets

The situation is different when the supply schedule in the secondary market is upward sloping. For example, in panel (c) of Figure 7.5 the supply schedule for fishing equipment is shown as S_E. (Perhaps the equipment is a special bait produced only in the local market.) Now price rises in the equipment market from P_{E0} to P_{E1}. This price rise is not taken into account in the consumer valuations represented in the demand schedule for fishing shown in panel (a). (Remember that the demand schedule for fishing assumes that the price of equipment remains unchanged.[13]) Therefore, the effect of the price rise must be taken into account in the equipment market. We do this by measuring social surplus effects of the price rise using the shifted demand schedule, D_{E1}, which takes account of the price change in the fishing days market. Producers gain surplus equal to the area of trapezoid $P_{E1}ceP_{E0}$. Consumers lose surplus equal to the area of trapezoid $P_{E1}cdP_{E0}$. Thus, the net loss in social surplus equals the area of triangle cde. We must subtract this loss from the social surplus gain in the fishing market to obtain the benefits of the project.

To see how market distortions complicate the valuation of effects in secondary markets, return to panel (b) of Figure 7.5. Imagine that the market price P_{E0} underestimates the marginal social cost by x cents. (Think of the equipment as lead sinkers, some of which eventually end up in the lake, where they poison ducks and other wildlife. The x cents would then represent the expected loss to wildlife from the sale of another sinker.) In this case, the expansion of consumption involves a social surplus loss equal to x times ($q_{E1} - q_{E0}$). This loss should be subtracted from the gain measured in the fishing market to obtain program benefits. In general, *quantity as well as price changes in distorted secondary markets are relevant in benefit-cost analysis.*

Despite these situations where the valuation of effects in secondary markets is conceptually correct, in practice you should be very cautious in including them in your benefit-cost analyses. Our advice is based on several considerations.

First, price changes in the secondary market are likely to be small. Most goods are neither strong complements nor strong substitutes so that large price changes in the primary markets are necessary to produce noticeable demand shifts in the secondary markets. Further, in the case of local policies, it is unlikely that demand shifts in secondary markets will be large enough to affect the prices of products sold in national markets.

Second, estimation problems usually preclude accurate measurement of welfare changes in secondary markets. Estimating own-price effects (how does the quantity demanded change as the price of the good changes?) is often difficult; estimating cross-price effects (how does the quantity of good Y demanded change as the price of good Z changes?) is more difficult yet. Consequently, we are rarely very confident of predictions of demand shifts in secondary markets.

---

[13]The change in price in the equipment market may induce a shift in the demand schedule for fishing. Taking account of the change in social surplus in the equipment market can be thought of as a way of correcting for the shift in the demand schedule. For more detailed discussions, see Robert Sugden and Alan H. Williams, *The Principles of Practical Cost-Benefit Analysis*, pp. 134–47; and Edward M. Gramlich, *Benefit-Cost Analysis of Government Programs*, pp. 83–87. For a more theoretical discussion that considers the limits of the basic supply and demand analysis, see Frank Camm, *Consumer Surplus, Demand Functions, and Policy Analysis* (Santa Monica, Calif.: Rand Corporation, R-3048-RC, 1983).

Third, it is tempting for advocates of the policy under consideration to claim benefits in secondary markets because the difficulty of predicting effects in these markets gives leeway for optimistic claims. Ironically, such claims cannot be justified unless the secondary market is distorted—when society is broadly defined, demand shifts in undistorted (efficient) secondary markets *always* involve social surplus losses.[14] Only when we restrict standing to some group smaller than society as a whole do undistorted secondary markets appear as sources of positive benefits. For example, if you are evaluating the stocking project from the perspective of the local county, then you might include as a benefit increases in sales tax revenue resulting from nonresidents buying fishing equipment in the county. Keep in mind, however, that from the broader social perspective these revenues simply represent a transfer from nonresidents to residents and therefore appear in the social benefit-cost analysis as exactly offsetting costs and benefits.

Summary.   Changes in social surplus serve as the basis for measuring the costs and benefits of policies. The concept of opportunity cost helps us value the inputs that policies divert from private use; the concept of willingness to pay helps us value policy outputs. The key to valuing outputs is to identify the primary markets in which they appear. When the outputs are not traded in organized markets, ingenuity is often needed to infer supply and demand schedules (remember the market for "fishing days"). Effects in undistorted secondary markets should be treated as relevant costs and benefits only if they involve price changes.

Discounting for Time and Risk

Policies often have effects far into the future. For example, deepening a harbor this year will allow large ships to use the harbor for perhaps a decade before dredging is again necessary. In determining the desirability of the harbor project, should we treat a dollar of benefit accruing next year as equivalent to a dollar of benefit accruing ten years from now? How should we take account of the possibility that dredging will be needed as soon as five years instead of the predicted ten? The concept of *present value* provides the basis for comparing costs and benefits that accrue at different times. The concept of *expected value* provides the commonly used approach to dealing with risky situations.

The Concept of Present Value.   Most of us would be unwilling to lend someone $100 today in return for a promise of payment of $100 in a year's time. We generally value $100 today more than the promise of $100 next year—even

---

[14]Panel (c) in Figure 7.5 illustrated the case of an outward shift in demand in a secondary market. We can use the same figure to illustrate the case of an inward shift in demand. Simply take D_{E1} as the original demand schedule and D_{E0} as the postproject demand schedule. Using the postproject demand schedule for measuring social surplus changes, we see that the price decline from P_{E1} to P_{E0} results in a producer surplus loss equal to the area of trapezoid $P_{E1}ceP_{E0}$ and a consumer surplus gain equal to the area of $P_{E1}feP_{E0}$ so that social surplus falls by the area of triangle fce. For further discussion, see Edward M. Gramlich, *Benefit-Cost Analysis of Government Programs*, Appendix to Chapter 5, pp. 83–87.

if we are certain that the promise will be carried out and that there will be no inflation. Perhaps $90 is the most that we would be willing to lend today in return for a promise of payment of $100 in a year's time. If so, we say that the present value of receiving $100 next year is $90. We can think of the $90 as the future payment *discounted* back to the present. Discounting is the standard technique for making costs and benefits accruing at different times commensurate.

Imagine that you are the economics minister of a small country. The curve connecting points X_1 and X_2 in Figure 7.6 indicates the various combinations of current (period 1) and future (period 2) production that your country's economy could achieve. By using available domestic resources to their fullest potential, your country could obtain any combination of production on the curve connecting X_1 and X_2. (The locus of these combinations is what economists call the *production possibility frontier* for your economy.) If all effort is put into current production, then X_1 can be produced and consumed in period 1, but production and consumption will fall to zero in period 2. Similarly, if all effort is put into preparing for production in period 2, then X_2 will be available in period 2 but there is no production in period 1. You undoubtedly find neither of these extremes attractive. Indeed, let us assume that you choose point i on the production possibility frontier as the combination of production and consumption in the two periods that you believe makes your country best-off. The curve labeled I_1 gives all the other hypothetical combinations of production and consumption in the two periods that you find equally satisfying to combination (q_1, q_2). You consider any point to the northeast of this indifference curve better than any point on it. Unfortunately, combination (q_1, q_2) is the best you can do with domestic resources alone.

Now suppose that you identify foreign banks that are willing to lend or borrow at an interest rate r. That is, the banks are willing to either lend or borrow one dollar in period 1 in return for the promise of repayment of $(1 + r)$ dollars in period 2. You realize that, with access to this capital market, you can expand your country's consumption possibilities. For instance, if you choose point j on the production possibility frontier in Figure 7.6, then you could achieve a consumption combination anywhere along the line with slope $-(1 + r)$ going through point j by either borrowing or lending. This line is shown as connecting points R_1 and R_2, where R_2 equals $(1 + r)R_1$. Each additional unit of consumption in period 1 costs $(1 + r)$ units of consumption in period 2; each additional unit of consumption in period 2 costs $1/(1 + r)$ units of consumption in period 1. Once these intertemporal trades are possible, your country's consumption possibility frontier expands from the original production possibility frontier connecting X_1 and X_2 to the discount line connecting R_1 and R_2.

The most favorable consumption possibility frontier results from choosing the production combination such that the discount rate line is just tangent to the production possibility frontier. Point j happens to be the point of tangency. The most desirable consumption opportunity is shown as point k, which is on your indifference curve I_2, the one with the highest utility that can be reached along the consumption possibility frontier (the line connecting R_1 and R_2). Thus your best policy is to set domestic production at x_1 and domestic consumption at c_1 in period 1, lending the difference $(x_1 - c_1)$ so that in period 2 your country can consume c_2, consisting of x_2 in domestic production and $(c_2 - x_2)$ (equal to $[1 + r]$ times $[x_1 - c_1]$ in repaid loans).

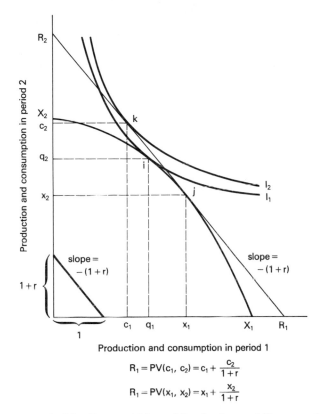

$$R_1 = PV(c_1,\ c_2) = c_1 + \frac{c_2}{1+r}$$

$$R_1 = PV(x_1,\ x_2) = x_1 + \frac{x_2}{1+r}$$

Figure 7.6   The Present Value of Production and Consumption

Note that the most desirable point on the production possibility frontier gives us the largest possible value for R_1. But R_1 can be interpreted as the present value of consumption, which is defined as the highest level of consumption that can be obtained in the present period (period 1). We write the present value of consumption as $PV(c_1,c_2)$ and the present value of production as $PV(x_1,x_2)$. Each of these present values equals R_1.

We can arrive at an algebraic expression for the present value of consumption as follows: First, note that the present value of c_1 is just c_1. Second, note that the maximum amount that could be borrowed against c_2 for current consumption is $c_2/(1 + r)$. Third, adding these two quantities together gives

$$PV\ (c_1,c_2)\ =\ c_1\ +\ \frac{c_2}{(1\ +\ r)}.$$

Similarly, we can express the present value of production as

$$PV\ (x_1,x_2)\ =\ x_1\ +\ \frac{x_2}{(1\ +\ r)}.$$

The present value formula is easily extended to more than two periods. For example, consider the present value of consumption in three periods, $PV(c_1,c_2,c_3)$.

If we are in the second period, the present value of future consumption is $a_2 = c_2 + c_3/(1 + r)$, the maximum quantity of consumption in the second period that can be obtained from c_2 and c_3. Now step back to the first period. The present value of consumption equals $c_1 + a_2/(1 + r)$, which by substitution gives

$$PV\ (c_1, c_2, c_3)\ =\ c_1\ +\ \frac{c_2}{(1 + r)}\ +\ \frac{c_3}{(1 + r)^2}.$$

In general, we can write the present value for N periods as

$$PV(c_1, c_2, c_3, \ .\ .\ .\ , c_N)\ =\ c_1\ +\ \frac{c_2}{(1 + r)}\ +\ \frac{c_3}{(l + r)^2}\ +\ .\ .\ .\ +\ \frac{c_N}{(1 + r)^M},$$

where $M = N - 1$.

The key to understanding the use of present value in benefit-cost analysis is to recognize that at point k in Figure 7.6 you are indifferent between having one additional unit of consumption in period 1 and $(1 + r)$ additional units in period 2. (The slope of I_2 at k, which gives your marginal rate of substitution between consumption in the two periods, equals the slope of the discount line.) Thus, in evaluating policies that make small changes to your consumption in the two periods, you should treat one dollar of change in period 1 as equivalent to $1/(1 + r)$ dollars of change in period 2. This is equivalent to taking the present value of the changes.

In an economy with a perfect capital market, all consumers see the same interest rate so that they all have the same marginal rates of substitution between current and future consumption. Because everyone is willing to trade current and future consumption at the same rate, it is natural to interpret the interest rate as the appropriate social rate for discounting changes in social surplus occurring in different periods so that they can be added to measure changes in social welfare. Later in this chapter we discuss the appropriateness of interpreting market interest rates as social discount rates.

When doing benefit-cost analysis, we apply the discounting procedure by converting benefits and costs to present values. So, for instance, if benefits B_t and costs C_t occur t periods beyond the current period, then their contribution to the present value of net benefits equals $(B_t - C_t)/(1 + d)^t$ where d is the social discount rate. The present value of net benefits equals the sum of the discounted net benefits that occur in all periods.

We illustrate discounting with a simple example. Consider a city that uses a rural landfill to dispose of solid refuse. By adding larger trucks to the refuse fleet, the city would be able to save $100,000 in disposal costs during the first year after purchase and a similar sum each successive year of use. The trucks can be purchased for $500,000 and sold for $200,000 after four years. (The city expects to open a resource recovery plant in four years that will obviate the need for landfill disposal.) The city can currently borrow money at an interest rate of 10 percent. Should the city buy the trucks? Yes, if the present value of net benefits is positive.

To calculate the present value of net benefits, we must decide whether to work with *real* or *nominal* dollars—either one will lead to the same answer as long as we use it consistently.

Real, or constant, dollars control for changing purchasing power by adjusting for price inflation. When we compare incomes in different years, we typically use the purchasing power in some base year as a standard. For example, nominal per capita personal income in the United States was $3,945 in 1970 and $9,503 in 1980. If you have ever listened to an older person reminisce, you know that a dollar purchased more in 1970 than it did in 1980. The Consumer Price Index (CPI) is the most commonly used measure of changing purchasing power.[15] It is based on the cost of purchasing a standard market basket of goods. The cost in any year is expressed as the ratio of the cost of purchasing the basket in the current year to the cost of purchasing it in some base year. For instance, using 1972 as the base year, real per capita personal income was $4,265 in 1970 and $5,303 in 1980. Thus, while nominal per capita personal income rose over the decade by 141 percent, real per capita income rose by only 24 percent.

In benefit-cost analysis, we are looking into the future. Obviously, we cannot know precisely how price inflation will change the purchasing power of future dollars. Nevertheless, if we take the nominal market interest rate facing the city as its discount rate, then we must estimate future costs and benefits in inflated dollars. The reason is that the market interest rate incorporates the expected rate of inflation—lenders do not want to be repaid in inflated dollars. Thus *one appropriate approach to discounting is to apply the nominal discount rate to future costs and benefits that are expressed in nominal dollars*.

The righthand side of Figure 7.7 shows nominal benefits assuming a 4 percent annual rate of inflation. Assuming that the projected annual savings of $100,000 in years two, three, and four represent a simple extrapolation of the savings in the first year, and that the $200,000 liquidation benefit is based on the current price of used trucks, we can interpret these amounts as being expressed in constant dollars. (We are implicitly assuming that wage rates, gasoline prices, and other prices that figure into the benefit calculations increase at the same rate as the general price level.) To convert from real to nominal dollars, we simply multiply the amount in each year by $(1 + i)^M$, where i is the assumed rate of inflation and M equals the number of years beyond the current year that the costs and benefits accrue. For instance, the $100,000 of real savings in the fourth year would be $112,490 in nominal fourth-year dollars if the inflation rate held steady over the period at 4 percent. Using the 10 percent market interest rate seen by the city as the nominal discount rate, the present value of net benefits from purchasing the new trucks is $28,250. Thus, as long as no alternative equipment configuration offering a greater present value of net benefits can be identified, the city should purchase the trucks.

An alternative method of discounting leads to the same present value of net benefits: *apply a real discount rate to future costs and benefits that are expressed in constant (real) dollars*. Projecting costs and benefits in constant dollars (that is, ignoring inflation) is natural. The difficulty arises in determining the appropriate discount rate. Nominal interest rates are directly observable in the marketplace; real in-

---

[15]A broader measure is the *implicit deflator for gross national product* (GNP), which is the ratio of GNP measured at current prices to GNP measured at prices in some base year. Whereas CPI is based on a standard market basket of consumer goods, the implicit deflator for GNP is a comprehensive price index.

	Yearly Net Benefits Based on Real Dollars	Yearly Net Benefits Assuming 4% Annual Inflation
Year 1: Purchase	− $500,000	− $500,000
Savings	$100,000	$100,000
Year 2: Savings	$100,000	$104,000
Year 3: Savings	$100,000	$108,160
Year 4: Savings	$100,000	$112,490
Year 5: Liquidation	$200,000	$233,970

	Present Value of Net Benefits Using Real Discount Rate (d) of 5.77%:	Present Value of Net Benefits Using Nominal Discount Rate (r) of 10%:
	$28,250	$28,250

Let r = nominal discount rate
 d = real discount rate
 i = expected inflation rate

then $(1 + r) = (1 + d)(1 + i)$ If r = .10 and i = .04, then d = 5.77%
$d = (r - i)/(1 + i)$

Figure 7.7   The Present Value of the Net Benefits of Investment in New Garbage Trucks

terest rates are not. So when we decide that the interest rate facing the decision maker is the appropriate discount rate, we must adjust the observable nominal rates to arrive at real rates. This requires us to estimate the expected inflation rate just as we must if we decide to work with nominal costs and benefits. The real interest rate approximately equals the nominal interest rate minus the expected rate of inflation. More precisely:

$$d = (r - i)/(1 + i)$$

where d is the real discount rate, r is the nominal discount rate, and i is the expected rate of inflation.[16]

For our city, which sees a nominal discount rate of 10 percent and expects a 4 percent inflation rate, the real discount rate is 5.77 percent. Applying this real discount rate to the yearly real costs and benefits in the lefthand column of Figure 7.7 yields a present value of net benefits equal to $28,250. Thus, discounting real costs and benefits with the real discount rate is equivalent to discounting nominal costs and benefits with the nominal discount rate. As long as we use either real dollars and real discount rates or nominal dollars and nominal discount rates, we will arrive at the same present value.

---

[16]The real discount rate equals the nominal rate less the expected inflation rate when discounting is done continuously rather than by discrete period. (Think of the distinction between annual and continuous compounding of interest.) In discounting by discrete period, we can separate the nominal discount factor $(1 + r)$ into the product of the real discount factor $(1 + d)$ and the constant dollar correction $(1 + i)$. From the expression $(1 + r) = (1 + d)(1 + i)$, we can solve for $d = (r - i)/(1 + i)$.

The desirability of a policy often depends critically on the choice of discount rate. Policies that involve building facilities, establishing organizations, or investing in human capital usually accrue costs before benefits: *when costs precede benefits, the lower the discount rate used, the greater is the present value of net benefits*. Because analysts always have some uncertainty about the precise value of the appropriate discount rate, advocates of policies often argue for the lower discount rates than those who oppose them.

As an illustration, look at the present value of net benefits of the truck purchase. The curve in Figure 7.8 displays the present value of net benefits as a function of the real discount rate. Note that the present value is greatest when the real discount rate is zero. Indeed, it is more than three times larger than the present value based on the 5.77 percent real discount rate used in Figure 7.7. Also note that, for discount rates greater than about 8.4 percent, the present value becomes negative. We can think of 8.4 percent as the break-even point—present value is positive for smaller discount rates and negative for larger ones.

When disagreement about the appropriate discount rate is likely, we recommend that you generate a curve, similar to that in Figure 7.8, showing the present value of net benefits as a function of the discount rate. (You can do so fairly easily by using a spreadsheet program on a personal computer.) You can then indicate to your client how small the discount rate must be for the policy under consideration to offer positive net benefits.[17]

The Concept of Expected Value.   Future costs and benefits can never be known with absolute certainty. Often, however, we know that certain future conditions, or contingencies, will influence costs and benefits. If we know which contingencies will arise, then we can make a much more accurate prediction. For example, if at least one major flood occurs in a river valley sometime over the next twenty years, then we might predict the present value of net benefits of building a dam to be, say, $25 million. If, on the other hand, a major flood does not occur, then we might predict the present value of net benefits of building the dam to be − $5 million. Of course, we do not know with certainty which of these contingencies will actually occur.

When dealing with contingencies in benefit-cost analysis, the standard approach is to assign probabilities to the various contingencies so that expected net benefits can be calculated. In common terminology, we convert the decision problem from one of uncertainty to one of risk by specifying contingencies and their probabilities of occurrence.

Once we have converted the problem to one of risk, we can apply the standard techniques of decision analysis.[18] Specifically, we follow a four-step pro-

---

[17]The discount rate at which the present value of net benefits equals zero is called the *internal rate of return*. Some analysts advocate the following decision rule: choose the project with the highest internal rate of return. Edward Gramlich gives good reasons why this decision rule should *not* be used: First, it is possible that a project will have more than one internal rate of return, raising the question of which is the appropriate one for comparative purposes. Second, because the internal rate of return is not defined for projects that involve only current period costs and benefits, it does not always allow us to rank all alternative projects. Edward M. Gramlich, *Benefit-Cost Analysis of Government Programs*, p. 93.

[18]For introductions to decision analysis, see Robert D. Behn and James W. Vaupel, *Quick Analysis for Busy Decision Makers* (New York: Basic Books, 1982); and Howard Raiffa, *Decision Analysis* (Reading, Mass.: Addison-Wesley, 1968).

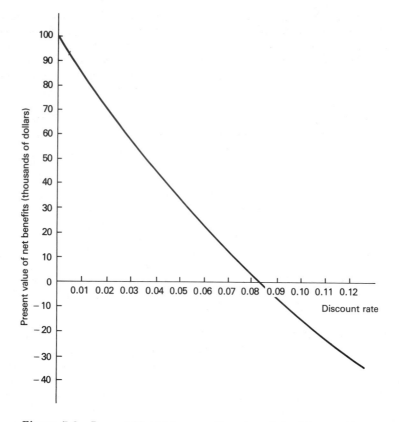

Figure 7.8   Present Net Value as a Function of the Discount Rate

cedure: First, identify a set of mutually exclusive contingencies that cover all possibilities. For example, "one or more major floods in the next twenty years" and "no major floods in the next twenty years" are mutually exclusive and exhaust the possibilities. Second, for the policy being evaluated (the dam), estimate the present value of net benefits under each contingency ($25 million if one or more major floods, – $5 million if no major floods). Third, assign a probability of occurrence to each contingency such that the probabilities sum to one. For instance, if, over the last 100 years, there were two major floods in the river valley, then we might estimate the annual probability of a major flood occurring as 0.02 so that the probability of one or more floods in the next twenty years is 0.33;[19] the probability of a major flood not occurring would be one minus the probability of a major flood occurring, or 0.67. Fourth, multiply the present value of net benefits for each contingency by the probability that the contingency will occur and sum to arrive at the expected value of present net benefits. To find the ex-

---

[19]The probability of no flooding in any year equals 1 – .02 = 0.98. Assuming that the probability of flooding in any year is independent of the probability in any other year, then the probability of at least one flood in the next twenty years is 1 – .98^{20} = .33.

pected value of present net benefits for the dam, for example, we evaluate the expression,

$$(0.33)(\$25 \text{ million}) + (0.67)(- \$5 \text{ million}),$$

which equals \$4.9 million.

In evaluating policies that have effects extending over a number of years, it is often appropriate to calculate the expected net benefits for each year and then discount to arrive at the present value of expected net benefits. For example, if we are evaluating a dam, we would almost certainly want our measure of net benefits to reflect when in the dam's twenty-year useful life the major flood would occur. (Only if we believe that the value of avoided loss from a major flood grows at a yearly rate exactly equal to the discount rate would the timing of the flood be irrelevant.) To do this, we use our estimate of the annual probability of there being a major flood (.02—two flood years in the last century) so that we can calculate the expected value of net benefits for the ith year as: $ENB_i = (0.02)NB_{Fi} + (0.98)NB_{NFi}$ where NB_{Fi} equals the net benefits accruing in the ith year if a major flood occurs and NB_{NFi} equals the net benefits accruing in the ith year if a major flood does not occur. The present value of expected net benefits for the dam is the sum of these yearly expected values discounted back to the present.

When we calculate expected net benefits on a yearly basis, we can allow for changing probabilities. For instance, if we believe that deforestation accompanying population growth in the river valley will gradually increase the chances of a major flood above the historical frequency, we can estimate yearly probabilities on the basis of either a hydrological model or some expert opinion and use them in our yearly calculations. Obviously, the more speculative the probabilities that we use, the more important it is that we test the sensitivity of the present value of expected net benefits to changes in the probabilities. (Again, you will find this relatively easy if you use a spreadsheet program on a personal computer.)

For most of us, the use of expected net benefits makes intuitive sense. Is its use conceptually valid as well? If we imagine society choosing among a large number of independent policies with relatively small marginal impacts, then the answer is Yes—adopting policies with positive expected net benefits will generally increase economic efficiency. As the number of policies adopted according to the expected value rule increases, the probability that their aggregate effect will be an increase in efficiency approaches certainty.

When the net benefits that will actually result from policies are not independent, the averaging process will not necessarily reduce the probability of an aggregate efficiency loss to a vanishingly small level.[20] For example, imagine a dozen industrial development projects, each of which offers positive expected net benefits but will actually yield only positive net benefits if no flood occurs in the

---

[20]In situations involving collective risk, the appropriate benefit measure at the individual level is the *option price*, the maximum certain payment that the person would make to obtain the project. Social benefits would then be the sum of individual option prices. See Daniel A. Graham, "Cost-Benefit Analysis under Uncertainty," *American Economic Review*, Vol. 71. No. 4, September 1981, pp. 715–25. Unfortunately, it is generally not possible to estimate option prices from market data.

river valley over the next twenty years. If the river valley were the one in our previous example, there would remain a .33 chance that the collection of projects will result in a net efficiency loss.

Special care should be taken when using the expected net benefits rule in the evaluation of projects from the perspective of local governments. Telling a mayor that a project offers positive expected net benefits may not be as important as telling her that, if 100 cities like hers adopt a particular type of project, about sixty will enjoy large benefits and about forty will suffer large costs. The mayor may be unwilling to accept such a high probability of project failure. Generally, local jurisdictions have less opportunity to spread risk through pooling than do central governments. We should therefore not be surprised to find local decision makers exhibiting risk aversion in the evaluation of major projects. Our analyses, therefore, should not only report the expected net benefits but also our estimates of the probabilities that projects will actually yield positive net benefits.

Summary. People generally value a dollar today more than the promise of a dollar tomorrow; they generally prefer a certain dollar more than the chance of receiving a dollar. Therefore, benefit-cost analysis requires us to discount for time and risk. Costs and benefits accruing in different time periods should be discounted to their present values. We can use either the real discount rate with constant dollars or the nominal discount rate with nominal dollars to arrive at present values. When we are able to express our uncertainty about costs and benefits in terms of contingencies and their probabilities, we can calculate expected net benefits. Adopting only policies with positive expected net benefits will generally lead to increased aggregate efficiency. Caution is warranted, however, when a jurisdiction risks substantial loss from policy failure.

Choosing among Policies

Our discussion so far has largely considered the evaluation of single policies in isolation. If, after appropriately discounting for time and risk, a policy offers positive net benefits, then it satisfies the Kaldor-Hicks criterion and should be adopted. (Assuming, of course, that efficiency is the only relevant goal.) A more general rule applies when we confront multiple policies that may enhance or interfere with each other: *choose the combination of policies that maximizes net benefits.* Physical, budgetary, and other constraints may limit the feasibility of generating such combinations.

Physical and Budgetary Constraints. Policies are sometimes mutually exclusive. For example, we cannot drain a swamp to create agricultural land and also preserve it as a wildlife refuge. *When all of the available policies are mutually exclusive, we maximize efficiency by choosing the one with the largest positive net benefits.* For example, consider the list of projects in Figure 7.9. If we can choose any combination of projects, we simply choose all those with positive net benefits—namely, projects A, B, C, and D. Assume, however, that all the projects are mutually exclusive except C and D, which can be built together. By taking the combination of C and D to be a separate project, we can consider all the projects on the

	Costs	Benefits	Net Benefits	Benefits/Costs
No project	0	0	0	—
Project A	1	10	9	10
Project B	10	30	20	3
Project C	4	8	4	2
Project D	2	4	2	2
Projects C and D	7	21	14	3
Project E	10	8	− 2	0.8

(1) No constraints: Choose projects A, B, C, and D
   (net benefits equal 43)
(2) All projects mutually exclusive: Choose project B
   (net benefits equal 20)
(3) Costs cannot exceed 10: Choose projects A, C, and D
   (net benefits equal 23)

Figure 7.9   Choosing Among Projects on the Basis of Economic Efficiency

list to be mutually exclusive. Looking down the column labeled Net Benefits, we see that project B offers the largest net benefits and therefore should be the one that we select.

Analysts often compare programs in terms of their benefit-cost ratios. Note that project B, which offers the largest net benefits, does not have the largest ratio of benefits to costs. Project A has a benefit-cost ratio of 10 while project B only has a benefit-cost ratio of 3. Nevertheless, we select project B because if offers larger net benefits than project A. This comparison shows that the benefit-cost ratio can sometimes confuse the choice process.[21] Therefore, *we recommend that you avoid using benefit-cost ratios altogether*.

Also note that projects C and D are shown as synergistic. That is, the net benefits from adopting both together exceed the sum of the net benefits from adopting each independently. Such might be the case if project C were a dam that created a reservoir that could be used for recreation and D were a road that increased access to the reservoir. Of course, projects can also interfere with each other—for instance, the dam might reduce the benefits of a downstream recreation project. The important point is that care must be taken to determine interactions among projects so that the combination of projects providing the greatest net benefits in aggregate can be readily identified.

Returning to Figure 7.9, interpret the listed costs as public expenditures and the listed benefits as the monetized value of all other effects. Now assume that, while none of the projects are mutually exclusive in a physical sense, total public expenditures (costs) cannot exceed 10. If project B is selected, the budget constraint is met and net benefits of 20 result. If projects A, C, and D are selected instead, the budget constraint is also met but net benefits of 23 result. No other feasible combination offers larger net benefits. Thus, under the budget constraint, net benefits are maximized by choosing projects A, C, and D.

[21]Another disadvantage of the benefit-cost ratio is that it depends on how we take account of costs and benefits. For example, consider project B in Figure 7.9. Imagine that the costs of 10 units consist of 5 units of public expenditure and 5 units of social surplus loss. We could take the 5 units of social surplus loss to be negative benefits so that costs would then be 5 units and benefits 25 units. While net benefits still equal 20 units, the benefit-cost ratio increases from 3 to 5.

Distributional Constraints. The Kaldor-Hicks criterion requires only that policies have the potential to produce Pareto improvements; it does not require that people actually be compensated for the costs that they bear. One rationale for accepting potential, rather than demanding actual, Pareto improvements for specific policies is that we expect different people to bear costs under different policies so that over the broad range of public activity few, if any, people will actually bear net costs. Another rationale is that, even if some people do end up as net losers from the collection of policies selected on the basis of efficiency, they can be compensated through a program that redistributes income or wealth.

These rationales are less convincing for policies that concentrate high costs on small groups. If we believe that the losers will not be indirectly compensated, then we may wish to consider redesigning policies so that they either spread costs more evenly or provide direct compensation to big losers. We can think of limits on the size of losses as a constraint that must be met in applying the Kaldor-Hicks criterion. Alternatively, we can imagine applying weights to costs and benefits accruing to different groups—this would lead us to the modified benefit-cost analysis we discussed in Chapter 6. Using distributional constraints and weights obviously introduces values beyond efficiency. We should be careful to make these values explicit. Indeed, the best approach would be to treat net benefits as the measure of efficiency within a multigoal analysis.

Of course, the inclusion of distributional values requires that costs and benefits be disaggregated for relevant groups. This entails doing separate benefit-cost analyses from the perspective of different income classes, geographic regions, ethnic groups, or whatever other categories that have distributional relevance. When you begin your analyses, err on the side of overdisaggregation. It may not be possible to gather necessary information to do distributional analysis at the end of a study. In addition, it may be that a distributional value will become important to you or your client only after you have seen the estimated distribution of net benefits. If efficiency does turn out to be the only relevant value, then aggregation is no more difficult than addition.

Disaggregation of net benefits by interest groups may be valuable in anticipating political opposition.[22] While the estimation of aggregate net benefits enables us to answer the normative question, Is the policy efficient?, the estimation of net benefits by interest groups helps us answer the positive question, Who will oppose and who will support the policy? For example, Lee S. Friedman estimated net benefits from several perspectives in his evaluation of the supported work program in New York City.[23] In addition to the social perspective, he estimated net benefits from the perspectives of taxpayers (Will the program continue to be politically feasible?), the welfare department (Will the program continue to be administratively feasible?), and a typical program participant (Will people continue to be willing to enter the program?). In this way, disaggregated benefit-cost analysis can serve as a first cut at predicting political and organizational feasibility.

[22]For a general discussion, see Harold S. Luft, "Benefit-Cost Analysis and Public Policy Implementation: From Normative to Positive Analysis," *Public Policy*, Vol. 24, No. 4, 1976, pp. 437–62.

[23]Lee S. Friedman, "An Interim Evaluation of the Supported Work Experiment," *Policy Analysis*, Vol. 3, No. 2, 1977, pp. 147–70.

Summary   When efficiency is the only relevant goal, we should choose the feasible combination of policies that maximizes net benefits. We should be especially careful in applying the net benefits rule when policies have interdependent effects. We should also anticipate the possible introduction of distributional values by developing disaggregated net benefit estimates where practical. Finally, disaggregating net benefits by interest groups may enable us to anticipate political and organizational feasibility.

AN ILLUSTRATION: TAXING ALCOHOL TO SAVE LIVES

Alcohol is a widely used—and abused—substance. While some evidence suggests that moderate use of alcohol may actually improve health,[24] the medical literature reports that excessive use contributes to brain damage, cirrhosis of the liver, birth defects, heart disease, cancer of the liver, and a number of other adverse health conditions.[25] These alcohol-related conditions play at least some role in over 100,000 deaths per year in the United States.[26] Yet the most dramatic consequence of alcohol abuse is the large number of highway fatalities caused by alcohol-involved drivers. In 1980, for example, over 23,000 of the approximately 53,000 highway fatalities in the United States were caused by drivers who had been using alcohol.[27] Young drivers, who have higher accident rates than adults, are especially dangerous when they have been drinking. Drivers under the age of 22 years are 100 times more likely to die in fatal crashes when they are under the influence of six or more drinks than when they are sober.[28]

Not all of these adverse consequences of alcohol consumption fall on the drinker. On average, each 100 alcohol-involved drivers who die in automobile accidents take with them about 77 victims. Nonfatal accidents caused by alcohol-involved drivers inflict injury and property damage on nondrinkers. Publicly subsidized health insurance programs pay for some fraction of the costs of the morbidity caused by alcohol abuse. These external effects suggest that the market price of alcohol does not fully reflect its marginal social cost.

Recognizing these adverse external effects of alcohol consumption, and seeing a potential for generating substantial public revenue, a number of economists advocate that federal excise taxes on alcoholic beverages be raised.[29] They note that per-unit taxes on beer and liquor have fallen greatly in real terms since the 1950s.

---

[24]A. L. Klatsky, G. D. Friedman, and A. B. Siegleaub, "Alcohol and Mortality: A Ten-Year Kaiser-Permanente Experience," *Annals of Internal Medicine,* Vol. 95, No. 2, August 1981, pp. 139–45.

[25]National Institute on Alcohol Abuse and Alcoholism, *Fourth Special Report to the U.S. Congress on Alcohol and Health* (Washington, D.C.: U.S. Department of Health and Human Services, January 1981), pp. 42–79.

[26]E. P. Noble, *Alcohol and Health* (Washington, D.C.: Department of Health, Education and Welfare, 1978), pp. 9–10.

[27]National Highway Traffic Safety Administration, *Alcohol Involvement in Traffic Accidents: Recent Estimates from the National Center for Statistics and Analysis* (Washington, D.C.: U.S. Department of Transportation DOT-HS-806-269, May 1982), Appendix C.

[28]Charles E. Phelps, "Risk and Perceived Risk of Drunk Driving among Young Drivers," *Journal of Policy Analysis and Management,* Vol. 6, No. 4, Summer 1987, pp. 708–14.

[29]George A. Hacker, "Taxing Booze for Health and Wealth," *Journal of Policy Analysis and Management,* Vol. 6, No. 4, Summer 1987, pp. 701–8.

Returning excise taxes to their previous real levels would not only raise revenue but also internalize within the price of alcohol some portion of its external costs. Evaluating the economic efficiency of any particular tax increase requires us to identify and monetize the external effects of alcohol consumption. One of the more important effects is highway fatalities. How many highway fatalities will be avoided if people consume less alcohol because increased taxes raise the retail price? Can these lives be reasonably monetized? We concentrate on these questions in the context of a benefit-cost analysis of an increase in the excise tax on alcohol. Our analysis relies heavily on estimates made by Charles Phelps of the impact of tax increases on the highway fatality rates of young drivers.[30]

Estimating the Effects of a Tax on Alcohol

We consider the following impacts of an increase in alcohol taxes: social surplus losses in the alcohol markets (the major cost of the tax), reductions in fatalities caused by young and older drivers (benefits), reductions in the number of nonfatal highway accidents (benefits), and reductions in health and productivity losses (benefits). We discuss yearly effects with specific reference to a 30 percent tax on the retail prices of beer, wine, and liquor.

Social Surplus Losses in Alcohol Markets. In general, an excise tax reduces both consumer and producer surplus. If we assume that supply is perfectly elastic, however, the entire burden of the tax is borne by consumers. Figure 7.10 illustrates this case for the beer market. The current retail price of beer averages about $0.63 per 12-ounce drink across the United States. At this price, 54 billion drinks are consumed annually in the United States. We assume that the beer industry would supply more or less at the same price—that is, the supply schedule is flat (perfectly elastic). If we impose a $0.19 tax per drink (30 percent of the current retail price), the retail price seen by consumers would rise to $0.82 per drink. In other words, the assumption of a flat supply schedule implies that the entire burden of the tax falls on consumers.

How will consumers respond? To answer this question, we must make assumptions about the demand schedule. Following the approach used by Phelps, we assume that demand is isoelastic.[31] Relying on a review of the empirical

---

[30]Charles E. Phelps, "Death and Taxes: An Opportunity for Substitution," Public Policy Analysis Program Working Paper No. 8702, University of Rochester, May 1987.

[31]In particular, we assume that the demand schedule has the following form
$$q = ap^{-b}$$
where q is the quantity demand, p is the price, and a and b are parameters. In particular, the elasticity of this demand schedule equals $-b$, a constant. By taking the logarithm of both sides of the equation, we obtain
$$\log(q) = \log(a) - b \log(p)$$
which, with some additional assumptions, permits the estimation of the parameters a and b by applying linear regression to the transformed price and quantity data. (In practice, an estimation would include other variables that might affect demand besides price.) When researchers report that they transformed their data by taking the logarithms of their raw data, you should interpret their reported elasticity as the negative of parameter b in the equations above. If they based their estimation on the raw quantities and prices, then the underlying demand schedule is linear in price and therefore does not have constant elasticity.

literature, Phelps assumes that the price elasticity of demand for beer equals − 0.5 (a 1 percent increase in the price leads to a 0.5 percent reduction in the quantity demanded).[32] As indicated in Figure 7.10, increasing the price to $0.82 under these assumptions reduces consumption to 47.4 billion drinks per year. The area of the shaded figure equals $9.538 billion, which is the loss in consumer surplus (equal to the sum of tax revenue and deadweight loss) in the beer market.[33] The area of the shaded rectangle equals $8.951 billion, the portion of consumer surplus loss that is gained by the government as tax revenue. Thus, the net loss in social surplus in the beer market equals $0.586, the difference between the consumer surplus loss and the government's revenue gain.[34] It is the "deadweight" loss we discussed in Chapter 3.

We follow the same procedure for estimating the social surplus losses in the wine and liquor markets.[35] For the wine market, we assume that the price elasticity of demand equals − .75. Given the current average retail price of $0.46 per 5-ounce drink and current consumption of about 16 billion drinks per year, we find that a 30 percent tax on the current retail price yields a consumer surplus loss of $1.996 billion, a revenue gain of $1.814 billion, and a deadweight loss of $0.182 billion. Assuming an elasticity of − 1.0 in the liquor market, a 30 percent tax on the average retail price of $0.63 per 1.5-ounce drink, reduces annual consumption from 32 billion to 24.5 billion drinks and results in a consumer surplus loss of $5.205 billion, a revenue gain of $4.578 billion, and a deadweight loss of $0.627 billion.

Adding effects across the beer, wine, and liquor markets, we find that the 30 percent tax on retail prices reduces the consumption of alcoholic drinks by 16.6 percent, inflicts consumer surplus losses of $16.739 billion, generates tax revenue equal to $15.343 billion, and results in deadweight losses of $1.396

---

[32]The empirical literature suggests a demand elasticity of between − 0.3 and − 0.4. Wishing to be conservative in his estimations of the costs of tax increases, Phelps selected − 0.5 as his base case. (The higher the absolute value of the elasticity, the greater the consumer surplus loss in the beer market.) For a review of the empirical literature, see Stanley I. Ornstein, "Control of Alcohol Through Price Increases," *Journal of Studies on Alcohol*, Vol. 41, 1980, pp. 807–18.

Given an elasticity (− b), the current price (p), and the current quantity (q), we can solve for the appropriate value of the constant (a) in the demand schedule, $q = ap^{-b}$.

[33]Mathematically, this area equals the integral of the demand schedule between the initial price (p_0) and the new price (p_1). For our isoelastic demand schedule, the area equals

$$[a/z][\, p_1^{\,z} - p_0^{\,z}]$$

where z equals (1 − b).

[34]If we were to assume a price elasticity of demand for beer of − .25 instead, we would find a social surplus loss of $0.306. Assuming a demand elasticity of − .75 we would find a social surplus loss of $0.842. When doing benefit-cost analyses, it is standard practice to test the sensitivity of our conclusions to changes in our assumptions. In other words, repeat the analysis, keeping all assumptions the same except the one under consideration. Given the consensus in the empirical literature, a range as large as − .25 to − .75 almost certainly covers the true value.

[35]We measure quantities in terms of drinks with approximately the same alcohol content: 12 ounces of beer, 5 ounces of wine, and 1.5 ounces of liquor.

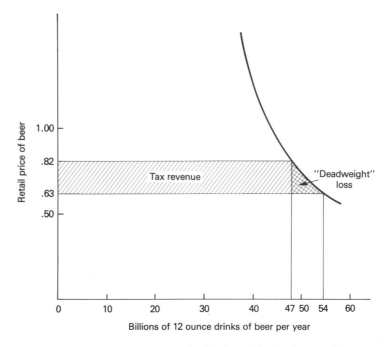

Figure 7.10   Social Surplus Loss in the Beer Market from a 30% Tax

billion.[36] We can either simply report the deadweight losses as the net cost of the policy in the alcohol markets or report the total consumer surplus losses as a cost and the total tax revenue as a benefit. Although the choice of approach will not alter our estimate of net benefits, the latter approach preserves information that may be relevant later if we decide that, along with economic efficiency, reducing the federal deficit is a relevant goal.

Reductions in Fatalities Caused by Young Drivers.   The connection between alcohol taxes and fatal accidents caused by young drivers follows an intuitively straightforward chain: taxes raise the retail price of alcohol; higher prices

[36]The figures for alternative tax rates are as follows (in billions of dollars):

Tax Rates (percent)	Consumer Surplus Losses	Tax Revenue Gains	Social Surplus Losses
10	5.922	5.733	0.189
20	11.485	10.802	0.683
30	16.738	15.343	1.395
40	21.725	19.457	2.268
50	26.477	23.217	3.260

lead young drivers to drink less; because they drink less, young drivers are involved in fewer fatal accidents. Until recently, however, we have not had very good estimates of the strengths of the links in the chain. New information has been provided by Michael Grossman, Douglas Coate, and Gregory M. Arluck on the price elasticity of youth drinking.[37] Phelps combines this information with data from autopsies on the blood-alcohol levels of drivers killed in automobile accidents to estimate the effect of consumption changes on accident risks.

Grossman, Coate, and Arluck analyzed data from the U.S. Health and Nutrition Survey to estimate the effects of price, the legal drinking age, and other variables on the frequency and intensity of drinking by youths aged 16 to 21. They found that the frequency and intensity of drinking were highly sensitive to price. Indeed, they estimated that a 7 percent increase in the price of beer and liquor would have about the same effect as raising the minimum legal drinking age by one year. (Wine consumption appeared not to depend on price.) Their estimates permit the calculation of the probability of drinking level i, P(drinking level i), and the probability of drinking frequency j, P(drinking frequency j), for any set of assumed alcohol prices.[38]

In order to calculate the number of driver fatalities, we need the probability of a young driver dying in an automobile accident conditional on drinking level, P(death/drinking level i). That is, what is the probability that a youthful driver will be killed, given that he or she has had i drinks? Several states do autopsies, which measure blood-alcohol levels, on all highway fatalities.[39] Data from these states permit the estimation of P(drinking level i|death), the probability that a young driver killed in a highway accident was drinking at level i. Phelps realized that he could find the probability of death conditional on drinking level by using the following property of conditional probabilities:

$$P(\text{death}|\text{drinking level } i)P(\text{drinking level } i) =$$
$$P(\text{drinking level } i|\text{death})P(\text{death})$$

where P(death) is the unconditional probability that a young driver will die in a highway accident. Because P(death) can be determined from aggregate statistics, it is possible to solve for the probability of death, given drinking level i:

$$P(\text{death}|\text{drinking level } i) =$$

$$\frac{P(\text{drinking level } i|\text{death})P(\text{death})}{P(\text{drinking level } i)}$$

[37]"Price Sensitivity of Alcoholic Beverages in the United States," in H. D. Holder, ed., *Control Issues in Alcohol Abuse Prevention: Strategies for States and Communities* (Greenwich, Conn.: JAI Press, 1987) pp. 169–98.

[38]The levels of drinking intensity indicate the number of drinks taken on a typical drinking day: 6 and over, 3 to 5, 1 to 2. The levels of drinking frequency indicate how often youths drink: every day, 2 to 3 times per week, 1 to 4 times per month, 4 to 11 times per year, and never (fewer than 3 drinks in previous year).

[39]National Highway Traffic Safety Administration, *Alcohol Involvement in Traffic Accidents: Recent Estimates from the National Center for Statistics and Analysis* (Washington, D.C.: U.S. Department of Transportation DOT-HS-806-269, May 1982), Appendix B.

which is simply a statement of Bayes' theorem.[40] These probabilities change as the tax on alcohol changes because P(drinking level i) depends on the price of drinks.

Phelps next used the conditional probabilities of death and the probabilities of drinking frequencies estimated by Grossman, Coate, and Arluck to calculate the reduction in the number of young drivers who would die as the tax on beer is increased. Phelps concentrated on beer for two reasons: first, it is by far the drink of choice of youths; and second, the price elasticity for beer estimated by Grossman, Coate, and Arluck was much more statistically precise than their estimates for wine and liquor. As long as the tax is actually imposed on wine and liquor as well as beer, Phelps's approach leads to conservative estimates of the number of lives saved.

Phelps found that a 30 percent tax would result in 1,650 fewer drivers 16 to 21 years of age dying in highway fatalities per year.[41] These driver fatalities are avoided because the tax decreases both the intensity and frequency of drinking. Because 77 nondriver fatalities are associated on average with each 100 driver fatalities, the 1,650 avoided driver deaths would result in an additional 1,270 lives saved per year. Thus, the 30 percent tax would reduce the number of highway fatalities caused by young drivers by about 2,920 per year.[42]

[40]A stylized example may be helpful to readers who have not encountered Bayes' theorem before:

Imagine that you are playing a game that involves guessing the proportion of red (R) and white (W) balls in an urn. Assume that you know that the urn contains either 8 W and 2 R balls (Type 1 urn) or 2 R and 8 W balls (Type 2 urn). Also assume that you believe that the prior probability of the urn being Type 1 is one-half—that is, before you sample the contents of the urn, you believe that P(Type 1) = P(Type 2) = 0.5. Now imagine that you draw one ball from the urn and observe that it is white. What probability should you assign to the urn being Type 1, *given* that you have observed a white ball? In other words, what is P(Type 1|W)? Bayes's theorem tells you that

$$P(\text{Type 1}|W) = P(W|\text{Type 1})P(\text{Type 1})/P(W).$$

But you know that $P(W)$ = $P(W|$Type 1$)P($Type 1$)$ + $P(W|$Type 2$)P($Type 2$)$

$$= (8/10)(.5) + (2/10)(.5) = .5.$$

(In other words, because the urn types are equally likely before you sample, you can assume that you are drawing from their combined contents of 10 W and 10 R so that the probability of drawing a white ball is .5.)

Applying Bayes' theorem thus gives

$$P(\text{Type 1}|W) = (8/10)(.5)/(.5) = .8.$$

Thus, if you draw a white ball, then you should believe that the probability of the urn being Type 1 is .8.

[41]Phelps, "Death and Taxes," Table 11.

[42]Phelps' estimates for a range of tax rates are as follows:

Tax Rates (percent)	Fatalities Avoided per Year		
	Drivers	Victims	Total
10	825	635	1460
20	1340	1031	2371
30	1650	1270	2920
40	2475	1906	4381
50	3299	2540	5839

Reductions in Fatalities Caused by Older Drivers. Unfortunately, no study comparable to that of Grossman, Coate, and Arluck is available for quantifying the behaviors of older drinkers in the United States. Consequently, we must use an ad hoc procedure that reflects two factors: first, on average adults have a much less elastic demand for alcohol than do youths; and second, for any given intensity of drinking, adults on average are less likely than youthful drivers to be involved in a fatal accident. As is often the case in benefit-cost analysis, we must do the best we can with available information.

We start by noting that the 30 percent tax reduces the number of alcohol-involved fatalities of young drivers by about 40 percent (a reduction of about 1,650 on a base of about 4,120). Ignoring that adults have less elastic demand for alcohol and that alcohol-involved adult drivers are less dangerous, we might simply assume that the 30 percent tax would reduce the number of alcohol-involved fatalities of older drivers by the same fraction. With about 8,000 alcohol-involved fatalities each year among drivers over 21, the simple estimate would be 3,200. Obviously, this approach would lead to an overstatement of the number of fatalities involving drivers over 21 that would be avoided by the 30 percent tax.

In order to take account of the less-elastic demand of adults, we might scale the simple estimate by the ratio of the adult elasticity of demand to the youth elasticity of demand. Using the Grossman, Coate, and Arluck results, Phelps calculates the elasticity of demand for beer for those 16 to 21 to be − 2.3. The elasticity of demand for older drinkers approximates the aggregate market elasticity because older drinkers constitute the large majority of the market. So the market elasticities we used in estimating effects in the alcohol markets (− .5 for beer, − .75 for wine, and − 1.0 for liquor) are reasonable approximations for the elasticity of drinkers older than 21. The ratio of the weighted average of these elasticities to the youth elasticity equals 0.3. Applying this ratio to the simple estimate of 3,240 adult drivers saved yields an adjusted estimate of 972 per year.

A lack of relevant data makes it more difficult to adjust further for the lower propensity of older drivers to be involved in fatal accidents at any given drinking level. We do know that while those 21 and younger constitute about 13 percent of licensed drivers, they account for about 26 percent of all alcohol-involved accidents.[43] For lack of more relevant data, we assume that, at any given drinking level, drivers over 21 are only 50 percent as likely to have fatal accidents as younger drivers. Adjusting for this factor reduces the estimate of adult drivers saved to 486. Applying the victim-to-driver ratio of 0.77 yields another 375 lives saved. Thus, we estimate the total number of lives saved due to changes in the behavior of drivers over 21 to be 861 per year.

Reductions in Injuries and Property Damage. Phelps estimates the injury and property damage costs of highway accidents involving alcohol-involved drivers to be about $3.75 billion per year, one-third of which is attributable to drivers 21 and younger.[44] To estimate the injury and property damage savings

---

[43]National Highway Traffic Safety Administration, Appendix B, Table 6.

[44]Estimates of the percentage of accidents that involve alcohol-involved drivers can be found in National Highway Traffic Safety Administration, Appendix B. An earlier report provides estimates

associated with changes in youth drinking behavior, we assume that nonfatal accidents fall in the same proportion as fatal accidents. Multiplying the percentage reduction in alcohol-related deaths of young drivers from a 30 percent tax (a 40 percent reduction) by the total costs of alcohol-involved nonfatal accidents ($1.25 billion) yields annual savings of $0.5 billion. Following the same procedure for older drivers (a 0.06 reduction times $2.50 billion) yields annual savings of $0.15 billion. Thus we estimate the total annual injury and property damage savings from imposition of the 30 percent tax to be $0.65 billion.

Health and Productivity Gains. We expect reductions in alcohol consumption to contribute to better health. We also expect reductions in alcohol consumption to increase productivity— better health and greater sobriety contribute to reductions in absenteeism and workplace accidents. For lack of more appropriate information, we assume that health and productivity losses are proportional to alcohol consumption.[45] Therefore, because we expect the 30 percent tax to reduce alcohol consumption by 16.6 percent, we predict that health and productivity losses would also fall by 16.6 percent.

We must rely on previous studies for estimates of the yearly health and productivity costs associated with alcohol consumption. The best available estimates appear to be for the year 1975.[46] Converting these estimates to 1986 dollars gives annual health costs equal to $25.92 billion and annual productivity costs equal to $39.96 billion. Therefore, under our assumption of proportionality between consumption and costs, we estimate $4.29 billion in annual health savings and $6.61 billion in annual productivity savings from the 30 percent tax.

Monetizing and Interpreting Effects

We have measured all effects in dollars except lives saved. We might think, therefore, that our only remaining task is to assign a dollar value to lives saved. Unfortunately, we must also question whether all the effects we have quantified belong in our calculation of net benefits. Do any of the effects involve double counting?

---

of the average cost of accidents, which can be inflated to 1986 dollars. National Highway Traffic Safety Administration, *1975 Societal Costs of Motor Vehicle Accidents* (Washington, D.C.: U.S. Department of Transportation, December 1976). Phelps combines these estimates to arrive at the annual cost of injury and property damage caused by alcohol-involved drivers.

[45]Proportional reduction would be unlikely if most of the reduction in alcohol consumption was by light rather than heavy drinkers. Evidence suggests, however, that even heavy drinkers do alter their behavior in the face of higher prices. See George A. Hacker, "Taxing Booze for Health and Wealth," *Journal of Policy Analysis and Management*, Vol. 6, No. 4, Summer 1987, pp. 701–8.

[46]R. E. Berry, Jr., J. P. Boland, C. N. Smart, and J. R. Kanak, "The Economic Costs of Alcohol Abuse and Alcoholism, 1975," Final Report to the National Institute on Alcohol Abuse and Alcoholism, ADM 281-760016, August 1977.

Which Lives Count?   We estimated lives saved in four categories: young drivers, victims of young drivers, older drivers, and victims of older drivers. We can think of the victims of alcohol-involved drivers as suffering an externality of the drivers' alcohol consumption. The costs borne by victims are not reflected in alcohol markets. In contrast, the costs borne by the drivers themselves may be reflected in their demand for alcohol. We expect that someone fully informed about the risks of driving under the influence of alcohol will consider these risks in deciding when and how much to drink. Other things equal, the higher the implicit values that drivers place on their own lives or the higher the probabilities of having fatal accidents after drinking, the less alcohol drivers will demand at any given price. To the extent that drivers are uninformed about the risks of driving under the influence of alcohol, their demand for alcohol will not fully reflect their risk of being an alcohol-involved driver fatality.

Think back to our earlier discussion of the measurement of costs and benefits in secondary markets. We can think of the alcohol markets as the primary markets and the "markets for victim and driver fatalities" as secondary markets. In the "fatality markets" people demand personal highway safety as a function of the "price" of safety, which can be thought of as the monetary equivalent of the level of effort expended on avoiding accidents. Now the market for victim fatalities is clearly distorted by the external effects of alcohol consumption. Therefore, we should count effects in the "victim market" in our benefit-cost analysis. The "driver market" is not distorted as long as drivers fully realize the increased risks they face from their alcohol consumption. If we believe that drivers are fully informed, then we should not count reductions in their fatality rate as benefits—they are already counted in the alcohol markets. If we believe, however, that they do not fully take account of the increased risks, then the "driver market" is distorted by an information asymmetry and we should count all or part of the avoided fatalities as benefits.

We estimate benefits under three different sets of assumptions about how well young and older drivers are informed about the risks of drinking and driving. First, we assume that all drinkers are uninformed. Under this assumption, we count all avoided driver and victim fatalities as benefits. We can treat our estimate of benefits under this assumption as an upper bound on the true benefits. Second, we assume that all drinkers are fully informed. In this case, we count only avoided victim fatalities as benefits. This case provides a lower bound on benefits. Third, we make a "best guess" about the extent to which young and older drivers are informed. We assume that young drivers are only about 10 percent informed so that we count 90 percent of avoided young-driver fatalities as benefits.[47] We also assume that older drivers are about 90 percent informed so that we count 10 percent of avoided older-driver fatalities as benefits. As in the other cases, we count all avoided victim fatalities as benefits.

---

[47]Phelps reports that the college students he surveyed underestimated the increase risks of driving after heavy drinking by a factor of more than ten. Charles E. Phelps, "Risks and Perceived Risk of Drunk Driving among Young Drivers," *Journal of Policy Analysis and Management*, Vol. 6, No. 4, Summer 1987, pp. 708–14.

Monetizing the Value of Life.   What dollar value should we assign to avoided fatalities? This question may strike you as crass, especially if you think about putting a dollar value on the life of a specific person. Many of us would be willing to spend everything we have to save the life of someone we love. But we all implicitly put finite values on lives when we make decisions that affect risks to ourselves and those we love. Do you always buckle your seat belt? Do you make all your passengers buckle theirs? Do you have a smoke detector on every floor of your house? Do you have a working fire extinguisher? Do you always wear a helmet when riding your bicycle? Do you always drive within the legal speed limit? If you answer No to any of these questions, you are implicitly saying that you do not put an infinite value on lives—you have decided to accept greater risks of fatality in order to avoid small certain costs.

The key distinction is between actual and statistical lives. Most of us are willing to spend great sums to save the lives of specific persons. For example, we spare no cost in trying to rescue trapped miners. Yet we are less willing to take actions that reduce the probability of accidents—as a society we do not take all possible precautions to prevent miners from becoming trapped. Indeed, miners themselves sometimes knowingly accept higher risks by ignoring inconvenient safety rules. In other words, as long as we are dealing with probabilities rather than certainties, people seem willing to consider trade-offs between dollars and lives. By observing these trade-offs, we can impute a dollar value to a statistical life— the problem we face in our benefit-cost analysis of the alcohol tax.[48]

A number of studies have attempted to measure how much people implicitly value their lives by seeing how much additional wage compensation they demand for working at riskier jobs.[49] Imagine two jobs with identical characteristics except that one involves a 1/1,000 greater risk of fatal injury per year. If we observe people willing to take the riskier job for an additional $2,000 per year in wages, then we can infer that they are placing an implicit value on their (statistical) lives of $2,000/(1/1,000), or $2 million. The validity of our inference depends on the jobs differing only in terms of risk and the workers fully understanding the risk.

In practice, researchers use econometric techniques to control for a wide range of job and worker characteristics. In his review of ten major studies of wage-risk trade-offs, W. Kip Viscusi found estimates of the value of life ranging from about $600,000 to over $8 million (in 1986 dollars).[50] We take $1 million, near

---

[48]The risk-premium approach is conceptually well grounded in the economic concept of willingness to pay. The other major approach, used by courts in deciding compensation in wrongful death cases, is to value life at the present value of forgone future earnings. While this approach provides abundant consulting opportunities for economists, it does not have as clear a conceptual basis in economic theory as the risk-premium approach and therefore should be avoided in benefit-cost analysis.

[49]This approach was pioneered by Richard Thaler and Sherwin Rosen, "The Value of Saving a Life: Evidence from the Labor Market," in Nestor E. Terleckyj, ed., *Household Production and Consumption* (New York: Columbia University Press, 1976), pp. 265–98.

[50]W. Kip Viscusi, "Alternative Approaches to Valuing the Health Impacts of Accidents: Liability Law and Prospective Evaluations," *Law and Contemporary Problems*, Vol. 46, No. 4, Autumn 1983, pp. 49–68. More recent work using more accurate data on industrial accident rates suggests a value of life in the $5 million range. See Michael J. Moore and W. Kip Viscusi, "Doubling the Estimated Value of Life: Results Using New Occupational Fatality Data," *Journal of Policy Analysis and Management*, Vol. 7, No. 3, Spring 1988, pp. 476–99.

the lower end of this range, as a conservative estimate of the value of life. Obviously, with such a wide range of estimates we should check the sensitivity of our results to different assumptions about the value of lives saved. As we discuss below, it is usually desirable to determine the smallest dollar value of life that we must assume to generate positive net benefits.

Apportioning Other Effects. We must determine how much of the injury, property damage, health, and productivity effects to count as benefits under our uninformed demand, informed demand, and best guess cases. We follow the same line or argument that we used in deciding which avoided fatalities to count.

In the *uninformed demand* case, we assume that people do not consider the accident, health, and productivity costs of drinking so that we count the entire savings in these categories as benefits. This approach is consistent with treating the uninformed demand cases as an upper bound on benefits from the tax.

In the *informed demand* case, we assume that drinkers fully anticipate and bear these costs so that we do not count them as benefits. With respect to accident costs, for instance, we assume that the drinkers pay for the property damage and injuries they inflict on others through either higher insurance premiums or loss of coverage. Similarly, we assume that workers who are less productive because of their drinking bear most of the productivity losses in the form of lower wages. To the extent that insurance and wage rates do not fully reflect accident propensities, health risks, and productivity losses associated with drinking, our accounting will underestimate benefits—an approach consistent with treating the informed demand case as a lower bound on benefits.

In the *best guess* case, we apportion costs under the assumption that young drinkers are about 10 percent informed, and older drinkers are about 90 percent informed, of the health, productivity, and accident costs associated with their drinking. Because the majority of health and productivity losses accrue to older drinkers, we take 10 percent of the total savings in these categories as benefits. With respect to accidents, we count as benefits all the costs avoided by nondrivers as well as 90 percent of costs avoided by young drivers and 10 percent avoided by older drivers. Although lack of better information forces us to adopt these ad hoc assumptions, they probably provide a reasonable intermediate estimate of benefits.

Estimating Net Benefits

Having apportioned and valued effects, we are ready to estimate net benefits under each of the three cases. As long as we expect the same pattern of costs and benefits to persist over time, we need only look at the net benefits in the single year. If we think that costs and benefits will change substantially over time, then we should estimate net benefits for a number of years into the future and discount them back to the present. For instance, stricter enforcement of driving-while-intoxicated laws might reduce the frequency with which people drink and drive so that over time the number of lives saved from the tax will fall. When we expect costs and benefits to change over time, we should adopt a horizon as long as we expect the policy to be in effect.

Net Benefits of the 30 Percent Tax.   Figure 7.11 displays the costs and benefits of a 30 percent tax on the retail prices of beer, wine, and liquor. Note that the tax appears to offer positive net benefits in each of the three cases. We should be careful in our interpretation, however.

First consider the net benefits in the informed demand case. The reported net benefits of $0.24 billion are quite small when compared to the size of the costs and benefits. If we have underestimated consumer surplus losses by as little as 2 percent, then the true net benefits under the informed demand case would be negative instead of positive. Because we have been conservative in counting benefits in this case, it is probably reasonable for us to conclude that the tax at least breaks even. Nevertheless, the general point is that we should not put false confidence in the accuracy of our specific estimates.

Next consider the uninformed demand case. Here we report large positive net benefits of $13.95 billion annually. In inspecting the benefit categories, we note that almost 80 percent of the net benefits come from benefits under the heading of avoided health and productivity costs. Yet the estimates underlying these benefits were pulled somewhat uncritically out of the literature. Lack of time and access to primary data forced us to take at face value the yearly health and productivity costs estimated by other analysts. Our uncertainty about the accuracy of these estimates should give us concern. We may be victim to what has been called the problem of horse and rabbit stew.[51] When we mix our fairly accurate estimates of avoided fatalities (rabbit) with the larger but less certain estimates of health and productivity savings (strong-flavored horse), our net benefits (stew) will be dominated by the less-certain estimates (our stew will taste primarily of horse). The general point is that the uncertainty of the larger costs and benefits will largely determine the uncertainty of our net benefit estimate.

Fortunately, these problems are not as serious for the best guess case. Net benefits equal $3.41 billion, a fairly substantial amount even when compared to the large consumer surplus losses. Health and productivity benefits comprise less than one-third of net benefits, reducing the danger that we have cooked horse and rabbit stew. Of course, whether or not our estimate of net benefits under the best guess is close to the true value of net benefits depends on the reasonableness of the various assumptions we have already discussed.

Net Benefits of Other Tax Rates.   We focused on the 30 percent tax rate for purposes of exposition. Does the 30 percent rate offer the largest net benefits? Figure 7.12 shows net benefits for lower and higher rates for each of the three cases. Under the informed demand case, net benefits peak at the 20 percent tax rate. Thus, if we see this case as the appropriate one (because either we think it is the most likely or we wish to be conservative), then we should recommend 20 percent as the most efficient rate.

Under either the uninformed demand or best guess case, net benefits continue to rise up to 50 percent, the highest rate analyzed. This indicates that an even higher rate than 50 percent may be optimal. Two considerations, one methodological and the other substantive, suggest caution in this interpretation. First, the further we move from current policy, the less confidence we should have

[51]E. J. Mishan, *Cost-Benefit Analysis* (New York: Praeger, 1976), pp. 160–64.

	Uninformed Demand	Best Guess	Informed Demand
Lives saved ($1 million/life)			
Young drivers	1.65	1.49	0
Victims of young drivers	1.27	1.27	1.27
Older drivers	.49	.05	0
Victims of older drivers	.37	.37	.37
Total	3.78	3.18	1.64
Injury and property damage avoided			
Young drivers	.50	.47	0
Older drivers	.15	.07	0
Total	.65	.54	0
Health and productivity costs avoided			
Health	4.29	.43	0
Productivity	6.61	.66	0
Total	10.90	1.09	0
Tax revenue			
(beer, wine, liquor)	15.34	15.34	15.34
Consumer surplus change			
(beer, wine, liquor)	−16.74	−16.74	−16.74
Net benefits	13.95	3.41	0.24

Figure 7.11   Costs and Benefits of a 30% Tax on Alcohol (billions of dollars per year)

in our predictions of effects. Our assumption of isoelastic demand, for instance, may be quite reasonable for small, but not large, price changes. Second, as we move toward prohibitive taxes, we may encounter radically different behavioral responses. Think of the ways people responded to Prohibition in the United States during the 1920s: they smuggled alcohol into the United States from other countries; they formed criminal organizations, which corrupted officials and practiced violence, to supply alcohol to the illegal market; they made alcohol at home; they developed a taste for more concentrated, and therefore more easily smuggled, forms of alcohol.[52] Along with these sorts of behaviors, substantially higher taxes might induce greater use of other recreational drugs and perhaps trigger other

[52]For discussions of the costs of prohibition, see Irving Fisher, *Prohibition at Its Worst* (New York: Macmillan, 1926), and Malvern Hall Tillitt, *The Price of Prohibition* (New York: Harcourt, Brace and Company, 1932).

Tax Rate (tax revenue)	Uninformed Demand	Best Guess	Informed Demand
.10 (5.73)	6.24	2.09	0.63
.20 (10.80)	10.72	3.12	0.65
.30 (15.34)	13.95	3.41	0.24
.40 (19.46)	17.99	4.68	0.20
.50 (23.22)	21.60	5.79	0.03

Figure 7.12   Net Benefits of Alcohol Taxes (billions of dollars per year)

important, but unanticipated, effects. Because we did not consider these possible effects, we should be cautious about advocating very high tax rates on the basis of our benefit-cost analysis alone.

Reconsidering the Value of Life: Switching to Cost-Effectiveness.   If we are unwilling to assign a dollar value to lives saved, then we must abandon benefit-cost analysis because we have incommensurable goals: saving lives and increasing economic efficiency. As long as we have only two goals, we can apply cost-effectiveness analysis instead. We ask the basic question: How many dollars of economic efficiency must be given up for each life saved? For example, consider the informed demand case for the 30 percent tax. At a net cost of $1.4 billion, 1,645 lives can be saved, yielding a cost per life saved of $0.85 million.

We should compare the 30 percent tax rate with other tax rates in terms of cost per life saved. As the tax rate increases beyond 30 percent in the informed demand case, the number of lives saved goes up but so too does the cost per life saved. It is only when we compare alternatives that save the same number of lives that we can unequivocally say that the one with the lowest cost per life saved is best. Nevertheless, the cost per life saved indicates how high a dollar value of life we have to assume in a benefit-cost analysis to yield positive net benefits.

We can also compare the 30 percent tax with other regulatory programs in terms of cost per life saved. Does the tax appear as cost-effective as other life-saving programs that have been adopted? Figure 7.13 shows estimates of the cost per life saved for forty-four proposed, rejected, or final rules analyzed by the U.S. Office of Management and Budget. Our estimate of $0.85 million puts the cost per life saved for the 30 percent tax among the most cost-effective of the analyzed rules. Comparing it to other highway safety regulations, we see that it is not as cost-effective as the 1984 Passive Restraints/Belts rule, which is predicted to save a comparable number of lives but at about one-third the cost.[53] On the other hand, we see that it saves more lives and is more cost-effective than the 1970 rule on standards for side doors. Thus, the cost-effectiveness of the tax does not seem out of line with other safety regulations that have been adopted.

Summary

Our analysis of alcohol taxation illustrates the basic craft and art of benefit-cost analysis. Basic concepts for measuring costs and benefits constitute the craft; drawing together fragmentary evidence from disparate sources to predict and monetize effects constitutes the art. Our conclusion that a 30 percent tax offers positive net benefits appears fairly robust to changes in assumptions about the measurement of benefits. Thus we could be fairly confident in concluding that it would increase economic efficiency if adopted. Yet we remain highly uncertain about whether 30 percent is close to the optimal rate.

A CLOSER LOOK AT SEVERAL SELECTED TOPICS

So far we have limited our attention to the basic concepts that underlie the practical application and interpretation of benefit-cost analysis. Here we offer brief discussions of a few additional topics that deserve attention: the choice of discount rate, the measurement of consumer surplus in the presence of income effects, and the estimation of demand for nonmarketed goods. A full discussion of these topics is beyond the scope of this text. Instead, we briefly indicate why each topic is important and where it can be pursued in greater depth.

Determining the Social Discount Rate

In our discussion of discounting for time we noted that lower discount rates generally make public investments appear more efficient. It should not be surprising, therefore, that the appropriate method for choosing the discount rate has been and continues to be hotly debated among theoretical and applied economists.[54] Unfortunately, policy analysts do not have the luxury of waiting until a clear consensus develops.

[53]For excellent examples of cost-effectiveness analysis applied to highway safety issues, see Fred Thompson, "Regulating Motor Vehicle Safety Maintenance: Can We Make It Cost-Effective?" *Journal of Health Politics, Policy and Law*, Vol. 9, No. 4, Winter 1985, pp. 695–715; Dana B. Kamerud, "Benefits and Costs of the 55 MPH Speed Limit: New Estimates and Their Implications," *Journal of Policy Analysis and Management*, Vol. 7, No. 2, Winter 1988, pp. 341–52; and Robert W. Crandall, Howard K. Gruenspecht, Theodore E. Keeler, and Lester Lave, *Regulating the Automobile* (Washington, D.C.: Brookings Institution, 1986).

[54]For an excellent introduction to the discount rate controversy, see Robert C. Lind, "A Primer on the Major Issues Relating to the Discount Rate for Evaluating National Energy Projects," in Robert C. Lind et al., *Discounting for Time and Risk in Energy Policy* (Washington, D.C.: Resources for the Future, 1982), pp. 21–94. Other articles in the same volume provide detailed discussions of particular conceptual issues.

Figure 7.13 The Cost of Various Risk-Reducing Regulations Per Life Saved

Regulation	Year	Agency	Status*	Initial Annual Risk**	Annual Lives Saved	Cost Per Life Saved (thousands of 1984$)
Steering column protection	1967	NHTSA	F	7.7 in 10^5	1,300.000	$100
Unvented space heaters	1980	CPSC	F	2.7 in 10^5	63.000	100
Oil & gas well service	1983	OSHA-S	P	1.1 in 10^3	50.000	100
Cabin fire protection	1985	FAA	F	6.5 in 10^8	15.000	200
Passive restraints/belts	1984	NHTSA	F	9.1 in 10^5	1,850.000	300
Fuel system integrity	1975	NHTSA	F	4.9 in 10^6	400.000	300
Trihalomethanes	1979	EPA	F	6.0 in 10^6	322.000	300
Underground construction	1983	OSHA-S	P	1.6 in 10^3	8.100	300
Alcohol & drug control	1985	FRA	F	1.8 in 10^6	4.200	500
Servicing wheel rims	1984	OSHA-S	F	1.4 in 10^5	2.300	500
Seat cushion flammability	1984	FAA	F	1.6 in 10^7	37.000	600
Floor emergency lighting	1984	FAA	F	2.2 in 10^8	5.000	700
Crane suspended personnel platform	1984	OSHA-S	P	1.8 in 10^3	5.000	900
Children's sleepware flammability	1973	CPSC	F	2.4 in 10^6	106.000	1,300
Side doors	1970	NHTSA	F	3.6 in 10^5	480.000	1,300
Concrete & masonry construction	1985	OSHA-S	P	1.4 in 10^5	6.500	1,400
Hazard communication	1983	OSHA-S	F	4.0 in 10^5	200.000	1,800
Grain dust	1984	OSHA-S	P	2.1 in 10^4	4.000	2,800
Benzene/fugitive emissions	1984	EPA	F	2.1 in 10^5	0.310	2,800
Radionuclides/uranium mines	1984	EPA	F	1.4 in 10^4	1.100	6,900
Asbestos	1972	OSHA-H	F	3.9 in 10^4	396.000	7,400
Benzene	1985	OSHA-H	P	8.8 in 10^4	3.800	17,100

Figure 7.13 (Continued)

						**
Arsenic/glass plant	1986	EPA	F	8.0 in 10^4	0.110	19,200
Ethylene oxide	1984	OSHA-H	F	4.4 in 10^5	2.800	25,600
Arsenic/copper smelter	1986	EPA	F	9.0 in 10^4	0.060	26,500
Uranium mill tailings/inactive	1983	EPA	F	4.3 in 10^4	2.100	27,600
Acrylonitrile	1978	OSHA-H	F	9.4 in 10^4	6.900	37,600
Uranium mill tailings/active	1983	EPA	F	4.3 in 10^4	2.100	53,000
Coke ovens	1976	OSHA-H	F	1.6 in 10^4	31.000	61,800
Asbestos	1986	OSHA-H	F	6.7 in 10^5	74.700	89,300
Arsenic	1978	OSHA-H	F	1.8 in 10^3	11.700	92,500
Asbestos	1986	EPA	P	2.9 in 10^5	10.000	104,200
DES (cattlefeed)	1979	FDA	F	3.1 in 10^7	68.000	132,000
Arsenic/glass manufacturing	1986	EPA	R	3.8 in 10^5	0.250	142,000
Benzene/storage	1984	EPA	R	6.0 in 10^7	0.043	202,000
Radionuclides/DOE facilities	1984	EPA	R	4.3 in 10^6	0.001	210,000
Radionuclides/elemental phosphorus	1984	EPA	R	1.4 in 10^5	0.046	270,000
Acrylonitrile	1978	OSHA-H	R	9.4 in 10^4	0.600	308,000
Benzene/ethylbenzenol styrene	1984	EPA	R	2.0 in 10^6	0.006	483,000
Arsenic/low-arsenic copper	1986	EPA	R	2.6 in 10^4	0.090	764,000
Benzene/maleic anhydride	1984	EPA	R	1.1 in 10^6	0.029	820,000
Land disposal	1986	EPA	P	2.3 in 10^6	2.520	3,500,000
EDB	1983	OSHA-H	P	2.5 in 10^4	0.002	15,600,000
Formaldehyde	1985	OSHA-H	P	6.8 in 10^7	0.010	72,000,000

*Proposed, rejected or final rule

**Annual deaths per exposed population. An exposed population of 10^3 is 1,000, 10^4 is 10,000 etc.

Source: John F. Morrall, III, "A Review of the Record," Regulation, November/December 1986, pp. 25–34; table 4, p. 30.

283

The Conceptual Issues. In a world with perfect capital markets, like the one illustrated in Figure 7.6, every consumer is willing to trade between marginal current and marginal future consumption at the market rate of interest. At the same time, the rate at which the private economy transforms marginal current consumption into marginal future consumption (the marginal rate of return on investment) also equals the market rate of interest. Thus, the market rate of interest would appear to be the appropriate social discount rate.

The situation becomes immensely more complicated when we relax our assumption of a perfect capital market.

First, because individual consumers have finite lives, they may not sufficiently take into account the consumption possibilities of future generations. Those yet unborn do not have a direct voice in current markets, yet we may believe that they should have standing in our benefit-cost analysis. The willingness of people to pass inheritances to their children and to pay to preserve unique resources gives indirect standing to future generations. Further, future generations inherit a growing stock of knowledge that will compensate at least somewhat for current consumption of natural resources. Nevertheless, to the extent that the interests of future generations remain underrepresented in current markets, an argument can be made for using a discount rate lower than the market interest rate.

The argument is particularly relevant when evaluating projects, like the storage of nuclear wastes, that have consequences far into the future. Even very low positive discount rates make negligible the present value of costs and benefits occurring in the far future. Rather than trying to adjust the discount rate so that these far-off costs and benefits carry weight in a benefit-cost analysis, we believe that it is more appropriate to treat net benefits, discounted in the standard way, as the measure of one goal in a multigoal policy analysis.

Second, taxes and other distortions lead to divergence between the rate of return on private investment and the rate at which consumers are willing to trade current and future consumption. Suppose that consumers are willing to trade marginal current and marginal future consumption at a rate of 6 percent.[55] If they face an income tax of 25 percent and firms face a profits tax of 50 percent, then they will invest only in projects that earn a return of at least 16 percent. (The firm returns 8 percent to the investor after the profits tax is paid; the investor retains 6 percent after paying the income tax.)

Which, if either, of these rates should be interpreted as the social discount rate? Economists have generally answered this question in terms of the opportunity costs of the public project.[56] If the public project is to be financed entirely at the expense of current consumption, then the private discount rate for consumption is appropriate. If the public project is to be financed at the expense of private investment, then the rate of return on private investment is appropriate. More generally, the average of the investment and consumption rates, weighted in proportion to the costs of projects in terms of lost private investment and consumption, has been advanced as the appropriate social discount rate.

[55]We take this example from Robert C. Lind, *Discounting for Time and Risk in Energy Policy*, pp. 28–29.

[56]See ibid., pp. 32–33.

Controversy still remains, however, because economists disagree about whether public investment detracts primarily from current consumption or private investment. Arnold Harberger, for instance, argues that because marginal public expenditures are typically financed by borrowing, public investment fully displaces private investment.[57] Accepting this "crowding out" hypothesis, we might use some market measure, such as the rate of return on corporate Aaa bonds, as the first approximation for the social discount rate.[58] Of course, we would adjust for expected inflation to arrive at a real social discount rate.

A discount rate based on the rate of return on corporate Aaa bonds would generally be considered riskless. Should a further adjustment be made for risk? Again, there is no clear consensus among economists on the answer.[59] In general, the answer depends on the expected correlation between the returns on the project and the level of national income. Upward adjustments to the riskless rate are in order if returns from the project are positively correlated with national income; downward adjustments if returns are negatively correlated with national income. We very rarely have adequate information for making such adjustments, however.

Practical Approaches.   What can we do in the absence of a consensus on the appropriate social discount rate? One approach is to report net benefits for a range of discount rates. Analysts should also explain why they believe the range they have used is reasonable. A related approach, which we illustrated in Figure 7.8, is to report the largest discount rate that yields positive net benefits. Clients can then be advised to adopt the project if they believe the correct discount rate is smaller than the reported rate.

Another approach is to use the same discount rate for all projects being considered by the decision-making unit. With this approach, at least all projects are evaluated using the same standard. The U.S. Office of Management and Budget followed this approach in 1972, requiring all federal agencies to use a real discount rate of 10 percent.[60] Congress exempted water projects, however, because many politically favored projects needed a lower discount rate to show positive net benefits—even benefit-cost analysis itself can be subverted by government failure! Of course, there may be losses rather than gains in efficiency from using a common standard if it is far from the correct value.

Finally, there are some situations where market interest rates represent the opportunity cost of public investment and therefore are the appropriate discount

[57]Arnold C. Harberger, "The Discount Rate in Public Investment Evaluation," in *Conference Proceedings of the Committee on the Economics of Water Resource Development* (Denver, Colo.: Western Agricultural Economics Research Council, Report No. 17, 1969).

[58]For a demonstration of how to move from market rates to the social discount rate under the Harberger hypothesis, see Steve H. Hanke and James Bradford Anwyll, "On the Discount Rate Controversy," *Public Policy*, Vol. 28, No. 2, Spring 1980, pp. 171–83.

[59]See Martin J. Bailey and Michael C. Jensen, "Risk and the Discount Rate for Public Investment," in Michael C. Jensen, ed., *Studies in the Theory of Capital Markets* (New York: Praeger, 1972), pp. 269–93.

[60]U.S. Office of Management and Budget, "To the Heads of Executive Departments and Establishments, Subject: Discount Rates to Be Used in Evaluating Time-Distributed Costs and Benefits," Circular A-94, March 27, 1972.

rates. For example, if we are doing a benefit-cost analysis from the perspective of a local government, then the opportunity cost of public investment is the rate at which the local government can borrow. A similar argument can be made for small countries that borrow in international capital markets.

Measuring Consumer Surplus in the Presence of Income Effects

All of our discussion of consumer surplus has been in terms of market demand schedules. A *market*, or *Marshallian, demand schedule* indicates the relationship between the price of a good and the quantity of the good demanded, holding consumers' incomes and the prices of all other goods constant. We refer to it as a market demand schedule because it can often be estimated from directly observable market data. We have assumed throughout our discussion that consumer surplus changes measured under the Marshallian demand schedule exactly correspond to the aggregate of individuals' compensating variations for the price change being considered. That is, we have equated consumer surplus loss with sums of payments that would be just sufficient to return consumers to the utility levels they enjoyed prior to the price increase. In fact, surplus changes measured under Marshallian demand schedules only approximate the sums of individuals' compensating variations. Discrepancies arise because price changes induce income effects that also change consumers' utility levels.

Compensated Demand Schedules.   Instead of drawing the Marshallian, or constant income, demand schedule, we can draw demand schedules that hold the utility levels of consumers constant. That is, for a given price change, give consumers enough additional income so that they are as well-off after the price change as before. In other words, compensate consumers for their utility losses to obtain what is called a *Hicksian demand schedule*. The consumer surplus measured under the Hicksian demand schedule exactly equals the sum of compensating variations.

Figure 7.14 shows the relationship between the Marshallian and Hicksian demand schedules. The line labeled D_{M} is the Marshallian demand schedule. The line labeled D_{C} is the Hicksian demand schedule drawn to hold utility constant at the level obtained at the original price P_0. The vertical distance under D_{C} measures the maximum amount that consumers could pay for an additional, or marginal, unit of the good and still have the utility level that they enjoy when price is P_0. The difference between this vertical distance and the price they actually have to pay represents the surplus they enjoy from the marginal unit. If we took the marginal unit away, we would have to give them the surplus amount to return them exactly to the initial level of utility. By adding the marginal surpluses over a quantity change, we obtain a total surplus change that exactly equals the compensating variation for the quantity change.

In light of this interpretation of the Hicksian demand schedule D_{C}, the area of trapezoid $P_1 b d P_0$ exactly equals the compensating variation for a price change from P_0 to P_1. Using the consumer surplus measure with the Marshallian demand schedule underestimates the compensating variation by the area of triangle abd.

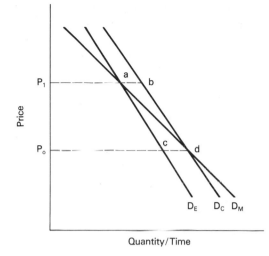

Figure 7.14   Constant Income and Constant Utility Demand Schedules

We could also construct a Hicksian demand schedule that corresponds to equivalent variation, which answers the question: What change in income at the initial price level, P_0, would change the utility level to that resulting from the move to price P_1? Because we are holding utilities constant at the levels obtained at P_1, the Hicksian demand schedule corresponding to equivalent variation crosses the Marshallian demand schedule at P_1. It is shown as D_E in Figure 7.14.

The consumer surplus change measured using D_E exactly equals the equivalent variation for the price increase from P_0 to P_1. Therefore, the Marshallian consumer surplus change overestimates the equivalent variation by the area of triangle adc.

The greater the income effect of the price change, the steeper are the slopes of the Hicksian demand schedules relative to the slope of the Marshallian demand schedule. If the income elasticity for the good were zero, then the Hicksian demand schedules would be coincident with the Marshallian demand schedule. In this case, compensating variation, equivalent variation, and consumer surplus based on the Marshallian demand schedule would be exactly equal. Even if the income elasticity were not zero, as long as the fraction of income spent on the good after the price increase is small, the income effect will be negligible so that equivalent and compensating variation will be closely approximated by the Marshallian consumer surplus.[61]

[61]The relevant quantity for determining the size of the income effect is the proportion of income spent on the good multiplied by the income elasticity of the good. If this quantity is small relative to the price elasticity of the Marshallian demand schedule, then Marshallian consumer surplus will closely approximate compensating and equivalent variation. For a clear discussion of income and substitution effects, see Lee S. Friedman, *Microeconomic Policy Analysis* (New York: McGraw-Hill, 1984), pp. 88–96, 143–52.

Dealing with Large Income Effects.   When income effects are large, the Marshallian consumer surplus substantially underestimates compensating variation, the basic measure of willingness to pay in benefit-cost analysis.[62] One approach, developed by Robert D. Willig, uses estimates of the upper and lower bounds on income elasticities to place bounds on the divergence between Marshallian consumer surplus and compensating variation.[63] Another approach, developed by George W. McKenzie and Ivor F. Pearce, approximates equivalent variation using information that can be derived from Marshallian demand schedules.[64]

These approaches are fairly complicated to execute and difficult to explain. Should they be more commonly used? We think not for two reasons. First, estimation errors in Marshallian consumer surplus are likely to be larger than theoretical divergences from either compensating or equivalent variation for even fairly large income effects—we generally do not have very precise estimates of price and income elasticities. For example, consider the wide range of price elasticities for beer found in the literature. Second, benefit-cost analysis is unlikely to be the appropriate technique for evaluating any policy that involves extremely large income effects—distributional values are almost certain to come into play. For example, a policy that greatly increased the price of housing, a major component of most family budgets, would almost certainly not be analyzed solely in terms of economic efficiency. Once we move to multigoal analysis, errors in our estimate of net benefits are likely to have less influence on the policy choice.

Estimating the Demand for Nonmarketed Goods

Public projects often produce goods that are not traded in markets. Indeed, market failures involving public goods provide the primary rationale for direct public supply. Consequently, we frequently encounter situations where we cannot directly infer demand schedules from market data. Two general approaches are sometimes useful in assessing the demand for nonmarket goods: hedonic price models and survey assessments.

Hedonic Price Models.   Levels of nonmarketed goods sometimes affect the prices of goods that are marketed. For example, a housing price not only reflects the characteristics of the house, but also such locational factors as the quality of the public school district, the level of public safety, and accessibility. (Remember the old saying: "There are three important factors in real estate— location, loca-

---

[62]We have selected compensating variation as the money metric for measuring welfare changes because it has a slightly more natural interpretation than equivalent variation. George W. McKenzie argues, however, that only equivalent variation satisfies all the desirable properties of a money metric for social welfare. See George W. McKenzie, *Measuring Economic Welfare: New Methods* (New York: Cambridge University Press, 1983).

[63]Robert D. Willig, "Consumer Surplus Without Apology," *American Economic Review*, Vol. 66, No. 4, September 1976, pp. 589–97.

[64]George W. McKenzie and Ivor F. Pearce, "Welfare Measurement—A Synthesis," *American Economic Review*, Vol. 72, No. 4, September 1982, pp. 669–82.

tion, and location.'') Now, if we could find houses that were identical in all these factors except, say, the level of public safety, then we could interpret any price difference as the value the market places on the difference in safety levels.

In practice, we are almost never fortunate enough to find groups that are identical in every way except for the particular characteristic of interest. Nevertheless, statistical techniques can often be used to identify the independent contribution of the characteristic of interest on price. The theoretical foundation for such estimation is the *hedonic price model*.[65] We have already discussed use of the hedonic price model to estimate the value of life implicit in risk-wage trade-offs. Other applications include using intercity salary differences to estimate the benefits of air quality improvements;[66] using housing values to estimate the value of air quality improvements;[67] and using housing price differences to estimate implicit values placed on health risks.[68]

Lack of appropriate data severely limits the widespread applicability of the hedonic price model. Unless data describing all the major characteristics affecting price are available, a reliable estimate of the independent contribution of the characteristic of interest cannot be made. Even when data on all major characteristics are available, it may still be difficult to separate the independent effects of characteristics that tend to vary in the same pattern. Nonetheless, the hedonic price model offers a conceptually attractive approach even if its practical applicability is limited.

Opinion Surveys.[69]   A direct approach to estimating the benefits of public goods is to ask a sample of people how much they would be willing to pay to obtain them. By comparing the demographic characteristics of the sample to that of the general population, an estimate of the aggregate willingness to pay for specific levels of public goods can be made. A major advantage of this approach is that it permits estimation of the benefits of a wide range of public goods, including

[65]See Zvi Griliches, ed., *Price Indexes and Quality Change* (Cambridge, Mass.: Harvard Univerity Press, 1971); and Sherwin Rosen, "Hedonic Prices and Implicit Markets: Product Differentiation in Pure Competition," *Journal of Political Economy*, Vol. 82, No. 1, January-February 1974, pp. 34-55.

[66]Mark Bayless, "Measuring the Benefits of Air Quality Improvements: A Hedonic Salary Approach," *Journal of Environmental Economics and Management*, Vol. 9, No. 1, 1982, pp. 81-89.

[67]Ronald Ridker and John Henning, "The Determinants of Residential Property Values with Special Reference to Air Pollution," *Review of Economics and Statistics*, Vol. 49, No. 2, May 1967, pp. 246-56. This early application preceded the explicit development of the hedonic price model. For a more recent treatment, see A. Mitchell Polinsky and Daniel L. Rubinfeld, "Property Values and the Benefits of Environmental Improvements: Theory and Measurement," in Lowdon Wingo and Alan Evens, eds., *Public Economics and the Quality of Life* (Baltimore: Johns Hopkins University Press, 1977), pp. 154.-80.

[68]Paul Portney, "Housing Prices, Health Effects, and Valuing Reductions in Risk of Death," *Journal of Environmental Economics and Management*, Vol. 8, No. 1, 1981, pp. 72-78.

[69]For an excellent review, see Ronald G. Cummings, Louis Anthony Cox, Jr., and A. Myrick Freeman, III, "General Methods for Benefits Assessment," in Judith D. Bentkover, Vincent T. Covello, and Jeryl Mumpower, eds., *Benefits Assessment: The State of the Art* (Boston: D. Reidel, 1986), pp. 161-91; also see V. Kerry Smith and William H. Desvousges, *Measuring Water Quality Benefits* (Boston: Kluwer-Nijhoff, 1986), pp. 71-116.

national ones like defense that do not vary at the local level.[70] It also permits estimates of the benefits people derive from the provision of public goods to others.[71]

Obviously, this approach suffers from all the well-known problems of survey research: answers are sensitive to the particular wording of questions; nonrandom sampling designs or nonresponses can lead to unrepresentative samples; respondents have limited attention spans; and respondents often have difficulty putting hypothetical questions into meaningful contexts. There is also the danger that respondents will behave strategically. For example, because I know that I will not actually have to pay the amount that I state, I may inflate my true willingness to pay for public goods I prefer so as to increase the chances that the survey will value them highly. While strategic behavior can be limited somewhat by forcing respondents to make trade-offs among competing public goods, it remains an unavoidable problem of the survey approach.[72]

Activity Surveys: The Travel Cost Method.   Some of the problems of opinion surveys can be avoided by questioning people about their actual behavior. The most common application of this approach is the estimation of the value of recreation sites from people's use patterns.[73] For example, imagine that we wish to estimate the value people place on a regional park. We could survey people who live various distances from the park about how frequently they visit it. We then would statistically relate the frequency of use to the travel costs (the effective price of using the park) and the demographic characteristics of the respondents. These relationships enable us to estimate the population's demand schedule for park visits so that we can apply standard consumer surplus analysis. Of course, the accuracy of the estimated demand curve depends on how well wage rates measure the opportunity cost of travel time; it will not be a good measure for people who view the travel itself as desirable.

CONCLUSION

Benefit-cost analysis provides a framework for evaluating the economic efficiency of policies. The calculation of net benefits answers the question: Does the policy generate sufficient benefits so that those who bear its costs could at least potentially be compensated so that some people could be made better-off without making anyone worse-off? In order to calculate net benefits, we must decide which effects are relevant and how they can be made commensurable. The general con-

[70]See, for example, Daniel Hewitt, "Demand for National Public Goods: Estimates from Surveys," *Economic Inquiry*, Vol. 23, No. 3, July 1985, pp. 487–506.

[71]W. Kip Viscusi, Wesley A. Magat, and Anne Forrest, "Altruistic and Private Valuations of Risk Reduction," *Journal of Policy Analysis and Management*, Vol. 7, No. 2, Fall 1987, pp. 227–45.

[72]For a conceptual approach to limiting strategic behavior, see Edward H. Clarke, *Demand Revelation and the Provision of Public Goods* (Cambridge, Mass.: Ballinger, 1980). Unfortunately, Clarke's approach does not seem feasible for collective choice by large numbers of people.

[73]See Marion Clawson and Jack L. Knetsch, *Economics of Outdoor Recreation* (Baltimore: Johns Hopkins University Press, 1966).

cepts of opportunity cost and willingness to pay guide us in the application of the craft of benefit-cost analysis. The art lies in making reasonable inferences from data that are usually fragmented and incomplete. The art also lies in realizing when inadequate data or social values other than efficiency make the narrow benefit-cost approach inappropriate.

8

THINKING STRATEGICALLY ABOUT ADOPTION AND IMPLEMENTATION

The adoption and execution of collective decisions inherently involve cooperation. Collective decisions begin as proposals in political arenas and culminate in effects on people. We can divide this process into two phases: adoption and implementation. The adoption phase begins with the formulation of a policy proposal and ends, if ever, with its formal acceptance as a law, regulation, administrative directive, or other decision made according to the rules of the relevant political arena. The implementation phase begins with the adoption of the policy and continues as long as the policy remains in effect. While policy analysts typically make their contributions by formulating and evaluating proposals during the adoption phase, they cannot do so effectively without anticipating the entire process from proposal to effect.

Yet the distinction between adoption and implementation does not do justice to the complexity that typically characterizes the policy process. Adopted policies, especially laws, rarely specify exactly what is to be done. Instead, they may require policy decisions to be made in other arenas. For example, a county legislature might adopt an ordinance that prohibits smoking in certain public places, makes violations punishable by fines, and delegates enforcement responsibility to the county health department. Now the county's health department must adopt an enforcement policy. Should it simply wait for complaints about violations from the public, or should it institute spot checks? Should it issue warnings, or immediately impose fines? Although the head of the health department may have legal authority to answer these questions as she sees fit, her decisions probably would be influenced by the (perhaps conflicting) advice of her staff. If spot checks are to be instituted, then the chief inspector would face the task of designing a sampling procedure that his deputies could and would execute. Thus, the smoking policy that the public encounters results from a series of decisions following adoption of the ordinance.

We naturally think of values and interests coming into play during the adoption phase, and we are not surprised when those who oppose policies attempt to block their adoption. By thinking of the implementation phase as a series of adoptions, we prepare ourselves for the intrusion of the values and interests of those whose cooperation is needed to move the adopted policy from a general statement of intent to a specific set of desired impacts. In other words, we begin to think strategically about process as well as substance: How can we take advantage of the interests and values of others to further our ends?

We believe that our discussion of strategic thinking in this chapter is valuable from a number of perspectives. First, as we discussed in Chapter 6, we cannot make accurate predictions of the consequences of candidate policies without paying careful attention to their implementation. Strategic thinking is valuable, therefore, because it enables us to understand better the implementation process.

Second, clients often want their analysts to consider the political feasibility of policy alternatives. Sometimes political feasibility is explicitly treated as one goal in a multigoal policy analysis. Other times clients ask analysts to prepare confidential analyses of the political feasibility of particular policy alternatives. In either case, good analysis requires strategic thinking.

Third, as we discussed in Chapter 6, designing effective policy alternatives requires a certain amount of creativity. Strategic thinking helps us to be more creative by drawing our attention to ways of taking advantage of the self-interested behaviors of others. Similarly, it helps us to be more perceptive about potential problems and opportunities in designing implementation plans.

Fourth, analysts themselves often participate in adoption and implementation efforts. Clients sometimes solicit advice from analysts about day-to-day maneuvering in political arenas, invite them to participate as "technical experts" in negotiations, or send them as representatives to meetings where issues are discussed and perhaps even decided. Analysts are sometimes called upon to advise, direct, oversee, or even manage implementations. These sorts of "hands-on" activities require analysts to put strategic thinking into practice.

THE ADOPTION PHASE

Political scientists offer surprisingly little advice about how to predict and influence political feasibility.[1] Recent work applying expected utility theory to the study of international relations and national coalitions offers promise for making accurate and nonintuitive predictions.[2] In practice, however, politicians and businessmen who desire political predictions usually turn to *area experts*, people

[1]On the paucity of scholarly work on political feasibility, see David J. Webber, "Analyzing Political Feasibility: Political Scientists' Unique Contribution to Policy Analysis," *Policy Studies Journal*, Vol. 14, No. 4, June 1986, pp. 545-53.

[2]For a summary of the expected utility approach, see Bruce Bueno de Mesquita, David Newman, and Alvin Rabushka, *Forecasting Political Events: The Future of Hong Kong* (New Haven, Conn.: Yale University Press, 1985), pp. 11-54. The approach has already been employed with some success to explain international conflict. See Bruce Bueno de Mesquita, *The War Trap* (New Haven, Conn.: Yale University Press, 1981); and his article, "The War Trap Revisited," *American Political Science Review*, Vol. 79, No. 1, March 1985, pp. 156-77.

who are familiar with the relevant actors in local, national, or regional settings. For example, someone interested in the prospects for passage of U.S. legislation on trade may hire an expert on Congress. A firm considering capital investments in some country may consult an expert on the institutions of that country about the prospects for political stability. Of course, politicians usually consider themselves to be experts on the particular political arenas in which they operate. Policy analysts who have long tenure in institutional settings likewise tend to develop contextual knowledge that is useful in predicting political feasibility.

Finding the sort of information that an area expert provides is a reasonable starting point for predicting political feasibility. But this information by itself is often descriptive and dated. To put it to effective use, we need a theory about how people behave so that we can develop strategies for improving the chances of obtaining the outcomes we desire. Hence, after reviewing the sorts of information that are relevant to understanding the political environment, we turn to the basic elements of political strategy.

Assessing and Influencing Political Feasibility

One of the few political scientists to speak directly to the question of how policy analysts can predict and influence the political feasibility of policy proposals is Arnold Meltsner.[3] He provides a checklist of the information needed to assess political feasibility: Who are the relevant actors? What are their motivations and beliefs? What are their political resources? In which political arenas will the relevant decisions be made? Although we discuss these questions sequentially, in practice we answer them iteratively, moving among them as we learn more about the political environment.

Identifying the Relevant Actors.   Which individuals and groups are likely to voice an opinion on an issue? Two, usually overlapping, sets of actors need to be identified: those with a substantive interest in the issue and those with official standing in the decision arena. For example, imagine a proposal before a city council that would prohibit firms within the city from subjecting their employees to random tests for detecting the use of illegal drugs. We expect unions to support the measure and business groups to oppose it. Further, we expect unions and business groups that have been politically active in the past to be the ones most likely to become active on this issue—say, the Labor Council and the Chamber of Commerce as shown in Figure 8.1. At the same time, we identify the members of the city council as actors by virtue of their rights to vote on legislation and the mayor by virtue of her veto power.

We expect union and business leaders to be active because their direct interests are at stake. Civil libertarians might become involved because values they perceive as important are at issue. (Some may see the ordinance as necessary to protect the right of workers to privacy; others may view it as an unwarranted interference in the decisions of firms.) Perhaps certain community groups such as the Urban League will become active either because they have a direct interest or because they usually ally themselves with one of the interested parties.

---

[3] "Political Feasibility and Policy Analysis," *Public Administration Review*, Vol. 32, No. 6, November/December 1972, pp. 859–67.

Actors	Motivations	Beliefs	Resources
Interest groups:			
Labor Council	Protect workers from harassment	Testing will be used unfairly	Large membership; ties to Democratic party
Chamber of Commerce	Protect firms' rights to weed out dangerous and unproductive workers	Testing may be necessary to detect and deter employee drug use	Influential membership; ties to Republican party
Civil Liberties Union	Protect right of individuals	Testing infringes on right to privacy	Articulate spokesmen
Libertarian party	Protect right of contract	Testing limits should be matter of negotiation between labor and management	Vocal membership
Urban League	Protect minority employees	Testing disproportionately hurts minorities	Can claim to speak for minority interests
Daily News	Support business community	Testing ban not appropriate at city level	Editorials
Nonelected officials			
City Attorney	Support mayor	Ban probably legal	Professional opinion
Director of Public Health	Fight drug abuse	Testing probably desirable if not punitive	Professional opinion; evidence on accuracy of tests
Elected officials			
Council member A (Dem.)	Support labor	Ban desirable	Vote
Council member B (Dem.)	Support labor	Ban probably desirable	Vote
Council member C (Dem.) (President of Council)	Support community groups	Ban probably desirable	Vote, agenda control

Figure 8.1 A Political Analysis Worksheet: Feasibility of a Ban on Random Drug Testing in the Workplace

Figure 8.1   (continued)

Actors	Motivations	Beliefs	Resources
Council member D (Rep.)	Support business	Ban probably undesirable	Vote
Council member E (Rep.)	Support business	Ban undesirable	Vote
Mayor (Dem.)	Maintain good relations with labor and business	Ban probably not desirable	Veto power, media attention

Other public figures besides the members of the city council may also be relevant. For example, although the city attorney does not have a vote on the council, his opinion on the legality of the proposal may carry considerable weight with council members. The opinion of the director of public health on the accuracy of testing may also be influential. The editor of the local newspaper has no official standing whatever, yet may be an important participant by virtue of the editorials he writes and the influence he exerts over the coverage of the news.

How should analysts compile lists of potential actors? Obviously, *assume that anyone with a strong interest—whether economic, partisan, ideological, or professional—will become actors*. Also, include those in official positions. If you are new to the issue or arena, then try to find an experienced person to be your informant. Use newspapers or other written accounts to discover who participated in public debates on similar issues in the past. Finally, contact potential actors directly to question them about their views and to assess the likelihood that they will become active participants when doing so will not adversely affect your client or the future prospects for your proposal.

Understanding the Motivations and Beliefs of Actors.   The motivations and beliefs of organized interest groups will often be apparent. When they are not, you can usually make a reasonable guess about how they will view particular proposals by comparing the costs and benefits that the leaders of the groups are likely to perceive. If their perceptions are based on what you think are incorrect beliefs, then you may be able to influence their positions by providing information. For example, the president of the local Urban League chapter may support a ban on random drug testing because he believes that the ban would protect minority workers, one of his constituencies. He might decide to oppose the ban, however, if he comes to believe that the ban will result in a net loss in minority jobs because some firms will leave the city to avoid its restrictions.

It may be more difficult to determine the relevant motivations and beliefs of those in official positions. Elected officials, political appointees, and members of the civil service all have a variety of motivations. As we discussed in Chapter 4, elected officials are likely to be concerned with reelection or election to higher office as well as with representing the interests of their constituencies and promoting the social good. Political appointees may be motivated by their substantive values as well as by their loyalties to their political sponsors, by their desire to maintain their effectiveness in their current positions, and by their interest in opportunities for future employment. In addition to substantive values, civil servants are often motivated by their sense of professionalism and by their desire to secure resources for their organizational units.

It should not be surprising that it is often difficult to predict which motivations will dominate. Indeed, such conflicting motivations can lead the officials themselves to the sort of personal ethical dilemmas that we described in Chapter 2. How can we understand the relative importance of officials' various motivations concerning a particular issue? We can begin by heeding the insight in the aphorism: *where you stand depends on where you sit.*[4] In other words, put yourself in the position of the relevant officials. What would you want if you were in their place? What actions would you be willing to take to get what you want?

Obviously, the more you know about particular officials, the better you will be able to answer these questions. If an official holds a strong substantive value relevant to the issue, for instance, then she may be willing to act against even vocal constituent interests. On the other hand, she may be willing to go against her own substantive values if the issue is of fundamental concern to one of her important constituencies. Of course, such factors as the safety of her district and the nearness to an election can also affect the position that she takes on the issue.

Assessing the Resources of Actors.   Actors have a variety of political resources. Interest groups can claim to speak for a constituency. They may have financial resources that can be used to pay for lobbying, analysis, publicity, and campaign contributions. Their leaders may have ongoing relationships with relevant officials. By virtue of their memberships, analytical capacity, or track record, the information they provide may command attention or carry weight. All these resources can be thought of as potentially relevant. Whether they actually come into play depends on the motivations of the groups and their leaders.

Officials have resources based on their positions and relationships. Legislators can vote, hold hearings, and influence the agenda; elected executives like mayors usually have veto power as well as considerable discretion in interpreting laws that are adopted; unelected executives often have influence by virtue of their professional status, programmatic knowledge, and ties to clientele groups. Any of these actors may be able to influence others through personal relationships based on trust, loyalty, fear, or reciprocity.

Figure 8.1, which presents a simple worksheet that identifies the actors who may be relevant in predicting the political feasibility of a city ordinance to ban random drug testing of employees, also notes their likely motivations, beliefs, and resources. Many of the entries may be little more than guesses. The entries in the worksheet should be updated as more information becomes available. For example, the actors' actual responses to the proposal once they learn about it may very well change your assessment of their beliefs and their willingness to use resources.

[4]Some view this aphorism as the central element of effective strategic thinking. For example, see Donald E. Stokes, "Political and Organizational Analysis in the Policy Curriculum," *Journal of Policy Analysis and Management*, Vol. 6, No. 1, Fall 1986, pp. 45–55, at p. 52.

Choosing the Arena.   Each political arena has its own set of rules about how decisions are made. The basic rules are generally written—legislatures have "rules of order" and agencies have administrative procedures. But unwritten traditions and standard practices may be just as relevant to understanding how decisions are typically reached. Becoming familiar with these rules, both formal and informal, is important for political prediction and strategy.

To use the information in Figure 8.1 to make a prediction about the likelihood of adoption of the testing ban, we must first determine the arenas in which the proposal will be considered. As suggested by the entries in Figure 8.1 under "elected officials," we expect that the city council will be the primary arena. Assuming that the council members vote according to their constituencies' apparent interests, the ban would pass on a party-line vote of three to two. The mayor would then be in a difficult situation. If she vetos the ordinance, then she may alienate her fellow Democrats. If she does not veto it, then she will alienate business interests.

The mayor might be able to get out of this difficult political position by trying to change the arena. She might argue that, although restrictions on testing are desirable, they are more appropriately imposed at the state level. If she can find a state assemblyman or senator to propose the ban in the state legislature, then she could argue that a vote by the city council should be delayed until the prospects for state action become clear. Perhaps she would ask the council to pass a resolution urging state action. If the council agrees, then she will have been successful in changing arenas.

More generally, we should expect that actors who lose, or anticipate losing, in one arena will try to move the issue to another. As illustrated by the mayor's maneuver, unfavorable outcomes at one level of government can sometimes be avoided by shifting the issue to another level. For example, one reason why labor unions pushed for the federal legislation that became the Occupational Safety and Health Act of 1970 was their dissatisfaction with their ability to influence the setting and enforcement of health standards at the state level.[5] The arena can also shift from one branch of government to another. For instance, when the Food and Drug Administration published a proposed rule that would prohibit the use of saccharin as a food additive, opponents succeeded in getting Congress to pass a moratorium on finalization of the rule.[6] Often those who lose in the legislative and executive branches try to shift the arena to the courts. For instance, during the 1970s advocates of busing to reduce the racial segregation in schools caused by housing patterns routinely achieved their objectives through the courts. Of course, the ability to make a credible threat to move the issue to another arena can itself be a political resource.

---

[5]John Mendeloff, *Regulating Safety: An Economic and Political Analysis of Occupational Safety and Health Policy* (Cambridge, Mass.: MIT Press, 1979), pp. 15–16.

[6]Richard A. Merrill, "Saccharin: A Regulator's View," in Robert W. Crandall and Lester B. Lave, eds., *The Scientific Basis of Health and Safety Regulation* (Washington, D.C.: Brookings Institution, 1981), pp. 153–70.

Political Strategies Within Arenas

Trying to shift issues to more favorable arenas is not the only political strategy that can be used to achieve policy outcomes. We can often use one or more of four other general strategies: co-optation, compromise, heresthetics, and rhetoric. We briefly consider each of these in turn.

Co-optation.   People, especially the types with strong egos who typically hold public office (and teach at universities), tend to take pride in authorship. Indeed, we are sometimes reluctant to admit the weaknesses in what we perceive to be *our* ideas. Getting others to believe that your proposal is at least partly their idea is perhaps one of the most common political strategies.[7] In legislative settings it often takes the form of cosponsorship—across aisles and chambers. In administrative settings, it often involves creating an advisory group that is constituted so as to arrive at the desired recommendation. Potential adversaries, who believe that they have contributed to the recommendation as committee members, may be less likely to become active opponents. Public officials with strong interpersonal skills can sometimes successfully co-opt potential opponents with as little as a seemingly heart-to-heart conversation or other gesture of personal attention. (Didn't you wonder why the dean invited you and the other student leaders to those dinners?)

Co-optation may be useful when your proposal infringes on the "turf" of other political actors.[8] Politicians and bureaucrats often stake out areas of interest and expertise. Although some of them may be "natural allies" by virtue of their interests and beliefs, they may nevertheless feel threatened by proposals originated by other people that appear to fall within their areas. Unless you involve them to some extent in the design of policy proposals, they may voice opposition without seriously considering substantive merits. Further, other actors who take their cues on the issue from the experts may decline to give the proposals close attention. For example, council members may not give serious attention to a proposal for the establishment of a particular type of drug rehabilitation program unless the director of public health says that it is worthy of consideration.

Of course, you cannot use co-optation as a strategy unless you are willing to share credit. As an analyst, the nature of your job demands that you allow your client to take credit for your good ideas (and that you save any discredit

[7]More generally, it may be that radical policy change is possible only when elites from the major political cultures perceive the change as consistent with their fundamental values. For a discussion of such nonincremental change, see Dennis Coyle and Aaron Wildavsky, "Requisites of Radical Reform: Income Maintenance Versus Tax Preferences," *Journal of Policy Analysis and Management*, Vol. 7, No. 1, Fall 1987, pp. 1–16.

[8]For a discussion of the use of co-optation at the organizational level, see Philip Selznick, *TVA and the Grass Roots* (Berkeley: University of California Press, 1949), pp. 13–16. Harvey M. Sapolsky identifies co-optation of potential critics both inside and outside the Navy as one of the factors contributing to the success of the Polaris missile project. See his *The Polaris System Development: Bureaucratic and Programmatic Success in Government* (Cambridge, Mass.: Harvard University Press, 1972), pp. 15, 47–54.

for bad ideas for yourself)—remember you earn your keep by providing good ideas. Co-optation strategies, therefore, should be based on your client's explicit willingness to give credit in return for progress toward policy goals.

Compromise.   We use the word *compromise* to refer to substantive modifications of policy proposals intended to make them more politically acceptable. When our most preferred policy lacks adequate support, we can consider modifying it to gain the additional support needed for adoption—in terms of multigoal policy analysis, we trade progress toward some goal to achieve greater political feasibility. Compromise is desirable if we prefer the resulting adoptable proposal to any others that are also feasible. Generally, desirable compromise involves making the smallest modifications necessary to attract the minimal number of additional supporters required for adoption.[9]

One approach to compromising is to remove or modify those features of the proposal that are most objectionable to its opponents. Do any features appear as "red flags" to opponents? Sometimes offending features can be removed without great change in the substantive impact of the proposal. For example, imagine that you have made a proposal that the county hire private firms to provide educational services to inmates in the county jail. Some opponents, who object on ideological grounds to profit-making activity in connection with criminal corrections, may be willing to support your proposal if you specify that only nonprofit organizations can be service providers. With this restriction, you may be able to gain adoption of a policy with most of the benefits of your original proposal.

Another approach to compromising is to add features that opponents find attractive. In Chapter 4 we discussed logrolling, a form of compromise that is characterized by the packaging together of substantively unrelated proposals. The engineering of logrolls is usually the purview of clients rather than analysts. More commonly, analysts are in a position to give advice about the composition of a single proposal. For example, consider again the proposal to ban random drug testing in the workplace. Matched against the status quo, it appears that the ban would be adopted by the city council. If you opposed the ban, then you might try to stop it by proposing that firms be banned not from testing but from firing, demoting, or disciplining an employee on the basis of a single test. Assuming that the two council members (D and E) who are opposed to the ban would support this compromise position, it might get the necessary votes by attracting the support of one of the less-enthusiastic supporters of the stronger ban (B or C). You

[9]In arenas where the gains of winners come at the expense of losers (zero-sum games), Riker's size principle predicts such behavior: "In social situations similar to *n*-person, zero-sum games with side-payments, participants create coalitions just as large as they believe will ensure winning and no larger." William H. Riker, *The Theory of Political Coalitions* (New Haven, Conn.: Yale University Press, 1962), pp. 32–33.

In some circumstances, however, compromising more to obtain a broader coalition may be desirable if the greater consensus will deter opponents from seeking to overturn the policy at a later time or in another arena. For example, Justice Felix Frankfurter successfully delayed the Supreme Court decision in *Brown v. Board of Education*, 347 U.S. 483 (1954), so that a unanimous opinion could be achieved. Bernard Schwartz with Stephan Lesher, *Inside the Warren Court* (Garden City, N.Y.: Doubleday, 1983), pp. 21–27.

might be able to get the mayor and the director of public health to support the compromise position and help secure the third vote.

In organizational settings, compromise often takes the form of *negotiation*, whereby interested parties attempt to reach agreement through bargaining. For example, local implementation of a state law requiring teachers and health professionals to report suspected cases of child abuse may require an agreement to be reached between the police chief and the director of social services on how reports are to be investigated.

What factors are likely to influence the character and outcomes of negotiations?[10] One factor is the frequency with which the participants must deal with each other—if they must deal with each other often, then it is likely that they will be more flexible and amicable than they would be in an isolated negotiation.[11] Another factor is the political resources that each brings to the negotiations. Is either one in a better position to appeal to outside parties such as the county executive or the mayor? Can either one use precedent as an argument? Can either party inflict costs on the other by delaying agreement?

Roger Fisher and William Ury provide a useful practical guide for negotiating effectively.[12] We note here two of their themes that can be thought of as general strategies for successfully negotiating compromise.

First, remember that you are dealing with people who have emotions, beliefs, and personal interests. The presentation as well as the content of proposals can be important for reaching mutually satisfactory agreements. For example, if your counterpart in the negotiation has gone on record as opposing a tax increase, then, even if you convince him that additional revenue is needed, he is unlikely to agree to something called a tax increase. Look for a compromise that allows him to "save face." Perhaps what we would normally describe as a gasoline tax could be called a "road user's fee" instead. Maybe just substituting the euphemism "revenue enhancement" will be an adequate face saver—perhaps even if everyone knows that it is just a different phrase for the same thing! The general point is to always keep in mind that you are dealing with people, who, like yourself, want to feel good about what they are doing.

Second, try to negotiate interests rather than positions so that mutually beneficial compromises can be found. For example, Fisher and Ury point to the negotiations between Egypt and Israel over the Sinai, which was captured by Israel in the Six-Day War of 1967.[13] As long as both sides approached the issue positionally—Egypt demanding return of the entire Sinai and Israel demanding that the boundary line be redrawn—there was little possibility of agreement. By looking at interests, however, a solution became possible. While Egypt, after centuries of domination, was unwilling to cede sovereignty to any of its territory, Israel did not desire the territory per se. Rather, it wanted to keep Egyptian forces

[10]For a more comprehensive listing, see Howard Raiffa, *The Art and Science of Negotiation* (Cambridge, Mass.: Harvard University Press, 1982), pp. 11–19.

[11]On reciprocity as a source of social cooperation, see Robert M. Axelrod, *The Evolution of Cooperation* (New York: Basic Books, 1984).

[12]Roger Fisher and William Ury, *Getting to Yes: Negotiating Agreement Without Giving In* (New York: Penguin Books, 1983).

[13]Ibid., pp. 42–43.

away from its border. The solution was to return the Sinai to Egyptian sovereignty but to demilitarize those areas that could be used as staging areas to threaten Israel. The general point to keep in mind is that the ultimate purpose of negotiations should be to satisfy the interests of the parties involved. In other words, approach negotiations as a sort of on-the-spot policy analysis—get agreement on the facts in the dispute (define the problem), identify interests (determine goals), agree on criteria for determining a fair solution (specify evaluation criteria), brainstorm for possible solutions (develop policy alternatives), and only then consider specific solutions (evaluate alternatives in terms of criteria).[14]

Heresthetics.   William H. Riker has coined the word *heresthetics* to refer to strategies that attempt to gain advantage through manipulation of the circumstances of political choice.[15] Heresthetical devices fall into two categories: those that operate through the agenda and those that operate through the dimensions of evaluation.

In Chapter 4 we illustrated the paradox of voting with the hypothetical example of a determination of U.S. policy toward Nicaragua through pairwise votes on three alternatives (war, peace, and support of the Contras). The preferences of the voters were such that, if everyone voted their true preferences, the order in which policies were considered—the agenda—determined the one that would be selected. Thus, manipulating the agenda can be a powerful political strategy.

The holders of specific offices often have the opportunity to manipulate the agenda directly. Such officials as the speaker of the legislature, the committee chairman, or the administrator running a meeting may be able to influence the policy outcome by the way they structure the decision process. Sometimes they can bluntly structure the decision process to their advantage by refusing to allow certain alternatives to be considered—perhaps justifying their actions by a call for further study. Other times they can achieve their ends by determining the order in which the alternatives will be considered.

Obviously, agenda setters are especially important actors in any political arena. If your client is an agenda setter, then you are in an advantageous position for seeing your accepted recommendations adopted as policy. If your client is not an agenda setter, then you must find ways to increase the chances that your client's proposals receive favorable agenda positions. One approach is to design your proposals so that they appeal to the agenda setters.

Another approach is to mobilize other political actors on your behalf to make it politically costly for agenda setters to block your proposals. For example, in 1962 Senator Estes Kefauver found that the legislation he introduced to amend the laws governing the regulation of drugs was stalled in the Judiciary Committee by its chairman, Senator James Eastland, who opposed it. Only by generating criticism of inaction in the press and mobilizing the support of the AFL-CIO did Kefauver succeed in getting President John F. Kennedy to pressure Eastland to report out a version of Kefauver's bill.[16] Obviously, such tactics must be used

---

[14]Ibid., pp. 10–14.

[15]William H. Riker, *The Art of Political Manipulation* (New Haven, Conn.: Yale University Press, 1986), p. ix.

[16]Richard Harris, *The Real Voice* (New York: Macmillan, 1964), p. 166.

with care, especially when the goodwill of the agenda setter may be important on other issues in the future.

Once your proposal gets a place on the agenda, you may be able to improve its prospects by *sophisticated voting*—that is, by not voting your true preferences at some stage to achieve a better final outcome. For example, in 1956 the Democratic leadership of the U.S. House of Representatives proposed that federal aid be given directly to local school districts for the first time. If everyone had voted their true preferences, then the bill would have been passed by the Democratic majority. Representative Adam Clayton Powell introduced an amendment to the bill, however, that would have prevented funds from going to segregated schools. The amendment was supported by Northern Democrats, but it was opposed by Southern Democrats. Riker argues that a number of Republicans, who preferred no bill to the unamended bill and the unamended bill to the amended bill, nevertheless voted for the amendment because they expected that Southern Democrats would vote against the amended bill.[17] Their expectations were correct and the amended bill did not pass.

Assuming that the Northern Democrats preferred the unamended bill to no bill, why didn't they counter the Republicans' sophisticated voting with their own by voting against the Powell amendment so that the Southern Democrats would join with them to pass the unamended bill? Perhaps, as Riker suggests, the Northern Democrats saw taking a stand against segregation more valuable to them in terms of constituent support than obtaining a more preferred policy outcome. In other words, their position was complicated by the need to consider a second dimension of evaluation.

The situation of the Northern Democrats suggests the second category of heresthetical devices: those that alter the *dimension of evaluation*. When you are in a minority position, you can sometimes introduce a new consideration that splits the majority. For example, in 1970 several West Coast senators proposed amendments to the pending military appropriations bill that would have prohibited the Department of Defense from shipping nerve gas from Okinawa to the United States. Although they initially did not have enough votes to prevent the shipments, Senator Warren Magnuson helped them gain a majority by arguing that what was really at stake was the dignity of the Senate. The Senate had earlier passed a resolution saying that the President could not change the status of any territory involved in the peace treaty with Japan without consulting the Senate. Magnuson asserted that the gas shipments were part of preparations to return Okinawa to Japan—an unconstitutional usurpation of the Senate's right to ratify treaties. By casting the issue in terms of the rights of the Senate, Magnuson was able to gain passage of the amendment by attracting enough votes from those who would otherwise have favored the gas shipments.[18]

Rhetoric. Perhaps the most common political strategy is *rhetoric*, the use of persuasive language. At one normative extreme, rhetoric provides correct and relevant information that clarifies the probable impacts of proposed policies. At the other normative extreme, it provides incorrect or irrelevant information that

[17]William H. Riker, *Art of Political Manipulation*, pp. 114–28.
[18]Ibid., pp. 106–13.

obfuscates the probable impacts of proposed policies. As a policy analyst, you are likely to face ethical questions concerning the extent to which you should participate in your client's use of rhetoric that obfuscates rather than clarifies.

As an illustration of the ethical use of rhetoric, return to the proposal to ban random testing for drug use. In Figure 8.1, Council member C is listed as likely to vote for the ban because she sees her major constituency as community groups, which favor the ban. The director of the Urban League, for instance, favors the ban because he believes that testing might be used unfairly against minority workers. If you opposed the ban, then you might provide information to the Urban League director indicating that the ban would discourage some employers from staying or expanding in the city—the net effect on minority employment may actually be negative. If convinced, the director might then convince Council member C to change her position so that the ban would not pass.

Often the most effective rhetoric influences political actors indirectly through public opinion rather than directly through persuasion. As we discussed in Chapter 4, there seem to be policy windows—periods when public opinion and media attention are sensitive to political initiatives in specific policy areas. Public figures may be moved to act by the opportunity to gain publicity.[19] To keep policy windows open, or perhaps even to create them, policy advocates can provide information to the media through such mechanisms as press conferences, news releases, hearings, planted stories, and leaks. Obviously, information that can be portrayed as sensational will be more likely to get into the media than information that appears mundane.

A common, but ethically questionable, rhetorical strategy is to emphasize very negative, but unlikely, consequences.[20] This strategy takes advantage of the apparent tendency of people to overestimate the likelihood of very low probability events and to be more sensitive to potential losses than to potential gains.[21] For example, in discussions of health and safety, opponents of nuclear power tend to emphasize the consequences of a meltdown in combination with a containment structure failure. Now such an accident would indeed be catastrophic. But it is hard to imagine peacetime scenarios that would result in the failure of a containment structure.[22] Despite the very low probability of such a disaster, the public

[19]For a general overview on how federal officials interact with the press, see Martin Linsky, *Impact: How the Press Affects Federal Policymaking* (New York: Norton, 1986), pp. 148–68.

[20]Riker labels this strategy, *induced dread*, and explains how it operates in "Rhetoric in the Spatial Model," Paper Presented to the Conference on Coalition Government, European Institute, Florence, Italy, May 28, 1987. Also see R. Kent Weaver, "The Politics of Blame Avoidance," *Journal of Public Policy*, Vol. 6, No. 4, October-December 1986, pp. 371–98.

[21]See Daniel Kahneman and Amos Tversky, "Prospect Theory: An Analysis of Decision under Risk," *Econometrica*, Vol. 47, No. 2, March 1979, pp. 263–91; and Amos Tversky and Daniel Kahneman, "The Framing of Decisions and the Psychology of Choice," *Science*, Vol. 211, 30 January 1981, pp. 453–58.

[22]For a discussion of the possibilities see Bernard L. Cohen, *Before It's Too Late: A Scientist's Case for Nuclear Energy* (New York: Plenum Press, 1983), pp. 62–68; and Nigel Evans and Chris Hope, *Nuclear Power: Futures, Costs and Benefits* (New York: Cambridge University Press, 1984), pp. 4–5. For a highly partisan but nevertheless provocative view on the public debate over nuclear power, see Samuel McCracken, *The War Against the Atom* (New York: Basic Books, 1982).

tends to focus on it in discussions of nuclear safety to the exclusion of more mundane risks inherent in the mining and transportation of fuels and the disposal of wastes.

In Chapter 2 we discussed analytical integrity as one of the values that should be considered by policy analysts. We argued that the professional ethics of policy analysts should generally preclude participation in the injection of false or grossly misleading information into public debates. If you decide to place responsibility to client or furthering your conception of the good society above analytical integrity, then you might still want to avoid rhetorical dishonesty in most circumstances so that you will be credible when you do sacrifice analytical integrity. As Machiavelli suggests, for political actors the appearance of honesty is more important than the virtue itself.[23] But, generally, the best way to appear honest is to be honest.

THE IMPLEMENTATION PHASE

If policy adoption is courtship, then implementation is marriage. Courtship is a sort of coalition building—in times gone by the couple manuevered to gain the support of their parents; now they often must seek the support of their own children from previous marriages. Not all courtships are successful. Those that are, however, have a formal conclusion (the wedding). With the wedding begins implementation of the marriage agreement. Unless the couple admit failure and divorce, implementation goes on and on. The couple must constantly work to keep the marriage healthy in an ever-changing environment. At some point, however, they may become so accommodated to each other that the marriage stays healthy with little conscious effort. Perhaps achieving this latter condition, though not always permanent, represents the closest we can come to declaring a successful implementation.

In drawing the analogy between implementation and marriage, we hope that we have inspired neither dread of marriage among our single readers nor dread of implementation among our married readers. We hope that we have conveyed the generally open-ended nature of implementation and the need to think seriously about it when proposals are being developed.

Implementation: Factors Affecting Success and Failure

What factors influence the likelihood of successful implementation? A large literature attempts to answer this question.[24] We consider three general factors

[23]Niccolò Machiavelli, *The Prince* (New York: Appleton-Century-Crofts, 1947), Chapter XVIII, pp. 50–52.

[24]The seminal work in the literature is Jeffrey L. Pressman and Aaron Wildavsky, *Implementation* (Berkeley: University of California Press, 1973). For overviews of the literature that followed, see Paul A. Sabatier, "Top-Down and Bottom-Up Approaches to Implementation Research: A Critical Analysis and Suggested Synthesis," *Journal of Public Policy*, Vol. 6, No. 1, 1986, pp. 21–48; and Robert Nakamura and Frank Smallwood, *The Politics of Policy Implementation* (New York: St. Martin's, 1980), pp. 12–18.

that have been the focus of much of this literature: the logic of the policy, the nature of the cooperation it requires, and the availability of skillful and committed people to manage its implementation. An awareness of these factors is the first step toward designing policies that can be successfully implemented.

Logic of the Policy: Is the Theory Reasonable?   Compatibility is important in marriage. We often question the logic of marriages between people who appear to be incompatible. We should do the same for policies. What theory underlies the connection between policy and intended outcomes? Is the theory reasonable?

We can think of the logic of a policy as a chain of hypotheses. For example, consider a state program to fund locally initiated experiments intended to identify promising approaches to teaching science in high schools. For the program to be successful, the following hypotheses must be true: first, that school districts with good ideas for experiments apply for funds; second, that the state department of education select the best applications for funding; third, that the funded school districts actually execute the experiments they proposed; fourth, that the experiments produce valid evidence on the effectiveness of the approaches being tested; and fifth, that the department of education be able to recognize which successful approaches can be replicated in other jurisdictions.

Now it is easy to imagine that any of these hypotheses could be false, or at least not universally true. For instance: applicants may be predominantly school districts with experience in applying for grants rather than school districts with good ideas; the education department may face political pressure to distribute funds widely rather than to the school districts with the best ideas; school districts may divert some of the funds to other uses—say, paying for routine classroom instruction; school districts may lack skilled personnel to carry out evaluations or they may be reluctant to report evaluation results that do not support the efficacy of their approaches; the department of education may not have sufficient personnel to look closely at the evaluations to determine which ones are valid. The more likely it is that these hypotheses are false, the less likely it is that the program will produce useful information about how to do a better job teaching science in high schools.

The characteristics of the policy, and the circumstances of its adoption, determine the hypotheses underlying implementation and the likelihood that they will be true. In general, the greater the legal authority the adopted policy gives implementors, the greater their capacity to compel hypothesized behavior. Similarly, the stronger the political support for the adopted policy and its putative goals, the greater the capacity of the implementors to secure hypothesized behavior. For example, a department of education is in a better position to get school districts to provide competent evaluations of their experiments if it can require selected grant recipients to hire external evaluators. With respect to political support for policy goals, this department of education is in a better position to ward off pressure for widespread distribution of grants if most of the supporters of the program in the legislature hold the putative goal of improving high school science education as more important than using program funds to provide general aid to school districts.[25]

Obviously, we should view a policy as illogical if we cannot specify a plausible chain of behaviors that leads to the desired outcomes.[26] Later we discuss scenario writing as a way of discovering plausible chains. But first, we turn to the other factors that affect the likelihood that the hypothesized behaviors will occur.

Assembly: Who Has the Essential Elements?   As we noted in Chapter 4, Eugene Bardach provides a useful metaphor for implementation: an assembly process involving efforts to secure essential elements from those who control them.[27] His metaphor suggests the generalization that the more numerous and varied are the elements that must be assembled, the greater the potential for implementation problems. More usefully, it suggests important questions to ask when considering the prospects for successful implementation: Exactly what elements (the hypotheses linking policy to desired outcomes) must be assembled? Who controls these elements? What are their motivations? What resources does the implementor have available to induce them to provide the elements? What consequences will result if the elements cannot be obtained either on a timely basis or at all?

These questions are essentially the same ones we ask in order to determine political feasibility. Indeed, the efforts to secure the elements needed for implementation typically involve politics—although rarely decided by votes, those controlling the necessary elements must nevertheless be convinced to provide them. In other words, as we noted at the beginning of this chapter, we can think of implementation as a series of adoptions.

Clear legal authority is almost always a valuable resource for implementors. It may not be sufficient by itself to guarantee cooperation, however. For example, imagine a mayor opposed to the transportation of nuclear wastes on the railroad running through her city. Assume that she is required by law to prepare a plan for the evacuation of her city in the event of an accident involving the release of nuclear waste into the environment. Also assume that the transportation through the city cannot begin until an evacuation plan is accepted. The mayor might hinder

---

[25]As Pressman and Wildavsky note, it is not clear what successful implementation means without specification of a goal: "Implementation cannot succeed or fail without a goal against which to judge it." Jeffrey L. Pressman and Aaron Wildavsky, *Implementation*, p. xiv. In practice, we often face the problem that policies are adopted without explicit agreement about their goals. See Charles Lindblom, "Some Limitations on Rationality: A Comment," in Carl J. Friedrich, ed., *Rational Decision* (New York: Atherton, 1964), pp. 224–28.

[26]Note that politicians sometimes support policies as symbolic statements and really do not expect the putative consequences to result. For a discussion of position taking by members of Congress, see David R. Mayhew, *Congress: The Electoral Connection* (New Haven, Conn.: Yale University Press, 1974), pp. 61–73.

[27]Eugene Bardach, *The Implementation Game: What Happens after a Bill Becomes a Law* (Cambridge, Mass.: MIT Press, 1977), pp. 57–58.

implementation of the shipment program by following one of three tactics: tokenism, delayed compliance, or blatant resistance.[28]

The mayor might intentionally have her staff prepare an evacuation plan that meets the letter of the law but falls short substantively. If the implementor—say, the state public utilities commission—accepts the inadequate plan, then it risks not only public safety but also bad publicity and a court challenge from interest groups who oppose the shipment program. Of course, if the implementor does not accept the evacuation plan, then the program cannot go forward. Because the mayor has complied in form, the implementor may have difficulty gaining the political or legal support needed to force the mayor to comply in spirit. Indeed, tokenism is so difficult to deal with because the implementor generally bears the burden of showing that the compliance was inadequate.

The mayor might have her staff prepare the required evacuation plan but have them delay completing it as long as they can without inviting a legal challenge from the implementor. During the period of delay, the mayor may be able to mobilize political support to block the program from shipping through her city. Perhaps an intervening election or change in public opinion will make it possible to repeal the legislation that authorized the program. Or perhaps the implementor will give up and choose another shipment route. In any event, the mayor probably has little to lose from a strategy of delay and at least some hope of a favorable change in political circumstances.

Finally, instead of making a token response, the mayor might simply refuse to allow her staff to prepare an evacuation plan. Such blatant resistance may be costly for the mayor if the implementor decides to seek legal sanctions. But taking the mayor to court may be politically costly for the implementor and would probably involve considerable delay. On the other hand, not challenging the mayor's noncompliance might encourage other mayors also to refuse to prepare evacuation plans, throwing the whole shipment program into jeopardy.

While massive resistance is generally rare—it takes fortitude and works best from a position that makes it costly for the implementor to force compliance—tokenism and purposeful delay are common tactics for those who oppose the policy being implemented. Employees, especially those with civil service protection, can often slow, or even stop, implementation with halfhearted or leisurely contributions.[29] Their ability to impede implementation is particularly great when they must be relied upon to make continuing contributions over an extended period. For instance, management information systems typically require a steady and accurate flow of input data to provide information benefits—delays or inattention to accuracy by a few data providers may be enough to undermine the value of the entire system.[30]

---

[28]For excellent discussions of tokenism and massive resistance and ways to counter them, see Eugene Bardach, *The Implementation Game,* pp. 98–124.

[29]On the resources available to employees and lower-level managers, see David Mechanic, "Sources of Power of Lower Participants in Complex Organizations," *Administration Science Quarterly,* Vol. 7, No. 3, December 1962, pp. 348–64.

[30]For a discussion of the problems encountered in implementing information systems, see David Leo Weimer, "CMIS Implementation: A Demonstration of Predictive Analysis," *Public Administration Review,* Vol. 40, No. 3, May/June 1980, pp. 231–40.

So, even when implementors have the legal authority to demand compliance, they will not necessarily get it at levels adequate for successful implementation. Implementors should expect that their efforts to secure program elements will be political—allies must be mobilized and agreements must be reached with people who have contrary interests. Therefore, implementors should be prepared to use political strategies, especially co-optation and compromise, to assemble program elements and keep them engaged. For example, to increase the chances that mayors will produce acceptable evacuation plans on a timely basis, the implementors might offer to discuss limitations on the frequency and circumstances of the shipments before the mayors commit themselves to noncompliance through their public stands. Perhaps the implementor can offer a concession on an entirely different issue of mutual concern.[31]

Noncompliance need not be purposeful to hinder the implementation process. Someone holding a necessary program element may have every intention of providing it but fail to do so because of incompetence or an inability to get others to provide necessary support. For example, the mayor may believe that the preparation of an evacuation plan as required by law is a duty that should be discharged. Yet her staff may lack the necessary skills to produce an adequate plan. Or, perhaps the staff is competent but cannot complete their task quickly because local procedure requires that the plan be discussed in public hearings and reviewed by the city attorney, the city and county planning boards, and the city council. Even without strong opposition to the plan, scheduling problems and routine delays may prevent the plan from being approved in what the implementor considers a reasonable period of time.

Diversity among those providing similar elements makes it difficult to estimate how much inadvertant noncompliance will be encountered. For example, imagine that the shipment program requires that evacuation plans be prepared by twenty cities. Perhaps most have staffs with adequate skills to comply. But even if only a few are incapable of complying, the implementation may be jeopardized—because, say, the authorization for the program requires that all evacuation plans be filed before shipments can begin.

In summary, legal authority alone may not be sufficient to guarantee the compliance of those who control necessary program elements. If they view the program, or their specific contributions to it, as contrary to their interests, then the implementor should expect them to try to avoid full compliance through tokenism, delay, or even blatant resistance. Further, the implementor should hold realistic expectations about the capabilities of those who nominally control the elements to provide them.

Availability of "Fixers:" Who Will Manage the Assembly?   So far we have been vague about the identity of the implementor. Our examples suggest

---

[31]For example, when the governor of Louisiana held up construction of facilities for the U.S. Strategic Petroleum Reserve program by objecting to the issuing of permits by the Army Corps of Engineers, the Department of Energy got the governor to drop his objections by making several concessions, including a promise that DOE would not store nuclear wastes in Louisiana. David Leo Weimer, *The Strategic Petroleum Reserve: Planning, Implementation, and Analysis* (Westport, Conn.: Greenwood Press, 1982), pp. 50–51.

someone who favors the policy and is willing to expend time, energy, and resources to see it put into effect—in other words, someone who behaves as we think we would. But as policy analysts, we are rarely in a position to manage an implementation ourselves. Indeed, if our clients are legislators or high-ranking executives, it is unlikely that they will be willing or able to attend to the day-to-day management of implementations. Instead, the responsibility for managing implementations typically goes to the administrators of organizational units that provide related services. For example, the implementor of the nuclear waste shipment program would probably be the director of the office within the public utilities commission that oversees the state's nuclear power plants.

In light of the importance of politics in the implementation process, understanding the motivations and political resources of the implementor is obviously important for predicting the likelihood that the policy will produce the intended consequences. An implementor who views the policy as undesirable or unimportant is less likely to expand personal and organizational resources during the assembly process than one who views the policy more favorably. One reason that organizational units are sometimes created to implement new policies is the perception that the administrators of existing units will not be vigorous implementors because of their commitments to already-existing programs.[32]

The failings of the implementor can sometimes be compensated for by people who Bardach calls *fixers*—those who can intervene in the assembly process to help gain needed elements that are being withheld.[33] For example, the staff of the legislative sponsor of the policy may oversee the implementation process, perhaps helping to negotiate compromises with noncompliers. Oversight by the staff may also help motivate a less than enthusiastic implementor.

The availability of fixers at the local level can be especially helpful in adjusting centrally managed policies to local conditions. Sometimes local fixers can be found among interest groups who support the policy; sometimes local administrators become effective fixers. In their evaluation of the implementation of youth employment programs, for instance, Martin Levin and Barbara Ferman found that the most successful local programs usually had executives who were willing to intervene in administrative detail to correct problems. Some of these fixers were especially effective in using incentives to turn the mild interest of other local actors into active support. Other fixers had official and personal connections that enabled them to facilitate interorganizational cooperation.[34]

Allies at the local level can also serve as "eyes and ears" for the implementor.[35] Information about local contexts is often costly for a central implementor to gather without willing informants. Local supporters of the policy may be able to provide information that is useful in anticipating and countering noncompliance tactics. For example, if the state attorney general's office is attempting to implement more stringent medical care standards for local jails, it might find local groups

[32]Erwin C. Hargrove, *The Missing Link: The Study of the Implementation of Social Policy* (Washington, D.C.: Urban Institute, 1975), p. 113.

[33]See Eugene Bardach, Implementation Game, pp. 273–78.

[34]Martin A. Levin and Barbara Ferman, *The Political Hand: Policy Implementation and Youth Employment Programs* (New York: Pergamon, 1985), pp. 102–4.

[35]Eugene Bardach, Implementation Game, pp. 277–78.

interested in judicial reform or county medical societies as sources of valuable information on whether the standards are actually being followed. Such information could help the attorney general's office target limited enforcement resources on the worst offenders.

In summary, policies do not implement themselves. In assessing the chances for successful implementation, we should consider the motivations and resources of those who will be managing the implementation. We should also look for ways to mobilize supporters of the policy who can serve as fixers.

Anticipating Implementation Problems

Despite the extensive literature on implementation, social scientists have offered relatively little practical advice on how to anticipate and avoid implementation problems.[36] Nevertheless, we believe that two general approaches provide useful frameworks for thinking systematically about implementation in practical situations. The most basic is *scenario writing*, which involves specifying and questioning the chain of behaviors that link policies to desired outcomes. Because scenarios move from policies to outcomes, they can be thought of as "forward mapping." In contrast, the other general approach, "backward mapping," begins with the desired outcomes, determines the most direct ways of producing them, and then maps actions backward (effects to causes) through the organizational hierarchy to the highest-level policy that must be adopted to realize the desired outcomes. Whereas forward mapping is most useful for anticipating the problems that are likely to be encountered during the implementation of already-formulated policy alternatives, backward mapping is most useful for generating policy alternatives that have good prospects for successful implementation.

Forward Mapping: Scenario Writing. *Forward mapping* is the specification of the chain of behaviors that link a policy to desired outcomes. We emphasize the "specific" in specification—exactly what must be done by whom for the desired outcomes to occur? We join with Bardach in recommending scenario writing as a method for analysts to organize their thinking about the behaviors that must be realized for successful implementation.[37] Scenario writing helps analysts discover implicit assumptions that are unrealistic. It may also help them discover alternative approaches to implementation with better prospects for success.

Effective forward mapping requires cleverness and a certain amount of courage. The forward mapper must think about how those involved in the implementation will behave and how their behavior might be influenced. It requires what has been referred to as *dirty mindedness*—the ability to think about what could possibly go wrong and who has an incentive to make it go wrong.[38] In other words, one must be able to visualize the worst case. The forward (and backward)

[36]For a review of the prescriptive literature, see Laurence J. O'Toole, Jr., "Policy Recommendations for Multi-Actor Implementation: An Assessment of the Field," *Journal of Public Policy*, Vol. 6, No. 2, May 1986, pp. 181–210.

[37]Eugene Bardach, Implementation Game, pp. 250–67.

[38]Martin Levin and Barbara Ferman, "The Political Hand: Policy Implementation and Youth Employment Programs," *Journal of Policy Analysis and Management*, Vol. 5, No. 2, Winter 1986, pp. 311–25, at p. 322.

mapper must be courageous about making predictions. Many predictions will be incorrect, especially in their details. But much of the value of forward mapping comes from the thinking that goes into being specific. Therefore, the forward mapper must not become paralyzed by fear of being wrong.

We recommend a three-step approach to forward mapping: (1) write a scenario linking the policy to outcomes; (2) critique the scenario from the perspective of the interests of its characters; and (3) revise the scenario so that it is more plausible. Figure 8.2 highlights these steps, which we discuss in turn.

1. Write the Scenario.   Scenarios are stories. They are narratives about futures as you see them. They have beginnings and ends that are linked by plots involving essential actors. Plots should be consistent with the motivations and capabilities of the actors. Plots should also be "rich" in the sense that they convey all the important considerations that are relevant to implementation.[39]

The plot consists of a series of connected actions. Your narrative should answer four questions for each action: What is the action? Who does the action? When do they do it? Why do they do it? For example, suppose that you are writing a scenario for the implementation of a Neighborhood Sticker Plan (NSP) that would limit long-term on-street parking in specified neighborhoods to residents who yearly purchase stickers to identify their automobiles. An element of your plot might read as follows:

> Upon passage of the NSP (the previous "what"), the director of parking in the police department (the "who") designs procedures for verifying that applicants are bona fide residents of participating neighborhoods and that their out-of-town guests qualify for temporary permits (the "whats"). As requested by the police chief (the "why"), he submits an acceptable procedure to the planning department within one month (the "when").

By putting together a series of such elements, you can connect the adopted policy (the NSP) with the desired outcome (neighborhood residents and their out-of-town guests having convenient access to on-street parking).

By writing scenarios that read well, you may be able to get the attention of clients and colleagues who might otherwise be distracted—most people like stories and easily learn from them. You may be able to make your scenarios more convincing and more lively by inserting quotes from interviews and noting past behaviors that are similar to the ones you are predicting. For example, if the director of parking has told you in an interview that his staff could easily design verification procedures, weave his statement into the plot. Even if you are preparing the scenario for your own exclusive use, write it out. It is the discipline of writing a coherent story that forces you to consider the obvious questions about what must happen for the implementation to be successful.

---

[39]For a discussion of richness and other desirable characteristics of policy narratives, see Thomas J. Kaplan, "The Narrative Structure of Policy Analysis," *Journal of Policy Analysis and Management*, Vol. 5, No. 4, Summer 1986, pp. 761–78. Also see Martin H. Krieger, *Advice and Planning* (Philadelphia: Temple University Press, 1981), p. 75.

Scenario: Write a narrative that describes all the behaviors that must be realized for the policy to produce the desired outcome. Be specific about who, what, when, and why.

Critique: Is the scenario plausible?

For each actor mentioned:

1. Is the hypothesized behavior consistent with personal and organizational interests?

2. If not, what tactics could the actor use to avoid complying?

3. What countertactics could be used to force or induce compliance?

Thinking of the direct and indirect effects of the policy, what other actors would have an incentive to become involved?

1. How could they interfere with hypothesized behaviors?

2. What tactics could be used to block or deflect their interference?

Revision: Rewrite the narrative to make it more plausible.

Figure 8.2 Thinking Systematically about Implementation: Forward Mapping

2. Critique the Scenario.   Is the scenario plausible? Are all the actors capable of doing what the plot requires? If not, your plot fails the basic test of plausibility and should be rewritten. Of course, if you cannot specify a plausible plot, then you can be fairly certain that the policy is doomed to fail.

The more interesting test of plausibility lies in considering the motivations of the actors. Will they be willing to do what the plot requires?

For each actor mentioned in the plot, ask yourself if the hypothesized behavior is consistent with personal and organizational interests. If not, what tactics could the actor use to avoid complying? For example, the director of parking may view the verification procedures as an undesirable burden of his already over-worked staff. He might therefore produce a token plan that will not adequately exclude nonresidents from purchasing stickers—the result could be that parking congestion will remain a problem in the participating neighborhoods. Perhaps he opposed the NSP in the first place and sees inadequate verification procedures as a way of undermining the whole program.

Can you think of any ways of countering the noncompliance? For example, would a memorandum from the police chief clearly stating the director's responsibility for designing effective verification procedures be sufficient to get the director to do a good job? Would he be more cooperative if he were allocated additional overtime hours for his staff? If inducements such as these appear ineffectual, then you should consider writing him out of the plot by assigning the task to some other organizational unit.

After considering the motivations of actors who are in the plot, think about the dogs that didn't bark. Who not mentioned in the plot will likely view the policy, or the steps necessary to implement it, as contrary to their interests? How might they interfere with the elements of the plot? What tactics could you employ to block or deflect their interference?

For instance, what will the commuters who have been parking in the participating neighborhoods do when they are excluded? Will they park in other residential neighborhoods or on commercial streets closer to the downtown? This might create pressure for the creation of additional sticker-parking areas or lead adversely affected city residents to oppose continued implementation. Perhaps arranging more convenient bus service from parking lots on the outskirts of the city could help absorb the displacement of nonresident parking from the participating neighborhoods.

3. Revise the Scenario.   Rewrite the scenario in light of the critique. Strive for a plot that is plausible—even if it does not lead to the desired outcome. If it still does lead to the desired outcome, then you have the basis for a plan of implementation. If it does not lead to the desired outcome, then you can conclude that the policy is probably unfeasible.

Backward Mapping: Bottom-Up Policy Design.   Richard Elmore describes the logic of backward mapping as follows:

> Begin with a concrete statement of the behavior that creates the occasion for a policy intervention, describe a set of organizational operations that can be expected to affect that behavior, describe the expected effect of those operations, and then describe for each level of the implementation process what effect one would expect that level to have on the target behavior and what resources are required for that effect to occur.[40]

In other words, begin thinking about policies by looking at the behavior that you wish to change. What interventions could effectively alter the behavior? What decisions and resources are needed to motivate and support these interventions? The candidate policies are then constructed from alternative sets of decisions and resources that will achieve the interventions and that can be controlled by the policy maker.

Backward mapping is really nothing more than using your model of the policy problem to suggest alternative solutions (remember our discussion of designing alternatives in Chapter 6). It adds something to our thinking about policy alternatives, however, by drawing our attention to the organizational processes that give them form. Also, by focusing initially on the lowest organizational levels, it may help us discover less-centralized approaches that we might have otherwise overlooked.

The development of an implementation plan for neighborhood sticker parking in San Francisco (which we discuss more fully in Chapter 10) provides an example of the usefulness of backward mapping. By the early 1970s parking con-

---

[40]Richard F. Elmore, "Backward Mapping: Implementation Research and Policy Design," *Political Science Quarterly*, Vol. 94, No. 4, Winter 1979–80, pp. 601–16, at p. 612.

gestion had become a serious problem in many San Francisco neighborhoods as single-family homes were split into multiple units and percapita rates of car ownership increased. The congestion was aggravated in many neighborhoods by commuters who parked near access points to public transportation and by users of public facilities like hospitals. Several neighborhood associations and the City Planning Department favored the introduction of neighborhood sticker parking (like the NSP discussed in the previous section). One of the major issues was determining which neighborhoods would participate in the plan. The City Planning Department originally thought in terms of a top-down approach: planners in the department would designate the neighborhoods that would participate as part of the policy proposal. But an analyst convinced them to use a bottom-up approach instead: establish a procedure for neighborhoods to self-select.

The analyst reached his recommendation through a backward mapping of the political problem faced by the City Planning Department. Many residents wanted to participate in the sticker plan and expressed their support for it through their neighborhood associations. Some residents, however, preferred the status quo to having to pay for the privilege of using off-street parking in their neighborhoods. Until they realized that their neighborhoods were to be included in the plan, these latent opponents would probably have remained silent and unknown to the City Planning Department. Therefore, the City Planning Department was faced with the prospect of some local opposition when it made public the neighborhoods designated for participation. Viewing the dissatisfaction with the status quo on the part of the currently vocal residents as the behavior that would be the policy target, the analyst thought of a procedure that would allow them to seek participation—that way the City Planning Department would not be seen as imposing its preferences on the neighborhoods. Because there was already a procedure in place that allowed neighborhoods to self-select for designation as two-hour parking zones, the analyst specified an adaptation of that procedure as the appropriate "organizational operation."

THINKING STRATEGICALLY ABOUT POLICY DESIGN

Backward mapping aside, we have so far considered strategic thinking primarily in the context of predicting and influencing the political and organizational feasibility of specific policy proposals. We now turn to strategic thinking in the context of policy design. In particular, we look at ways of making our policies less sensitive to errors in our assumptions about behavior and more effective in helping us learn about how to design better policies in the future.

Uncertainty and Error Correction

Policy analysis inherently involves prediction. Because the world is complex, we must expect to err. Our theories about human behavior are simply not powerful enough for us to have great confidence in most of our predictions. Changing economic, social, and political conditions can make even our initially accurate predictions about the consequences of adopted policies go far astray as time elapses. Our design of policies should acknowledge the possibility of error. In particular, can we design policies that facilitate the detection and correction of error?[41]

Redundancy and Slack. Duplication and overlap generally carry the negative connotation of inefficiency. In a world with perfect certainty, this connotation has validity: Why expand more than the minimum amount of resources necessary to complete a task? In our uncertain world, however, some duplication and overlap can be very valuable. We don't consider redundant safety systems on airplanes as necessarily inefficient—even the best engineering and assembly cannot guarantee perfect performance from all primary systems. We should not be surprised, then, that redundancy can be valuable in many organizational contexts. Redundancy can provide a safety margin, serve as a source of resources for dealing with anomalous situations, and make available slack resources for organizational experimentation.[42] Thus, designing redundancy into policies can sometimes make them more feasible and robust.

Consider the problem of critical links in the implementation process. If one link in a chain of behaviors connecting the policy to desired outcomes seems especially tenuous, then you should look for ways to make the link redundant, recognizing the trade-off between costs and the probability of successful implementation. For instance, return to our earlier example of the program to ship nuclear wastes on railroads running through the state. Rather than simply asking mayors of cities along the most preferred route to prepare evacuation plans, you might simultaneously have evacuation plans prepared along a few alternative routes as well. If a mayor along the preferred route failed to comply, then you might be able to switch to one of the alternative routes without great loss of time. Whether the higher administrative (and probably political) costs of such a parallel approach were warranted would depend on the value of the reduction in expected delay it would provide.

Redundancy can also be useful in facilitating experimentation and the reduction of uncertainty. For example, imagine you are designing a county-funded program to purchase counseling services over the next year for 100 indigent drug abusers. Conceivably, a single firm could provide all the services. While the administrative costs of contracting with one firm for the entire 100 participants might be lower, hiring more than one firm would offer the potential for comparing their performance. It also would enhance competition by increasing the chances that more than one firm will bid to provide services in future years.

Using redundant suppliers also makes it easier to cope with the unexpected loss of one supplier. For instance, one of the counseling firms may unexpectedly go bankrupt early in the year and default on its contract. It would probably be

---

[41]For insights on error and error correction, see Aaron Wildavsky, "The Self-Evaluating Organization," *Public Administration Review*, Vol. 32, No. 5, September/October 1972, pp. 509–20.

[42]For a development of these ideas, see Martin Landau, "Redundancy, Rationality, and the Problem of Duplication and Overlap," *Public Administration Review*, Vol. 29, No. 4, July/August 1969, pp. 346–58.

faster, and perhaps more desirable, to shift participants to other firms already under contract than to try to hire new firms.

Finally, building redundant resources (slack) into programs may be desirable if supplementing initial allocations during implementation will be difficult. For instance, if the credibility of the state transportation department's proposal to replace a series of bridges hinges critically on completing the first replacement in the promised six months, then the department would probably be wise to pad the budget for this first project with some reserve funds to deal with such unlucky circumstances as exceptionally bad weather or construction accidents. The political trade-off is between the lower initial support because of the higher budget and a reduced risk of lower future support due to loss of credibility.

Anticipating Evaluation.   Often the effectiveness of adopted policies is not directly observable. For example, consider a program that provides intensive supervision for certain parolees. How would we determine if the participants had lower recidivism rates? We could fairly easily observe the number of arrests and the number of months of street-time (time in community after release from prison) for the group. We could interpret the ratio of total arrests to total street-time as a crude measure of the recidivism rate for the participants. But how would we interpret this rate? We might compare it to the recidivism rate for a sample of nonparticipants. The comparison could be misleading, however, if participants differed substantially from the controls in terms of age, criminal history, education level, or some other factor potentially relevant to recidivism. We would have to worry that one of these factors may be confounding our results. (In Chapter 12 we show how statistical techniques can sometimes be used to take account of confounding.)

To guard against confounding, we might have designed the intensive supervision program as an experiment—randomly select participants and controls to increase the chances that the only systematic difference between the groups is the intensive supervision.[43] We could then more confidently attribute any measured differences in recidivism rates between the participant and control groups as due to the intensive supervision. Of course, the random selection of participants and controls must be part of the original program design.[44]

[43]We generally evaluate experiments in terms of their internal and external validity. *Internal validity* holds when the measured difference between the control and experimental groups can be reasonably attributed to the treatment. *External validity* holds when the measured difference can be generalized to some population of interest. For an excellent discussion of internal validity and external validity and the factors that jeopardize them, see Donald T. Campbell and Julian C. Stanley, *Experimental and Quasi-Experimental Designs for Research* (Chicago: Rand McNally, 1963), pp. 5–6.

[44]Randomized selection from among the target population and randomized assignment to treatment and control groups greatly enhances the internal and external validity of evaluations. Implementing randomization, however, is often difficult. Administrators and professionals often do not want to give up discretion over assignment of subjects. For an illustration, see Leslie L. Roos, Jr., Noralou P. Roos, and Barbara McKinley, "Implementating Randomization," *Policy Analysis*, Vol. 3, No. 4, Fall 1977, pp. 547–59.

Even nonexperimental evaluations of policy effects generally require some forethought.[45] For example, if we want to know whether improvements at a public park have increased use, then we had better plan on measuring use levels *before* the improvements are made so that we have a benchmark for comparing measurements made *after* the improvements. If we are worried that changes in the local economy over the period of the improvements may influence use, then we would be wise to take contemporaneous measurements at another park not being improved to help us spot any area-wide changes.

Building the prerequisites for evaluation into policy designs is not costless. Such preparations as random selection of participants and collection of baseline data can involve substantial administrative costs, perhaps consuming scarce managerial resources needed for implementation. Preparations for future evaluations can also delay implementation. So, before bearing these costs (or inflicting them on administrators), it is important to think carefully about the feasibility of actually carrying out the evaluation and the value of the resulting information.

Several questions are relevant to determining if planning for evaluation is likely to be worthwhile.[46] First, can you imagine the results influencing a future decision? If the costs of the park improvements are sunk (there are no ongoing costs) or if no other park improvements are likely to be considered in the near future, then an evaluation is unlikely to be worthwhile. Second, will personnel with appropriate skills be available to conduct the evaluation? The parks department may be unable or unwilling to provide staff to collect and analyze data. Third, could the evaluation be completed soon enough to influence any decisions? Perhaps the county legislature will consider making similar improvements in another park next year—if an evaluation of the current improvements cannot be ready in time, then it will be irrelevant. Fourth, will the results of the evaluation be credible? If the county legislature does not trust the parks department to provide reliable information, then the evaluation is not likely to have much effect.

[45]Nonexperimental designs attempt to draw inferences about program effects when the use of randomly selected intervention and control groups is not possible. The two most commonly used nonexperimental designs are:

1. *The before-after comparison.* Measurements of the variable of interest are taken before and after the policy intervention. The internal validity of the before-after comparison is questionable because other things beside the intervention may have caused the observed change.

2. *The nonequivalent comparison group.* Measurements of the variable of interest are taken before and after the policy intervention for two groups: a group subjected to the intervention and a group not subjected to the intervention. The changes in the variable of interest for each group are then compared. The more similar the intervention and comparison groups, the more closely this design approximates a true experiment.

For more thorough treatments of nonexperimental designs, see Carol H. Weiss, *Evaluation Research: Methods of Assessing Program Effectiveness* (Englewood Cliffs, N.J.: Prentice Hall, 1972), pp. 60–91; David Nachmias, *Public Policy Evaluation: Approaches and Methods* (New York: St. Martin's, 1979, pp. 47–73; Peter H. Rossi and Sonia R. Wright, "Evaluation Research: An Assessment of Theory, Practice, and Politics," *Evaluation Quarterly*, Vol. 1, No. 1, February 1977, pp. 5–52; and Carl V. Patton and David S. Sawicki, *Basic Methods of Policy Analysis and Planning* (Englewood Cliffs, N.J.: Prentice Hall, 1986), pp. 304–28.

[46]For a review of the literature on the use of evaluations, see Laura C. Leviton and Edward F. X. Hughes, "Research and Utilization of Evaluations: A Review and Synthesis," *Evaluation Review*, Vol. 5, No. 4, August 1981, pp. 525–48.

Short of evaluation requirements, it is sometimes desirable to build reporting requirements into policy designs.[47] Program administrators are commonly required to provide accounting data on expenditures and revenues. If activity levels (types of clients served, for instance) are routinely reported as well, executive and legislative oversight may be better able to spot anomalous performance and perhaps take corrective action.

Reporting requirements may also have educational value—they let the administrator know of factors that are likely to be given attention by overseers. For example, if you are concerned that the state employment office avoids trying to help releasees from prison, then you might require that, along with total clients, they report the number of clients with serious criminal records. If the administrator of the employment office believes that the budget committee or the governor's office is paying attention to the reports, then it is likely that more clients with criminal records will be served. Of course, all the warnings we raised in Chapter 6 about the dangers of dysfunctional behavioral responses to evaluation criteria should be kept in mind.

Facilitating Termination. Once policies are adopted, it is often difficult to repeal them. As we noted in Chapter 4, even policies with large net social costs usually have vocal constituencies who receive benefits. Policies embodied in programs typically enjoy the support of their employees, clientele, and political sponsors. The public organizations that house programs on the whole enjoy great longevity.[48] Even if we are fairly certain that a proposed policy is desirable, and will remain desirable for a long time, the inherent persistence of policies should give us some pause. When the consequences of a policy are very uncertain, we should design it with the possibility of termination in mind.

The most common way for policy designs to anticipate the possibility of termination is through *sunset provisions*, which set expiration dates for policies. Unless policies are legislatively renewed prior to their expiration dates, they automatically terminate. In this way, sunset provisions force explicit reconsideration of policies at specified times. We expect sunset provisions to be most effective when coupled with evaluation requirements that provide evidence on effectiveness during the consideration of renewal.

Given the limited capability of governments to conduct evaluations and the limited time available on legislative calendars, the widespread use of simple sunset provisions may not elicit serious reconsideration of policies. Garry Brewer argues that, if they are to be effective in commanding attention in the legislative arena, sunset provisions should be selectively employed. He further suggests that sunset provisions be used in conjunction with *success thresholds* that, if not met, call for intensive evaluation.[49] Success thresholds alter the burden of proof somewhat

[47]For a conceptual discussion of the design of management control systems, see Fred Thompson and L. R. Jones, "Controllership in the Public Sector," *Journal of Policy Analysis and Management*, Vol. 5, No. 3, Spring 1986, pp. 547–71.

[48]Herbert Kaufman, *Are Government Organizations Immortal?* (Washington, D.C.: Brookings Institution, 1976), pp. 70–77.

[49]Garry D. Brewer, "Termination: Hard Choices—Harder Questions," *Public Administration Review*, Vol. 38, No. 4, July/August 1978, pp. 338–44.

during renewal decisions. While sunset provisions have the virtue of getting recon-sideration of policies on the legislative agenda, even when coupled with evalua-tion requirements, they do not directly affect the interests supporting them.

Support for continuation of policies should be expected from employees and other people whose livelihoods or careers depend on them. Further, others may oppose termination because they feel a moral repugnance against disrupting ar-rangements upon which such people have come to rely.[50] By designing organiza-tional arrangements that keep the cost of termination to employees low, we reduce the likelihood of strong opposition. One approach to keeping costs of termination low is to avoid designing permanent organizations to implement and administer policies. Instead, consider using ad hoc groups like task forces that temporarily assign employees from elsewhere in the organization to the implementation of the policy.[51] If these employees see termination as simply a return to their former duties without loss of career status, they may be less likely to oppose it than if it involves the loss of jobs or status. Note that contracting out for services rather than producing them in-house also reduces the direct cost of termination to public organizations.

The use of temporary organizational structures is not without its disadvan-tages, however. Ad hoc groups of employees may not be willing to invest the extra effort needed for successful implementation if they do not associate their personal interests with the programs. Also, at some point ad hoc groups in effect become permanent as people become accustomed to new positions and lose interest in the old. Therefore, it probably makes sense to use ad hoc groups for implement-ing new programs only if any attempts at termination are likely to come in months rather than years.

What can we say about designing termination policies? A general strategy is to try to buy off the beneficiaries of the policy you hope to terminate.[52] In Chapter 5 we described "grandfathering" as one way of overcoming opposition to policy change. Another is to provide direct compensation to those who will bear costs as a consequence of the termination. For example, say we wanted to remove an agricultural price support that was becoming increasingly expensive and socially costly. We might be able to lessen opposition by proposing to pay

[50]Eugene Bardach, "Policy Termination as a Political Process," *Policy Sciences*, Vol. 7, No. 2, June 1976, pp. 123–31. Bardach also notes that people may oppose termination out of a reluctance to damage the existing program apparatus that may have future value. Also on the psychological im-pediments to termination, see Peter DeLeon, "Public Policy Termination: An End and a Beginning," *Policy Analysis*, Vol. 4, No. 3, Summer 1978, pp. 369–92.

[51]Robert P. Biller, "On Tolerating Policy and Organizational Termination: Some Design Con-siderations," *Policy Sciences*, Vol. 7, No. 2, June 1976, pp. 133–49. Biller offers a number of other provocative ideas about how to make policy termination more acceptable to members of organiza-tions. He suggests the following sorts of institutional mechanisms: savings banks (allow organizations to keep part of the savings from terminated programs); trust offices (keep a skeleton crew to preserve institutional memory and provide a home for some program employees); and receivership referees (encourage organizations to reorganize voluntarily to eliminate ineffective programs).

[52]For a discussion of this strategy and others, see Robert D. Behn, "How to Terminate a Public Policy: A Dozen Hints for the Would-be Terminator," *Policy Analysis*, Vol. 4, No. 3, Summer 1978, pp. 393–413.

current recipients at current levels for some period following removal of the price support.

Coping with Diversity

Analysts often face the problem of designing policies for diverse circumstances. Uniform policies that usually accomplish their goals may nevertheless fail badly with respect to specific localities, communities, categories of people, or firms. Central governments typically face the problem of diversity in connection with policies that influence the provision of local public goods or regulate local externalities. Sometimes such diversity can be accommodated by decentralizing certain aspects of policy. Other times diversity can be exploited in the design of implementation strategies.

Bottom-Up Processes.   Rather than mandating participation in centrally established policies, it is sometimes advantageous to allow for self-selection. The implementation of sticker parking in San Francisco illustrates the use of a selection process as part of a policy design: neighborhoods had to apply for designation as sticker-parking areas. This bottom up process avoided the opposition that might have arisen if the areas had been designated by the City Planning Department.

More generally, processes that permit the participation of interest groups in aspects of implementation may be valuable in forestalling political attacks on the entire policy. The basic idea is to provide a mechanism that permits the policy to be altered somewhat to accommodate local interests. Requiring public hearings, establishing local advisory boards, and providing resources for discretionary uses may offer opportunities for making policies more attractive to local interests. From the perspective of the policy designer, the trick is to structure such mechanisms so that they promote acceptable program adaptations and co-opt potential political opponents without creating bottlenecks or veto points that can threaten implementation.

Where local governments and organizations lack the capability to deal with local policy problems, higher levels of government may find it worthwhile to adopt long-run strategies of *capacity building*—that is, facilitate improvements in the managerial and analytical capabilities of local organizations so that they will be better able to initiate bottom-up policies.[53] For example, if a state department of transportation were concerned that cities were failing to consider improved traffic control technologies, then it might adopt policies to make local personnel more aware of available technologies (through state-sponsored training, information networks, personnel exchanges, and direct information) and more capable of implementing them (through funding and technical assistance programs). Such programs are intended to increase the capability of local organizations to choose improvements that best fit local conditions.

---

[53]See Bruce Jacobs and David L. Weimer, "Inducing Capacity Building: The Role of the External Change Agent," in Beth Walter Honadle and Arnold M. Howitt, eds., *Perspectives on Management Capacity Building* (Albany: State University of New York Press, 1986), pp. 139–60.

Phased Implementation.   Limited resources, including the time and attention of implementors, often make phased implementation desirable or necessary. How should the sites for the first phase be selected? One strategy is to select a representative set of sites so that the full range of implementation problems will likely be encountered. Seeking diversity in the first phase makes sense when the implementors are confident of their ability to deal with the problems that do arise. Assuming that the program survives the first phase, knowing the full range of problems that are likely to be encountered will permit reevaluation of its desirability and its implementation plan.

An alternative strategy for selecting sites for the first phase of implementation is to stack the deck in favor of the implementors by picking sites where the conditions for success seem most favorable. By starting with easier sites, the implementor is better able to avoid failure and build an effective staff for dealing with the later stages of implementation. Stacking the deck in the first phase makes sense when an early failure will make the program vulnerable to political attack. The trade-off is between more realistic information about future problems and better prospects for immediate success. Make a conscious choice.

CONCLUSION

Analysts who want to affect public policy should know the political environment. Clients are more likely to embrace policy proposals that promote their political interests. Strategies that take account of the interests of actors in the relevant political arenas can influence the likelihood that policies will be adopted. Anticipating and solving implementation problems requires an understanding of the interests of those who bear the consequences of the means and ends of policies. Thus, if analysts are to provide useful advice, then they cannot avoid paying attention to the political environment.

9

A STYLIZED ANALYSIS: CANADIAN AIRLINE DEREGULATION

In the preceding chapters, we laid conceptual foundations for thinking about policy problems and we gave practical guidance for doing policy analysis. Although we provided illustrations throughout our discussions, they were necessarily brief. We now turn to some more extended illustrations to better prepare you for your own first attempts at policy analysis.

In the three chapters following this one, we present cases that look at the conduct of analysis in political and organizational settings. The story of neighborhood sticker parking in San Francisco (Chapter 10) illustrates how policy advocates can use analysis to advantage. The debate over the appropriate size of the U.S. petroleum stockpile (Chapter 11) shows the tribulations and rewards of doing benefit-cost analysis in bureaucratic settings. The analysis supporting the revision of the lead standard for gasoline (Chapter 12) illustrates the process of moving from back-of-the-envelope calculations to major studies employing sophisticated statistical methods. From these cases you should get a feel for what it is like to be a policy analyst in a variety of environments.

Before we turn to these cases on the process of analysis, however, we provide an example of the product of analysis. Thinking back to our first graduate workshop on policy analysis, we remember being put in the position of having to prepare analyses for clients without ever having read any! Of course, we had seen numerous government reports and published studies, but we had not read any policy analyses in the form of direct communications from analysts to clients. Our purpose in this chapter is to spare you the frustration that we experienced. Our approach is to provide a stylized analysis that you can use as a rough template for your initial analytical efforts.

The example, an analysis of the Canadian airline industry, is based on an exercise for an introductory course on policy analysis. It represents the sort of analysis that you should be able to do in a relatively short period—between one and three weeks—with only library research. It does not necessarily present the "right" answer. Nor is it an exceptionally skillful or creative analysis. Rather, it shows that someone with limited experience can competently cover the bases in a very limited period of time.

Our example represents the sort of briefing paper that analysts often prepare on very short notice for high-level decision makers. Indeed, many busy executives and legislators rely almost exclusively on briefing papers for learning about technical issues and policy options. They sometimes expect their analysts to produce them within hours. For example, a department secretary who is going to testify before a congressional committee in the afternoon may see something in the morning newspaper that suggests a possible line of questioning; he may ask his staff to prepare a one-page briefing paper that he can read over lunch. He is unlikely to be pleased if his analysts fail to meet either the deadline or the page limit!

The following analysis is based on course exercises completed by Eric E. Irvine, Nancy Briden, and S. Stuart Maynes at Simon Fraser University. We gave Irvine a fairly free hand in preparing this version so that it would serve as a realistic model for the sort of product a neophyte analyst might produce on an unfamiliar topic with only library research. It was written before the National Transportation Act of 1986 (Bill C-18)—which substantially deregulated much of the Canadian airline industry—was passed by the House of Commons on June 18, 1987.

THE REPORT

Report to: Minister of Transport
From: Eric E. Irvine, Transport Policy Consultants
*Regarding:*Deregulation of the Canadian Airline Industry
Date: May 1987

Executive Summary

The three main assumptions under which the Canadian airline industry
has been regulated are no longer valid. The deregulatory experience
in the United States has demonstrated that: (1) the airline industry
is not a natural monopoly—it can possess a competitive market structure; (2) safety will not be affected by variations in price and route
regulation; and (3) regulation is not required to maintain air service
to small communities.

Regulation has led to nonprice competition that protects inefficient firms and causes overcapitalization (operation of larger aircraft
than economically efficient), both of which increase costs to consumers.
Under current forms of regulation, airline employees are able to obtain restrictive work rules and wages above competitive levels.

Considerable empirical research is now emerging on the benefits
and costs of the U.S. experience with airline deregulation. Recent
studies suggest substantial efficiency gains. Competition has increased,
fares are lower, and pricing has become more closely related to costs.
The increased efficiency resulting from deregulation in the United
States is relevant to Canada.

This policy analysis recommends: (1) deregulation as a means
of increasing efficiency in the Canadian airline industry; (2) airline-
specific anticombines legislation to ensure that the airline industry remains contestable over the long term; and (3) a subsidy program to
ensure air service in Canada's small and remote communities.

The Issue

The Minister of Transport has asked me to consider whether he should
continue with the planned deregulation of the Canadian airline industry as he proposed in pending legislation (Bill C-18). He has asked
me **not** to address the issues of government ownership of airlines or
airports. My analysis follows.

Historical Background on Airline Regulation

From the early days of aviation until the 1970s, successive Canadian
governments have maintained both substantial regulation of commercial aviation and government ownership of airlines. While it is diffi-

cult to impute motivation to unstated rationales for this intervention, they appear to be of several kinds:

1. An unregulated market will not work efficiently. There appears to have been two different strands to this market failure argument: (i) the airline industry was thought to have some characteristics of a natural monopoly (or at least that there are substantial economies of scale); (ii) entangled with this argument was some general sense that an unregulated market would lead to "destructive competition" or predatory behavior by some firms.

2. Information about safety will not be adequately provided by airlines.

3. Many communities, especially in remote locations, will not receive airline service in a competitive, unregulated market.[1]

Are these assumptions still valid in the contemporary market?

Could an Unregulated Market Work in Canada?

Given the historical importance of the market failure rationale for intervention, the crucial issue is whether the Canadian airline market would be contestable if unregulated. It is clear that a completely deregulated Canadian airline market would not be served by a large number of carriers. This is not the appropriate test, however. Rather, the appropriate test is whether the market is contestable—would attempts to charge higher than competitive prices attract new entrants? If the market is contestable the current regulatory regime imposes considerable costs on the Canadian economy. In order to assess this, I look at relevant theory and review the recent experience of the United States. With respect to the latter, there are two questions: (1) Has deregulation conferred benefits or imposed costs on the U.S.? (2) Is the U.S. experience relevant to the somewhat different Canadian context?

The Theory of Contestability Theory suggests that a deregulated Canadian airline market would be contestable. Airlines have few sunk costs, even if there are some economies of scale. Consequently, entry and exit can easily occur. Thus, even if a particular route only has one airline, the market will be contestable (provided, that is, that the government does not discourage competition). The airline industry, perhaps better than any other, illustrates the difference between fixed and sunk costs. The airplane market is highly liquid on a global level, as illustrated by the "secondhand" market for airplanes and the pervasiveness of leasing.

---

[1] G. B. Reschenthaler and W. T. Stanbury, "Deregulating Canada's Airlines: Grounded by False Assumptions," *Canadian Public Policy*, Vol. 9, No. 2, 1983, pp. 210–22, at p. 216; also see Anthony P. Ellison, *U.S. Airline Deregulation: Implications for Canada*, Technical Report No. 11 (Ottawa: Economic Council of Canada, 1981), p. 3.

The U.S. Experience with Deregulation   Considerable empirical research is now emerging on the benefits and costs of the deregulation that has occurred in the United States since the Airline Deregulation Act of 1978. Unfortunately, a "pure" assessment of the impact of deregulation has been complicated by the fact that it occurred at the same time as the recession (see Appendix A for a discussion of this issue). In spite of this methodological difficulty, recent studies suggest considerable efficiency gains, mostly accruing to airline customers.

Steven Morrison and Clifford Winston find that consumer gains range between $1.3 billion and $8.7 billion annually, with a best estimate of approximately $6 billion. They also estimate that gains to airlines in the order of $2.5 billion annually.[2]

Elizabeth Bailey, David Graham, and Daniel Kaplan also report major efficiency gains from deregulation: competition has increased, fares are lower, and pricing has become more closely related to costs.[3] Nearly all other recent studies come to similar conclusions. The only real caveat about contestability that emerges from this literature is whether the emergence of "hub and spoke" systems may constitute a barrier to entry.[4] For a more complete review of the available evidence on efficiency gains, see Appendix A.

The substantial U.S. airline losses during the recession have caused concern that deregulation may be leading to the emergence of a cartelized industry that will engage in predatory pricing and prevent new airlines from forming. Alfred Kahn, who as chairman of the Civil Aeronautics Board helped pioneer airline deregulation, said recently that: "The industry may be headed toward an uncomfortably tight oligopoly."[5]

The experience of the United States with deregulation reveals very few examples of predation. This is not surprising, as contestability theory suggests that it is restrictions on competitors that invite predation. Open competition in an industry with modest economics of scale and easy entry and exit makes predation unproductive. There is some evidence, however, that potential competition is not quite as effective as actual competition in restraining prices. Fares in markets with two equal competitors have been estimated to be on average about 6 percent lower than in monopoly markets, while those with four equal com-

[2]Steven Morrison and Clifford Winston, *The Economic Effects of Airline Deregulation* (Washington, D.C.: Brookings Institution, 1986), pp. 35–36.

[3]Elizabeth E. Bailey, David R. Graham, and Daniel P. Kaplan, *Deregulating the Airlines* (Cambridge, Mass.: MIT Press, 1985), p. 66.

[4]See Michael E. Levine, "Airline Competition in Deregulated Markets: Theory, Firm Strategy, and Public Policy," *Yale Journal on Regulation*, Vol. 4, No. 2, Spring 1987, pp. 393–94; and Clinton V. Oster, Jr., "Airline Deregulation," *Journal of Policy Analysis and Management*, Vol. 6, No. 3, Spring 1987, pp. 469–73.

[5]*The Globe and Mail*, September 9, 1986, p. B23.

petitors were found to be 11 percent lower. The presence of a new entrant typically reduced fares about 20 percent.[6]

Moving to the distributional question, the evidence demonstrates that regulation is not required to ensure service to small communities in the United States. Bailey, Graham, and Kaplan conclude that the provision of services to small communities has only declined slightly.[7] Morrison and Winston's analysis of deregulation found that travelers in all market categories gained, including travelers to and from small communities.[8]

How Relevant Is the U.S. Experience to Canada?   I believe that the U.S. experience has considerable relevance to Canada, especially with respect to economic efficiency. There is no reason to believe that Canada would not receive benefits similar to those in the United States, although, of course, of a different magnitude. There are only two caveats to this general conclusion: (1) the Canadian airline industry is now considerably more concentrated than the U.S. industry was prior to deregulation (this is in itself more a result of government actions than market forces); (2) it is hard to extrapolate U.S. experience in small communities to Canada because of differences in geography and population density. On the other hand, Reschenthaler and Stanbury note evidence that only a few small communities are actually receiving an internal cross-subsidy from Canadian airlines under current regulations.[9] This suggests that few communities would lose service under deregulation.

What Has Been the Impact of Regulation?

The government currently limits who can fly where, how often, in what type of plane, and at what price. This has left the Canadian industry with two major transcontinental airlines (i.e., Air Canada and Canadian Airlines International) and a number of smaller regional airlines. When the threat of entry is removed and there are very few competitors, inefficiency is likely to occur. Firms facing reduced competition with respect to price shift to competition with respect to quality of service. Costs increase through overcapitalization and higher wages, and inefficient firms survive.[10]

Under current forms of regulation, airline employees capture a significant share of the *potential* excess returns that might accrue to shareholders by obtaining restrictive work rules and progressively

---

[6]Bailey, Graham, and Kaplan, *Deregulating the Airlines*, p. 164. Morrison and Winston, *Economic Effects of Airline Deregulation*, reach the similar conclusion that airline markets are not perfectly contestable but that potential competition does have an influence.

[7]Bailey, Graham, and Kaplan, *Deregulating the Airlines* p. 111.

[8]Economic Effects of Airline Deregulation, pp. 41–52.

[9]"Deregulating Canada's Airlines," p. 216.

[10]G. W. Douglas and James C. Miller, *Economic Regulation and Domestic Air Transport: Theory and Policy* (Washington, D.C.: Brookings Institution, 1974), p. 43.

higher wages.[11] Regulation reduces incentives to negotiate low-cost labor contracts because airlines that are able to achieve a cost advantage are prohibited from translating it into a fare advantage, and because airlines with high costs do not have to fear competition from airlines with lower costs. As an airline executive told the Canadian Transport Commission: "Regulation has afforded us the luxury of passing on our costs along to the consumer."

Appropriate Policy Goals

What does the above analysis suggest about the appropriate goals for assessing alternative federal policies? Most importantly (and most clearly), the government should strive to promote efficiency of operation in the Canadian airline industry. Additionally, it is necessary to recognize the special needs of Canada's northern and remote communities, which rely on regular air service as the primary method for passenger and cargo transportation.

The issue of safety will not be addressed directly because, on the basis of the U.S. experience, there is no reason to believe that safety will be affected by variations in the regulation of routes and fares.

Approaching a Solution

In light of the limited time you have given to me to report, I have not attempted to collect any original data. The approach I take in the rest of this report is to assess qualitatively the potential efficiency gains and losses of major policy alternatives. As I believe that you consider the distributional impacts on small Canadian communities to be of vital importance, I also attempt to qualitatively assess the impact of the policy alternatives on service to these communities. Although I know that you are primarily concerned with improving the efficiency of the industry and the impact on small communities, I also briefly assess the political feasibility of the alternatives.

Also, given the scope of this topic and the time frame of this analysis, I use broad concepts of efficiency and equity, rather than more specific evaluation criteria, to assess the potential impacts of policy alternatives.

Policy Alternatives

I consider several alternatives to the current regulatory regime. Each involves replacing "public convenience and necessity" with "fit, willing, and able" as the test for participation in the airline market. Beyond this basic change, the alternatives include a subsidy program to ensure at least current levels of service to small communities, airline-specific antitrust restrictions, or both.

[11]David R. Graham and Daniel P. Kaplan, "Airline Deregulation Is Working," *Regulation*, May/June 1982, pp. 26–32, at p. 27.

1. Maintain the Status Quo   (i.e., the current regulatory system). In Canada there is an elaborate system of regulatory controls on entry, exit, fare levels, mergers, acquisitions, safety of operations, and types of service offered that apply to all carriers. In addition, there have been government subsidies to certain air carriers to provide specific services desired by the government. One of the primary instruments of government intervention has been government ownership, notably through Air Canada.

2. A Pure Competitive Market Policy   (i.e., essentially U.S.-style airline deregulation). Price and entry controls would be removed entirely, along the lines of the phased U.S. deregulation. As with each of the following alternatives, "fit, willing, and able" would replace "public convenience and necessity" as the test for market participation.

3. A Competitive Market Policy with a Special Subsidy Program for Small Communities.   (i.e., essentially deregulation but with *direct* subsidies, rather than internal airline cross-subsidies, to small communities). The federal government would provide operating subsidies to ensure continued air service to any community now being served. The crucial element of this proposal is that subsidies be direct. I would caution that a major problem with this alternative may be opportunistic behavior by airlines (i.e., claiming that service to many communities will not be economic without such subsidies). This alternative, therefore, should include an auction mechanism, whereby the airline that is prepared to accept the lowest subsidy provides the service. Funding should be out of general revenues rather than out of a dedicated revenue source so as not to attract unjustified subsidy seeking.

4. An Anticombines-Oriented Competitive Market Policy.   (i.e., deregulation with airline-specific antitrust provisions). In light of the expressed, and to some extent unresolved, concerns about market structure, it may make sense to allow the Canadian Transport Commission to enforce appropriate competitive behavior once direct exit, entry, and price regulations are removed. There are dangers here, however. Powers must be restricted to fostering, not restricting, long-run competition. I recommend that a "one-way gate" policy be the primary tool for ensuring competition.[12] The one-way gate would allow any carrier to freely enter any point now served by Air Canada and Canadian Airlines International, but disallow either of these two national carriers from entering any point now served by any other carrier. Air Canada and Canadian Airlines International would be free to enter any point without service or any point currently being served by the other.

5. An Anticombines Competitive Market Policy with a Subsidy Program (alternatives 3 and 4 in combination).

---

[12]A similar proposal can be found in Anthony P. Ellison, *U.S. Airline Deregulation: Implications for Canada*, p. 150.

Evaluation of the Alternatives

I have already noted the severe costs that almost certainly occur under the current regulatory regime. Canadian regulators defend higher costs, citing severe weather, the dispersed population, and geography; but William Jordan demonstrates that these factors do not significantly add to costs.[13] Other inadequacies that have resulted from government regulation include cross-subsidization between international and domestic routes and a perception of high cost by air travelers in Canada as they become aware of the costs that they bear in comparison to U.S. travelers.[14]

How do the other four alternatives compare in terms of efficiency? Either the pure competitive market (alternative 2) or the anticombines competitive market (alternative 4) offer greater efficiency than the current regulatory system. Airline deregulation with direct subsidies (alternatives 3 and 5) also dominate the status quo, despite the fact that subsidies impose some efficiency losses. Given that there appears to be relatively little cross-subsidization of routes under the current regulatory regime, I do not expect the costs of the subsidy program to be large.

How do the pure competitive market (alternative 2) and the anticombines competitive market (alternative 4) compare in terms of efficiency? Choosing between the two depends on whether the problems associated with concentration are expected to be serious. Because the Canadian airline industry is already highly concentrated, the anticombines policy would probably lead to the greatest efficiency.

The problem with either the purely competitive alternative or the anticombines alternative is that there is no mechanism to ensure service to Canada's small and remote communities. While the evidence from the United States shows that small communities have not been adversely affected, there are geographical and population differences between Canada and the United States that may invalidate the comparison. The political ramifications of actual, or anticipated, reductions in service to small communities might give opponents, primarily airline workers, an opportunity to stop deregulation. Therefore, inclusion of the subsidy program would substantially increase the political feasibility of deregulation.

In order to provide you with a summary of (1) the impacts that I predict for each alternative, and (2) how I believe the alternatives "score" in terms of the goals I have outlined, I have attached Appendix B. An examination of the table in Appendix B suggests that the best policy is alternative 5, a combination of a competitive market policy with direct subsidies and an anti-combines-oriented competitive

---

[13]William A. Jordan, *Performance of Regulated Canadian Airlines in Domestic and Transborder Operations* (Ottawa: Bureau of Competition Policy, Consumer and Corporate Affairs Canada, 1982), Research Monograph No. 12, pp. 177–80.

[14]Reschenthaler and Stanbury, "Deregulating Canada's Airlines," p. 17.

market policy. This combination policy would achieve most of the potential for increased economic efficiency while ensuring service, and the expectation of service, to small communities. It would be the most politically feasible of the deregulation alternatives. Given the overall benefits, I believe that you should support this proposal. The details are outlined below.

While I have not examined the public ownership of Air Canada, I feel it relevant to mention its status. It may have a transitory role during deregulation, but the rationale for a public airline in an open, mature, and competitive market is obscure.

Recommendations

I recommend a combination of airline-specific anticombines legislation and direct subsidies to small communities as a replacement for the current regulatory regime. The specific elements of the proposal are as follows:

- Allow all national, regional, and local carriers to set fares as they see fit.
- Employ a "one-way gate" approach under which any carrier may freely enter any point now served by Air Canada and Canadian Airlines International, but neither of these two national airlines may enter routes now served by any other carrier. Air Canada and Canadian Airlines International should be free to serve any point without service or any point currently being served by the other.
- Amendments should be made to the Combines Investigation Act specifically regulating competition in the airline industry. All accommodations or informal understandings that reduce competition among carriers should be prohibited. Predatory pricing and predatory flight scheduling should also be disallowed.
- New legislation should replace "public convenience and necessity" (PCN) with a "fit, willing, and able" test that focuses on the safety of carrier operations and adequate liability insurance.[15]
- Subject the abandonment of existing points to the following conditions: Public notice of intention to abandon service should be given no less than 60 days prior to the proposed date of abandonment. If no other carrier indicates its desire to serve the point after abandonment, the Canadian Transport Commission may, upon the request of the Minister of Transport, subsidize a level of service as specified by the Minister.

---

[15]As you know, Minister, this proposal is already before the House. The PCN test has been used to control entry and restrict competition.

Appendix A:
Evidence on Benefits and Costs of Airline
Deregulation in the United States

As mentioned in the report, a major problem in assessing the U.S. experience is separating the impact of deregulation from the impact of the recession. Reschenthaler and Stanbury[16] argue that the U.S. industry's problems were caused by the recession and other external factors unrelated to deregulation per se, specifically: (1) rapidly rising energy prices, which caused large cost increases; (2) the deep recession, which reduced travel demand; (3) high interest rates, which hit the airline industry particularly hard as airlines attempted to finance their larger, more fuel-efficient aircraft; (4) unrealistic market growth expectations; (5) reductions in flights due to the air traffic controllers' strike; (6) overexpansion by some carriers at the time of deregulation; and (7) overinvestment in aircraft due to unreasonable market growth projections during the 1978-80 period.

Morrison and Winston reach a similar conclusion that recession and fuel price increases are largely responsible for industry losses and that deregulation helped rather than hurt the industry's financial state.[17]

On the contestability issue, Reschenthaler and Stanbury state that while system-wide economies of scale do not appear to be important in the airline industry, city-pair market economies are such that many airline markets will be served by only one or two carriers because of the economies of aircraft size.[18] Bailey, Graham, and Kaplan, and Morrison and Winston, argue that carriers can use hub and spoke networks to generate cost savings because of scale economies of larger aircraft.[19] Oster argues, however, that scale economies would have been much more modest if the analysis included the newest generation of narrow-body aircraft, and that no evidence suggests that large aircraft have substantial, inherent economies over small aircraft. Oster asserts that while hub and spoke systems allow the use of larger aircraft, this was attractive to the airlines more because they entered deregulation with a surplus of large aircraft than because of any economies of scale.[20]

Some of the most important efficiency gains from deregulation may not even be discernable in the short run. Meyer and Clinton mention many of these potential ''dynamic'' gains that accrue from

[16]"Deregulating Canada's Airlines," p. 210-22.

[17]*Economic Effects of Airline Deregulation*, p. 2.

[18]"Deregulating Canada's Airlines," p. 216.

[19]*Deregulating the Airlines*, p. 74; *Economic Effects of Airline Deregulation*, pp. 4-10.

[20]"Airline Deregulation," p. 472.

deregulation, including the use of new technology and secondary airports.[21]

Appendix B: A Summary of Predicted Outcomes and Valuations

	Efficiency	Service to Small Communities	Political Feasibility
Status quo	*Low efficiency:* protection of inefficient firms and overcapitalization	*High service:* service guaranteed	*High feasibility:* status quo politically attractive
Competitive market	*Medium efficiency* concentration may result in efficiency losses	*Medium service:* service not guaranteed but not likely to diminish greatly	*Low feasibility:* some expect service loss
Competitive market with subsidies	*Medium efficiency:* direct subsidies better than cross-subsidization but attract subsidy seekers	*High service:* essentially guaranteed	*Medium feasibility:* service removed as issue
Competitive market with anticombines	*High efficiency:* industry kept under competitive forces	*Medium service:* service not guaranteed but not likely to diminish greatly	*Low to medium feasibility:* some expect service loss
Competitive market with anticombines and subsidies	*Medium efficiency:* industry kept under competitive forces; cost of subsidies	*High service:* essentially guaranteed	*Medium feasibility:* service removed as issue

Bibliography

Other useful background sources not directly cited in the report include:
BAUMOL W. J. "Contestable Markets: An Uprising in the Theory of Industry Structure." *American Economic Review*, Vol. 72, No. 1, March 1982, pp. 1–15.

[21]John R. Meyer and ClintonV. Oster, Jr., eds., *Deregulation and the New Airline Entrepreneurs* (Cambridge, Mass.: MIT Press, 1985).

COHEN, MARVIN S. "The Antitrust Implications of Airline Deregulation." *Antitrust Bulletin*, Vol. 27, No. 1, Spring 1983, pp. 131–50.

GOMEZ-IBANEZ, JOSE A., CLINTON V. OSTER, and DON H. PICKELL. "Airline Deregulation: What's Behind the Recent Losses?" *Journal of Policy Analysis and Management*, Vol. 3, No. 1, Fall 1983, pp. 74–89.

KAHN, ALFRED E. "Applying Economics in an Imperfect World." *Regulation*, Vol. 2, No. 3, Nov./Dec. 1978, pp. 17–27.

CONCLUDING COMMENTS

We conclude with a few brief comments. Notice that the analyst only briefly mentions the solution method that he has used. This is quite common. Sometimes it is clear which method the analyst has selected, especially in the case of a quantitative benefit-cost analysis. Yet analysts often do not explicitly specify the solution method when using qualitative benefit-cost analysis or multigoal analysis. Unfortunately, it may be difficult in some circumstances to infer what basic approach is being used. This is often a "flag" to you to treat the conclusions of such an analysis especially cautiously. If you cannot infer which of the five basic approaches set out in Chapter 6 (multigoal, standard benefit-cost, modified benefit-cost, cost effectiveness, or qualitative benefit-cost) is being used, then there is likely to be some muddle in the analysis.

The report also illustrates the value of examining evidence from analogous jurisdictions. In this case, the Canadian analyst was fortunate to have the U.S. airline deregulation experience as a model. He could, at least to some extent, use the U.S. experience to test alternative hypotheses concerning the contestability of the airline market under deregulation. Notice that the analyst chose not to discuss this evidence extensively in the body of the report. Does this seem appropriate for his client?

As indicated in the report, the crucial question for interpreting U.S. data is: How comparable are Canada and the United States? Indeed, this is always the problem with evidence from analogous jurisdictions. Clearly, Canada is quite different from the United States: first, its population is much smaller and more dispersed; second, its small communities are more distant and peripheral (for example, along the Arctic) than those in the United States; third, the degree of pre-deregulation concentration in Canada is much higher than it was in the United States. An analyst working for the European Economic Community or one of its member countries would face the same issue of comparability in interpreting the U.S. experience.

If you have read the preceding chapters, then you should be ready to produce an analysis comparable to the one presented here. Remember, it was done by a student like yourself in a few weeks' time. In the next chapter, we discuss another student analysis and the impact that it had. Together, these student analyses should convince you that you are ready to try your hand as policy analysts.

10

POLICY ANALYSIS AND ADVOCACY IN LOCAL SETTINGS: PREFERENTIAL PARKING IN SAN FRANCISCO[1]

Many people in government, especially at the local level, do policy analysis in the context of broader responsibilities. Public administrators and planners often do policy analyses for their supervisors, but sometimes they serve as their own clients, analyzing problems that they themselves face in their areas of responsibility. Rather than viewing analysis as a final product, they are likely to see it as only instrumental to the implementation of desired policies. Thus they are *policy entrepreneurs*—people who use analysis as a resource in advocacy.[2]

The story we present in this chapter illustrates the use of analysis by a policy entrepreneur (Arthur D. Fulton of the Transportation Planning Section of the San Francisco City Planning Department). His policy problem was parking congestion in San Francisco residential neighborhoods, and his solution was the granting of preferential parking privileges to neighborhood residents. He sought advice on designing a politically, administratively, and legally feasible preferential parking plan from a student analyst (David Weimer). He then followed political strategies to put the advice into practice.

Our story does not lend itself to the classification of actors into "proponents" and "opponents." As expected, the neighborhood associations representing the

[1]Much of this chapter originally appeared as Arthur D. Fulton and David L. Weimer, "Regaining a Lost Policy Option: Neighborhood Parking Stickers in San Francisco," *Policy Analysis*, Vol. 6, No. 3, Summer 1980, pp. 335–48. Reprinted here with permission of the Association for Public Policy Analysis and Management.

[2]Arnold Meltsner uses the term *entrepreneur* to describe someone who combines analytical and political skill to pursue policy preferences. Arnold J. Meltsner, *Policy Analysts in the Bureaucracy* (Berkeley: University of California Press, 1976), pp. 48–49. Policy entrepreneurs tend to have worldviews similar to the issue advocates described in Chapter 2.

residents who would be the direct beneficiaries of preferential parking privileges played the role of proponents; but those who would lose from the privileges—the nonresidents who were to be excluded from parking in the neighborhoods—did not participate in the policy debate.[3] Rather, opposition came from politicians and bureaucrats who thought that the privileges would not be legally valid. As will become clear, our story is not about a struggle between opposing groups of political actors. Instead, it describes an effort to overcome the initial negative perceptions that intensified the often-encountered bureaucratic resistance to change. To be a successful policy analyst, you must learn to anticipate such organizational inertia; to be a successful policy entrepreneur you must learn how to deal with it.

THE POLICY PROBLEM

Several circumstances interact to produce intensive use of on-street parking in San Francisco residential neighborhoods. High-density residential neighborhoods without adequate off-street parking facilities developed because of historically lax zoning laws.[4] More automobiles per household led to more intensive use of on-street parking. When residents are the only major source of on-street parking demand for an area, neighborhood on-street parking spaces can usually accommodate it. A large source of nonresidential parking demand, however, can result in high-peak occupancy rates (the maximum percentage of parking spaces filled during the day) that are considered unreasonable by the San Francisco Department of Public Works.[5]

Four sources of demand for nonresidential parking can be found in San Francisco's neighborhoods: hospitals, educational institutions, access points to public transportation, and direct walking access to business districts. Hospitals and educational institutions generate long-term parking demand through their employees and short-term demand through their patients and students. Commuters often park in residential neighborhoods surrounding public transportation access points, then continue their trips to the central business district by bus or trolley. As a result, a commuter's automobile occupies a residential parking space for periods generally longer than eight hours. The consequent high rate of occupancy for on-street parking often forces residents and their guests to park long distances from the residents' homes. Parking congestion itself causes ill effects. Traffic flow can become impeded because service vehicles cannot leave the traffic lane when stopping. In addition, the congested street has a cluttered appearance that detracts from its residential character.

[3]The lack of commuter opposition is not surprising. In the absence of an organization, any single commuter is likely to expect costs in excess of benefits from active political opposition. The transaction costs of forming an organization for the geographically dispersed commuters probably would have been high.

[4]In 1955 the code was revised to require one new off-street parking space for each new dwelling built. See Clyde O. Fisher, "Land Use Control Through Zoning: The San Francisco Experience," *Hastings Law Journal*, Vol. 13, February 1962, pp. 322–43.

[5]The San Francisco Department of Public Works considers a peak occupancy rate under 70 percent to be reasonable for residential neighborhoods.

We can view on-street parking as a common property resource. Commuters do not have to pay the marginal consumption costs of their on-street parking. The result is that they consume too much on-street parking, inflicting congestion costs on neighborhood residents. A possible solution is to establish effective property rights to longterm on-street parking.[6] One way to distribute property rights is to give preferential parking privileges to neighborhood residents.

THE INITIAL POLICY PROPOSAL

When the residential parking problem became acute in the early 1970s, the need arose for a desirable regulatory plan that would reduce peak-hour parking demand, guarantee residents (and their visitors) access to on-street parking in close proximity to their homes, and do both without excessive administrative costs or enforcement problems. The standard regulatory approach used by the San Francisco Department of Public Works in nonresidential parts of the city was a two-hour restriction on all parkers. This would reduce parking demand in the neighborhoods, but would also deny long-term parking to neighborhood residents. Understandably, few of the neighborhoods viewed two-hour restrictions for all parkers as a desirable solution. Eventually several neighborhood associations representing the Sunset and Richmond districts proposed that residents be given preferential parking privileges. Although no detailed plan was developed at the time, what the neighborhood associations had in mind was identification stickers that permit residents to use on-street parking denied to nonresidents. Such a preferential parking scheme would reduce parking congestion without denying long-term parking to neighborhood residents. In 1972, prompted by enthusiastic support from neighborhood associations, the San Francisco Board of Supervisors passed by a vote of seven to three a request to the California legislature for permission to establish a preferential parking system. The city attorney's office and the state legislative council held that any preferential treatment of neighborhood residents with respect to parking would be unconstitutional. In the face of these opinions, the Board of Supervisors declined to take further action.

THE POLICY ENTREPRENEUR

The preferential parking idea continued to be of interest to the Area Planning Program of the San Francisco Department of City Planning. From a practical point of view, this program serves as an information-gathering arm of the department. At its best, it keeps the department in touch with the desires of neighborhood residents. At its worst, it helps the department determine how it can play on neighborhood desires to advance its own favored projects and programs. Shortly after joining the Transportation Planning Section of the City Planning Department in 1973, our policy entrepreneur-to-be was approached by one of the area planners, who indicated that there was considerable neighborhood sentiment in

[6]Another solution would be to charge for on-street parking by installing parking meters. Unfortunately, the meters would discourage even low levels of long-term parking that did not inflict marginal consumption costs on others. Also, the meters would probably detract from the attractiveness of the neighborhoods.

favor of some form of regulation limiting the parking congestion generated by nonresidents. The neighborhood associations continued to express interest in the idea of using identification stickers to grant special parking privileges to residents.

The department's Transportation Planning Section thought that a neighborhood sticker plan could contribute significantly to some major planning goals. First by reducing the congestion caused by nonresident vehicles, the plan might improve neighborhood environments in many respects. Second, by diminishing the supply of convenient parking for automobile commuters, preferential parking might force a number of commuters to switch to mass transit or car pools. Finally, support of the plan seemed to offer the department and the section some potential for good public relations with the neighborhoods. This conceptual agreement within the section, along with some strong encouragement from a number of neighborhood organizations, led the policy entrepreneur to decide to develop a preferential parking proposal, even though it was not an official project of the department and would not become so until most of the work had been completed and the legislation was imminent.

The policy entrepreneur outlined the possibilities for a preferential parking program in a memorandum to his immediate supervisor and was given permission to work on the plan during lulls in other projects. He then contacted faculty members at the University of California at Berkeley who might have professional interests in problems related to parking congestion or to the legal issues involved in parking regulation. A professor in the Graduate School of Public Policy (C. B. McGuire) suggested that the parking congestion problem might be an appropriate spring-quarter project for the policy analysis workshop course taken by all first-year graduate students. A student analyst volunteered and began work on the problem in April 1974.

SUPPORTING EVIDENCE: THE STUDENT ANALYSIS

The student analyst was asked to address the following question: How can a preferential parking plan be designed so that it will be legally, politically, and administratively feasible? The student's report considered several alternative regulatory approaches, but focused attention on the neighborhood sticker plan (NSP). The NSP was a detailed specification of the preferential parking plan envisioned by the neighborhood associations.[7] It would establish a procedure for designating neighborhoods where time-restricted parking zones would be established. Residents of a neighborhood would be eligible to purchase (for an administrative fee of approximately $10) a sticker exempting their vehicles from the time-limit restrictions of the NSP parking zones in their neighborhood.

The analysis supporting the NSP focused on the following major questions: Would the NSP be an effective regulatory approach? What restrictions should be placed on nonresidential parkers? Would the NSP be legally valid? Which neighborhoods should be designated as NSP participants?

---

[7]At the time of the student analysis, the only city known to be operating a preferential parking plan was Richmond, Virginia. The traffic order creating Richmond's preferential parking zone was used as a model for the development of a sample ordinance for the NSP. Unfortunately, the legality of the Richmond traffic order had not yet been tested in the courts.

Effectiveness

Unlike the standard regulatory approach that established two-hour zones for all parkers, the NSP would reduce congestion without denying parking to residents. Its use would involve enforcement costs and costs to the displaced commuters, who would have to switch to less-desirable parking or public transportation. The analysis implicitly assumed that benefits to residents resulting from the NSP would exceed the costs inflicted on the displaced commuters. It concluded that the fees charged to residents would cover administrative and enforcement costs as well as be acceptable to the residents. The analysis also considered other types of sticker plans, but did not consider nonregulatory approaches such as increasing bridge tolls, building parking lots, or expanding public transportation, because these options involved issues much more complex and less direct than the allocation of parking in residential neighborhoods.[8]

The neighborhood associations advocating preferential parking had generally assumed that two-hour time zones would be established for nonresident parkers. The student analyst pointed out, however, that ease of enforcement and convenience of visitor parking might be increased through the use of other types of time zones. For example, one-hour zones are much easier to enforce than two-hour zones, although less convenient for short-term visitors to neighborhood residents. But in neighborhoods where congestion was due primarily to all-day nonresident parkers, one-hour zones might be put into effect solely during the midday peak demand period or for one side of the street during the morning and the other side during the afternoon. Combinations of restrictions such as these would reduce the inconvenience to visitors as well as aid enforcement.

Legality

Interviews with members of the San Francisco Board of Supervisors and their administrative assistants indicated that their perception of the legal validity of the NSP would determine its political feasibility. If potential NSP supporters, a clear majority of the board, believed the NSP to be legally valid, its adoption would be highly probable. Unfortunately, the unfavorable opinions by the city attorney's office had led to a general perception among board members that any form of preferential parking would be unconstitutional. The student analyst, therefore, made a review of the NSP in terms of the city attorney's objections a central part of his analysis.[9]

---

[8]The cost of San Francisco's automobile-related services each year was an estimated $13 million more than revenues collected from automobile users (Douglas Lee, "The Costs of Private Automobile Usage in the City of San Francisco," Working Paper 171 [Berkeley: University of California, Institute of Urban and Regional Development, 1972]. This meant that the city paid an average of $65 per year to provide services related to the 200,000 on-street parking spaces. The $65 could have been used as a sticker charge to be applied only to nonresident parkers. The nonresident fee, however, would still have been substantially less than downtown parking costs, which suggested that it might be more effective in generating revenue than in reducing parking congestion in neighborhoods.

[9]Drafts of his analysis of the legality of the NSP were reviewed by several members of the University of California's School of Law before the student analyst completed his report. The student analyst was also encouraged in his efforts when he discovered that the city attorney had apparently misquoted the opinion in a case particularly relevant to parking regulation.

According to the city attorney, a preferential parking plan such as the NSP might be challenged as a violation of the equal protection clause of the Fourteenth Amendment to the U.S. Constitution. This challenge could be countered by the argument that the problem (parking congestion) and the alternative regulatory remedy (two-hour limits for all parkers) would inflict higher costs on residents than on nonresidents. Consequently, the classification of parkers into residents and nonresidents could be viewed as reasonable and not arbitrary.

The city attorney's opinions also included the assertion that preferential parking would violate the constitutionally guaranteed right to travel. But the right to travel has generally been used by the courts to mean migration in and among the states rather than what might be called the "right to commute." The NSP obviously would not interfere with residential choice, nor would it prevent commuting. The NSP would only hinder automobile travel that required long-term parking in certain residential neighborhoods. The NSP would therefore not interfere with the right to travel or the right to commute any more than the commonly employed two-hour parking zones.

Participant Neighborhoods

The Planning Department originally envisioned that it would specify the neighborhoods included in any preferential parking plan at the time the plan was adopted. The student analyst convinced his client, however, that it would be politically better and more analytically feasible to allow neighborhoods to self-select. Therefore, the NSP would provide a procedure for neighborhoods to become preferential parking areas (a bottom-up policy) rather than a direct specification of the covered areas (a top-down policy).

The student analyst recommended a number of criteria for determining which residential neighborhoods could participate in the NSP. He proposed that included areas have a peak daytime occupancy rate of 70 percent for legal on-street spaces. The 70-percent criterion, long used by the San Francisco Department of Public Works to define parking congestion, would help limit the NSP to those neighborhoods with a severe and (by administrative tradition) legally definable problem. Other criteria proposed to ensure the effectiveness of the NSP included the requirement that a substantial proportion of the congestion be due to long-term nonresident parkers, because it would be undesirable to incur administrative costs for the operation of the NSP in neighborhoods where the NSP would provide little relief from parking congestion.

The student analyst recommended that the Board of Supervisors be asked to adopt an enabling ordinance that would allow the criteria to be applied through a procedure similar to that used by the Department of Public Works for the establishment of two-hour parking zones. The existing procedure offered several advantages. First, its use would minimize administrative start-up costs. Second, the procedure provided the recognized mechanisms of petitions and public hearings to take into account neighborhood residents' sentiments, an important feature if the NSP were not to be viewed as interference by the City Planning Department in neighborhood life. Finally, the procedure would be readily accepted as part of a regulatory proposal and consequently would not generate debate that might detract from the potential support for the entire proposal.

INTRAORGANIZATIONAL DELAY

Two aspects of the student analysis encouraged the policy entrepreneur to continue working on preferential parking. First, he felt that the legal arguments presented in support of the NSP were persuasive, especially those dealing with the right to travel. Second, the suggested use of one-hour zones and alternate-side-of-street parking in addition to two-hour zones could reduce the enforcement and short-term visitor problems anticipated in association with preferential parking schemes.

Using the student analysis as a major source, the policy entrepreneur prepared a report that could be used to describe the NSP to other city agencies, the Board of Supervisors, and neighborhood organizations. Neither the outgoing director of the City Planning Department nor his successor were enthusiastic about supporting the NSP, however. The main reason for this was procedural more than substantive. Under the San Francisco City Charter, the City Planning Department, along with almost all city departments, is directed to have all its legal affairs handled by the city attorney's office. Because the city attorney had already issued several opinions saying that preferential parking was unconstitutional, many departmental officials thought it would be inappropriate to continue any kind of work on the idea, not to mention publishing a report on the subject. This feeling was reinforced by the practical consideration that the City Planning Department necessarily maintains a close working relationship with the city attorney's office in order to fulfill its function of administering and updating the city planning code. If a published report on preferential parking were interpreted as an affront to the city attorney's office, this working relationship might be strained. The department's reluctance to release the report manifested itself in repeated requests for successive report drafts mainly involving format changes, a process the policy entrepreneur called "perpetual rewrite mode."

In the meantine, the City Planning Department, in response to a U.S. Environmental Protection Agency (EPA) promulgation in the fall of 1973, had undertaken with the Department of Public Works and a private consultant a comprehensive "parking management" study for the city. This study was well underway in the summer of 1975 when the successive drafts of the preferential parking report were being written. As fall approached, the director of the City Planning Department decided that the preferential parking report should become an addendum to the parking management study and be issued the following spring, whether or not the city attorney had changed his opinion.

Because the director of the City Planning Department was now willing to risk offending the city attorney, the only reason for delay seemed to be a desire for the conceptual tidiness of integrating the parking management study and the preferential parking report. To the policy entrepreneur the fact that a number of neighborhood organizations, already weary from delays in publication of the report, were anxious to bring the issue once again to the attention of the Board of Supervisors seemed more compelling. In the fall of 1975, the policy entrepreneur released a pirate version of the report under a blank letterhead to the neighborhood organizations in an attempt to focus their attention on a specific proposal. Shortly thereafter, representatives from a number of neighborhood organizations had the matter put before the Board of Supervisors (for hearings only, no legislation was submitted), and it was referred to the board's Fire, Safety, and Police Committee. The chairman of the committee declined to hold a hearing until the city attorney had ruled on the matter again. The proponents of preferential parking were back at square one.

OVERCOMING LEGAL OBJECTIONS

Back in 1973, when he first got started on the preferential parking proposal, the policy entrepreneur visited the deputy attorney in the city attorney's office who had written the most recent opinion ruling against preferential parking. The deputy, although he had written the negative opinion, was open to the possibility that preferential parking might have a constitutional basis. As a result, he directed the policy entrepreneur to a number of precedent cases that might be helpful in establishing the proposal's legality. The policy entrepreneur included as a major part of his original report a section on the legal questions, drawing from the student analysis and his own legal research as directed by the deputy attorney. The legal section did not become a part of the final version, but in the fall of 1975, when the constitutionality issue was resubmitted to the city attorney by the Board of Supervisors, the legal section was rewritten by a staff attorney at the City Planning Department and sent to the city attorney, along with the final version of the preferential parking report. The hope was that the city attorney would use these materials in preparing his new opinion. (Incidentally, this was the first official surfacing of the report.)

The request made to the city attorney's office for an opinion on the legality of the NSP called for an element of bureaucratic diplomacy. The request was therefore written in a way that would allow the city attorney to reverse his opinion without "losing face." The transmittal letter suggested that the NSP was significantly different from the previously proposed preferential parking schemes. While the NSP was different in that it presented a detailed specification of how a neighborhood sticker plan would operate, nothing made it legally distinct from other preferential parking proposals. The transmittal letter also suggested that recent court decisions in other states approving plans similar to the NSP necessitated a review of the outdated opinions. These new court decisions directly testing preferential parking schemes and other schemes involving legislative classification had not been available when the city attorney's original opinions were written. The legal memorandum was not presented as a legal analysis better than the city attorney's previous opinions, but rather as something the city attorney's office might find helpful in preparing a new opinion.

An unplanned circumstance may also have helped to encourage a favorable legal opinion on the NSP. The University of California Medical Center had been concerned in recent years about its employees' contribution to parking congestion in the surrounding neighborhoods. It had been especially concerned in the winter of 1976-77 because its building expansion program had been encountering strong neighborhood opposition, partly due to the likelihood of increased parking congestion. The U.C. Medical Center held a number of public meetings on the problem, at one of which the NSP was discussed. A representative of the Citizens' Action League an organization sympathetic to neighborhood interests, attended the meeting and observed strong neighborhood support for the NSP. (Ironically, one neighborhood organization that had long been a supporter of preferential parking switched its position when its members realized that the university would support the NSP—the organization feared that the NSP might undercut its court suit against university expansion.) The league's observer got the impression that a representative of the city attorney's office who attended the meeting did not think that the NSP would be legal. After reviewing the accumulated material on the NSP, the Citizens' Action League decided to support it. In February 1976, the league arranged to have a large delegation meet with the city attorney. When the delegation arrived, the city attorney announced that his office would give an opinion favorable to the NSP. Although the delegation may not have influenced the opinion, it definitely helped stimulate a prompt response to the City Planning Department's request.

A LEGISLATIVE SPONSOR

The Citizens' Action League also was able to secure enthusiastic support of the NSP from a member of the San Francisco Board of Supervisors. This supervisor was planning to run for the California Senate in the next election and saw support of the NSP as a way of strengthening his appeal in the neighborhoods. His interest in the NSP was genuine, and he continued to work for it after he was defeated in the Senate race. The immediate effect of his sponsorship, when he demanded that the City Planning Department prepare an ordinance for the establishment of an NSP, was to bring into the open the NSP report previously prepared by the policy entrepreneur. The supervisor received the NSP ordinance in April. After it was rewritten by the city attorney's office, the ordinance was placed on the agenda of the July 1976 meeting of the Fire, Safety, and Police Committee of the Board of Supervisors.

Prior to the committee hearing, the supervisor invited representatives of the City Planning Department, the Police Department, and the Department of Public Works to a meeting in his office. He made clear that he wanted all three departments to support the NSP at the hearing that afternoon. When the representative of the Police Department said that the department did not want to administer the issuing of stickers, the supervisor called the tax collector to see if he would object to issuing the stickers. The tax collector happened to be out of his office when the supervisor called; the proposed ordinance was altered to specify the tax collector as the administrator of the stickers. (The attraction of the path of least resistance should not be underestimated!)

The chairman of the Fire, Safety, and Police Committee saw the NSP as a tool for generating revenue. At the committee hearing he insisted that the proposed ordinance be modified to require a $12 yearly fee for stickers, whereas only a $6 fee had been recommended in the City Planning Department's report. Most of the testimony against the proposed ordinance came from neighborhood organizations who supported the NSP but opposed the sticker fee. When the ordinance was reported out of committee, it included a provision for a $10 sticker fee as a compromise.

The NSP flew through the Board of Supervisors. It passed unanimously on its first reading, and became an ordinance by passing the second reading ten to one. The lone negative vote may have been a backlash against the City Planning Department's ill-fated attempt to install traffic diverters in one of San Francisco's residential neighborhoods.

BEGINNING IMPLEMENTATION

The day the NSP ordinance was passed, one of the neighborhood organizations that had been instrumental in supporting it at the Fire, Safety, and Police Committee hearing presented a petition for establishing the NSP in its neighborhood. The city departments were not ready to handle such requests. The City Planning Department's representative on the Interstaff Committee on Traffic and Transportation had tried to convince the other departmental representatives that the ordinance would be passed; they had ignored his repeated suggestions that preparations for implementation be discussed. An interdepartmental committee, including a representative of the mayor's office and the administrative assistant to the supervisor who sponsored the ordinance, was eventually established to guide implementation of the NSP. The need to develop administrative procedures for actually establishing the NSP in neighborhoods delayed consideration of the first neighborhood request to participate. In addition, funds had to be secured to cover the initial administrative costs borne by each department. (Sticker fees and parking ticket fines were expected to generate enough revenue to offset or exceed subsequent administrative costs.) Final hearings on the first two neighborhood requests were held in May 1977; both were approved. By that time, nine other neighborhoods had requested participation in the NSP.

CONCLUSION

The history of the NSP illustrates the difficulties that may be encountered by policy entrepreneurs. It also illustrates the role of analysis in an organizational context. We conclude by offering aspiring policy entrepreneurs some simple advice and encouragement. First, do not allow yourself to be blocked by "expert" advice or opinion. Bureaucratic "experts," especially lawyers, are always able to advance some technical or legal objections to proposals they oppose for reasons of inertia, if not of self-interest. Second, keep in close contact with the constituency of potential beneficiaries. Their input helps the policy entrepreneur package the proposal in a politically feasible form, and their active support may be needed to overcome bottlenecks during the adoption and implementation phases. Third, be persistent and watch for favorable times (policy windows) to introduce or reintroduce proposals into the political arena. At some point, taking personal risks, such as releasing private reports, may be necessary to get the proposal moving again. Finally, do not isolate yourself from administrative departments or political forces that are necessary to the proposal. Allow others to share credit for policy ideas; give opponents an opportunity to save face.

11

BENEFIT-COST ANALYSIS
IN A BUREAUCRATIC SETTING:
THE STRATEGIC PETROLEUM RESERVE

Benefit-cost analyses alone rarely pay decisive roles in the resolution of important policy issues. Although benefit-cost analysis speaks to aggregate economic efficiency, the pluralistic and decentralized political systems of Canada, the United States, and most of the other Western democracies give voice to the organized interests that expect to be winners and losers. Lest aspiring analysts despair, however, they should realize that sound benefit-cost analyses can make important contributions to better policy by informing statesmen and by giving support to partisans whose interests happen to be consistent with aggregate economic efficiency. Thus, benefit-cost analysis may serve as a political resource as well as a normative guide.

In this chapter we look at the role benefit-cost analysis had in affecting decisions concerning the size of the Strategic Petroleum Reserve program (SPR), a fundamental element of U.S. energy policy since the oil price shocks of the 1970s. Our story illustrates the use of benefit-cost analysis to evaluate programs whose future benefits are inherently uncertain. It also illustrates the process of doing quantitative analyses in bureaucratic settings and the role that such analyses can play in influencing political decisions. We hope to be both encouraging and sobering to aspiring analysts about the potential usefulness of their technical skills.

BACKGROUND: ENERGY SECURITY AND THE SPR[1]

After the Second World War, the United States became a net importer of crude oil. In 1959 the United States instituted mandatory quotas on oil imports to limit

---

[1]For a more detailed discussion of the U.S. stockpiling program, see David Leo Weimer, *The Strategic Petroleum Reserve: Planning, Implementation, and Analysis* (Westport, Conn.: Greenwood Press, 1982). Our account here draws heavily on this source.

its growing dependence on foreign sources and to support higher prices for domestically produced oil. Throughout the 1960s, the Texas Railroad Commission stabilized domestic prices by regulating the quantity of oil produced in Texas, the major oil-producing state.[2] Thus, even though U.S. *dependence* on foreign oil continued to grow, the United States was not directly *vulnerable* to changes in the world oil market because the Texas Railroad Commission could adjust domestic production to compensate for shifts in import levels.

The picture had changed by the early 1970s. As countries asserted sovereignty over their natural resources during the 1960s, the international oil companies, anticipating eventual loss of control over oil reserves, favored high rates of current production that led to falling real prices. The years of falling real oil prices and a growing world economy contributed to a steady growth in world oil consumption. By the time national governments had achieved direct control over their domestic oil production, they were in a favorable position to exercise some market power through the Organization of Petroleum Exporting Countries (OPEC).

Meanwhile, in the United States two factors were contributing to greater dependence on imported oil and greater vulnerability to swings in the world market. Ceilings on wellhead prices of domestic crude oil had come into effect as part of the general wage and price controls instituted in August 1971 by President Richard Nixon. Although the ceilings had provisions to encourage the development of new oil fields, their overall effect was to slow the growth in domestic oil production and thereby increase import levels. By this time, the Texas Railroad Commission was allowing wells to produce at their maximum efficient rates, and therefore it no longer controlled excess capacity that could be used to increase domestic production rapidly.

Recognizing that a large fraction of oil supplied to the world market originated in the politically unstable Middle East, a small but growing number of analysts and political leaders in Congress and the executive agencies began to worry about the growing vulnerability of the United States to disruptions of the world oil market. By the summer of 1973, there were several proposals that the United States establish petroleum stockpiles. For example, the National Petroleum Council, an industry advisory group to the Department of Interior, raised the possibility of protecting the United States from supply disruptions by storing ninety days of oil imports in salt dome caverns by 1978.[3] Senator Henry Jackson held hearings before the Interior and Insular Affairs Committee on legislation he had introduced that would establish government-owned petroleum stocks.[4] Although administration witnesses offered cautious support for the idea of creating petroleum reserves, they argued that more time was needed to study the options.

Events did not allow much time for quiet study. On October 6, 1973, Egypt attacked Israeli positions along the Suez Canal. Led by Saudi Arabia, the Organization of Arab Petroleum Exporting Countries (OAPEC) tried to use the

[2]For an overview of the contribution of the Texas Railroad Commission to price stability, see Arlon R. Tussing, "An OPEC Obituary," *The Public Interest*, No. 70, Winter 1983, pp. 3–21.

[3]National Petroleum Council, "Emergency Preparedness for Interruptions of Petroleum Imports into the United States," Proposed Interim Report, July 24, 1973.

[4]U.S. Congress, Senate, "Strategic Petroleum Reserves," Hearings before the Committee on Interior and Insular Affairs, 93rd Congress, 1st Session, May 30 and July 26, 1973.

"oil weapon" in support of Egypt. When the United States began to resupply arms to Israel through bases in The Netherlands, OAPEC embargoed oil shipments to the two countries. More significantly, OAPEC members reduced their total oil production so that total world supply fell by about 5 percent in the last quarter of 1973 and the first quarter of 1974. The result was a quadrupling of oil prices. The spot price of Mideast light crude, for example, went from $2.70 per barrel in the third quarter of 1973 to $13.00 per barrel in the first quarter of 1974. This price shock triggered a deep recession that extended well into 1975. The "policy window" for energy security was clearly open.

Initiation of the SPR Program

In response to the Arab oil embargo, President Nixon announced Project Independence, a national effort to achieve energy self-sufficiency by the end of the decade. An interagency task force, eventually headed by the newly created Federal Energy Administration (FEA), began to analyze ways of implementing Project Independence. The task force eventually realized that reducing U.S. vulnerability to disruptions of the world oil market was a much more appropriate goal than self-sufficiency.[5] Yet most of the report was devoted to modeling domestic supply and demand to predict future import levels. Relying heavily on the earlier National Petroleum Council analysis, the Project Independence Report nevertheless suggested that petroleum stockpiles of a billion barrels or more might be justified on grounds of economic efficiency.

The creation of a strategic petroleum reserve was one of the few recommendations of the Project Independence Report included by the new Ford Administration in its legislative proposals of January 1975. Of all the proposals, it received the warmest reception in Congress. The Energy Policy and Conservation Act (P.L. 94-163), which was passed and signed into law in December 1975, gave the FEA administrator one year to submit to Congress a plan for the implementation of a Strategic Petroleum Reserve program (SPR) that would have 150 million barrels of petroleum in storage within three years and eventually store up to one billion barrels. Although there was a presumption in the legislation that the SPR would hold about ninety days of petroleum imports (then about 500 million barrels) within seven years, the details of program design and implementation were left to the FEA administrator.

Basic Program Structure

The SPR Plan, which was submitted to Congress in December 1976, called for 150 million barrels of oil to be in storage by December 1978, 325 million barrels by December 1980, and 500 million barrels by December 1982. The choice of 500 million barrels was the result of a compromise with the Office of Management and Budget (OMB). OMB analysts favored a smaller reserve. Although FEA analysts believed that a larger reserve could be justified on efficiency grounds with reasonable assumptions about the likelihood of future disruptions, they did not wish to reopen the issue with OMB.

[5]Federal Energy Administration, Project Independence Report, November 1974, p. 19.

The SPR Plan identifies salt dome caverns and mines as the most desirable storage facilities. They were expected to be much cheaper than the major alternatives: steel tanks, floating tankers, and shut-in wells.[6] The writers of the plan anticipated that about 200 million barrels of salt dome storage capacity could be purchased from firms that had created caverns as a by-product of brine production and salt mining. Additional capacity would be created through solution mining (making caverns by dissolving salt with fresh water), which permitted new caverns to be filled with oil as they were being created. The salt dome formations were conveniently located along the Gulf Coast near existing transportation facilities so that oil taken out of storage could be easily distributed.

The SPR Plan was generally well received in Congress. The only major criticism came from a few senators who wanted the plan to include the storage of petroleum products in regional locations as well as the storage of crude oil along the Gulf Coast. The FEA administrator under the new Carter Administration was able to deflect this criticism by promising further study. Consequently, the Senate and House allowed the plan to go into effect without amendment in April 1977.

Implementation Problems

The SPR program appeared to get off to a good start. Within one week of the plan's going into effect, three of the major sites for solution mining were acquired. Within a few months, oil was being injected into caverns at one site; by the end of the year, oil was being injected at all three sites and a conventionally mined site had been acquired. Soon, however, problems arose that frustrated efforts to keep the program on schedule and under budget. In 1979, when oil purchases were stopped in response to the increases in price growing out of the Iranian Revolution, only 92 million barrels were in storage. The resulting general perception of failure, and some of the specific reasons for it, left the program vulnerable to later attempts to limit its size.

Here we briefly sketch some of the major sources of implementation failure at the outset of the SPR program.[7]

Problems Inherent in Program Design. The SPR Plan was overly optimistic about how much existing storage capacity could be purchased and immediately put to use. Several caverns did not have as much capacity as expected. The capacity that was available required the disposal of a barrel of brine for each

[6]Storage in the form of surge capacity from shut-in oil wells is the most expensive of the alternatives. For each barrel of surge capacity, about eight barrels of proven reserves must be shut in. To have the capacity to increase production by one billion barrels per year would require eight billion barrels of proven reserves, or about 25 percent of total U.S. proven reserves. Further, transportation facilities and production crews would have to be kept at the ready.

Whereas new solution-mined caverns were expected to cost between $1.35 and $2.15 per barrel (actual costs turned out to be closer to $3.00 per barrel) and new steel tanks between $8 and $12 per barrel, in situ storage was estimated to cost between $45 and $100 per barrel. Strategic Petroleum Office, "Strategic Petroleum Reserve Plan," December 15, 1976, Table IV-1, p. 75.

[7]For a fuller discussion, see David Leo Weimer, "Problems of Expedited Implementation: The Strategic Petroleum Reserve," *Journal of Public Policy*, Vol. 3, No. 2, May 1983, pp. 169–90.

barrel of oil put in storage. Deep wells, which would eventually be replaced by planned pipelines to the sea, proved inadequate for disposing of the brine. The deficit of existing capacity, which necessitated more solution mining of new capacity, greatly exacerbated the problem of brine disposal—the mining of each barrel of new capacity produces seven barrels of brine as a by-product.

The SPR Plan also failed to anticipate the difficulty of initiating and monitoring the large number of contracts—eighty-five major construction contracts alone during the first year—with a small staff based in Washington, D.C. The task was overwhelming. The eventual solution, a limited privatization of the contracting function, was to hire a prime contractor who in turn contracted for the necessary construction services and materials. Nevertheless, the initial contracting problems slowed implementation, contributed to cost overruns, and diverted attention from building a management infrastructure.

Should these problems have been foreseen by program planners? Undoubtedly, the limited technical experience of the planners contributed to their over-optimistic assumptions about the availability and feasible rate of developing storage capacity. But without taking time to do field experiments, it is not obvious how they could have made better estimates. In contrast, if they had prepared detailed implementation scenarios, then they might have anticipated the difficulty of administering so many contracts with such a small staff in an organization with no prior experience in procuring construction services.

Unrealistic Expectations. James R. Schlesinger, who later became secretary of the new Department of Energy, served as President Jimmy Carter's chief energy advisor in the early days of the new administration. He viewed reliance on Middle Eastern oil as a serious weakness in the U.S. defense posture. He also believed that the then ''soft'' world oil market would become ''tight'' in the early 1980s, so it would be better to accumulate oil for the reserve sooner rather than later. He therefore convinced the president that development of the SPR should be accelerated by two years and its ultimate size increased to one billion barrels.

These decisions were made, however, without consulting the SPR office about their feasibility. The SPR staff argued for a more modest acceleration; but Schlesinger insisted on changing the schedule so that 250 million barrels would be in storage by the end of 1978 and 500 million barrels by the end of 1980. So at a time when the SPR Office was straining to keep the implementation on the old schedule, it had to divert scarce managerial resources to devising a plan for meeting a more ambitious one. The plan was transmitted to Congress in May as an amendment to the original SPR Plan.

Aside from using scarce managerial resources at a critical stage in the implementation, the acceleration decision forced the SPR Office to take a number of gambles in order to meet the new schedule. For example, to avoid delays in deliveries of oil, purchases were made in anticipation of facilities being completed. When they were not ready, demurrage charges had to be paid for the unaccepted deliveries. The acceleration decision also contributed to a loss of credibility that hurt the program in its future efforts to secure needed resources. Thus, because of the failure to consider the feasibility of implementation, the acceleration decision actually decelerated the program. The decision to expand the size of the SPR to one billion barrels opened the bureaucratic battles that we discuss later in the chapter.

Lack of Organizational Support.   When the SPR Office was located within the FEA, it enjoyed a favored position. The head of the SPR Office was an assistant administrator who reported directly to the FEA administrator. This access enabled the SPR Office to obtain fast decisions from the administrator and elicit his support in securing cooperation from other agencies and other units within the FEA. For example, when the magnitude of the contracting problem became apparent, the administrator helped set up a special procurement board to expedite the signing of construction contracts.

All this changed with the creation of the Department of Energy (DOE) in October 1977. Instead of reporting directly to the FEA administrator, the director of the SPR Office now reported to a deputy assistant secretary, who reported to an assistant secretary, who reported to the undersecretary, who reported to a deputy secretary, who reported to the secretary. No longer was it possible to get fast decisions. Further, each substantive office within the department competed for the attention of the new hierarchy.

Three serious problems arose. First, the SPR Office could not easily mobilize the DOE leadership to intervene with other agencies, such as the Environmental Protection Agency and the Army Corps of Engineers, whose procedures for issuing environmental and water use permits were slowing construction. Second, when the Department of Energy was created by merging the FEA, the Federal Power Commission, and the Energy Research and Development Administration, the number of employees exceeded the limit for the new agency. The response was a department-wide hiring freeze—just at the time that the SPR Office needed to add personnel with experience in contract administration. The director of the SPR Office had to devote staff time to making special requests for new hires. Third, all procurement responsibilities were transferred to what had been the procurement office of the Energy Research and Development Administration. Its cumbersome procedures were designed to handle procurements for large and complex research and development projects. Contracts that the FEA would have processed in weeks or months now took as long as nine months. Indeed, a critical six-month period passed with virtually no contracts for the SPR being let.

These problems highlight the importance of considering organizational structure in designing new programs. Perhaps many of the problems could have been avoided if the SPR Office had been established as either an independent agency or a unit reporting directly to the secretary. The necessity of winning support within the large DOE bureaucracy also became relevant in later battles with OMB over funding for program expansion.

Summary.   The SPR program failed to meet either its original or accelerated schedule. At the end of 1978 only 68.5 million barrels were in storage—far less than the 150 million barrels called for by the old schedule or the 250 million barrels called for by the accelerated schedule. The 500-million-barrel mark was not reached until 1986, four years later than under the original schedule and six years later than under the accelerated schedule.

The implementation problems that led to these delays had been largely solved by 1980. But were (and are) the objectives of the SPR program appropriate? It is to this question that we turn next.

ANALYTICAL APPROACHES TO THE SIZE ISSUE

The intuitive logic behind stockpiling is simple: buy oil when prices are low (in normal markets) and sell oil when prices are high (in disrupted markets). Such speculation has the potential for generating profits, suggesting the possibility of private stockpiling. Why then should the government be involved in oil stockpiling? In other words, what market or government failures justify publicly owned oil stocks? There are two major rationales for public stockpiling: one based on market failure and the other based on government failure.[8]

First, stockpiling involves external effects. Firms do not bear the full costs and benefits of their stockpiling decisions. When firms purchase oil stocks, they increase the world demand for oil, which may in turn increase the price. While the stockpilers must pay the higher price, so too must all buyers of oil. The economic costs of the higher prices, however, are external to the profit calculations of the stockpilers. Thus, the social costs of building stocks may be higher than the private costs. With respect to drawdowns that reduce price, the social benefits may be higher than the private benefits. Also, the mere existence of a large stockpile may provide political benefits, such as the deterrence of purposeful disruptions, that do not show up in the profits of private stockpilers. In general, we expect the positive externalities to be greater than the negative externalities. The reason is that stock accumulations usually occur gradually, so that small price increases with negligible economic effects result; drawdowns are likely to occur during price shocks, when even small price reductions can have noticeable economic benefits.[9]

Second, because of government price controls and mandatory petroleum allocations in the recent past, firms may anticipate the possibility that the government will prevent them from selling speculative stocks at market prices during future oil price shocks. In other words, past government actions have undermined the security of property rights to stockpiled oil. Therefore, too little oil will be

---

[8]George Horwich and David Leo Weimer, *Oil Price Shocks, Market Response, and Contingency Planning* (Washington, D.C.: American Enterprise for Public Policy Research, 1984), pp. 112–14. A third rationale is based on the recognition that firms may be risk averse. For an individual firm, stockpiling in anticipation of a major price shock is like gambling—if the price shock occurs, the firm profits; if it does not, the firm suffers a loss. Therefore, from the firm's perspective stockpiling is like gambling—a sure payment is made in return for the small probability of a big gain. From the social perspective, however, stockpiling is like insurance—a sure payment is made in return for avoiding the small probability of a big loss.

[9]The major exception occurs in situations in which firms attempt to build their stocks once disruptions have already begun. Such behavior may be consistent with the maximization of profits if firms anticipate higher prices in the future, but it contributes to the magnitude of the price shock that the economy suffers.

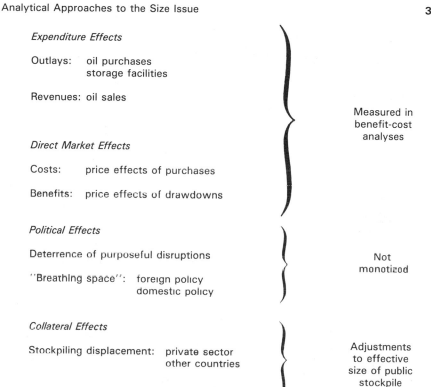

Expenditure Effects

Outlays: oil purchases
            storage facilities

Revenues: oil sales

)

Direct Market Effects

Costs: price effects of purchases

Benefits: price effects of drawdowns

Measured in
benefit-cost
analyses

Political Effects

Deterrence of purposeful disruptions

"Breathing space":   foreign policy
                     domestic policy

Not
monetized

Collateral Effects

Stockpiling displacement: private sector
                            other countries

Adjustments
to effective
size of public
stockpile

Figure 11.1   Impacts of a Public Oil-Stockpiling Program

privately stockpiled for use during oil supply disruptions.[10] These rationales suggest the desirability of a public role in oil stockpiling. But how big a role? Assuming that stockpiling is to be supplied directly by government, how big should the stockpile be? How quickly should it be built? And under what circumstances should it be used? The benefit-cost framework helps us begin to answer these questions.

Impacts of a Stockpiling Program

As shown in Figure 11.1, we divide the impacts of a public stockpiling program into four categories: expenditures, direct market, political, and collateral effects.

Expenditure Effects.   The most visible costs of an oil-stockpiling program are the outlays that must be made to secure storage facilities and purchase oil. Estimates of the costs of building storage facilities can be based on engineering data or on the costs of similar facilities built in the past. Estimating the cost of

[10]We can think of this as an institutional common property resource problem—because firms are not able with certainty to exclude others from using their stockpiled oil when it is most valuable, they will undersupply speculative stocks.

oil requires projections of future prices—including the effects of the purchases themselves. Because purchases generally will not be made in disrupted markets, such projections can take the form of assumptions about long-run rates of price growth (or decline).

When the government sells oil from the stockpile, it realizes revenue. Large sales will depress the price of oil—the intended effect when stocks are used to counter a disruption. We may assume that the program will be terminated at some future date by selling facilities and any remaining stocks at projected prices. These revenues constitute the anticipated scrap value of the program.

Market Effects.   The left-hand panel of Figure 11.2 illustrates the market effects of a drawdown of stocks during a disruption of the world oil market. Prior to the disruption, the world price of oil is P_0, the price at which the supply schedule S_{WN} and the demand schedule D_W intersect. A disruption, which suddenly removes supply from the market, shifts the supply schedule to S_{WD}. This shift causes price to rise to P_1. (The sudden jump in price from P_0 to P_1 is the *oil price shock*.) A drawdown of oil stocks shifts the supply curve back to the right. A drawdown of size d shifts the postdisruption supply schedule horizontally to the right by d units to $S_{WD} + d$, so that price P_2 results. Thus, the drawdown keeps the postdisruption price from rising all the way to P_1. The difference between P_1 and P_2 is the source of the economic benefits of the drawdown for net oil importers like the United States.

A purchase of oil for the stockpile shifts the demand schedule in the world market to the right. If the supply schedule is horizontal over the range of the shifting demand schedule, then the purchase does not cause the price to rise. If the

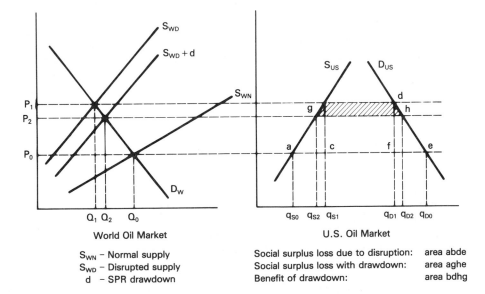

Figure 11.2   Measuring the Direct Economic Benefits of an SPR Drawdown

supply schedule is upward sloping, however, the shift in demand does cause price to rise. This rise in price results in economic losses for net oil importers that can be measured in the same way as the economic losses caused by the oil supply disruption.

Political Effects.   A large stockpile may deter embargoes and politically motivated reductions in supply. The larger the stockpile, the more political opponents must reduce supply in order to impose any particular level of economic loss on importers. As long as the exporting countries anticipate that they also will suffer economic losses by reducing supply, the existence of a large stockpile will deter somewhat the use of supply disruptions for political purposes.

A large stockpile also expands the range of options that the United States can pursue in carrying out domestic and foreign policy. Because a stockpile drawdown provides "breathing space" between the time when supplies from an exporting region are disrupted and the time when the full impact of the resulting price increase is felt, diplomatic initiatives can be launched in a less politically volatile domestic environment than otherwise. If the disruption coincides with, or leads to, military intervention, the stockpile will enhance operational flexibility by reducing the costs to the United States and its allies of temporary damage that they might inflict collaterally to oil-producing facilities. In terms of domestic policy, drawdowns may lessen the political panic that can lead to price controls and mandatory allocations of the sort that exacerbated the economic costs of disruptions during the 1970s.[11]

Collateral Effects.   Public stockpiling may discourage private stockpiling. The existence of a large stockpile controlled by the government may displace stockpiling that would otherwise be done by the private sector. Firms will expect government drawdowns during disruptions to reduce the price at which their own stockpiles could be sold. Although this price-reducing effect will tend to lower the size of private stockpiles, the marginal reduction is likely to be small because firms already anticipate that price controls and mandatory allocations of private stockpiles will be reimposed during disruptions large enough to trigger use of the government stockpile. Indeed, if firms believe that larger government stockpiles reduce the likelihood that price controls and allocations will be reimposed, increasing the size of the government stockpile may actually encourage private stockpiling. Overall, the displacement of private stockpiling is probably insignificant.

A large U.S. stockpile may also discourage the stockpiling efforts of foreign governments. Because oil consumers worldwide gain from drawdowns of the U.S. stockpile, other importing nations may take a "free ride" on large U.S. stocks. If this happens, then each barrel added to the U.S. stockpile will result in less than a barrel in net additions to world stocks. A factor that constrains free riding is the International Energy Agency. Its members, including the United States,

---

[11]For a discussion of the impact of the U.S. regulations during the 1970s, see Horwich and Weimer, *Oil Price Shocks*, pp. 57–110.

Canada, Japan, West Germany, and most of the other countries in Western Europe, have agreed to hold minimum levels of petroleum stocks for use during supply disruptions. Even without such an agreement, fear that the United States may fail to use its reserves is likely to restrain countries somewhat from free riding.

The standard approach for taking account of these displacement effects in benefit-cost analyses is to assume that the public stockpile has a smaller effective, than physical, size. So, for example, if analysts believed that private stocks would be reduced by one barrel for each five barrels put in the public stockpile, then a 500-million-barrel reserve would have an effective size of only 400 million barrels.

Quantifying Costs and Benefits

We can employ the standard tools of economics to quantify the budgetary and market effects of a stockpiling program. Unfortunately, the political and collateral effects are not as easily quantified. It is probably reasonable to assume that the displacement effects of a U.S. stockpiling program are small. Although the political benefits cannot be quantified, they nevertheless may be important— especially to a president who must make politically sensitive decisions, such as those concerning the resupply of Israel during a Middle East war or the use of military force to aid the government of Saudi Arabia against foreign-supported insurgents. In excluding political benefits from our benefit-cost analysis, we understate the net benefits of stockpiling. As we discussed in Chapter 6, the benefit-cost analysis becomes one component of a larger multigoal analysis.

We must also consider the issue of standing. As we have already mentioned, acquisitions and drawdowns affect the price of oil in the world oil market. One approach is to measure the costs and benefits accruing not just to the United States, but also to its allies who import oil at the world price. Instead, the standard practice for analysts in the U.S. government has been to measure only costs and benefits accruing domestically. In other words, they give standing in their benefit-cost analyses only to U.S. residents.

Changes in Social Surplus.   We return to Figure 11.2 to illustrate the measurement of the benefits of drawdowns and the costs of acquisitions.

The right-hand panel shows the effect of the rise in price from P_0 to P_1 on the U.S. oil market. At the predisruption price P_0, q_{D0} is domestically consumed (point e on the U.S. demand schedule, D_{US}) and q_{S0} is domestically produced (point a on the U.S. supply schedule, S_{US}). The difference between domestic consumption and domestic production equals the level of imports prior to the disruption. When the price rises to P_1, domestic consumption falls to q_{D1} and domestic production rises to q_{S1}. The resulting loss in social surplus equals the area of trapezoid $abde$; the area of triangle def represents the consumer surplus lost because less is being consumed; the triangle abc represents the real resource costs of increasing domestic production; and the area of rectangle $bdfc$ represents the additional amount that consumers must pay to foreign suppliers for the imports that they continue to consume.

The postdisruption price with a drawdown of size d is only P_2. The social surplus loss of a rise in price from P_0 to P_2 equals the area of a trapezoid $aghe$, which is smaller than the social surplus loss without the drawdown by the area of trapezoid *bdhg*. Thus, the avoided social surplus loss from the drawdown equals the area *bdhg* (which is shaded in the figure). Applying the rule we developed in Chapter 7, the benefits of the drawdown equal the realized revenue (*d* times P_2) plus the change in social surplus in the primary market (area *bdhg*).

Oil acquisitions that increase world price also cause a social surplus loss in the U.S. domestic oil market. Imagine that the rise in price from P_0 to P_1 had been caused by a very large oil purchase. It would cause the same loss in social surplus as the disruption. To calculate the costs of the acquisition, we would add expenditures for the purchased oil to the change of social surplus in the domestic market. Only if price did not rise as a result of the oil purchase would the cost of the acquisition just equal the budgetary cost.

What information is needed to calculate these direct social surplus changes? To locate the positions of the supply and demand schedules, we need projections of price, world consumption, domestic consumption, and domestic supply for the period of time when the stockpiling program is to be in existence. Such long-run projections are typically based on historical trends. To measure the effect of supply interruptions on price, we need estimates of the price elasticities of supply and demand in the world oil market; to measure social surplus losses we need estimates of the price elasticities of supply and demand in the U.S. oil market. Econometric analyses of historical or cross-national data indicate reasonable ranges for these elasticities.

Adjustment Costs. The social surplus analysis assumes that the economy can move from one equilibrium to another without cost. While this is a reasonable assumption for moderate price changes, it may not be for steep price changes in a commodity, such as oil, that is a basic input to important sectors of the economy. The higher price of oil requires that relative prices throughout the economy change to achieve efficient allocation at the new equilibrium. Not all prices are perfectly flexible, however. Nominal wages, for instance, tend to be downwardly sticky so that during a large price shock we may see greater involuntary unemployment rather than an immediate fall in wages. Although inflation may eventually permit an appropriate adjustment by reducing real wages, the short-term consequences may be greater inefficiency than estimated by the direct changes in social surplus.

Similarly, sharp oil price shocks induce immense transfers in wealth from domestic consumers to domestic and foreign oil producers; this shifts demand schedules throughout the economy. Uncertainty about the new composition of demand can slow investment needed to produce a capital stock consistent with the new relative prices. Delayed investment and reduced aggregate consumption can lead to recession. The inefficiency of idle resources during recession and the loss in future output caused by delays in current investment are not reflected in the direct changes in social surplus.

In light of these adjustment costs, do benefit-cost analyses based on direct changes in social surplus have any systematic biases? Because adjustment costs grow disproportionately with the size of the price shock, direct measures of social surplus changes contribute more to an underestimation of the benefits of drawdowns than an underestimation of the costs of acquisitions. Therefore, benefit-cost analyses based on direct social surplus changes in the oil market generally underestimate the true net benefits of stockpiling.

Macroeconomic Simulations.   Given that an oil price shock sets in motion price changes throughout the economy, a dynamic model of the entire economy would provide an attractive tool for estimating the full economic costs of oil price shocks and thereby the costs and benefits of stockpiling. Large-scale macroeconomic models employ hundreds of interrelated equations to represent various sectors of the economy and their interactions. A variety of these models are used in government and business for predicting GNP, inflation, unemployment, and other measures of aggregate economic performance. For example, the Department of Energy relied on the commercial forecasting models developed by Data Resources Incorporated (DRI) and Wharton Econometric Forecasting Associates in many evaluations of the SPR.

To measure the benefits of a stockpile drawdown, an analyst would employ the following procedure: First, specify a disruption scenario—the price path of oil over a number of three-month periods. Second, using the specified price path of oil, simulate the response of the economy and measure the present value of GNP over a period of several years. Third, specify a new price path of oil that reflects the assumed drawdown and measure the present value of GNP. Fourth, interpret the difference in the present value of GNP as the benefit of the drawdown.

Aside from the limitations of GNP as a measure of social welfare, two important practical problems inherent in this procedure make it analytically unattractive.[12]

First, the most commonly used macroeconomic models are not well designed to estimate the effects of supply-side shocks like oil supply disruptions. The models focus primarily on aggregate demand with only implicit accounting of supply flows; thus they often produce internally inconsistent results that must be corrected with ad hoc procedures. Also, the econometrically estimated relationships in the models may not hold for large disruptions beyond the range of historical data.

Second, the great complexity of the models, and the numerous assumptions that must be made in using them to simulate something extraordinary like an oil price shock, provide a great opportunity for the modeler to manipulate the results. For example, small changes in assumptions about government monetary and fiscal policies can have large effects on the estimated costs of disruptions. Because numerous ad hoc corrections are needed to achieve internal consistency, even a well-trained macroeconomist may have difficulty in finding inappropriate assumptions hidden in the complexity. Given that the cost of using the model is high (in terms of both human and computer time), it is often not feasible to test the sensitivity of all major assumptions. All these features invite analytical abuse by those already committed to policies.

Dealing with Uncertainty

Uncertainty about the timing, frequency, duration, and magnitude of oil supply disruptions provides an interesting challenge for anyone wishing to do a

---

[12]Exactly offsetting shifts in domestic consumption and exports would not change GNP. Yet the social surplus of U.S. residents would certainly go down—foreigners are now consuming goods that they previously consumed. The measure of changes in economic efficiency should be the sum of changes in GNP and changes in foreign claims on GNP. For a comparison of GNP and social surplus as measures of welfare, see Horwich and Weimer, *Oil Price Shocks*, pp. 8–14.

benefit-cost analysis of a stockpiling program. If no disruption occurs, or one occurs before significant stocks can be accumulated, then the stockpiling program will almost certainly involve net costs. But this possibility must be weighed against the possibility that a drawdown during a major disruption will yield huge benefits that greatly exceed the costs of building the stockpile.

We briefly discuss here the two major approaches that have been used to deal with uncertainty in benefit-cost analyses of the SPR: scenario/break-even analysis and dynamic stochastic programming.

Scenario/Break-Even Analysis.   Early benefit-cost analyses of the SPR were based on specified scenarios of program development and future market conditions. Each analysis compared two scenarios with identical program schedules: a disruption scenario with a specified supply interruption and a base-case scenario without it. After measuring the costs and benefits incurred under each scenario, the analysts then calculated how likely the scenario with the supply interruption would have to be for the program to barely pass the benefit-cost criterion with zero expected net benefits. For example, the scenarios might call for the addition of sixty million barrels of oil to the SPR in each of the next five years. The disruption scenario might then call for the drawdown on all 300 million barrels in response to a major supply interruption (say the loss of six million barrels per day to the world market for a period of six months) in the seventh year. The base-case scenario might assume that oil would be held for another ten years and then sold. If the present value of the costs of acquiring and storing the oil under the base-case scenario equalled C, and if the present value of benefits from the drawdown during the disruption equalled a larger amount B, then the break-even probability, P_b, would equal C/B.[13] If you believe that the probability of an interruption similar to the one in the disruption scenario is greater than the break-even probability, then you would conclude that the proposed program schedule offered positive net expected benefits.

The scenario/break-even approach oversimplifies the stockpiling problem in a number of important ways. It does not allow for uncertainty over the timing, magnitude, and duration of disruptions. It ignores the possibility of there being more than one disruption over the life of the program. In considering the break-even probability, decision makers must subjectively account for these limitations in determining how large a probability to assign to the occurrence of the disruption. In addition, the scenario/break-even methodology provides little insight into the optimal timing of acquisitions and drawdowns.

---

[13]The break-even probability solves the following equation for zero net expected benefits:

$$0 = p_b (B - C) + (1 - p_b)(0 - C)$$

where B is the present value of benefits if the interruption occurs and C the present value of costs. Of course, this simple formulation implies a world with only two contingencies: the supply interruption in the scenario occurs and the supply interruption in the scenario does not occur. It also assumes that the costs of developing the reserve are identical with and without the supply interruption, or that B is adjusted to make the costs equal. For example, B would equal the drawdown benefits plus the present value of the avoided costs of future acquisitions and minus the present value of forgone scrap value.

Simple Decision Analysis

Decision analysis, which we briefly discussed in Chapter 7, provides a framework for expressing the various dimensions of uncertainty in terms of combinations of simple risks. The basic tool of decision analysis is the *decision tree*. Figure 11.3 illustrates a very simple decision tree that corresponds to a stylized break-even analysis. The tree consists of two types of nodes connected by lines representing outcomes. The square at the left of the tree is a *decision node*, where we begin by making one of two choices: adopt the proposed stockpiling program or do not adopt it. If we do not adopt it, then we move to the lower circle representing a *chance node*, which leads to a disruption (an economic cost of 100) with probability p and no disruption (an economic cost of zero) with probability $1 - p$. If instead we decide to adopt the proposed stockpiling program, then we pay for the program (an economic cost of 10) and move to the upper circle, which leads to a disruption (an economic cost reduced to 60 by drawdown) with probability p and no disruption (an economic cost of -8 because of liquidation of stocks) with probability $1 - p$.

To calculate a break-even probability, we compare the expected value of stockpiling with the expected value of not stockpiling. These expected values are shown at the bottom of Figure 11.3. By equating the expressions for the expected values and solving for p, we find that stockpiling offers positive net expected benefits if the probability of disruption is greater than one in sixteen.

Now imagine that we let the tree grow decision nodes at the end of each of the chance branches. We could interpret the resulting structure as representing two successive time periods. It would be possible to have no disruption over the two periods, one disruption lasting one period, or one disruption lasting the entire two periods. As we add more and more periods, the tree allows for the possibility of ever-greater patterns of disruptions. Thus, by constructing a multiperiod decision tree, we create a model that incorporates a large number of scenarios involving disruptions of varying length and frequency.

Also imagine that we expand the chance nodes to include several levels of disruption. Now the tree permits the possibility of scenarios with the magnitude of a disruption changing over time. We can allow for flexibility in the schedule of the stockpiling program by modifying the decision nodes to have multiple choices about increments and decrements to stocks.

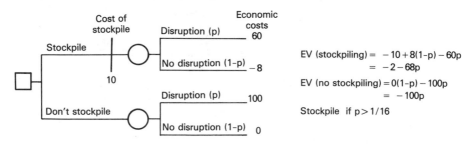

Figure 11.3   A Simple Decision Tree

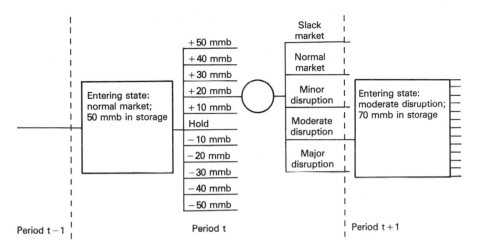

Figure 11.4   A Sample Node in the Decision Tree for the Stockpiling Problem

Figure 11.4 shows a close-up of a small portion of an expanded decision tree for the stockpiling problem. As shown, we enter period *t* under normal market conditions with 50 million barrels of oil already in the stockpile. We are then faced with the decision of how much oil to acquire or drawdown. Eleven possible decisions are shown. They range in 10-million-barrel increments from drawing down the entire stockpile (– 50 million barrels) to adding another 50 million barrels. If we add, say, 20 million barrels then we move to the chance node with 70 million barrels in the stockpile. Now one of five possible market conditions occurs: a slack market in which some oil could be purchased without driving up that price; a normal market in which purchases drive the price up somewhat; a minor disruption; a moderate disruption; and a major disruption. The market condition and the stockpile size define the entering state at the beginning of period *t* + 1.

The decision tree for a stockpiling problem with, for instance, fifteen time periods, five market states, and stockpile increments of 10 million barrels would be literally impossible to draw or solve by hand. Fortunately, a general solution method called *stochastic dynamic programming* can be applied with the aid of a computer.

Stochastic Dynamic Programming.   If we were to solve a decision tree by hand, we would start at the last period, calculating expected values over the outcomes of the last chance nodes. We would then replace the chance nodes with these expected values and prune off all but the chance node with the largest expected value for each decision node. We would then discount the dominant nodes back to the previous period. Continuing this process of taking discounted expected values and pruning off dominated chance nodes, we would eventually work back to the decision node in the initial period. As a result of this pruning process, we would be able to select the decision in the initial period that had the largest present value of expected net benefits. Reading through the pruned tree from the first to last period would give us the optimal strategy for any sequence of market conditions.

Stochastic dynamic programming employs a similar solution method, identifying the optimal sequence of drawdowns and acquisitions for any scenario of market conditions. Constraints on the allowable size of the stockpile in each period can be incorporated to model proposed schedules of storage capacity development. To compare alternative schedules, the stockpiling model would be solved for each schedule separately. The schedule offering the largest present value of expected net benefits would be selected as most efficient.

What assumptions must be made to employ stochastic dynamic programming? First, for each alternative program we require a specification of a schedule of storage capacity availability and the present value of the costs of providing it. Second, assumptions about prices, quantities, and elasticities for the world and U.S. oil markets are necessary for each period so that costs and benefits can be calculated. Third, a social discount rate must be selected. Fourth, the probabilities of each market condition arising in each period contingent on the market condition of the previous period are needed for calculating expected values. For example, given a normal market in the current period, what is the probability that the next period will also have a normal market?

The first three of these categories comprise the sorts of assumptions that we normally make in doing benefit-cost analysis. Therefore, we have fairly standard approaches for making them. Assumptions about the probabilities of market conditions are much more subjective. If we allow only two possible market conditions, then we can easily do sensitivity analysis by varying the two assumed probabilities.[14] For a model with five market conditions, however, sixteen independent probabilities must be specified. The greatest weakness in the stochastic dynamic programming approach is the difficulty analysts face in selecting these probabilities and communicating their significance to clients.

Stochastic dynamic programming was first applied to the oil-stockpiling problem by Thomas J. Teisberg, then a member of the economics faculty at the Massachusetts Institute of Technology.[15] He worked with policy analysts in the Department of Energy to develop a model that became the standard tool for evaluating economic costs and benefits of alternative stockpiling policies. In the story that follows, we look at the role played by this model in the debate between the Department of Energy and the Office of Management and Budget over the appropriate size of the SPR.

[14]For two market conditions, the following transition matrix displays the probabilities:

		Market Condition in Period $t + 1$	
		Normal	Disrupted
Market Condition	Normal	p_N	$1 - p_N$
in Period t	Disrupted	p_D	$1 - p_D$

[15]For a description of his model, see Thomas J. Teisberg, "A Dynamic Programming Model of the U.S. Strategic Petroleum Reserve," *Bell Journal of Economics*, Vol. 12, No. 2, Autumn 1981, pp. 526–46.

THE ROLE OF ANALYSIS IN THE SPR SIZE CONTROVERSY[16]

The Energy Policy and Conservation Act mandated the creation of an SPR of between 150 million and one billion barrels, with a strong presumption that the SPR would be sufficient to replace 90 days of petroleum imports (then about 500 million barrels). Although work completed by the Institute of Defense Analyses suggested that a much larger SPR was economically justified, the billion-barrel figure was selected as a round number larger than the largest size that the administration anticipated recommending to Congress in the SPR plan.[17] The lower level of 150 million barrels represented an estimate by the FEA of the amount of existing salt dome storage capacity that it could obtain for the program. The presumed size of 500 million barrels, consistent with the National Petroleum Council recommendation, was selected by President Ford as a compromise between the positions of the OMB and the FEA. Presaging later battles, the OMB had argued for a smaller SPR to reduce program costs, while the FEA had argued for the greater security that would be provided by a larger reserve.

The SPR Plan submitted by the FEA to Congress in December 1976 included a cost-effectiveness analysis in support of the 500-million-barrel size.[18] The analysis concluded that under optimistic assumptions about import levels and the likelihood of disruptions, a reserve of 500 million barrels or larger was cost effective. Agreement in favor of the 500-million-barrel size was tenuous, however. Analysts at OMB wanted to limit the size to 200 million barrels, but they could not gain sufficient support to override the legislative presumption for 500 million barrels. For their part, most FEA analysts believed that a larger size could be justified on economic grounds, but they decided not to press their case in view of anticipated opposition from OMB.

The Billion-Barrel Initiative

In the early days of the new administration, James R. Schlesinger served as President Carter's chief energy advisor. As a former secretary of defense, he was familiar with the national security aspects of energy policy. Believing that reliance on Middle Eastern oil was a weak link in the American defense posture, he favored a larger SPR—whether or not it could be shown to be economically cost effective. During the preparation of the National Energy Plan, the energy policy overview for the new administration, he persuaded President Carter to seek expansion of the SPR to one billion barrels.

[16]This section is based on Hank C. Jenkins-Smith and David L. Weimer, "Analysis as Retrograde Action: The Case of Strategic Petroleum Reserves," *Public Administration Review*, Vol. 45, No. 4, July/August 1985, pp. 485–94, which provides a full documentation of sources. Parts are reprinted with permission from *Public Administration Review*, © 1985 by the American Society for Public Administration, 1120 G Street, N.W., Suite 500, Washington, D.C. All rights reserved.

[17]Robert E. Kuenne, Gerald F. Higgins, Robert J. Michaels, and Mary Sommerfield, "A Policy to Protect the U.S. Against Oil Embargoes," *Policy Analysis*, Vol. 1, No. 4, Fall 1975, pp. 571–97.

[18]The analysis employed an estimated relationship between oil import reductions and GNP. It is summarized in Randall Holcombe, "A Method of Estimating the GNP Loss from a Future Oil Embargo," *Policy Sciences*, Vol. 8, No. 2, June 1977, 217–34.

Development of the National Energy Plan was tightly controlled by Schlesinger. His staff tapped the agencies and departments for information but remained secretive about policy options. Operating efficiency was selected over "the more time-consuming process of consensus building."[19] The National Energy Plan draft was circulated within the administration for comments only a short time before President Carter released the final version on April 29, 1977. Consequently, OMB career staffers concerned with the SPR did not have time to convince their new director to seek presidential reconsideration of the billion-barrel goal. In bureaucratic slang, Schlesinger had successfully "rolled" OMB on the SPR issue.

OMB found an opportunity to blunt the billion-barrel initiative during the preparation of the administration's FY 1979 budget proposals in the fall of 1977. Schlesinger, as secretary of the newly created Department of Energy, had requested funding for construction of the second 500 million barrels (Phase III would take the SPR to about 750 million barrels and Phase IV to one billion barrels) of storage capacity. When OMB cut these funds, Schlesinger appealed to the president. Schlesinger presented his case to the president at a White House meeting with the OMB director. OMB staffers, armed with flipcharts, began to make the case that a reserve size larger than 500 million barrels was unjustified. They were cut short by President Carter, however, who stated that the size of the SPR was not at issue; he was still committed to an ultimate reserve size of one billion barrels. The real issue was how much would be spent in FY 1979 for phases III and IV. As a compromise, the president allowed planning funds to be included for Phase III only.

The results of this meeting might be viewed as a Pyrrhic victory for Schlesinger. He secured presidential reaffirmation of the billion-barrel goal. (Congress endorsed the expanded goal by approving an amendment to the SPR Plan the following June.) In the process, however, OMB staffers, who would be involved in future budget fights over the SPR, were embarrassed in front of the president. It is possible that the incident influenced their attitudes toward the SPR program.

In these initial rounds, then, DOE analysts under Schlesinger had successfully mounted an initiative to expand the SPR size. Persistent opposition from OMB had been temporarily overcome. Given widespread support within both Congress and the administration, as well as the repeated analytic justification for a large SPR, how can the continued opposition of OMB be explained?

OMB analysts had legitimate reasons to question the analytic justification for the larger SPR size. The analysis presented in the SPR plan was unsophisticated in the way it measured the benefits of drawdowns and dealt with uncertainty. Within the analytical framework employed, ample room existed for disagreement over assumptions about future conditions. These assumptions, in turn, were critical to estimates of future SPR benefits. Thus, at this stage of the controversy, OMB opposition on analytic grounds was clearly defensible.

Institutional factors may also have contributed to opposition by OMB staffers. OMB is responsible for the overall budget and is concerned with limiting

[19]James L. Cochrane, "Carter Energy Policy and the Ninety-fifth Congress," in Craufurd B. Goodwin, ed., *Energy Policy in Perspective* (Washington, D.C.: Brookings Institution, 1981), pp. 547–600, at p. 555.

expenditures wherever possible. The SPR made an attractive target for several reasons: First, its benefits are diffuse, with no strong constituency to oppose budget cuts; its aggregate benefits may be large, but no politically active group anticipates a large enough share to make it worthwhile to take political action. Second, the SPR resembles an insurance policy in that the costs are certain but the full benefits accrue only from events that may not occur. Because the initial costs for SPR facilities and stock purchases are relatively large, those who are most responsible for the budget may be willing to accept higher levels of risk for reduced premiums. Third, the costs must be borne today while the benefits result sometime in the future. Those responsible for this year's budget may have a higher subjective discount rate than other decision makers. Thus the institutional mission of OMB, coupled with the diffuse benefits and high start-up costs of the SPR, made the initiative to expand the SPR a particularly attractive target for budget cutters.

Analytical Trench Welfare, Round One: 1978

In February of 1978, OMB organized an interagency task force to study contingency planning issues. It consisted of personnel from the Office of Contingency Planning in the Policy and Evaluation Office of DOE, the Special Studies Division for Natural Resources, Energy, and Science in OMB, and the Council of Economic Advisors (CEA). DOE agreed to consider alternatives for implementation of the expanded reserve, implicitly reopening the size issue.

By mid-April, participants reached tentative agreement on the assumptions that would be employed to measure the macroeconomic costs of oil supply disruptions. With these assumptions, DOE and CEA analysts used the Wharton and DRI macroeconomic models to estimate a relationship between reductions in oil imports and quarterly losses in GNP. The relationship was used by DOE analysts in a benefit-cost analysis of the fourth 250 million barrels (Phase IV) of the SPR. When OMB analysts discovered that the DOE analysis supported implementation of Phase IV, they began to attack the assumptions used—including some to which they had previously agreed. Although DOE made a number of concessions on assumptions, Phase IV still appeared to be justified. Finally, OMB presented its own analysis arguing against Phase IV in a memorandum to the president.

Secretary Schlesinger prepared to argue the issue with OMB during meetings on the FY 1980 budget. Schlesinger had been informed by his staff that OMB had argued that the probability of a severe disruption (the loss of approximately 60 percent of Persian Gulf exports for six months) would have to be between 10 percent and 25 percent per year over twelve years to justify Phase IV. With CEA concurrence, Schlesinger presented the DOE case that a yearly break-even probability of only 1 percent would justify Phase IV. When OMB agreed (its figures had been for the entire twelve-year period), Schlesinger seemed to be thrown off balance. Rather than threaten to take the issue to the president, he agreed not to press for Phase IV planning funds for FY 1980 and to recommend that the issue of ultimate size be referred to the National Security Council. One OMB analyst who attended the meeting believes that OMB would have backed down if Schlesinger had demanded a meeting with the president in which he would have asked the secretaries of defense and state if they would be willing to assume that the probability of a major disruption would be less than 1 percent per year.

Perhaps Schlesinger might have taken this approach if his analysts had not focused his attention on the apparent discrepancy between DOE and OMB conclusions.

Round Two: 1979

In January of 1979, OMB began to pressure DOE to participate in another joint study of the economic costs and benefits of implementing the billion-barrel goal. DOE analysts who had been involved in the previous joint study argued against participation. They believed the OMB analysts would not be satisfied with any analysis that supported SPR expansion. But institutional relationships within the federal bureaucracy make it difficult for a department to refuse an OMB request. Beyond its influence in a given budgetary dispute, OMB must be dealt with on numerous budget issues, and the costs of noncooperation can extend beyond the particular issue involved. DOE committed about twenty staff-months of professional time and approximately $80,000 for consultants to the project.

The first project task was to complete simulations of the macroeconomic effects of disruptions based on the DRI and Wharton macromodels. Although initially agreement was reached on a set of assumptions to be used, the OMB and CEA representatives continually required modifications of assumptions. This was frustrating for the DOE analysts who had to implement them, particularly because it appeared to them that OMB staffers were consistently looking for ways to make disruptions appear less costly—and hence the SPR less valuable.

DOE completed a first draft of the study report in October 1979. It assumed that the first 550 million barrels of the SPR would be drawn down only for disruptions involving losses to the United States of over one billion barrels per year. It also assumed that private industry would draw down its stocks by 125 million barrels during a severe disruption. The expected benefits from SPR drawdowns were estimated for a number of disruption scenarios and their assumed probabilities of occurrence. The report concluded that the economically desirable reserve was 2.1 billion barrels or larger.

OMB staff participating in the study project were outraged. OMB had been preparing to argue not only against Phase IV, but also against Phase III on grounds that new capacity should not be added while existing capacity was not being filled. (In light of the long lead time needed to construct storage facilities, the OMB position seemed to assume that the then-current tight market conditions caused by Iranian production reductions would prevail for five or six years.) Also, the revelations over the preceding year of cost overruns and schedule delays encountered during the implementation of Phases I and II made the SPR an even more tempting and perhaps more vulnerable target for budget cuts.

Focusing on the least certain (and therefore most vulnerable) techniques and assumptions included in the analysis, OMB raised four major objections to the draft report. First, the use of assumed probabilities for the disruption scenarios was attacked as arbitrary. DOE countered by arguing that, although arbitrary, the probabilities were viewed as conservative by most experts consulted. Second, OMB wanted the GNP loss function to be estimated on the basis of more accommodating monetary and fiscal assumptions that would yield lower real GNP losses but higher inflation rates. DOE responded that the more extreme the monetary and fiscal policy assumptions made, the more suspect the results of the macroeconomic models. Third, OMB objected to the assignment of a salvage value to

SPR oil. DOE analysts thought it was obvious that the sale of remaining assets at the termination of the program should be counted as benefits. Finally, OMB argued that SPR drawdowns would not replace lost imports barrel per barrel— an objection that DOE analysts had to admit as valid. (Note that in Figure 11.2, the price effect of a drawdown depends on the price elasticities of supply and demand in the world market. Drawdowns of the SPR do not replace lost imports barrel for barrel.)

After it became clear that OMB was attempting to cut funds for Phase III from the budget, the DOE analysts decided to redo their analysis with a set of assumptions that OMB would not be able to attack. Successfully accomplished, such a move would reduce the opportunity for further delays based on demands for better analysis. The resulting new study, which even included an arbitrary across-the-board reduction of 25 percent of benefits to reflect possible inefficiencies in SPR use, found that expansion of the SPR to 750 million barrels was justified if one believed that the probability of a disruption of moderate size (less than two million barrels per day for one year) was greater than 3.5 percent per year.

This effort was to no avail. Not only did OMB cut funding for implementation of Phase III from the FY 1980 supplementary budget and the FY 1981 budget, but the DOE leadership decided not to appeal the decision to the president. Schlesinger, the strongest SPR supporter among the DOE leadership, was no longer secretary. The new secretary, Charles W. Duncan, and his assistant secretary for policy and evaluation, William Lewis, were not yet familiar with the issue. The remaining leadership in the past had emphasized long-run energy policy, such as conservation, over contingency planning measures, such as the SPR. Consequently, there was no one to lead a fight against OMB cuts. In fact, DOE undersecretary John Deutch agreed to yet another joint OMB/DOE study to be conducted in 1980 for the FY 1982 budget decision on Phase III.

Round Three: 1980

While the Office of Contingency Planning was struggling with OMB over the 1979 study, the Office of Oil, also under the assistant secretary for policy and evaluation, was developing a methodology for investigating the optimal timing of oil acquisitions and drawdowns and of capacity expansions. Recognizing the weakness of methods previously used to handle the uncertainty about supply interruptions in prior studies, Lucian Pugliaresi, director of the Office of Oil, encouraged economist Thomas Teisberg to work on the problem.

Teisberg developed a stochastic dynamic programming formulation of the stockpiling problem. For each year of the SPR, his model determines the oil acquisition or drawdown, subject to technical constraints, that minimizes the discounted sum of expected future net social surplus losses. Uncertainty is converted to risk by assuming probabilities of moving from each market condition to each of the other possible market conditions in future periods. Using the model to look ahead, at some point the stockpiling reaches a size where it is not longer optimal to make additions. This plateau level is an indication of the "optimal" stockpile size for planning purposes.

In December of 1979, Glen Sweetnam, Steven Minihan, George Horwich, and other staff members in the Office of Oil completed a major study of acquisition and drawdown analyses using the Teisberg model. Over a range of assumptions, the plateau level was found to vary from 800 million to 4.4 billion barrels. More importantly, the study suggested that large net benefits were associated with rapid expansion of the SPR toward the plateau.

The new assistant secretary for policy and evaluation intensively reviewed the Office of Oil study and concluded that it employed a more appropriate methodology than that used in the joint OMB/DOE studies. He argued in a memorandum to the undersecretary that future joint studies with OMB be based on modifications and extensions of the Teisberg model rather than on macro-economic simulations.

Introduction of the new modeling technique added a fresh element to the struggle over the size of the SPR. On one hand, the new technique was widely recognized as a more appropriate approach to the problem of public stockpiling than previously used methods. At the same time, however, introduction of the Teisberg model created opportunities for OMB to demand analysis as a delaying tactic.

In the spring of 1980, representatives from OMB and CEA objected to the use of the Teisberg model on a variety of grounds. Though some of the criticisms struck DOE analysts as gratuitous, and most of the others could easily be handled by revisions of the model, the most serious and fundamental objection concerned the probabilities assumed in the model. OMB complained that the assumed matrix of probabilities of going from each market condition to each of the others was ". . . so complex and theoretical as to have no meaning to policy-makers."[20] The DOE analysts admitted that the Teisberg model appeared complex, but argued that it was conceptually straightforward. They argued further that it provided a method to deal with uncertainty that was much more systematic than the scenario approach.

A compromise of sorts that permitted use of the Teisberg model was reached at a July meeting of the DOE assistant secretary for policy and evaluation, the OMB assistant director for natural resources, energy, and science, a council member of CEA, and their respective staffs. The assistant secretary for policy and evaluation made it clear that DOE would include an analysis based on the Teisberg model in its FY 1982 budget request. He indicated that his staff would modify and run the model as requested by OMB but would not attempt to find mutually acceptable assumptions. He also committed $100,000 in contractor support (the former undersecretary had promised up to $1 million for the study) and four person-months of staff time to assist OMB and CEA in the proposed macro-economic simulation study.

The DOE analysts provided energy projections and other advice as requested by OMB, but they refused to be drawn into battles about assumptions. Within a short time, it became apparent that the assumptions made by CEA and passively agreed to by OMB were going to yield results even more supportive of SPR expansion than the 1979 joint study. OMB and CEA never completed the proposed macroeconomic simulation study.

In the meantime, DOE had modified the Teisberg model to focus explicitly on the Phase III question. The results were presented in October at an OMB

---

[20]Chuck Miller, "Questions/Issues Regarding DOE (Teisberg) B/C Model: Memorandum of CEA and OMB Comments to Lou Pugliaresi, DOE," Office of Management and Budget, May 27, 1980.

hearing on the SPR budget. Perhaps because the macroeconomic analysis had not turned out as they had expected, OMB finally expressed an interest in analyses from the Teisberg model. The analyses were completed with the understanding that DOE did not necessarily endorse the assumptions that OMB had requested.

To summarize the debate through 1980, the presidential decision in 1977 to expand the SPR to one billion barrels was not based primarily on economic analysis. In 1978 OMB forced DOE to evaluate the economic benefits of the expanded reserve with a somewhat more sophisticated methodology. Although the resulting analysis supported the expansion, OMB cut planning funds for Phase IV and secured agreement from DOE to reconsider the size issue in the next budget cycle. During 1979 OMB analysts attempted to force DOE to agree to combinations of assumptions in the previously used macroeconomic simulations that would lead to results not supporting expansion of the SPR. Even though fairly conservative assumptions were employed, the results favored expansion. Nevertheless, OMB delayed funding of Phase III from FY 1980 to FY 1982. In 1980, OMB analysts again attempted to draw DOE into a battle over assumptions in the macroeconomic approach. Failing, they reluctantly expressed interest in the dynamic programming model that DOE intended to use in support of its FY 1982 budget request.

Apparent Resolution

By mid-November of 1980, it had become clear that OMB would not oppose funding in the Carter Administration's FY 1982 budget request for implementation of Phase III. Did analysis finally carry the day? Perhaps. In light of the extended fight over Phase III, however, a more plausible explanation is that analysis was a secondary factor. Most likely, the OMB staff anticipated that the assistant secretary for policy and evaluation, who enjoyed the confidence of the secretary, would recommend that the issue be taken to the president if Phase III funding was not included in the FY 1982 budget proposal. Unlike the previous two years, it appeared that the DOE leaders were confident of their analysis and willing to take OMB to the mat. At the time, the SPR program had begun to reestablish its managerial credibility, undercutting implied arguments that it could not handle implementation of Phase III. Finally, perhaps with excessive hindsight, one cannot help but wonder if the presidential election was not a factor. As it turned out, President-elect Ronald Reagan appointed David Stockman, a strong congressional supporter of the SPR, as director of OMB. It may be that the career staff at OMB anticipated this possibility and did not wish to be seen by the new administration as being responsible for further delay of the SPR program. In fact, during the early months of the Reagan Administration, the same OMB staffers who had led the fight against expansion of the SPR throughout the Carter Administration directed a joint study with DOE of options for accelerating Phase III. Thus it appears that changing political factors, as much as analysis, resolved the debate over the appropriate size of the SPR.

But analysis played an important role in several ways. First, if any of the benefit-cost studies conducted during the period of controversy had failed to find that expansion of the SPR was justified on economic grounds, then OMB would almost certainly have been able to stop Phase III. Second, without the Teismodel, the Office of Oil staff probably would not have been able to convince the new assistant secretary to support SPR expansion. Absent his willingness to take the question of Phase III funding to the president—something usually done only for the most important issues—OMB might have continued to stall. Finally, the introduction of the Teisberg model drew attention to acquisition and drawdown strategies. One result was the consideration of acceleration options. Another was the later development within the Reagan Administration of a policy calling for early use of the SPR to counter oil price shocks.

CONCLUSION

Our story of the controversy over the size of the SPR should be both encouraging and sobering for aspiring analysts. It should be encouraging because it shows that participants in policy debates do consider the results of formal analyses to be important—at least sometimes—and because it demonstrates that new analytical insights can make a difference. It should be sobering because it shows analysis to be a political resource that can be abused.

The opportunity for abuse is especially great in situations where no consensus exists about the reasonableness of analytical assumptions. Political decision makers rarely have the time, inclination, or expertise to resolve analytical disputes. So when analysts disagree about assumptions and methods, analysis is unlikely to play a decisive, or perhaps even an informative, role. From a practical perspective, analysts should be prepared for attacks on their assumptions and methods by advocates of opposing policies. They should anticipate such attacks in choosing models, gathering supporting evidence, and eliciting support from neutral experts. From an ethical perspective, analysts should remember their responsibility to the value of analytical integrity in deciding whether to attack the analysis of others.

12

WHEN STATISTICS COUNT: REVISING THE LEAD STANDARD FOR GASOLINE

Policy analysts must deal with many kinds of empirical evidence. Often the constraints of time and resources, as well as the nature of the policy problem under consideration, force analysts to rely on qualitative and fragmentary data. Sometimes, however, analysts can find data that enable them to estimate the magnitudes of the effects of policy interventions on social, economic, or political conditions. The estimates may permit the analysts to calculate the likely net social benefits of proposed policies or even apply formal optimization techniques to find better alternatives.

The effective use of quantitative data requires an understanding of the basic issues of research design and a facility with the techniques of statistical inference. Even when analysts do not have the resources available to do primary data analysis, they often must confront quantitative evidence produced by other participants in the policy process or extracted from the academic literature. If they lack the requisite skills for critical evaluation, they risk losing their influence in the face of quantitative evidence that may appear more objective and scientific to decision makers. Well-trained analysts, therefore, need some facility with the basic concepts of statistical inference for reasons of self-defense, if for no others.

The basics of research design and statistical inference cannot be adequately covered in an introductory course in policy analysis. Similarly, we cannot provide adequate coverage in this book. Yet we can provide an example of a policy change where quantitative analysis was instrumental: the decision by the U.S. Environmental Protection Agency in 1985 to reduce dramatically the amount lead permitted in gasoline. The story of the new lead standard has a number elements frequently encountered when doing quantitative analysis in organizational settings: replacement of an initial "quick and dirty" analysis with sophisticated versions as more time and data become available; repeated n to rule out alternative explanations (hypotheses) offered by opponents of posed policy; and serendipitous events that influence the analytical strategy. Although our primary purpose is to tell what we believe to be an intrinsically interesting and instructive story about the practice of policy analysis, we hope to offer a few basic lessons on quantitative analysis along the way.

BACKGROUND: THE EPA LEAD STANDARDS

The Clean Air Amendments of 1970 give the administrator of the Environmental Protection Agency authority to regulate any motor fuel component or additive that produces emission products dangerous to public health or welfare.[1] Before exercising this authority, however, the administrator must consider "all relevant medical and scientific evidence available to him" as well as alternative methods that set standards for emissions rather than for fuel components.[2]

In 1971 the EPA administrator announced that he was considering possible controls on lead additives in gasoline.[3] One reason given was the possible adverse health effects of emissions from engines that burned leaded gasoline, the standard fuel at the time. Available evidence suggested that lead is toxic in the human body, that lead can be absorbed into the body from ambient air, and that gasoline engines account for a large fraction of airborne lead. The other reason for controlling the lead content of gasoline was the incompatibility of leaded fuel with the catalytic converter, a device seen as having potential for reducing hydrocarbon emissions from automobiles. The first reason suggests considering whether reductions in the lead content of all gasoline might be desirable; the second argues for the total removal of lead from gasoline for use by new automobiles equipped with catalytic converters.

Without going any further one might ask: Why should the government be concerned with the level of lead in gasoline? And why had the federal government already decided to require the installation of catalytic converters? The following analysis does not explicitly deal with the desirability of catalytic converters. As we have argued, however, it is always important to make sure that there is a convincing rationale for public action. The interventions at hand, the catalytic converter and the related lead restrictions, deal with market failures—viewed as problems of either negative externalities or public goods (ambient public goods). In addition, another market failure may come into play with respect to lead—imperfect consumer information about the impacts of lead on health and the maintenance cost of vehicles. Because the health and maintenance impacts may not manifest themselves for many years (leaded gasoline is a post - experince good), markets may be inefficient because of information asymmetry. These apparent market failures make a case for considering government intervention.

But intervention itself may be costly. It is quite conceivable that the costs of intervention could exceed the benefits. Several questions must be answered before the comparison of costs and benefits can be made: What are the impacts gasoline lead additive on people, the environment, and property (including lytic converters)? How do these physical impacts change under alternative

The Clean Air Act Amendments of 1970, Public Law 91–604, December 31, 1970.

ction 211(c)(2)(A), 42 U.C. @ 1857f-6c(c)(2)(A).

Fed. Reg. 1468 (January 1971).

public interventions? What are the dollar costs associated with these interventions and what are the dollar benefits associated with the changes they produce? Finally, which alternative, including no intervention, appears to offer the greatest excess of benefits over costs?

The EPA explored these questions for a limited number of alternative lead regulations. About one year after raising the possibility of lead restrictions, the EPA administrator proposed formal regulations for lead reductions in 1972.[4] After an extended period of comment and several public hearings, the EPA was ready to issue final regulations requiring refiners to make available some unleaded gasoline for use by new automobiles, which, beginning with the 1975 model year, would be equipped with catalytic converters.[5] At the same time, the EPA reproposed reductions in lead content for public health reasons.

The health-based standards were controversial. Refiners valued lead as a gasoline additive because it increased octane without affecting vapor pressure or other fuel properties that had to be balanced in the blending process. Refiners were joined in their opposition to the proposed regulations by manufacturers of the lead additives. Supporting the regulations were a number of environmental organizations, including the Natural Resources Defense Council, which successfully sought a court order that forced EPA to issue final regulations on November 28, 1973.[6]

The final regulations called for phased reductions over a five-year period in the average lead content of all gasoline sold. By 1979 the average would fall to 0.5 grams of lead per gallon (gpg) of gasoline. Implementation of the phasedown, however, was slowed first by a court challenge to the regulation[7] and later by concerns about gasoline availability during the 1979 oil price shock following the Iranian Revolution.[8] Consequently, the 0.5 gpg standard was not put into effect until October 1, 1980.

By 1982 some analysts in EPA became concerned that, as relatively more unleaded gasoline was sold to meet the demand from the growing number of automobiles in service with catalytic converters, refiners would be able to increase the concentration of lead in leaded gasoline and still meet the 0.5 gpg average. In February EPA announced a general review of the 1973 standards[9] and in August proposed new standards that would limit the content of lead in leaded gasoline rather than the average content of lead in all gasoline.[10] The final rules, issued in October 1982, set 1.10 grams per leaded gallon as the new standard.[11] (The new standard was roughly equivalent to the old standard in terms of total lead emissions—0.5 gpg on 100 percent of total gasoline sales versus 1.10 gpg on the approximately 45 percent of total gasoline sales that were leaded at the time. Because the quantity of leaded gasoline sold was expected to continue to

[4] 37 *Fed. Reg.* 1178 (February 23, 1972).

[5] 38 *Fed. Reg.* 1254 (January 10, 1973).

[6] 38 *Fed. Reg.* 33734 (November 28, 1973).

[7] *Ethyl Corporation v. Environmental Protection Agency*, 541 F.2d 1 (1976).

[8] 44 *Fed. Reg.* 33116 (June 8, 1979).

[9] 47 *Fed. Reg.* 4812 (February 22, 1982).

[10] 47 *Fed. Reg.* 38070, 38072, 38078 (August 27, 1982).

[11] 47 *Fed. Reg.* 49331 (October 29, 1982).

decline, corresponding reductions in lead emissions were projected.) Although implementation was slowed somewhat by the courts, the new regulations phased-out special provisions that had been added to reduce the impact of the 1973 standards on small refiners. The regulations also allowed "trading" of additional reductions across refineries. For example, a refinery would be allowed to produce gasoline with 1.20 gpg if it "traded" with another refinery producing an equivalent quantity with 1.00 gpg so that the pooled average would be 1.10 gpg.

ORIGINS OF THE 1985 STANDARDS

Several factors prompted reconsideration of the lead standard in the summer of 1983. EPA Administrator William D. Ruckelshaus and Deputy Administrator Alvin L. Alm were concerned that many cities would not achieve the 1987 ozone standards. Ozone, a major component of smog, results when emissions of hydrocarbons and nitrogen oxides chemically react in the atmosphere. Well-maintained catalytic converters greatly reduce these emissions from motor vehicles. The converters, designed to be used only with unleaded gasoline, lose their effectiveness when exposed to lead. Because leaded gasoline was both cheaper and offered higher performance than unleaded, many consumers were fueling their converter-equipped vehicles with leaded gasoline. A 1982 EPA survey estimated that 13.5 percent of vehicles were being misfueled.[12] Lowering the permissible level of lead in gasoline could reduce the misfueling problem in two ways. First, it would reduce the economic incentive to misfuel by raising the relative price of leaded to unleaded gasoline. Second, the lower lead levels would result in slower degradation of converters that were misfueled.

Another factor was continuing concern about the health effects of lead emissions. As new scientific evidence became available, the apparent connection between lead emissions and lead levels in blood became ever stronger. The growing evidence increased the chances that a more stringent standard could be adequately supported.

The external environment also seemed favorable. Many environmental groups had long advocated a total ban on lead; they would undoubtedly support further tightening of the standards. So too would alcohol fuel advocates, who hoped restrictions on lead would make alcohol more attractive as an octane-boosting fuel additive. In addition, the U.S. Court of Appeals for the District of Columbia Circuit, in a case challenging the provisions of the 1982 lead standards, had given an opinion that currently available evidence "would justify EPA in banning lead from gasoline entirely."[13] Although not a guarantee of judicial acceptance of stricter standards, the opinion was encouraging.

The EPA leadership decided that another look at the lead standard would worthwhile. Robert Wolcott, special assistant to the deputy administrator, was the task of overseeing the project. He turned to Joel Schwartz, an analyst Economic Analysis Division who had worked on the 1982 regulations.

S. Environmental Protection Agency, *Motor Vehicle Tampering Survey 1982* (Washington, al Enforcement Investigation Center, EPA, April 1983).

Refiner Lead Phase-Down Task Force v. EPA, 705 F.2d 506 (D.C. Cir. 1983), p. 531.

Schwartz used his accumulated knowledge from previous analyses to complete in two or three days a quick and dirty benefit-cost analysis of a total ban on lead additives.

Because a total ban was one of the options considered in 1982, it was fairly easy for Schwartz to come up with a reasonable estimate of cost. As is often the case in evaluating health and safety regulations, the more difficult problem was estimating the benefits of a total ban. Schwartz looked at two benefit categories: increased IQ scores of children due to lower levels of blood lead and the avoided damage to catalytic converters.

Schwartz used estimates from a variety of sources to piece together a relationship between lead emissions and the present value of lifetime earnings of children. The first step involved using estimates from the 1982 analyses of the relationship between lead emissions and blood lead levels in children. He next turned to epidemiological studies that reported a relationship between blood lead levels and IQs. Finally, he found econometric studies that estimated the contribution of IQ points to the present value of future earnings.

As a first cut at quantifying the benefits resulting from the more effective control of other emissions, Schwartz estimated the cost of catalytic converters being contaminated under the current standards that would not be contaminated under a total ban. He used the number of converters saved multiplied by the price per converter as the benefit measure. Assuming that converters themselves have benefit-cost ratios greater than one, this benefit measure would be conservative.

These "back-of-the-envelope" calculations suggested that the benefits of a total ban on lead additives would be more than twice the costs. Schwartz discussed the results with his branch chief, G. Martin Wagner, who sent word to the office of the administrator that further analysis of a lead ban seemed worthwhile. A few weeks later Schwartz and fellow analyst Jane Leggett began a two-month effort to move from the back of an envelope to a preliminary report.

PULLING THE PIECES TOGETHER

The most urgent task facing Schwartz and Leggett was to develop better measures of the benefits of a lead ban. The key to improving the measure of benefits from avoided converter poisonings was a more sophisticated accounting of the future age composition of the U.S. vehicle fleet. The key to improving the measure of benefits from reduced lead emissions was a better quantitative estimate of the relationship between gasoline lead and blood lead. Modeling and statistical analysis would be an important part of their work.

The age composition of the vehicle fleet continually changes as old vehicles, some of which have contaminated or partially contaminated converters, are retired and new ones, with fresh converters, are added. A ban on lead would have different effects on different vintage vehicles. For instance, it would be irrelevant for vehicles that already have contaminated converters, but very important for vehicles that would otherwise be contaminated and remain in service for a long time.

The analysts developed an inventory model that tracked cohorts of vehicles over time. Each year a new cohort would enter the fleet. Each successive year a fraction of the vehicles would be retired because of accidents and mechanical failures. In addition, a fraction would suffer converter poisoning from misfueling. By following the various cohorts over time, it was possible to predict the total number of converters that would be saved in each future year from specified reductions in the lead content of leaded gasoline today and in the future. Avoided loss of the depreciated value of the catalytic converters (later avoided costs of the health and property damage from pollutants other than lead) could then be calculated for each future year. With appropriate discounting, the yearly benefits could then be summed to yield the present value of the lead reduction schedule being considered.

Two important considerations came to light during work on the vehicle fleet model. One was a body of literature suggesting that lead increases the routine maintenance costs of vehicles. Subsequently, a new benefit category, avoided maintenance costs, was estimated using the vehicle fleet model. The other consideration was the possibility that some engines might suffer premature valve-seat wear if fueled with totally lead-free gasoline. Although the problem was fairly limited (primarily automobile engines manufactured prior to 1971 and some newer trucks, motorcycles, and off-road vehicles), it suggested the need to consider alternatives to a total ban.

Efforts to quantify better the link between gasoline lead and blood lead focused on analysis of data from the second National Health and Nutrition Examination Survey (NHANES II). The NHANES II survey was designed by the National Center for Health Statistics to provide a representative national sample of the population between ages 6 months and 74 years. It included 27,801 persons sampled at sixty-four representative sites from 1976 to 1980. Of the 16,563 persons who were asked to provide blood samples, 61 percent complied.[14] The lead concentrations in the blood samples were measured, providing data that could be used to track average blood levels over the four-year survey period. The amount of lead in gasoline sold over the period could then be correlated with the blood lead concentrations.

A positive relationship between blood lead concentrations from the NHANES II data and gasoline lead had already been found by researchers.[15] The positive correlation is apparent in Figure 12.1, which was prepared by James Pirkle of the Centers for Disease Control to show the close tracking of blood lead concentrations and total gasoline lead.[16] Much more than the apparent correlation, however, was needed for the benefit-cost analysis. Schwartz used multiple regression techniques, which we will discuss in detail later in our story, to estimate the increase in average micrograms of lead per deciliter of blood ($\mu g/dl$) due to each additional 100 metric tons per day of lead in consumed gasoline. He also employed

---

[14] There appeared to be no nonresponse bias in the sample. R. N. Forthofer, "Investigation of Nonresponse Bias in NHANES II," *American Journal of Epidemiology*, Vol. 117, No. 4, April 1983, pp. 507–15.

[15] J. L. Annest, J. L. Pirkle, D. Makuc, J. W. Neese, D. D. Bayse, and M. G. Kovar, "Chronological Trends in Blood Lead Levels between 1976 and 1980," *New England Journal of Medicine*, No. 308, June 9, 1983, pp. 1373–77.

[16] Joel Schwartz, Jane Leggett, Bart Ostro, Hugh Pitcher, Ronnie Levin, *Costs and Benefits of Reducing Lead in Gasoline: Draft Final Proposal* (Washington, D.C.: Office of Policy Analysis, EPA, March 26, 1984), p. V–26.

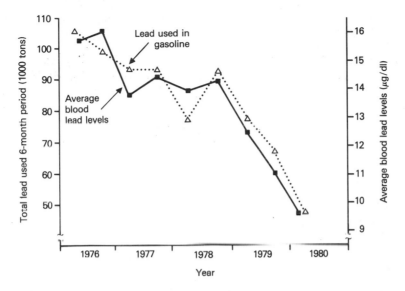

Figure 12.1 Lead Use in Gasoline Production and Average NHANES II Blood Lead Levels. *Source:* J. Schwartz, et al., *Costs and Benefits of Reducing Lead in Gasoline: Final Regulatory Impact Analysis,* Publication No. EPA-230-05-85-006 (Washington, D.C.: EPA, 1985), p. E-5.

models that allowed him to estimate the probabilities that children with specified characteristics will have toxic levels of blood lead (then defined by the Centers for Disease Control as greater than 30 µg/dl) and gasoline lead. These probabilities could then be used to predict the number of children in the population who would avoid lead toxicity if a ban on gasoline lead were imposed.

In early November of 1983, Schwartz and Leggett pulled together the components of their analyses and found a ratio of benefits to costs of a total ban to be greater than Schwartz's original back-of-the-envelope calculation. Together with their branch chief, they presented their results to Deputy Administrator Alm, who found them encouraging. He gave the green light for the preparation of a refined version that could be presented to the administrator as the basis for a new regulation. Alm also wanted the various components of the refined study to be subjected to peer review by experts outside the EPA. At the same time, he urged speed in order to reduce the chances that word would get out to refiners and manufacturers of lead additives, the primary opponents of a ban, before the EPA had an opportunity to review all the evidence.

The branch chief expanded the analytical team in order to hasten the preparation of the refined report that would be sent to the administrator. Joining Schwartz and Leggett were Ronnie Levin; Hugh Pitcher, an econometrician; and Bart Ostro, an expert on the benefits of ozone reduction. In little more than one month the team was ready to send a draft report out for peer review.

The effort involved several changes in analytical approach. Because of the valve-head problem, the analysis focused on a major reduction in grams of lead per leaded gallon (from 1.1 gplg to 0.1 gplg) as well as a total ban. The available evidence suggested that the 0.1 gplg level would be adequate to avoid excessive valve-head wear in the small number of engines designed to be fueled only with leaded gasoline. At the same time, considerable effort was put into quantifying the maintenance costs that would be avoided by owners of other vehicles if the lead concentration were reduced. It soon appeared that the maintenance benefits consumers would enjoy would more than offset the higher prices they would have to pay for gasoline. Finally, the team decided that the benefits based on the blood lead (through IQ) to future earnings relationship would be too controversial. Instead, they turned their attention to the costs of compensatory education for children who suffered IQ losses from high blood lead levels.

In late December, sections of the report were sent to experts outside the EPA for comments. The list included automotive engineers, economists, biostatisticians, toxicologists, clinical researchers, transportation experts, and a psychologist. During January 1984, the team refined their analysis and incorporated, or at least responded to, the comments made by the external reviewers.

Finally, in early February, the team was ready to present its results to Administrator Ruckelshaus. He agreed that their analysis supported a new standard of 0.1 gplg. He told the team to finalize their report without a proposed rule and release it for public comment. Ruckelshaus also directed the Office of the Assistant Administrator for Air and Radiation to draft a proposed rule.

The team's *Draft Final Report* was printed and eventually released to the public on March 26, 1984.[17] The team continued to refine the analysis in the following months. It also had to devote considerable time to external relations. Executive Order 12291 requires regulatory agencies to submit proposed regulations that would have annual costs of more than $100 million to the Office of Management and Budget for review. The team met with OMB analysts several times before securing their acceptance of the benefit-cost analysis of the tighter standard.

The political environment was taking shape pretty much as expected. Opposition would come from refiners and manufacturers of lead additives. The refiners, however, generally seemed resigned to the eventual elimination of lead from gasoline. Their primary concern was the speed of implementation. Some refiners seemed particularly concerned about the first few years of a tighter standard, when they would have difficulty making the required reductions with their existing configurations of capital equipment. In response, the team began exploring the costs and benefits of less stringent compliance schedules.

The manufacturers of lead additives were ready to fight tighter standards. In May, Schwartz attended a conference at the Centers for Disease Control in Atlanta, Georgia, on the proposed revision of the blood lead toxicity standard for children from 30 μg/dl to 25 μg/dl. Representatives of the lead manufacturers were also there. They openly talked about their strategy for challenging tighter standards. They planned to argue that refiners would blend more benzene, a suspected carcinogen, into gasoline to boost octane if lead were restricted. Schwartz investigated this possibility following the conference. He found that, even if more benzene were added to gasoline, the total emissions of benzene would decline

---

[17]Joel Schwartz, Jane Leggett, Bart Ostro, Hugh Pitcher, and Ronnie Levin, *Costs and Benefits of Reducing Lead in Gasoline: Draft Final Report* (Washington, D.C.: Office of Policy Analysis, EPA, March 26, 1984).

because of the reduction in the contamination of catalytic converters, which oxidize the benzene if not contaminated. The day that the proposed rule was published Schwartz put a memorandum on the docket covering the benzene issue, thus preempting the manufacturers' main attack.

The EPA published the proposed rule on August 2, 1984.[18] It would require that the permitted level of gasoline lead be reduced to 0.1 gplg on January 1, 1986. The proposal stated the EPA assumption that the new standard could be met with existing refining equipment, but indicated that alternative phase-in schedules involving more gradual reductions also were being considered in case this assumption proved false. Finally, the proposal raised the possibility of a complete ban on gasoline lead by 1995.

A CLOSER LOOK AT THE LINK BETWEEN GASOLINE LEAD AND BLOOD LEAD

Calculation of the direct health benefits of tightening the lead standard requires quantitative estimates of the contribution of gasoline lead to blood lead. The NHANES II data, combined with information on gasoline lead levels, enabled the study team to make the necessary estimates. Their efforts provide an excellent illustration of how statistical inference can be used effectively in policy analysis.

The Need for Multivariate Analysis

A casual inspection of Figure 12.1 suggests a strong positive relationship between gasoline lead and blood lead. Why is it necessary to go any further? One reason is the difficulty of answering, directly from Figure 12.1, the central empirical question: How much does the average blood lead level in the United States decline for each 1,000-ton reduction in the total gasoline lead used over the previous month? Figure 12.1 indicates a positive correlation between gasoline lead and blood lead—changes in blood lead track changes in gasoline lead quite closely. But for the same correlation in the data, we could have very different answers to our central question.

Figure 12.2 illustrates the difference between correlation and magnitude of effect with stylized data. If our data were represented by the triangles, we might "fit" line one as our best guess at the relationship between blood lead and gasoline lead. The effect of reducing gasoline lead from 500 tons per day to 400 tons per day would be to reduce average blood lead from 10.1 μg/dl to 10.0 μg/dl, or 0.1 μg/dl per 100 tons per day. An alternative sample of data is represented by the dots, which are plotted to have approximately the same correlation between gasoline lead and blood lead as the data represented by triangles. The slope of line two, the best fit to the dots, is 1.0 μg/dl per 100 tons per day—ten times greater than the slope of line one. That is, although the two data sets have the same correlation, the second implies a much greater contribution of gasoline lead to blood lead than the first.

[18]49 *Fed. Reg.* 31031 (August 2, 1984).

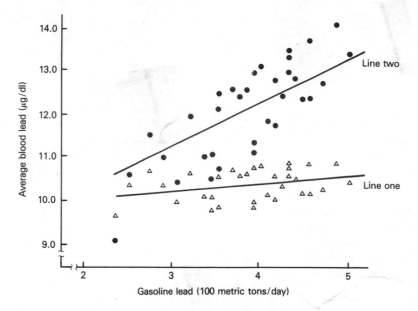

Figure 12.2   Data Samples with Identical Correlations but Different Regression Lines

Even after we display the data in Figure 12.1 as a plot between blood lead and gasoline lead, our analysis is far from complete because the apparent relationship (the slopes of lines one and two in our example) may be spurious. Blood lead and gasoline lead may not be directly related to each other but to some third variable that causes them to change together. The classic illustration of this problem is the correlation sometimes found between the density of stork nests and the human birth rate. If one were to plot birth rates against the density of stork nests for districts in some region, one might very well find a positive relationship and perhaps conclude that there might be something to the myth about storks bringing babies.

Of course, there is a more plausible explanation. A variable measuring the degree to which a district is rural "intervenes" between birth rate and nest density—rural areas have farmers who want a lot of children to help with chores as well as lot of open land that provides nesting grounds for storks; more urbanized areas tend to have people who want smaller families as well as less hospitable nesting grounds. Looking across a sample that included both rural and urban districts could yield the positive correlation between birth rate and nest density. If we were to "control" statistically for the intervening variable by looking at either rural or urban districts separately rather than pooled together, we would expect the correlation between birth rate and nest density to become negligible.

Returning to our analysis of lead, we must be concerned that one or more intervening variables might explain the positive correlation between gasoline lead and blood lead. For example, there is some evidence that cigarette smokers have higher blood lead levels than nonsmokers. It may be that over the period th the NHANES II data were collected the proportion of smokers in the sample declined, so that much of the downward trend in average blood lead levels should be attributed to reductions in smoking rather than reductions in gasoline lead.

To determine whether smoking is an intervening, or confounding, variable, we might construct separate diagrams like Figure 12.2 for smokers and nonsmokers. In this way, we could control for the possibility that changes in the proportion of smokers in the sample over time were responsible for changes in blood lead levels. If we fit lines with similar positive slopes to each of the samples, we would conclude that smoking behavior was not an intervening variable for the relationship between gasoline lead and blood lead.[19]

With unlimited quantities of data, we could always control for possible intervening variables in this way. Unfortunately, with a fixed sample size, we usually stretch our data too thin if we try to form subsets of data that hold all variables constant (e.g., everyone is a nonsmoker) except the dependent variable (blood lead levels) we are trying to explain and the independent variable (gasoline lead) we are considering as a possible explanation. For example, occupational exposure, alcohol consumption, region, and age are only a few of the other variables that might be causing the relationship in our data between gasoline lead and blood lead. If we selected from our sample only adult males living in small cities in the South who are moderate drinkers and nonsmokers and have no occupational exposure to lead, we might have too few data to reliably fit a line as in Figure 12.2. Even if we had adequate data, we would end up with estimates of the relationship between gasoline lead and blood lead from all of our subsets. (The number of subsets would equal the product of the number of categories making up our control variables.) We might then have difficulty combining these subset estimates into an overall estimate.[20]

The Basic Linear Regression Model

Linear regression provides a manageable way to control statistically for the effects of several independent variables.[21] Its use requires us to assume that the effects of the various independent variables are additive. That is, the marginal effect on the dependent variable of a unit change in any one of the independent

---

[19]If the two lines coincided, we would conclude that smoking did not contribute to blood lead. If the lines were parallel but not identical, the difference between their intercepts with the vertical axis would represent the average effect of smoking on blood lead. If the lines were not parallel, we might suspect that smoking interacted with exposure to gasoline lead so that their effects are not additive. That is, smokers were either more or less susceptible to exposure to gasoline lead than nonsmokers.

[20]If the relationship truly varies across our subsets, then it would generally not make sense to make an overall estimate. As we will explain later, however, we never really observe the true relationship—it always contains some unknown error. Therefore, we may not be sure if it is reasonable to combine our subsample data. Because the variance of the error will be larger the smaller the size of our subsamples, the more we divide our data, the more difficult it is to determine whether observed differences reflect true differences.

[21]For clear introductions, see Eric A. Hanushek and John E. Jackson, *Statistical Methods for the Social Sciences* (New York: Academic Press, 1977); and Christopher H. Achen, *Intrepreting and Using Regression* (Beverly Hills, Calif.: Sage Publications, 1982).

variables remains the same no matter what the values of the other independent variables.[22] We can express a linear regression model in mathematical form:

$$y = b_0 + b_1 x_1 + b_2 x_2 + \ldots + b_k x_k + e$$

where y is the dependent variable, $x_1, x_2, \ldots, x_k$ are the k independent variables, $b_0, b_1, \ldots, b_k$ are parameters (coefficients) to be estimated, and e is an error term that incorporates the cumulative effect on y of all the factors not explicitly included in the model. If we were to increase x_1 by one unit while holding the values of the other independent variables constant, y would change by an amount b_1. Similarly, each of the coefficients measures the marginal effect of a unit change in its variable on the dependent variable.

Imagine that we set the values of all the independent variables except x_1 equal to zero. We could then plot y against x_1 in a graph like Figure 12.2. The equation $y = b_0 + b_1 x_1$ would represent the line fit to our sample of observations. The slope of the line is b_1, the magnitude of the change in y that will result from a unit change in x_1, other things equal. The actual observations do not lie exactly on the line, however. Their vertical distances from the line will be equal to the random error, represented in our model by e, incorporated in each of the observations of y. If the values of e are small, our line will fit the data well in the sense that the actual observations will lie close to it.

How should we go about fitting the line? The most commonly used procedure is the method of *ordinary least squares* (OLS). When we have only one independent variable, so we can plot our data on a two-dimensional graph like Figure 12.2, the OLS procedure picks the line for which the sum of squared vertical deviations from the observed data is smallest. When we have more than one independent variable, OLS determines the values of the coefficients $(b_0, b_1, \ldots, b_k)$ that minimize the sum of squared prediction errors.[23] As long as the number of observations in our sample exceeds the number of coefficients we are trying to estimate, and none of our independent variables can be expressed as a linear combination

---

[22]This assumption is not as restrictive as it might at first seem. We can create new variables that are functions of the original independent variables to capture nonlinearities. For example, if we thought smokers were likely to absorb environmental lead faster than nonsmokers, we might include in our linear regression model a new variable that is the product of the number of cigarettes smoked per day and the level of gasoline lead. This new variable, capturing the interaction of smoking and gasoline lead, would have an effect that would be additive with the other independent variables in the model, including the smoking and gasoline lead variables. The marginal effect of gasoline lead on blood lead would consist of the contribution from the gasoline lead variable and the contribution from the variable representing its interaction with smoking, which will change, depending on the particular level of smoking.

[23]The *prediction error* is the observed value of the dependent variable minus the value we would predict for the dependent variables based on our parameter estimates and the values of our independent variables. For the ith observation the prediction error is given by:

$$y_i - (b_0 + b_1 x_{1i} + b_k x_{ki})$$

The prediction error is also referred to as the *residual of the observation*. OLS selects the parameter estimates to minimize the sum of the squares of the residuals.

of the other independent variables, the commonly available regression software packages will enable us to use computers to find the OLS fitted coefficients.[24]

The estimates of coefficients that we obtain from OLS will generally have a number of very desirable properties. If the independent variables are all uncorrelated with the error term (e), then our coefficient estimators will be *unbiased*.[25] (NOTE: an *estimator* is the formula we use to calculate a particular estimate from our data.) To understand what it means for an estimator to be unbiased, we must keep in mind that our particular estimate depends upon the errors actually realized in our sample of data. If we were to select a new sample, we would realize different errors and hence different coefficient estimates. When an estimator is unbiased, we expect that the average of our estimates across different samples will be very close to the true coefficient value. For example, if gasoline lead had no true effect on blood lead, we would almost certainly estimate its coefficient to be positive or negative, rather than exactly zero. Repeating OLS on a large number of samples and averaging our estimates of the coefficient of gasoline lead, however, would generally yield a result very close to zero.[26] Indeed, by adding more and more samples, we could get the average as close to zero as we wanted.

Unfortunately, we usually only have a single sample for estimating coefficients. How do we decide if an estimate deviates enough from zero for us to conclude that the true value of the parameter is not zero? Making the fairly reasonable assumption that the error term for each observation can be treated as a draw from

---

[24]When one independent variable can be written as a linear combination of the others, we have a case of *perfect multicollinearity*. A related and more common problem, which we can rarely do anything about, occurs when the independent variables in our sample are highly correlated. This condition, called *multicollinearity*, is not a problem with the specification of our model but with the data we have available to estimate it. If two variables are highly correlated, positively or negatively, OLS has difficulty identifying their independent effects on the dependent variable. As a result, the estimates of the parameters associated with these variables will not be very reliable. That is, they will have large variances, increasing the chances that we will fail to recognize, statistically speaking, their effects on the dependent variable. One way to deal with multicollinearity is to add new observations to our sample that lower the correlation. For example, if we had a high positive correlation between smoking and drinking in our sample, we should try to add observations on individuals who smoke but do not drink and who drink but do not smoke. Unfortunately, we often have no choice but to work with the data that are already available.

[25]Strictly speaking, we must also assume that our independent variables are fixed in the sense that we could construct a new sample with exactly the same observations on the independent variables. Of course, even if the independent variables are fixed, we would observe different values of the dependent variable because of the random error term. In addition, for complete generality, we must assume that the expected value of the error term is constant for all observations.

[26]Our average will not be close to zero if gasoline lead is correlated with a variable excluded from our model that does have an effect on blood lead. In this case, gasoline lead stands as a proxy for the excluded variable. Other things equal, the stronger the true effect of the excluded variable on blood lead and the higher the absolute value of the correlation between gasoline lead and the excluded variable, the greater will be the bias of the coefficient of gasoline lead. We might not worry that much about the bias if we knew that it would approach zero as we increase sample size. (If the variance of the estimator also approached zero as we increased sample size, we would say that the estimator is *consistent*.) Although OLS estimators are consistent for correctly specified models, correlation with an important excluded variable makes an estimator inconsistent.

a Normal distribution with constant variance, the OLS estimators will be distributed according to the Student-t distribution.[27] That is, we can interpret the particular numerical estimate of a coefficient as a draw from a random variable distributed as a Student-t distribution centered around the true value of the coefficient. (The OLS estimator is the random variable; the actual estimate based on our data is a realization of that random variable.)

Knowing the distribution of the OLS estimator enables us to interpret the *statistical significance* of our coefficient estimate. We determine statistical significance by asking the following question: How likely is it that we would observe a coefficient estimate as large as we did if the true value of the coefficient were zero? We answer this question by first assuming that the true value of the coefficient is zero (the null hypothesis) so that the distribution of our estimator is centered around zero. We then standardize our distribution to have a variance of one by dividing our coefficient estimate by an estimate of its standard error (a by-product of the OLS procedure). The resulting number, called the t-ratio, can then be compared to critical values in tabulations of the standardized Student-t distribution found in the appendix of almost any statistics text. For example, we might decide that we will reject the null hypothesis that the true value of the coefficient is zero if there is less than a 5 percent probability of observing a t-ratio (in absolute value sense) as large as we did if the null hypothesis is true. (The probability we choose puts an upward bound on the probability of falsely rejecting the null hypothesis.)[28] To carry out the test, we look in the standardized tabulations of the Student-t distribution for the critical value corresponding to 5 percent.[29] If the absolute value of our estimated t-ratio exceeds the critical value, then we reject the null hypothesis and say that our estimated coefficient is statistically significantly different from zero.

Fortunately, most regression software saves us the trouble of looking up critical values in tables by directly calculating the probability under the null hypothesis of observing a t-ratio as large as that estimated. To do a classical test of hypothesis on the coefficient, we simply see if the reported probability is less

---

[27] The *Central Limit Theorem* tells us that the distribution of the sum of independent random variables approaches the Normal distribution as the number in the sum becomes large. The theorem applies for almost any starting distributions—the existence of a finite variance is sufficient. If we think of the error term as the sum of all the many factors excluded from our model, and further, we believe that they are not systematically related to each other or the included variables, then the Central Limit Theorem suggests that the distribution of the error terms will be at least approximately Normal.

[28] Falsely rejecting the null hypothesis is referred to as Type I error. Failing to reject the null hypothesis when in fact the alternative hypothesis is true is referred to as Type II error. We usually set the probability of Type I error at some low level like 5 percent. Holding sample size constant, the lower we set the probability of Type I error, the greater the probability of Type II error.

[29] The Student-t distribution is tabulated by degrees of freedom. In the basic OLS framework, the degrees of freedom is the total number of observations minus the number of coefficients being estimated. As the degrees of freedom becomes larger, the Student-t distribution looks more like a standardized Normal distribution.

You should also note the difference between a one-tailed and two-tailed test. Because the standardized Student-t is a symmetric distribution centered on zero, a 5 percent test usually involves setting critical values so that 2.5 percent of area lies under each of the tails (positive and negative). A one-tailed test, appropriate when the null hypothesis is that the true coefficient value is zero or less than zero, puts the entire 5 percent in the positive tail.

than the maximum probability of falsely rejecting the null hypothesis that we are willing to accept. If it is smaller, we reject the null hypothesis.

Consider the regression results presented in Figure 12.3. They are based on data from 6,534 whites in the NHANES II survey for whom blood lead measurements were made.[30] The dependent variable is the individual's blood lead level measured in $\mu g/dl$. The independent variables are listed under the heading "Effect." The independent variable of primary interest is the national consumption of gasoline lead (in hundreds of metric tons per day) in the month prior to the individual's blood lead measurement. The other independent variables were included in an effort to control statistically for other factors that might be expected to affect the individual's blood lead level. With the exception of the number of cigarettes smoked per day and the dietary factors (vitamin C, riboflavin, and so on), these other statistical controls are indicator, or "dummy," variables that take on the value one if some condition is met and zero otherwise. So, for example, if the individual is male, the variable "male" will equal one; if the individual is female, it will equal zero. The variables "vitamin C," "phosphorus," "riboflavin," and "vitamin A," which are included as proxy measures for dietary intake of lead, each measure dietary intake in milligrams. Otherwise, the other variables are intended to capture demographic, income, occupational exposure, drinking habit, and locational effects. The reported R^2 indicates that, taken together, the independent variables explain about 33 percent of the total variation in blood lead levels.[31]

The estimated coefficient for gasoline lead is 2.14 $\mu g/dl$ of blood per 100 metric tons per day of national gasoline lead consumption. Dividing the coefficient estimate by its estimated standard error of 0.192 yields a t-ratio of about 11. The probability of observing a t-ratio this large or larger if the true value of the coefficient were actually zero is less than one chance in 10,000 (the 0.0000 entry in Figure 12.3 under "P-value"). We would thus reject the null hypothesis in favor of the alternative hypothesis that gasoline lead does contribute to blood lead. In other words, we would say that gasoline lead has a *statistically significant effect* on blood lead.

After finding a statistically significant effect, the next question to ask is whether the size of the coefficient is *substantively significant*. That is, does the variable in question have an effect that is worth considering?[32] One approach to answer-

---

[30]The analysts estimated similar models for blacks and for blacks and whites together. Their estimates of the coefficient for gasoline lead never deviated by more than 10 percent across the different samples. To conserve space, they reported in detail only their regression results for whites. They chose whites because it was the largest subgroup and because it preempted the assertion that the relationship between blood lead and gasoline lead was due to changes in the racial composition of the sample over time.

[31]R^2 is a measure of the *goodness of fit* of the model to the particular sample of data. It is the square of the correlation between the values of the dependent variable predicted by the model and the values actually observed. An R^2 of one would mean that the model perfectly predicted the independent variable for the sample; an R^2 of zero would mean that the model made no contribution to prediction.

[32]The standard errors of the coefficient estimates decrease as sample size increases. Thus, very large samples may yield large t-ratios even when the estimated coefficient (and its true value) are small. We refer to the power of a statistical test as 1 minus the probability of failing to reject the null hypothesis in favor of the alternative hypothesis. Other things equal, larger sample sizes have greater power, increasing the chances that we will reject the null hypothesis in favor of alternatives very close to 0.

Effect	Coefficient	Standard Error	P-value
Intercept	6.15		
Gasoline	2.14	.142	0.0000
Low income	0.79	.243	0.0025
Moderate income	0.32	.184	0.0897
Child (under 8)	3.47	.354	0.0000
Number of cigarettes	0.08	.012	0.0000
Occupationally exposed	1.74	.251	0.0000
Vitamin C	−0.04	.000	0.0010
Teenager	−0.30	.224	0.1841
Male	0.50	.436	0.2538
Male teenager	1.67	.510	0.0026
Male adult	3.40	.510	0.0000
Small city	−0.91	.292	0.0039
Rural	−1.29	.316	0.0003
Phosphorus	−0.001	.000	0.0009
Drinker	0.67	.173	0.0007
Heavy drinker	1.53	.316	0.0000
Northeast	−1.09	.332	0.0028
South	−1.44	.374	0.0005
Midwest	−1.35	.500	0.0115
Educational level	−0.60	.140	0.0000
Riboflavin	0.188	.071	0.0186
Vitamin A	0.018	.008	0.0355

[a] *Dependent variable*: Blood lead (μg/dl) of whites in NHANES II Survey

Figure 12.3   Basic Regression Model for Estimating the Effects of Gasoline Lead on Blood Lead.[a] *Source:* Joel Schwartz, et al., *Costs and Benefits of Reducing Lead in Gasoline: Final Regulatory Impact Analysis* (Washington, D.C.: EPA, 1985), p. III–15. The original document reported incorrect standard errors. The standard errors reported here were provided by Joel Schwartz.

ing this question is to multiply the estimated coefficient by the plausible change in the independent variable that might occur. For example, by the end of the NHANES II survey, gasoline lead was being consumed at a rate of about 250 metric tons per day nationally. A strict policy might reduce the level to, say, 25 metric tons per day. Using the estimated coefficient of gasoline lead, we would expect a reduction of this magnitude to reduce blood lead levels on average by about 4.8 μg/dl (the reduction of 225 metric tons per day times the estimated coefficient of 2.14 μg/dl per 100 metric tons per day).

To get a better sense of whether a 4.8 μg/dl reduction is substantively important, we can look at the blood lead levels for representative groups at the 250 and 25 metric ton levels. For example, at the 250 metric ton level a nonsmoking (number of cigarettes equals zero), moderate drinking (drinker equals one; heavy drinker equals zero), nonoccupationally exposed (occupationally exposed equals zero), adult female (child, teenager, male, male teenager, and male adult equal zero), living in a large Northeastern city (Northeast equals one; small city, rural, South, and Midwest equal zero), with moderate income, a college degree, and a high-nutrition diet (low income equals zero; moderate income, educational level, vitamin C, phosphorus, riboflavin, and vitamin A equal one) would be expected to have a blood lead level of 10.6 μg/dl. We would expect the same person to have a blood lead level of only 5.8 μg/dl if the gasoline lead level were cut to 25 metric tons per day—a reduction of about 45 percent. Thus, the effect of gasoline lead on blood lead appears substantively as well as statistically significant.

The study team was especially interested in estimating the contribution of gasoline lead to blood lead in children. As a first cut, they developed a logistic regression model[33] for predicting the probability that a child between the ages of six months and eight years will have blood levels in excess of 30 μg/dl, the definition of lead toxicity used by the Centers for Disease Control at the time. *Logistic regression*, which assumes a nonlinear relationship between the dependent and the independent variables,[34] is usually more appropriate than linear regression when the dependent variable is dichotomous (Y equals one if the condition holds, Y equals zero is it does not).[35] The study team found a strong relationship in the NHANES II data between gasoline lead and the probability that a child has a toxic level of blood lead. In fact, they estimated that the elimination of gasoline lead would have reduced the number of cases of lead toxicity in the sample by 80 percent for children under eight years of age. The study team used logistic regression and other probability models to estimate how reductions in gasoline lead would change the number of children having various blood lead levels. These estimates were essential for their subsequent valuation of the effects of gasoline lead reductions on the health of children.

Reconsidering Causality

Finding that an independent variable in a regression model has a statistically significant coefficient does not by itself establish a causal relationship. That is, it does not guarantee that changes in the independent variable cause changes in the dependent variable. Even if the independent variable has no direct effect on the dependent variable, some other variable, not included in the model, may be correlated with both so as to produce an apparent relationship in the data sample (remember the apparent relationship between birth rates and the density of stork nests). Should the strong relationship between gasoline lead and blood lead be interpreted as causal?

The study team considered this question in detail. Although its demonstration was not legally necessary, they believed that adoption of the proposed rule would be more likely if a strong case for causality could be made. Their approach was to apply the criteria commonly used by epidemiologists to determine the

---

[33]For an introduction to logistic regression, see Hanushek and Jackson, *Statistical Methods*, pp. 179–216.

[34]The logistic regression model is written

$$P(Y) = e^Z/(1 + e^Z)$$

where $P(Y)$ is the probability that condition Y holds, e is the natural base, and $Z = b_0 + b_1 x_1 + \ldots + b_k x_k$ is the weighted sum of the independent variables $x_1, x_2, \ldots, x_k$. The coefficients, $b_0, b_1, \ldots, b_k$, are selected to maximize the probability of observing the data in the sample. Note that the marginal contribution of x_i to the value of the dependent variable is not simply b_i, as would be the case in a linear regression model. Rather, it is $b_i[1 - P(Y)]P(Y)$, which has its greatest absolute value when $P(Y) = 0.5$.

[35]The logistic regression model, unlike the linear regression model, always predicts probabilities that lie between zero and one (as they should).

likelihood of causality. Not all of the criteria are directly applicable outside of the health area. Nonetheless, the way the study team applied the criteria illustrates the sort of questioning that is valuable in empirical research. Therefore, we briefly review the six criteria that they considered.

Is the Model Biologically Plausible?   The study team noted that lead can be absorbed through the lung and gut. They pointed out that gasoline lead, the major source of environmental lead, is emitted predominantly as respirable particulates in automobile exhaust. These particulates can be absorbed directly through the lungs. They also contaminate dust that can be inhaled through the lungs and absorbed through the gut. Therefore, they argued, it is biologically plausible that gasoline lead contributes to blood lead.

Biological plausibility is the epidemiological statement of a more general criterion: Is the model theoretically plausible? Prior to looking through data for empirical relationships, you should specify a model (your beliefs about how variables are related). If you find that your data are consistent with your model, then you can be more confident that the relationships you estimate are not simply due to chance.[36]

Is There Experimental Evidence to Support the Findings?   The study team found reports of several investigations specifically designed to measure the contribution of gasoline lead to blood lead. One was an experiment conducted in Turin, Italy, by researchers who monitored changes in the isotopic composition of blood lead as the isotopic composition of gasoline lead varied.[37] They found that at least 25 percent of the lead in the blood of Turin residents originated in gasoline. Thus, the experiment not only confirmed the biological plausibility of the contribution of gasoline lead to blood lead, but also suggested an effect on the order of magnitude of that estimated by the study team.

Being able to find such strong and directly relevant experimental support is quite rare in policy research, much of which deals with the behavioral responses of people. Controlled experiments in the social sciences are rare, not only because they are costly and difficult to implement, but also because they often involve tricky ethical issues concerning the assignment of people to "treatment" and "control" groups. Nevertheless, there have been a number of policy experiments in

---

[36]Imagine that you regress a variable on twenty other variables. Assume that none of the twenty independent variables has an effect on the dependent variable. (The coefficients in the true model are all zero.) Nevertheless, if you use a statistical test that limits the probability of falsely rejecting the null hypothesis to 5 percent, then you would still have a 0.64 probability $[1 - (.95)^{20}]$ of rejecting at least one null hypothesis. In other words, if you look through enough data you are bound to find some statistically significant relationships, even when no true relationships exist. By forcing yourself to specify theoretical relationships before you look at the data, you reduce the chances that you will be fooled by the idiosyncrasy of your particular data sample. For a brief review of these issues, see David L. Weimer, "Collective Delusion in the Social Sciences: Publishing Incentives for Empirical Abuse," *Policy Studies Review*, Vol. 5, No. 4, May 1986, pp. 705–8.

[37]S. Fachetti and F. Geiss, *Isotopic Lead Experiment Status Report*, Publication No. EUR8352ZEN (Luxembourg: Commission of the European Communities, 1982).

the United States over the last twenty years.[38] It is unlikely, however, that any of these experiments will be directly applicable to your policy problem. Therefore, you must typically broaden your search for confirmation beyond experiments to other empirical research.

Do Other Studies Using Different Data Replicate the Results?   The study team reviewed several studies that also found relationships between gasoline lead and blood lead. These studies were based on data collected in conjunction with community-wide lead-screening programs funded by the Centers for Disease Control during the 1970s[39] and on data collected from the umbilical cord blood of over 11,000 babies born in Boston between April 1979 and April 1981.[40] These studies reported statistically significant relationships between gasoline lead and blood lead, and thus supported the study team's analysis based on the NHANES II data.

Does Cause Precede Effect?   The study team used information about the half-life of lead in blood to make predictions about the strengths of relationships between lagged levels of gasoline lead and blood lead that would be expected if gasoline lead contributes to blood lead. Lead has a half-life of about thirty days in blood. Noting that the average NHANES II blood test was done at mid-month, they predicted that the previous month's gasoline lead (which on average represents emissions occurring between fifteen and forty-five days before the test) should have a stronger impact on blood lead than that of either the current month (average exposure of zero to fifteen days) or the month occurring two months prior (average exposure of forty-five to seventy-five days). They tested their predictions by regressing blood lead levels on current, one-month lagged, and two-month lagged gasoline lead levels. As predicted, one-month lagged gasoline lead was the most significant of the three. Also, consistent with the thirty-day half-life, two-month lagged gasoline lead had a coefficient approximately one-half that of one-month lagged gasoline lead. Thus, cause did appear to precede effect in the expected way.

Does a Stable Dose-Response Relationship Exist?   The regression model used by the study team assumed a linear relationship between gasoline lead and blood lead. Did this relationship remain stable as the level of gasoline lead changed? To answer this question, the study team took advantage of the fact that, on average, gasoline lead levels were about 50 percent lower in the second half of the NHANES II survey than in the first half. If the relationship between gasoline lead and blood lead is stable and linear, then reestimating the regression model using only data from the second half of the survey should yield a coefficient for gasoline lead comparable to that for the entire sample. They found that the coefficients were in-

---

[38]For a review of the major policy experiments conducted in the United States, see David H. Greenberg and Philip K. Robins, "The Changing Role of Social Experiments in Policy Analysis," *Journal of Policy Analysis and Management*, Vol. 5, No. 2, Winter 1986, pp. 340–62.

[39]Irwin H. Billick, et al., *Predictions of Pediatric Blood Lead Levels from Gasoline Consumption* (Washington, D.C.: U.S. Department of Housing and Urban Development, 1982).

[40]Michael Rabinowitz and Herbert L. Needleman, "Petrol Lead Sales and Umbilical Cord Blood Lead Levels in Boston, Massachusetts," *Lancet*, January 1/8, 1983, p. 63.

deed essentially the same. In addition, estimation of regression models that directly allowed for the possibility of nonlinear effects supported the initial findings of a linear relationship between gasoline lead and blood lead.

Is it Likely That Factors Not Included in the Analysis Could Account for the Observed Relationship?   The study team considered several factors that might confound the apparent relationship between gasoline lead and blood lead: dietary lead intake, exposure to lead paint, seasonality, and sampling patterns.

The basic regression model included nutrient and demographic variables as proxy measures for the intake of lead in the diet. Yet these variables may not adequately control for a possible downward trend in dietary lead that could be causing the estimated relationship between gasoline lead and blood lead. Market basket studies conducted by the Food and Drug Administration over the survey period, however, showed no downward trend in dietary lead intake. Also, lead intake from drinking water is largely a function of acidity, which did not change systematically over the survey period. Evidence did suggest that changes in solder reduced the content of lead in canned foods over the period. But the study team was able to rule out the lead content in canned foods as a confounding factor when they added the lead content in solder as an independent variable, reestimated the basic regression model, and found that the coefficient of gasoline lead remained essentially unchanged.

The study team recognized changing exposure to lead paint as another potential confounding factor. They dismissed the possibility on three grounds.

First, paint lead is a major source in blood lead for children (who eat paint chips) but not for adults. If declining exposure to lead paint were responsible for the estimated relationship between gasoline lead and blood lead, we would expect the reduction in blood lead to be much greater for children than for adults. In fact, the average reduction over the survey period for adults was only slightly smaller than that for children (37 percent versus 42 percent).

Second, the ingestion of paint lead usually results in large increases in blood lead levels. If reduced exposure to paint lead were responsible for declining blood lead levels, then we would expect to observe the improvement primarily in terms of a reduction in the number of people with very high blood lead levels. In fact, blood lead levels declined over the survey period even for groups with low initial levels.[41]

Third, declining exposure to paint lead should be a more important factor in central cities than in suburbs because the latter tend to have newer housing stocks with lower frequencies of peeling lead paint. Yet the gasoline lead coefficient was essentially the same for separate estimations based on central city and suburban subsamples.

Blood lead levels in the United States are on average higher in the summer than in the winter. To rule out the possibility that seasonal variation confounds the relationship between gasoline lead and blood lead, the study team reestimated the basic model with indicator variables included to allow for the possibility of independent seasonal effects. The coefficients of the seasonal variables were not

---

[41]The study team also used data from the lead-screening program in Chicago to estimate the probability of toxicity as a function of gasoline lead for children exposed and not exposed to lead paint. They found that gasoline lead had statistically significant positive coefficients for both groups.

statistically significant when gasoline lead was kept in the model. Thus, it appeared that changes in gasoline lead could adequately explain seasonal as well as long-term changes in blood lead levels.

As already mentioned, the study team estimated the basic model on a variety of demographic subsamples and found no more than a 10 percent difference across any two estimates of the gasoline lead coefficient. They were also concerned, however, that changes in NHANES II sampling locations over the survey period might have confounded the estimation of the gasoline lead coefficient. Therefore, they reestimated the basic model with indicator variables for forty-nine locations and found that the gasoline lead coefficient changed by only about 5 percent. Further, they found that, even when including variables to allow for different gasoline lead coefficients across locations, the coefficient representing the nationwide effect of gasoline lead was statistically and substantively significant. Together, these tests led the study team to dismiss the possibility of serious sampling bias.

The Weight of the Evidence

The study team produced a very strong case in support of an important causal relationship between gasoline lead and blood lead. In many ways their efforts were exemplary. They draw relevant evidence from a wide variety of sources to supplement their primary data analysis. They gave serious attention to possible confounding factors, considering both internal tests (such as subsample analyses and model respecifications) and external evidence to see if they could be ruled out. As a consequence, opponents of the proposed policy were left with few openings for attacking its empirical underpinnings.

FINALIZING THE RULE

The primary task facing the analytical team after publication of the proposed rule was to respond to comments made by interested parties. Team members participated in public hearings held in August and spent much of the fall of 1984 responding to comments placed in the public docket, which closed on October 1. During this process they became more confident that the proposed rule would produce the large net benefits they predicted. At the same time they discovered another benefit category—reductions in adult blood pressure levels—that could potentially swamp their earlier estimates of benefits.

In 1983 Schwartz chanced upon a research article reporting a correlation between blood lead and hypertension.[42] He began work with researchers at the Centers for Disease Control and the University of Michigan to determine if a relationship existed between blood lead and blood pressure levels. By the summer of 1984 their analysis of the NHANES II data suggested a strong link.[43] Because high blood pressure contributes to hypertension, myocardial infarctions,

---

[42]V. Batuman, E. Landy, J. K. Maesaka, and R. P. Wedeen, "Contribution of Lead to Hypertension with Renal Impairment," *New England Journal of Medicine*, No. 309, 1983, pp. 17–21.

[43]The results of their research were later published in J. L. Pirkle, J. Schwartz, J. R. Landes, and W. R. Harlan, "The Relationship Between Blood Lead Levels and Blood Pressure and Its Cardiovascular Risk Implications," *American Journal of Epidemiology*, Vol. 121, No. 2, 1985, pp. 246–58.

and strokes, the potential benefits from blood lead reductions were enormous. Although the final rule was ultimately issued without reference to quantitative estimates of the benefits of lower adult blood lead levels, the team provided estimates in the supporting documents.

The one remaining issue was the compliance schedule. The costs of various lead standards were estimated, using a model of the U.S. refining sector originally developed for the Department of Energy. The model represents the various types of refining capabilities that are available to convert crude oils to final petroleum products. It employs an optimization procedure for finding the allocations of crude oils and intermediate petroleum products among refining units that maximizes social surplus, the sum of consumer and producer surpluses. This allocation corresponds to that which would result from a perfectly competitive market operating without constraints on the utilization of available units. Cost was estimated by looking at the decline in social surplus resulting when the lead constraint was tightened—for instance, from 1.1 gplg to 0.1 gplg. The manufacturers of lead additives challenged these results on the grounds that the model assumed more flexibility in capacity utilization across different refineries than was realistic.

The analytical team held meetings with staffers from other EPA offices to consider alternative compliance schedules. Although a tentative decision was reached to set an interim standard of 0.5 gplg, to be effective July 1, 1985, and a final standard of 0.1 gplg, to be effective January 1, 1986, several staffers feared that some refiners would be unable to comply with their existing equipment. If these fears were realized, the economic costs of the new rule would be higher than estimated and perhaps raise political problems.

A consultant to the project, William Johnson of Sobotka and Company, suggested a solution. If the physical distribution of equipment among refineries interfered with the flexibility in petroleum transfers assumed in the model, he reasoned, perhaps a secondary market in lead rights could be created to facilitate trading to get around specific bottlenecks. Taking the total permitted lead content from July 1, 1985, to January 1, 1988, as a constraint, the key was to create an incentive for refiners who could make the least costly reductions in lead additives below the interim 0.5 gplg standard to do so. Their additional reductions could then be used to offset excess lead in gasoline produced by refiners who could not easily meet the basic standards with the equipment they had in place. Because current reductions below the standard create a right to produce above the standard some time in the future, the trading process was called "banking of lead rights." Refiners would be free to buy and sell lead rights at prices that were mutually beneficial. As a result, the aggregate cost of meeting the new standard would be reduced.

Representatives from the various EPA offices involved with the lead rule agreed that banking seemed to be a good way to deal with concerns about the compliance schedule. Because it had not been discussed in the proposed rule published in August, banking could not be part of the final rule. Nevertheless, by moving quickly to propose banking in a supplemental notice, it would be available shortly after the new standard became final.[44]

[44]50 *Fed. Reg.* 718 (January 4, 1985); and 50 Fed. Reg. 13116 (April 2, 1985).

The remaining task for the team was to prepare the *Final Regulatory Impact Analysis*, which would be published in support of the final rule.[45] The resulting document began by discussing the misfueling and health problems associated with lead additives along with alternatives (public education and stepped-up local enforcement to deal specifically with misfueling, pollution charges to deal generally with lead as a negative externality, and other regulatory standards) to the final rule. It then detailed the methods used to estimate the costs of tighter lead standards, the link between gasoline lead and blood lead, the health benefits of reducing the exposure of children and adults to lead, the benefits of reducing pollutants other than lead, and the benefits from reduced vehicle maintenance costs and increased fuel economy.

The present value of the net benefits of the final rule was presented with various assumptions about misfueling (the use of leaded gasoline in vehicles with catalytic converters). The lower level of permitted lead would reduce the price differential between leaded and unleaded gasoline, thereby reducing the economic incentive for misfueling. It was not possible to predict with confidence, however, how much misfueling would actually decline. Therefore, the reasonable approach was to consider net benefits over the range of possibilities. Figure 12.4 presents the results of this sensitivity analysis. Note that net benefits were given both including and excluding the adult blood pressure benefits. Although the blood pressure benefits appeared huge, they were the last of the benefit measures considered and hence had the least-developed supporting evidence. Nevertheless, even assuming that the standard would produce no reduction in misfueling and no health benefits for adults, the present value of benefits appeared to be more than double the present value of costs. Indeed, it appeared that maintenance benefits alone would more than cover higher refining costs.

The *Final Regulatory Impact Analysis* was released in February 1985. On March 7, 1985, the final rule was published in the *Federal Register*.[46] The 0.1 gplg standard would take effect on January 1, 1986, almost three years after work on the supporting analysis began.

CONCLUSION

We have described a case where statistical analysis made an important contribution to changing policy. Is this case typical? Yes and No. You should not expect that such a confluence of skill, time, data, resources, and interest will often arise to produce such definitive empirical findings. At the same time, you should expect to encounter empirical questions that at least can be approached, if not con-

[45]Joel Schwartz, Hugh Pitcher, Ronnie Levin, Bart Ostro and Albert L. Nichols, *Costs and Benefits of Reducing Lead in Gasoline: Final Regulatory Impact Analysis*, Publication No. EPA-230-05-85-006 (Washington, D.C.: Office of Policy Analysis, EPA, February, 1985). By the time the final report was prepared, Jane Leggett left the project team. In the meantime, Albert Nichols, a Harvard University professor who was visiting the EPA as the acting director of the Economic Analysis Division, began working closely with the team to produce the final document.

[46]50 *Fed. Reg.* 9386 (March 7, 1985).

	No Misfueling	Full Misfueling	Partial Misfueling
Monetized benefits			
Children's health effects	2,582	2,506	2,546
Adult blood pressure	27,936	26,743	27,462
Conventional pollutants	1,525	0	1,114
Maintenance	4,331	3,634	4,077
Fuel economy	856	643	788
Total monetized benefits	37,231	33,526	35,987
Total refining costs	2,637	2,678	2,619
Net benefits	34,594	30,847	33,368
Net benefits excluding blood pressure	6,658	4,105	5,906

Figure 12.4   Present Values of Costs and Benefits of Final Rule, 1985–1992 (Millions of 1983 Dollars). *Source:* Joel Schwartz, et al., *Costs and Benefits of Reducing Lead in Gasoline* (Washington, D.C.: EPA, 1985), table VIII–8, p. VIII–26.

fidently answered, with the sort of statistical methods used by the EPA analysts. Consider a few prominent examples from recent years: Does the death penalty deter homicide?[47] Do higher minimum legal drinking ages and the 55-mile-per-hour speed limit reduce traffic fatalities?[48] Do smaller class sizes improve student performance?[49] Although widely accepted answers to these empirical questions would not necessarily be decisive in resolving policy debates, they would

[47]See Isaac Ehrlich, "The Deterrent Effect of Capital Punishment: A Question of Life and Death," *American Economic Review*, Vol. 65, No. 3, June 1975, pp. 397–417; and Alfred Blumstein, Jacqueline Cohen, and Daniel Nagin, eds., *Deterrence and Incapacitation: Estimating the Effects of Criminal Sanctions on Crime Rates* (Washington, D.C.: National Academy of Sciences, 1978).

[48]See Charles A. Lave, "Speeding, Coordination, and the 55 MPH Limit," *American Economic Review*, Vol. 75, No. 5, December 1985, pp. 1159–64; and Peter Asch and David T. Levy, "Does the Minimum Drinking Age Affect Traffic Fatalities?" *Journal of Policy Analysis and Management,* Vol. 6, No. 2, Winter 1987, pp. 180–92.

[49]See Eric A. Hanushek, "Throwing Money at Schools," *Journal of Policy Analysis and Management*, Vol. 1, No. 1, Fall 1981, pp. 19–41.

at least move the debates beyond disputes over predictions to explicit considerations of values. Such highly controversial issues aside, you are likely to find that making empirical inferences and critically consuming those of others often contribute in important ways to the quality of your policy analyses.

13

DOING WELL AND DOING GOOD

The preceding chapters set out what we believe to be the important elements of an introduction to policy analysis. As a faithful reader, you should now be ready to begin to produce your own analyses with some success. As you gain practical experience, we hope you will find it useful to return to some of the chapters for reference and reinterpretation. We conclude with a few thoughts about how you should view your role as a policy analyst.

Our first exhortation: Do well! Keep your client in mind! Policy analysts earn their keep by giving advice. Always strive to give useful advice by keeping in mind the range of actions available to your client. But, like a doctor, one of your guiding principles should be "Do no harm." This demands skepticism and modesty. Be skeptical about information provided by others and be modest about the accuracy of your own predictions so as to avoid leading your client into costly or embarrassing mistakes. As a professional advice giver, you should be prepared to allow your client to take credit for your popular ideas while keeping the blame for unpopular ones for yourself. Beyond the satisfaction of knowing that you have done a job well, you are likely to be rewarded with the trust of your client and the opportunity to continue to be heard.

But, as we tried to make clear in Chapter 2, your duties as a policy analyst go beyond responsibility for the personal success of your client. You have responsibilities to the integrity of your craft and to contributing to a better society. Thus our second exhortation: Do good!

Doing good requires some basis for comparing alternative courses of action. At the most general level, promoting human dignity and freedom are values widely shared in Western societies. Unfortunately, these values sometimes conflict, and they often do not provide direct guidance for dealing with the majority of issues that most analysts confront in their day-to-day work. As a practical matter, analysts must employ less abstract values in their search for good policy.

Throughout this book we have emphasized economic efficiency as an important goal in the evaluation of alternative policies. Aside from the intuitive appeal of efficiency (if we can make someone better-off without making anyone else worse-off, then shouldn't we do so?), we believe that it often receives too little attention in political arenas because it generally lacks an organized constituency. As a society we might very well be willing to sacrifice considerable efficiency to achieve redistributional or other goals, but we should do so knowingly. Introducing efficiency as a goal in the evaluation of policies is one way that policy analysts can contribute to the "public good" (for once not used in the technical sense!).

Beyond raising efficiency as a goal, you can contribute to the public good by identifying other values that receive too little attention in political arenas. Are there identifiable groups that consistently suffer losses from public policies? Is adequate consideration being given to the future and the interests of future generations? Are dangerous precedents being set? Your social responsibility as an analyst is to make sure that questions such as these get appropriately raised.

Is raising politically underrepresented values consistent with providing useful, presumedly politically feasible, advice? Unfortunately, the answer is often No—self-interest dominates. But at other times people, including politicians, respond to analysis in a public spirit, putting aside their narrow personal and political interests for the greater good.[1] Also, ideas that are not immediately politically feasible may become so in the future if they are repeatedly raised and supported with substantively sound analysis; witness the role of economic analysis in setting the stage for the eventual deregulation of the U.S. telephone, trucking, and airline industries.[2] Sometimes doing good simply requires analysts to advise their clients to forgo some current popularity or success to achieve some important value. You are doing exceptionally well when you convince your client to accept such advice!

---

[1] For a provocative development of this point, see Steven Kelman, " 'Public Choice' and Public Spirit," *The Public Interest*, No. 87, Spring 1987, pp. 80–94.

[2] See Martha Derthick and Paul J. Quirk, *The Politics of Deregulation* (Washington, D.C.: Brookings Institution, 1985), pp. 246–52.

INDEX

taxes and subsidies, effect on, 133
value of, 15–16
Egypt, Israel and, 301–2, 347–48
Ehrenwald, Jan, 180
Ehrlich, Isaac, 394
Eismeier, Theodore J., 146
Ekwurzel, Drucilla, 223
Electoral cycles in representative
government, 110–11
Electric utilities, 162, 174, 208
Elkin, Stephen L., 136
Elliott, Kimberly Ann, 137
Ellison, Anthony P., 326, 330
Ellwood, David T., 172
Elmore, Richard, 201, 314
Endogenous preferences, 77–78
Endowments, participation in markets and,
90–91
Energy, Department of, 120, 206, 224, 351,
358, 362, 364, 392
Energy crisis, 106
Energy Policy and Conservation Act, 348,
363
Energy Research and Development
Administration, 351
Energy sector, journals associated with, 222
Energy security, Strategic Petroleum
Reserve and, 346–52
Entoven, Alain C., 179, 199
Entrepreneurs, policy, 336, 338–39
Environmental Protection Agency (EPA),
120, 342, 351
lead standards for gasoline, 371, 372–74
Epstein, Richard A., 149
Equality of outcomes, increasing, 91–93
Equilibrium model, general, 31
Equity
as goal, 190, 191–93
of opportunity, 89–91
value of, 15–16
vertical and horizontal, 92
Equivalent variation, 34
ERIC (Educational Resources Information
Center), 224
Erickson, P., 128
Errors
correction of, 315–21
prediction, 382
Type I and II, 384
Estimator, 383–84
Ethics, professional, 13, 14–28
analytical roles and, 15–18
ethical code vs. ethos, 26–28
rhetoric and, 304–5
value conflicts and, 18–26
examples of, 24–26
responses to, 19–24
Etzioni, Amitai, 185
European Economic Community, 100
Evaluation
of alternatives, 210–12

anticipating, 317–19
dimension of, 303
Evans, Nigel, 304
Evans, Robert G., 156
Evens, Alan, 289
Evidence, gathering and organizing, 219–38
Excise (commodity) tax, 33–34, 135, 146–47
Excludability, 40
costs of exclusion, 43–44
of marketable public goods, 44, 45–47
of private goods, 44, 45
unfeasibility of exclusion, 52
Executive summary, 214, 325
Exhaustible resources, 86
Exit, concept of, 20–24
Exit, Voice and Loyalty (Hirschman), 20
Expected utility hypothesis, 83
Expected value, 210, 255, 261–64
Expenditure effects of oil-stockpiling
program, 353–54
Experience goods, 69, 71–74
Experts, area, 293–94
Externalities, 56–61
defined, 56
divergence between aggregate social
welfare and welfare of local
government, 241–42
economic, 242
efficiency losses of, 57–59
fiscal, 121–22, 242
internalizing, 144, 154
market responses to, 60–61
negative, 56–59, 139–40, 146
positive, 57–59, 144, 251
problem, 56
in production or consumption, 57
Externality taxes, 135
External validity, 317

Fachetti, S., 388
Facilitating markets, 126, 129–30
Factor markets, 244–48
Facts, gathering and organizing, 219–38
document research, 220–34
field research, 234–37
putting document and field research
together, 237
Fama, Eugene F., 118, 162
Fare, R., 174, 176
Farris, Paul W., 77
FDA, 75, 155, 298, 390
Feasibility
goals and program, 192–93
political, 294–98
Federal agencies, policy analysts in, 10–11
Federal Deposit Insurance Corporation, 162
Federal Emergency Management Agency,
168
Federal Energy Administration (FEA), 348,
351, 363

Federal government, policy analysts in, 9–11
Federal National Mortgage Association, 162
Federal Power Commission, 351
Feigenbaum, Susan, 174, 176
Fenno, Richard F., Jr., 234
Ferman, Barbara, 213, 310, 311
Field research, 234–37
Final Regulatory Impact Analysis (lead standard), 393
Financial institutions, 175
Finsinger, Jorg, 174, 176
Fire services, 175
Fiscal externalities, 121–22, 242
Fiscal policies, 89
Fisher, Anthony C., 86
Fisher, Clyde O., 337
Fisher, Irving, 279
Fisher, Roger, 301
Fixed costs, 35
"Fixers," availability of, 309–11
Fixler, Philip E., Jr., 164
Fleishman, Joel L., 15
Flood Control Acts of 1926 and 1936, U.S., 239
Flood Disaster Protection Act of 1973, 168
Floors on consumption, 89–91
Flowers, Marilyn R., 164
Food and Drug Administration (FDA), 75, 155, 298, 390
Food Stamp Act, 144
Food stamps, 142, 144
Ford Administration, 348
Forrest, Anne, 290
Forsyth, P.J., 175, 176
Forthofer, R.N., 376
Forward mapping, 311–14
Forward markets, 84
Framework rules, 148–50
Frank, Robert H., 78
Frankfurter, Felix, 300
Frech, H.E., III, 174, 176
Frederickson, H. George, 7
Freedman, Lee S., 132
"Free" goods, 54–55. *See also* Public goods
Freeing markets, 125–29
Freeman, A. Myrick, III, 86, 289
Free rider problem, 43, 48–51, 355–56
French, Peter A., 23
Frequency of purchase, 70–71
Frey, B.S., 174, 177
Friedman, G.D., 267
Friedman, James W., 76
Friedman, Lee S., 34, 139, 158, 266, 287
Friedman, Milton, 145, 156
Fujii, Edwin T., 147
Full price, 70
Fulton, Arthur D., 336
Futures markets, 84

Garbage truck purchase, benefit-cost analysis of, 258–61
Gardner, B. Delworth, 55, 130
Gardner, Bruce L., 170
Gasoline, lead standard for. *See* Lead standard for gasoline, revising
Geiss, F., 388
General Accounting Office, 10
General equilibrium model, 31
General Possibility Theorem, 97–98
Generic policies, 124–78
  alternatives, 201
  cushions, providing, 166, 169–72
  establishing rules, 147–57
    frameworks, 148–50
    regulations, 150–57
  facilitating markets, 126, 129–30
  freeing markets, 125–29
  insurance, providing, 166–68
  searching for, 173
  simulating markets, 126, 130–32
  subsidies and taxes to alter incentives, 132–47
    demand-side subsidies, 142–46
    demand-side taxes, 146–47
    supply-side subsidies, 138–42
    supply-side taxes, 135–38
  supplying goods through nonmarket mechanisms, 157–65
    contracting out, 128, 164–65
    direct supply by government bureaus, 159–61
    independent agencies, 161–64
Geographic impact of policy, 241–42
Gibbard, Allan, 98
Gibbs, Curtis, 139
Ginsberg, R., 83
Ginsburg, Paul B., 174, 176
"Go, no go" rule, 211–12
Goals
  categories of, 190–91
  choosing and explaining, 188–94
  conversion to objectives and constraints, 198–200
  distinction between policies and, 193–94
  efficiency as, 189–93, 397
  as outputs, 188–93
  program feasibility and, 192–93
  putting policy alternatives together with, 203–12
  vagueness, 188–93
Goehlert, R.U., 230
Goetz, Charles J., 121
Goldberg, Victor, 131
Goldman, Alan H., 27
Gomez-Ibanez, Jose A., 153, 335
Good, adherence to one's concept of, 16–18
Goodfellow, Gordon, 168
Goodin, Robert E., 15, 85
Goodness of fit, 385

Weintraub, E. Roy, 30
Weisbrod, Burton A., 86, 171
Weiss, Carol H., 318
Whalley, John, 31
Wharton Econometric Forecasting
    Associates, 58
Whistle-blowing, 23–24
White, William D., 156, 157
White House staff, analysts on, 18
Whiteneck, Gale G., 11
Whittington, Dale, 79, 241
Wicks, John H., 174, 177
Wildasin, David E., 172
Wildavsky, Aaron, 5, 6, 7, 12, 118, 120,
    188, 189, 299, 305, 307, 316
Wilentz, Amy, 226
Williams, Alan H., 240, 254
Williams, Arlington W., 131
Williams, Walter, 2, 201
Williamson, Oliver E., 114, 131, 162
Willig, Robert D., 34, 64, 288
Willingness to pay, 248–55
Wilson, George W., 174, 178
Wilson, James Q., 112, 194
Wilson, Thomas A., 77
Wilson, Woodrow, 7
Wingo, Lowdon, 289

Winston, Clifford, 64, 127, 327, 328, 333
Wintrobe, Ronald, 117
Wise, David A., 144
Wiseman, J., 79
Wittfogel, Karl, 159
Wohl, Martin, 147
Wolcott, Robert, 374
Wolf, Charles, Jr., 94, 118
Wolkoff, Michael, 170, 197–98
Wright, Brian D., 170
Wright, Sonia R., 318
Wu, Chi-Yuen, 6

X-inefficiency, 66–67, 151
  in public agencies, 115
  public executives use of discretionary
      budget and, 118

Yondorf, Barbara, 128

Zambia, Bank of, 132
Zardkoohi, Asghar, 174, 176
Zarnowitz, Victor, 88
Zeckhauser, Richard J., 80, 82, 154, 179
Zerbe, R., 162
Zwirn, J., 228